Teaching and Learning Mathematics

315-1
19

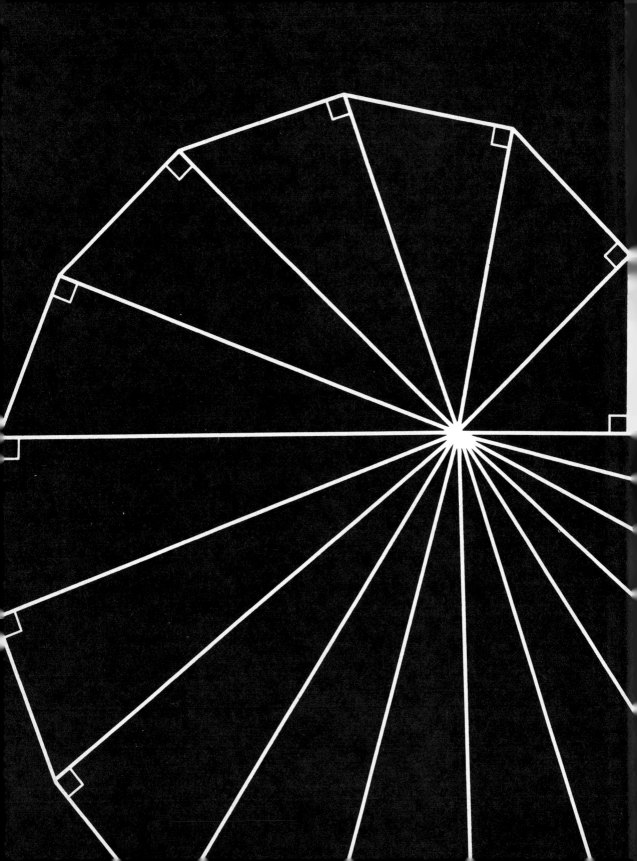

Teaching and Learning Mathematics
(In Secondary Schools)

Frederick H. Bell
University of Pittsburgh

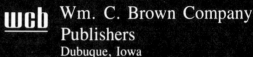 Wm. C. Brown Company
Publishers
Dubuque, Iowa

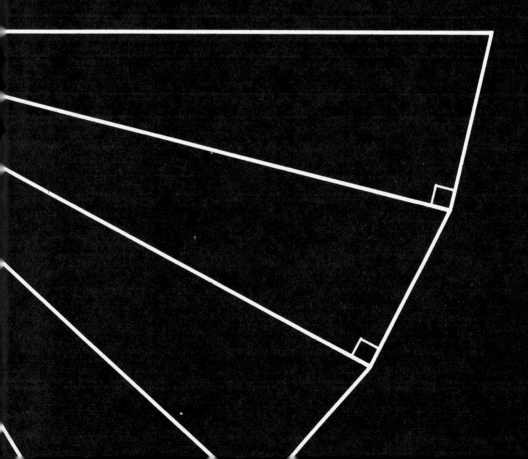

Copyright © 1978 by Wm. C. Brown Company Publishers

Library of Congress Catalog Card Number: 77—92108

ISBN 0—697—06017—9

Contents

4 Preparing to Teach Mathematics Lessons 167

5 Models for Teaching and Learning the Direct Objects of Mathematics 221

8 Professional Considerations Outside the Classroom   453

9 Teaching Exceptional Students 501

Preface

Mathematics teaching can be a difficult, challenging, and exciting profession. This book was written to assist secondary school mathematics teachers in resolving many of the day-to-day problems that they encounter in our rapidly changing educational system. The primary objective of this textbook is to assist prospective teachers and practicing teachers to become more effective teachers by synthesizing and applying the teaching and learning variables of mathematics content, secondary school curriculum, theories of learning, teaching methods, classroom management techniques, and professional activities outside the classroom. Although this book is directed to teachers, student learning in both the cognitive and affective areas is emphasized in each chapter. The nature of learning, as well as methods of teaching, is emphasized because teaching is viewed not as an end in itself but as a means of facilitating learning.

A **Selected Bibliography** of readily obtainable reference and resource materials is included at the end of each chapter to assist the reader in locating additional materials related to the topics presented in the chapters. A dynamic approach to references is taken; that is, the reader is told how to locate continuing, current sources of information and is encouraged to obtain, read, and use in his or her own classroom teaching a variety of current professional publications. For instance, in addition to suggesting that the reader study a specified set of references on a particular topic, he or she is directed to browse through recent issues of several journals such as *The Arithmetic Teacher, The Mathematics Teacher,* and *School Science and Mathematics* to find the current literature on the topic being considered.

A set of suggested supplementary activities for the reader is presented near the end of each chapter in a section titled **Things to Do.** The "things to do" for each chapter are activities to assist the reader in reviewing, analyzing, synthesizing, evaluating, and extending the ideas and methods that are discussed and illustrated in each chapter. Both the text material and the **Things to Do** sections emphasize active involvement and participation by the reader, who is directed to evaluate, use, and extend the teaching/learning activities that are suggested in each chapter.

This textbook is designed to help mathematics teachers become independent professionals who are able to plan, organize, and implement their own informal programs of continuing education and professional development. Throughout the book the mathematics teacher or prospective teacher is shown how to carry out a variety of teaching/learning activities. A rationale, based upon tested principles of teaching and learning, is given for suggested activities; numerous examples, illustrations, and scenarios are presented throughout the book.

An Introduction to Mathematics Education, is an introduction to the book. This chapter presents many of the specific objectives of the book in the context of those things that a mathematics teacher should know and be able to accomplish in his or her classroom.

Chapter 1, **The Nature of Mathematics,** summarizes several important developments throughout the history of mathematics and contains topics on the philosophy, foundations, and methods of mathematics. This chapter is a brief history of mathematics and is designed to motivate the reader to continue his or her study of the history and content of mathematics as they were influenced by the outstanding men and women of mathematics.

Chapter 2, **The School Mathematics Curriculum,** presents the "new math/old math" controversy in its historical context; discusses past, present, and probable future influences upon the school mathematics curriculum; and contains a comparative description of the school mathematics curricula before 1960 and after 1970.

Chapter 3, **Using Learning and Instructional Theories in Teaching Mathematics,** provides a summary of seven important theories of learning and teaching, and illustrates the applications of each theory in secondary school mathematics classrooms.

Chapter 4, **Preparing to Teach Mathematics Lessons,** contains a model for planning mathematics lessons that includes formulating objectives, selecting mathematics content, obtaining teaching/learning resources, assessing learning readiness, evaluating learning, and choosing teaching/learning strategies.

Chapters 5 and 6 contain twelve models for teaching and learning mathematics. Among the models discussed and illustrated are expository teaching, discovery learning, educational games, individualizing instruction, theorem proving, problem solving, mathematics laboratories, working in groups, and computer-assisted learning. These two chapters, together with Chapter 4, comprise the nucleus of this textbook and contain many methods for teaching mathematics together with example lesson plans to illustrate various teaching/learning strategies.

Chapter 7, **Developing and Maintaining an Effective Learning Environment,** deals with selecting and using textbooks, obtaining classroom resources, assigning homework, using classroom questioning techniques, assessing student learning difficulties, dealing with discipline problems, testing and grading students, and evaluating teacher effectiveness.

Chapter 8, **Professional Considerations Outside the Classroom,** presents and discusses non-classroom activities of teachers which can have an indirect influence upon their effectiveness in the classroom. Among the topics considered in this chapter are teachers' rights and responsibilities, extracurricular activities of teachers, cooperation with other teachers and school administrators, continuing education and professional development, and the future of mathematics education.

Chapter 9, **Teaching Exceptional Students,** contains a discussion of the characteristics and needs of slow learners and gifted students. It also deals with special methods for teaching mathematics to slow learners and gifted students. In addition, this chapter has a section on teaching reading in the mathematics classroom. Although slow learners are most likely to have reading problems, the section on reading mathematics is appropriate for teaching reading to students of all ability levels.

This textbook contains sufficient content for two one-semester courses on teaching and learning secondary school mathematics. Since the book was written to help teachers or prospective teachers improve their teaching effectiveness, it can also be used as a basis for a graduate mathematics teacher-education course. Each chapter is a relatively self-contained unit, and brief (from one day to two weeks) inservice teacher education programs can be developed around any of the chapters in the book. For example, a two-week workshop on applying learning theory in teaching mathematics could be centered around Chapter 3. Chapters 4, 5, and 6 could be the basis for a one-semester undergraduate course for people who are preparing to become mathematics teachers. Chapters 1, 2, 3, 7, 8 and 9 might form the nucleus for a second one-semester course for undergraduates. I have also used material from selected chapters as the basis for an in depth study of teaching and learning in a one-semester graduate course. Each college or university instructor, or school curriculum coordinator of mathematics, can make an appropriate selection of topics to suit his or her own purposes for undergraduate or graduate courses or inservice workshops on teaching and learning mathematics.

Special thanks are extended to Barbara Lindenberg who typed the classroom trial manuscript for this book and to Ellen Bell who proofread the manuscript. I also wish to recognize two outstanding mathematics educators—Mr. Martin Valenti and Dr. George Lewis. The photographs in this book were taken by Margot Critchfield, Project Solo, University of Pittsburgh.

F. H. Bell

To Ellen

An Introduction to Mathematics Education

Teaching and learning are very complex, interrelated processes which have not yet been precisely specified. It would seem that an effective teacher education and training program, or a training program for any vocation or profession, should be based upon a set of answers to these questions: What must one know and be able to do in order to effectively practice the profession? What are the criteria for evaluating a person's level of success in his or her profession? What are the elements of a successful program to prepare people for the profession? Unfortunately there are no comprehensive sets of answers for each of these three questions with respect to the teaching profession. We do not know exactly what knowledge and skills are necessary to guarantee success as a teacher. It is very difficult to list all the criteria for evaluating teacher effectiveness or even to agree upon the appropriateness of those criteria which have been specified. Consequently, there is no one model for teacher education which can be shown to be better than all the others and which can assure the preparation of outstanding teachers.

There are several reasons for this less than ideal state of affairs in teacher education. First, there are so many variables involved in both teaching and learning, and these variables interact with each other in such complex ways, that even when sets of teaching/learning variables have been identified, it is not usually possible to determine how they influence each other. Second, there are so many different teaching/learning situations, both within and outside the classroom, that even if it were possible to identify all of them, it would not be practical to specify procedures for dealing with each situation. Third, human variation is so great, and each person is so distinct, that optimum teaching and learning strategies appear to be different for each teacher and each student in each learning environment. Fourth, the science of measurement and evaluation of human beings is still in a rather primitive state. Although good tests and measurements—which are fairly reliable and valid—have been developed for evaluating learning of knowledge and skills, it is quite difficult to design tests to assess higher level mental processes such as concept formation, the ability to analyze and synthesize knowledge, learning how to learn, and the ability to evaluate information. It is

1

even more difficult to design good instruments for accurately assessing changes in attitudes, perceptions, feelings, and emotions, which are also important objectives of teaching and learning.

The complexity of teaching and learning and the variation among teachers and students indicate that teaching, learning, and learning how to teach are highly individualized and personalized activities. To avoid frustration and disillusionment, it is important to realize that no teacher education program, teacher, or book can teach how to teach, or mold an outstanding teacher. What teacher education programs, teachers, and books can do is to help you become an adequate (even effective) mathematics teacher if you are now preparing for that profession. If you are already a mathematics teacher, these resources can assist you in improving your teaching effectiveness. However, to become more than merely adequate as a teacher, you must assume most of the responsibility for your own professional development. You must be willing to try different teaching strategies for different students, to critically evaluate the effectiveness of your strategies, and to modify or discard ineffective procedures. It is equally important that every teacher continue his or her professional development through college courses, inservice programs, activities in professional societies, and reading the professional literature in mathematics education. Even the person who graduates from a teacher education program as an outstanding teacher will soon become mediocre or worse as a teacher if he or she merely applies what was previously learned. We certainly would not want to entrust our welfare to a doctor who hadn't read a medical journal since he graduated from medical school, a lawyer who hadn't read any law for ten years, or an automobile mechanic who specialized in Edsels in his training program and learned nothing new since then. In summary, teaching is not an exact, well-defined activity; it is a very difficult and demanding profession; it requires a continuing program of self-improvement and professional development if it is to be practiced effectively.

The Objectives of Mathematics Teacher Education

One of the strategies usually associated with effective teaching is to explicitly state your goals and objectives and share them with the learner before he or she begins to study the course or unit. The goals of this book about teaching and learning mathematics are (1) to help people who are preparing to become mathematics teachers learn and practice some of the knowledge, skills, and activities which have been found by many teachers to be relatively effective in helping students learn and enjoy mathematics, and (2) to assist those people who are now teaching mathematics to become better teachers. Although these goals would be acceptable to most people as appropriate for a methods of teaching mathematics textbook, they are stated much too generally. In order for the author to have written a book to meet these goals, and for the people who use this book to evaluate the success of the book in achieving the goals of mathematics education, it is necessary to specify these general goals in more detail by considering specific objectives of mathematics education programs. There are several ways to determine objectives. One way is to select a personalized, idealized set of objectives which may be good but which may not be practical to achieve in a less than ideal educational system. A second method may be to select a "safe" list of objectives which would be acceptable to nearly everyone but which may not aim for excellence. Then there is the "middle ground" of selecting objectives which are somewhat idealistic, which aim for excellence, which have a good chance of being achieved, and which will be acceptable to most mathematics educators—the approach used in determining the objectives for this book. Since the general goal of the book is to improve mathematics teaching, the objectives were selected to reflect those things which teachers should know and those things which teachers should be able to do. The objectives were drawn from several sources—(1) the author's experience in directing teacher education programs, (2) the *Recommendations on Course Content for the Training of Teachers of Mathematics* prepared by the Committee on the Undergraduate Program in Mathematics, (3) *Guidelines and Standards for the Education of Secondary School Teachers of Science and Mathematics* prepared by the Project on the Education of Secondary School Teachers of Science and Mathematics, (4) *Guidelines for the Preparation of Teachers of Mathematics* by the Commission on Preservice Education of Teachers of the National Council of Teachers of Mathematics, (5) *Recommendations Regarding Computers in High School Education* by the Conference Board of the Mathematical Sciences Committee on Computer Education, (6) *Report of the Conference on the K-12 Mathematics Curriculum* which was held at Snowmass, Colorado, and (7) the *Report of the Cambridge Conference on School Mathematics*. These objectives are not only the objectives of this book, but in a larger sense they represent the objectives of the entire mathematics education community which are reflected in the six publications listed above. You can view the following set of objectives as a guide to those things which a secondary school mathematics teacher should know and should be able to do. The people who were responsible for developing these objectives realize that no beginning mathematics teacher will know all the information suggested in the objectives nor be able to do everything specified in the objectives. A dedicated and intelligent mathematics teacher might expect to achieve most of these objectives at a high level of competency through a good college or university mathematics teacher education program and five to ten years of conscientious teaching.

Mathematical Content

Although it is a fact that there are many people who have an excellent knowledge of mathematics but who are not very good teachers of mathematics, there are few, if any, good mathematics teachers who do not know mathematics. Among the many characteristics of a good mathematics teacher, the primary requisite is a sound knowledge and understanding of mathematics. Every teacher should know and understand the mathematics contained in the textbooks which are commonly used in secondary school mathematics courses, but a good teacher will know much more mathematical content. The teacher who has both breadth and depth in his or her understanding of college level mathematics will be better prepared to teach high school mathematics in a manner which is accurate, interesting, and useful to every student.

Most mathematicians and mathematics teacher educators agree that secondary school mathematics teachers should have a sound understanding of the structure of the real number system, abstract algebra, linear algebra, modern trigonometry, modern geometry, probability and statistics, differential and integral calculus, analysis, and the structure and logical foundations of mathematics. This means that junior and senior high school and middle school teachers should be able to:

Real Number System

1. Use and explain the base ten numeration system.
2. Carry out and explain the four basic operations on real numbers.
3. Use and explain equality and inequality relations.
4. Relate the number line to the measurement concept, and explain basic concepts of measuring quantities such as length, area, capacity, weight, etc. in both the U.S. customary and metric systems of units.
5. Present and explain the extended real number system, and discuss orders of infinities and infinite sets.
6. Determine ordinal and cardinal numbers for finite and infinite sets.
7. Show that the real number system is a complete ordered field.

Abstract Algebra

1. Develop the properties of the real and complex number systems.
2. Perform algebraic operations on rational forms and functions.
3. Explain and give examples of polynomial functions and rings of polynomials over a field.
4. Define and illustrate group, ring, integral domain, field, normal subgroup, and ideal.
5. Develop iterative procedures.
6. Solve Diophantine equations, use the Euclidean algorithm, and work in modular systems of arithmetic.
7. Derive the complex numbers as residue classes of polynomials modulo $x^2 + 1$.
8. Know the fundamental theorem of algebra.
9. Use various methods to solve polynomials.

Linear Algebra

1. Define and give examples of vector spaces.
2. Carry out the operations of matrix algebra.
3. Define and illustrate transformations and linear mappings.
4. Use matrices to solve systems of linear equations.
5. Explain matrix properties, matrices of transformations, and change of base.
6. Define and work with the triangular form of matrices, diagonal form of symmetric matrices, invariant subspaces, and quadratic forms.
7. Prove and illustrate the Cayley-Hamilton theorem.
8. Explain inner products and orthogonal transformations.

Modern Trigonometry

1. Develop the trigonometric functions as functions on a unit circle.
2. Solve trigonometric equations.
3. Graph trigonometric functions and their inverses.
4. Prove the law of sines and the law of cosines.
5. Discuss polar coordinates.
6. Put complex numbers in trigonometric form.
7. Prove and apply DeMoivre's theorem.

8. Define and use logarithmic and exponential functions.
9. Apply trigonometry to the solution of physical problems.
10. Discuss uniform circular motion and radian measure.

Modern Geometry

1. Demonstrate a thorough understanding of Euclidean synthetic geometry.
2. Explain and apply the Cartesian plane and space geometries of lines, planes, circles, and spheres.
3. Know and understand the analytic geometry of the conic sections.
4. Define and explain motions in Euclidean space, groups of motions, matrices and linear transformations, vectors, and linear independence.
5. Use rotations in the plane and in space.
6. Explain properties of n-dimensional vector spaces.
7. Know and understand projective geometry and affine geometry.
8. Give examples of non-Euclidean geometries.

Probability and Statistics

1. State the basic definitions in probability theory for finite sample spaces.
2. Discuss procedures for sampling from a finite population.
3. Explain independence and conditional probability.
4. Explain random variables and discuss their distributions.
5. State and explain applications of Chebychev's inequality.
6. Discuss joint distribution of random variables and independent variables.
7. Explain the Poisson distribution.
8. Discuss the differences between descriptive and inferential statistics and the difference between data and statistics.
9. Carry out hypothesis testing and draw appropriate conclusions about populations based upon samples drawn from the populations.
10. Know the difference between parametric and nonparametric statistical techniques and when to use each.
11. Discuss relation and correlation.

Differential and Integral Calculus

1. Use techniques of differentiation and integration to solve standard applied problems.
2. Extend the processes of one-variable calculus to the calculus of more than one variable.
3. Understand and apply the mean value theorem, the fundamental theorem of calculus, and the implicit function theorem.
4. Understand the limiting processes that occur in calculus such as infinite sequences, infinite series, improper integrals, interchange of limits, convergence, and uniform convergence.
5. State and prove theorems about limits of sums, differences, products, and quotients of functions.
6. Derive the formulas for differentiating and integrating special functions.

Analysis

1. Solve simple differential equations.
2. Explain the concepts of open set, closed set, limit point, connected set, measure, and metric space.

3. Understand what it means for a function to be Riemann integrable.
4. Give examples of functions which are not Riemann integrable.
5. Explain the elements of intuitive measure theory and Lebesgue integration.
6. Use the differential geometry of space curves.
7. Know and apply multidimensional integral and differential calculus.
8. Use interpolation, difference methods, indeterminant forms, and Taylor's series.
9. Use Fourier series to solve simple boundary value problems.
10. Solve integral equations and know Green's functions and variational and iterational methods.
11. Apply techniques from numerical analysis.

Structure and Foundation of Mathematics

1. Present a general discussion of the history, philosophy, nature, and cultural significance of mathematics.
2. Give specific historical examples of mathematical events and mathematicians which relate to specific topics in each area of mathematics.
3. Discuss the relationships and common techniques among the various areas of mathematics.
4. Explain the structure of various branches of mathematics by discussing the axiomatic system and the unifying concepts found in each branch.
5. Present logical difficulties which have been discovered in various branches of mathematics and explain how these difficulties have either been partly or completely resolved.
6. Describe the common elements found in axiomatic systems.
7. Give examples of logical paradoxes found in mathematics and explain how they were resolved.
8. Understand and explain the elements of propositional calculus and logical implications.
9. Discuss how much of mathematics can be axiomatized using elements of set theory.
10. Discuss the chronological development of each of the several branches of mathematics.

Two characteristics of this lengthy list of mathematical competencies which are expected of teachers should be emphasized. First, the list is not necessarily complete; there are other mathematical topics which some mathematicians and educators believe people should know in order to be outstanding secondary school mathematics teachers. Second, most mathematics teachers will not learn everything on this competency list in a typical four year undergraduate degree and teacher certification program. Since most states require additional inservice courses and programs for continuing teacher certification, many teachers acquire some of their knowledge of more advanced mathematics topics in post-baccalaureate courses, or in master's degree programs, or in self-initiated, independent professional study. Self-directed reading and study is an excellent way for teachers to improve their skills and knowledge, and can be just as effective as taking college or university courses.

Applications of Mathematics

Although some mathematicians believe that sufficient justification for their study and research in mathematics can be found within the field of mathematics, other mathematicians and most users of mathematics think that the major value of mathematics lies in its applications in other fields of study and in its contributions to the improvement of our physical world. Therefore, a good teacher should motivate his or her students' learning of mathematics through both its inherent aesthetic appeal and its many uses in society. Some of the objectives of this book, and of people concerned with preparing mathematics teachers, deal with the applications of mathematics and the study of other subjects which are related to mathematics. The good middle school, junior high, or high school mathematics teacher should be prepared to:

1. Apply the real number system to problems in ratio, proportion, variation, scaling, and approximation.
2. Use the techniques of statistics and probability to solve problems pertaining to central tendency, dispersion, expectation, prediction, relationships, and differences between distributions of measurements.
3. Formulate a research question as a scientifically or statistically testable hypothesis and collect and analyze data relative to the hypothesis.
4. Plan for, make, and record observations and present data in a well-organized, clear, and orderly form.
5. Solve practical problems in two and three dimensional geometry.
6. Use integral and differential calculus and techniques of analysis to solve problems in the physical, biological and social sciences.
7. Have sufficient depth of knowledge in one or two quantitative sciences to solve problems and build mathematical models in those sciences.
8. Explain the role of mathematics in the development of contemporary culture.
9. Discuss the role of mathematics in defining a particular social or technological problem.
10. Explore the potential and limitations of mathematics for solving problems associated with human welfare.
11. Describe how mathematics and related technology might interact with social, political, and economic forces to influence future social development.
12. Demonstrate understanding of the methods, logical processes, and explanatory systems characterizing the natural sciences and mathematics.
13. Compare mathematical "truth" with other kinds of "truths" which people have formulated.
14. Illustrate how mathematical models can be used to organize knowledge about a known phenomenon.
15. Identify essential elements of a mathematical model, describe the assumptions of the model, distinguish among competing models, identify appropriate models for particular problems, and modify the model to accommodate new information.

Uses of Computers in Mathematics Education

Within the past ten years computers and computer-related technology have become important aids to teaching in many secondary schools. Computers are used by teachers to provide drill and practice lessons for students, to test students, to store and analyze information about students' learning progress, and to schedule various learning activities. School teachers and students also write and use computer programs to solve mathematical problems, to model scientific and social processes, and to simulate complex physical situations. Computers are being used in a variety of ways in many schools to make learning more efficient, meaningful, and interesting for students. Computer-centered learning laboratories have been used to give students significant control over their own learning and to broaden the scope of school-based learning activities.

Contrary to the concerns of some people, the use of computers in schools does not dehumanize and depersonalize learning. When students and teachers have control of the computer they can construct learning situations which personalize learning for each student. Many people believe that computer-related technology can be used to effect the positive revolution in education which other learning technologies have failed to do.

All teachers should have some degree of computer literacy; however mathematics teachers should be uncommonly well-informed about computers and their use in education. This is so because when a school begins to use computers to augment learning, it is usually the mathematics teachers who are given responsibility for maintaining and using the computer-oriented learning facility. Consequently, each mathematics teacher should have the following computer-related competencies:

1. Explain and illustrate the uses of computers in society.
2. Discuss the several components required for a computer facility and show how the components interact.
3. Be able to discuss the capabilities and limitations of computers.
4. Understand the potential of computers for unethical purposes, and know how to guard against uses of computers which may be detrimental to society and which may subvert individual rights and freedoms.
5. Explain both the physical and conceptual operations of computers.
6. Be familiar with the history of computer technology.
7. Have a basic knowledge of the several fields of computer science such as hardware development, system analysis, automata theory, artificial intelligence, numerical analysis, and programming languages.
8. Be able to write computer programs in at least two programming languages; for example, BASIC and FORTRAN.
9. Be able to use computers in a variety of instructional situations.
10. Be able to write computer-related curriculum modules for drill, practice, testing, data analysis, games, simulations, and models.
11. Teach computer programming and assist students in using computers for interesting and useful purposes.
12. Help other teachers learn about computers and use computers in their own teaching.
13. Be able to evaluate and select computer hardware, software and courseware.
14. Be able to integrate computer-related learning strategies with other instructional procedures to create an effective total learning environment.
15. Be able to develop and teach high school computer literacy and computer programming courses.
16. Be familiar with the variety of computer-related vocations available to students and be able to advise them in selecting one of these vocations.
17. Use computers to involve students in a variety of problem-solving activities and to assist them in analyzing the nature of their own learning.

The Modern Mathematics Curriculum

There is somewhat of a controversy concerning the effectiveness of the so-called modern or "new" mathematics curriculum; therefore every mathematics teacher should be familiar with the differences in content, philosophy, techniques, and consequences between the previous mathematics curriculum and the modern curriculum. Teachers are frequently called upon by students, parents, and administrators to justify the mathematical content which they are teaching as well as the teaching methods which they are using. A good mathematics teacher should be able to:

1. Compare the content of the modern mathematics curriculum to the content of the curriculum which it replaced.
2. Evaluate the strengths and limitations of the "new" and "old" mathematics curricula.
3. Describe and evaluate the forces which set the scene for a new mathematics curriculum.
4. Identify the major mathematics curriculum development projects and discuss the curriculum produced by each one.
5. Compare recent methods of teaching mathematics to older methods and evaluate each method.
6. Know and evaluate the various claims for success and failure of the modern mathematics curricula.
7. Explain to parents what modern mathematics is and why it is being taught in schools.
8. Analyze and evaluate various secondary schools textbooks and select a textbook which is most appropriate for his or her students.
9. Identify ways in which the present mathematics curriculum could be improved.
10. Explain to students the value and applications of the mathematics which they are required to study in school.

Learning Theories

As we noted previously, a sound knowledge of mathematics is necessary for good teaching, but understanding of content is not sufficient. An outstanding teacher will know, understand, and apply various theories about how people learn mathematics in his or her teaching, and will evaluate the success of each application of a learning theory. Among the proficiencies appropriate for a mathematics teacher are:

1. Know and understand the major theories of learning and mental development such as those of Jerome Bruner, Jean Piaget, Benjamin Bloom, J. P. Guilford, B. F. Skinner, Z. P. Dienes, George Polya, and Robert Gagné.
2. Describe the nature of physical, intellectual, and emotional development of children and adolescents.
3. Describe the behavior of high school students both in classroom situations and away from school.
4. Know what research indicates about learning and apply research findings in teaching mathematics.
5. Analyze processes and structures in learning mathematics and synthesize methods to accommodate individual student learning styles.
6. Plan teaching and learning experiences to create a relevant learning en-

vironment which promotes questioning, exploration, problem solving,
and learning how to learn.

7. Select and prepare methods and teaching materials which are based
    upon professional knowledge of learning and which are appropriate for
    special teaching situations.

8. Evaluate procedures and curriculum materials used to teach mathematics.

9. Know and observe the stages of mental, physical, and attitudinal development in students and recognize individual differences among children which affect learning of mathematics.

10. Diagnose common learning disabilities and know what methods are
    available to assist in correcting these disabilities.

11. Recognize developmental and behavioral problems that require special
    assistance and know what help is available and how it can be obtained.

12. Read, evaluate, and apply significant studies in mathematics education
    which are relevant for improving teaching and learning.

13. Know and apply major theories of motivation to help children from
    differing social, economic, and ethnic backgrounds enjoy learning
    mathematics.

14. Know the philosophies held by educators such as Carl Rogers, Erik
    Erikson, and John Dewey and develop a personal philosophy of
    mathematics education.

Models for Teaching Mathematics

Most good teachers know a variety of teaching/learning strategies and select
effective strategies according to the characteristics of students in their classrooms. Research studies show that there is no one best way to teach. Exclusive
use of any single teaching model can become ineffective due to its inappropriateness for certain learning situations and for specific students. Among the instructional competencies that a mathematics teacher should develop are:

1. Knowing and understanding the elements of teaching/learning models
    such as expository teaching, using group activities, individualizing
    learning, discovery and inquiry approaches, spiral learning, problem-solving strategies, concept learning, using advance organizers, mathematics laboratories, games, and computer-based instruction.

2. Selecting models which are appropriate for teaching mathematical facts,
    skills, principles, or concepts.

3. Choosing appropriate models for each of the following mental activities—learning facts, understanding information, developing computational skills, applying knowledge, analyzing or synthesizing information, and evaluating information.

4. Preparing instructional strategies that permit students to learn by hearing, seeing and doing.

5. Planning activities for students which will permit them to create things,
    make things work, obtain recognition, and feel a sense of satisfaction,
    pride and accomplishment in their work.

6. Planning lessons which provide for pre-assessment of student readiness,
    mental and attitudinal activities, the use of a variety of methods and
    materials, student learning objectives, postassessment strategies and
    evaluation of the effectiveness of the lessons.

7. Evaluating the achievement of individual students and prescribing appropriate remedial and enrichment work for each person according to the evaluation.
8. Using techniques of audio and video recordings, micro-teaching, interaction analysis, pupil comments, student success, supervisor's evaluation and self evaluation to analyze and improve his or her teaching.
9. Evaluating the entire mathematics program from goals and objectives through procedures for evaluation.
10. Choosing appropriate and interesting individualized homework assignments.

Managing A Learning Environment

Many of the teacher competencies listed above pertain in general to providing and managing an appropriate learning environment, however there are several specific competencies which teachers need for effective classroom management:

1. The ability to select mathematics topics appropriate for different student ability levels and various grade levels.
2. An ability to plan lessons, units, and entire mathematics courses.
3. Know ways to create an attractive and interesting classroom by using posters, bulletin boards, models, and examples of student work.
4. Be able to obtain, use and evaluate commercially-produced learning resources such as books, magazines, films, models, games and audio tapes.
5. Use the community as a teaching and learning resource.
6. Help students develop self-confidence and take responsibility for their own learning.
7. Be able to ask good questions, listen to students' responses, and encourage students to discuss mathematics with each other.
8. Relate to, understand, and communicate with children of different ages, races, ethnic backgrounds and geographic origins.
9. Be aware of negative non-school influences on students and compensate for these influences in your teaching.
10. Be able to deal individually with student discipline problems in a sympathetic, professional manner.
11. Develop fair and equitable methods for evaluating students.

Personal and Professional Growth

There are hundreds of personal and professional characteristics which are usually possessed by outstanding mathematics teachers, many of which are enumerated above. Every teacher should be aware that education and professional preparation for mathematics teaching, while usually originating in a four- or five-year teacher preparation program in a college or university, are a continuing lifetime endeavor. Any teacher who views completion of a degree and certification program as sufficient and terminal preparation for teaching will become, in a few years, a poor or at best, a mediocre mathematics teacher. The following list contains activities in which every mathematics teacher should participate in order to maintain and improve his or her professional and personal ability to motivate and teach students interesting and useful topics in mathematics.

1. Ask relevant questions about mathematics and teaching mathematics and listen to, accept, and respond to questions and ideas from students, colleagues and laypeople.
2. Continue to study mathematics and teaching through college courses, inservice programs in secondary schools and informal reading activities.
3. Become a member of several mathematics and education professional organizations such as the National Council of Teachers of Mathematics, the School Science and Mathematics Association, the Mathematical Association of America and state and local teacher groups.
4. Take an active role in organizations which are concerned with improving teaching and learning conditions in schools and communities.
5. Observe other mathematics teachers, as well as teachers of other subjects; borrow and modify their successful teaching methods for your own classes.
6. Design and carry out small research programs to prepare and evaluate new methods and programs.
7. Share your best ideas and techniques with other teachers through speeches at professional meetings and articles in newsletters and journals.
8. Assist in the preservice and inservice professional development of other teachers.
9. Become active in community affairs and be concerned with improving the total environment of your students.
10. Work with individual parents and groups of parents of your students in order to learn more about each student and to impove your methods of teaching individual students.
11. Use your school principal and other administrators as resource people to help you become a better mathematics teacher.
12. Use appropriate techniques to evaluate and modify your philosophy of teaching and learning.
13. Become aware of decisions which are made at national, state, and local levels which may influence mathematics education and classroom teaching.
14. Plan and carry out activities to influence legislators and administrators in making decisions that affect mathematics education.
15. Be aware of and use community agencies and resources which can assist you in dealing more effectively with students.
16. Know the rights and responsibilities of teachers and students and various laws and regulations concerning schools, parents, teachers and students.
17. Evaluate your professional activities according to their consequences on you and your students.
18. Participate in extracurricular school activities.
19. Participate in curriculum development and evaluation activities.
20. Keep adequate records of your many professional activities and share them with colleagues and administrators as a means of self- and peer-evaluation.

The lengthy list of objectives in this section is somewhat idealistic and rather awesome. These competencies are presented as a goal toward which every mathematics teacher should aim, and it is expected that only the best teachers will attain a high level of proficiency in each of the competencies. A beginning teacher might be expected to be quite proficient in approximately one-fourth of the competencies, somewhat proficient in another one-half, and not very proficient in the remaining competencies. There also may be many skills and characteristics which good teachers possess that are not included in this list of objectives. Teaching is a very personalized endeavor, and each teacher must attempt to develop individual abilities according to his or her own strengths and weaknesses and the needs of his or her students.

Acquiring Mathematics Teaching Competencies

Preservice Education

Although there are several ways to obtain the necessary competencies to become a secondary school mathematics teacher, most teachers become certified through a four-year degree program in a college or university. Such programs usually are approved by a state department of education and a teaching certificate is issued by the state through the college. Many colleges and universities have alternative teacher education programs for people who have already earned a bachelors degree in mathematics or a related field and want to complete additional requirements for mathematics teacher certification. Most mathematics teaching certificates permit a teacher to teach mathematics in any public middle school, junior high school, or high school. Private schools are not bound by state certification regulations and they set their own requirements for the teachers they employ.

While teacher education and certification programs differ somewhat from state to state, and from college to college, most have many common requirements and most states recognize a teaching certificate from another state as a sufficient prerequisite for obtaining a license to teach in that state. There is no standard set of college course requirements; however a typical, average program would require mathematics teacher education students to take courses or demonstrate competencies in various fields and to demonstrate minimal teaching skills under the direction of an experienced secondary school mathematics teacher and a supervisor and/or advisor from the college.

One might expect a prospective mathematics teacher to become proficient in *mathematical content* by taking courses in college algebra and geometry, calculus and analytic geometry, probability and statistics, abstract and linear algebra, Euclidean and non-Euclidean geometry, the structure of mathematical systems and applied mathematics. Optional mathematics courses might include number theory, topology, differential equations, analysis and special topics in mathematics. Teacher education program requirements vary from a minimum of 18 semester hours of mathematics to as many as 42 hours.

While some *applications of mathematics* are learned in mathematics and methods of teaching courses, others are studied in courses in physics, chemistry, computer science, and other science courses. Some, but not all, teacher preparation programs require courses in computer programming and applications and a course or two in the *uses of computers in mathematics education*. A prospective mathematics teacher might expect to take from 12 to 24 semester hours of science and computer science courses.

13

Most college programs require from three to six courses in general education such as educational psychology, instructional technology, history and philosophy of education, school law, methods of educational testing and evaluation, and educational research methods. Usually mathematics education students will study one to three courses in specific methods of teaching mathematics. These courses will include topics in the *modern mathematics curriculum, learning theories, models for teaching mathematics,* and *personal and professional growth.*

Nearly all colleges and state certification agencies require teachers to have a broad liberal education in addition to specific competencies in a teaching field. Therefore, a prospective teacher might expect to study courses in English, history, philosophy, urban studies, Black studies, social work, economics, sociology, women's studies and other fields.

The amount of time spent learning and teaching in a secondary school, junior high school, or middle school (usually called practicum, internship, practice teaching, or student teaching) varies from several weeks to a year or more. Some colleges leave student teaching until all college courses have been completed, and others integrate student teaching and course studies. In some programs a student teacher will be assigned to an experienced mathematics teacher in a school and will see very little of his or her university supervisor. Other programs integrate some of their academic and professional courses with student teaching; college professors and staff conduct seminars, courses, and supervisory sessions in schools where groups of students are centered. There are many different approaches to teacher preparation and certification ranging from college-centered education, where nearly all learning experiences are conducted at the college or university, to school-centered education, where up to half of the program takes place in school and community sites. Both college-centered and school-centered approaches have their proponents and critics. Some people find that college-centered programs result in teachers with higher standards of scholarship and better knowledge of their subjects, and others find that school-centered programs develop teachers who are better able to cope with the many variables and problems found in a "real" school mathematics classroom.

Some states do issue teaching certificates to people who show exceptional potential for teaching, but who have not participated in a formal teacher preparation program. Few people obtain mathematics teaching certificates in this manner. Only people who have unique and extensive life experiences or professional background qualify for certification without completing an approved college or university program.

Inservice Education

Since some states require additional college or university coursework beyond the bachelors degree and initial certification, many teachers are required to continue their formal education through evening courses and summer programs. Another incentive for continuing studies is that most school systems provide salary increases to teachers for completion of blocks of additional college credits. Some school systems conduct teacher education programs either by themselves or in partnership with a college or university; these programs may be recognized by the state for continuing certification and by the school system for salary increases. Each state sets its own requirements for initial and continuing teacher certification. Each school system has its own policies regarding inservice studies for its teachers, which may be negotiated year by year with a teacher bargaining organization. Even within a single state, teacher education and certification programs may differ considerably from college to college, with minimum requirements specified by the state for all colleges. Since the control of teacher education and certification requirements may be shared within each state by professional organizations, state departments of education, local school districts, teacher bargaining organizations and colleges and universities, anyone who is preparing to become a teacher or who is seeking a teaching position should check local and state requirements through the various organizations which share in the control of standards.

Models for Educating Teachers

Before 1970 nearly all secondary school mathematics teachers prepared for teaching through what has come to be called an *experience-based teacher education model*. Since 1970 a number of teacher educators and several state departments of education have been developing, implementing, evaluating, and promoting what is called a *competency-based teacher education model*. In 1975 most teachers still were prepared for teaching through an experience-based model; however after 1975 the only new teacher education programs which were being approved by several states were competency-based programs. By the middle of the nineteen seventies, an increasing number of colleges and universities were offering competency-based teacher education programs; although the majority of teachers were still being prepared to teach in experience-based programs. By the mid-nineteen eighties enough teachers will have been educated in competency-based teacher education programs and will be teaching in schools so that the effects of such programs can be evaluated. At this time it is in no way certain that competency-based teacher education programs will be widely accepted throughout the educational system; however, after 1980, it is becoming more likely that people entering a college or university to prepare for teaching careers will be educated in a competency-based program.

Also some secondary schools (most schools had experience-based programs before 1975) have changed to competency-based *student* education programs. In fact, the number of competency-based secondary (and elementary) schools will likely increase during the nineteen eighties. There are other models for educating students and for preparing people to teach students; however, in the foreseeable future, it appears that a large majority of elementary school, middle school, junior high school, high school and college students will receive their education through either experience-based or competency-based programs. Therefore, it is important that teachers and prospective teachers be familiar with the components of these two models for education.

Experience-Based Education

What is meant by experience-based education? In general, an experience-based program for teacher education or for schools is based upon identifying and selecting appropriate experiences for students which have been shown to meet the goals and objectives of the education program for the majority of students. At times administrators and teachers select goals and objectives which may not be specifically stated, but which are implied through the textbook and the teaching/ learning activities that take place in the classroom. Experience-based learning is usually somewhat teacher-centered and textbook-oriented with approximately the same activities and experiences being provided for each student in the class for the same amount of time. Students are usually evaluated through activities such as tests and assignments which are given to the entire class at the same time, and everyone is expected to complete these activities at nearly the same time. Evaluation tends to be *norm referenced,* which means that students are evaluated and graded according to how well they did with respect to other students. Usually a student must go on to the next unit of the subject after the teacher has completed the previous unit, irrespective of how well he or she did on the test. Some teachers tend to design learning experiences directed toward the ''average student'', with the poorer and better students having to learn through the same experiences. However, many other teachers do design varied experiences for individual students, even though instruction in each subject unit is completed at the same time for all students.

Experience-based (traditional) education, as it is practiced today, evolved from procedures which were shown to be relatively effective for teaching groups of diverse students in fixed locations with limited resources. This model for teaching provides for efficient use of resources and is an effective way for many, but not all, people to learn in a compulsory, mass-education system. Even though experience-based education does tend to be teacher and group-centered, it can be implemented very effectively by a good teacher who provides for individual differences among students and uses a variety of well-tested teaching/learning strategies.

Competency-Based Education

Since experience-based education has been a relatively successful (albeit less than perfect) way to educate many people, what is the purpose of an alternative competency-based model for education; what is competency-based education; and what are the outcomes of competency-based education programs? Competency-based education was conceptualized for several reasons. Many students were unable to keep up in learning basic skills in traditional education programs and others were being held back by these same programs, which resulted in a movement to individualize instruction. In many classrooms in many schools, some students didn't seem to be learning much about anything except how to hate schools and teachers. The higher cost of education, and increased public awareness of some of the poor outcomes of education for many students, resulted in a call for accountability of schools and teachers for their students' successes and failures in the classroom. New concepts of school management and recent technological developments made new methods and resources for teaching and learning available to school personnel. Recent advances in the art and science of teaching and increased public awareness of the right of everyone to obtain a good education (especially a good compulsory education) provided additional reasons for trying a revised model for education. New public school curricula and new methods of teaching seemed to suggest the appropriateness of a new system for implementing these new developments in education. Also, some of the components which are found in competency-based programs were already being tried in experience-based programs.

In summary, competency-based education programs evolved from the need to correct deficiencies in traditional education, the appropriateness of preserving the best elements of the experience-based model, a desire to combine some of the new instructional methods into a single process, and the human drive to try something different.

Competency-based education programs were developed through attempts to explicitly state the objectives of learning in small chunks so that each student's success in meeting each learning objective could be evaluated through observable changes in his or her behavior. There may be as many definitions of competency-based education as there are practitioners of this model; however, most competency-based education programs at least attempt to maintain a common philosophy and some common procedures. For instance, students are expected to be involved in setting goals and objectives and to be responsible for managing their own learning. Students have a choice of alternative methods, experiences, and materials to use in meeting each learning objective. Students learn how to do things, and the amount of time spent on learning to do each thing is permitted to vary from student to student. Teachers try to assure that the evaluation procedures are consistent with the objectives, and students may be given alternative ways to demonstrate their competencies for each objective. Students take tests when they are ready and continue working on each set of objectives until they can demonstrate mastery. Students are evaluated according to their success in attaining a predetermined and explictly-stated level of competency (criterion level) which is called *criterion-referenced evaluation;* not according to how well they did with respect to other students, the norm-referenced method. Each student is encouraged to compete with himself or herself rather than with other students.

In their book *Competency-Based Teacher Education,* Houston and Howsam (the editors) list the following characteristics which should be present in a competency-based education program:

(1) specification of learner objectives in behavioral terms; (2) specification of the means for determining whether performance meets the indicated criterion levels; (3) provision for one or more modes of instruction pertinent to the objectives, through which the learning activities may take place; (4) public sharing of the objectives, criteria, means of assessment, and alternative activities; (5) assessment of the learning experience in terms of competency criteria; and (6) placement on the learner of the accountability for meeting the criteria. Other concepts and procedures—such as modularized packaging, the systems approach, educational technology, and guidance and management support—are employed as means in implementing the competency-based commitment. For the most part, these contributory concepts are related to individualization. (pp. 5-6)

Competency-based programs emphasize the importance of setting learning objectives, developing alternative ways for students to meet the objectives, and devising appropriate methods to determine whether students have attained mastery of each objective. Most competency-based programs identify five categories of learning objectives according to the criteria which will be used to assess student performance. (1) *Cognitive objectives* specify knowledge, understanding, skills, and general mental abilities that are to be demonstrated by students. (2) *Affective objectives* specify attitudes, beliefs, and values that students are expected to develop. (3) *Performance objectives* require students to demonstrate an ability to do something; that is to carry out some activity. Students are expected to apply their skills and knowledge in actually completing a task. (4) *Consequence objectives* relate to the effects and consequences of students' actions. The concern here is with how students use their skills and knowledge in performing tasks in a way which will have an appropriate influence upon other people and upon their environment. (5) *Exploratory objectives* are experience objectives. They specify activities which should be engaged in and which promise to promote significant learning, but which can't be specified or measured. Visiting an art gallery or a museum are examples of exploratory objectives. Something valuable is expected to happen there, but that something is impossible to specify and measure.

Most competency-based programs divide the subject to be learned into small units called *learning modules*. Each learning module usually contains at least five parts. (1) The *rationale* explains the importance of the module and gives reasons for learning the material contained in the unit. (2) The *learning objectives* of the module state those things which are to be learned and, in criterion-referenced terms, specify the level of mastery which will be required. (3) The *preassessment* specifies ways to measure the learner's readiness for the module and his or her previous mastery of the learning objectives of the module. (4) *Enabling activities* specify alternative materials, activities, and procedures for meeting the objectives of the module. (5) The *postassessment* specifies ways to measure whether the learner has met the objectives of the module. After the learner has met the objectives he or she moves on to another module. If the objectives have not been achieved, the learner proceeds with additional activities designed to assist him or her in achieving mastery.

Both competency-based and experience-based education programs have strengths and weaknesses. An intelligent, knowledgeable, perceptive and patient teacher will probably be able to use either model to promote learning. A teacher who has little regard for students and professional development will no doubt be an ineffective teacher regardless of the educational model used. Teaching and learning are very personal activities and there are few pat answers and guaranteed approaches to each. Every teacher must develop a repertoire of attitudes and behaviors that he or she can draw upon in various teaching/learning situations. The repertoire will be different for every teacher, although there will be many common elements, and no teacher will become competent automatically.

The complexity and difficulty of teaching is well stated in an article about accountability in education by Stephen S. Willoughby, which was published in the November, 1972 *Mathematics Teacher:*

> Unfortunately, education is . . .more difficult than the other professions. The human mind is undoubtedly the most remarkable and complex object on earth, and the processes by which it learns are, at best, imperfectly understood. Furthermore, many people perceive the educator as doing the entire job

of education, but everyone recognizes the fact that the physician and lawyer do only part of the job of keeping people healthy and out of legal trouble. Everybody is expected to know something about health and the law and to behave in a reasonably rational way regarding both, but education is thought by many people to be entirely the province of the schools. Both common sense and scientific studies tell us that the schools are responsible for only a small part of education, but the schools are still blamed or praised for the educational level of children in a community as though they were solely responsible. Thus, while the other professionals tend to treat the emergencies of individuals, the teachers are responsible for the total welfare of many individuals at the same time and seldom have the opportunity to try to diagnose and solve the problems of specific individuals one at a time. (p. 589)

Things To Do

1. Locate several references on competency-based education programs (some are listed in the **Selected Bibliography** at the end of this chapter) and read about this model for educating teachers and school children. Make a list of the distinguishing characteristics of both competency-based education and experience-based education. Compare the strengths and weaknesses of these two models for education.

2. Select several of the many teacher education objectives listed in this chapter and describe appropriate activities for a prospective teacher to carry out in order to attain each objective. How could a teacher demonstrate competency in meeting each objective?

3. Obtain catalogs from several colleges or universities which offer mathematics teacher education programs and compare their requirements for teaching mathematics. Determine whether each program is competency-based or experience-based. Are activities required of each program which will insure that a prospective mathematics teacher will attain many of the objectives in this chapter?

4. Check the list of objectives given near the beginning of this chapter, under the heading THE OBJECTIVES OF MATHEMATICS TEACHER EDUCATION, against what you feel are your own competencies. Design a future plan of courses and experiences that will help you attain the objectives which you think are very important for you as a mathematics teacher.

Selected Bibliography

Bell, Frederick H. "Building a Conceptual Computer." *The Mathematics Teacher* 65 (1972): 57-60.

Bell, Frederick H. "Why is Computer-Related Learning So Successful?" *Educational Technology* 14 (December, 1974): 15-18.

Cambridge Conference on School Mathematics. *Goals for School Mathematics*. Boston: Houghton Mifflin Company, 1963.

Commission on Preservice Education of Teachers. *Guidelines for the Prepara-*

tion of Teachers of Mathematics. Reston, Virginia: National Council of Teachers of Mathematics, 1973.

Committee on Computer Education. *Recommendations Regarding Computers in High School Education.* Washington, D.C.: Conference Board of the Mathematical Sciences, April, 1972.

Committee on the Undergraduate Program in Mathematics. *Recommendations on Course Content for the Training of Teachers of Mathemtics.* Berkeley, California: Mathematical Association of America, August, 1971.

Elfenbein, Iris M. *Performance-Based Teacher Education Programs: A Comparative Description.* Washington, D.C.: American Association of Colleges for Teacher Education, 1972.

Houston, W. Robert and Howsam, Robert B. (Editors) *Competency-Based Teacher Education.* Chicago: Science Research Associates, 1972.

PBTE Newsletters. Albany, New York: Multi-State Consortium on Performance-Based Teacher Education, June 1972 to September 1974.

Project on the Education of Secondary School Teachers of Science and Mathematics. *Guidelines and Standards for the Education of Secondary School Teachers of Science and Mathematics.* Washington, D.C.: American Association for the Advancement of Science, 1971.

Springer, George (Conference Director). *Report of the Conference on the K-12 Mathematics Curriculum, Snowmass, Colorado, June 21-June 24, 1973.* Washington, D.C.: Educational Resources Information Center, June, 1973.

Teacher Education Development Service. *Glossary of Terms, Competence-Based Teacher Education.* Albany, New York: State University of New York, 1974.

Willoughby, Stephen S. "Accountability Threat and Opportunity." *The Mathematics Teacher* 65 (1972): 589, 661-63.

Weber, Wilford A., Cooper, James M. and Houston, Robert W. *A Guide to Competency Based Teacher Education.* Westfield, Texas: Competency Based Instructional Systems, 1973.

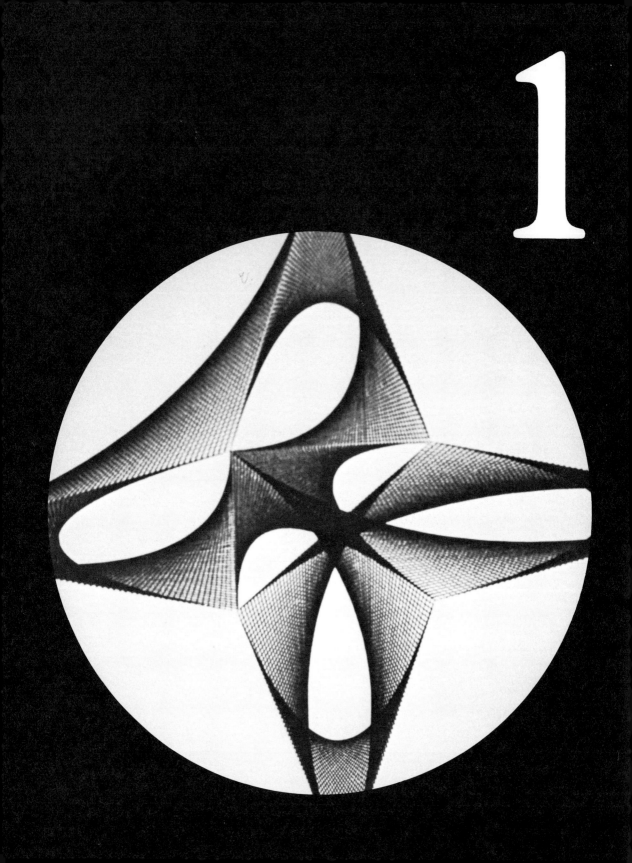

The Nature of
Mathematics

Philosophy of Mathematics

It has been said quite seriously that mathematicians, people who either discover
or invent mathematics, don't know if their mathematical objects exist and don't
know if the theorems they prove are true. To include such a pessimistic statement
about the nature of mathematics in a book about mathematics and mathematics
teaching is somewhat risky. I hope that the mathematics teacher or prospective
teacher will not be prompted to consider another professional field, such as history, where the state of affairs is more precise and definite. Or is it? Since
historical truths are viewed differently by various historians and it is not known
for sure that all the famous, and infamous, personalities in history actually did
exist, this discouraging indictment could be applied to historians as well as to
mathematicians.

Although mathematics has been called the queen of the sciences and is
reputed to be beyond reproach in its methods, validity, and logic, it does have
problems in its logical foundations, is only partially developed, and is continually changing in its methods and content. While mathematics may be much more
exact than the social sciences and somewhat more exact than the physical sciences, it is not exact in any absolute sense. For one who has been indoctrinated
in the absolute truth and perfection of mathematics, a study of mathematicians
and the history of mathematics can be both disheartening and enlightening. The
development of mathematics has been disorganized, repetitious, and downright
messy. Probably the second most important activity (the first is producing new
mathematics) of mathematicians is cleaning up (removing inconsistencies in and
completing development of) the mathematics created by their predecessors. Even
though the process of developing mathematics has been tumultuous, the final
products are quite good; mathematics contains few inconsistencies and logical
paradoxes. In spite of the fact that logical difficulties still exist in the foundations
of mathematics, especially in the mathematics of infinite sets, mathematics has
been an accurate and indispensable tool in social, economic, and technological
development.

The validity of the statement "mathematicians don't know if their creations exist'' is illustrated in the fact that mathematical systems are based upon definitions which assume the existence of mathematical entities. For instance, even such an intuitively appealing set as the set of *natural numbers* (the counting numbers) is defined as a set whose existence is stated in the following *postulates* (statements assumed to be *true*). These postulates were first formulated by the Italian logician Giuseppe Peano (1858-1932).

(a) 1 is a natural number.
(b) The successor of any natural number is a natural number.
(c) No two natural numbers have the same successor.
(d) 1 is not the successor of any natural number.
(e) Any property of 1, and also of the successor of every natural number having that property, is a property of all natural numbers.

The last of these assumptions is called the *principle of mathematical induction*. If the word successor means *add one,* then these five postulates define the natural numbers 1, 2, 3, · · · . However, since successor is an undefined term, if we decide that it will mean *divide by three,* then the postulates generate the set of numbers

$$1, \frac{1}{3}, \frac{1}{9}, \frac{1}{27}, \frac{1}{81}, \quad \cdot \cdot \cdot \quad .$$

So, even after defining the natural numbers, it appears that we don't know precisely what we are talking about.

Using Postulate (e) and assuming the addition and multiplication rules for natural numbers, the theorem

$$1 + 2 + 3 + \cdot \cdot \cdot + n = \frac{n}{2}(1 + n)$$

is true, because $1 = \frac{1}{2}(1 + 1)$.

Also, if it is assumed that

$$1 + 2 + 3 + \cdot \cdot \cdot + k = \frac{k}{2}(1 + k), \text{ then it follows that}$$

$$(1 + 2 + 3 + \cdot \cdot \cdot + k + (k + 1)) = \frac{k}{2}(1 + k) + (k + 1)$$

$$= k\left(\frac{k + 1}{2}\right) + 2\left(\frac{k + 1}{2}\right)$$

$$= \frac{k + 1}{2}(1 + (k + 1)).$$

It follows from Postulate (e) that the theorem is true. That is, the theorem is true if Postulate (e) is true. Since Postulate (e) was assumed to be true without proof, we don't really know that the theorem is true. What can be said is that logic and the procedures of mathematics imply the truth of the theorem, assuming Postulate (e) is true.

In summary, Peano defined the natural numbers, which may not exist, and we proved a theorem, which may not be true, about these numbers. While this may all seem like an argument by the Mad Hatter from *Alice in Wonderland,* it does illustrate important issues in the foundations of mathematics which are studied and debated by mathematicians, logicians, and philosophers. Lewis Carroll was, in fact, the mathematician Charles Dogson (1832-1898)—who was also somewhat of a philosopher.

The idea, at the beginning of this chapter, that mathematicians are people who either discover or invent mathematics illustrates a deep philosophical issue, dividing those mathematicians who are concerned with such issues into two schools of thought. One school believes that mathematics exists in nature, just as certain laws of physics exist in nature, and that mathematicians discover the elements and laws of mathematics. The other school feels that mathematics is more like a work of art, a painting that doesn't exist until the artist, in this case the mathematician, *creates* it. There are still others who believe, as did the German mathematician Leopold Kronecker (1823-1891), that ''God made the integers; all the rest is the work of man.''

Recently it has been shown, though it had long been suspected, that all traditional mathematics can be derived from the natural numbers. The Greek mathematician Pythagoras, who lived in the sixth century B.C., believed that not only mathematics, but everything else could be deduced from numbers. The Pythagoreans may have discovered the most serious obstacle to their dreams of *arithmetising* mathematics. It is thought that one of the Pythagoreans probably discovered the irrational numbers, called incommensurable numbers, none of which can be measured off using any rational unit, no matter how small. For example, the commensurable number 1.414 can be measured off using a small length of 0.001 unit; however there is no rational unit which can be used to measure off $\sqrt{2}$, a finding which greatly perplexed the Pythagoreans. The commensurable numbers, which can be represented as the quotient of two integers, are called *rationals* and the incommensurable numbers are called *irrationals.* The square root of 2 can be shown to be irrational; that is, not expressable as a quotient of integers. If $\sqrt{2}$ is rational, then $\frac{k}{m} = \sqrt{2}$ where k and m are *relatively prime* integers; that is $\frac{k}{m}$ is a fraction which has been reduced to lowest terms. Then

$$\frac{k^2}{m^2} = 2 \text{ and}$$

$$k^2 = 2m^2$$

Since $2m^2$ on the right of the equal sign is an even number, k^2 must also be an even number. If k^2 is an even number, then k is also an even number. Consequently, k^2 can be written as $4p^2$, and

$$4p^2 = 2m^2$$
$$2p^2 = m^2$$

By the reasoning used above, m^2 and m must be even numbers. Since both k and m are even numbers, k and m are *not* relatively prime. This contradicts the fact that k and m were selected to be relatively prime. Therefore the assumption that $\sqrt{2}$ is rational leads to a contradiction, which implies that $\sqrt{2}$ is irrational.

The method used in the above argument is called the indirect method of proof or proof by contradiction, which was avoided in the past by some famous mathematicians who considered it to be an illogical method. As an illustration of the possible logical difficulty of the indirect method of proof, suppose we had assumed that $\sqrt{2}$ is irrational, which it is, and were able to use valid statements of mathematics and logic to arrive at a contradiction of this assumption. What then? Should we assume that $\sqrt{2}$ is rational, which it is not? There are some *propositions* (possible theorems which may or may not be valid theorems) in mathematics that are *undecidable*. A proposition is undecidable if it can neither be proved nor disproved. This is not to say that no one has yet been clever enough to prove or disprove the proposition; rather it means that someone has proved the impossibility of either proving or disproving the proposition.

In 1921 the Polish mathematician Jan Lukasiewicz published a research paper on three-valued logic, and the American Emil Post prepared an article on general n-valued logical systems. In the two-valued logical system, the one with which most school mathematics students are familiar, statements are either true (T) or false (F). Using the calculus of propositions, several statements can be combined into a new statement whose truth or falsity depends upon the truth or falsity of the individual statements. For example, the two-valued truth table for the conjunction, **p and q**, of two statements p and q is shown below. This table has all possible truth values for p and q and the resulting truth values for the conjunction **p and q**.

p	q	p and q
T	T	T
T	F	F
F	T	F
F	F	F

If both p and q are true statements, then the statement **p and q** is true. If either p or q is false, then the statement **p and q** is false. While a two-valued logical system such as this is adequate for many formal mathematical systems, it is not satisfactory to illustrate the logic necessary for functioning in a world dominated by practical political decisions. Most alternative courses of action in politics, international affairs, economics, and social change do not have true or false values. Unfortunately the answer to most statements of the form *p is better than q* is undecidable. A truth table for all possible truth values of p and q and resulting truth values for the conjunction **p and q** is given below. In this three-valued logical system, the third value is undecidable (U).

p	q	p and q
T	T	T
T	F	F
F	T	F
F	F	F
T	U	U
U	T	U
F	U	F
U	F	F
U	U	U

By way of explanation of the situation where p is an undecidable statement and q is a false statement, **p and q** is a false statement; because either a true or false statement in conjunction with a false statement will result in a statement which is false.

While a two-valued logical system should be taught in school mathematics to help students deal with non-classroom applications of logic, it is equally important to illustrate and use a three-valued logical system for the same reason.

Structure of Mathematical Systems

Mathematics can be divided into four major areas—*higher arithmetic, algebra, geometry,* and *analysis.* The *queen of mathematics,* higher arithmetic (also called number theory) is the study of structure, relations, and operations in the set of integers. Higher arithmetic is probably the only area of mathematics whose issues form an unbroken sequence of study from earliest man to today's mathematicians. The Greek geometer Euclid, who lived around 300 B.C., proved that the number of primes is infinite. In the third century B.C. the Alexandrian Eratosthenes developed his well known sieve for removing the composite numbers from the set of natural numbers, leaving the primes. Excluding 1 which is called a *unit,* a *prime number* is one whose only factors are itself and 1. Those numbers having additional factors are *composite numbers.* Proving that there are an infinite number of primes is equivalent to demonstrating that there is no largest prime number p. The proof of this fact is another example of proof by contradiction. Suppose that there is a largest prime p; form the number N, which is a 1 plus the product of all the prime numbers.

$$N = 1 + (2 \cdot 3 \cdot 5 \cdot 7 \cdot 11 \cdot 13 \cdot 17 \cdot 19 \cdot \cdot \cdot p)$$

N is either prime or composite. If N is composite, it can be factored into primes. However, these primes could not be any of 2, 3, 5, $\cdot \cdot \cdot$, p; because none of these numbers are factors of N. N divided by each prime from 2 to p yields a remainder of 1; therefore if N is composite, one of its prime factors must be larger than p. If N is prime, and since N is larger than p, there must be a prime N larger than p. In either case the assumption that p is the largest prime leads to a contradiction; so there is no largest prime number.

Secondary school mathematics provides many other examples of procedures and theorems in the higher arithmetic of the integers as well as examples from algebra and geometry. One of the early and most important examples of analysis, the study of infinite processes, is the calculus of the Englishman Isaac Newton (1642-1727) and the German Gottfried Leibniz (1646-1716). Although mathematics can be separated into the four areas just mentioned, it can also be divided into the study of *discrete processes* (finite processes) and the study of *infinite processes*. Although most of the techniques of secondary school algebra and geometry deal with discrete processes and those of calculus with infinite processes, no branch of mathematics deals exclusively with either the finite or the infinite. Even in high school algebra infinite processes are used. For example the formula for the sum of an infinite geometric progression $S = \dfrac{a}{1-r}$, where a is the first term and r is the ratio in the progression, involves summing (finding the limit of) an infinite series.

Since the recent (within the previous 300 years) unification and modernization of mathematics, any attempt to partition mathematics into mutually exclusive branches, regardless of the scheme used, is doomed to failure. Mathematicians working in each of their many specialties use techniques and results from other special branches of mathematics. The applications of mathematics in engineering and sciences provide an additional hindrance to any attempt at subdividing mathematics. It is just not possible to fence in any single field of mathematics and to keep it pure from the rest of mathematics. The creation and validation of Albert Einstein's theories of special and general relativity would not have been possible without many of the eighteenth and nineteenth century developments in algebra, geometry and analysis. In addition to the unifying force from its applications, mathematical specialties are provided an additional cohesiveness by the underlying logical foundations in all of mathematics. In fact, logical foundations could be considered a fifth area to add to the four mathematical areas mentioned above.

One other unifying impetus in mathematics is provided by the common structure of all mathematical systems. Every mathematical system rests upon its own unique set of undefined terms and unproved *axioms*. In this book, as in some other books about mathematics, *axiom* and *postulate* will be used as synonyms for an accepted but unproved assumption in mathematics. Some books call the basic assumptions of geometry postulates and those of algebra axioms. Still others use axiom in reference to any basic assumption in mathematics, and postulates are those axioms which apply only to geometry.

It may appear to be useful to define all the terms in any subject area; in fact, the English language vocabulary, as defined in a dictionary, is an attempt to define every word. Although our intuition may cause us to be uneasy about undefined terms, their acceptance does avoid the circular reasoning which occurs when an attempt is made to define everything. In mathematics, circular reasoning is considered to be illogical reasoning; consequently mathematics must be cursed (or blessed according to your viewpoint) with undefined terms. Axioms, which are accepted (although unproven) statements about relationships among undefined and defined terms, provide a basis for drawing conclusions (proving theorems) about an hypothesized mathematical system. While it is possible to create an unbounded number of mathematical systems by randomly varying the set of undefined terms and axioms in each system, most unrestricted systems are not very useful. Mathematicians through the centuries have developed a set of rules for acceptable mathematical systems; these rules have been modified and probably will be modified again in the future. There are two kinds of rules or criteria for acceptable mathematical systems. One set of rules is based upon mathematical culture, which can be described less elegantly as mathematical fashion. The other set of rules is more stable, although subject to modification, because this set is grounded in logic.

Mathematical fashion is usually set by living mathematicians who are considered to be the best mathematicians by other mathematicians, and who are the most productive and influential mathematicians as measured by the quantity and quality of their publications and correspondences. Mathematical fashion is also determined in a more subtle way by national political leaders who, through allocation of resources, can provide or withhold support to individuals and fields of study. Napoleon's support of the French mathematician Gaspard Monge (1746-1818), who invented the descriptive geometry of engineering, positively directed and influenced the course of Monge's mathematical endeavors. The brilliant French mathematician Évariste Galois (1811-1832), whose discoveries revolutionized algebra, seemed to find *no* support for his mathematical work in the political aftermath of the French Revolution. Galois' passionate political views culminated in a senseless duel which extinguished his life at the age of 21 and the world was robbed of his ability to produce mathematics of the highest order. E. T. Bell's fascinating book, *Men of Mathematics,* provides more than a score of examples of both positive and negative influences of politics and politicians upon the work of mathematicians and the development of mathematics. Georg Cantor (1845-1918), who was born in Russia and emigrated to Germany as a boy, was profoundly and negatively influenced by other mathematicians of his period. Cantor's revolutionary invention, the theory of infinite sets, was attacked by other mathematicians. Chief among Cantor's detractors was Kronecker, who objected to the non-constructive nature of Cantor's methods and proofs. These attacks and other pressures on the hypersensitive Cantor led to a series of nervous collapses which culminated in Cantor's death in a mental hospital. After Cantor's death, his work came to be accepted as a major contribution to the foundations of mathematical analysis.

To return to the nature of non-constructive methods for which Cantor was so unmercifully criticized, a *non-constructive proof* may establish the existence of solutions for a certain class of equations but will not specify a method for finding those solutions. For example, the proof of the quadratic formula that

$$y = \frac{-b \pm \sqrt{b^2 - 4ac}}{2a} \text{ is the solution set of } y = ax^2 + bx + c \text{ is a}$$

constructive proof because it yields a procedure *(algorithm)* whereby the solu-

29

tion to any quadratic equation can be produced in a finite number of steps. There have been and still are (Kronecker being a prime example) many mathematicians who find it difficult to accept mathematical procedures for dealing with infinite processes and infinite sets.

Cantor's methods for defining and working with infinite sets are embodied in the proof of the theorem, which defies intuition, that the set of natural numbers contains precisely as many members as the set of perfect square numbers, which is a proper subset of the natural numbers. To prove that two finite sets have the same number of elements, we merely need to count the elements in each set. If our count is the same for both sets, then the sets have the same number of elements. If the counts differ, then the sets differ in their number of elements. This straightforward procedure for comparing finite sets is useless in comparing infinite sets, because it is impossible to complete the job of counting off the elements in an infinite set. The technique of attempting to set up a one-to-one correspondence between the elements of two infinite sets proves to be an appropriate procedure for comparing the sizes of infinite sets. If the elements of two infinite sets can be paired so that every element of one set is matched with exactly one element of the other set, and no elements are left over in either set, then the sets are said to have the same number of elements, or more precisely to have the same *cardinal number*. As was previously stated, the set of perfect square natural numbers has the same cardinal number as the set of natural numbers. A one-to-one correspondence between the elements of these two sets is shown by listing the perfect square numbers under the natural numbers which are paired with them.

$$1 \quad 2 \quad 3 \quad 4 \quad 5 \cdot \cdot \cdot n \cdot \cdot \cdot$$
$$1 \quad 4 \quad 9 \quad 16 \quad 25 \cdot \cdot \cdot n^2 \cdot \cdot \cdot$$

By pairing each natural number with its square, a one-to-one correspondence has been established between the elements of the two sets.

The cardinal number of any finite set is the number of elements in the set. The cardinal number of the set of natural numbers, or any set whose elements can be put in one-to-one correspondence with the natural numbers, is denoted by the symbol $\aleph_0$, called *aleph null,* where aleph is the first letter of the Hebrew alphabet and null is zero. As can be seen in the previous example, one property of every infinite set is that its elements can be put in one-to-one correspondence with the elements of some of its proper subsets. There are infinite sets larger than the set of natural numbers. The set of real numbers is one example of a set whose cardinal number is greater than $\aleph_0$. A method for generating larger and larger infinite sets is to generate all the subsets of an existing infinite set. The set of all distinct subsets of an infinite set will be a set whose cardinal number is larger than the original set.

Basing an abstract, deductive mathematical system upon undefined terms, which are empty symbols, and unprovable axioms has the advantage of being general and efficient. For instance, the abstract concept of a mathematical group is general enough to be useful in unifying a number of other concepts in each of number theory, algebra, geometry, and analysis. Many different mathematical structures have the four properties of a group in common:

(1) A *group* is a non-empty set of elements having a *binary operation* on its elements. The binary operation is a rule for combining two elements in the set to obtain an element of the set.
(2) There is an *identity element* in the set which combined with any element of the set yields that element.
(3) Each element of the set has an *inverse* which combines with that element to give the identity element.
(4) The binary operation is an associative operation.

Every mathematical system is made up of undefined terms, defined terms, axioms and theorems. If an abstract mathematical system is to be of maximum efficiency and usefulness, it should also be complete, independent, categorical and consistent.

A mathematical system is *complete* if it is possible to either prove or disprove every proposition about the undefined terms and axioms of the system. If some propositions are undecidable, the mathematical system is incomplete.

In the interest of efficiency, some mathematicians are concerned about the mutual independence of the postulates for a mathematical system. If it is possible in a mathematical system to prove an axiom from other axioms, then that system is *not* an independent mathematical system. An *independent* mathematical system is one in which no axiom is a logical consequence of other axioms. It is not extremely important that a mathematical system have a set of mutually independent axioms; however an independent system is more concise and is more logically appealing to the mathematician who is searching for perfection in his or her mathematics. Sometimes it is easier for students to learn mathematics if dependent axioms are included in a mathematical system to make it clearer and more understandable. This is especially true if proofs of certain theorems in an independent system are very difficult and tedious, or require mathematical techniques beyond the knowledge of high school students.

Before defining categoricalness in a mathematical system, it is useful to give a mathematical interpretation of the word *model*. A model of a mathematical system is an interpretation of the undefined terms of the system which converts the axioms of the system into *true* statements. A mathematical model can be either a physical interpretation of the undefined terms and axioms or it can be an interpretation in another mathematical system. A mathematical system is *categorical* if every pair of models for the system is *isomorphic;* that is, the elements of pairs of models are in one-to-one correspondence and all the relations among elements in each system are preserved between systems.

While completeness, independence, and categoricalness are not necessary for the validity of a mathematical system, consistency of the axioms is a critical property. A system is *consistent* if no theorem and its contradiction can both be proven from the system's axioms. The proof of two contradictory theorems could lead to a large set of other contradictory theorems which would greatly impair the validity and usefulness of the mathematical system. Since in most mathematical systems it is impossible to state all possible theorems, a less rigorous but more useful definition of consistency is that a system is consistent if a model of the system can be found which converts all the axioms into true statements.

One of the most frustrating dilemmas in mathematics results from the extreme difficulty (maybe even impossibility) of building an unrestricted mathematical system that is consistent. In 1931 Kurt Gödel proved that every mathematical system must be incomplete. Since being able to prove or disprove every proposition is not vital for the validity of a mathematical system, this discovery is not catastrophic for mathematical foundations. However it is somewhat disconcerting to find that one of Gödel's undecidable propositions in any system is that of the consistency of that mathematical system.

Omitting the complex and technical symbolism of Gödel's proof, the intuitive basis of the proof is similar to that which follows.

(1) If a proposition and its contradiction are both provable, then the proposition is inconsistent. Consequently, the mathematical system containing the proposition is inconsistent.

(2) If a proposition and its contradiction are both undecidable then the impossibility of either proving or disproving the proposition and its contradiction can be established. As a result, the consistency of the proposition and its contradiction is undecidable, and the consistency of the system containing the proposition is also undecidable.

(3) For the consistency of a mathematical system to be undecidable is *not* the same as for the system to be inconsistent. For a system's consistency to be undecidable means that it can *not* be determined if the system is consistent.

Gödel showed that every mathematical system has propositions which are undecidable. Using the argument in (1), (2), and (3) above, this establishes that the consistency of every system is undecidable.

Since the natural number system defined by Peano's postulates is regarded as the most nearly perfect mathematical system, it will be used to illustrate the procedure for generating undecidable propositions. Each of the properties of the natural numbers can be defined in a sentence containing a finite number of letters of the alphabet. These definitions can be ordered by assigning each one a distinct index number, which is a natural number, as follows. One is assigned to the property defined in the fewest number of letters, two to the property with the next fewest number of letters, and so forth. If several properties are defined using the same number of letters, they are indexed in alphabetical order. An index number is called *nice* if it does *not* have the property described in the definition it indexes. For example if 228 indexes the statement *An even number is one that can be divided into two sets having the same cardinal number,* then 228 is *not* nice; because it has the property of evenness which it defines. If 246 indexes *An odd number is one that can **not** be divided into two sets having the same cardinal number,* then 246 is nice. Consider the definition *A number is **nice** if it does **not** have the property described in the statement it indexes.* This definition describes a property of certain natural numbers, so it has an index number. Let n be this index number. Is the proposition n *is nice* true? If the answer is *yes*, then n cannot have the property that it indexes. Since n indexes the property of being nice, then *n* is not nice. But this contradicts our assumption that *n* is nice. Taking the opposite viewpoint, suppose the answer is *no*. Then *n* is *not* nice which means that it has the property which it indexes; but this is the property of being nice. Therefore *n* is nice, which contradicts our supposition that *n* is not nice. We have a paradox, because either of the two possible answers leads to a contradiction. Since the method of indirect proof led to the paradox, we can either eliminate that method of proof from mathematics or accept the theorem that the consistency of the natural number system is undecidable and that the natural number system is incomplete.

What is the purpose of pointing out these imperfections in the foundations of mathematics which have been presented to this point in Chapter 1? First, a well-informed mathematics teacher should know something about the nature and foundations of his or her subject, even though it is less than perfect. Throughout the history of mathematics, attempts to eliminate these and other imperfections in mathematics have caused mathematicians to discover (create?) many large volumes of very important and useful mathematics. The few remaining problems in the foundations of mathematics are of small consequence compared to the many and varied applications of mathematics. Second, a perceptive and compassionate mathematics teacher who knows what mathematics is, as well as what it is not, can exercise patience in helping his or her students understand those so-called *obvious* concepts which so perplexed some of the most brilliant mathematicians in history. If Kronecker couldn't accept infinite mathematical processes and Cantor's thoughts about infinite sets contributed to his nervous collapse, we should not expect that our students will understand and accept these and other mathematical ideas based solely upon our assurance that everything is all right. Students who question the validity of the indirect method of proof in geometry, and many will, may be showing a high level of mathematical intuition. While some politicians and teachers (Galois was surrounded by some of the worst examples of both) attempt to suppress heretical thinking, a good teacher will accept and even encourage students to question common mathematical *truths*.

Modern Approaches to Mathematics

Around 1960 a number of separate projects were underway to produce new school mathematics textbooks containing some of the recent developments in mathematics and modern approaches to mathematical problem-solving. Many of these new textbooks were completed and in use in schools by 1965, and by 1970 criticisms of the so-called *modern school mathematics* were being heard from a minority of mathematics teachers and mathematicians. By 1975 research and evaluation studies indicated that students using the new mathematics textbooks were doing about the same on tests of mathematical concepts as were those people who studied mathematics from the older texts containing classical mathematics. However, large-scale testing programs of arithmetic skills showed that students studying new mathematics were not doing as well in arithmetic as previous students who had studied traditional mathematics. It was also found that a large proportion of adults were unable to solve problems containing fractions and decimals. Even though this apparent decline in mathematical ability could not be directly attributed to the changes in school mathematics and methods of teaching mathematics, it did result in a wave of criticism of modern mathematics and a renewed emphasis on teaching basic arithmetic skills. More will be said in Chapter 2 about the development of the modern mathematics curriculum and its strengths and weaknesses.

Although modern secondary school mathematics textbooks do contain some of the mathematics developed within the previous two-hundred years, they do not present a completely accurate picture of the nature of modern mathematics. Many people, even some mathematics teachers, have mistakenly been led to believe that *old math* is the study of arithmetic; whereas *new math* is the study of sets. The purpose of the rest of this chapter is to describe the development and nature of modern mathematics from the viewpoint of professional mathematicians. After reading this description you will be better able to answer the question frequently asked of mathematics teachers—"What is modern mathematics?" The answer to this question, although it might be similar in some details, is not precisely the same as the answer to the question—"What is the nature of school mathematics?" This second question will be answered in Chapter 2. Although modern methods developed concurrently in the four major areas of mathematics, we will discuss each area—arithmetic, algebra, geometry, and analysis—separately. Since this division of mathematics corresponds to the division of mathematics in secondary school courses, this approach will better aid you in selecting topics from this chapter for discussion in your own classes. According to E. T. Bell in his book *The Development of Mathematics* (1945), a conventional division of mathematical history contains seven periods:

(1) From the earliest times to ancient Babylonia and Egypt, inclusive.
(2) The Greek contribution, about 600 B.C. to about A.D. 300, the best being in the fourth and third centuries B.C.
(3) The Oriental and Semitic peoples—Hindus, Chinese, Persians, Moslems, Jews, etc., partly before, partly after (2), and extending to (4).
(4) Europe during the Renaissance and the Reformation, roughly the fifteenth and sixteenth centuries.
(5) The seventeenth and eighteenth centuries.
(6) The nineteenth century.
(7) The twentieth century.

This division follows loosely the general development of Western civilization and its indebtedness to the Near East. Possibly (6), (7) are only one, although profoundly significant new trends became evident shortly after 1900. (p. 16)

Some mathematical historians consider the time before 1800 to be the *classical period* of mathematical history, while the period after 1800 is called the *modern period;* hence the term *modern mathematics.* The mathematics developed from 1637, the date of publication of the Frenchman René Descartes' analytic geometry, to 1800 can also be considered modern, since it provided the basis for a complete break with classical methods and set the stage for modern approaches to mathematical development. Although Descartes (1596-1650) is usually credited with the invention of analytic geometry, his French contemporary Pierre Fermat (1601-1665) independently, and at about the same time, also invented the subject.

Classical arithmetic began before history was recorded when humans first recognized that some sets contain more objects than do others and when primitive counting proceeded one, two, and many. The classical or traditional approach to arithmetic methods included the development of ingenious algorithms for computing products and quotients, the search for symmetries in certain numbers and sets of numbers, and the production of lists of numerical tables to assist in calculations. Since most of the *history of mathematics* books listed at the end of this chapter contain standard examples of these techniques which are now of only historical interest, only one example will be given here. The well-known sieve of Eratosthenes for separating the prime numbers from the composite numbers is mentioned on page 27. His scheme for sifting the primes is to start with 2 and list the natural numbers to any large number n. Then cross out every second number after 2, every third number after 3, every fifth number after 5, every seventh number after 7, and so forth, until every p^{th} number after the prime number p has been crossed out. Although the procedure is not extremely efficient, many numbers will be crossed out several times, its completion does result in a list of all prime numbers from 2 to n.

Two factors which severely retarded the development of arithmetic, as well as other areas of mathematics, were the lack of an efficient system of symbolism for arithmetic, and the tendency of useful discoveries to remain isolated in one country or to be lost for centuries, only to be discovered again in a different place. A symbol for zero, which is critical for an efficient place-value system of numeration, was probably invented by the Babylonians before 700 B.C., was discovered independently by the Mayas of Central America around 400 A.D., and is traditionally credited to the Hindus around 800 A.D. Before the fourth century B.C. the Babylonians accepted negative numbers as legitimate numbers and even used the correct rules of signs for multiplication problems in astronomy. The Babylonians' acceptance of negatives as part of the number system was lost for centuries following the demise of Babylonia. Even as late as 1600, some mathematicians refused to accept negative numbers as a legitimate part of the number system.

The German Carl Friedrich Gauss (1777-1855), who was the greatest pure mathematician in the history of the world, did his best work in number theory and contributed greatly to the development of this branch of mathematics. Although it is now popular to call arithmetic by the more sophisticated name number theory, Gauss was quite satisfied to make his greatest mathematical contributions in the subject he called arithmetic. Gauss is credited with saying that "mathematics is the queen of the sciences, and **arithmetic** the queen of mathematics." While some people may argue that Isaac Newton was a greater mathematician than Gauss, it is usually conceded by those who quantify greatness that Newton was the greatest scientist in history and Gauss the greatest mathematician. Gauss did mathematics for his own enjoyment and was little interested in publishing his results; consequently some of his most important findings were filed away among his papers only to be reproduced independently by mathematicians who came after him. He is sometimes credited with being less than encouraging to young mathematicians of his time. While this criticism is not entirely true, it may be due to his already having previously discovered, and filed among his papers, some of the mathematical creations which were submitted by other mathematicians for his approval. However Gauss did befriend, through his mathematical correspondence, a certain French mathematician known to him as Monsieur Leblanc, who it turned out was the brilliant woman Sophie Germain (1776-1831). Reflecting a rather liberal viewpoint for his time, Gauss was delighted when Monsieur Leblanc revealed her true identity, which she had secreted from him out of fear that a famous mathematician would think poorly of mathematics produced by a woman. The fact that there were very few recognized woman mathematicians until the twentieth century is due to the lowly intellectual roles societies usually assigned to women throughout history. This exclusion of women from mathematics no doubt resulted in the retardation of mathematical development.

One of the important problems of higher arithmetic is finding integer solutions of equations having more than one variable. Such equations, called indeterminate equations, and their integral solutions were first studied by the Alexandrian mathematician Diophantus who lived sometime between the birth of Christ and 250 A.D. The study of indeterminate equations, now called *diophantine analysis,* has occupied many great mathemticians, Gauss and Fermat being two of the greatest. Attempts by mathematicians to solve the well-known *Fermat's Last Theorem,* that there is no solution in natural numbers of the diophantine equation $x^n + y^n = z^n$ if n is a natural number greater than 2, led to a number of important developments in number theory. This theorem has not yet been proved or disproved; however Fermat, who had the habit of writing theorems and proofs in the margins of pages of his books, wrote in his copy of Bachet's *Diophantus* ''I have found a truly marvelous proof of this theorem but this margin is too narrow to contain it.'' The frustrations of many mathematicians in not being able to see Fermat's ''marvelous proof'' may be a good reason for requiring students not to write in the margins of their textbooks.

One branch of modern arithmetic which sprang from diophantine analysis is the theory of congruences that Gauss developed. Gauss defined two integers as being *congruent* with respect to a natural number *modulus n* if their difference is exactly divisible by n. For example, if $n = 3$, 1 and 121 are congruent modulo 3; because $121 - 1 = 120$ is exactly divisible by 3. This statement is written $1 \equiv 121 \pmod 3$. In fact, each integer in the set

$\{ \cdot \cdot \cdot \ -11, -8, -5, -2, 1, 4, 7, 10, \cdot \cdot \cdot \}$ is equivalent to 1 modulo 3.
Each of the integers
$\{ \cdot \cdot \cdot \ -10, -7, -4, -1, 2, 5, 8, 11, \cdot \cdot \cdot \}$ is equivalent to 2 modulo 3,
and each integer
$\{ \cdot \cdot \cdot \ -12, -9, -6, -3, 0, 3, 6, 9, \cdot \cdot \cdot \}$ is equivalent to 0 modulo 3.

These three infinite sets of integers can be represented by the symbols [0], [1], [2]. Equivalence modulo 3 has partitioned the set of integers into three subsets called *equivalence classes.* All the integers in [0] are considered to be equivalent, the integers in [1] are considered to be equivalent, and the integers in [2] are equivalent. To *partition* a set is to separate it into subsets so that each element of the set appears in one and only one subset. Every natural number n partitions the integers into n equivalence classes. It is possible to define operations on these equivalence classes and to study the algebraic properties of the set of equivalence classes with respect to these operations. In so doing, one is led from modern arithmetic into modern algebra. Gauss and others studied equations containing variables and equivalences modulo n. For instance, $x^2 + x \equiv [2] \pmod 3$ has the solution $x = [1]$, because

$[1]^2 + [1] = [2]$ if we define
$[1] \times [1] = [1 \times 1] = [1]$, and
$[1] + [1] = [1 + 1] = [2]$.

Equivalence classes of integers modulo n, together with addition and multiplication of equivalence classes, are important in modern algebra because they provide a way to indirectly study the properties of the infinite set of integers and operations on integers through finite sets of equivalence classes.

The efforts of mathematicians in developing a logical, postulational foundation for the real number system provide another example of the modern approach to numbers. We have seen that the natural numbers are a model characterizing Peano's postulates and modular arithmetic is a generalization of the arithmetic of the integers. Starting with the natural numbers as postulated by Peano, it is possible to define the integers, which contain the negative whole numbers as ordered pairs of natural numbers. Having produced the integers, the rational numbers can be defined as ordered pairs of integers. The ordered pair process does *not* provide a method for generating the real numbers. However, the reals can be defined as the set of numbers which are limits of certain infinite sequences, *Cauchy sequences,* named for the first great French mathematician, Augustin-Louis Cauchy (1789-1857), whose work belongs to the modern age of mathematics. The real numbers also can be defined as Dedekind cuts (partitions) of the rational numbers into two distinct infinite sets. Dedekind cuts were named for their developer, the German mathematician Richard Dedekind (1831-1916). Since both Cauchy and Dedekind's methods use infinite processes, our discussion of real numbers will lead us out of the realm of arithmetic and into analysis. Finally, the complex numbers can be defined as ordered pairs of reals. Surprisingly enough, we're still not finished. There are numbers even more general than the real numbers; that is, ordered n-tuples of real numbers which are called vectors. Now we are leaving arithmetic and venturing into algebra, geometry, and analysis.

Once again we see the difficulty of working exclusively in one area of mathematics. Although a comprehensive introduction to all of these sets of numbers would require a course or two in college mathematics, a brief intuitive discussion will be presented in the remainder of this section. In studying the history of mathematics, it is surprising to find that numbers were not axiomitized in an orderly chronological sequence proceeding from the natural numbers to the generalized n-dimensional vectors. Mathematicians had settled the issue of what are complex numbers, years before negative numbers were established upon a solid foundation.

Starting with the natural numbers which are defined on page 24, and addition and multiplication of natural numbers, the integers can be defined as ordered pairs (m, n) of natural numbers; or more precisely, they are defined as equivalence classes of ordered pairs. The integer 0 is defined as the set of all ordered pairs of natural numbers of the form (k, k); that is,

$$\{(1, 1), (2, 2), (3, 3), \cdots (k, k), \cdots \}.$$

The integer -5 is the set of pairs of the form $(m, m + 5)$, which is the set $\{(1, 6), (2, 7), (3, 8), \cdots (m, m + 5), \cdots \}$. The integer $+5$ is the set of natural number pairs of the form $(m + 5, m)$ which is $\{(6, 1), (7, 2), (8, 3), \cdots (m +5, m), \cdots \}$. Each pair in a set is considered to be equivalent to every other pair in that set. These last two examples illustrate that a negative integer is a set of equivalent pairs of natural numbers, the first number of each pair being smaller than the second number. The natural number pairs for positive integers have larger first elements. The symbolism can be reduced by representing an integer $\{ \cdots , (p, q), \cdots \}$ by the symbol $[p, q]$. Integers $[m, n]$ and $[p, q]$ are equivalent if $p + n = q + m$.

Using the condensed notation, addition of integers is defined by

$$[m, n] + [p, q] = [m + p, n + q] \text{ and subtraction by}$$
$$[m, n] - [p, q] = [m + q, n + p].$$
So, $[5, 2] + [6, 1] = [5 + 6, 2 + 1] = [11, 3]$
$\qquad [3] + [5] \quad = [8]$
and $[5, 2] - [6, 1] = [5 + 1, 2 + 6] = [6, 8]$
$\qquad [3] - [5] \quad = [-2].$

The natural numbers are *closed* under both addition and multiplication because the sum or product of two natural numbers is a natural number. Although the natural numbers are not closed under subtraction, the integers are. Neither natural numbers nor integers are closed under division. You might be interested in trying to use only addition and multiplication of natural numbers to define multiplication of integers.

The set of *rational numbers* can be defined as equivalence classes of ordered pairs of integers. The rational number $\frac{p}{q}$ where q is not zero is $\{ \cdots , (p, q), \cdots \}$, which is shortened to $[p, q]$. If p and q are relatively prime, the set $\{ \cdots , (p, q), \cdots \}$ contains all pairs of integers of the form $(\pm np, \pm nq)$ where n is any natural number. The rational $[p, q]$ is equivalent to $[r, s]$ if $ps = rq$. The sum of $\frac{p}{q}$ and $\frac{r}{s} = [p, q] + [r, s]$ is $[ps + qr, qs]$ and the difference is $[ps - qr, qs]$. The product $[p, q] \times [r, s] = [pr, qs]$ and the quotient $[p, q] \div [r, s] = [ps, qr]$. As is true for integers, rational numbers are closed under addition, subtraction, and multiplication. However, the rationals are also closed under division, provided we exclude division by zero.

As examples of the arithmetic of rational numbers, consider $\frac{2}{5} = [2, 5]$ and

$$\frac{-3}{7} = [-3, 7].$$

$$[2, 5] + [-3, 7] = [(2 \times 7) + (5 \times (-3)), 5 \times 7]$$
$$= [-1, 35]$$
$$= \frac{-1}{35}$$
$$[2, 5] \div [-3, 7] = [(2 \times 7), (5 \times (-3))]$$
$$= [14, -15]$$
$$= \frac{14}{-15}$$

The real numbers can *not* be defined as ordered pairs of rational numbers. One definition is that a real number is an equivalence class of infinite Cauchy sequences of rational numbers. A *Cauchy sequence* is a sequence whose terms become arbitrarily close together as the sequence progresses. A Cauchy sequence is similar to a convergent sequence; however there is a subtle difference between the two. A *convergent sequence* is one whose terms become arbitrarily close to some number, called the limit of the sequence, as the sequence progresses. The distinction between these two types of sequences can be seen in the following example.

Let R be the set of all rational numbers and S be the subset of rationals which are not integers. The sequence $\frac{1}{2}, \frac{2}{3}, \frac{3}{4}, \cdots, \frac{n}{n+1}, \cdots$ converges to the natural number one which belongs to R. This sequence is a convergent sequence in R, because it has a limit in R. It is also a Cauchy sequence in R. However, this sequence does not converge in S; although it is a Cauchy sequence in S. It fails to converge in S because the only candidate, one, for its limit is not an element of S. Our example supports the general theorem that every convergent sequence is Cauchy, but not every Cauchy sequence is convergent.

The sequence of rational numbers

$$\left(\frac{3}{2}\right)^2, \left(\frac{4}{3}\right)^3, \left(\frac{5}{4}\right)^4, \left(\frac{6}{5}\right)^5, \cdots, \left(\frac{n+1}{n}\right)^n, \cdots$$

can be shown to be a Cauchy sequence which does not have a limit in the set of rational numbers. The limit of this sequence is the irrational number e, which is the base for natural logarithms and is a common number in calculus.

Many different Cauchy sequences converge to the same limit. For example, the sequences $\frac{1}{2}, \frac{2}{3}, \frac{3}{4}, \cdots, \frac{n}{n+1}, \cdots$

$$\frac{2}{1}, \frac{3}{2}, \frac{4}{3}, \cdots, \frac{n+1}{n}, \cdots$$

$$\frac{1+k}{n}, \frac{2+k}{n}, \frac{3+k}{n}, \cdots, \frac{n+k}{n}, \cdots \text{(for } k \text{ a constant) all}$$

converge to the real number one. For any rational number r, it is possible to construct an infinite number of sequences converging to r; consequently the real number r is defined as the equivalence class containing all sequences which converge to r. If the Cauchy sequences in an equivalence class converge to *no* rational number, then an irrational number is represented by that equivalence class. Since infinite sequences can be added, subtracted, multiplied, and divided, these operations can be defined on Cauchy sequences, resulting in an arithmetic for real numbers so defined.

Using Cauchy sequences to define real numbers may appeal to mathematicians who like to work with infinite sequences. However, the method of Richard Dedekind, who defined the reals as partitions of the set of rational numbers, may be preferred by set theorists. Dedekind regarded the rational numbers as points on a number line. He observed that every rational number "cuts" the number line into two parts, with either the left or right part of the line containing the rational number producing the cut. For example $\frac{7}{8}$ cuts the number line into one set of rationals less than $\frac{7}{8}$ and another set greater than $\frac{7}{8}$. If $\frac{7}{8}$ is put into the lesser set, the greater set has no smallest rational. If $\frac{7}{8}$ is in the greater set, the lesser set has no largest rational. These two facts can be established by observing that if r is the largest rational in the lesser set and s the smallest in the greater set, then the rational number $\frac{r + s}{2}$ is in neither set, which contradicts the definition of a cut. Dedekind observed that some cuts on the number line result in lower sets with no largest rational number and upper sets with no smallest rational. These cuts produce holes in the number line, and Dedekind defined the irrational numbers as those numbers which fill up these holes. The result is a continuous number line. An example of a cut through a hole in the number line is the partition of the number line into two sets, one set containing all negative rationals and all positive rationals whose squares are less than 5. The upper set contains all the other rational numbers. Since the lower set contains no rational upper bound and the upper set contains no rational lower bound, this cut defines an irrational number which is called $\sqrt{5}$. By paying sufficient attention to the different results obtained when operating with positive and negative numbers, the four arithmetic operations can be defined for Dedekind cuts.

Addition of Dedekind cuts can be defined thus. Let r be the real number defined by the cut which divides the rationals into lower and upper sets R_1 and R_2, respectively. Let s be the real number defined by the cut which yields sets S_1 and S_2. Then $r + s$ is the cut whose lower set contains precisely those rational numbers $a + b$ where a belongs to R_1 and b belongs to R_2. For example, $-3 + 2$ is the cut whose lower set contains all rational sums $a + b$ where a is less than -3 and b is less than 2. You might find it interesting to make definitions for subtraction and multiplication of real numbers by using the Dedekind cut concept. However, take care not to overlook the facts that subtractions of negative numbers can result in positive numbers, and the product of two negative numbers is a positive number.

After the real numbers have been defined, complex numbers can be dispensed with rather quickly. A complex number is defined to be an ordered pair of real numbers; or more precisely, a number of the form $a + bi$ where a and b are real and $i = \sqrt{-1}$. Of course the arithmetic of complex numbers is nearly the same as the arithmetic of binomials of the form $a + bx$. The exception being that the square of the symbol $\sqrt{-1}$ is the real number -1. Never being satisfied with their inventions, mathematicians went beyond the complex numbers to hyper-complex numbers and vectors.

The Irish mathematician William Hamilton (1805-1865) regarded complex numbers as ordered pairs of reals. Then after many years of thought about or-dered quadruples of real numbers, Hamilton found that he could not define an arithmetic of quadruples satisfying the laws of physical space and which also satisfied the commutative law for multiplication. The arithmetic operations which he finally defined on quadruples of real numbers is known as *quaternion algebra*. Hamilton defined a hypercomplex number as a number $a + bi + cj + dk$ where a, b, c, and d are real numbers and i, j and k are symbols whose products are defined in the following multiplication table. It can be seen from the table that multiplication is not commutative. For instance $ij = k$ but $ji = -k$.

$\times$	1	i	j	k
1	1	i	j	k
i	i	-1	k	$-j$
j	j	$-k$	-1	i
k	k	j	$-i$	-1

Using the products in this table and appropriate simplifications, multiplication of quaternions is the same as multiplication of polynomials. For example (being careful not to commute i, j, and k)

$$(j + k)(1 + 2i + k) = j + 2ji + jk + k + 2ki + k^2$$
$$= j - 2k + i + k + 2j - 1$$
$$= -1 + i + 3j - k$$

However,

$$(1 + 2i + k)(j + k) = j + k + 2ij + 2ik + kj + k^2$$
$$= j + k + 2k - 2j - i - 1$$
$$= -1 - i - j + 3k$$

Vector algebra, vector geometry, and vector analysis use even more general numbers which are n-tuples of real numbers. Sets of real n-tuples have arith-metic operations defined upon them and have various algebraic structures such as group or ring structures. We can even generalize beyond n-tuples to $n \times m$ matrices which can be considered number forms; although a more useful in-terpretation is that of *transformations*. For example, the matrix $\begin{bmatrix} 2 & 1 \\ 3 & 7 \end{bmatrix}$ trans-forms the pair $\begin{bmatrix} x \\ y \end{bmatrix}$ into the new pair $\begin{bmatrix} 2x + 1y \\ 3x + 7y \end{bmatrix}$, according to the standard definition of matrix multiplication.

Ordered n-tuples have a geometric interpretation which is illustrated in two-dimensional space where pairs of numbers are used to represent points in a coor-dinate plane. In three-dimensional geometry, points are located using ordered triples of numbers. And, in n-dimensional geometry, which obviously can not be visualized, ordered n-tuples represent points in n-space.

Even though these examples have barely hinted at the vastness of modern number theory, and in spite of the fact that I frequently strayed from arithmetic to other mathematics fields, several very important concepts from modern arithmetic were discussed in this section. We will now leave arithmetic and take a brief look at modern algebra.

Modern Algebra

The primary distinction between the classical and modern approaches to algebra is found in the nature of the elements of algebra and the approach to stating and solving algebraic problems. Classical mathematicians regarded the elements of algebra as numbers or points in a plane; whereas modern algebraists consider algebra to be an abstract, deductive postulational system. The elements of modern algebra are not defined as numbers or points; but are abstractions which can be interpreted in a variety of ways consistent with the postulates of the system. The questions which were formulated by classical algebraists were stated in concrete terms and were answered by using methods which were appropriate for specified problems or sets of problems. However these methods were not necessarily useful for solving problems of a more general nature.

For instance, the four postulates of a mathematical group which are stated on page 31 are true in the set of integers; however many other mathematical and physical structures are also groups. Certain sets of transformations in geometry and physics have the four properties of a group. The modern mathematician would state and prove theorems of the form: *In a group, the truth of statement p implies the truth of statement q.* Then he or she would study mathematical and physical systems by looking for group structures. Any system, no matter where it is found (be it in electronics, chemistry or geometry), which can be shown to have the properties of a group, will also have all the characteristics that have been proved in the theorems about groups. However, the classical mathematician who stated theorems in the form *In the integers, the truth of statement p implies the truth of statement q* would not be able to use these theorems for any structure other than the integers.

Usually, modern mathematicians define very general mathematical structures. They prove theorems about these general structures, look for very specific mathematical or physical systems having such structures, and apply the theorems for general structures to the specific structures. In mathematical terminology, mathematicians look for *isomorphisms* (one-to-one, operation preserving correspondences) among mathematical and physical systems. This modern approach is a much more useful and efficient way to attack problems in mathematics and the sciences. Traditional algebra is sometimes called generalized arithmetic because its structure and theorems are based upon the real numbers.

Hypatia, who is credited as being the first woman mathematician in history, was influenced in her work in algebra by Diophantus who was the first mathematician to use a shorthand notation in place of the lengthy verbal arguments of algebra. Although little is known about the Alexandrian Hypatia's mathematical work, it is known that she was murdered by a fanatical mob as a consequence of her unpopular beliefs and ideals. From Hypatia's time until the sixteenth century, the development of algebra progressed slowly; however it had emerged as a discipline of its own by 1300, due to Moslem and Hindu influences. The sixteenth and seventeenth centuries, while being a productive period for algebra, mark the beginning of the end for classical algebra. These two centuries found many mathematicians hard at work producing algorithms for solving polynomials of certain degrees having special characteristics. The methods of the Italian mathematicians Niccolo Fontana (1500-1557), Girolamo Cardano (1501-1576), and Lodovico Ferrari (1522-1565) illustrate the traditional algebraic approach to finding ways of solving polynomials.

While it is a fact that the Italians developed the method for finding exact solutions for any cubic polynomial, it is less clear who should be given the credit for this algorithm. According to Edna Kramer (1970) in her book *The Nature and Growth of Modern Mathematics,* the situation may have been as follows:

> Around 1535 a mathematics contest was proposed by Antonio Mario Fior of Bologna. Each contestant was to deposit a certain stake with a notary, and whoever could solve the problems in a collection of thirty propounded by his opponent was to get the stakes, thirty days being allowed for the solution of the questions proposed. Fior had learned to solve a special type of cubic from his teacher, Scipione del Ferro (1465-1526). It is believed that Del Ferro may have obtained his method from Arab sources. Fior's opponent in the contest was a Venetian mathematics professor, Niccolo Fontana (1500-1557), commonly known as Tartaglia, a nickname meaning "stammerer" but nevertheless adopted by Fontana, whose impediment was due to an injury suffered during the French sack of Brescia, his native town. Tartaglia suspected that the questions would all be cubics, and so developed a formula for solving cubic equations. He answered all the questions put to him, and in return gave Fior questions on cubics of a type the latter could not handle. (pp. 96-97)

Ferrari, who was a pupil of Cardano, developed a formula for solving the general fourth-degree polynomial equation. His method involves the use of substitutions and simplifications to reduce the solution of the fourth-degree equation to that of solving a cubic equation, which can be solved using Tartaglia's method. The procedure used by Tartaglia in developing a formula for solving cubics also uses techniques whereby the problem is simplified to that of solving an equation of lower degree. He was able to transform the problem of solving a cubic into that of solving a quadratic equation.

Although many mathematicians, both before and after Ferrari, attempted unsuccessfully to develop formulas for solving general polynomials of degree five or greater, it was left to Lagrange, Ruffini, Able, and Galois to settle the issue once and for all. In 1770 the Frenchman Joseph-Louis Lagrange (1736-1813), while attempting a solution of the general fifth-degree equation, examined the techniques that his predecessors used in solving equations of lower degree to discover why they succeeded while his own efforts failed. He found that in each case the technique used to solve a general polynomial is to reduce the problem to that of solving an equation of lower degree. In applying this seemingly universal method to the general quintic, Lagrange obtained a sixth-degree equation. Although his methods hinted at the impossibility of finding general solutions to polynomials of degree higher than fourth, Lagrange went no further. It was left for Able and Galois to provide the coup de grâce to traditional algebra.

In the early 1800's both the Norwegian mathematician Niels Henrik Abel

(1802-1829) and the Italian physician Paolo Ruffini (1765-1822), independently, proved the impossibility of finding solutions for general polynomial equations of degree greater than four. The work of Abel inspired Galois to look for the conditions under which a polynomial equation is solvable by radicals. Fortunately for mathematics, he found these conditions in the theory of groups and fields before his short life ended at the age of 21. The exact statement of Galois' fundamental theorem of algebra is: "An equation is solvable by radicals if and only if its group, for the field of its quotients, is solvable." While the verification of this theorem is not extremely difficult, no attempt will be made to illustrate the proof here. The proof involves concepts from higher algebra which are usually studied in a second graduate level course in mathematics.

The formulas which have been developed to solve polynomial equations of degree less than five use the coefficients of the polynomial together with the four operations of arithmetic and radical signs. An equation which can be solved using a formula containing only the operations of arithmetic and radical signs is said to be *solvable by radicals*. Galois did *not* establish that no equation of degree greater than four can be solved. Rather, he did prove that there are no general formulas containing arithmetic operations and radicals by which every equation of degree n ($n > 4$) can be solved. It is possible to solve many (but not all) equations of degree greater than four using arithmetic operations, and some equations of higher degree can be solved using trigonometric functions from advanced mathematics. It is also possible to use computers to find approximate solutions, to any reasonable degree of precision, for polynomial equations which are not solvable by radicals.

While many mathematicians have been responsible for improving and adding to the fine work of algebraic pioneers such as Abel and Galois, one of the most notable is the outstanding woman mathematician Emmy Noether (1882-1935). Born in Germany, she grew up in the university town of Erlangen where she lectured occasionally at the University as a substitute for her father, Max Noether, when he was ill. She later became a professor at the University of Göttingen, where she stayed until her death except for a short period of mathematical research and lectures in the United States. Some of her major work was in the theory of *rings* and an important class of rings, called noetherian rings, is named for her. While her own contributions to mathematics are significant, she was also an inspiring teacher; consequently many of her ideas took shape in the works of her pupils.

In summary, traditional (classical) algebra is generalized arithmetic where specific algorithms are developed to solve certain problems. Modern algebra is a postulational system of mathematics having traditional algebra as one of the many specific models of its undefined terms, postulates, and theorems.

Modern Geometries

The difference between classical and modern approaches to geometry is illustrated by the general, unifying structure of modern geometries as compared to the more specific axioms and postulates of the geometry of Euclid's time. The discovery that logically consistent geometries which are mutually contradictory can be postulated and applied in mathematics and science marked the end of the classical, intuitive period of geometry. Nevertheless traditional plane geometry, which was developed by the Greeks before 300 B.C., is still taught, with minor changes in structure, in schools today. This geometry, which was consolidated and refined by Euclid of Alexandria about 300 B.C., has the basic structure of all modern mathematical systems. The postulational foundation of Greek geometry provides the first significant example of a systematic deductive approach in the history of mathematics.

The plane geometry found in the thirteen books of Euclid's "Elements" had a profound influence on the intellectual development of the human race. Euclid based his geometry upon five "common notions" called axioms and five postulates. Although most mathematicians no longer differentiate between axioms and postulates, the difference was quite clear to early Greek mathematicians. They regarded axioms as common notions which must be accepted due to the nature of the logic of human thought. Postulates were regarded as more specific notions which have their basis in geometrical ideas. According to Cornelius Lanczos (1970) in his book *Space Through The Ages,* the best estimate of Euclid's list of the axioms and postulates of plane geometry is:

Axioms or "common notions" · · · :
1. Things which are equal to the same thing, are equal to one another.
2. If equals be added to equals, the remainders are equal.
3. If equals be subtracted from equals, the remainders are equal.
4. Things which coincide with one another are equal to one another.
5. The whole is greater than the part.

Postulates. Let it be granted:
1. To draw a straight line from any point to any point.
2. To produce a finite straight line continuously in a straight line.
3. To describe a circle with any center and any distance.
4. That all right angles are equal to one another.
5. That, if a straight line falling on two straight lines makes the interior angles on the same side less than two right angles, the two straight lines, if produced indefinitely, meet on that side on which are the angles less than the two right angles. (p. 25)

The fifth postulate is known as the *parallel postulate* which is usually stated: on a plane, one and only one line can be drawn, through a point not on a given line, parallel to the given line.

Euclid's axioms and postulates are not perfect. In fact, Postulate 1 should be stated: To draw *one and only one* straight line from any point to any point. The incompleteness of Euclid's geometry is shown in the fact that it can neither be proved nor disproved, using his axioms and postulates, that *all* triangles are isosceles. It is said that Euclid did not find Postulate 5 to be intuitively appealing and that he attempted unsuccessfully to prove it from the axioms and other postulates. Whether or not Euclid was concerned about this postulate, mathematicians for the next 2000 years tried unsuccessfully to prove the parallel postulate before it was shown to be independent of the other postulates and axioms. Although many other mathematicians (most notable among them being Archimedes (287-212 B.C.) and Hipparchus (180-125 B.C.)) contributed to geometry, no major changes were made in the subject until the seventeenth century.

In the first half of the seventeenth century, Descartes and Fermat made the first break with classical geometry when they invented the analytic geometry of a rectangular coordinate system—thus combining geometry and algebra. Nearly 200 years later, Gauss generalized coordinate geometry by introducing coordinate axes which are not perpendicular. Gauss developed these general coordinate systems for surfaces in space to assist him in the practical problem of conducting a geodetic survey of the land of the German Hanovers.

The period of classical geometry gave way to the modern era with the discovery that Euclid's parallel postulate is independent of the remaining postulates and axioms. In the second half of the eighteenth century, the German mathematician J. H. Lambert (1728-1777) found that geometry on a sphere provides a model of a non-Euclidean geometry where no two lines are parallel. He also suggested that a novel kind of surface would be necessary to model a geometry where there are an infinite number of lines, through a point, which are parallel to a given line. Nothing came of his suggestion that such a surface might exist until the Italian Eugenio Beltrami (1835-1900) showed that the surface conjectured by Lambert is the surface of a pseudosphere. Although Lambert had the idea for non-Euclidean geometries, he did not pursue his work very far. It remained for the Russian Nicholas Lobachevski (1793-1856), the Hungarian János Bolyai (1802-1860), and the Germans Bernhard Riemann (1826-1866) and Carl Gauss, and others to develop the geometries for a modern age. Almost simultaneously, and independently, Bolyai and Lobachevski produced consistent geometries in which Euclid's first four postulates are satisfied but the fifth is contradicted. Both mathematicians developed geometries in which the sum of the angles of a triangle is less than 180° and in which there are an infinite number of lines, through a point not on a given line, parallel to the given line. The work of Bolyai, Lobachevski and Gauss led to an interesting controversy among mathematical historians to determine who first created non-Euclidean geometry and whose work influenced whom. Lanczos (1970) offers the following account:

> The father of the Hungarian mathematician János (Johannes) Bolyai (1802-1860) was Farkas (Wolfgangus) Bolyai (1775-1856), a friend of Gauss during his student days in Goettingen. He later became professor at a secondary college in Transsylvania (now Rumania) where he wrote an elementary textbook on mathematics · · · . While this book was in no way extraordinary, his son Johannes contributed an ''Appendix'' of extraordinary brilliance, in which he exposits the ''Science of Absolute Geometry'', as he calls it, that is the principles and theorems of non-Euclidean geometry, if we adopt the name coined by Gauss. (The expression ''absolute geometry'' refers to the fact that the first four postulates of Euclid, which Bolyai considered as unassailable, were satisfied.) The father communicated this work to Gauss who recognized the outstanding qualities of the young author but tempered his praise by the remark that these results had been known to him for many years. The young Bolyai was naturally hurt by these remarks and Gauss was often criticized for his lack of generosity toward a brilliant, though little-known colleague. One has to acknowledge, however, that Gauss was for many years intensively interested in the question of the parallel postulate and that he actually solved the problem years earlier by a method which was deeper and far more comprehensive than the synthetic geometrical approach pursued by Bolyai (and also Lobachevski). That he did not publish his researches in this field was motivated by his unwillingness to offend old-established prejudices, since Euclid was sacrosanct in his time. (pp. 64-65)

Riemann, whose contributions in many areas of mathematics were ahead of his time, also contributed to the development of modern geometry. He is credited with developing a non-Euclidean geometry where no two lines are parallel and the sum of the angles of a triangle is greater than 180°. Riemann is also partly responsible for the development of *n*-dimensional geometry and curvature quantities called *tensors*. *Tensor algebra* deals with operations (in algebra, geometry, and analysis) in finite dimensions, and *tensor calculus* deals with operations in arbitrarily small areas which give rise to differentiation.

Following the developments of these pioneers mentioned above, geometry continued its march toward increased generality, leading to postulational systems based upon properties which remain invariant under certain types of transformations. The German mathematician Felix Klein (1849-1925) advanced the idea that any geometry is the study of invariants associated with a particular group of transformations. Klein's transformations are akin to one-to-one mappings of a set *onto* itself, and the elements of the sets are objects (sets of points) in *n*-dimensional spaces. Certain mappings, such as translations and rotations, preserve shape and size; that is, shape and size are invariant under the mapping. Other mappings, such as the stretching and shrinking of geometric objects, preserve closeness and continuity but distort shape and size. Although there are many other mathematicians who have contributed to modern geometry and there are numerous types of concrete and abstract geometries having a number of important applications in engineering and the sciences, we will close our discussion of modern geometries with two examples. To better understand the general, deductive, postulational nature of modern geometry in the context of its models and applications, our illustrations will be of Riemann's geometry on the surface of a sphere and Lobachevski's geometry on the surface of a pseudosphere.

On a plane surface the shortest path between two points is a straight line; in general, the shortest path between two points on a curved surface will be a curved line. For example, the shortest path from the base to the tip of some peoples' noses is a convex curve; while the shortest path on other peoples' noses is a concave curve. Complicated surfaces, such as human bodies, have varying degrees of curvature in different areas; consequently the shortest paths between pairs of points will be lines with different curvatures. The shortest paths between pairs of points on surfaces in space are called *geodesics*. Geodesics on plane surfaces are straight lines and goedesics on spherical surfaces are arcs of great circles. On a sphere a *great circle* is a circle whose plane passes through the center of the sphere. For instance on the surface of the earth's oceans, the shortest shipping route between two small islands is along the arc of the great circle whose plane passes through both islands and the center of the earth.

If "straight line" is replaced by "geodesic" in Euclid's Postulates 1 and 2, the first four postulates will be true for geometry on a spherical surface. Postulate 5, the parallel postulate, is false on a spherical surface. In spherical geometry this postulate must be replaced by the postulate that *through a point not on a given geodesic there is no geodesic parallel to the given geodesic*. This is equivalent to saying that all great circles intersect each other; in fact, any two great circles intersect at two points. The spherical model of Riemann's non-Euclidean geometry is quite useful in navigation on the oceans of the earth, and we also see that a geometry contradictory to Euclid's geometry is not necessarily a flight of fancy. Figure 1.1 illustrates the fact that great circles always intersect. The great circle **NRST** intersects the great circle **WRET** in the two points **R** and **T**. The spherical triangle **NPR** shows that the sum of the angles of a triangle is greater than 180° in this non-Euclidean geometry. You can see that the plane of each great circle contains the sphere's center point.

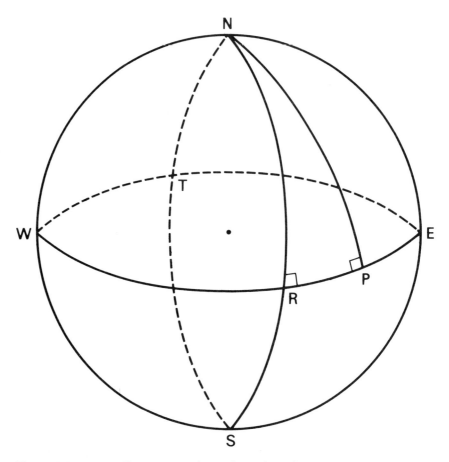

Figure 1.1.   Geometry on the surface of a sphere.

Lobachevski's non-Euclidean geometry can be obtained by replacing "straight line" with "geodesic" in Postulates 1 and 2, and by revising the fifth postulate so that *through a point not on a given geodesic there are an infinite number of geodesics which do not intersect the given geodesic*. Geometry on the surface of a pseudosphere provides the appropriate model for this set of postulates. A *pseudosphere* is formed by revolving a tractrix, shown in Figure 1.2, around the *x*-axis. The *tractrix* is a concave curve whose equations involve hyperbolic trigonometric functions.

A pseudosphere has a concave surface which makes it the concave analog of the sphere whose surface is convex. The pseudosphere, which extends infinitely

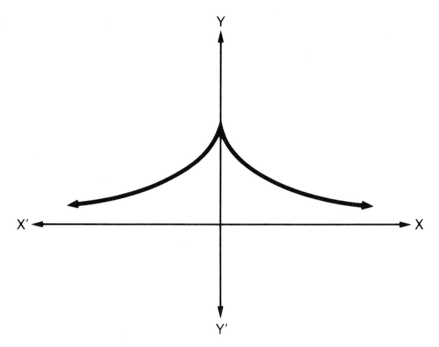

Figure 1.2.   A tractrix.

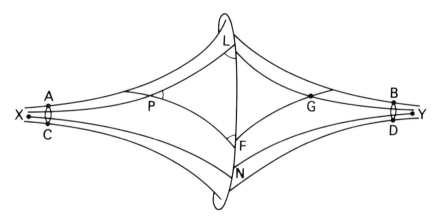

Figure 1.3.   Geometry on the surface of a pseudosphere.

in two opposite directions, is the double-trumpet shaped object shown in Figure 1.3. A plane passing through the center of the pseudosphere, from top to bottom, will cut the surface in lines **AB** and **CD**. These lines are geodesic lines (great tractrixes) which are analogous to great circles on a sphere. Although all great tractrixes are geodesics, there are other curves on the pseudosphere which are also geodesics. For example, the circle passing through points **L** and **F** is a geodesic. Through point **P**, the two geodesics **PFG** and **PLG** (neither of which are tractrixes) do not intersect the tractrix **XNY.** Thus we have an example of

49

two geodesics through a point not on a given geodesic being "parallel" to the given geodesic. The sum of the angles of the pseudospherical triangle **PFL** is less than 180°, contradicting the sum of the angles of a *plane* triangle being 180°.

As a closing remark to this section about modern geometry, Einstein's theories of relativity and much of modern physics would not have been possible without the work of the eighteenth and nineteenth century mathematicians who pioneered modern geometry.

Analysis

Analysis is the mathematical study of infinite processes, and since the fifth century B.C. mathematicians have been both interested in and disturbed by thoughts of the infinite. Zeno of Elea (490-430 B.C.) was perplexed by notions of the infinite and infinitesimal, and his four famous paradoxes about the "many" and the "movable" provided a basis for mathematical research from his time to the present. His first two paradoxes (*the Dichotomy* and *the Achilles*) came from the assumption that a line segment is infinitely divisible, and the last two (*the Arrow* and *the Stadium*) from the assumption that line segments are *not* infinitely divisible.

In the *Achilles* paradox, Zeno argued that Achilles could never win a race with a turtle which had a head start, because to do so he must first reach the turtle's starting point. By that time the turtle is at a new point ahead of its starting point, so Achilles is still behind. Then Achilles must get to the turtle's new position, but when he does, the turtle will be at a second new position. Achilles is still behind! Repeating this argument forever shows that Achilles will always be at some point behind the turtle, so he will never win a race. The problem here is that if Achilles must occupy an infinite number of points in a finite time period, he will never overtake the turtle. To resolve this paradox requires clarifying one's idea of infinity. The modern analysis of infinite sequences does resolve the paradox. If the turtle and Achilles run forever, their sequences of total distances covered, second by second, both will diverge to infinity. But, Achilles, being a faster runner, will have a sequence which diverges faster than the turtle's sequence. Consequently, at some finite time in the race the terms of Achilles' sequence will become and remain larger than the terms of the turtle's sequence, and Achilles will lead the race from that time until infinity. If the race lasts for a finite time which is long enough for Achilles' sequence to overtake the turtle's sequence, Achilles will win. The sequences could look like this, where the turtle has a 100-foot head start.

Elapsed time—	0	1	2	3	4	5
Distance traveled—Turtle —	100	100.5	101.0	101.5	102.0	102.5
Distance traveled— Achilles —	0	30	60	90	120	160

After four seconds, Achilles will be ahead and he will remain ahead to win the race.

In the *Arrow* paradox Zeno assumed that time is made up of infinitesimal instants, and at any instant of time a moving arrow is either at rest or it is not at rest. If an instant is indivisible, then the arrow is at rest, for if it were not the instant would be divisible. Therefore, since the arrow can not move at any single instant, it must always remain at rest.

The discovery of irrational numbers by the Pythagoreans is another example of a paradox discovered by ancient mathematicians which resulted from an incomplete understanding of the nature of the infinite. The discovery that the hypotenuse of a right triangle each of whose legs are one unit in length can not be measured by fractions, which at that time were the only acceptable numbers, was quite a shock to the Greek geometers. They were able to prove, as is shown on page 25, that the length of this hypotenuse is incommensurable. They also were able to use the Pythagorean theorem to produce many other incommensurable numbers (irrational numbers) as is illustrated in the right triangle spiral shown in Figure 1.4. It is believed that incommensurable numbers so disturbed the Pythagoreans that they kept their discovery secret from those outside their group.

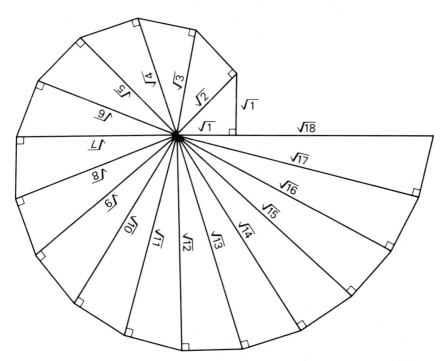

Figure 1.4.   A Pythagorean spiral for generating irrational numbers.

Georg Cantor's work, which is discussed briefly on page 29 and following pages, as well as the work of Kurt Gödel, which is referred to on page 32, did much to explain these and other paradoxes which could not be resolved previously, due to an incomplete understanding of the infinite. However, even with a better definition of the infinite, logical difficulties still existed in the foundations of infinite mathematics as is illustrated by the barber paradox formulated in 1902 by the English philosopher and mathematician Bertrand Russell (1872-1970). Russell hypothesized a certain town, having a male barber, where all the men were clean shaven. It was known that the town barber shaved all those men and only those men in town who did not shave themselves. Who shaved the barber? If the barber is one of the men who did not shave himself, then he was shaved by the barber—a paradox. If the barber shaved himself then he was not shaved by the barber—another paradox. This paradox is a special case of the more general paradox resulting from a consideration of the set of all sets. Is the set S of all sets a member of itself? If S is not a member of itself, then there must exist a set P which contains S as one of its elements and which is not in the set of all sets— still another paradox. The assumption that S is a member of itself results in a more obvious paradox. What would a set containing itself look like?

In 1908 Russell found a way to avoid these and other paradoxes. He proposed that certain restrictions should be placed upon the type of elements that are permitted to be members of certain *classes* of sets. He formulated a *theory of types* whereby individual elements are of type 0; classes of individuals are of type 1; classes of classes of individuals are of type 2; and so forth. Any class of type n is permitted to be an element of a class of type $n + 1$. However, classes of type $n + 1$, or of type k where k is greater than n, are *not* allowed to be members of classes of type n or less. As a result of this sequencing of sets into classes of higher and higher order, the set of all sets would not be allowed to be a member of itself, and the *set-of-all-sets paradox* could not exist. There is also a similar ordering of language types. Words referring to individuals are placed in level 0; statements about individuals are in level 1; statements about statements about individuals are in level 2; and so forth. If the levels are kept distinct from each other, no statement in a specific level can refer to itself; because every statement in a particular language level must refer to statements in a language level just beneath it. Without an ordering of language statements, the following paradox results. Consider the three statements *I always lie.*, *I always lie is a true statement.*, and *I always lie is a false statement.*. Without a language hierarchy, *I always lie.* is a paradox. If *I always lie.* is a true statement, then I don't always lie, because I just told the truth. If *I always lie.* is a false statement, then I don't always lie, which contradicts *I always lie.*. But, this paradox can not happen in a language system where a hierarchy of language levels has been formulated. *I always lie.* is a statement about individuals (consequently, it is in level 1). *I always lie is a true statement.* and *I always lie is a false statement.* are statements about statements about individuals (which are in level 2). Such statements about statements about individuals are excluded from arguments containing statements about individuals.

The preceding discussion of paradoxes, classes of classes, and language levels, while being concerned with infinite processes, is not analysis in the sense that mathematicians use the word today. Modern analysis is considered to have begun with the calculus of the great English mathematician Isaac Newton (1642-1727) and the German mathematician Gottfried Leibniz (1646-1716). Although a great controversy raged between English and German mathematicians during the lives of Newton and Leibniz—and for a century after their deaths—as to which man invented calculus, it is now known that they invented the subject independently and at nearly the same time. Since Leibniz employed a more efficient and useful notation for his version of calculus, those mathematicians who based their work in analysis upon the work of Leibniz produced better results.

The fact that little of consequence in analysis was produced by English mathematicians in the century following Newton's death is attributed, in part, to their insistence upon using Newton's notation for their work.

Even though good mathematicians rely upon intuition for important mathematical discoveries, they are still wary of results based solely upon intuition. Attempts to remove the foundations of infinite process from the intuitive realm, with its many paradoxes, to a firmer analytical foundation, marked the end of classical analysis and the beginning of modern analysis. For example, while the traditional intuitive notion of a *continuous curve* as one which doesn't have any breaks can be useful, it can also lead to difficulties. Intuitively speaking, a curve is continuous at a point if it isn't broken at that point. That this is not a sound definition for continuity at a point is seen from curves that are defined everywhere and are discontinuous at every point except one.

Consider the function defined as

$$y = f(x) = \left\{ \begin{array}{l} x \text{ if } x \text{ is irrational} \\ 0 \text{ if } x \text{ is rational} \end{array} \right\} \text{ on the interval } [-1, 1].$$

Intuition indicates that the graph of $y = f(x)$, represented in Figure 1.5, is everywhere discontinuous, but such is not the case. $y = f(x)$ is discontinuous for every

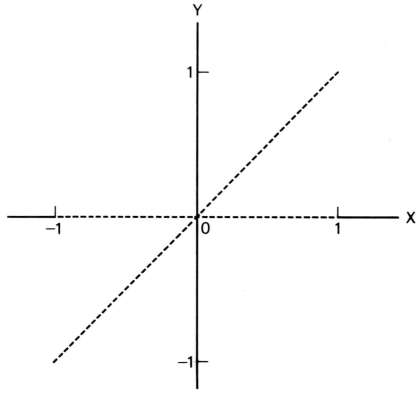

Figure 1.5. $\quad f(x) = \left\{ \begin{array}{l} x \text{ if } x \text{ is irrational} \\ 0 \text{ if } x \text{ is rational} \end{array} \right\}.$

value of x except $x = 0$. At $x = 0$ the function defies intuition and is continuous. To prove this we need a modern definition of *continuity at a point* which is: $y = f(x)$ is continuous at $x = a$ if the limit of $f(x)$, as x approaches a, exists and is equal to $f(a)$; that is,

$$\lim_{x \to a} f(x) = f(a).$$

The modern definition of the *limit of a function at a point* is: $\lim_{x \to a} f(x) = b$ if for every $\epsilon > 0$, no matter how small, there exists a $\delta > 0$ such that $|x - a| < \delta$ implies $|f(x) - b| < \epsilon$. The function whose graph is shown in Figure 1.5 has the limit 0 at the point $x = 0$, because for any $\epsilon > 0$, δ can be selected to be equal to ϵ and the inequalities in the limit definition will hold. Also the value of the function at $x = 0$ is 0 which is equal to the limit of the function as x approaches 0. So we have a function which is continuous at $x = 0$, and which can be shown to be discontinuous for every other value of x by using the definition of continuity at a point.

Leibniz and Newton's definitions of a definite integral put the notion of area on a sound general foundation, but their definitions did not cover every possible situation of area in mathematics. While Leibniz and Newton generalized and modernized the area concept, it was left to other mathematicians to further generalize their work and to put it on an even better mathematical foundation. After France's great modern analyst, Augustin-Louis Cauchy, put calculus on a sound logical basis, his definition of the definite integral as the limit of sums of rectangles was named the *Mengoli-Cauchy integral*, in honor of the pre-Newtonian Italian mathematician Pietro Mengoli (1626-1686) and Cauchy. Mengoli preceded Newton and Leibniz in systematically representing areas as limits of sums of rectangles. The Mengoli-Cauchy definition of a definite integral requires that the function to be integrated be continuous. In 1854 Riemann used upper and lower *Darboux sums* to generalize the Mengoli-Cauchy definition so that bounded functions with a finite number of discontinuities could be integrated. The Frenchman Gaston Darboux (1842-1917), for whom Darboux sums were named, showed that a bounded function over an interval will have a Riemann integral on the interval if and only if the set of discontinuities of the function on that interval is a set of measure zero. This means that a function having an infinite number of bounded discontinuities on an interval can be integrated using Riemann's definition of definite integral, provided the number of discontinuous points is no larger than $\aleph_0$, the infinity of the natural numbers. In 1902 the French mathematician Henri Lebesgue (1875-1941) further generalized, and revolutionized, the concepts of area and definite integral by defining what is now called the Lebesgue integral. Lebesgue's generalizations permit n-dimensional functions having huge infinities of discontinuities to be integrated. Lebesgue's methods can be used to integrate any function which could be integrated by previous methods; in addition, it can be used to integrate classes of functions which could not be integrated previously.

The Mengoli-Cauchy definition of the definite integral of $y = f(x)$ on the interval $[a, b]$, where $f(x)$ is continuous is

$$\int_b^a f(x)\, dx = \lim_{\Delta x_i \to 0} \sum_{i=1}^{n} f(x_i)\, \Delta x_i.$$

As shown in Figure 1.6, the Δx_i are intervals on the x-axis which cover the interval $[a, b]$, and the $f(x_i)$ are values of the function at points x_i in the intervals Δx_i.

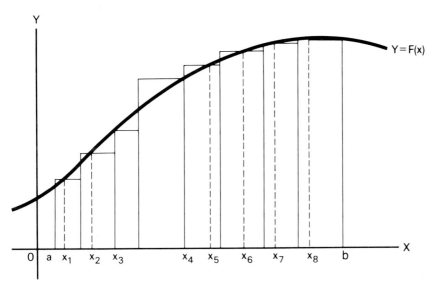

Figure 1.6.　　Approximating rectangles for the Mengoli-Cauchy integral.

The Riemann definition of the definite integral of $y = f(x)$ where $f(x)$ is bounded and has a finite number of discontinuities on the interval $[a, b]$ is defined as follows.

$$\int_b^a f(x)\, dx = \lim_{\Delta x_i \to 0} \sum_{i=1}^{n} L_i\, \Delta x_i$$ (where the Δx_i are small intervals partitioning the x-axis, and each L_i is a greatest *lower bound* of $f(x)$ in the interval Δx_i provided this limit is equal to the following limit.

$$\lim_{\Delta x_i \to 0} \sum_{i=1}^{n} U_i \Delta x_i,$$ where each U_i is a least *upper bound* of $f(x)$ in the interval Δx_i. This first limit is called a lower Darboux sum and the second an upper Darboux sum.

Lebesgue's definition of a definite integral is based upon the concept of the measure (size) of a set of points. The set of points in question may be the points on a line segment, a portion of a plane or three-dimensional space, or even a piece of n-dimensional space. Our intuition tells us that *measure* should be defined so that the measure of the line segment from the point zero to the point two will turn out to be 2 units. The measure of a square whose edge is 2 units should be 4 square units, of a cube of edge 2 units should be 8 cubic units, and of a hypercube of edge 2 units should be 16 hypercubic units. We also want such general ideas as the following to hold in our definition of measure:

1. The measure of any set is either zero or some positive real number.
2. The measure of an empty set is zero.
3. The measure of a set is either greater than or equal to the measure of any one of its subsets.
4. The measure of the union of non-overlapping sets is the sum of the measures of the individual sets.

In general the measure of a set containing a single point is zero, as is the measure of a set containing a finite or countably infinite number of points. This means that the measure of the countably infinite set of points represented by the rational numbers between 0 and 2 on the number line is zero. Therefore, since the measure of the entire set of points from 0 to 2 is two, the measure of the irrational points from 0 to 2 must be two.

Rather than defining the Lebesgue integral, which is not difficult but does require many pages of preliminary definitions, postulates, and theorems, we will look at an example of a function which has an uncountable number of discontinuities and is neither Mengoli-Cauchy integrable nor Riemann integrable. The function $f(x)$ shown in Figure 1.7 is defined as $y = f(x) = \begin{cases} 2 \text{ if } x \text{ is irrational} \\ 0 \text{ if } x \text{ is rational} \end{cases}$
and is everywhere discontinuous on the interval [0, 3].

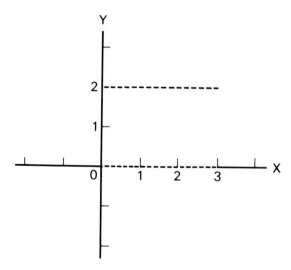

Figure 1.7. $f(x) = \begin{cases} 2 \text{ if } x \text{ is irrational} \\ 0 \text{ if } x \text{ is rational} \end{cases}$ on the interval [0, 3].

This function can not be Mengoli-Cauchy integrated on this interval because if all the x_i in each Δx_i interval are selected from the irrational numbers, all the $f(x_i)$ will be 2 and the Mengoli-Cauchy limit will be 6. If all the x_i are selected from the rational numbers, the limit will be 0. Using Riemann's definition, the lower Darboux sum will be 0 and the upper Darboux sum will be 6; so this function also does not have a Riemann integral. Lebesgue's method for integrating this function follows. Since the range of this function contains only two distinct values, 0 and 2, Lebesgue would have found the measure of all the x-values whose corresponding y-value is 2 and the measure of all those x-values whose corresponding y-value is 0. The first measure is the measure of the irrationals from 0 to 3 and that measure is 3. The second is the measure of the rationals from 0 to 3 and that measure is 0. The Lebesgue integral is the sum of the products of each y-value times the measure of the set of x's whose $f(x)$ value is that y-value. In this case the Lebesgue integral is

$$\int_L = (2 \times 3) + (0 \times 0) = 6.$$

The following example illustrates how a simple Riemann integrable function can be Lebesgue integrated.

As our intuition, which is correct in this instance, tells us, the Riemann integral of $y = f(x) = x$ on the interval $[0, 1]$ has the value $1/2$, which is the area of the triangle shown in Figure 1.8.

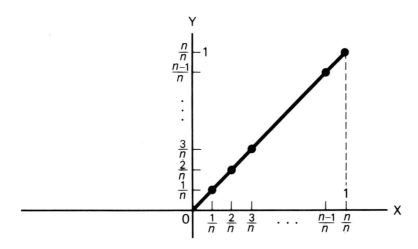

Figure 1.8. $f(x) = x$ on the interval $[0, 1]$.

For each value of x in the interval $[0, 1]$, the value of y is equal to x, and each distinct y-value has a distinct x-value yielding that y-value. Since the measure of a single point is zero, we might be tempted to reason that each of the infinite y-values should be multiplied by zero with the resulting infinite sum being zero. Although such reasoning may be valid for a finite set of points, it is not appropriate to use in considering an infinite sum. A better approach is to divide the x-axis into n equal intervals each one of measure $\frac{1}{n}$. The y-values for the

x-interval from 0 to $\dfrac{1}{n}$ range from 0 to $\dfrac{1}{n}$, and their average is $\dfrac{1}{2}\left(0 + \dfrac{1}{n}\right)$ $= \dfrac{1}{2n}$. In the next x-interval $\dfrac{1}{n}$ to $\dfrac{2}{n}$, the y-values range from $\dfrac{1}{n}$ to $\dfrac{2}{n}$ and average $\dfrac{3}{2n}$. In the next interval the y-values average $\dfrac{5}{2n}$, and so forth for successive intervals, until the nth interval has y-values averaging $\dfrac{2n-1}{2n}$. Since the measure of each x-interval is $\dfrac{1}{n}$, the Lebesgue integral for $y = x$ on $[0, 1]$ is

$$\left(\frac{1}{2n} + \frac{3}{2n} + \frac{5}{2n} + \cdots + \frac{2n-1}{2n}\right)\left(\frac{1}{n}\right) \text{ which equals}$$

$\dfrac{1}{2n^2}(1 + 3 + 5 + \cdots + (2n - 1))$. However the formula for the sum of an arithmetic progression shows that

$$(1 + 3 + 5 + \cdots + (2n - 1)) = \frac{n}{2}(1 + (2n - 1))$$

$$= n^2$$

Therefore the Lebesgue integral is $\dfrac{n^2}{2n^2} = \dfrac{1}{2}$, just as we know it should be.

Even as n is made to approach infinity, this Lebesgue sum will still be $\dfrac{1}{2}$.

The methods of integration developed by Riemann and Lebesgue, as well as methods for differentiating functions, form the basis of present-day analysis. Even though our examples have been from the calculus of two dimensions, modern analysts are also concerned with problems of limits, continuity, differentiation, and integration of functions in general n-dimensional spaces.

In this chapter I have illustrated some of the concepts and methods of classical mathematics as well as those of modern mathematics. It would be nice to conclude this chapter with a sentence, or even a paragraph, defining modern mathematics. Unfortunately the nature of modern mathematics is so multi-faceted, that no brief definition can do more than suggest what it is. Those ideas which you have assimilated from this chapter will serve as a good first approximation to the nature of modern mathematics. If you would like to know a great deal more about this topic and about the history of modern as well as classical mathematics, I suggest that you read sections from the books listed on pages 60-64, many of which are fine references on the subject.

Things To Do

1. Construct a proof showing that $\sqrt{5}$ is irrational which a high school algebra student would be able to understand. Consider how you could

prove that $\sqrt{n}$ for any natural number n which is not a perfect square is an irrational number.

2. Devise a proof which could be understood by junior high school students showing that the sum of any two even natural numbers is even and that the sum of any two odd natural numbers is even.

3. Construct a truth table for the disjunction *p or q* of two statements *p* and *q* in a two-valued logical system. Construct the *p or q* truth table for a three-valued logical system.

4. Find the limit of the sum of this series.

$$\frac{1}{3} + \frac{1}{6} + \frac{1}{12} + \frac{1}{24} + \cdots . \text{ Is the limit a rational number?}$$

5. Write an accurate, historical answer to the question "What is the difference between an axiom and a postulate?" which is frequently asked by mathematics students.

6. Explain how mathematical systems can be of any practical use, since they are based upon undefined terms and axioms.

7. Write a paragraph explaining and illustrating the difference between a *constructive proof* and a *nonconstructive proof*. Give an example of a constructive proof and an example of a nonconstructive proof in plane geometry. Be careful; constructing auxiliary lines in a geometric figure doesn't necessarily mean that the proof of a theorem about that figure is constructive.

8. Prove that the set of positive rational numbers has the same cardinal number as the set of even natural numbers.

9. Explain the term *mathematical model* in a manner that could be understood by secondary school students.

10. With regard to mathematical systems, write definitions and find illustrations for the concepts of *completeness, independence, categoricalness,* and *consistency.*

11. Prepare an explanation of *isomorphism* and tell why this is such an important idea in modern mathematics.

12. Use the definition of an *integer* as an ordered pair of natural numbers and define multiplication of integers using only addition and multiplication of natural numbers.

13. Use Dedekind's definition of a real number as a *cut* in the rational numbers to define subtraction in the set of real numbers.

14. List the equivalence classes of integers modulo 4 and the equivalence classes of integers modulo 5. Write addition and multiplication tables for these two sets. Is either set a *group* under addition? Under multiplication? Is either set a *ring? A field?*

15. Find two quaternions (quadruples of real numbers), neither of which is zero, whose product as defined by Hamilton is zero.

59

16. Decide if the product of two 2×2 matrices can be $\begin{pmatrix} 0 & 0 \\ 0 & 0 \end{pmatrix}$ if neither matrix is $\begin{pmatrix} 0 & 0 \\ 0 & 0 \end{pmatrix}$.

17. Find an old algebra book or theory of equations book which has Cardan's (Tartaglia's?) method for solving a cubic and use it to solve $3x^3 - 11x^2 + 5x - 1 = 0$.

18. Discuss the nature of geometry on a hemisphere, a hemi-pseudosphere, and an ellipsoid.

19. Develop a rational, mathematical argument that resolves *Zeno's Arrow paradox*.

20. Produce an example of a function which is defined on all the real numbers and which is everywhere discontinuous.

21. Determine whether the function $f(x) = \left\{ \begin{array}{l} x \text{ if } x \text{ is an integer} \\ 1 \text{ if } x \text{ is not an integer} \end{array} \right\}$ is continuous for integer values of x. Does $f(x)$ have a limit as x approaches each integer?

22. Show that $f(x) = \left\{ \begin{array}{l} x \text{ if } x \text{ is rational} \\ 1 \text{ if } x \text{ is irrational} \end{array} \right\}$ is neither Mengoli-Cauchy nor Riemann integrable, but that it is Lebesgue integrable. What is its Lebesgue integral on the interval $[0, 2]$?

23. Write a several page answer to the following question (with the blanks replaced by either arithmetic, algebra, or geometry) which would be suitable to give to the parents of your mathematics students or future students. Question: What is modern _____, and why is it being taught in school now instead of traditional _____?

24. Select a famous mathematician in history (either someone mentioned in this chapter or another person of your choice) and read about his or her life and mathematical works. The books listed in the following bibliography are useful resources for this activity.

25. Select one of the books listed in the bibliography at the end of this chapter, and set up a regular reading program so that you will have completed it within the next two months.

26. Construct a list of some notable mathematicians who are alive today and gather information about their lives and their research in mathematics.

Selected Bibliography

Books

Bell, E. T. *The Development of Mathematics*. New York: McGraw-Hill Book Company, 1945.

This interesting and informative book contains a broad account of the general development of the main concepts and methods in mathematics throughout the past 6000 years. It is a narrative of decisive epochs in mathematical history, including the nationalities, names, and dates of many mathematicians who made major contributions to mathematical progress. The influences of earlier periods of mathematical development upon later periods are traced and illustrated, and influences of individual mathematicians upon each other are discussed. Important applications of mathematics in the other sciences are presented, and mathematical discoveries are shown to have had a major influence upon scientific discoveries. This book is a valuable general reference on the history and development of mathematics.

————. *Mathematics: Queen and Servant of Science*. New York: McGraw-Hill Book Company, 1951.

Another history and nature of mathematics book containing some interesting mathematics, this work emphasizes the influence and application of mathematics in the sciences. According to the paper jacket of the book:

> Here is the absorbing story of the developments in pure and applied mathematics from the geometry of Euclid 2200 years ago to the most recent developments in mathematical physics.

and

> ...(This book) contains a wealth of fascinating information on the personalities and philosophies of the great mathematicians, and perceptive resumés of their specific contributions to the moving force of this great science.

This book is another good reference for mathematics teachers; however, some of the content is found in E. T. Bell's other books.

————. *Men of Mathematics*. New York: Simon and Schuster, 1965.

This book contains brief, yet fascinating, biographies of thirty-five mathematicians from Zeno to Cantor. The biographies are arranged in chronological order and are relatively independent of each other; therefore chapters can be selected and read at will without losing the historical continuity. Among the mathematicians whose lives and works are discussed are Descartes, Newton, Gauss, Galois, and Riemann. While this book is extremely interesting, the author liberally included his own early twentieth century prejudices among the historical narratives, which tends to reduce the book's credibility for a more liberal, present-day reader. Nevertheless, this is an excellent history of mathematicians book, with early editions containing portraits of many mathematicians.

Benacerraf, Paul and Putnam, Hillary (Editors). *Philosophy of Mathematics: Selected Readings*. New Jersey: Prentice-Hall, 1964.

A compilation of mathematical philosophy, here is a collection of articles and excerpts from books which were written by well-known philosophers and mathematicians. The articles in the book are grouped by subject into four sections: *foundations of mathematics, the existence of mathematical objects, mathematical truth,* and *Wittgenstein on mathematics.*

Birkhoff, Garrett and MacLane, Saunders. *A Survey of Modern Algebra*. New York: The Macmillan Company, 1965.

This book illustrates the nature of modern algebra. While emphasizing algebraic structure and proof, it also contains numerous concrete examples to illustrate the more abstract concepts. It is an interesting and readable book suitable for college sophomores.

Cohen, Leon W. and Ehrlich, Gertrude. *The Structure of the Real Number
System*. Princeton, N.J.: D. Van Nostrand Company, 1963.

> This book presents the structure of the real number system from the view-
> point of modern, abstract arithmetic. It begins with the undefined term *set*,
> and procedes through a rigorous, axiomatic development of the natural num-
> bers, the integers, the rationals, and the reals. The book provides an interest-
> ing view of the real number system as a pure axiomatic mathematical system.

Eves, Howard. *An Introduction to the History of Mathematics*. New York:
Rinehart and Company, 1953.

> This book was designed to be used in a one-semester undergraduate history
> of mathematics course, and the mathematical content does not extend beyond
> elementary calculus. Since the book was written for use as a textbook, it has a
> set of "problem studies" at the end of each chapter. Many of these problems
> can be used as assignments or projects to supplement the problems which are
> included in typical secondary school textbooks. This is another valuable re-
> source book for mathematics teachers.

Eves, Howard and Newsom, Carroll V. *An Introduction to The Foundations
and Fundamental Concepts of Mathematics*. New York: Holt, Rinehart and
Winston, 1965.

Kline, Morris. *Mathematics in Western Culture*. New York: Oxford University
Press, 1953.

———. *Mathematics and the Physical World*. New York: Thomas Y. Crowell
Company, 1959.

———. *Mathematics: A Cultural Approach*. Reading, Mass.: Addison-Wesley
Publishing Company, 1962.

> Although these three books by Morris Kline are independent of each other,
> they are related in the nature of their content; consequently they will be dis-
> cussed as a unit.

> The content of *Mathematics in Western Culture* is described in the book's
> jacket as follows:

>> This refreshing treatment of mathematics answers the question: What con-
>> tributions has mathematics made to Western life and thought aside from
>> techniques that serve the engineer? By presenting a remarkably fine ac-
>> count of the influences mathematics has exerted on the development of
>> philosophy, the physical and social sciences, religion, literature, and the
>> arts, the book amply supports the contention that *mathematics is a prime
>> molder and major constituent of our culture*.

> *Mathematics and the Physical World* presents mathematics in the context
> of its applications in the physical sciences. A number of interesting mathemat-
> ics and science problems are presented and explained. This book illustrates
> well the practical inseparability of mathematics and science.

> The Preface to *Mathematics: A Cultural Approach* begins with an ex-
> planation of the purpose of the book:

>> This text attempts to show what mathematics is, how mathematics has
>> developed from man's efforts to understand and master nature, what the
>> mathematical approach to real problems can accomplish, and the extent to
>> which mathematics has molded our civilization and our culture. (p. v)

All three books treat the history, philosophy, nature and content of mathematics. However, their distinctiveness is in the discussion of specific contributions of mathematics to the sciences and in showing the general contributions of mathematics to world culture.

Kramer, Edna E. *The Nature and Growth of Modern Mathematics.* New York: Hawthorn Books, 1970.

Although this excellent book contains more than seven-hundred pages, it is an economical (in terms of hours expended) book to read. The author has written a book that combines history of mathematics, biographies of mathematicians, mathematics, applications of mathematics, and the nature of mathematics into one volume which is as interesting as a best-selling novel. Here is one book that should be read by every mathematics teacher. The book's extensive mathematical content, while including many of the most important mathematical developments in history, is presented so as to be understandable to people having limited knowledge of mathematics. By all means read this book! It will make you a better mathematician and a better mathematics teacher.

Lanczos, Cornelius. *Space Through the Ages.* Academic Press: New York, 1970.

Here is a history and nature of mathematics book presenting the nature of modern geometry and related concepts with a heavy emphasis upon mathematics content. Although this book can be understood by people who have a good background in undergraduate level mathematics, it is somewhat technical, especially with regard to some of the notation. This is a good modern geometry reference book for high school geometry teachers.

MacDuffee, Cyrus Colton. *Theory of Equations.* New York: John Wiley & Sons, 1954.

Since theory of equations is seldom taught as a separate course in schools or colleges, and many of its topics are outdated by modern algebra, nearly all books with such a title were published before 1960. This book is representative of classical algebra as it was taught in traditional algebra courses in which specific techniques, rather than general structure, were emphasized. Within the book is the kind of algebra that was done by Cardan, Tartaglia, and the other sixteenth century algebraists.

National Council of Teachers of Mathematics. *Historical Topics for the Mathematics Classroom: Thirty-first Yearbook.* Washington, D.C.: National Council of Teachers of Mathematics, 1969.

This NCTM yearbook, while providing historical notes about mathematics and mathematicians, emphasizes the use of the history of mathematics in classroom teaching of mathematics. Among its strengths is an excellent and extensive bibliography of mathematical history. Two of the six principles used as a guide in preparing the book indicate its uses:

The book should include not only usable historical materials but also some indication of how they may be used by the teacher or student.

The general topics should include something of significant mathematical value for all different grade levels whenever possible. (p. ix)

Smith, David Eugene. *History of Mathematics*. New York: Dover Publications, 1958.

The first volume of this two volume set is titled *General Survey of the History of Elementary Mathematics* and the second volume is titled *Special Topics of Elementary Mathematics*. This 1300 page work is a more complete history of mathematics reference than the other books listed in this bibliography. It is distinctive in its many illustrations of mathematical artifacts, and for this (and other reasons) it should be in your school library for reference by you and your students. It also contains a good bibliography of other history of mathematics books, many of which are more specific histories; however some of these references are in other languages.

Stoll, Robert R. *Set Theory and Logic*. San Francisco: W. H. Freeman and Company, 1963.

Stoll's book is representative of mathematics books about the foundations of modern mathematics. It includes such topics as modern set theory, logic, ordinal and cardinal numbers, and propositional calculus. Most of the book requires little of the reader beyond a sound knowledge of high school mathematics and the mathematical maturity usually found in college juniors.

Magazines

The American Mathematical Monthly. Washington, D.C.: The Mathematical Association of America.

This journal is published ten times a year, and contains both technical and general articles about college level mathematics. Each year's volume contains several articles about the history of mathematics, mathematicians, or the nature of mathematics. Although some of the articles in each issue are of little interest to secondary school mathematics teachers, each journal contains a section on mathematics teaching. Browse through back issues and look for useful articles in current issues of this journal as they appear. Nearly all college and other technical libraries subscribe to the *Monthly*.

The Mathematics Teacher. Reston, Va.: National Council of Teachers of Mathematics.

This journal which is published monthly nine times a year is required reading for every mathematics teacher who wants to keep abreast of developments in secondary school teaching. Many back issues of the journal contain articles about the nature and history of mathematics. Membership in the National Council of Teachers of Mathematics, which includes this journal, is inexpensive; I recommend that you subscribe to *The Mathematics Teacher* as well as to its sister journal, *The Arithmetic Teacher*.

Other Sources

Many books have been written about the history of mathematics in various countries and about the lives and works of many of the best-known mathematicians in history. A good way to locate such books is to browse through the library shelves adjacent to the shelves where the books listed in this bibliography are stored. Public libraries usually have some books about mathematics and all college and university libraries, as well as many high school libraries, have books about the nature, history, and philosophy of mathematics. Some of your best book and magazine discoveries can be made by *browsing* through libraries.

2

...dents find SMP material relevant...
...teresting—and different in approach...
Secondary Texts.

Write us for a free Sampler and Secondary...

We specialize in mathematics

...from textbook programs to sup...

■ Cuisenaire® rods
■ Geoboards
■ Student Activity Cards

The School Mathematics Curriculum

The various modes of teaching Arithmetic may be resolved into two; the mere *didactic* or *descriptive,* and the *inductive* and *analytic.* The former method teaches abstract rules, instructing the learner in the *manner* of performing operations without any explanation of the *reasons* for it. It treats him as a kind of machine, appealing almost solely to the memory. The study, thus pursued, is dry and comparatively uninteresting. The learner may, to a certain extent, become acquainted with forms and rules; but a knowledge of general principles, and the improvement of the mind, form no part of the result of this plan. Fortunately, this method has been almost entirely abandoned by intelligent teachers.

On the other hand, instruction by *analysis* and *induction* leads the pupil to the principles from which rules are derived, and teaches him to regard rules as results, *rather* than *reasons.* He understands the *reason* for every operation he performs. This may be termed the *rational* method, by which both objects of this study are accomplished. A thorough knowledge of Arithmetic is acquired, while all the more important faculties of the mind are disciplined and strengthened. (p. 5)

A passage from the preface to a modern arithmetic textbook, offering good advice to the teacher? Not at all! This quotation is from an old mathematics textbook; in fact, it is from a book which was published in 1849, called *Ray's Arithmetic: Part Third.* From the nature of this pre-Civil War advice, it is obvious that there must be characteristics of the modern approach to mathematics teaching other than the emphasis upon understanding of principles.

As you will see in this chapter, the nature of recent secondary mathematics curriculum change is multi-faceted. The content of secondary mathematics textbooks has been changed considerably since 1849, and most of these changes have been made since 1950. The procedures for writing and disseminating mathematics textbooks have changed, and methods of teaching mathemtics have been modified as much as, and maybe even more than, the mathematics content of textbooks. Most of the modern mathematics textbooks in use in high schools today have either been produced from the work of several major curriculum development projects or are based upon curriculum materials from these projects. In varying degrees, the modern mathematics curriculum development projects which started to appear in the nineteen fifties have been concerned with three issues:

1. What mathematics should be taught in schools—*the content issue*.
2. How do people learn mathematics—*the learning psychology issue*.
3. How should teachers teach mathematics—*the instructional strategies issue*.

In this chapter we will consider four aspects of modern mathematics curricula, which are usually grouped together under the title "new math." First we will consider those influences which precipitated the so-called *revolution in school mathematics*. Next we will discuss some of the major curriculum development projects in somewhat of an historical vein. Then we will compare the characteristics of "old math" and "new math," and the contents of mathematics textbooks. Finally we'll look at the successes and failures of new math.

Influences on School Mathematics

Changes in Society and Education

In the years following World War II a number of diverse forces converged in a manner that made general curriculum reform inevitable in schools in the United States. A backlog of criticisms of the educational system had been building before and during the war, and at the conclusion of the war resources were released which made major and expensive changes in teaching methods and curricula possible. World War II with its development of and reliance upon complex weapons such as rockets, radar and nuclear bombs showed that the ability of a country to wage war was now closely related to the quality of its science and technology. The necessity for rapid training of large numbers of men and women in technological skills required for the war effort highlighted the inadequate scientific education that was being provided by the educational system. There appeared to be a consensus that the first and most important step in guaranteeing a reservoir of scientific personnel for the future was to increase the emphasis on science and mathematics in the public schools and to improve the teaching of these subjects. Dramatic post-war changes in society and the need to reconstruct a large portion of the world which had been destroyed by war reinforced the viewpoint that what was being taught in schools needed to be modified.

The war years, and even prewar years, witnessed a declining enrollment in colleges. In attempts to reverse this trend many colleges relaxed or eliminated admission requirements following the war. However, while easing entrance requirements, many college programs and courses set prerequisites in mathematics and science which were difficult for traditionally-educated high school graduates to meet. An increasing emphasis in society on the value of a college education, together with postwar economic prosperity, resulted in an influx of students into colleges. Many of these students had been poorly trained in mathematics in high school which caused additional pressures for curriculum reform. These factors together with labor shortages, the increased prestige of mathematics, and a new concern about preparing students for college made the revolution in school mathematics inevitable.

To respond to these concerns about the quality of scientific education in the schools, prestigious scientific and education organizations initiated a series of conferences and reports about mathematics education and the needs of society. In 1947 the Commission on Post War Plans of the National Council of Teachers of Mathematics called for new goals and methods for mathematics teaching and urged a comprehensive curriculum reform in school mathematics. In 1948 the Symposium on College Entrance Requirements, sponsored by the Mathematical Association of America, called for a reform in high school mathematics which would substitute newer, more interesting and more useful mathematics for outmoded topics in the curriculum. The Cooperative Committee on the Teaching of Science and Mathematics of the American Association for the Advancement of Science issued a report in 1947 calling for a new emphasis on mathematics and science in high schools to meet the scientific demands of postwar society.

As is illustrated in Chapter 1, the content of mathematics underwent drastic changes as a consequence of the work of seventeenth, eighteenth and nineteenth century mathematicians. By the middle of the twentieth century many of these modern mathematics concepts and methods were included in college level mathematics; however, most high school mathematics was still taught as though Galois, Riemann, Gauss, and Cantor had never existed. The new applications of mathematics and the content of college mathematics were mostly ignored in the high school curriculum of the nineteen forties. Postwar shortages, new social and urban problems, the demand for more and improved technology, and the need for more and better mathematicians to assist in solving these problems and meeting these demands created a situation whereby something had to be done about the state of high school mathematics. The topics being taught in school mathematics in the nineteen forties appeared to have little relevance for the new scientific and technological uses of a modernized mathematics.

At the time pressure was mounting to make school mathematics modern and relevant, new theories and research on how people learn were beginning to discredit some of the traditional methods of teaching, such as lecture, drill, and memorization. The theories and research of the Swiss psychologist and biologist Jean Piaget and his followers indicated that traditional teaching methods should be modified according to various age, heredity, and environmental-related stages of intellectual development in children. Research conducted by J. P. Guilford and his colleagues indicates that general intelligence is a combination of many specific intellectual abilities. Consequently, different methods of presenting mathematics (concrete versus abstract, or figural versus symbolic illustrations) may be appropriate for various people. Another learning theorist, Robert Gagné, developed and tested his theory that knowledge is organized hierarchically in the mind and that lower level skills and principles must be learned before higher order structures can be understood. Jerome Bruner, a learning psychologist, thought that transfer of one learning task to other learning tasks can be achieved through appropriate teaching and that people can be taught to "learn how to learn." Another psychologist, David Ausubel, said that verbal exposition (carefully presented lectures) and appropriately structured problem-solving experience is the most effective general method to use in teaching high-school students. B. F. Skinner and others have studied the effectiveness of various stimuli and responses and the effects of rewards and punishments upon learning. While these diverse (and sometimes contradictory) learning theories seemed to

69

indicate that there is no best way to teach, they did result in the realization that different people learn in different ways under different conditions. Although the people just mentioned worked on theories about learning in general, all of them used mathematical concepts and principles in testing their theories. As a result, the applications of these theories have been apparent in mathematics teaching, and have greatly influenced both the organization and structure of high-school textbooks and procedures for teaching mathematics. Such common new methods for teaching modern mathematics as individualized instruction, discovery learning, spiral approaches, mathematics laboratories, and computer-based instruction have their beginnings in the theories of these well-known psychologists. More will be said in subsequent chapters about learning theories and their influence upon methods of teaching mathematics. For now, it suffices to say that the interest in learning theory in the nineteen forties and fifties provided another important influence on the new mathematics curricula which were developed.

Curriculum Projects

Even though the creation of a new body of mathematical knowledge, new needs of a changing society and a better understanding of the nature of learning indicated the need for a revised school mathematics curriculum, it is doubtful that the development and implementation of this new curriculum would have been so rapid and far reaching had it not been for two additional influences. One of these influences was political and is exemplified in the creation by Congress in 1950 of the National Science Foundation. The other is concerned with the development of a new system (*the curriculum project approach*) for carrying out curriculum change. This first influence provided the money needed to produce a new mathematics curriculum and the second provided a mechanism for the efficient dissemination of the new curriculum.

Through an act of Congress in 1950 the National Science Foundation was created as an independent agency of the executive branch of government. Its primary purpose was to develop a national policy to promote basic research and education in the sciences. In 1951 the University of Illinois established the University of Illinois Committee on School Mathematics (UICSM) for the purpose of studying problems related to the content and teaching of mathematics in grades nine through twelve. The Carnegie Foundation of New York provided initial financial support for this project and later the U.S. Office of Education and the National Science Foundation contributed additional funds. UICSM was the first large-scale curriculum project to develop and distribute a modern mathematics curriculum for secondary-school mathematics; its director, the late Max Beberman, is sometimes referred to as the father of new math. The project set out to produce a curriculum emphasizing basic mathematical concepts containing a minimum of manipulative activities and emphasizing student discovery and understanding of mathematical concepts and principles. The UICSM staff produced and tested mathematics curriculum units for grades 9-12, tried these units in a number of schools, and conducted summer institutes to teach mathematics teachers how to use the new curriculum. According to the *Seventh Report*

Until 1962 the UICSM devoted its efforts to producing a highly self-consis-tent and inter-related series of texts for college bound students in grades 9-12. These texts are unusual in that they embody "discovery method" pedagogy; they were the first to introduce a strong deductive thread to the teaching of elementary algebra; and they introduce and use principles of logic and a level of precision in language which is not common to high school texts. Since 1962, our major curriculum development effort has been the development of unusual approaches to topics in junior high school mathematics appropriate for culturally disadvantaged students in large urban school systems. (pp. 589-90)

The UICSM mathematics curriculum is commercially available in textbook format, and many other modern secondary-school mathematics textbooks have been influenced by the UICSM curriculum. The UICSM model of a large cur-riculum project supported by private and public money to produce textbooks, train teachers in their use, and promote the use of their curriculum in schools became a pattern for later new mathematics curriculum projects. The success of such projects in establishing modern mathematics as a major school curriculum in the United States is good evidence of the efficiency of this model for dis-seminating curricula. This is in contrast to the model of a publishing company commissioning one or two authors to write a textbook for use in a particular subject.

No doubt the largest and best-known of the United States' mathematics cur-riculum projects is the School Mathematics Study Group (SMSG) which began at Yale University in 1958 and later moved to Stanford University. The director of this project was (it has been completed) Dr. E. G. Begle. According to the Clearinghouse report referenced above:

The primary purpose of the SMSG is to foster research and development in the teaching of school mathematics. The work of SMSG consists primarily in the development of courses, teaching materials and teaching methods. It is part of SMSG's task, in cooperation with other mathematical organizations, to encourage exploration of the hypotheses underlying mathematics educa-tion. (p. 516)

The project has had profound influence upon school mathematics; SMSG textbooks and textbooks based upon the SMSG curriculum are being used in a large percentage of American schools. In addition to producing and publishing mathematics textbooks for use in grades K-12, SMSG has produced 43 newslet-ters about its activities, programmed materials in mathematics and computer programming, supplementary and enrichment mathematical monographs, re-ports, articles, reprints, and a series of booklets on the National Longitudinal Study of Mathematical Abilities which it initiated. SMSG teacher training work-shops have been conducted all over the United States to prepare teachers to teach the new math. Although the SMSG faced criticism of its work from many people, it has been instrumental in carrying out the new mathematics revolution, and its books have served as models for many mathematics textbook writers.

A more recent new math project, which was begun in 1965 under the direction of Dr. Howard Fehr at Columbia University, is the Secondary School Mathematics Curriculum Improvement Study (SSMCIS). According to the clearinghouse report:

> The Project is unique in that it is building a curriculum in mathematics for the upper 20% in academic ability that will bring the instruction in line with contemporary conceptions of mathematics and on a par with recently established programs in the Nordic European and Russian States. (p. 548)

The SSMCIS is also unique in that the textbook series which it developed for grades 7-12 takes a completely unified view of secondary school mathematics. The usual separation of high school mathematics into arithmetic, algebra, geometry, trigonometry, and advanced mathematics is replaced by an integrated presentation where the branches of mathematics are unified through fundamental concepts (sets, functions, operations, etc.) and structures (groups, rings, fields, vector spaces, etc.). The program also contains topics from statistics, probability, computer science, and linear algebra. In addition to textbooks, several booklets containing more advanced mathematics topics have been developed by the SSMCIS.

It is common practice for most secondary school mathematics textbook publishers to offer a series of algebra, geometry, trigonometry, and advanced mathematics books, any one of which can be used for a single course without using the others for other courses. For example, you could use an SMSG book for an algebra course and a UICSM book for geometry without losing continuity. This cannot be done with the SSMCIS unified series. To use SSMCIS books it is best to start with the first course and continue sequentially from grade seven through grade twelve. Although a school which uses the SSMCIS curriculum locks its students into that series, SSMCIS does have one distinct advantage. That is, a student who uses SSMCIS texts and takes only one, two, or several courses in mathematics will have learned some algebra, geometry, trigonometry, number theory, and statistics, and will have a much broader (although not as deep in a single area) background in mathematics than he or she would have had by taking a year or two of algebra.

The initiators of SSMCIS followed some of the recommendations found in the publication *Goals for School Mathematics* which is the Report of The Cambridge Conference on School Mathematics that was held at Cambridge, Massachusetts. A group of 29 mathematicians and users of mathematics met in the summer of 1963 to propose a radically new mathematics curriculum for grades K-12. According to *Goals for School Mathematics:*

> The subject matter which we are proposing can be roughly described by saying that a student who has worked through the full thirteen years of mathematics in grades K-12 should have a level of training comparable to three years of top-level college training today; that is, we shall expect him to have the equivalent of two years of calculus, and one semester each of modern algebra and probability theory. (p. 7)

The program recommended by the Cambridge Conference appears to have been designed to prepare school students to become future research mathematicians. Since the participants were unable to agree on a single set of recommendations for the content of school mathematics, they proposed two alternative programs. A complete grade-by-grade list of the proposed topics for school mathematics is found in the Report. It suffices to say that the Cambridge Conference participants did propose that those mathematics topics taught in a *very* good college be included in secondary schools. The suggested program is quite visionary for most high school students and is even beyond the college mathematics education of many high school teachers as is illustrated by the inclusion of differential equations, differential geometry of space curves, multidimensional calculus, boundary value problems, and Fourier series in grades 11 and 12. Needless to say, no standard new mathematics curriculum, not even SSMCIS, follows all of the recommendations of the Cambridge Conference.

UICSM, SMSG, and SSMCIS are only a few of the many mathematics curriculum improvement projects which have been initiated since 1950. *The Eighth Report of the International Clearinghouse on Science and Mathematics Curricular Developments 1972* lists 33 mathematics curriculum development projects in the United States. Even this list is not complete, and some of the earlier projects, such as UICSM, which have been completed are no longer listed. Several of the projects listed are developing computer-based mathematics curriculum materials.

Two of the larger computer-oriented curriculum development projects, which are not referenced by the Clearinghouse, are PLATO at the University of Illinois, directed by Dr. Donald Bitzer, and Project Solo, directed by Dr. Thomas Dwyer at the University of Pittsburgh. PLATO is a computer-based instructional system containing some unique instructional technology including remote computer graphics terminals with audio, video, and standard remote computing capabilities. PLATO has a large number of computer-based lessons and courses in a variety of elementary, secondary, and college subjects; many of the lessons are in mathematics and science. Although the PLATO curriculum materials are quite good, access to them via a remote computer terminal connected to the PLATO computer installation is expensive. Project Solo has produced a number of excellent computer-related mathematics curriculum modules ranging from arithmetic, through algebra, to calculus and beyond. Modules have also been developed to illustrate applications of mathematics in science, engineering and computer science. Some of the Solo modules are available from commercial computer corporations.

Only a few of the many new math curriculum development projects have been mentioned and discussed briefly in this section. The **Things to Do** section and the **Selected Bibliography** at the end of the chapter suggest activities and resources which are appropriate for learning more about mathematics curriculum projects. While the Soviet launching of the Sputnik I satellite in 1957 is sometimes credited as being the event which also launched new math, such is not the case. Although the launching of Sputnik I did serve as a catalyst in the development of several modern mathematics curricula, new math was well on its way at this time. As part of the effort to maintain a technological advantage over the Soviets (which appeared to be slipping with the advent of Sputnik I), additional funds were made available for the improvement of mathematics as well as science education.

The New Mathematics Curricula

The influence of school mathematics curriculum development projects which were initiated in the nineteen fifties and sixties is apparent in nearly all secondary mathematics textbooks. But has there been a *revolution* in school mathematics? The best way to determine what changes have been made in school mathematics is to compare textbooks published around 1950 with those published after 1970. Depending upon which set of current high school textbooks is selected for comparison with older textbooks, one finds that the modern mathematics phenomenon ranges from modest change to a true revolution. Some textbooks have the word **MODERN** in boldface letters on their covers, while others, whose publishers may have been influenced by the continuing criticisms of new math, are careful to avoid using the words ''modern'' or ''contemporary.'' Some of the textbooks used in school classrooms today differ little from those used 20 years ago, and others contain changes which are radical enough to indicate that there has been a real revolution in school mathematics. Even those textbooks which are called *modern* are different enough from each other to indicate that there is no single modern mathematics curriculum, but that there are several modern curricula.

Are there any characteristics that all the newer secondary school mathematics textbooks have in common which make them different from their predecessors? First, nearly every textbook uses the word *set* in the mathematical sense and most discuss subsets and operations on sets such as union, intersection, and complement. Second, most high school textbooks contain mathematics topics which were reserved for college courses twenty-five years ago. In this respect the recommendation of the Cambridge Conference on School Mathematics that the first three years of college mathematics be included in high school mathematics has been partially fulfilled. Third, most mathematics books now emphasize the structure of mathematics and are concerned with student understanding of concepts; consequently, reliance upon rules and memorization has decreased. Fourth, many textbooks now use some of the vocabulary and symbolism used by modern mathematicians. Finally, many textbook publishers now reflect the growing concern for better teaching by offering teachers' editions of their textbooks. These editions contain goals and objectives for the mathematics topics, alternative ways to teach the material, and some more advanced mathematics concepts to improve the teacher's knowledge of mathematics.

Another way to gain some perspective on the changes in the content of secondary school mathematics is to study the changes in course requirements in colleges that prepare high school mathematics teachers. Prospective mathematics teachers are expected to learn in depth in college those mathematics topics which they may be assigned to teach in high schools.

In 1950 the typical minimum mathematics course requirements for college students in teacher education programs were 24 semester credits for mathematics as the major field and 18 credits for a minor in mathematics. In effect this meant that a person could be certified to teach any high school mathematics course by taking six college mathematics courses. At that time it was possible for a teacher to become certified (and many did in a four year college program) to teach four different high school subjects by judiciously choosing electives. It was not at all difficult to obtain certification in all of mathematics, science, English, and history in a four year teacher education program. The standard minimum mathematics program for teachers was composed of the following courses:

1. College Algebra, which contained most of the traditional mathematics topics usually taught in high school Algebra 2 today.
2. College Trigonometry, another of today's high school courses, but without the analytic approach to the trigonometric functions as functions on a unit circle.
3. College Geometry, a course containing traditional Euclidean plane geometry and a unit on solid geometry; however, there was no mention of coordinate geometry and transformations which are included in modern high school geometry texts.
4. Analytic Geometry, which was the geometry of the conic sections in a rectangular coordinate system.
5. Differential Calculus in two dimensions taught in the style of Leibniz with an emphasis upon manipulation.
6. Integral Calculus, also taught in the eighteenth century tradition, and also limited to two dimensions.

For a student interested in going beyond this minimum set of courses, there were electives such as:

7. Theory of Equations, which included complex number arithmetic and the solution of polynomial equations—topics now found in high school algebra and analysis.
8. An elementary, technique-oriented Statistics course.
9. Mathematics of Finance which dealt with interest rates, annuities and insurance.
10. A course in Surveying which served as an applied mathematics course.
11. A History of Mathematics course.
12. Possibly Differential Equations, which was considered to be quite advanced.

In contrast, today's school mathematics teachers usually are expected to take at least ten courses for a secondary teaching certificate, and many states require additional mathematics courses for continuing certification. In addition to taking more mathematics courses, teachers now study mathematics topics which are quite different from those studied in 1950. A representative list of courses might be:

1. Three courses in calculus are offered, including topics in analytic geometry. While manipulative skills are still taught, there is a new emphasis upon structure and proof, and the calculus has been modernized to be more in the tradition of Riemann's calculus. Also many calculus courses now include topics from *n*-dimensional calculus.

    Algebra and trigonometry are thought to be more appropriate for high school study, and if taken in college they may be classified as remedial courses or as not satisfying mathematics credit requirements.
2. Abstract Algebra is a required course in modern algebra which emphasizes structure and proof in the context of mathematical generalizations such as groups, rings, and fields.
3. Linear Algebra includes matrix algebra and the study of vector spaces. Again the emphasis is upon modern mathematical structures.

4. Probability and Statistics are now required studies, because topics (and even entire courses) in these subjects are being taught in secondary schools.

5. The narrow view of geometry as the province of Euclid has been replaced by a course, or courses, to illustrate the general structure of all geometries and to view geometries (as did Felix Klein) as the study of invariants associated with particular groups of transformations.

6. Differential Equations and Advanced Calculus are now regarded as appropriate courses to be taken in college by prospective secondary teachers.

7. The old Theory of Equations, Mathematics of Finance and Surveying courses have been replaced by Analysis, Topology, Graph Theory, Differential Geometry, Transformational Geometry, Projective Geometry, Logic and other courses representative of mathematics developed in the nineteenth and twentieth centuries.

8. Many colleges now require that people preparing to be mathematics teachers take courses in computer science—Computer Programming and Numerical Analysis—as well as other courses illustrating the applications of mathematics.

As one might expect, this new college mathematics curriculum is representative of modern secondary school mathematics, and it is still required that prospective teachers study, in depth, those mathematics topics which they may be expected to teach in secondary schools.

The most direct way to catalog the changes in the secondary school mathematics curriculum is to compare old algebra, trigonometry and geometry textbooks with their modern replacements. In the following paragraphs we will examine the topics usually found in textbooks in the ten year period following World War II, discuss the contents of the modern textbooks which were influenced by the work of the SMSG (representing a moderate approach to change), and look at the sequence of topics in the SSMCIS curriculum series (a more revolutionary approach to curriculum change).

Algebra

Before the mathematics curriculum development projects began to influence secondary school textbooks, a typical Algebra 1 course contained the following topics:

symbols and formulas	*solving linear equations*
algebraic expressions and equations	*factoring trinomials*
operations on negative numbers	*simplifying algebraic fractions*
adding and subtracting polynomials	*simplifying complex fractions*
multiplying and dividing polynomials	*fractional equations*
	statement problems for each topic

These topics were usually found in the first half of an algebra book, and emphasis was solely on rules and manipulative techniques, with no mention of algebraic structure or proof. The names given to the numbers used in problems were *whole numbers, negative numbers, fractions,* and *decimals.*

The second half of an algebra book was used for the Algebra 2 course, which began with a complete review of Algebra 1. Then the following new topics were taught, with the emphasis still being on rules and manipulations:

graphs of linear equations   *solving quadratic equations*
graphs of pairs of linear equations *graphing quadratic equations*
solving pairs of linear equations   *ratio, proportion, variation*
powers of algebraic expressions   *linear and quadratic functions*
operations on radical expressions   *numerical trigonometry*
                                      statement problems

Many algebra textbooks either ignored imaginary numbers or briefly mentioned their existence, and all quadratic equations in these books had real roots. Numbers under radical signs were called irrational expressions if the numbers were not perfect squares, but no explanation of irrational numbers was found in most textbooks. Complex numbers were left for college and were discussed there in Theory of Equations courses. The pre-new-math algebra books emphasized *how to do it* with little explanation of *why*.

Modern Algebra 1 textbooks influenced by the SMSG, while still being concerned with skills and applications of algebra, emphasize precise mathematical language and notation, understanding of algebraic structure, and use of deductive reasoning. A representative list of topics covered in a first course in modern algebra is:

algebraic symbols   *solving equations by factoring*
the vocabulary of modern algebra   *algebraic fractions*
sets and operations on sets   *graphing equations and inequalities*
variables and open sentences   *solving systems of linear equations*
solutions of equations and inequalities *properties of irrational numbers*
the foundational axioms of algebra *operations on radical expressions*
properties of arithmetic operations *structure of the real number system*
algebra of logic   *functions*
operations on the integers   *variation and proportions*
absolute value   *quadratic equations*
properties of inequalities   *quadratic inequalities*
rational numbers   *graphing quadratic functions*
polynomial arithmetic   *topics in geometry*
exponents and powers   *numerical trigonometry*
special products and factoring   *word problems*

Most modern mathematics textbook publishers now separate first and second year algebra into two textbooks. Topics which would probably be found in an Algebra 2 textbook influenced by the SMSG are:

a review of sets   *negative and fractional exponents*
axioms for the real numbers   *fractional equations*
properties of the real numbers   *repeating decimals*
mathematical proof   *relations*
equations in one variable   *functions*
systems of linear equations   *special functions*
coordinate geometry in 2 dimensions *quadratic functions*
coordinate geometry in 3 dimensions *radical expressions*

systems of linear inequalities	*quadratic inequalities*
factoring polynomials	*radical equations*
solving inequalities	*analytic geometry of conic sections*
arithmetic operations on polynomials	*exponential functions*
introduction to theory of equations	*logarithms*

Many of the topics from Algebra 1 are covered again in greater depth in Algebra 2; however, additional topics which used to be taught in college are now included in Algebra 2. For example, logarithms, exponential functions, analytic geometry, and theory of equations were generally taught only in college courses 30 years ago.

Many Algebra 2 textbooks also include some of the topics listed below which were generally taught in colleges 30 years ago. Some college preparatory Algebra 2 courses include these topics; however time may not permit teaching them in general algebra classes. Also, the SMSG and other projects have produced sets of monographs on special advanced algebra topics for high school students.

arithmetic progressions	*matrices and determinants*
geometric progressions	*permutations and combinations*
binomial theorem	*topics from probability*
infinite series	*topics from statistics*
complex numbers	*infinite sets*
theory of equations	*groups, rings, and fields*
graphing polynomials	*structure of the real number system*
mathematical induction	*propositional calculus*
Boolean algebra	

Geometry

Thirty years ago high school plane geometry differed little from the geometry which Euclid unified and structured about 300 B.C. For two thousand years after Euclid, geometry to mathematicians was Euclidean geometry, and for twenty-two hundred years the geometry studied by students was that of Euclid. Now there are two standard approaches to modern high school geometry. The approach which was developed first is that of the modern curriculum projects and is a modernized version of Euclidean geometry. Euclid's axioms and postulates have been enlarged and modified to remove most of the ambiguities and inconsistencies found in *old* Euclidean geometry. While the basic structure of geometry as a postulational mathematical system remains, emphasis is now given to applications of the inductive and deductive reasoning techniques of geometry in non-mathematical situations. The methods of coordinate geometry have been merged with the synthetic methods of Euclid to illustrate the relation between algebra and geometry.

The second approach is closer to Felix Klein's approach to geometry as the study of invariants associated with transformation groups. This approach is exemplified in high school geometry textbooks having the word *transformation* in their titles. Most transformational geometry textbooks maintain the content of Euclidean geometry, but use transformations such as reflections and rotations as a unifying concept for geometry and the other fields of mathematics. It is believed by some people that a transformational approach to geometry is easier and more understandable for students and provides them with a better foundation for future study of mathematics.

The contents of most thirty-year-old high school plane geometry books would resemble the following list of topics; however, a few older textbooks did include an algebraic approach to some geometric proofs:

points, lines, planes, and angles	*locus*
postulates and axioms	*congruency*
proving theorems	*circles*
constructions	*tangents*
parallel lines	*proportions*
congruent triangles	*similar triangles and polygons*
sides and angles of triangles	*Pythagorean theorem*
areas of triangles	*proportions of line segments*
quadrilaterals	*areas of plane closed figures*
distance	*proportional areas*
polygons	*regular polygons*
inequalities	*coordinate geometry*
	introduction to solid geometry

The topics found in a modern (nontransformational) geometry textbook would resemble those in this list:

sets and operations on sets	*theorems about trapezoids*
basic undefined terms	*equalities and inequalities*
basic defined terms	*ratio and proportion*
measuring angles	*similarity*
inductive reasoning	*similar polygons*
deductive reasoning	*properties of special triangles*
methods of geometric proof	*Pythagorean theorem*
truth tables and logic	*introduction to trigonometry*
basic postulates of algebra	*theorems about circles*
basic postulates of geometry	*theorems about parts of circles*
mathematical systems	*geometric constructions*
theorems about lines and angles	*locus*
parallelism	*coordinate geometry*
theorems about parallel lines	*symmetry*
theorems about parallel planes	*graphs and equations*
polygons	*coordinate geometry proofs*
congruent triangles	*transformations*
theorems about parts of triangles	*areas*
theorems about quadrilaterals	*volumes of solids*
	surface areas of solids

The following topics may be found in transformational geometry textbooks:

operations on real numbers	*size transformations—*
introduction to set theory	*expansions and contractions*
undefined terms	*ratios and proportions*
coordinates	*inverse transformations*
defined terms	*similarity transformations*
line segments and rays	*Pythagorean theorem*
angles and their measures	*coordinate geometry*
theorems about angles	*introduction to trigonometry*

geometric constructions	*circles and their parts*
transformations	*tangents and secants*
translations	*the power of a point*
reflections	*triangle inequality*
rotations	*shortest paths*
isometries	*incenter and circumcenter*
symmetry	*space geometry*
congruence	*matrices as transformations*
the nature of proof	*shear transformations*
congruent polygons	*determinants*
reflection-symmetric figures—	*perimeter*
* lines, angles, triangles,*	*area*
* quadrilaterals, circles*	*volume*
indirect proof	*limits*
parallel lines	*symmetry groups*
congruent triangles	*the congruence group*
trapezoids	*the similarity group*

Although many of the same topics are found in traditional Euclidean geometry, modern school geometry, and transformational geometry, both the objectives and the approaches differ. The primary objectives for studying Euclidean geometry are to learn how to do mathematical proofs and to improve one's logical reasoning techniques. The old math approach to Euclidean geometry was to learn geometric facts in isolation from other areas of mathematics and to prove theorem after theorem. In addition to learning how to do proofs and improving one's reasoning powers, modern geometry has the objectives of unifying algebra and geometry and improving spatial visualization. The modern approach to school geometry is to include topics from algebra, analytic geometry and solid geometry among the traditional topics of Euclidean geometry. This same set of goals applies to transformational geometry. In transformational geometry the unification of geometry with other mathematics subjects is accomplished by using topics from linear algebra, group theory, and transformations to present a more general formulation of geometry—a geometry one step closer to the work of the great "modernizer" of mathematics, Felix Klein.

Trigonometry

Some eighteenth century mathematicians and a few mathematicians of the nineteenth century worried that mathematics might be a dying subject because nearly everything of importance had been discovered. While this concern for the future of mathematics appears to be ludicrous in view of the fantastic growth of mathematics in this century, it is not inaccurate to say that trigonometry is a *dead* subject for mathematical research. New applications of trigonometry are being found every decade, but no research mathematician classifies himself as a *trigonometrist*. Trigonometry is still an important subject for study in school because of its many scientific and technical uses and applications in other areas of mathematics.

Traditional high school trigonometry was taught as a subject whose only purpose was the measurement of triangles. The trigonometric functions were defined as ratios of sides of right triangles; the standard unit of angular measure was the degree; and the major objective of trigonometry was to memorize facts and rules to be used for solving triangles. Modern trigonometry uses an analytic approach which begins by defining the trigonometric functions as functions on the set of real numbers. Then it uses the radian as the standard unit for measuring angles, and shows many applications of trigonometry in addition to triangle measurement.

The following list is representative of the set of topics taught in most pre-1950 high school trigonometry courses:

*definitions of the trigonometric
    functions as ratios of sides
    of triangles
reciprocal functions
basic identities
functions of special angles
approximate numbers
solving right triangles
interpolation
scientific notation
logarithms
using logarithms to solve
    right triangles
applied problems*

*general properties of
    trigonometric functions
radian measure
graphs of trigonometric functions
inverse trigonometric functions
graphs of inverse functions
proving identities
trigonometric formulas
trigonometric equations
solving oblique triangles
law of sines and law of cosines
law of tangents
oblique triangle applications
spherical trigonometry*

Topics which might be found in modern high school trigonometry textbooks are:

*sets, relations, and functions
circular functions
special values for trigonometric
    functions
relations among the
    trigonometric functions
reduction formulas
periodic properties
even and odd functions
graphing circular functions
    and their inverses
linear interpolation
period, amplitude, and
    phase shift
parametric equations
inverse trigonometric
    functions
identities*

*conditional equations
measure of an angle
uniform circular motion
trigonometric ratios and
    functions
the laws of sines and cosines
solving triangles
geometric vectors
n-dimensional vectors
polar coordinates
complex numbers
field properties
trigonometric form for
    complex numbers
De Moivre's theorem
logarithmic functions
exponential equations
properties of the real
    number system*

The modern school mathematics curriculum projects and textbook authors, influenced by these curriculum projects, included topics from modern mathematics in their versions of the new school mathematics curriculum and attempted to unify the various areas of school mathematics. Most modern algebra, geometry, and trigonometry textbooks include topics and applications from *each* of these three areas of mathematics with emphasis upon the structure as well as the techniques of mathematics. Rigor, structure, precision of language, deductive reasoning, unification, and applications are key terms in the philosophy and goals of most versions of the modern school mathematics curriculum.

The Secondary School Mathematics Curriculum Improvement Study

The Secondary School Mathematics Curriculum Improvement Study (SSMCIS) developed a completely unified mathematics curriculum for upper 20% ability level students in grades 7-12. The approach that the SSMCIS has taken to mathematics curriculum improvement is exemplified in the following quotations taken from its November, 1970 *Information Bulletin*.

> Now we are entering a second phase in the reconstruction of school mathematics which has as its purpose the presentation of mathematics as a unified body of knowledge reflecting the contemporary conception of the subject and the innovations that have occurred world-wide throughout the sixties. What is happening will have real significance for the continued improvement of mathematics during the decade of the seventies. (pp. 1-2)
>
> The realization that certain fundamental *concepts* are the structural backbone of all mathematical systems should be the basis for a new unified mathematics program. In the curriculum there should be built, with progressively increasing breadth and complexity, the ideas of set, relation, binary operation, and function (mapping); the fundamental structures of group, ring, field and vector space, as well as the most important examples of these abstract structures, i.e. the number systems, various geometries, probability, and the calculus, including numerical analysis related to digital computers. The resulting curriculum is (to borrow a term from modern biology) a kind of double helix in which the abstract concepts and structures develop simultaneously with the important realizations—the good old know-how of traditional mathematics.
>
> The algebraic structures that are studied should grow in complexity and abstractness from the very concrete beginnings in the study of operational systems up through groups, fields, and vector spaces, while at the same time, the illustrations of these structures should grow in complexity and importance from finite clock arithmetics to the real and complex number systems. (pp. 7-8)

True to its objectives and philosophy, the SSMCIS developed a secondary school curriculum which unifies modern school mathematics using a spiral approach to concept development. The 1972 revision of the SSMCIS program contains the following topics in the sequence given below:

Course 1.

finite number systems	*sets and relations*
operational systems	*number theory*
mathematical mappings	*rational numbers*
integers	*probability and statistics*
multiplying integers	*transformations in a plane*
lattice points	*using rational numbers*

Course 2.

measures and measurement	*fields*
sets and structure	*affine geometry*
mathematical reasoning and	*real number system*
language	*coordinate geometry*
groups	*descriptive statistics*
	real functions and graphs

Course 3.

matrix algebra	*rational functions*
linear systems	*probability and combinatories*
metric geometry	*circular functions*
polynomials	*informal solid geometry*
	vector spaces

Course 4.

computer programming	*vector algebra*
quadratic equations	*linear programming*
complex numbers	*sequences and series*
circular functions	*exponential functions*
conditional probability	*logarithmic functions*
random variables	*vector spaces*

Course 5.

continuity	*linear mappings*
limits	*linear programming*
linear approximations	*expectation*
derivatives	*Markov chains*
	integration

Course 6.

infinity	*analytic properties of*
conics	*logarithmic functions*
analytic properties of	*integration techniques*
circular functions	*applications of integration*
analytic properties of	*infinite outcome sets*
exponential functions	*problem solving strategies*

The New Math Curriculum: Success or Failure?

In the mid-nineteen sixties, when various modern mathematics curricula were being adopted in many schools throughout the country, a number of articles extolling the virtues of the new math appeared in newspapers and magazines. This new curriculum was praised as being modern, relevant, useful, and interesting for students. By learning about the structure of mathematics in addition to the techniques of computation, it was thought that students would find mathematics to be more meaningful and easier to understand. Students studying modern mathematics would be better prepared for college and for careers in science and technology. Ten years later in the mid nineteen seventies, when various modern mathematics curricula had become firmly established in a majority of the nation's schools, serious criticisms of the new math curriculum were appearing in these same newspapers and magazines. It was claimed that modern mathematics was only for the college-bound student. Basic arithmetic skills were being neglected. Overemphasis upon structure and symbolism was confusing and inappropriate for school students, and mathematics textbooks largely ignored the applications of mathematics. In fact, in 1973 Morris Kline (also an earlier critic of the proposed new mathematics curriculum) in his book *Why Johnny Can't Add* characterized most of the projects to improve school mathematics education as failures.

As the number of conflicting claims about the value of the modern mathematics curriculum continues to increase year by year, it is difficult to determine whether new math has been a success or a failure. In balancing the positive and negative assessments of the new math revolution, most well-informed people arrive at the conclusion that new math is neither a dismal failure nor an overwhelming success. The situation is not nearly as bad as the severest critics of new math claim. However, the mathematical competencies of a new generation schooled in modern mathematics are less than expected and somewhat disappointing. The new math curriculum has been a modest success, but it has not met all of the expectations of its supporters. Many students still dislike math, can't do arithmetic, and don't understand mathematical concepts.

The remaining paragraphs of this section contain some of the major arguments in support of and some arguments in opposition to the modern school mathematics curriculum. In reviewing the positive and negative opinions about new math (or any other subject) you should remember that rational opinions can be based upon conclusions resulting from two distinct processes. An opinion can be justified through an appeal to wisdom, insight, logical reasoning, and authority; however it can also be defended based upon empirical data gathered through careful research. Both methods of forming opinions and conclusions are useful and valid, but each method used in isolation from the other can result in spurious conclusions. For example, some of the negative statements about new math have been criticized by educational researchers because they are not based upon empirical evidence or even ignore existing empirical results; also some educational researchers are criticized for their excessive reliance upon data and statistics which may not accurately describe the situation which is being studied. There are many historical examples showing that an inept or unethical person can use both authoritative and empirical methods to justify inaccurate opinions and conclusions. Also, intelligent and ethical people can arrive at contradictory opinions and conclusions by using different methods and different sources of information—which is why two highly respected and honest mathematics educators can completely disagree about the value of the modern mathematics curriculum.

Even while the modern mathematics curriculum was still largely in the planning and experimental stages it was not without its critics. Morris Kline (1958), in a paper originally presented at the Thirty-sixth Annual Meeting of the National Council of Teachers of Mathematics, made a number of specific criticisms of the proposals for a new mathematics curriculum. He objected to proposals which included Boolean algebra, symbolic logic, set theory, abstract algebra and topology in the school mathematics curriculum. Some of these topics are peripheral to important mathematics; some are new and untried branches of mathematics; and some have limited applications. In fact one of Professor Kline's major objections to the proposed curriculum was the separation of mathematics from its many applications. He argued that the new curriculum would put abstract concepts before concrete materials; consequently mathematics would become less meaningful, to students. He also felt that school students were not sufficiently developed intellectually to understand or appreciate the proposed emphasis upon mathematical rigor, and that overemphasis upon rigor can hinder an intuitive understanding of concepts and can obscure the uses of mathematics. Professor Kline also thought that the proposed new math ignored the primary reason for the existence of mathematics (i.e., "the investigation of nature") and presented mathematics as an introverted, self-serving subject. He agreed that a drastic revision of the current school mathematics curriculum was needed, but that it should emphasize new approaches for presenting the standard content rather than substitute a different set of topics for those in the old curriculum. Any new approach should emphasize the role of mathematics in human activities, should give practice in intuitive thinking, and should arouse interest in mathematics.

Albert Meder, Jr. (1958) prepared a thoughtful and critical rebuttal to Morris Kline's remarks in which he argued that Professor Kline was poorly informed about what the new math curriculum developers intended to do and had misinterpreted some of their proposals. He also disagreed with Professor Kline regarding the importance of topics such as symbolic logic, topology, and Boolean algebra in mathematics and the appropriateness of including some topics from these areas of mathematics in secondary schools.

Although there were substantive differences of opinion as to which mathematics topics should be included in the proposed new curriculum, and whether mathematics should be presented as a discipline worthy of study in its own right or as a subject of use in other human endeavors, many of the disagreements seemed to have been the consequence of different people's interpretations of the same terms. For example, when one educator proposed including some symbolic logic in the curriculum, he or she may have meant including a brief section on propositional calculus and truth tables, together with a few of the symbols of symbolic logic. A research mathematician may have envisioned a theoretical college-level development of the subject. Also, what a professional research mathematician means by set theory, topology, and abstract algebra is usually not at all similar to what a high school mathematics teacher means by these terms. Even though the modern mathematics curriculum which was eventually produced did not meet with the approval of Morris Kline and other critics of the proposed curriculum, it appears that their criticisms did have a moderating effect upon the degree of change. No modern mathematics curriculum textbook series has come close to meeting the recommendations of the Cambridge Conference; however, some have been influenced by this Conference.

When the modern mathematics curriculum was still in the proposal stage, both its proponents and opponents had to justify their positions by using authoritative type arguments. Since the new curriculum did not yet exist, no one could try it out and compare the attitudes and competencies of students who studied new math to those of students who studied old math. What *was* known as a consequence of empirical research was that most high school students didn't like mathematics very well. Mathematics was regarded as a very difficult subject, and most high school students were ill prepared to study mathematics in college or to use it in technical vocations. Some attempts were made to compare the mathematical competencies of high school students in the United States to those of foreign students of the same age who were studying "modern" mathematics in their home countries. Such attempts were not very successful in settling the issue because most countries did not have a universal educational system where nearly everyone of ages 12-17 went to school for a general, liberal education. In many countries the intellectually elite studied college-level mathematics at a young age and less talented people prepared for a trade or did not attend school.

In 1967 when much of the new math curriculum had been developed and was being used in many schools, Herbert Fremont published an article titled "New Mathematics and Old Dilemmas." Compared to the writers of 1958, Mr. Fremont had the advantage of being able to base his opinions about new math upon the experience of teachers and students who were using the new curriculum. Also some, but not much empirical evidence concerning the effectiveness of new math had been gathered and reported in the journals. In his article Fremont reacted to what he viewed as an inordinate body of literature in single-minded, unsubstantiated praise of modern mathematics—something which **must** be good because it is **modern** and not old-fashioned. He criticized the new math emphasis upon the role of unification in mathematics as being impossible for students to appreciate when they have no understanding of what it is that is being unified. According to Fremont, the new math of 1967 appeared to have been built upon many of the shortcomings of the old math. Students still did not understand and appreciate mathematics, and meaningless manipulations were being carried out by students using the new symbols of modern mathematics. However, he did find some hope for the future of mathematics education: inertia had been overcome and change was continuing.

By 1974 both the critics and proponents of modern mathematics had new information to use in their arguments about the merits of the new curriculum. A number of empirical studies (some which were short-term doctoral dissertation research projects and others which were long-term evaluation projects) had been conducted to compare various new-math and old-math curricula and to assess student performance and attitudes. Most of the doctoral dissertations indicated that students who studied new math did about as well on tests of arithmetic skills, and did somewhat better on tests of understanding. Some state and local testing programs for arithmetic skills found that students were not learning arithmetic as well in 1974 as they had several years previously, and the inference was made that studying new math with its emphasis upon theory and structure may have caused the decrease in arithmetic scores. Although this may be a correct interpretation of the cause of the decrease in scores, it may also be incorrect. It is a fact that the decrease in arithmetic skills coincided with the adoption of the new math curriculum; however, it is not known whether new math or some other factor caused the decrease. Just because two events occur simultaneously, does not necessarily mean that one caused the other.

A large body of empirical data (test scores and statistical data) concerning mathematics achievement and related information such as student attitudes and teacher behavior has been gathered by two national projects—the National Longitudinal Study of Mathematical Abilities (NLSMA) and the National Assessment of Educational Progress (NAEP). The NLSMA which was a project directed by the School Mathematics Study Group (SMSG) is described in the SMSG *Newsletter No. 30* as follows:

The National Longitudinal Study of Mathematical Abilities was a five-year study, carried out during the years of 1962-1967. Over 112,000 students from 1,500 schools in 40 states participated in the Study. The primary purpose of

NLSMA was to identify and measure variables associated with the development of mathematical abilities (e.g., textbook effect, attitude, teacher background, etc.).

A large population of students at each of three grade levels was tested in the fall and spring of each year, beginning with grades 4 (X Population), 7 (Y Population), and 10 (Z Population) in the fall of 1962. The X-Population and Y-Population were tested for five years. The Z-Population was tested for three years and then followed with questionnaires after graduating from high school. The design stressed three features: (1) the long-term study of a group of students—up to five years, (2) study of the same grade level at different times—for instance, grades 7-8 in 1962-64 for the Y-Population and again in 1965-67 for the X-Population, and (3) extensive data on mathematics achievement and psychological variables for grades 4 through 12. (p. 17)

E. G. Begle, the director of SMSG, reported in 1973 on some of the findings of the NLSMA and other SMSG activities. The findings discussed in this article refute some of the arguments which were voiced in opposition to the early proposals for new mathematics curricula. Textbooks that concentrate on the structure of mathematics are not harmful to students. Students using such books did better on problem-solving tests and about the same on tests of mathematical skills. There is also abundant evidence that teachers should teach for understanding. It was found that higher-level mathematics topics, when presented in an appropriate manner, could be taught to students at younger ages than many people had anticipated. This indicates that specific topics don't necessarily have to be based upon the age of the student, but rather can be based upon the overall structure of mathematics. Some people thought that only the brighter students would be able to understand new math; such is not the case. Below average seventh-graders who were given two years to cover what superior students covered in one year did better than the superior students. This suggests that differences in ability may be more quantitative than qualitative. The SMSG data analysis indicated that, contrary to the concerns of some critics, both high and low IQ students can learn new math. It was also discovered that fourth graders have favorable attitudes toward mathematics which tend to increase until junior high school when attitudes drop slowly but steadily until the end of high school. The SMSG found that drill in arithmetic is not sufficient for improving higher level skills such as understanding and problem-solving.

In 1969 the National Assessment of Educational Progress began as an activity of the Education Commission of the States. The NAEP was created to measure the growth or decline in educational attainments throughout the United States over periods of several years. The following description of the NAEP is given in the Foward to *Math Fundamentals: Selected Results from the First National Assessment of Mathematics,* January, 1975.

The National Assessment of Educational Progress (NAEP) is an information-gathering project which surveys the educational attainments of 9-year-olds, 13-year-olds, 17-year-olds and adults (ages 26-35) in 10 learning areas: art, career and occupational development, citizenship, literature, mathematics, music, reading, science, social studies and writing. Different learning areas are assessed every year, and all areas are periodically reassessed in order to measure educational change.

Each assessment is the product of several years work by a great many educators, scholars and lay persons from all over the country. Initially, these people design objectives for each area, proposing specific goals which they feel Americans should be achieving in the course of their education. After careful reviews, these objectives are then given to exercise (item) writers, whose task it is to create measurement tools appropriate to the objectives.

When the exercises have passed extensive reviews by subject-matter specialists and measurement experts, they are administered to probability samples from various age groups. The people who comprise these samples are chosen in such a way that the results of their assessment can be generalized to an entire national population. That is, on the basis of the performance of about 2,500 9-year-olds on a given exercise, we can generalize about the probable performance of all 9-year-olds in the nation. (p. ix)

In 1972-73 the NAEP conducted its first survey of mathematics attainment and found that mastery of basic arithmetic skills does improve from ages 9 to 13 to 17. Most young Americans were found to be able to add, subtract, multiply, and divide, and people in the 26 to 35 age group do about the same as 17-year-olds. While it was found that most adults can add, subtract, multiply, and divide whole numbers, a significant number of people have trouble with fractions, decimals, and more complex combinations of arithmetic operations. However, it does appear that the formal educational system in the United States is successful in teaching basic arithmetic skills. One might infer from the fact that 17-year-olds and adults from 26 to 35 performed equally well on tests of arithmetic skills that the spread of new math has not resulted in a deterioration of basic skills. The people who were in the 26 to 35 age group in 1972 were likely to have completed high school before modern mathematics programs were implemented in their schools, and the 17-year-olds in 1972 probably studied some of their mathematics from modern mathematics textbooks. After the second national assessment of mathematics competencies has been completed, we will have a better measure of changes in student performance which may reflect changes in the effectiveness of our schools.

The criticisms of the modern mathematics school curriculum are epitomized in Morris Kline's book *Why Johnny Can't Add* which was published in 1973. Since the book is subtitled *The Failure of the New Math,* there is little doubt that Professor Kline has not changed his mind about new math between 1958 and 1973. Professor Kline does cite a number of valid general criticisms of new math in this book. However, he tends to base some of his generalizations upon horrible examples; for example, one new math book which overemphasizes structure and rigor or one case of a poor mathematics teacher. In offering suggestions as to what should be done about the shortcomings of new math, Professor Kline emphasizes the importance of good teaching:

The training of good teachers is far more important than the curriculum. Such teachers can do wonders with any curriculum. Witness the number of good mathematicians we have trained under the traditional curriculum, which is decidedly unsatisfactory. A poor teacher and a good curriculum will teach poorly whereas a good teacher will overcome the deficiencies of any curriculum. (p. 170)

and

I think that we owe what we have accomplished [in mathematics] to a few wise, mature, devoted teachers who by their care in choosing what to emphasize and by their personal charm and magnetism have attracted some students to mathematics. These noble souls have saved us from disaster. (p. 170)

Every mathematics teacher should read *Why Johnny Can't Add* which is a thoughtful criticism of new math based upon ''authoritative'' type arguments. However, no teacher should read this book without also reading Edward Begle's review of it, which was published in the 1974 January/February issue of *The National Elementary Principal*. Professor Begle used ''empirical'' type arguments to refute many of Professor Kline's criticisms of new math.

In summary, there are several lessons for the mathematics teacher in the continuing controversy over the successes and failures of new math. First, there is a genuine disagreement over what should be emphasized in school mathematics. Witness the fact that some opponents of new math criticize it because:

1. It is too abstract and deductive.
2. It is introverted and does not sufficiently emphasize the applications of mathematics.
3. It overemphasizes structure, rigor, and symbolism.
4. It includes topics such as sets, logic, inequalities, and number theory which should not be taught in elementary and secondary schools.
5. It overemphasizes relatively new and not very useful areas of mathematics such as topology and symbolic logic and underemphasizes important historical topics such as Euclidean solid geometry, theory of equations and arithmetic skills.

In contrast, some proponents of modern math praise it because:

1. It illustrates the abstract, deductive nature of modern mathematics.
2. It contains important topics from modern mathematics which have significant applications in other fields of study.
3. It illustrates the unifying structure of mathematics, is rigorous enough to show the sound foundations of modern mathematics and employs appropriate modern mathematical symbolism.
4. It contains topics such as set theory, logic, inequalities, and number theory which should be taught in schools.
5. It includes new and useful areas of mathematics such as topology and logic and de-emphasizes outmoded topics such as Euclidean geometry, theory of equations and rote memorization of arithmetic skills.

As you can see from these two lists, one person can use the same reasons to support new math as someone else might use to criticize it. This fact illustrates our second lesson for the teacher. A well-informed objective teacher should examine both sides of an issue (especially the new math issue), find out why supporters and opponents of the issue use the same ''facts'' to arrive at contradictory conclusions, and form a reasonable position on the issue which is based upon authoritative and empirical arguments on both sides of the issue.

A third lesson to be learned from the controversy about new math is that many people are concerned that our children obtain a good education in mathematics and these people are willing to expend a significant amount of resources to meet this objective. However, educational improvement is not easy and is never finished. Consequently, it is critical to mathematics education that every teacher learn how to make intelligent selections from the vast variety of curriculum materials available, and that he or she continue to gather new information to improve his or her classroom teaching.

Things To Do

1. Write a brief discussion of the forces which converged about 1950 to set the scene for a new school mathematics curriculum.

2. Select one or two of the following mathematics curriculum projects and discuss the factors influencing each project, the philosophy of the project, and the nature and content of the mathematics curriculum produced by the project:

    Comprehensive School Mathematics Program
    The Greater Cleveland Mathematics Program
    Madison Project
    Minnesota Mathematics and Science Teaching Project
    University of Illinois Arithmetic Project
    University of Maryland Mathematics Project

    Any one of the recent editions of *Report of the International Clearinghouse on Science and Mathematics Curricular Developments* (see the bibliography at the end of this chapter) will be helpful in locating information for this activity.

3. Carry out the following activity after placing the word *algebra, trigonometry,* or *geometry* in each of the blanks:

    Select a copy of a high school _____ textbook published before 1950 and a copy of a high school _____ textbook published after 1970 which is promoted as a *modern* book. Carefully browse through the books and list the similarities and differences between these two "old math" and "new math" textbooks. Be sure to look for differences in both content and methods of presenting topics. A good source for such textbooks is either a college curriculum library or a high school mathematics department.

4. Interview a high school mathematics teacher who was teaching mathematics both before 1950 and after 1970 and ask him or her about his or her opinions of new math and old math. You might ask such questions as:
    A. Which did you prefer teaching, new math or old math? Why?
    B. Do you think new math is better than old math? Why?
    C. Did students learn skills better when studying old math? Why?
    D. What are the differences between new and old math?
    E. Do students understand new math better than old math? Why?
    F. Do students studying new math appear to like mathematics better than those who studied old math? Why?
    G. If you could dictate another new math curriculum, what would you

delete from the present curriculum? What new topics would you include? Why?

5. List the criticisms and the positive comments about the modern mathematics curriculum and discuss the validity of both the praise and criticism. Why do you think there are so many contradictory opinions about the value of the new math curriculum?

6. Choose a college that prepares secondary school mathematics teachers and search through one of their older (before 1950) catalogs and their current catalog to find the differences between their former and current requirements for secondary school mathematics teacher certification. What courses are no longer required? What new courses are required? Compare the catalog descriptions of the courses required for mathematics teachers before 1950 and those required now.

Selected Bibliography

Aichele, Douglas B. and Reys, Robert E. (Editors) *Readings in Secondary School Mathematics.* Boston, Mass.: Prindle, Weber, & Schmidt, 1971.

A collection of articles on mathematics education, this book is divided into nine parts each of which contains several articles pertaining to a particular issue in mathematics education. Parts I and II deal with mathematics curriculum reform in the United States and other parts of the world. The book also contains an extensive bibliography on secondary school mathematics education.

Begle, E. G. "Some Lessons Learned by SMSG." *The Mathematics Teacher* 66 (1973): 207-214.

This article, based upon the National Longitudinal Study of Mathematical Abilities and other studies of the effectiveness of the modern mathematics curriculum, indicates which variables are related to student achievement in mathematics and which are not. Various teacher, student, and curriculum variables were studied in controlled experiments to determine which variables are related to student achievement and what effects the modern mathematics curriculum has had upon student performance.

Begle, Edward G. and Selfridge, Oliver. "What's All the Controversy About? Two Reviews of *Why Johnny Can't Add.*" *The National Elementary Principal* LIII, 2 (1974): 26-34.

This pair of reviews of *Why Johnny Can't Add,* the first quite critical and the second in qualified agreement, should be read after reading Morris Kline's book. They contain two thoughtful viewpoints of the successes and failures of new math. The entire issue of the journal containing this article is about mathematics education and contains other articles about modern mathematics.

Bidwell, James K. and Clason, Robert G. *Readings in the History of Mathematics Education.* Washington, D.C.: National Council of Teachers of Mathematics, 1970.

This book is a collection of original articles about mathematics education, which was compiled from many different sources. The articles were written between 1830 and 1970 and were selected to represent the nature of mathematics education throughout this 140 year period. The articles are grouped into four sections:

1. Beginnings of the Art of Teaching Mathematics, 1828-1890.
2. Emergence of National Organizations as a Force in Mathematics Education, 1891-1919.
3. The "1923 Report" and Connectionism in Arithmetic, 1920-1937.
4. Prewar and Postwar Reforms, 1938-1959.

Cambridge Conference on School Mathematics. *Goals for School Mathematics*. Boston: Houghton Mifflin Company, 1963.

The report of the Cambridge Conference, this one-hundred page paperbound book contains the recommendations of a group of 29 scientists and mathematicians for topics to be included in school mathematics from grades K-12. Two alternative lists of topics recommended for each grade level are included in the book. This report contains a very ambitious set of goals for school mathematics, and has served as a source for topics which have been included in several college preparatory mathematics curriculum projects.

Critchfield, Margot. "Recent Trends in Mathematics Curriculum Research." *Creative Computing* 1, 4 (1975): 64-69.

A brief review of mathematics curriculum change, the article also contains a useful chronological chart of most of the major mathematics curriculum projects from 1952 to 1974.

Fehr, Howard F., Fey, James T., and Hill, Thomas J. *Unified Mathematics*. Menlo Park, California: Addison-Wesley Publishing Company, 1972.

Fremont, Herbert. "New Mathematics and Old Dilemmas." *The Mathematics Teacher* 60 (1967): 715-719.

Griffiths, H. B. and Howson, A. G. *Mathematics: Society and Curricula*. London: Cambridge University Press, 1974.

This book presents a comprehensive discussion of new mthematics in the United States and Great Britain. It examines the objectives of modern mathematics as well as the factors influencing the development of modern mathematics programs. It also contains a detailed look at the topics taught in school mathematics in the United States and Great Britain, providing an excellent source for a comparison of the two countries' approaches to new math.

Johnson, David C. and Johnson, Donovan A. "Evaluating a School Mathematics Program." North Central Association Quarterly 41 (1966): 184-191.

Kline, Morris. "The Ancients Versus the Moderns." *The Mathematics Teacher* 51 (1958): 418-427.

―――. *Why Johnny Can't Add: The Failure of the New Math*. New York: St. Martin's Press, 1973.

Throughout the nineteen sixties Morris Kline was one of many critics of the developing new mathematics curriculum, and this book contains his view that new math is a failure. He briefly discusses the nature of modern mathematics, origins of the new math curriculum movement, the content of the new math curriculum, and recommendations for improving the school mathematics curriculum. Professor Kline, who is a severe critic of new math, is not without his own critics, and Professor Edward Begle who directed the SMSG offers a thoughtful rebuttal of *Why Johnny Can't Add* in his article which is referenced above.

Lockard, J. David (Editor). *Seventh Report of the International Clearinghouse on Science and Mathematics Curricular Developments 1970.* University of Maryland: American Association for the Advancement of Science and the Science Teaching Center, University of Maryland, 1970.

This Clearinghouse publication, which is revised and updated every two years, contains descriptions of many of the major (and not so major) science and mathematics curriculum development projects in the world. This is a convenient reference for mathematics teachers interested in where the current mathematics curriculum projects are located and what materials have been produced by each project.

———. *Eighth Report of the International Clearinghouse on Science and Mathematics Curricular Developments 1972.* University of Maryland: American Association for the Advancement of Science and the Science Teaching Center, University of Maryland, 1972.

Meder, Albert E., Jr. "The Ancients Versus the Moderns—A Reply." *The Mathematics Teacher* 51 (1958): 428-433.

National Assessment of Educational Progress. *Math Fundamentals: Selected Results from the First National Assessment of Mathematics.* Denver, Colo.: Education Commission of the States, 1975.

In the 1972-73 school year over 90,000 people of age levels 9, 13, 17, and 26-35 were tested for a wide variety of mathematical skills. Probability sampling procedures were used to assure that those people who were chosen to participate in the study of arithmetic skills were representative of the total population of the United States at each of the four age levels. Percentages of success on a variety of arithmetic skill questions are reported for the age groups tested.

Ray, Joseph. *Ray's Arithmetic: Part Third. On the Inductive and Analytic Methods of Instruction Embracing Cancellation and Factoring.* Cincinnati: Winthrop B. Smith & Co., 1849.

An interesting old arithmetic book which attempts to teach arithmetic skills with understanding of concepts and principles, this textbook contains interspersed among its topics hints to the teacher on how to teach arithmetic. It also contains "Notes to Teachers" at the beginning of each topic explaining why that topic is important for students to learn. This old mathematics textbook contains a very modern approach to teaching arithmetic.

School Mathematics Study Group. *Newsletter No. 30: Status Reports, Recent Publications.* Stanford, California: School Mathematics Study Group, March, 1969.

Secondary School Mathematics Curriculum Improvement Study. *Information Bulletin 5: Why a New Program in Mathematics.* Columbia University, New York: November, 1970.

———. *Unified Modern Mathematics.* Columbia University, New York: Teachers College Press, 1972.

The National Council of Teachers of Mathematics. *A History of Mathematics Education in the United States and Canada.* Washington, D.C.: National Council of Teachers of Mathematics, 1970.

The Thirty-second Yearbook of the National Council of Teachers of Mathematics, this book provides a comprehensive review of mathematics education from 1620 to 1970 in the United States and Canada. It contains just about everything that a person might want to know about the history of mathematics education with sections about the forces and issues related to curriculum and instruction, the development of and reaction to the new math curricula, and the education of mathematics teachers. This book is a fine reference on mathematics education, and contains an excellent bibliography of the history of mathematics education.

Wilson, James W. and Begle, Edward G. *NLSMA Reports, Numbers 1-30*. Leland Stanford Junior University, Stanford, California: School Mathematics Study Group, 1972.

This series of 30 paper-bound reports prepared by the School Mathematics Study Group presents the findings of the National Longitudinal Study of Mathematical Abilities (NLSMA). The NLSMA was organized as a long-term study of the effects on students of various school mathematics programs.

The Arithmetic Teacher and *The Mathematics Teacher*. Washington, D.C.: National Council of Teachers of Mathematics.

These two journals have charted the development and evaluation of the modern mathematics curriculum. Many of the past issues of both journals contain one or more articles about the new math curriculum. A quick browse through the tables of contents of issues of these journals will provide a good list of references on new math.

3

Using Learning and Instructional Theories in Teaching Mathematics

Understanding of theories about how people learn and the ability to apply these theories in teaching mathematics are important prerequisites for effective mathematics teaching. Many people have approached the study of intellectual development and the nature of learning in different ways; this has resulted in several theories of learning. Although there is still some disagreement among psychologists, learning theorists, and educators about how people learn and the most effective methods for promoting learning, there are many areas of agreement. The different theories of learning should not be viewed as a set of competing theories, one of which is true and the others false. Each theory can be regarded as a method of organizing and studying some of the many variables in learning and intellectual development, and teachers can select and apply elements of each theory in their own classes. You may find that some theories are more applicable to you and your students because they seem to be appropriate models for the learning environment and the students with whom you interact. However, a perceptive teacher will find some applications of each learning theory for his or her students. As a consequence of being able to appreciate the learning theoretic reasons for various forms of behavior exhibited by each student, he or she will be a more understanding and sympathetic teacher.

In the past many mathematics teachers and teacher educators neglected the application of theories about the nature of learning and centered their teaching methods around knowledge of the subject. Recent findings in learning theory, better understanding of mental development, and new applications of theory to classroom teaching now enable teachers to choose teaching strategies according to information about the nature of learning. The purpose of this chapter is to present several of the major theories about the nature of intellectual development, to discuss theories about learning, and to illustrate applications of each theory to teaching and learning mathematics.

First, we will look at the theory of **Jean Piaget** who has determined and studied the various stages through which humans progress in their intellectual growth from birth to adulthood. Next we will consider the work of **J. P. Guilford,** who has developed and tested a theoretical model of human intellectual structure. Guilford and his associates have identified *one hundred twenty* intellectual aptitudes which encompass many of the mental abilities which are capable of being measured and evaluated. We will also consider the work of **Robert Gagné** who has identified four phases of a learning sequence. These phases are the apprehending phase, the acquisition phase, the storage phase, and the retrieval phase. Gagné also has specified eight types of learning which can be distinguished from each other according to the necessary conditions for the occurrence of each learning type; they are signal learning, stimulus-response learning, chaining, verbal association, discrimination learning, concept learning, rule learning, and problem-solving. The theories and work of **Zoltan Dienes** are also relevant to teaching mathematics. Dienes regards mathematics as the study of structures and relationships among structures and has developed a system for mathematics education which is based upon a theory of learning and a process for teaching mathematics. **David Ausubel** has made significant contributions to the study of verbal learning, which he believes can be accomplished through careful consideration of the structure of the discipline and by using appropriate principles to order the subject matter for presentation to students. The psychologist **Jerome Bruner** has listed general theorems for instruction and has developed a philosophy of education centered around the structural framework essential for learning, student readiness for learning, intuition, and motivation to learn. His general theories are also relevant for mathematics teachers. **B. F. Skinner** has conducted extensive studies of behavior and has developed a science of human behavior based upon his work in behavioral analysis. His writings suggest ways in which teachers can create more effective learning situations by using appropriate techniques to elicit desirable behaviors from students.

Piaget's Theory of Intellectual Development

According to the theory of the noted Swiss psychologist Jean Piaget, human intellectual development progresses chronologically through four sequential stages. The order in which the stages occur has been found to be invariant among people; however the ages at which people enter each higher order stage vary according to each person's unique hereditary and environmental characteristics.

Sensory-Motor Stage

The first period of intellectual development, called the *sensory-motor stage,* extends from birth until about two years of age. In this period the infant's learning consists of developing and organizing his or her physical and mental activities into well-defined sequences of actions called *schemas.* From birth to two years of age children learn to coordinate their senses and movements, learn that an object which is removed from sight does not cease to exist, and learn to attach word symbols to physical objects. For example, near the end of this stage a child can recognize the sound of father closing the front door to leave for work, can totter to the window and watch him get on the bus, and understands that he will return later. In this period children progress from having only reflex abilities at birth to being able to walk and talk at two years of age.

Preoperational Stage

98

The second period, the *preoperational stage,* extends from approximately age two to age seven. In this stage children are very *egocentric;* that is, they assimilate most experiences in the world at large into schemas developed from their immediate environment and view everything in relation to themselves. Young children believe that all their thoughts and experiences are shared by everyone else, that inanimate objects have animate characteristics, and that the distinction between one and many is of little consequence. This explains why a young child does not question a different Santa Claus on every street corner and Santa Claus mannequins in every department store window. The preoperational thinker has difficulty reversing thoughts and reconstructing actions, can not consider two aspects of an object or a situation simultaneously, and does not reason *inductively* (from specific to general) or *deductively* (from general to specific). The young child reasons *transductively;* that is, from specific instances to specific instances. In this stage children can not differentiate fact and fancy, which is why their ''lies'' are not a consequence of any moral deficiency, but result from their inability to separate real events from the world of their imaginations. Through physical maturation and interacting with his or her environment, the child in the pre-conceptual stage is developing the necessary mental schemas to operate at a higher intellectual level. Near the end of this stage children become capable of giving reasons for their beliefs, can classify sets of objects according to a single specified characteristic, and begin to attain some actual concepts.

Concrete Operational Stage

The *concrete operational stage* of mental development extends from age seven to age twelve, thirteen or even later. At the beginning of this stage there is a substantial decrease in children's egocentricity; play with other children replaces isolated play and individualized play in the presence of other children. In this stage children become able to classify objects having several characteristics into sets and subsets according to specified characteristics, and they can simultaneously consider several characteristics of an object. They begin to understand jokes; however they still have trouble explaining proverbs and fail to see hidden meanings. They are now able to deal with complex relationships between classes, can reverse operations and procedures, and can understand and visualize intermediate states of a transformation such as the sun rising and setting. In the concrete operational period children become able to see another person's viewpoint and near the end of this period begin to reason inductively and deductively; however many still tend to regard successive examples of a general principle as unrelated events.

Although children in this stage do develop many of the intellectual abilities found in adults, they have difficulties understanding verbal abstractions. They can perform complex operations such as reversibility, substitution, unions and intersections of sets, and serial orderings on concrete objects, but may not be able to carry out these same operations with verbal symbols. Their powers of judgment and logical reasoning are not well developed, and they rarely can solve a problem such as: Jane is taller than Bill; Jane is shorter than Susan; who is shortest of the three? However, children in this stage can order a pile of sticks from shortest to longest. Before the end of this period children are seldom able to formulate a precise, descriptive definition; although they can memorize another person's definition and reproduce what they have memorized. In this stage children learn to differentiate between deliberate wrongdoing and inadvertent mistakes. Even after developing a conception of rules and morality, they still attach a mystical aura to the origin of rules, morals, laws, and conventions, as well as the origin of names. To preadolescent children, a rose is called a rose because it *is* a rose, not because someone named it a rose.

This developmental period is called concrete operational because psychologists have found that children between seven and twelve have trouble applying formal intellectual processes to verbal symbols and abstract ideas; even though by age twelve most children have become quite adept at using their intellect to manipulate concrete physical objects. In this period children like to build things, manipulate objects, and make mechanical gadgets operate.

Formal Operational Stage

When adolescents reach the *formal operational stage,* they no longer need to rely upon concrete operations to represent or illustrate mental abstractions. They are now able to simultaneously consider many viewpoints, to regard their own actions objectively, and to reflect upon their own thought processes. The formal operational thinker can formulate theories, generate hypotheses, and test various hypotheses. People who have reached this intellectual stage can appreciate degrees of good and evil and can view definitions, rules and laws in a proper, objective context. They can also think inductively and deductively and can argue by implication (i.e., if *x* then *y*). Adolescents are able to understand and apply complex concepts such as permutations and combinations, proportions, correlations, and probability; and they can conceive of the infinitely large and the infinitesimally small.

Factors in Intellectual Development

Piagetian theory explains intellectual development as a process of assimilation and accommodation of information into the mental structure. *Assimilation* is the process through which new information and experiences are incorporated into mental structure, and *accommodation* is the resulting restructuring of the mind as a consequence of new information and experiences. The mind not only receives new information but it restructures its old information to accommodate the new. For example, new information about a political personality is not only added to the mind's old information about that person. This information may also alter the individual's viewpoint of politics, politicians, and government in general, and may even change his or her moral and ethical values. Learning is not merely adding new information to the stack of old information, because every piece of new information causes the stack of old information to be modified to accommodate the assimilation of the new information.

According to Piaget's theory, there are several factors influencing intellectual development. First, the physiological growth of the brain and nervous system is an important factor in general intellectual progress. This growth process is called *maturation.* Piaget also recognizes the importance of experience in mental development and identifies two types of experience. *Physical experience* is the interaction of each person with objects in his or her environment, and *logico-mathematical experiences* are those mental actions performed by individuals as their mental schemas are restructured according to their experiences. Another factor, *social transmission,* is the interaction and cooperation of a person with other people and is quite important for the development of logic in a child's mind. Piaget believes that formal operations would not develop in the mind without an exchange and coordination of viewpoints among people. The last factor, *equilibration,* is the process whereby a person's mental structure loses its stability as a consequence of new experiences and returns to equilibrium through the processes of assimilation and accommodation. As a result of equilibration, mental structures develop and mature. Piaget believes that these five factors (maturation, physical experience, logico-mathematical experience, social transmission, and equilibration) account for intellectual development and that each one must be present if a person is to progress through the four stages of intellectual development.

The four stages of development (sensory-motor, preoperational, concrete operational, and formal operational) while sequential in nature, do not have well-defined starting and ending points. The progression from one stage to the next occurs over a period of time and each individual may vacillate in his or her ability to exhibit the higher order mental processes throughout this transitional period. Even after a person has completed the transition from one stage to the next, he or she may still use mental processes associated with the earlier stages. An adolescent who has developed his or her intellectual capabilities to the formal operational stage has the mental structures necessary to carry out formal operations, but will not always do so. Many formal operational adults frequently count on their fingers which is a preoperational trait. A young person who has entered the formal operational stage will continue to improve his or her formal operational skills for many years.

Piaget's Theory and Teaching Mathematics

Several years ago while discussing teaching methods with a young mathematics teacher, she remarked that she was appalled because most of her seventh graders could not understand even a simple proof. I asked if she had studied Piaget's learning theories in college, and she replied that she had but didn't see what that had to do with her seventh graders doing mathematical proofs. This incident illustrates the need for teachers to see the applications in their own teaching of the theories which they learn in college, and for teacher educators to show prospective teachers the applications of learning theory.

Since seventh graders are twelve or thirteen years of age, some of them are still in the concrete operational stage, others have just entered the stage of formal operations, and still others are in transition between these two stages of intellectual development. Consequently, many seventh grade students' intellectual development has not yet progressed to the point where they have the mental structures necessary for constructing formal mathematical proofs. Some of these students do not yet see the difference between a single instance of a general principle and a proof of that principle. This is not to say that a seventh grade teacher should not explore the nature of intuitive and formal mathematical proofs with students; however he or she should realize that a twelve year old adolescent has a different mental structure (as well as an obviously different physical structure) than a twenty-two year old teacher.

Since secondary level mathematics teachers are expected to be able to teach students in middle schools, junior high schools and high schools, they must prepare to teach students ranging in age from eleven to nineteen. Sixth, seventh, and eighth grade teachers can expect to find many concrete operational students in their classes, and even some high school juniors and seniors are still in this stage of intellectual development. Therefore, it is appropriate for us to examine the intellectual attributes which some secondary school students do not have, but which are required to carry out many standard school mathematics learning activities.

A teacher should expect certain complex abilities, skills and behaviors from a student who is in the formal operational stage and should be concerned if formal operational mental processes are not exhibited. However, at every secondary school grade level there are students who have not completely entered the formal operational stage, and teachers should be aware of the behaviors that can be expected from these students. Such students merely illustrate the fact that people mature mentally at different ages which is analogous to the different rates of physical maturation which we have come to expect. No teacher would regard a seventh grader who is small for his age group as a physical cripple, and neither should teachers regard children who mature intellectually at a later age as being mentally retarded. Every mathematics teacher, especially those who teach in grades six through nine, should expect many students to be in the concrete operational stage, should be understanding of students' mental inabilities in this stage, should provide learning strategies appropriate for concrete operations, and should plan activities to help students progress to the stage of formal operations.

Students in grades six through nine are difficult to teach because they are still testing their recently discovered concrete operational abilities while they are entering the formal operational stage. Concrete operational students have discovered that rules are not absolute, but are arbitrary. These students are trying out their own rules and challenging the teacher's rules, which results in what we usually call discipline problems. In this period children need to associate and talk to other children as an aid to entering the formal operational stage through the process of social transmission. As a result junior high school students may appear to teachers to be talkative, noisy, rowdy, and undisciplined. What seems to adults to be a lot of fooling around on the part of students is partly a means of fostering their intellectual development.

These students do not want to accept statements based only upon the teacher's authority and do not care to accept new concepts which are outside their ability to visualize and conceptualize. Consequently they would be unlikely to either believe or accept on faith the concept of different orders of infinities or the fact that the cardinal number of the set of counting numbers is the same as the cardinal number of the set of even counting numbers which is a proper subset of the counting numbers. In fact, most concrete operational students have trouble with the concept of infinity and indefinite subdivisions of a line segment into arbitrarily small segments.

Junior high school students enjoy working with diagrams, models, and other physical devices; they need to relate new abstract concepts to physical reality and their own experiences. New topics in mathematics should be introduced through concrete examples, and intuition and experimentation should play a large part in teaching strategies for new principles and concepts. In geometry one should expect that many students will have trouble visualizing three-dimensional objects and relationships among objects. They will need to construct and manipulate models of geometric figures. Geometry in the junior high school should be presented informally and intuitively and formal geometric proof should wait until students are well into their formal operational stage of intellectual development. For a few people this will not happen until their freshman or sophomore year in college.

Although concrete operational students can formulate and use concepts correctly they have trouble explaining concepts using mathematical and verbal symbols. As a result of this deficiency, many students (maybe even most younger students) can not solve mathematical word problems, and resort to memorizing patterns and trial and error problem-solving. Their trial and error attempts are so unsystematic that they may keep repeating incorrect trials. As might be expected, many younger high school students are unable to make meaningful definitions of mathematical terms and merely memorize definitions.

Concrete thinkers can not be expected to solve logical puzzles or to resolve mathematical paradoxes. Also they tend not to be able to arrive at generalizations based upon a number of similar instances. For instance, they would not arrive at the commutative principle for addition, $a + b = b + a$, from examples such as $2 + 3 = 3 + 2$ and $8 + 11 = 11 + 8$. These children will not be able to handle several variables simultaneously, and complex relationships such as proportions and functions of several variables are inappropriate for many middle school children. Mathematical symbols and manipulations involve formal operations, and many students learn algebra by memorizing rules for combining and manipulating symbols with little understanding of the meaning of algebraic techniques. For example, $(x + y)^2 = x^2 + y^2$, $\dfrac{a + b}{a} = b$, and $\sqrt{x^2 + y^2} = x + y$

are perfectly sensible statements for many algebra students. Even numerical counterexamples to illustrate the fallacy of these statements are not meaningful to students who are merely manipulating x's, y's, a's, and b's according to arbitrary rules.

In conclusion, it should be pointed out that Piaget and his close associates have been concerned with studying and defining the nature and development of human thought and have not attempted to specify methods for improving teaching and learning. It has been left to others to apply the theories and findings of the Piagetians to classroom teaching. Many of the experiments which were developed to determine the stages of intellectual development involve observing and recording children's responses when they are given tasks of a mathematical nature. Consequently, some of the types of mathematical problems which children can handle at different ages and intellectual levels have been specified by the Piagetians. Even though much work on Piaget's theory of intellectual development remains to be done, his theory has gained wide acceptance among psychologists, learning theorists, and educators. Every mathematics teacher should be familiar with Piaget's work and should apply his discoveries about mental readiness for various learning tasks to his or her own teaching. Heed the example at the beginning of this topic of the teacher who knew the theory but never thought to apply it in her own classes. Some of the **Things to Do** and

references in the **Selected Bibliography** at the end of this chapter will help you
learn more about applications of Piaget's theory in mathematics teaching.

J. P. Guilford's Structure of Intellect Model

While Jean Piaget and others have studied the stages of intellectual development,
J. P. Guilford and his colleagues have developed a three-dimensional model
containing 120 distinct types of intellectual abilities. These 120 intellectual factors appear to encompass most of the human mental abilities which can be
specified and measured. In formulating this model, Guilford and his associates
have attempted to define and structure general intelligence into a variety of very
specific mental aptitudes. Their findings verify what many perceptive teachers
have observed: even very intelligent students may have difficulty carrying out
certain mental tasks; whereas other students who have attained low scores on
general intelligence tests may do surprisingly well at some types of mental activities. It is quite important for teachers to understand that individual students
may possess a variety of specific mental strengths and weaknesses. Tests have
been designed to measure many of these factors of intelligence, and it is possible
to select appropriate tasks to assist people in strengthening their specific cognitive inadequacies.

When a teacher finds that a student seems to be unable to attain even a minimal level of mastery of certain skills, the school psychologist may be able to
determine which intellectual abilities are poorly developed in that student, and
may suggest activities to improve those abilities. Even a teacher who works in a
school where the services of a psychologist are unavailable, or are available only
for students with severe intellectual or emotional handicaps, can recognize certain inadequately developed mental skills in some students and can assist them in
developing these skills. Teachers can have a significant positive influence upon
the formation of each student's self image, and every teacher should recognize
and encourage those unique talents which each individual possesses. Teachers
can also negatively affect students. Some teachers indicate through covert and
overt actions that students who are not particularly proficient and interested in the
teacher's specialty have little prospect of leading a useful and happy life. Every
mathematics teacher should appreciate the value of mathematics and should encourage students to learn and enjoy mathematics; however each teacher should
be objective enough to understand that mathematics is only one small, and in
some cases unimportant, concern in the lives of many successful people.

Intellectual Variables

Guilford's model of intellectual aptitudes, which is called *The Structure of Intellect Model,* was developed at the University of California using a statistical
procedure called factor analysis to identify and classify various mental abilities.
The model was substantiated by testing people varying in age from two years
through adulthood. The Structure of Intellect Model, which has been used as a
tool by researchers studying the variables in intelligence, characterizes learning
and intellectual development as being composed of three variables. The first of
these variables, *operations,* is the set of mental processes used in learning. The
second variable, *contents,* categorizes the nature of the material being learned.

Products, the third variable in intelligence, refers to the manner in which information is organized in the mind.

Operations of the Mind

Guilford has identified five types of mental operations which he calls *memory, cognition, evaluation, convergent production,* and *divergent production. Memory* is the ability to store information in the mind and to call out stored information in response to certain stimuli. *Cognition* is the ability to recognize various forms of information and to understand information. *Evaluation* is the ability to process information in order to make judgments, draw conclusions, and arrive at decisions. *Convergent production* is the ability to take a specified set of information and draw a universally accepted conclusion or response based upon the given information. *Divergent production* is the creative ability to view given information in a new way so that unique and unexpected conclusions are the consequence. A student who immediately answers ½ when asked to give the sine of 30° is using his or her memory. A child who can separate a mixed pile of squares and triangles into separate piles of squares and triangles is exercising a degree of cognition. When a member of a jury sits through a trial, deliberates in a closed session with other jury members, and concludes that the defendant is guilty as charged, that person has used his or her mental ability of evaluation. An algebra student who finds the correct solution to a set of three linear equations in three unknowns has used his or her convergent production ability. A mathematician who discovers and proves a new and important mathematical theorem is exhibiting considerable ability in divergent production.

Contents of Learning

Guilford, in his Structure of Intellect Model, identifies four types of content involved in learning. He calls the things that are learned *figural, symbolic, semantic,* and *behavioral contents. Figural contents* are shapes and forms such as triangles, cubes, parabolas, etc. *Symbolic contents* are symbols or codes representing concrete objects or abstract concepts. ♀ is a symbolic representation for a woman, and + is the mathematical symbol for the operation of addition. *Semantic contents* of learning are those words and ideas which evoke a mental image when they are presented as stimuli. Tree, dog, sun, war, fear, and red are words which evoke images in people's minds when they hear or read them. The *behavioral contents* of learning are the manifestations of stimuli and responses in people; that is, the way people behave as a consequence of their own desires and the actions of other people. The concrete shapes and forms (figures), the character representations (symbols), the spoken and written words (semantics), and the actions of people (behaviors) combine to make up the information that we discern in our environment.

Products of Learning

In Guilford's Model, the six products of learning (the way information is identified and organized in the mind) are *units, classes, relations, systems, transformations,* and *implications.* A *unit* is a single symbol, figure, word, object, or idea. Sets of units are called *classes,* and one mental ability is that of classifying units. *Relations* are connections among units and classes. In our minds we organize units and classes into interrelated structures so that we are aware of the relationships among these two products of learning. A *system* is a composition of units, classes, and relationships into a larger and more meaningful structure. *Transformation* is the process of modifying, reinterpreting, and restructuring existing information into new information. The transformation abiliy is usually thought to be a characteristic of creative people. An *implication* is a prediction or a conjecture about the consequences of interactions among units, classes, relations, systems, and transformations. The way in which the real number system is structured illustrates how the mind organizes information into the six products of learning. Each real number can be considered as a *unit*, and the entire set of real numbers is a *class*. Equality and inequality are *relations* in the set of real numbers. The set of real numbers together with the operations of addition, subtraction, multiplication, and division and the algebraic properties of these operations is a mathematical *system*. Functions defined on the real number system are *transformations*, and each theorem about functions on the real numbers is an *implication*.

The 120 ($5 \times 4 \times 6$) distinct intellectual abilities defined in Guilford's Structure of Intellect Model result from taking all possible combinations of the five operations, four contents, and six products. For instance, one intellectual aptitude, memory for figural units, is the ability of a person to remember figural objects which he or she has seen. An example of this aptitude in mathematics is a student's ability to reproduce a geometric figure after he or she has been shown an example of that particular figure. The following list of operations, contents, and products indicates how the 120 intellectual aptitudes can be formed by combining any operation, with any content, with any product, to form an ordered triple:

Guilford's Factors of Intellectual Ability

Operations	*Contents*	*Products*
1. memory	1. figural	1. units
2. cognition	2. symbolic	2. classes
3. evaluation	3. semantic	3. relations
4. convergent production	4. behavioral	4. systems
5. divergent production		5. transformations
		6. implications

Although this model of human intelligence is useful in identifying variables in learning and helps to explain various learning aptitudes and abilities, one limitation of the Structure of Intellect Model should be noted. Any attempt to structure and categorize complex human abilities into a model must result in an oversimplification of reality. Most of the facts, skills, principles, and concepts which teachers teach and students learn require complex combinations of intellectual abilities. When a student is unable to construct proofs in plane geometry, it may be quite difficult to determine which mental aptitude (or set of aptitudes) is causing this learning problem. Proving theorems in plane geometry may require a unique combination of a large subset of the 120 intellectual abilities, and most mathematics teachers have neither the skills nor resources to identify and measure these specific mental variables in each student. Even though the services of a trained psychologist may be required to determine precisely the intellectual deficiencies in a particular student and prescribe remedial activities, every teacher should learn to recognize certain general learning insufficiencies and assist students in overcoming some of their learning problems. The first step in dealing with these natural human intellectual variations is to recognize that every student's intellect is comprised of many different factors which may be present in varying degrees in each student. The next step is to observe each student's individual performance in specified areas of mathematics and attempt to identify his or her distinct strengths and weaknesses. The third step is to provide individualized work (as students' needs require and time permits) for students so that they can both apply their stronger intellectual abilities in learning mathematics and improve their weaker intellectual aptitudes. This step suggests that there are two approaches to overcoming learning handicaps. One approach is for the learner to bypass his or her weaknesses and apply his or her intellectual strengths to each task. Another approach is to attempt to strengthen intellectual deficiencies. Both methods of attacking intellectual shortcomings are useful and both can be employed simultaneously in the classroom. Finally every teacher should strive to learn more about the nature of intelligence and learning by reading professional journals and participating in inservice workshops, college courses, and postbaccalaureate programs.

A good source for further study of Guilford's Structure of Intellect Model and its interpretation and applications in teaching is Mary Meeker's book (1969), *The Structure of Intellect*. In this book Dr. Meeker defines each one of the 120 intellectual factors, cites tests to measure most of the factors, and suggests classroom activities and experiences which may be useful in strengthening each cognitive factor. To illustrate the format in which Dr. Meeker presents each intellectual factor, her discussion of cognition of symbolic classes is quoted below:

COGNITION OF SYMBOLIC CLASSES (CSC) is the ability to recognize common properties in sets of symbolic information.

Tests

Number-Group Naming. State what it is that three given numbers have in common. · · ·

Number Classification. Select one of five alternative numbers to fit into each of four classes of three given numbers each. · · ·

Best Number Pairs. Choose one of three number pairs that makes the most exclusive (best) class. · · ·

Other than the factor tests, few group-achievement tests include items in which symbols are classified.

Curriculum Suggestions

Using the above tests as models, teachers at any grade level can develop exercises within the context of their arithmetic tasks. Classifications in algebraic symbols will differ from classifications in multiplication or geometry. The primary goal would be the recognition of common properties in the subject matter. Chemistry, which is composed primarily of symbolic information, is predicated upon a classification model. Even here, though, the symbols can be classified in other unique ways. A close visual inspection of the meanings of the formulae for the purpose of other ways to classify them can actually reinforce and condition the expected learning. (pp. 38-39)

Robert Gagné's Theory of Learning

The research of the psychologist Robert M. Gagné into the phases of a learning sequence and the types of learning is particularly relevent for teaching mathematics. Professor Gagné has used mathematics as a medium for testing and applying his theories about learning and has collaborated with the University of Maryland Mathematics Project in studies of mathematics learning and curriculum development.

The Objects of Mathematics Learning

Before examining Gagné's four phases of a learning sequence and eight types of learning, it is appropriate to discuss the *objects* of mathematics learning, which are considered in his theory. These objects of mathematics learning are those direct and indirect things which we want students to learn in mathematics. The direct objects of mathematics learning are facts, skills, concepts, and principles; some of the many indirect objects are transfer of learning, inquiry ability, problem-solving ability, self-discipline, and appreciation for the structure of mathematics. The direct objects of mathematics learning—facts, skills, concepts, and principles—are the four categories into which mathematical content can be separated.

Mathematical *facts* are those arbitrary conventions in mathematics such as the symbols of mathematics. It is a fact that 2 is the symbol for the word two, that + is the symbol for the operation of addition, and that sine is the name given to a special function in trigonometry. Facts are learned through various techniques of rote learning such as memorization, drill, practice, timed tests, games, and contests. People are considered to have learned a fact when they can state the fact and make appropriate use of it in a number of different situations.

Mathematical *skills* are those operations and procedures which students and mathematicians are expected to carry out with speed and accuracy. Many skills can be specified by sets of rules and instructions or by ordered sequences of specific procedures called *algorithms*. Among the mathematical skills which most people are expected to master in school are long division, addition of fractions and multiplication of decimal fractions. Constructing right angles, bisecting angles, and finding unions or intersections of sets of objects and events are examples of other useful mathematical skills. Skills are learned through demonstrations and various types of drill and practice such as worksheets, work at the chalkboard, group activities and games. Students have mastered a skill when they can correctly demonstrate the skill by solving different types of problems requiring the skill or by applying the skill in various situations.

A *concept* in mathematics is an abstract idea which enables people to classify objects or events and to specify whether the objects and events are examples or nonexamples of the abstract idea. Sets, subsets, equality, inequality, triangle, cube, radius and exponent are all examples of concepts. A person who has learned the concept of triangle is able to classify sets of figures into subsets of triangles and non-triangles. Concepts can be learned either through definitions or by direct observation. By direct observation and experimentation young children learn to classify plane objects into sets of triangles, circles, or squares; however few young children would be able to define the concept of a triangle. A concept is learned by hearing, seeing, handling, discussing, or thinking about a variety of examples and non-examples of the concept and by contrasting the examples and nonexamples. Younger children who are in Piaget's stage of concrete operations usually need to see or handle physical representations of a concept to learn it; whereas older formal operational people may be able to learn concepts through discussion and contemplation. A person has learned a concept when he or she is able to separate examples of the concept from nonexamples.

Principles are the most complex of the mathematical objects. Principles are sequences of concepts together with relationships among these concepts. The statements, "two triangles are congruent if two sides and the included angle of one triangle are equal to two sides and the included angle of the other" and "the square of the hypotenuse of a right triangle is equal to the sum of the squares of the other two sides" are examples of principles. Each of these principles involves several concepts and relationships among these concepts. To understand the principle about congruent triangles, one must know the concepts triangle, angle, and side. According to Gagné (1966) in a chapter appearing in the book *Analyses of Concept Learning* edited by Herbert J. Klausmeier and Chester W. Harris:

> It would appear, then, that principles can be distinguished from what have previously been called concepts in two ways. First, the performance required to demonstrate that a concept has been learned is simply an identification, that is, a choice from a number of alternatives; a principle, in contrast, must be demonstrated by means of performances that identify its component concepts and the operation relating them to one another. Second, this means that the inference to be made about mediating processes is different in the two cases. A concept is a single mediator that represents a class of stimuli (or objects), whereas a principle is a sequence of mediators, each one of which is itself a concept. (pp. 86-87)

Principles can be learned through processes of scientific inquiry, guided discovery lessons, group discussions, the use of problem solving strategies and demonstrations. A student has learned a principle when he or she can identify the concepts included in the principle, put the concepts in their correct relation to one another, and apply the principle to a particular situation.

It probably would not be a very precise or useful activity to classify all the objects of secondary school mathematics into the four object categories—facts, skills, concepts and principles. Even the experts in mathematics and learning theory would disagree about the proper category for many mathematical objects. In general, the objects progress in order of complexity from simple facts, to skills and concepts, through complex principles. Also the classification of many (maybe even most) mathematical objects is relative to the observer's own viewpoint, which is an important fact (or is that a principle!) for every mathematics teacher to know. A student who merely memorizes the quadratic formula knows a fact. A student who can plug numbers into the quadratic formula and come up with two answers has learned a skill. A student who can classify 5, 3, and 4 as constants and x as a variable for the quadratic equation $5x^2 + 3x + 4 = 0$ is demonstrating acquisition of a concept. And, a person who can derive (or prove) the quadratic formula and explain his derivation to someone else has mastered a principle. Consequently, the quadratic formula which *is* a principle may be regarded as either a fact, a skill, or a concept by a student whose viewpoint of the quadratic formula is not as sophisticated as that of a mathematician.

As a mathematics teacher, you should develop testing and observation techniques to assist you in recognizing students' viewpoints of the concepts and principles which you are teaching. All of us have at times memorized the proofs of theorems, with no understanding of the concepts and principles involved in the proof, in order to pass tests. While this subterfuge is a form of learning, it is not what teachers hope to have students learn by proving theorems. The point to recognize here is that many times when teachers are teaching what they view as mathematical principles, students are internalizing as facts or skills the information which is being presented.

The Phases of A Learning Sequence

Gagné has identified eight sets of conditions that distinguish eight learning types which he calls signal learning, stimulus-response learning, chaining, verbal association, discrimination learning, concept learning, rule learning, and problem solving. Gagné believes that each one of these eight learning types occurs in the learner in four sequential phases. He calls these phases the apprehending phase, the acquisition phase, the storage phase, and the retrieval phase.

The first phase of learning, the *apprehending phase,* is the learner's awareness of a stimulus or a set of stimuli which are present in the learning situation. Awareness, or attending, will lead the learner to perceive characteristics of the set of stimuli. What the learner perceives will be uniquely coded by each individual and will be registered in his or her mind. This idiosyncratic way in which each learner apprehends a given stimulus results in a common problem in teaching and learning. When a teacher presents a lesson (stimuli) he or she may perceive different characteristics of the content of the lesson than are perceived by students, and each student may have a somewhat different perception than every other student. This is to say that learning is a unique process within each student, and as a consequence each student is responsible for his or her own learning because of the unique way in which he or she perceives each learning situation. The uniqueness of individual perceptions explains why students will interpret facts, concepts, and principles differently from the way a teacher meant for them to be interpreted. Although this situation may make teaching and learning somewhat imprecise and unpredictable, it does have many advantages for society. Each person is able to apply his or her unique perceptions of a problem and its solution to a group discussion of the problem, which results in more appropriate solutions of problems in our society.

The next phase in learning, the *acquisition phase,* is attaining or possessing the fact, skill, concept, or principle which is to be learned. Acquisition of mathematical knowledge can be determined by observing or measuring the fact that a person does not possess the required knowledge or behavior before an appropriate stimulus is presented, and that he or she has attained the required knowledge or behavior immediately after presentation of the stimulus.

After a person has acquired a new capability, it must be retained or remembered. This is the *storage phase* of learning. The human storage facility is the memory, and research indicates that there are two types of memory. Short-term memory has a limited capacity for information and lasts for a short period of time. Most people can retain seven or eight distinct pieces of information in their short-term memories for up to thirty seconds. An example of how short-term memory operates is our ability to look up a seven digit telephone number, remember it for a few seconds while we are dialing, and forget the number as soon as someone answers our call. Long-term memory is our ability to remember information for a longer period of time than thirty seconds, and much of what we learn is stored permanently in our minds.

The fourth phase of learning, the *retrieval phase,* is the ability to call out the information that has been acquired and stored in memory. The process of information retrieval is very imprecise, disorganized, and even mystical. At times desired information such as a name can not be retrieved from memory upon demand, but will "pop up" later when one is thinking about something that appears to be completely unrelated to the moment when the name was wanted. Other information is stored so deeply in memory that special techniques such as electrical stimulation of the brain or hypnosis are required to initiate retrieval.

These four phases of human learning—apprehending, acquisition, storage, and retrieval—have been incorporated into the design of computer systems, although in a much less complex form than they appear in human beings. A computer apprehends electronic stimuli from the computer user, acquires these stimuli in its central processing unit, stores the information present in the stimuli in one of its memory devices, and retrieves the information upon demand. The infinitely (?) more complex learning process in people is illustrated every day in mathematics classrooms. If students are to learn a procedure for finding an approximation to the square root of any number which is not a perfect square, they must apprehend the method, acquire the method, store it in memory, and retrieve the square root algorithm when it is needed. To aid students in progressing through these four stages in learning the square root algorithm, the teacher evokes apprehension by working through an example on the chalkboard, facilitates acquisition by having each student work an example by following, step-by-step, a list of instructions, assists storage by giving problems for homework, and evokes retrieval by giving a quiz the next day.

Types of Learning

The eight types of learning which Gagné has identified and studied (signal learning, stimulus-response learning, chaining, verbal association, discrimination learning, concept learning, rule learning, and problem-solving) will be presented and explained below. Some of the conditions appropriate for facilitating each learning type will be discussed.

Signal Learning

Signal learning is involuntary learning resulting from either a single instance or a number of repetitions of a stimulus which will evoke an emotional response in an individual. When a person says "I can't eat shrimp anymore because I once had a traumatic experience while eating them," that person is describing an example of undesirable signal learning. Signal learning is emotional learning and just as emotions can be either positive or negative, so also can the outcomes of signal learning be pleasant or unpleasant. Driving past your childhood home may evoke a flood of pleasant memories, while walking into your high school chemistry laboratory could be rather unpleasant if chemistry was difficult and frustrating for you. The examples in the previous sentence illustrate that signal learning can occur over a long period of time with a number of stimuli evoking a variety of pleasant or unpleasant responses. Signal learning can also occur from a single instance of an event which evoked intense emotional response; that was the case for the person who disliked shrimp. Another example of signal learning happening from a single event is that of a person who will not sing with other people present as a consequence of a first grade music teacher shouting at a little girl and slapping her with a ruler because she violated a rule during a group sing. The reason why many high school students dislike mathematics may be that they have experienced a set of unpleasant events in elementary school which they associate with a mathematics classroom. The cliché that ''success breeds success and failure breeds failure'' is a statement of the consequences of signal learning.

In order for signal learning to occur, there must be a neutral signal stimulus and a second, unexpected stimulus that will evoke an emotional response in the learner which he or she will associate with the neutral stimulus. In the example of the person who learned to fear group singing in a first grade music class, the neutral signal stimulus was singing in a group and the unexpected stimuli were a shout and a slap. People who have a high anxiety level tend to acquire responses through signal learning more rapidly than do nonanxious people. A few harsh remarks by the teacher to a shy, nervous seventh grader sitting in a mathematics classroom may condition a dislike for mathematics in that person. Signal learning cannot be easily controlled by the learner and can have considerable influence on his or her actions. Consequently, you as a mathematics teacher, should attempt to generate unconditioned stimuli which will evoke pleasant emotions in your students and hope that they will associate some of these pleasant sensations with the neutral signal which is your mathematics classroom. While many conscious attempts to generate positive, unexpected stimuli may fail to evoke the desired positive associations with neutral signals, inadvertently generated negative stimuli can at times do considerable damage to a student's desire to learn the subject which you teach.

Stimulus-Response Learning
Stimulus-response learning is also learning to respond to a signal; however, this form of learning differs in two ways from signal learning. Signal learning is involuntary and emotional; whereas stimulus-response learning is voluntary and physical. Stimulus-response learning involves voluntary movements of the learner's skeletal muscles in response to stimuli so that the learner can carry out an action when he or she wants to. This form of learning requires an external stimulus, which causes an internal muscular stimulation, followed by the desired response with a single, direct connection between the stimulus and the response. In stimulus-response learning a stimulus is presented to an individual who may react to the stimulus in several different ways. Each time the desired response occurs, the individual receives a positive reinforcement, which may be a word of

praise or a satisfying experience. As a result of a series of reinforcements for a desired response, the individual learns to discriminate the appropriate response from a set of other less desirable responses which could also follow the occurrence of the stimulus.

Most examples of pure stimulus-response learning in people are found in young children. They are learning to say words, carry out various life-supporting functions, use simple tools, and display socially acceptable behaviors. Learning to say the appropriate names of people and inanimate objects, holding a bottle at the proper angle so that milk can be sucked from it, and picking up a block are examples of stimulus-response learning. In order to learn a desired response, the learner must be physically capable of carrying out the appropriate muscular acts, and the correct response must result in an immediate reinforcement of the response from the learner's surroundings. Of course undesirable responses can be learned if they result in satisfying reinforcements, and desirable actions can be suppressed if their occurrence is accompanied by punishment.

Chaining

Chaining is the sequential connection of two or more previously learned nonverbal stimulus-response actions. Although stimulus-response learning can involve either verbal or nonverbal muscular responses, Gagné chooses to call sequences of nonverbal stimulus-response actions *chaining* and sequences of verbal stimulus-response actions *verbal association* which will be discussed as a separate learning type. Tying a shoe, opening a door, starting an automobile, throwing a ball, sharpening a pencil, and painting a ceiling are examples of chaining. In each of these situations it is necessary to chain an ordered sequence of previously learned stimulus-response skills in order to complete the task. Opening a door involves the four separate stimulus-response muscular actions of grasping the doorknob, turning the knob, holding the knob in the turned position, and pulling the door open.

In order for chaining to occur, the learner must have previously learned each stimulus-response link required in the chain. If each link has been learned, chaining can be facilitated by helping the learner establish the correct sequence of stimulus-response acts for the chain. Pulling on a doorknob before turning it is not the proper sequence of stimulus-responce actions for opening a door. Also for most chaining, the learner must be taught to execute the links in close time succession. For example, the chain of activities required for shifting gears in an automobile with a standard transmission requires a very close time sequence. It is usually necessary to practice a chain of stimulus-response actions in order for the chain to be completely mastered and remembered. If chaining is not accompanied by a satisfying reinforcement, learning can become more difficult and will take longer. Since chaining requires complex physical and mental interactions, fear of ridicule or punishment for failure to properly execute the chain may block these interactions and interfere with chain learning. In chaining, the completion of one stimulus-responce link may provide an intermediate stimulus to evoke the next stimulus-response link.

Most activities in mathematics which entail manipulation of physical devices such as rulers, compasses, and geometric models require chaining. Learning to bisect an angle with a straightedge and a compass requires proper sequencing and implementing of a set of previously learned stimulus-response type skills. Among these skills are the ability to use a compass to strike an arc and the ability to construct a straight line between two points.

In teaching mathematical skills requiring muscular activities, two characteristics of stimulus-responce learning and chaining should be understood and exploited. First, chaining, which involves appropriate sequencing of a set of individual stimuli and responses, cannot be accomplished by students who have not mastered the separate skills through appropriate stimulus-response learning situations. A student who can not learn to carry out a chain of stimulus-response activities may not have learned some of the links in the chain. Second, stimulus-response learning and chaining can be facilitated by a teacher who provides rewards and reinforcement for desired behaviors. Even though punishment can be used to promote certain types of stimulus-response learning, it can interfere with chaining and can negatively influence emotional development, attitudes and motivation to learn.

Verbal Association

Verbal association is chaining of verbal stimuli; that is, the sequential connection of two or more previously learned verbal stimulus-response actions. The simplest type of verbal chain is the association of an object with its name which involves chaining the stimulus-response of connecting the appearance of an object with its characteristics and the stimulus-response of observing the object and responding by saying its name. More complicated chains of verbal associations are forming sentences, learning poetry, memorizing the lines of a character in a play and learning a foreign language.

The mental processes involved in verbal association are very complex and not completely understood at present. Most researchers do agree that efficient verbal association requires the use of intervening mental links which act as codes and which can be either verbal, auditory, or visual images. These codes usually occur in the learner's mind and will vary from learner to learner according to each person's unique mental storehouse of codes. For example, one person may use the verbal mental code "*y* is determined by *x*" as a cue for the word *function,* another person may code *function* symbolically as "*y = f(x),*" and someone else may visualize two sets of elements enclosed in circles with arrows extending from the elements of one set to the elements of the other set. Other codes can be taught. For instance, a commonly used memory code for the order in which arithmetic operations in algebra are carried out is "*My Dear Aunt Sally*" which is a code for "*Multiply, Divide, Add, then Subtract.*" Research and observation suggest that an efficient method for memorizing long verbal passages such as poetry is to progressively learn each new part by rehearsing the previously learned older parts up to the new part and then rehearse the new part. For instance, the fifth line of a poem may best be learned by repeating the first four lines in sequence and then including line five.

The most important use of the verbal association type of learning is in verbal dialogue. Good oratory and writing depend upon a vast store of memorized verbal associations in the mind of the orator or writer. To express ideas and rational arguments in mathematics it is necessary to have a large store of verbal associations about mathematics. You can assist students in improving their verbal associations in mathematics by encouraging them to express facts, definitions, concepts, and principles correctly and concisely and to discuss mathematical ideas with each other. Many teachers inadvertently discourage verbal associations in their students by rephrasing every student's answers and comments. Students should be encouraged (even required) to communicate important mathematical concepts and processes to each other without having to use the teacher as an intermediary or interpreter. In so doing they will improve their mathematical verbal associations and will learn to influence others through effective communication.

Discrimination Learning

As you may have observed, each successive learning type which we have discussed is more complex than the type preceding it. Characteristics of the simpler types of learning are found in the more complex types. Discrimination learning is no exception to this building-block pattern of growth and increasing complexity. After stimulus-response connections have been learned, they can be sequenced into chains of more complex learning behaviors. *Discrimination learning* is learning to differentiate among chains; that is, to recognize various physical and conceptual objects. There are two kinds of discrimination—single discrimination and multiple discrimination. As an illustration, a young child may be given practice in recognizing the numeral **2** by viewing fifty **2's** on a page and by drawing a page of **2's.** Through a simple stimulus-response chain the child learns to recognize (not, in this case, the name ''two'' for the concept of two), but the physical appearance of the numeral **2.** This is an example of single discrimination where the child can recognize the numeral **2.** At the same time the child may be learning to recognize the numerals **0, 1, 3, 4, 5, 6, 7, 8,** and **9** and to discriminate among them, which is an example of multiple discrimination. On Tuesday the child may work with only the numeral **6** and on Wednesday he or she may learn to discriminate a **9.** However, when all of the single digit numerals are presented together, the same child may have trouble discriminating between the **6** and the **9.** If the child has previously learned each of the chains making up each numeral to be learned, can identify each numeral by itself, can say the names of each numeral, and has appropriate mental codes for the names and numeral symbols, then he or she is ready to learn to discriminate among the numerals.

As students are learning various discriminations among chains, they may also be forming these stimulus-response chains at the same time. This somewhat disorganized learning situation can, and usually does, result in several phenomena of multiple discrimination learning—generalization, extinction, and interference.

Generalization is the tendency for the learner to classify a set of similar but distinct chains into a single category and fail to discriminate or differentiate among the chains. The greater the similarity among chains, the more difficult is multiple discrimination among the chains. For example, a one-to-one mapping and an onto mapping have enough common characteristics so that many algebra students have trouble discriminating one from the other.

If appropriate reinforcement is absent from the learning of a chain of stimuli and responses, *extinction* or elimination of that chain occurs. Incorrect responses can be eliminated by withholding reinforcement; however, the occurrence of incorrect responses (even without reinforcement) can extinguish correct responses which must then be relearned. The problem of extinction is apparent in some methods of dealing with homework assignments. If students are not told whether their solutions to homework problems are appropriate, correct responses may become extinct and incorrect responses may interfere with learning of correct responses. Consequently, for many less complex types of learning, immediate teacher feedback concerning the correctness of student solutions of problems is desirable.

Forgetting previously learned chains of stimuli and responses can result from interference generated by learning new chains. The new information may also interact with the old information causing some previously learned responses to be forgotten and making it more difficult to learn the new responses. *Interference* can be a problem in learning a foreign language such as French, which has many words similar in meaning and spelling to English words. In learning to read and write French some people forget how to spell many English words and have trouble learning to spell some French words due to interference. These generalization and interference factors can create learning problems in algebra when students are taught a number of similar, but slightly different, techniques in close succession for simplifying different types of algebraic expressions containing exponents and radical signs. Many students can apply each technique for simplifying a particular type expression when that technique and those expressions are studied in isolation from the other techniques and problem types. However, on a unit test where each of forty different problems must be solved by selecting the correct procedure from the ten previously learned procedures, many students have little success because their learning of the ten different techniques interferes with their attempts to discriminate among the different problem types. Some students generalize the ten different techniques into several hybrid methods which they use indiscriminately (and improperly) in attempting to simplify different types of algebraic expressions.

Concept Learning

Concept learning is learning to recognize common properties of concrete objects or events and responding to these objects or events as a class. In one sense concept learning is the opposite of discrimination learning. Whereas discrimination learning requires that the learner distinguish among objects according to their different characteristics, concept learning involves classifying objects into sets according to a common characteristic and responding to the common property.

In order for students to learn a concept, simpler types of prerequisite learning must have occurred. Acquisition of any specific concept must be accompanied by prerequisite stimulus-response chains, appropriate verbal associations, and multiple discrimination of distinguishing characteristics. For example, the first step in acquiring the concept **circle** might be learning to say the word circle as a self-generated stimulus-response connection, so that students can repeat the word. Then students may learn to identify several different objects as circles by acquiring individual verbal associations. Next, students may learn to discriminate between circles and other objects such as squares and triangles. It is also important for students to be exposed to circles in a wide variety of representative situations so that they learn to recognize circles which are imbedded in more complex objects. When the students are able to spontaneously identify circles in unfamiliar contexts, they have acquired the concept of **circle.** This ability to *generalize* a concept to new situations is the ability which distinguishes concept learning from other forms of learning. When students have learned a concept, they no longer need specific and familiar stimuli in order to identify and react to new instances of the concept. Consequently, the way to show that a concept has been learned is to demonstrate that the learner can generalize the concept in an unfamiliar situation.

When new mathematics concepts are being taught to students it is important to (1) present a variety of dissimilar instances of the concept to facilitate generalizing, (2) show examples of different but related concepts to aid in discrimination, (3) present non-examples of the concept to promote discrimination and generalization, and (4) avoid presenting instances of the concept all of which have some common characteristic that may interfere with proper classification of examples of the concept. The importance of these four procedures in teaching a concept can be illustrated by discussing some of the pitfalls in teaching and learning the **triangle** concept. First, if all the examples of triangles are of the same variety (for instance, if all examples are drawn on the chalkboard), then students may not be able to identify triangular faces of solids or recognize triangular shapes outside of the classroom. If this is the case, the triangle concept has not been learned. Second, if students are not shown examples of other geometric objects such as trapezoids and pyramids, they may have trouble discriminating among different objects having some common characteristics. Third, plane objects which are not triangles should be presented and discussed to assist students in identifying the characteristics of triangles and the features of other objects which distinguish them from triangles. Fourth, if all of the triangle models shown to students happen to be colored red, then some students may associate the property of redness with the triangle concept and fail to recognize triangles which are not colored red.

All people acquire many concepts through teaching and learning strategies employing verbal chains; however if an acquired concept is to be of much use to a person, it must be identifiable in real-world stimulus situations. Students can memorize the verbal chain ''a triangle is a three-sided closed plane figure having straight sides,'' but this definition will be of little value if they can not use it to classify triangles into the triangle concept category. Also, if students do not have a large repertoire of words and sentences (verbal chains) available for use in concept learning, their facility to acquire concepts will be lessened and the time required to learn each concept may be greatly extended. Even though concept learning is usually based upon verbal cues, the value of a learned concept in thought and communication comes from the concrete references that people have for each concept name. One problem in communication and interpretation, and in teaching and learning, is that various people may have different viewpoints (verbal stimulus-response chains and concrete references) of the same concept, which can lead to misunderstanding, argument, and even conflict. If it were not for concept learning with the ability to generalize, all learning in the formal educational system would be extremely inefficient and of little practical use because every instance of each concept would have to be experienced directly in order for that instance to be learned.

Rule Learning

The six types of learning which we have just discussed (signal learning, stimulus-response learning, chaining, verbal association, discrimination learning, and concept learning) are basic learning types that must precede the two higher order learning types (rule learning and problem solving) which are the primary concern of formal education. *Rule learning* is the ability to respond to an entire set of situations (stimuli) with a whole set of actions (responses). Rule learning appears to be the predominant type of learning to facilitate efficient and coherent human functioning. Our speech, writing, routine daily activities, and many of our behaviors are governed by rules which we have learned. In order for people to communicate and interact, and for society to function in any form except anarchy, a huge and complex set of rules must be learned and observed by a large majority of people. Much of mathematics learning is rule learning. For example, we know that $5 \times 6 = 6 \times 5$ and that $2 \times 8 = 8 \times 2$; however without knowing the rule that can be represented by $a \times b = b \times a$, we would not be able to generalize beyond those few specific multiplication problems which we have already attempted. Most people first learn and use the rule that multiplication is commutative without being able to state it, and usually without realizing that they know and apply the rule. In order to discuss this rule, it must be given either a verbal or a symbolic formulation such as ''the order in which multiplication is done doesn't make any difference in the answer'' or ''for all numbers a and b, $a \times b = b \times a$.'' This particular rule, and rules in general, can be thought of as sets of relations among sets of concepts.

Rules may be of different types and of different degrees of complexity. Some rules are definitions and may be regarded as defined concepts. The defined concept $n! = n(n\text{-}1)\,(n\text{-}2)\,\cdots\,(2)\,(1)$ is a rule explaining how to treat the symbol $n!$ Other rules are chains of connected concepts, such as the rule that *in the absence of symbols of grouping arithmetic operations should be carried out in the ordered sequence* $\times$, $\div$, $+$, $-$. Still other mathematical rules provide sets of responses for sets of stimuli. The quadratic formula provides for an infinite set of responses, one response for each of an infinite set of quadratic equations. Each particular quadratic equation is a stimulus consisting of a concept chain, and each solution is a response made up of a chain of concepts.

As was noted previously, there is also a distinction between stating a rule and correctly using the rule. Just because a student can state a rule does not mean that he or she has learned the rule in the sense that the capability to use the rule is present in the person. Conversely, it is quite possible to correctly apply a rule without being able to state it. Nearly everyone can memorize the sequence of symbols $x = \dfrac{-b \pm \sqrt{b^2 - 4ac}}{2a}$, but without additional learning few people could apply it correctly. Most people use the rule that multiplication is commutative, but few people can state this rule as ''multiplication is commutative'' or $a \times b = b \times a$.

Mathematics teachers need to be aware that being able to state a definition or write a rule on a sheet of paper is little indication of whether a student has learned the rule. If students are to learn a rule they must have previously learned the chains of concepts that constitute the rule. The conditions of rule learning begin by specifying the behavior expected of the learner in order to verify that the rule has been learned. A rule has been learned when the learner can appropriately and correctly apply the rule in a number of different situations. In his book *The Conditions of Learning,* Robert Gagné (1970) gives a five step instructional sequence for teaching rules:

Step 1: Inform the learner about the form of the performance to be expected when learning is completed.

Step 2: Question the learner in a way that requires the reinstatement (recall) of the previously learned concepts that make up the rule.

Step 3: Use verbal statements (cues) that will lead the learner to put the rule together, as a chain of concepts, in the proper order.

Step 4: By means of a question, ask the learner to ''demonstrate'' one of (sic) more concrete instances of the rule.

Step 5: (Optional, but useful for later instruction): By a suitable question, require the learner to make a verbal statement of the rule. (p. 203)

Problem-Solving

As one might expect, problem-solving is a higher order and more complex type learning than rule-learning, and rule acquisition is prerequisite to problem-solving. *Problem solving* involves selecting and chaining sets of rules in a manner unique to the learner which results in the establishment of a higher order set of rules which was previously unknown to the learner. Words like discovery and creativity are often associated with problem-solving. In rule-learning, the rule to be learned is known in a precise form by the teacher who structures activities for the student so that he or she will learn the rule in the form in which the teacher knows it and will apply it in the correct manner at the proper time. The rule exists outside the learner who attempts to internalize the existing rule. In problem-solving the learner attempts to select and use previously learned rules to formulate a solution to a novel (at least novel for the learner) problem. Routine substitution of numerical values into the quadratic formula is not regarded by Gagné, and most other learning theorists, as an example of problem-solving. Such routine activities involve merely using a previously learned rule.

An example of novel problem-solving is that of a student, who has never seen the quadratic formula, developing this formula for the solution of the general quadratic equation $ax^2 + bx + c = 0$. Such a student would have to select the skill of completing the square of a trinomial from his stock of skills and apply that skill in the proper way to develop the quadratic formula. A student who derives the quadratic formula by carrying out a set of instructions from his or her teacher is learning a rule. The criterion for problem-solving is that the student has not previously solved that particular problem, even though the problem may have been solved previously by many other people.

Real-world problem solving usually involves five steps—(1) presentation of the problem in a general form, (2) restatement of the problem into an operational definition, (3) formulation of alternative hypotheses and procedures which may be appropriate means of attacking the problem, (4) testing hypotheses and carrying out procedures to obtain a solution or a set of alternative solutions, and

(5) deciding which possible solution is most appropriate or verifying that a single solution is correct. A novel problem for most people would be that of determining how much water flows from the Mississippi River in a year which is step 1, a general statement of the problem. Assuming one would attempt solving the problem rather than looking for the answer in a book of trivia, the second step is to restate the problem in a more precise, operational manner which may suggest how to solve the problem. After considering the general problem for a time, the problem solver may decide to carry out step 2 by restating the problem as "What is the approximate area of the land mass drained by the Mississippi River and what is the approximate average yearly rainfall over this land mass?" Another operational definition is "What is the approximate area of a cross-section of the Mississippi near its mouth and what is its approximate rate of flow at that point?" Now the problem is stated in terms which suggest methods of solution. In step 3, the problem-solver may decide to estimate the cross-section of the river to be one mile wide by an average of thirty feet deep and the rate of flow to be one and one-half miles per hour. He or she may also make an estimate of the area of the river's watershed and the average yearly rainfall over the watershed. It may be decided that other variables are negligible or will average each other out and have no significant influence on the problem. Step 4 is to solve the problem using each operational definition; this necessitates using previously learned measurement conversion rules, rules for finding volume, and several different rules of arithmetic. In this example, step 5 could be carried out by comparing the solutions obtained through using each of the operational definitions. If these two solutions are close to each other, the problem-solver may decide that the solution is acceptable for non-technical purposes.

It can be seen from this example of problem-solving that previously learned rules are needed to solve problems, but that the problem-solver also formulates a unique (for that person) higher-order rule which is the method of proceeding from the general statement of the problem to a reasonable solution. If the person who solved the Mississippi River problem were asked to determine the amount of water flowing from the Ohio River in one year, he or she could use the general problem-solving strategy, developed in solving the Mississippi River problem, to solve the Ohio River problem. Solving this second problem about the Ohio River would be a problem solving-situation for another student who never had been confronted with this type problem, but would be a routine application of a previously learned skill for the first problem-solver.

Learning Hierarchies

Gagné has applied his theory, parts of which have been discussed in this section, to structuring specific mathematics learning hierarchies for problem-solving and rule-learning. A *learning hierarchy* for problem-solving or rule-learning is a structure containing a sequence of subordinate and prerequisite abilities which a student must master before he or she can learn the higher order task. Gagné describes learning as observable changes in people's behaviors, and his learning hierarchies are composed of abilities which can be observed or measured. According to Gagné, if a person has learned, then that person can carry out some activity that he or she could not do previously. Since most activities in mathematics require definable and observable prerequisite learning, mathematics topics lend themselves to hierarchical analyses. When specifying a learning hierarchy for a mathematical skill, it is usually not necessary to consider all of the subordinate skills. Usually, but not always, a mathematics teacher is correct in assuming that all students in the class have acquired certain basic mathematics abilities that are prerequisite to mastering higher order skills.

Constructing a learning hierarchy for a mathematical topic is more than merely listing the steps in learning the rule or solving the problem. Preparing a list of steps is a good starting point; however the distinguishing characteristic of a learning hierarchy is an up-side-down tree diagram of subordinate and superordinate abilities which can be demonstrated by students or measured by teachers. Figure 3.1 contains an ordered list of steps which can be used to derive the quadratic formula, and Figure 3.2 is a learning hierarchy of prerequisite abilities needed for deriving the quadratic formula. You will notice that Figure 3.1 is nothing more than a list of steps. Neither the abilities necessary for implementing the steps nor the prerequisite abilities for these superordinate abilities are given in this list.

PROBLEM TO BE SOLVED
Derive the Quadratic Formula

Step 1. Write the general form of a quadratic equation.
$$ax^2 + bx + c = 0$$

Step 2. Add negative c to both sides of the equation.
$$ax^2 + bx = -c$$

Step 3. Divide both sides of the equation by a.
$$x^2 + \frac{bx}{a} = -\frac{c}{a}$$

Step 4. Complete the square of $x^2 + \dfrac{bx}{a}$ by adding $\dfrac{b^2}{4a^2}$ to both sides of the equation.
$$x^2 + \frac{bx}{a} + \frac{b^2}{4a^2} = -\frac{c}{a} + \frac{b^2}{4a^2}$$

Step 5. Factor the left side of the equation and add the terms on the right side.
$$\left(x + \frac{b}{2a} \right)^2 = \frac{b^2 - 4ac}{4a^2}$$

Step 6. Take the square root of both sides of the equation.
$$x + \frac{b}{2a} = \pm \sqrt{\frac{b^2 - 4ac}{4a^2}}$$

Step 7. Add $\dfrac{-b}{2a}$ to both sides and simplify the right side.
$$x = \frac{-b \pm \sqrt{b^2 - 4ac}}{2a}$$

Figure 3.1. A list of steps used to derive the quadratic formula.

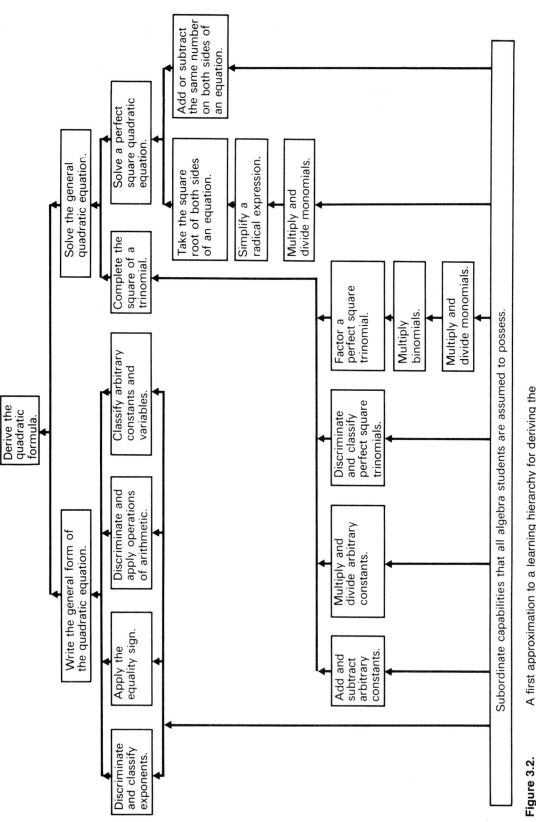

Figure 3.2. A first approximation to a learning hierarchy for deriving the quadratic formula.

Figure 3.2 is a learning hierarchy, because both superordinate and subordinate abilities are specified in their appropriate relationships to each other. Figure 3.2 can be thought of as a first approximation to the learning hierarchy for solving a quadratic equation. A more careful consideration of prerequisite abilities and research with students might result in a more precise hierarchy for this problem-solving ability. However, the hierarchy shown in this figure, as well as other hierarchies, can easily be developed by mathematics teachers and can be helpful in determining student readiness for this and other problem-solving-activities. Good learning hierarchies, even very informal ones, can be quite useful to teachers for preparing preassessment strategies to evaluate student readiness for learning mathematics topics.

A Final Note on Gagné

Gagné's division of learning into eight types from the simplest (signal learning), through the progressively more complex types (stimulus-response learning, chaining, verbal association, discrimination learning, and concept learning), to the higher order types (rule learning and problem-solving) is a useful and valid way to view learning. However, learning does not usually progress in a sequence of easily definable and identifiable steps, and the various learning types do not occur in chronological sequence as do Piaget's stages of intellectual development. All of these eight learning types can, and do, occur nearly simultaneously in all but a few people through most of their lives. As a teacher you should understand Gagné's different types of learning and select teaching strategies and classroom activities which promote each learning type when that particular type seems to be appropriate for learning the mathematics topic that you are teaching. Most teaching/learning sequences will require several of these eight types of learning which may interact in very complex ways.

Dienes on Learning Mathematics

Zoltan P. Dienes, who was educated in Hungary, France and England, has used his interest and experience in mathematics education and learning psychology to develop a system for teaching mathematics. His system, which is based in part upon the learning psychology of Jean Piaget, was developed in an attempt to make mathematics more interesting and easier to learn. In his book *Building up Mathematics,* Professor Dienes summarized his view of mathematics education as follows:

> At the present time there can hardly be a single member of the teaching profession concerned with the teaching of mathematics at any stage, from infants upwards, who can honestly say to himself that all is well with the teaching of mathematics. There are far too many children who dislike mathematics, more so as they get older, and many who find great difficulty with what is very simple. Let us face it: the majority of children never succeed in understanding the real meanings of mathematical concepts. At best they become deft technicians in the art of manipulating complicated sets of symbols, at worst they are baffled by the impossible situations into which the present mathematical requirements in schools tend to place them. An all too common attitude is 'get the examination over', after which no further thought is given to mathematics. With relatively few exceptions, this situation is quite general

and has come to be taken for granted. Mathematics is generally regarded as difficult and tricky, except in a few isolated cases where enthusiastic teachers have infused life into the subject, making it exciting and so less difficult. (p.1)

Mathematical Concepts

Dienes regards mathematics as the study of structures, the classification of structures, sorting out relationships within structures, and categorizing relationships among structures. He believes that each mathematical concept (or principle) can be properly understood only if it is first presented to students through a variety of concrete, physical representations. Dienes uses the term concept to mean a mathematical structure, which is a much broader definition of concept than Gagné's definition. According to Dienes there are three types of mathematics concepts—pure mathematical concepts, notational concepts, and applied concepts.

Pure mathematical concepts deal with classifications of numbers and relationships among numbers, and are completely independent of the way in which the numbers are represented. For instance, *six,* 8, XII, 1110 (base two), and $\triangle \triangle \triangle \triangle$ are all examples of the concept of even number; however each is a different way of representing a particular even number.

Notational concepts are those properties of numbers which are a direct consequence of the manner in which numbers are represented. The fact that in base ten, 275 means 2 hundreds, plus 7 tens, plus 5 units is a consequence of our positional notation for representing numbers based upon a powers-of-ten system. The selection of an appropriate notational system for various branches of mathematics is an important factor in the subsequent development and extension of mathematics. The fact that arithmetic developed so slowly is due in large part to the cumbersome way in which the ancients represented numbers. We have already mentioned the problems which occurred in the development of mathematical analysis in England as a consequence of the English mathematicians' insistence upon using Newton's cumbersome notational system for calculus, rather than the more efficient system of Leibniz.

Applied concepts are the applications of pure and notational mathematical concepts to problem solving in mathematics and related fields. Length, area and volume are applied mathematical concepts. Applied concepts should be taught to students after they have learned the prerequisite pure and notational mathematical concepts. Pure concepts should be learned by students before notational concepts are presented, otherwise students will merely memorize patterns for manipulating symbols without understanding the underlying pure mathematical concepts. Students who make symbol manipulation errors such as $3x + 2 = 4$ implies $x + 2 = 4 - 3, \frac{x + 2}{2} = x, a^2 \cdot a^3 = a^6$, and $\sqrt{x^2 + 5} = x + \sqrt{5}$ are attempting to apply pure and notational concepts which they have not adequately learned.

Dienes regards concept learning as a creative art which can not be explained by any stimulus-response theory such as Gagné's stages of learning. Dienes believes that all abstractions are based upon intuition and concrete experiences; consequently his system for teaching mathematics emphasizes mathematics laboratories, manipulative objects, and mathematical games. He thinks that in order to learn mathematics (that is, to be able to classify structures and identify relationships) students must learn to:

(1) *analyze* mathematical structures and their logical relationships,
(2) *abstract* a common property from a number of different structures or events and classify the structures or events as belonging together,
(3) *generalize* previously learned classes of mathematical structures by enlarging them to broader classes which have properties similar to those found in the more narrowly defined classes, and
(4) use previously learned abstractions to *construct* more complex, higher order abstractions.

Stages in Learning Mathematical Concepts

Dienes believes that mathematical concepts are learned in progressive stages which are, somewhat analogous to Piaget's stages of intellectual development. He postulates six stages in teaching and learning mathematical concepts: (1) free play, (2) games, (3) searching for communalities, (4) representation, (5) symbolization, and (6) formalization.

Stage 1, Free Play

The free play stage of concept learning consists of unstructured and undirected activities which permit students to experiment with and manipulate physical and abstract representations of some of the elements of the concept to be learned. This stage of concept learning should be made as free and unstructured as possible; however, the teacher should provide a rich variety of materials for students to manipulate. Even though this unregulated period of free play may appear to be of little value from the point of view of a teacher who is accustomed to teaching mathematics using very structured methods, it is an important stage in concept learning. Here students first experience many of the components of a new concept through interacting with a learning environment which contains concrete representations of the concept. In this stage students form mental structures and attitudes which prepare them to understand the mathematical structure of the concept.

Stage 2, Games

After a period of free play with representations of a concept, students will begin to observe patterns and regularities which are embodied in the concept. They will notice that certain rules govern events, that some things are possible and that other things are impossible. Once students have found the rules and properties which determine events, they are ready to play games, experiment with altering the rules of teacher-made games and make up their own games. Games permit students to experiment with the parameters and variations within the concept and to begin analyzing the mathematical structure of the concept. Various games with different representations of the concept will help students discover the logical and mathematical elements of the concept.

Stage 3, Searching for Communalities

Even after playing several games using different physical representations of a concept, students may not discover the mathematical structure which is common to all representations of that concept. Until students become aware of the common properties in the representations, they will not be able to classify examples and nonexamples of the concept. Dienes suggests that teachers can help students see the communality of structure in the examples of the concept by showing them how each example can be translated into every other example without altering the abstract properties which are common to all the examples. This amounts to pointing out the common properties found in each example by considering several examples at the same time.

Stage 4, Representation

After students have observed the common elements in each example of the concept, they need to develop, or receive from the teacher, a single representation of the concept which embodies all the common elements found in each of the examples. This representation could be either a diagrammatic representation of the concept, a verbal representation, or an inclusive example. Students need a representation in order to sort out the common elements which are present in all examples of the concept. A representation of the concept will usually be more abstract than the examples and will bring students closer to understanding the abstract mathematical structure underlying the concept.

Stage 5, Symbolization

In this stage the student needs to formulate appropriate verbal and mathematical symbols to describe his or her representation of the concept. It is good for students to invent their own symbolic representations of each concept; however, for the sake of consistency with the textbook, teachers probably should intervene in students' selections of symbol systems. It may be well to permit students to first make up their own symbolic representations, and then have them compare their symbolizations with those in the textbook. Students should be shown the value of good symbol systems in solving problems, proving theorems, and explaining concepts. For example, the Pythagorean theorem may be easier to remember and use when it is represented symbolically as $a^2 + b^2 = c^2$, rather than verbally as "for a right triangle, the square of the hypotenuse is equal to the sum of the squares of the other two sides." One difficulty caused by some symbolic representations of rules, formulas, and theorems is that the conditions under which each rule, formula, or theorem can be used are not always apparent from the symbolism. Our symbolic statement of the Pythagorean theorem does not state the conditions under which the theorem can be used; however the verbal statement does specify that the theorem applies to right triangles. Many students who are quite good at remembering rules have trouble matching the appropriate rule to each specific problem-solving situation.

Stage 6, Formalization

After students have learned a concept and the related mathematical structures, they must order the properties of the concept and consider the consequences. The fundamental properties in a mathematical structure are the axioms of the system. Derived properties are the theorems, and the procedures for going from axioms to theorems are the mathematical proofs. In this stage students examine the consequences of the concept and use the concept to solve pure and applied mathematics problems.

Dienes believes that games are useful vehicles for learning mathematical concepts throughout the six stages of concept development. He calls the games
played in the undirected play stage, where students are doing things for their own
enjoyment, *preliminary games*. Preliminary games are usually informal and unstructured and may be made up by students and played individually or in groups.
In the middle stages of concept learning, where students are sorting out the elements of the concept, *structured games* are useful. Structured games are designed for specific learning objectives and may be developed by the teacher or
purchased from companies which produce mathematics curriculum materials. In
the final stages of concept development, when students are solidifying and applying the concept, *practice games* are useful. Practice games can be used as drill
and practice exercises, for reviewing concepts, or as ways to develop applications of concepts.

Principles of Concept Learning

Dienes (1971), in his book *Building up Mathematics,* summarizes his system of
teaching mathematics in four general principles for teaching concepts. His six
stages in concept learning are refinements of these four principles:

1. *Dynamic Principle*. Preliminary, structured and practice and/or reflective type of games must be provided as necessary experiences from which
mathematical concepts can eventually be built, so long as each type of game is
introduced at the appropriate time. We shall see that this break-up can be
further refined.

Although while children are young these games must be played with concrete material, mental games can gradually be introduced to give a taste of
that most fascinating of all games, mathematical research.

2. *Constructivity Principle*. In the structuring of the games, construction
should always precede analysis, which is almost altogether absent from children's learning until the age of 12.

3. *Mathematical Variability Principle*. Concepts involving variables
should be learned by experiences involving the largest possible number of
variables.

4. *Perceptual Variability Principle* or *Multiple Embodiment Principle*.
To allow as much scope as possible for individual variations in concept-for-
mation, as well as to induce children to gather the mathematical essence of an
abstraction, the same conceptual structure should be presented in the form of
as many perceptual equivalents as possible. (pp. 30-31)

Applying Dienes' Theory in a Lesson

In applying Dienes' six stages for concept learning to planning a mathematics
lesson, you may find that one stage (possibly the free play stage) is not appropriate for your students or that the activities for two or three stages could be combined into a single activity. It may be necessary to plan unique learning activities
for each stage when teaching younger elementary school students; however older
secondary school students may be able to omit certain stages in learning some
concepts. Dienes' model for teaching mathematics should serve as a guide, and
not a set of regulations to be followed slavishly.

The concept of multiplying negative integers will be discussed here as an example of how Dienes' stages can be used as a guide in planning teaching/learning activities. Since nearly all students learn to add, subtract, multiply and divide natural numbers, and to add and subtract integers before learning to multiply integers, we will assume that these concepts and skills have been mastered by our hypothetical students.

For students who are in sixth or seventh grade, one could begin the *free play* session by informally discussing the arithmetic operations on the natural numbers and the algebraic properties of natural numbers. The teacher might also discuss adding and subtracting integers and the commutative and associative properties for addition. He or she may even choose to substitute an informal review for free play. Or the *free play* and *game* stages could be combined into several games such as the following simple card game: The teacher should prepare enough decks of standard playing cards with the face cards removed so that there is one deck for every five students in the class. Students playing in groups of five would each be dealt four cards. Each student would group his or her cards into pairs, then take the product of the numbers showing on the cards in each pair, and then add the two products. The student who is able to pair his or her cards to obtain the greatest product-sum is the winner of that hand in his or her group. The numbers on black cards (clubs and spades) are considered to be positive numbers, and numbers on red cards (hearts and diamonds) are negative numbers. Consequently students would immediately be confronted with the problem of how to group negative cards to get large positive products and sums. Various groups may agree upon different rules for handling the product of two negative numbers. For instance, a black 2 and 4 and a red 7 and 5 could be used to make $(2 \times 4) + (-7 \times -5) = 43$, if the correct rule that the product of two negative integers is a positive integer is formulated. If not, then negative numbers would be of no help in organizing a winning hand. Some students will certainly ask each other or the teacher about how to score negative integers.

To decide how to handle the product of two negative numbers, the teacher could present a series of problems involving a *search for communalities*. For instance, these problems could be discussed in class:

1. Assume that bad people are negative and good people are positive. Also assume that moving into a community is a positive act and leaving a community is a negative act. What is the net effect of five bad people leaving two different communities? The class should decide that these events constitute ten positive happenings.

2. What is the effect on your cash balance of subtracting four, three dollar debts from your newspaper route account book? Several students should immediately observe that the effect is positive twelve dollars.

3. Finish this table:
   $$-3 \times 3 = -9$$
   $$-3 \times 2 = -6$$
   $$-3 \times 1 = -3$$
   $$-3 \times 0 = 0$$
   $$-3 \times -1 = ?$$

$-3 \times -2 = ?$

$-3 \times -3 = ?$

4. $-3 \times (7 + -2) = (-3 \times 7) + (-3 \times -2) = -21 + \boxed{?}$

but

$-3 \times (7 + -2) = -3 \times 5 = -15$

so

What number is $\boxed{?}$?

As a mathematics teacher, you may be able to construct other examples showing that the product of two negative intergers is a positive integer.

In the *representation stage* of forming the concept of multiplying negative integers, students should be able to observe a diagram representing the concept and describe the general property of multiplication of two negative integers. The following diagram, shown in Figure 3.3, is one way to represent that the product of two negative integers is a positive integer.

In the *symbolization stage,* each student should be able to explain the diagram in Figure 3.3 and use it to show examples of the concept. Each student should also explain that the diagram shows that the product of two negative integers must be a positive integer in order for the distributive property to be true for multiplication and addition of integers. Finally, the class should adopt the symbol system that for any natural numbers *a* and *b,* $(-a)(-b) = +ab$; and for any integers *x, y, z, x(y + z) = xy + xz.*

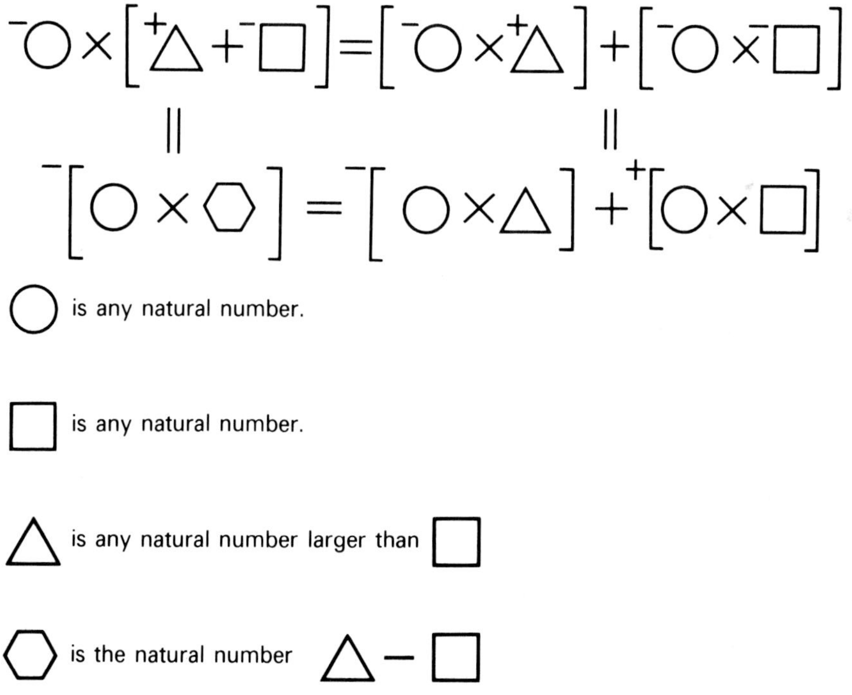

$$^{-}\bigcirc \times \left[{}^{+}\triangle + {}^{-}\square \right] = \left[{}^{-}\bigcirc \times {}^{+}\triangle \right] + \left[{}^{-}\bigcirc \times {}^{-}\square \right]$$

$$\| \qquad\qquad\qquad \|$$

$$^{-}\left[\bigcirc \times \hexagon \right] = {}^{-}\left[\bigcirc \times \triangle \right] + {}^{+}\left[\bigcirc \times \square \right]$$

$\bigcirc$ is any natural number.

$\square$ is any natural number.

$\triangle$ is any natural number larger than $\square$

$\hexagon$ is the natural number $\triangle - \square$

Figure 3.3. A representation of the concept that the product of two negative integers is a positive integer.

This concept can be *formalized* by recognizing that the statement, "the product of two negative integers is a positive integer," is an axiom. Theorems such as $y \times z = z \times y$ and $x(y + z) = xy + xz$ can also be stated and proved.

Diene's approach to teaching and learning mathematics can be summarized in the following list of subprinciples which are inherent in his four principles for concept learning.

1. All of mathematics is based upon experience and students learn mathematics by abstracting mathematical concepts and structures out of real experiences.
2. There is a fixed natural process that students must carry out in order to learn mathematical concepts. The process must include:
    a. A play and experimental period involving concrete materials and abstract ideas.
    b. An ordering of experiences into a meaningful whole.
    c. A flash of insight and understanding when the student suddenly comprehends the concept.
    d. A practice stage to anchor the new concept so that the student can apply it and use it in new mathematical learning experiences.
3. Mathematics is a creative art and it must be taught and learned as an art.
4. New mathematics concepts must be related to previously learned concepts and structures so that there is a transfer of old learning to new learning.
5. In order to learn mathematics, students must be able to translate a concrete situation or event into an abstract symbolic formulation.

Ausubel's Theory of Meaningful Verbal Learning

During the nineteen fifties many mathematics educators came to believe that the prevailing lecture method for teaching mathematics was resulting in rote learning which was not meaningful to students. As new mathematics programs with an emphasis upon understanding of concepts were developed and implemented in schools during the nineteen sixties, verbal expository teaching began to fall into disrepute. Many people felt that expository teaching resulted in rote learning, and teaching models such as discovery learning, inquiry, and mathematics laboratories were thought to be more appropriate methods for fostering meaningful learning. However, there were people who still believed that since the lecture method of teaching had worked reasonably well in the past, it should not be discarded as a bad teaching strategy. Throughout this period, the learning theorist David P. Ausubel argued that expository teaching was the only efficient way to transmit the accumulated discoveries of countless generations to each succeeding generation, and that many of the recently popular methods were not only inefficient, but were also ineffective in promoting meaningful learning. Ausubel's theory of meaningful verbal learning contains a procedure for effective expository teaching resulting in meaningful learning. To Ausubel, the lecture or expository method is a very effective teaching strategy, and he believes that educators should devote more effort toward developing effective expository teaching techniques.

Now that studies of mathematics skills in children and young adults (for example, studies conducted by the National Assessment of Educational Progress, NAEP) indicate that all is not well in applying arithmetic skills, many people are beginning to question the new mathematics programs and the new teaching methods. A study completed in 1975 by the NAEP and reported in the August, 1975 *NAEP Newsletter* showed that fewer than half of the 17-year-olds and young adults between the ages of 26-35 could solve simple consumer arithmetic problems. An earlier NAEP study found that people in these same age groups were reasonably proficient in solving textbook-type arithmetic problems, so there appears to be a problem in teaching meaningful, real-world applications of arithmetic. This unfortunate dilemma for mathematics education may lend some support to Ausubel's contention that the popular non-expository teaching methods do not necessarily result in the learning of meaningful problem-solving procedures.

Reception and Discovery Learning, Meaningful and Rote Learning

Ausubel's theory of meaningful verbal learning contains a rationale for expository teaching and shows how lecture-type lessons can be organized to teach the structure of a discipline to make learning more meaningful to students. As a proponent of expository teaching and verbal learning, Ausubel shows how reception learning can be both efficient and meaningful. However, some critics of reception learning and some proponents of discovery learning claim that reception learning usually is rote learning and discovery learning usually is meaningful for students. Consequently, many of Ausubel's writings contain a discussion of reception learning versus discovery learning and meaningful learning versus rote learning, in which he refutes these claims.

In an article in the February 1968 *Arithmetic Teacher,* Ausubel describes *reception learning* and *discovery learning* as follows:

> The distinction between reception and discovery learning is not difficult to understand. In reception learning the principal content of what is to be learned is presented to the learner in more or less final form. The learning does not involve any discovery on his part. He is required only to internalize the material or incorporate it into his cognitive structure so that it is available for reproduction or other use at some future date. The essential feature of discovery learning on the other hand, is that the principal content of what is to be learned is not given but must be discovered by the learner before he can internalize it; the distinctive and prior learning task, in other words, is to discover something. After this phase is completed, the discovered content is internalized just as in receptive learning. (p. 126)

The following explanation of Ausubel's distinction between rote and meaningful learning is taken from his article in the January 1961 issue of *Educational Theory*.

> The distinction between rote and meaningful learning is frequently confused with the reception-discovery distinction · · · . This confusion is partly responsible for the widespread but unwarranted belief that reception learning is invariably rote and that discovery learning is invariably meaningful. Actually, each distinction constitutes an entirely independent dimension of learning. Hence, both reception and discovery learning can each be rote or meaningful depending on the conditions under which learning occurs.
>
> By "meaningful learning" we also refer primarily to a distinctive kind of learning process, and only secondarily to a meaningful learning outcome—at-

tainment of meaning—that necessarily reflects the completion of such a process. Meaningful learning as a process presupposes, in turn, *both* that the learner employs a meaningful learning set and that the material he learns is potentially meaningful to him. Thus, regardless of how much potential meaning may inhere in a given proposition, if the learner's intention is to memorize it verbatim, i.e., as a series of arbitrarily related words, both the learning process and the learning outcome must necessarily be rote and meaningless. And conversely, no matter how meaningful the learner's set may be, neither the process nor outcome of learning can possibly be meaningful if the learning task itself is devoid of potential meaning. (pp. 17-18.)

Ausubel has observed that discovery learning and problem-solving teaching techniques can result in rote learning, just as poor expository teaching can cause students to memorize material which has no meaning to them. When learning to solve statement problems in algebra, many students memorize problem types and sets of rules for solving each type, with little meaningful understanding of why the rules lead to solutions. Good expository teaching, whereby a teacher structures and explains a mathematics topic so that students can organize the topic and relate it to previous meaningfully learned topics, can result in efficient and effective learning. Since people are able to memorize and retain limited quantities of arbitrary verbatim materials and must devote a great deal of time and effort to rote learning, the most efficient learning is meaningful learning. Ausubel believes that good expository teaching is the *only* efficient way to promote meaningful learning. He thinks that inquiry models, discovery lessons, and laboratory exercises are very inefficient learning strategies and should be used infrequently in schools. Although Ausubel concedes that some attention should be given to teaching problem-solving, inquiry methods and creative and critical thinking. However, he believes that schools should concentrate on teaching specific information which is useful for social survival and cultural progress, and the basic skills which are teachable to and learnable by the majority of students.

Preconditions for Meaningful Reception Learning
According to Ausubel there are two preconditions for meaningful reception learning. First, meaningful reception learning can only occur in a student who has a meaningful learning set. This is to say that the student's conditioning and attitudes are such that he or she approaches the learning task with the appropriate intentions. If a student approaches the learning task with the attitude that he or she intends to understand the learning material, and apply the new learning and relate it to previous learning, that student is likely to learn the new task in a meaningful manner. However, a student who regards the new learning task as an arbitrary, verbatim set of words having little inherent meaning or value will merely attempt to memorize the new material as an isolated set of verbal symbols. If the learner does not want to translate the new information into terminology consistent with his or her own vocabulary, does not attempt to evaluate how well he or she understands the information, and does not relate it to previously learned information, then meaningful learning will not occur. There are several reasons why students do not have appropriate learning sets for meaningful learning of mathematics. Many students have given up hope for ever understanding mathematics due to chronic failure and frustration in mathematics classes. Other students have

found that their mathematics teachers expect definitions to be reproduced in a verbatim manner, steps in solving homework problems to be carried out in a strict, unalterable sequence, and rules to be obeyed without question. For these students, attempts to relate new mathematics concepts to their own unique mental structures result in failure to satisfy teachers; so they memorize the material in exactly the same form as their teachers present it. Other students with good memories may temporarily find that memorizing new information and processes is easier than attempting to understand underlying concepts. Eventually these students will forget much of the mathematics which they have memorized and will confuse new information with previously memorized mathematical structures. For example, a bright student can get part way through a Euclidean plane geometry course by memorizing theorems and their proofs; however this "straw house of geometry" usually collapses long before the final test.

The second precondition for meaningful reception learning is that the learning task be potentially meaningful through its relation to the learner's existing cognitive structure. By relating new mathematical concepts and principles to previously learned (in a meaningful way) mathematical structures, the student can assimilate new materials into older cognitive structures. Earlier meaningful learning provides an anchor for new learning so that new learning and retention do not require rote learning of arbitrary associations. According to Ausubel, this anchoring process keeps newly learned material from interfering with previously learned similar materials, which is a hazard of rote learning. The new mathematics learning task must be nonarbitrarily and substantively related to the learner's existing structure of mathematical knowledge. Whether a learning task is potentially meaningful depends upon the nature of the material to be learned, the way in which the teacher structures his or her presentation of the mathematics topic, and the learner's unique cognitive structure, which is the manner in which the learner's existing knowledge is organized.

There are several factors that may hinder meaningful verbal learning. First, the learner may not possess the necessary level of mental development for meaningful learning of some mathematical concepts to occur. Those students in junior high school who are still in Piaget's stage of concrete operations may not be able to learn highly abstract mathematical principles and concepts without concurrent concrete examples of the principles and concepts. Second, students may not be sufficiently motivated to attempt to learn mathematics in a meaningful way. Poorly motivated students may not consciously resort to rote learning, but may delude themselves and their teachers into believing that their vague and imprecise verbal statements about mathematical concepts and principles are genuinely meaningful. Third, some teachers delude themselves into believing that their lists of definitions, problem solving rules and steps in the proofs of theorems are meaningful to students. Being able to define congruence and prove three theorems about congruent triangles does not necessarily mean that a student understands congruence and geometric proof in any meaningful way. Definitions and proofs can be memorized as sequences of words which have little meaning for students. The teacher who usually insists that students define a concept in the teacher's words, use the teacher's sequence of steps to solve problems, and give the teacher's sequence of statements and reasons in the proof of a theorem is inadvertently promoting meaningless rote learning.

133

Strategies for Meaningful Verbal Learning

Ausubel regards each academic discipline as having a distinct organizational and methodological structure and each individual as having a distinct cognitive structure. He conceptualizes the information-processing structure of the discipline and the information-processing structure of the mind as analogous. Both a discipline such as mathematics and a human mind contain a hierarchical structure of ideas in which the most inclusive ideas are at the top of the structure and subsume progressively less inclusive and more highly differentiated sub-ideas. Since each discipline has its unique structure, Ausubel thinks that disciplines should not be taught using an interdisciplinary approach; rather, each subject should be taught separately. Ausubel does not approve of unified science courses in which biology, physics, and chemistry are taught together; neither does he regard unified mathematics-science programs as an appropriate way to teach these two subjects. He regards the structure as the most important part of a discipline, and combining the teaching of two disciplines will cause the unique structure of each one to be obscured from the learner. Since geometry, algebra and analysis have different structures, it is doubtful that Ausubel would approve of unified mathematics programs such as Howard Fehr's unified modern mathematics textbook series for secondary school students.

Since, as Ausubel believes, the major job of education is to teach the disciplines, two conditions must be satisfied. First, the discipline must be presented to students so that the structure of the discipline is stabilized within each student's cognitive configuration and not absorbed and obliterated as a unique structure. According to Bruce Joyce and Marsha Weil (1972) in their book *Models of Teaching:*

> Ausubel's insistence on stabilization of new ideas rather than integrating and absorbing them comes from his position that the hierarchical organization of ideas within each discipline is extremely powerful and that the learner can make maximal use of these ideas by having them stabilized within his structure, rather than by integrating them with his old ideas and making new kinds of structures. (p. 168)

The second condition in teaching a discipline is to make the material meaningful to the learner. To insure meaningful learning, the teacher must help students build linkages between their own cognitive structures and the structure of the discipline being taught. Each new concept or principle within the discipline must be related to relevant, previously learned concepts and principles which are in the learner's cognitive structure.

Ausubel has developed two principles for presenting content in a subject field—progressive differentiation and integrative reconciliation. The principle of *progressive differentiation* is described by Ausubel (1963) in his book *The Psychology of Meaningful Verbal Learning:*

> When subject matter is programed in accordance with the principles of progressive differentiation, the most general and inclusive ideas of the discipline are presented first, and are then progressively differentiated in terms of detail and specificity. · · · The assumption we are making here, in other words, is that an individual's organization of the content of a particular subject-matter discipline in his own mind, consists of a hierarchical structure in

which the most inclusive concepts occupy a position at the apex of the structure and subsume progressively less inclusive and more highly differentiated subconcepts and factual data. (p. 79)

The *integrative reconciliation* principle implies that new information about the discipline being studied should be reconciled and integrated with previously learned information from that discipline. The teaching/learning sequence should be structured so that each new lesson is carefully related to previously learned materials. New learning in a discipline should be related to and built upon previous learning. It should be noted that although Ausubel says that each part of a discipline should be integrated with other parts, he does not support integrating the structures of various disciplines, thus obscuring the unique structure of each discipline.

The teaching strategy that Ausubel suggests in order to promote meaningful verbal learning through progressive differentiation and integrative reconciliation is the use of advance organizers. An *advance organizer* is a preliminary statement, discussion, or other activity which *introduces* new material at a higher level of generality, inclusiveness, and abstraction than the actual new learning task. The organizer is selected for its appropriateness in explaining and integrating the new material. Its purpose is to provide the learner with a conceptual structure into which he or she will integrate the new material. Advance organizers set the stage for meaningful reception learning and provide a top-down approach to learning new concepts and principles. The advance organizer is structured as an anchoring vehicle which subsumes the new material to be learned as a consequence of its high degree of generality and inclusiveness. Advance organizers are not merely outlines, overviews, or summaries which are usually presented at the same level of abstraction and generality as the material to be learned. Rather, they are inclusive subsumers which prepare students to meaningfully learn new materials by helping to organize abstract cognitive structures in their minds.

The purposes of advance organizers as stated by Ausubel (1968) in his book *Educational Psychology, A Cognitive View* are:

Advance organizers probably facilitate the incorporability and longevity of meaningfully learned material in three different ways. First, they explicitly draw upon and mobilize whatever relevant anchoring concepts are already established in the learner's cognitive structure and make them part of the subsuming entity. Thus, not only is new material rendered more familiar and potentially meaningful, but the most relevant ideational antecedents in cognitive structure are also selected and utilized in integrated fashion. Second, advance organizers at an appropriate level of inclusiveness, by making subsumption under specifically relevant propositions possible (and drawing on other advantages of subsumptive learning), provide optimal anchorage. This promotes both initial learning and later resistance to obliterative subsumption. Third, the use of advance organizers renders unnecessary much of the rote memorization to which students often resort because they are required to learn the details of an unfamiliar discipline before having available a sufficient number of key anchoring ideas. Because of the unavailability of such ideas in cognitive structure to which the details can be nonarbitrarily and substantively related, the material, although logically meaningful, lacks potential meaningfulness. (pp. 137-138)

An Advance Organizer Lesson

The following *Model for Teaching*[1] is an advance organizer teaching strategy which was written to prepare secondary school students to study a unit on the operation of computers and computer programming. The purpose of this organizer is to help students anchor an abstract, general and inclusive model of a computer operating system in their cognitive structures before studying more concrete and specific concepts and principles of computer operations. Most advance organizer lessons are expository; however this particular example combines expository teaching and a class activity.

Let's Make a Computer

This model will describe a lesson that illustrates the process used by computers to solve mathematical problems, by having students play the roles of components in a computer system. It will also motivate students into further inquiry about specific methods of computer programming and the devices needed in a computer system.

Performance Objective

Students will list in writing the general components needed for a computer system and describe the function of each component. They will also orally describe the process a computer uses in solving a mathematical problem.

Preassessment

The students should be able to solve mathematical problems by following specified algorithmic procedures (sets of instructions). Have them solve the following problems, each of which requires the use of an algorithm: $7431 - 874,236$ times 487, 867/32. If your students don't know the definition of $n!$, explain this definition by using examples such as $2! = 2 \times 1 = 2$; $3! = 3 \times 2 \times 1 = 6$; and $5! = 5 \times 4 \times 3 \times 2 \times 1 = 120$. This will enable you to review and identify any weaknesses.

Teaching Strategies

Explain to the class that a computer solves mathematical problems not by inventing or learning a method of solution, but by very rapidly and without error following a set of instructions called a computer program. These instructions were written and given to the computer by a human being who had to know the procedure for solving the problem, but did not have sufficient time to carry out the many mathematical operations necessary to finding the solution. Tell the students that several of them will be selected to act as parts of a computer to solve a problem the way a computer would.

Ditto, distribute and briefly explain the following parts of a computer:

Computer People Call It	We Will Call It	Its Use
Input device	INSTRUCTION READER	Puts instructions and data into the computer
Memory	MAILBOXES	Place to store instructions and data supplied by instruction reader
Arithmetic unit	ARITHMETICKER	Place where the arithmetic is done
Output device	ANSWER WRITER	Prints the answer to the problem after the computer has solved it
Central processing unit	CHIEF	Makes the other parts do their work at the proper time

Two additional operations that must be done by a computer are carried out in the circuits. LOOK-AND-TELL is the ability to look into the mailboxes and tell the chief what is stored in them; and RUN-AND-CHANGE is the ability to take information out of mailboxes and replace it with new information.

Before the next class session prepare six cardboard name signs for students to wear around their necks: INSTRUCTION READER, ARITHMETICKER, ANSWER WRITER, CHIEF, LOOK-AND-TELL and RUN-AND-CHANGE.

Also prepare a large poster or ditto and distribute as illustrated at the conclusion of this model, the set of instructions (computer program) which your human computer will use to find 8!. Each instruction is boxed in a "mailbox." You will also need two small boxes without tops and a package of 3×5 cards or paper slips for writing numbers to be placed in the mailboxes. Prepare two more name cards, FACTORIAL and COUNTER, for the boxes. (Be sure that the printing on the poster and the name cards is large enough to read from the rear of the room.)

Post the instruction poster on a wall in the front of the classroom and place the boxes on your desk so that the name cards face the class. According to the instructions the card numbered 1 is to be stored in the mailbox named FACTORIAL and the card numbered 2 in the mailbox

1. Reprinted by permission of the publisher, Croft-NEI Publications, Waterford, Connecticut, Copyright Croft Educational Services, Inc.

named COUNTER. Again, according to the instructions in BOX 3 the current numbers stored in FACTORIAL and COUNTER are to be multiplied, the product to replace the current number in FACTORIAL. Note the equal sign is not used here in the sense of equivalence. In the instructions for BOX4, when COUNTER contains an 8 skip BOX5 and BOX6 and obtain the next instruction from BOX7; otherwise the next instruction comes from BOX5. BOX5 causes the contents of COUNTER to be replaced with one more than its current contents. BOX6 sends you back to BOX3 for the next instruction. When BOX7 is reached, the contents of FACTORIAL, which will be 8!, are printed and BOX8 causes the computer to halt.

Ask for student volunteers to play the roles and give each one a sign. Since you are the chief, wear the CHIEF sign around your neck. The problem your human computer will solve is that of computing 8! (eight factorial).

Now position the student computer components in the same configuration as shown on the drawing. You and the five components should executive the instructions until BOX8 is reached and the problem is solved.

As CHIEF be sure to instruct each student computer part in precisely what he is to do and when he is to act. READER's job is to read each instruction from the boxes, one at a time, when CHIEF tells him to do so. Then ARITHMETICKER will multiply the current contents of FACTORIAL and COUNTER and tell CHIEF the answer. ANSWER WRITER's only job is to write the contents of FACTORIAL when BOX7 is finally reached. (CHIEF gives the instruction to write.) Each time CHIEF needs to know what numbers are in either FACTORIAL or COUNTER, he instructs LOOK-AND-TELL to look into the appropriate box and tell him what is there. When an instruction indicates that the number in either FACTORIAL or COUNTER is to be replaced with a new number, CHIEF tells RUN-AND-CHANGE to make the appropriate replacement. CHIEF writes the number on a 3 × 5 card and hands the card to RUN-AND-CHANGE with the instruction to replace the old card in a box with a new card. Be sure to have RUN-AND-CHANGE discard each old card when making a replacement, as computer mailboxes can only contain one number at a time.

You may have enough time in a single class period to run through the computer in action twice. This will give a second group of student volunteers the opportunity to be active participants. To capitalize upon the motivational aspects of the model, continue discussion about computers in the following class meeting, or invite a guest computer expert to talk with the students and answer their questions. You might also take the class on a field trip to see a computer in operation.

Postassessment

Have the students list the general components of a computer system and describe the function of each. Then have them describe the procedure a computer follows in solving a math problem.

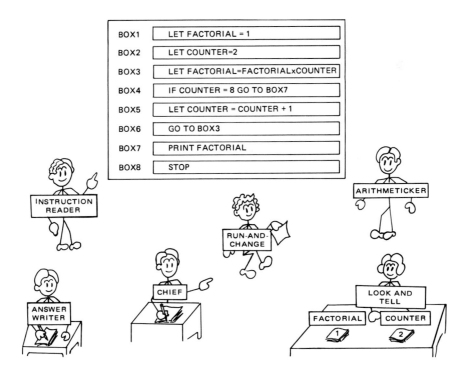

Jerome Bruner on Learning and Instruction

The well-known psychologist, Jerome Bruner, has written extensively on learning theory, the instructional process and educational philosophy. Since he has modified his position on the nature of instruction and his philosophy of education between 1960 and 1970, any comprehensive consideration of Bruner's work must include a comparison of his changing attitudes. In the late nineteen fifties Bruner and many other educators, notably those people who were beginning to develop the new curricula in mathematics and science, appeared to regard the structure of the disciplines as a very important factor (maybe even the most important factor) in education. At least, it would not be incorrect to say that the content issue was of major concern to many of the developers of the several variations of a modern mathematics curriculum. Bruner's highly acclaimed book, *The Process of Education,* which was written in 1959-60, reflects the then current thinking of the scholarly community with regard to primary and secondary education. This book is a synthesis of the discussions and perceptions of 34 mathematicians, scientists, psychologists and educators who met for ten days at Woods Hole on Cape Cod to discuss ways to improve education in schools in the United States. Their discussions centered around the importance of teaching the structure of disciplines, readiness for learning, intuitive and analytic thinking, and motives for learning. General principles such as those stated in the following list emerged from the Woods Hole conference:

1. Proper learning under optimum conditions leads students to "learn how to learn."
2. Any topic from any subject can be taught to any student in some intellectually honest form at any stage in the student's intellectual development.
3. Intellectual activity is the same anywhere, whether the person is a third grader or a research scientist.
4. The best form of motivation is interest in the subject.

Studying the structure of each subject was thought to be so important that four reasons for teaching structure were formulated. First, it was thought that an examination of the fundamental structure of a subject makes the subject more comprehensible to students. Second, in order to remember details of a subject, the details must be placed in a structured pattern. Third, the optimum way to promote transfer of specific learning to general applications of learning is through understanding of concepts, principles and the structure of each subject. Fourth, if the fundamental structures of subjects are studied early in school, the lag between current research findings and what is taught in school will be reduced.

These general principles of instruction and the more specific arguments for teaching structure were thought to constitute the basic rational for the curriculum changes which were under way in 1960. However, in his article "The Process of Education Revisited," which appeared in 1971 in the *Phi Delta Kappan* journal, Bruner assessed the major notions about education which were prevelant ten years previous and found them to be quite inadequate. In reference to the educational thinking of 1959, Bruner, in comments critical of that type of thought, stated in 1971 that:

> The prevailing notion was that if you understood the structure of knowledge that understanding would then permit you to go ahead on your own; you did not need to encounter everything in nature in order to know nature, but by understanding some deep principles you could extrapolate to the particulars as needed. Knowing was a canny strategy whereby you could know a great deal about a lot of things while keeping very little in mind. (p. 18)

and

> The movement of which *The Process of Education* was a part was based on a formula of faith: that learning was what students wanted to do, that they wanted to achieve an expertise in some particular subject matter. Their motivation was taken for granted. It also accepted the tacit assumption that everybody who came to these curricula in the schools already had been the beneficiary of the middle-class hidden curricula that taught them analytic skills and launched them in the traditionally intellectual use of mind.
>
> Failure to question these assumptions has, of course, caused much grief to all of us. (p. 19)

In this same *Phi Delta Kappan* article, Bruner states his more recent viewpoint of the school curriculum as follows:

> If I had my choice now, in terms of a curriculum project for the seventies, it would be to find a means whereby we could bring society back to its sense of values and priorities in life. *I believe I would be quite satisfied to declare, if not a moratorium, then something of a de-emphasis on matters that have to do with the structure of history, the structure of physics, the nature of mathematical consistency, and deal with it rather in the context of the problems that face us.* We might better concern ourselves with how those problems can be solved, not just by practical action, but by putting knowledge, wherever we find it and in whatever form we find it, to work in these massive tasks. (p. 21)

Bruner's Theory of Instruction

In his book *Toward a Theory of Instruction,* Bruner presents his viewpoint of the nature of intellectual growth and discusses six characteristics of growth. He also gives two general characteristics which he believes should form the basis of a general theory of instruction and discusses four specific major features which he thinks should be present in any theory of instruction.

Characteristics of Intellectual Growth

According to Bruner, intellectual growth is characterized by a person's increasing ability to separate his or her responses from immediate and specific stimuli. As people develop intellectually, they learn to delay, restructure and control their responses to particular sets of stimuli. One might understand, and even expect, a seventh grader's uncontrolled, angry response in the form of harsh, vulgar words and unacceptable physical actions to criticisms from his or her teacher. However, one would neither expect nor tolerate a teacher's swearing at or striking a student in response to the student's criticisms of the teacher. One of the general objectives of education is to assist students in learning to control their responses and to make socially acceptable responses to a variety of stimuli.

A second characteristic of growth is development of the ability to internalize external events into a mental structure which corresponds to the learner's environment and which aids the learner in generalizing from specific instances. People learn to make predictions and to extrapolate information by structuring sets of events and data. In one sense, the totality of a person's capabilities to extend and apply his or her previous learning is greater than the sum of that person's specific learning activities. Mathematical theorem-proving and problem-solving require this somewhat intuitive and creative ability to generalize specific learning.

A third characteristic of mental development is the increasing ability to use words and symbols to represent things which have been done or will be done in the future. The use of words and mathematical symbols permits people to go beyond intuition and empirical adaptation and to use logical and analytical modes of thought. The importance to mathematics of appropriate symbol systems has already been illustrated. Without symbolic notation, mathematics would develop very slowly and would have limited applications for modeling physical and conceptual situations.

The fourth growth characteristic is that mental development depends upon systematic and structured interactions between the learner and teachers; a student's ''teachers'' are other students, parents, school teachers, or anyone who chooses to instruct the learner. According to both Bruner and Piaget, intellectual development will be severely retarded if children do not have a variety of contacts with other people. One thing that many school teachers tend not to do is to exploit the unique abilities which students have for teaching each other. On many occasions, students are better able to learn concepts by discussing them with each other and explaining them to each other than through exclusive instruction from the teacher.

Bruner's fifth characteristic of growth is that teaching and learning are vastly facilitated through the use of language. Not only is language used by teachers to communicate information to students, language is necessary for the complete formulation of most concepts and principles. In mathematics classrooms, one of the primary ways for students to demonstrate knowledge and understanding of mathematical ideas is through the use of language to express their conceptions of the ideas.

The sixth characteristic is that intellectual growth is demonstrated by the increasing ability to handle several variables simultaneously. People who are intellectually mature can consider several alternatives simultaneously and can give attention to multiple, and even conflicting, demands at the same time. The influence of Piaget's work upon Bruner's thinking is apparent in Bruner's formulation of this characteristic of intellectual growth. You will recall that Piaget's research has shown that small children who are still intellectually immature are able to deal with only a single characteristic of an object at one time.

Features of a Theory of Instruction
According to Bruner, a theory of instruction should be prescriptive and normative. A theory of instruction is *prescriptive* if it contains principles for the most

effective procedures for teaching and learning facts, skills, concepts, and principles. That is, within the theory there are prescribed processes and methods for attaining the learning objectives of instruction. In addition, the theory should contain processes for evaluating and modifying teaching and learning strategies. A theory of instruction is *normative* if it contains general criteria of learning and states the conditions for meeting the criteria. That is, the theory should contain general learning objectives or goals and should specify how these objectives can be met.

Bruner distinguishes between a theory of learning, or a theory of intellectual development, and a theory of instruction. Learning theories are descriptive, not prescriptive. A theory of learning is a description of what has happened and what can be expected to happen. For example, Piaget's theory of intellectual development describes the stages through which mental growth progresses and even identifies mental activities which people are or are not able to carry out in each stage. However, Piaget's learning theory does not prescribe teaching procedures. A theory of instruction is prescriptive and does have learning objectives. A theory of learning will describe those mental activities which children are able to carry out at certain ages, and a theory of instruction will prescribe how to teach students certain capabilities when they are intellectually ready to learn them. For example, Piaget's learning theory describes the fact that young children can not understand one-to-one correspondence; however, an instructional theory might prescribe methods for teaching one-to-one correspondence to students who are intellectually ready to master this concept.

Theories of learning and theories of instruction are important in education and are, in fact, inseparable. While Piaget's major research efforts are designed to describe the nature of learning, he is not unconcerned with theories of instruction. Much of Bruner's work has been devoted to developing theories of instruction, but his theories of instruction are related to and compatible with elements of certain learning theories.

Bruner believes that any theory of instruction should have four major features which prescribe the nature of the instructional process.

The first feature is that a theory of instruction should specify the experiences which predispose or motivate various types of students to learn; that is, to learn in general and to learn a specific subject such as mathematics. The theory should specify how the student's environment, social status, early childhood, self image, and other factors influence his or her attitudes about learning. Predisposition for learning is an important aspect of any theory of instruction.

Second, the theory should specify the manner in which general knowledge and particular disciplines must be organized and structured so that they can be most readily learned by different types of students. Before it is presented to students, knowledge should be organized so that it relates to the characteristics of learners and embodies the specific structure of the subject. Bruner believes that the structure of any body of knowledge can be described in three ways: its mode of representation, its economy, and its power; each of which varies according to learner characteristics and disciplines.

The *mode of representation* of a body of knowledge can be either sets of examples or images of the concepts and principles contained in the body of knowledge, or sets of symbolic and logical propositions together with rules for transforming them. For seventh graders, the concept of a function could be represented quite appropriately by sets of actions such as adding 2 to a specified set of numbers, halving each measurement in a set of measurements, or converting a set of Fahrenheit measurements to the Centigrade scale. High school sophomores could be given examples of functions such as sets of ordered pairs of objects, or could be shown linear relations such as $y = 2x$, $y = \frac{x}{5}$, and $y = -x$, all of which are appropriate examples of functions for students in high school. High school students in advanced mathematics classes could be given a symbolic representation of the function concept in the form: $y = f(x)$ is a function of x if for every element a belonging to a set X there exists a *unique* element b belonging to a set Y such that a is mapped into b according to $b = f(a)$.

Economy in representing the structure of a discipline is the quantity of information which must be stored in memory in order to understand elements of the discipline. The less information one must remember in order to understand a concept, principle, or process in mathematics, the more economical is the representation of that particular idea or procedure. It is more economical to remember the formula for converting a Fahrenheit scale measurement to a Centigrade scale measurement than it is to remember a table of specific conversions. Economy of representation depends upon the way in which information is organized and sequenced, the manner in which it is presented to students, and the unique learning style of each student.

The *power* of the structure of a body of knowledge for each learner is related to the mental structure which he or she forms in learning the information and is the learner's capacity to organize, connect, and apply information which has been learned. A learner who has structured his or her learning of the mathematical concepts *group, ring,* and *field* in such a way that he or she sees no relationship among these three mathematical ideas, has mentally structured the concepts in a manner which is not very powerful.

The third feature of a theory of instruction is that the theory should specify the most effective ways of sequencing material and presenting it to students in order to facilitate learning. Dienes believes that material in mathematics should be sequenced so that students manipulate concrete representations of the concepts in the form of games before they proceed to more abstract representations. Gagné's hierarchical sequencing of mathematics topics suggests that some material should be sequenced using a bottom-to-top approach with prerequisite and simple material being presented first. In contrast to Gagné's sequencing of material, Ausubel suggests a top-down approach which begins with an advance organizer to subsume subordinate material and provide an anchoring mental structure. The problem of sequencing material in mathematics is very complex and is closely related to each student's individual learning characteristics.

Bruner's fourth feature of a theory of instruction is that the theory should specify the nature, selection, and sequencing of appropriate rewards and punishments in teaching and learning a discipline. Certain students, especially younger children, may require immediate teacher-centered rewards such as praise and grades on a frequent basis; whereas many older students may learn more effectively when the rewards are intrinsic, such as self-satisfaction and the joy of learning a new skill. Some high school students regard grades and school awards as artificial and not very meaningful; however other students are motivated to a large extent through their desire to obtain high grades and teacher approval.

These four features of a theory of instruction (developing a predisposition to learn, structuring knowledge, sequencing the presentation of materials, and providing rewards and reinforcement) suggest corresponding activities which mathematics teachers should engage in when preparing to teach courses, units, topics and lessons in mathematics. Motivating students to learn mathematics, while not within the exclusive control of the teacher, usually is the responsibility of the teacher. Structuring of knowledge and sequencing of topics in mathematics has been done, in part for teachers, by the writers of mathematics textbooks. However, many perceptive teachers find that student learning can be improved by some judicious resequencing of textbook topics, by selecting supplementary topics, and even by changing textbooks. The primary extrinsic reward system in schools is the grading system; although many good teachers encourage students to learn mathematics by developing learning activities which provide internal rewards such as satisfaction in work well done and appreciation of the nature and structure of mathematics as an interesting intellectual activity.

Theorems on Learning Mathematics

In order to identify factors involved in teaching and learning mathematics, Bruner and his associates have observed a large number of mathematics classes and have conducted experiments on teaching and learning mathematics. As a consequence of these observations and experiments, Bruner and Kenney (April, 1963) formulated four general "theorems" about learning mathematics which they have named the construction theorem, the notation theorem, the theorem of contrast and variation, and the theorem of connectivity.

Construction Theorem

The *construction theorem* says that the best way for a student to begin to learn a mathematical concept, principle, or rule is by constructing a representation of it. Older students may be able to grasp a mathematical idea by analyzing a representation which is presented by the teacher; however Bruner believes that most students, especially younger children, should construct their own representations of ideas. He also thinks that it is better for students to begin with concrete representations which they have a hand in formulating. If students are permitted to help in formulating and constructing rules in mathematics, they will be more inclined to remember rules and apply them correctly in appropriate situations. Bruner has found that giving students finished mathematical rules tends to decrease motivation for learning and causes many students to become confused. In the early stages of concept learning, understanding appears to depend upon the concrete activities which students carry out as they construct representations of each concept.

Notation Theorem

The *notation theorem* states that early constructions or representations can be made cognitively simpler and can be better understood by students if they contain notation which is appropriate for the students' levels of mental development. Efficient notational systems in mathematics make possible the extension of principles and the creation of new principles. Until efficient notational systems for representing equations were formulated, the development of general methods for solving polynomial equations and systems of linear equations progressed very slowly. Students should have a say in creating and selecting notational representations for mathematical ideas; simpler and more transparent notations should be used when concepts are being learned by younger students. Since seventh and eighth graders have just learned to use parentheses as symbols of grouping in arithmetic representations such as $(2 + 3) + (5 - 7) = (7 - 4)$, they are not yet ready to use the notation $y = f(x)$ to represent the concept of a mathematical function. For students in these grades, a better way of representing functions is to use a notation such as $\square = 2\triangle + 3$; where $\square$ and $\triangle$ denote natural numbers. Students in a beginning algebra class will be able to understand and apply representations such as $y = 2x + 3$ for functions, and students in advanced algebra courses will use $y = f(x)$ to represent functions. This sequential approach to building a notational system in mathematics is representative of the spiral approach to learning. *Spiral teaching and learning* is an approach whereby each mathematical idea is introduced in an intuitive manner and is represented using familiar and concrete notational forms. Then, month-by-month or year-by-year, as students mature intellectually, the same concepts are presented at higher levels of abstraction using less familiar notational representations which are more powerful for mathematical development.

Contrast and Variation Theorem

Bruner's *theorem of contrast and variation* states that the procedure of going from concrete representations of concepts to more abstract representations involves the operations of contrast and variation. Most mathematical concepts have little meaning for students until they are contrasted to other concepts. In geometry, arcs, radii, diameters and chords of circles all become more meaningful to students when they are contrasted to each other. In fact, many mathematical concepts are defined according to their contrasting properties. Prime numbers are defined as numbers which are neither units nor composite numbers, and irrational numbers are defined as numbers which are not rational. In order for any new concept or principle to be fully understood, it is necessary that its contrasting ideas be presented and considered. Contrast is one of the most useful ways to help students establish an intuitive understanding of a new mathematical topic and to aid them in progressing to more abstract representations of each topic.

If students are to learn general concepts in mathematics, each new concept must be represented by a variety of examples of that concept. If not, a general concept may be learned in close association with specific representations of itself. There have been cases in elementary school where children learned the concept of a set through examples of sets, all of which were represented in the textbook and by the teacher as being enclosed in braces, i.e. $\{\quad\}$. Consequently, students who were shown sets of objects such as $\triangle\ \bigcirc\ \square\ \bigcirc$ would not identify the collection as a set because the objects were not enclosed in braces. When teaching mathematics, it is necessary to provide many and varied examples of each concept so that students will learn that each general, abstract mathematical structure is quite different from more specific and more concrete representations of that structure.

Connectivity Theorem

The *connectivity theorem* can be stated as follows: each concept, principle, and skill in mathematics is connected to other concepts, principles, or skills. The structured connections among the elements in each branch of mathematics permit analytic and synthetic mathematical reasoning, as well as intuitive jumps in mathematical thought. The result is mathematical progress. One of the most important activities of mathematicians is the search for connections and relationships among mathematical structures. In teaching mathematics it is not only necessary for teachers to help students observe the contrasts and variations among mathematical structures, but students also need to become aware of connections between various mathematical structures. Gagné's development of learning hierarchies for structuring the teaching of mathematical content involves searching for connections in mathematics. The structure of mathematics is condensed and simplified and learning mathematics is made easier by identifying connections such as one-to-one correspondences and isomorphisms. In fact, many of the modern mathematics curriculum projects have attempted to illustrate the connections within each branch of mathematics and connections among various branches such as algebra, geometry, and analysis. Not only are connections important for the progress of mathematics, but awareness of connections is also important in learning mathematics. Since very few mathematics topics exist in isolation from all other mathematics topics, connections among topics must be illustrated and understood if progressive, meaningful learning is to be accomplished by students.

Applications of Bruner's Work

Bruner's earlier works, as well as his recent writings, are relevant and useful for teachers and students of mathematics. His viewpoint regarding the importance of intuition and discovery learning for meaningful learning provides mathematics teachers with a balanced contrast to the structured, expository approach to teaching and learning which Ausubel has promoted. In closing our discussion of Bruner's contributions to mathematics education, we will consider an illustration showing how his four theorems for teaching and learning mathematics can be applied to a topic in mathematics—the topic of limits.

Calculus is a difficult subject for many students, and some people who complete high school or college calculus courses do so by memorizing rules and problem types and have little understanding of the conceptual nature of the subject. The creation of calculus was motivated by the need for mathematical techniques to handle continuous processes in nature, such as the movement of bodies in our universe. While algebraic concepts and skills are quite satisfactory for dealing with discrete, finite processes, the concept of a limit is needed to attack those continuous and infinite processes in nature which are now commonly studied in calculus and related subjects. The fundamental concept of calculus, that of limits, is also the fundamental source of many difficulties in learning and applying the subject. Throughout school, until calculus comes along, little is said about limits in spite of the fact that the limit concept is indispensable to any serious consideration of continuous natural processes.

For each year in school from seventh grade on, Bruner's theorems of construction, notation, contrast and variation and connectivity suggest a spiral procedure for teaching and learning the very important mathematical concept of limit. It should be noted that Bruner's four theorems are not meant to be a chronological sequence of steps in the teaching/learning process. In teaching different mathematics topics, it may be appropriate to apply several of his theorems simultaneously or to use them in various sequences depending upon the characteristics of your students and the nature of the mathematics topic being studied. Consequently, the following discussion of limits, although based upon Bruner's theorems, is not organized as a four step process in one-to-one correspondence with the four theorems.

Seventh graders can be introduced to the limit concept through intuitive discussions of representations of limits such as the number sequences:

(a) $\frac{1}{2}, \frac{2}{3}, \frac{3}{4}, \cdots$ which "heads for 1."

(b) 1, 2, 3, 2, 1, 2, 3, 2, 1, $\cdots$ which "bounces around."

(c) 1, 1, 2, 2, 3, 3, $\cdots$ which "gets bigger and bigger."

Geometric representations such as the Pythogrean spiral shown in Figure 1.4 of Chapter 1 or the following sequences exemplify representational variations which are appropriate for a discussion of geometry in seventh grade:

(d) $\triangle, \square, \hexagon, \bigcirc, \cdots$ to a circle.

(e) $\bigcirc, \bigcirc, \bigcirc, \bigcirc, \bigcirc, \bigcirc, \bigcirc, \bigcirc, \bigcirc, \cdots$ to a point.

More abstract representations for seventh or eighth graders include sums of infinite sequences such as the series:

(f) $\frac{1}{2} + \frac{1}{4} + \frac{1}{8} + \cdots$ whose sum "goes toward 1."

(g) $1 + \frac{1}{2} + \frac{1}{3} + \cdots + \frac{1}{n} + \cdots$ which increases without bound;

however a computer may be needed to convince seventh graders of this fact.

Later, in algebra classes, students can consider more abstract representations of limits such as:

(h) $x, x^2, x^3, \cdots$ under the conditions $x = 1$ or -1, $-1 < x < 1$, or $|x| > 1$.

(i) $s = \dfrac{a}{1 - r}$ for $r^2 < 1$ where s is the sum of a geometric progression,

a is the first term, and r is the common ratio.

In a geometry classroom, the limit concept could be represented by sequences of geometric figures similar to those shown in (d) and (e) above or by the series:

(j) $1 - \dfrac{1}{3} + \dfrac{1}{5} - \dfrac{1}{7} + \dfrac{1}{9} - \dfrac{1}{11} + \cdots$ which converges to $\dfrac{\pi}{4}$.

In a trigonometry class, it would be appropriate to discuss the following sequences which converge to values of the trigonometric functions:

(k) $x - \dfrac{x^3}{3!} + \dfrac{x^5}{5!} - \dfrac{x^7}{7!} + \cdots$ which converges to $\sin x$ for all values of x.

(l) $x - \dfrac{x^3}{3} + \dfrac{x^5}{5} - \dfrac{x^7}{7} + \cdots$ which converges to $\tan^{-1}x$ for $x^2 < 1$.

In an advanced mathematics course such as senior analysis, these sequences would be appropriate for students to consider:

(m) $1 + \dfrac{1}{1} + \dfrac{1}{2!} + \dfrac{1}{3!} + \dfrac{1}{4!} + \cdots$ which converges to e.

(n) $(x - 1) - \dfrac{1}{2}(x - 1)^2 + \dfrac{1}{3}(x - 1)^3 - \dfrac{1}{4}(x - 1)^4 + \cdots$ which converges to $\log_e x$ for $0 < x < 2$.

In an advanced mathematics course, notation such as

$$\lim_{x \to 1} \frac{x^2 - 1}{x - 1} = 2,$$

$$\lim_{n \to \infty} \sqrt[n]{n} = 1, \text{ and}$$

$$\lim_{n \to \infty} \left(1 + \frac{1}{n} \right)^n = e$$

is appropriate for students to use, provided they understand and can explain this type of symbolic notation.

Of course, in calculus, limits such as the limiting value of a sequence of secant lines through a point on a curve, which is a representation of the concept of a derivative, and the sums of sequences of rectangles bounded by a curve, which represents the definite integral concept, are appropriate representations for the limit concept. Students in more advanced mathematics courses, such as real analysis, deal with representations and notational systems for limits of sequences of functions and limits of sums of sequences of functions.

Even though this example merely contains a set of representations and does not have specifications for teaching strategies and learning activities, we can observe that Bruner's four theorems for teaching mathematics are exemplified in the sequence of examples irrespective of the specific teaching/learning strategies which teachers may choose to use. A variety of concrete and abstract examples of the limit concept are given above, and the notation becomes more abstract and symbolic as the examples progress from seventh grade level to college level. The representations are varied enough so that the limit concept is freed from any particular type of representation or subject in mathematics; the concept of limit is connected to concepts from algebra, geometry, trigonometry, and higher mathematics. When teaching the limit concept, it also would be necessary to encourage students to construct their own representations of limits, to present them to each other, and to discuss the differences and similarities among the various embodiments of the concept.

B. F. Skinner on Teaching and Learning

For many years philosophers and psychologists have formulated and debated alternative viewpoints about the nature of human beings. There now are two generally accepted models of human actions—the *behaviorist model* and the *phenomenological model.* Those philosophers and psychologists who subscribe to the behaviorist viewpoint regard people as being somewhat passive organisms who are primarily controlled by stimuli from their environments. Proponents of this behaviorist model of human nature believe that people's behaviors can be controlled by properly controlling their environments, and that scientific methods are appropriate for the study of human behavior.

The phenomenological viewpoint proposes that people are inherently and primarily in control of their own actions. People are regarded as being free to make their own choices and to control their own behaviors. A philosopher or psychologist who agrees with the phenomenological model of mankind would center a study of human behavior around human consciousness, awareness, and self expression.

Although these two viewpoints of human behavior stem from contrasting philosophies, they do have some common elements: perhaps human behavior is, paradoxically, both capable and incapable of being studied scientifically. It may be that much of human behavior is subject to certain laws which are fixed for the time being, but which change through an evolutionary process as humanity gains new information and knowledge about itself. Frank Milhollan and Bill Forisha (1972), in their book *From Skinner to Rogers,* develop these contrasting models of human behavior by contrasting two psychologists' (B. F. Skinner and Carl Rogers) approaches to human behavior and education.

In this section we are going to study the scientific behavioral approach to teaching and learning which B. F. Skinner has described and researched. Skinner is regarded as one of the most influential of the modern psychologists. His work has provided a basis for many programmed instruction and individualized learning packages, and, more recently, for some computer-based instructional systems. Skinner's work has also had considerable impact upon society in general, through his development and promotion of strategies for the effective and efficient modification of human behavior. One of Skinner's major contributions to education is his experimental and scientific analysis of behavior, which has important implications for teaching and learning. In fact, according to Milhollan and Forisha (1972):

> One of the most influential positions regarding the nature of psychology and how it can be applied to education is exemplified by the work of B. F. Skinner. Skinner's system probably represents the most complete and systematic statement of the associationist, behaviorist, environmentalist, determinist position in psychology today. (p. 44)

While Piaget, Guilford, and Ausubel are primarily concerned with the development of the mind or the way the mind receives and structures information (that is, what goes on in the mind), Skinner believes that a study of teaching and learning depends primarily upon the observable behaviors of teachers and students. Since the scientific method has been quite successful in advancing knowledge in the physical sciences, Skinner thinks that a scientific approach can be used equally well for studying the social sciences. Milhollan and Forisha interpret Skinner's thoughts on this issue as follows:

> Skinner believes that the methods of science should be applied to the field of human affairs. We are all controlled by the world, part of which is constructed by men. Is this control to occur by accident, by tyrants, or by ourselves? A

scientific society should reject accidental manipulation. He asserts that a specific plan is needed to promote fully the development of man and society. We cannot make wise decisions if we continue to pretend that we are not controlled.

As Skinner points out, the possibility of behavioral control is offensive to many people. We have traditionally regarded man as a free agent whose behavior occurs by virtue of spontaneous inner changes. We are reluctant to abandon the internal ''will'' which makes prediction and control of behavior impossible. (p. 45)

and

Skinner notes that a scientific conception of human behavior dictates one practice and a philosophy of personal freedom another. Until we adopt a consistent view we are likely to remain ineffective in solving our social problems. A scientific conception entails the acceptance of an assumption of determinism, the doctrine that behavior is caused and that the behavior which appears is the only one which could have appeared. (p. 46)

Types of Behavior and Learning

According to Skinner, nearly all identifiable human behavior falls into two categories, respondent behavior and operant behavior. *Respondent behaviors* are involuntary (reflex) behaviors and result from special environmental stimuli. In order for a respondent behavior to occur, it is *first* necessary that a stimulus be applied to the organism. The stimulus of a bug flying toward your eyes will cause you to blink, an embarrassing event may cause you to blush, and a bright flash of light will result in your blinking your eyes. Only a few of our behaviors are respondent behaviors.

Most of our behaviors are *operant behaviors,* which are neither automatic, predictable, nor related in any known manner to easily identifiable stimuli. Skinner believes that certain behaviors merely happen, and even if they are caused by specific (but hard to identify) stimuli, these stimuli are inconsequential to the study of behavior. The word ''operant'' describes an entire set of specific instances of behaviors which *operate* upon the environment to generate events or responses within the environment. If these events or responses are satisfying, the probability that the operant behavior will be repeated is usually increased.

Both respondent and operant behaviors can be taught and learned. Teaching and learning a respondent behavior requires the presentation of a stimulus which will cause the desired behavior to occur; whereas an operant behavior is learned through an appropriate reinforcement (either a positive or a negative reinforcement) which is administered immediately or shortly after the spontaneous occurrence of the operant behavior. The administration of a reinforcement to a person following the occurrence of a desirable behavior usually increases the probability that he or she will repeat the behavior. If the reinforcement is a punishment, it is hoped that the individual will learn to refrain from the undesirable behavior which evoked the punishment.

For each type of behavior, respondent behavior and operant behavior, Skinner has identified a type of conditioning, a generalized teaching/learning strategy, which will facilitate learning the desired behavior. Classical *respondent conditioning* for *respondent learning* (which is similar to what Gagné calls signal learning) results when a new stimulus is presented simultaneously with an older stimulus which elicits the expected response. After a variable number of pairings, the new stimulus will elicit the response without being paired with the old stimulus. The classical example of respondent conditioning is provided in the work of the Russian physiologist Ivan Pavlov. Pavlov conditioned dogs in his laboratory to salivate at the sound of a tone by first sounding the tone simultaneously with the presentation of food to the dogs. After a number of paired presentations of food and tone sounding, the dogs salivated upon hearing the tone, even though they were not given food when the tone was sounded.

Operant conditioning, as specified by Skinner, can be used to promote operant learning. *Operant conditioning* for *operant learning* is controlled by following a behavior with a stimulus. This stimulus, which is presented after the response, is usually called a *reinforcement*. It can be either a positive or negative reinforcement, since both positive and negative reinforcements can be used to increase the likelihood that a behavior will be repeated. As an example of operant conditioning and operant learning, consider a hypothetical student sitting in the rear of the classroom who usually is shy, quiet, and unresponsive in class. The following alternative dialogs might occur between this student and his teacher:

(1) Teacher: "Jim, what does a^4 mean?"
    Jim: (no response)
    Teacher: "Well students, Jim must have forgotten how to talk." (Loud, laughter from the class, and Jim turns red with embarrassment.)

or

(2) Teacher: "Jim, what does a^4 mean?"
    Jim: "It means take four factors of a, which is a times a times a times a."
    Teacher: "That's quite good Jim, it's obvious that you have read the assignment and understand the meaning of exponents. Thank you." (Several students turn and give Jim looks of approval.)

Now, what type of *operant learning* might take place in Jim as a consequence of a series of events, over a two month period between Jim and his teacher, where most of the events are like (1)? Where most are like (2)? Obviously, the situation in case (1) is likely to result in a negative outcome for Jim. In this situation which of Jim's behaviors was made more likely to occur? The teacher probably hoped that Jim was more likely to respond to questions. However, Jim's embarrassment, together with his shyness, probably caused him to dislike mathematics class even more and made it *less* likely that he would respond to future questions from the teacher. So the teacher's negative response had an undesirable effect upon Jim and further conditioned Jim to exhibit the "undesirable behavior" of not responding to questions. A series of events such as those stated in case (2), where the teacher and the class presented Jim with a positive stimulus following his behavior, would be likely to improve Jim's attitude toward mathematics class, reduce his shyness, and cause him to volunteer answers in class—all of which are "desirable" behaviors.

Each of these situations is an example of operant conditioning resulting in operant learning. In the first case the operant learning was undesirable, and in the second case it was desirable. Note that in both of these operant learning situations the stimulus (the teacher's and students' reactions to Jim's response or lack of response) came after Jim's behavior (Jim's action in response to the teacher's question).

Let us reiterate the distinction between respondent conditioning and operant conditioning. Respondent conditioning results in the learner being conditioned to exhibit a particular behavior in response to a specific stimulus. In respondent conditioning a new stimulus is presented together with an old stimulus which causes a reflexive reaction. After a series of simultaneous presentations of the two stimuli, the learner gives the same reaction to the new stimulus (in the absence of the old stimulus) which he or she previously gave in response to the old stimulus by itself. In respondent learning, the learner *responds* to environmental stimuli.

In operant conditioning, the learner's unpredictable response (action) is followed by a stimulus. It is hoped that the stimulus will either help to suppress the response if it is undesirable or will increase the future likelihood of the response if it is desirable. Respondent learning is stimulus-response learning; whereas operant learning is response-stimulus learning. In respondent learning the learner responds to environmental stimuli; whereas in operant learning the learner *operates* on his or her environment and has these operations reinforced through appropriate stimuli or changes in the environment as a consequence of his or her actions.

Promoting Learning and Changing Behavior

Reinforcement

Reinforcers, which are happenings or stimuli that follow a response and which tend to increase the probability of that response, can facilitate learning and changes in behavior. In a school learning environment with classrooms and teachers, we find that grades, teacher and peer approval, punishment, and various means of recognizing and rewarding certain behaviors function as reinforcers. The many different environmental stimuli which act as reinforcers fall into two general categories, positive reinforcers and negative reinforcers.

Skinner defines *positive reinforcers* as stimuli which, when presented following a behavior by the learner, tend to increase the probability that that particular behavior will be repeated; that is, the behavior is strengthened. When our hypothetical student Jim answered correctly in class, the teacher's praise increased the likelihood that Jim would again respond to the teacher's questions; consequently the teacher's pleasant reaction functioned as a positive reinforcer for Jim. The teacher's unpleasant remark following Jim's failure to respond to the teacher's question also acted as a positive reinforcer, because it reinforced Jim's behavior which was to remain silent when questioned by the teacher. Any stimulus, pleasant or unpleasant, which follows the behavior that elicited it, and strengthens that behavior, is considered to be a positive reinforcer by Skinner.

Negative reinforcers are stimuli whose removal tends to strengthen behaviors. Many times the student behavior of attentiveness to appropriate classroom activities can be increased by removing distracting stimuli such as undesirable noise, a disruptive student, or distracting teacher mannerisms.

Forgetting and Extinction

If a learned behavior is not used for a long period of time it will be forgotten and will have to be relearned. In *forgetting,* the effect of operant conditioning is simply lost with the passage of time. Many students forget many of their algebraic skills if they do not practice them between their freshman year in high school and graduation from school. Even though most secondary school teachers learn calculus in college, we may forget many of the details and skills of this subject if we work in a school where we are not assigned to teach a calculus course for several years.

Skinner considers extinction to be a process of "unlearning" conditioned responses, this is distinct from forgetting. Many times students initially learn incorrect responses and behaviors and need to "unlearn" them later in school, while other conditioned responses are naturally "unlearned" as a consequence of the withdrawal of expected reinforcements. Skinner defines *extinction* as the process through which conditioned responses become less and less frequent when reinforcements are no longer forthcoming. Fortunately for learning desirable conditioned responses and behaviors (but unfortunately for "unlearning" undesirable behaviors), research studies have shown that operant extinction takes place much more slowly than operant conditioning. Several reinforcements may suffice in learning a response; however hundreds of unreinforced instances of the response may be necessary in order to "unlearn" the response; that is, to refrain from exhibiting the behavior.

Extinction of desirable student behaviors such as reviewing for quizzes and completing homework assignments may occur if quiz grades are not averaged into period grade reports and assignments are not graded by the teacher and returned to the students shortly after they have been handed to the teacher. In some secondary schools and colleges where letter grading systems have been replaced with Satisfactory/Unsatisfactory student evaluations, students, who had been conditioned to expect letter grades as reinforcements, became frustrated and lacked motivation as a consequence of being denied their previously expected letter grade reinforcements.

Extinction of undesirable behaviors, such as using incorrect mathematics techniques or indulging in cigarette smoking, which have been repeated many times with occasional reinforcement, is very difficult to accomplish. I once tutored a young man who was having trouble in higher level mathematics courses because he had learned a number of incorrect algebra techniques such as $(a + b)^2 = a^2 + b^2$. Even after being corrected many times, he continued to make this same error when carrying out more complex problem-solving algorithms. Each time I merely pointed to this error on his paper. He would slap himself on his head and make a comment similar to: "I know that $(a + b)^2 = a^2 + 2ab + b^2$, but why do I keep making this same mistake?" The answer to his question, although quite simple, was not very satisfying to him. That is, it is sometimes very difficult to "unlearn" something which has been learned incorrectly the first time and has been reinforced through repeated use. One of the hazards of assigning sets of similar drill and practice homework problems to reinforce a particular skill is that an inadvertent incorrect procedure may be reinforced through repeated repetition until it becomes very difficult to extinguish. It should be noted that the young man who finally learned the correct product for $(a + b)^2$, as well as the person who *extinguished* his or her cigarette smoking behavior, did not forget the undesirable behavior. Both people became conditioned to refrain from the undesirable behavior or to replace it with a more desirable behavior.

Aversion and Avoidance

A negative reinforcer is a stimulus whose withdrawal results in the strengthening of a response. An unpleasant, annoying, or frustrating negative reinforcer is called an *aversive stimulus* by Skinner. There are two ways to deal with aversive stimuli. One can *escape* an aversive stimulus either by removing the stimulus after he or she has come in contact with it, or by leaving the environment where the aversive stimulus exists. An aversive stimulus can be *avoided* by anticipating its occurrence and staying away from it. Note that avoidance is accomplished by never contacting the aversive stimulus and that escape is accomplished by removing the aversive stimulus after coming in contact with it. Many people *avoid* an upset stomach by refraining from over-eating spicy fried foods, while others go ahead and eat improperly and *escape* the resulting indigestion by taking an antacid preparation.

If a person is always successful in avoiding an aversive situation, the situation may lose its aversion for that person. Eventually the person may fail to emit the avoidance response to stimuli preceding the aversive stimulus and the aversive situation is not avoided. A person may avoid eating oysters due to a previously diagnosed allergic reaction to oysters long enough to be tempted into eating some more oysters. The resulting illness will reestablish the aversive response to oysters, and that person will then avoid oysters for some time until his or her aversion to oysters has weakened once more.

Many examples of aversion, escape, and avoidance are found in students in mathematics classes. For example, after unsuccessfully trying to solve the problems on a test, a student may attempt to *escape* failure by copying answers from the paper of a student seated nearby. Some students *avoid* failing tests by staying away from school on test days. Of course from the teacher's point of view, the desired method for avoiding failure may be to complete all the homework assignments and to prepare for tests through concentrated review sessions. Many so-called discipline problems are in fact students' attempts to escape from the boredom and failures which they associate with mathematics classes. Some not-so-subtle attempts to escape aversive classroom stimuli are student actions which disrupt the teacher's planned activities. More subtle escape attempts are questions from students which are asked in order to "get the teacher off the subject."

Punishment

Throughout history punishment has been a common technique for attempting to control behavior, and Skinner (1953) discusses the effects and by-products of punishment in his book *Science and Human Behavior*. His general viewpoint regarding the use of punishment to control behavior is summarized in the following quotation from this book:

> ...concern [about punishment] may be due to the realization that the technique has unfortunate by-products. In the long run, punishment, unlike reinforcement, works to the disadvantage of both the punished organism and

the punishing agency. The aversive stimuli which are needed generate emotions, including predispositions to escape or retaliate, and disabling anxieties. (pp. 182-83)

Skinner regards *punishment* as the deliberate presentation of a negative reinforcer (a negative reinforcer is a stimulus whose removal will strengthen a behavior) or the deliberate removal of a positive reinforcer (a positive reinforcer is a stimulus whose presentation will strengthen a behavior). Skinner and others have shown in laboratory experiments with both animals and humans that punishment does not have the opposite effect of reward. An equal number of punishments will not extinguish the effects of a given number of rewards. While punishment, and even prolonged punishment, can be effective in suppressing "unwanted" behaviors, this supression is usually only temporary. After a time the punished behaviors tend to reappear at a level not much lower than if no punishment had been administered. Even if punishment were effective in supressing or removing undesirable behaviors, it can generate unpredictable social and emotional consequences.

Skinner (1953) has identified three effects of punishment upon the person being punished. First, punishment suppresses behavior. Since a person's response to punishment is usually incompatible with the behavior being punished, the behavior is changed, at least temporarily. A student who is reprimanded by his or her teacher for arguing in class with another student may stop talking or may direct the argument toward the teacher.

The second effect of punishment is to evoke incompatible behavior resulting in anxiety and accompanying physiological changes such as increased heart rate, higher blood pressure, and muscle tension. People who know when they are lying and who have been punished for lying, will exhibit such physiological changes when lying, even in the absence of punishment. This suggests the principles which were used in developing lie-detecting devices.

The third and most important effect of punishment is to condition the punished person to do something other than the act for which he or she is being punished. Whatever this alternative behavior may be, it will be reinforced and it may be as undesirable in its long-range effects as the behavior being suppressed. At times students who are severely punished in school will develop an aversion to schools and structured learning in general. They may even perpetrate acts of vandalism against the school or the teacher's property. In extreme cases a student who has been punished by a teacher may even physically assault that teacher.

There is little evidence to suggest that the consequences of severe or repeated punishment are desirable or are even predictable. Even relatively mild punishment such as assigning extra homework or making students stay after school may not necessarily suppress the behavior which is being punished. It may even reinforce an aversion for mathematics and for school in general. Mild punishment may be temporarily effective is suppressing certain responses; however most types of punishment appear to be relatively ineffective in promoting permanent modification of behavior. Furthermore, severe or frequent punishment may produce emotional side effects which may prove to be even less desirable than the original behavior.

General Conditions of Learning

In Skinner's view, three variables make up the contingencies under which learning takes place. First there must be a *situation* in which a behavior occurs. The second contingency is the *behavior* itself, and the third contingency is the *consequence* of the behavior. If in a certain situation a person exhibits a particular behavior or response from a class of responses called an operant, and if he or she is reinforced as a consequence of the response, then it is likely that learning will take place. That is, it becomes more probable that a similar response from the same class of responses will be given by that person in a similar situation. Even though the situation did not initially act as a stimulus for the response, the learner, after receiving reinforcement for the response, will tend to associate the behavior which evoked the reinforcement with the initial situation. Operants (classes of responses) do acquire relationships to previous sets of stimuli (called *discriminated stimuli*); but the relationships between stimuli and responses are different from those found in classical stimulus-response conditioning. The prior situation (set of stimuli), when encountered again, becomes the occasion for the operant behavior, but does not cause the behavior as is the case in respondent learning. An unexpected finger in the ribs (stimulus) will usually cause most people to jump (response). A word of praise or extra credit toward a final grade for solving mathematics problems which were not assigned by the teacher may cause a student to continue to do extra work in mathematics. In the future, the more difficult textbook problems (which may not usually be assigned for homework by the teacher) act as discriminated stimuli for the student and become the occasion for his or her response of doing extra work.

The Art of Teaching

Skinner's research on the science of learning and the art of teaching suggests several reasons why many students leave elementary school without having learned simple arithmetic skills, and why they fail to learn these skills after repeated attempts in secondary school. First, some "reinforcements" for learning mathematics skills are still aversive. That is, many students still learn (or attempt to learn) arithmetic to escape punishment or the threat of punishment. Instead of studying and learning arithmetic in order to obtain positive reinforcements, many students do their schoolwork to avoid negative consequences: the teacher's displeasure, ridicule from classmates, poor grades resulting in punishment from parents, or poor results in competition with other students. Second, even when appropriate positive reinforcements are used in attempts to promote learning in arithmetic, the reinforcements are usually not optimized. In schools, reinforcement from teachers for students' correct written solutions to problems may occur infrequently in large classes. Or, when it does occur, may be given several minutes following a student's response. Skinner has found that in learning certain types of skills, such as basic arithmetic, some students require immediate reinforcement of their responses. Even a time lapse of a minute or two between a response and a reinforcement can, at times, remove much of the positive effects of an immediate reinforcement. Since homework assignments and tests are marked by the teacher and returned a day or more after students complete them, much of the learning value of these activities can be lost for many students. A third reason why so many students fail to learn in schools, even where immediate reinforcement is given to them, is that the frequency of reinforcement is inadequate. Skinner (1968, p. 17) in his book *The Technology of Teaching* estimates that a student throughout his or her first four years of school requires something on the order of 25,000 reinforcements and may be given only a few thousand.

Skinner's proposed solution for overcoming the impossiblity of teachers' being able to provide immediate reinforcement to every student on a regular basis, is to use programmed instructional materials and teaching machines to assist the teacher in reinforcing students. Printed programmed instructional modules and textbooks are usually structured so that information is presented in very small pieces. After each piece of information is given, the reader is asked a question, after which he or she immediately compares his or her answer to the correct answer which is printed following the question. The student may slide a card down the page in order to hide new information and answers to questions until each piece of information is read, and a corresponding question about that particular bit of information is answered. The principles which are used in preparing programmed materials are that information should be presented in small pieces and that the learner should show that he or she has learned each piece of information by answering a question, followed by immediate feedback concerning the student's answer. Some programmed materials are linear; that is, regardless of the student's response, he or she continues on. Other materials contain branches so that each student's next step in the program is determined by his or her response to a question, or responses to a sequence of questions. There are a number of programmed instructional materials for mathematics on the market. Samples can be obtained for previewing by contacting various publishing companies. The following passage is an example of a small part of a programmed instructional sequence in mathematics:

> Frame 59. A prime number is a number whose only divisors are one and the number itself. For example 7 is a prime number because only one and seven divide 7 without a remainder.
>
> Question 1. Is 29 a prime number? _____
> > You should have said *yes*. 29 is a prime number because its only divisors are one and twenty-nine.
>
> Question 2. What are the only divisors of a prime number?
>
> _____
>
> > You should have answered that the only divisors of a prime number are *one and the number itself.*
>
> If you answered both Question 1 and Question 2 correctly go on to Frame 60. If either of your answers was incorrect go back to Frame 59.

In the past Skinner and others developed and used ingenious mechanical teaching machines which presented printed sequences of instructional materials to students and which branched to new or previous material according to the responses which students selected to questions. Although these teaching machines did provide a medium for testing and evaluating Skinner's theories of instruction, they have become historical relics. Students now can interact with a computer-based instructional program at a remote teaching terminal and can obtain a variety of instructional "frames" based upon a computer analysis of their responses to computer generated questions and problems. The flexibility of PLATO computer terminals, which were developed at the University of Illinois as part of a very complex and sophisticated computer-based instructional system, is so great that students can select and use both audio and video programs at the computer terminal. They can "talk" to the computer by either typing commands or responses at the remote terminal or touching objects displayed on a television-like screen. They can also communicate with human teachers and other students via the computer network when they have a problem that the computer is not programmed to deal with. Rather than serving as a replacement for teachers, complex educational computing systems can free teachers to give more attention to the learning problems of individual students: problems which are complex enough to require the assistance of a human being who can be much more flexible, perceptive, and sympathetic than a computer.

In conclusion, much of Skinner's research on the science of learning and the art of teaching is useful to mathematics teachers. His principles of teaching and learning are particularly helpful in developing strategies for teaching facts and basic arithmetic skills to both elementary and secondary school students. Some of Gagné's work in structuring hierarchies of mathematical facts, skills, concepts, and principles to aid students in learning mathematics has its theoretical foundation in the theories of Burrhus Frederic Skinner. Even though individual chapters of Skinner's book, *The Technology of Teaching,* were written between 1954 and 1968, his analysis of teaching is still relevant—even for teaching "modern mathematics" in modern secondary schools.

Summary

The seven theories which are presented and discussed in this chapter are attempts by their developers to structure and explain the very complex processes of instruction and learning. No single theory provides a complete model of either teaching or learning, and there are areas of disagreement among the several theories. In spite of the limitations of these theories, each has applications for teaching and learning secondary school mathematics.

Piaget and Skinner have formulated two very different models of human learning. Piaget has developed a theory of intellectual maturation and development, whereas Skinner has studied the conditions under which human behaviors take place. Although they are different approaches to the study of learning and behavior, these two theories do complement each other; each has many applications in teaching mathematics.

Guilford has determined what he believes to be the 120 mental abilities which comprise general intelligence, and his findings can be of considerable use to teachers in identifying and dealing with specific learning problems in individual students.

Bruner's theory of instruction is useful to teachers in helping them formulate general approaches to teaching, and much of his work has been shown to be directly applicable to teaching mathematics.

Based, in part, upon Piaget's theory of intellectual development, Dienes has developed a theory of teaching mathematics which contains a sequence of strategies for teaching mathematics concepts. He has also described how specific topics from secondary school mathematics can be approached by using his six stages in concept development as a general model for teaching and learning mathematics.

Gagné and Ausubel, while concerned with refining theories of learning and instruction, have developed techniques and strategies for classroom teaching. Both of these men have formulated models for structuring the content of a discipline such as mathematics. Gagné has taken a bottom-to-top approach to structuring content into learning hierarchies which build upon simpler, prerequisite facts, skills, and concepts to learn more complex skills, concepts and principles. Ausubel has developed a theory of meaningful verbal learning which can be used by teachers when presenting material in a lecture or expository mode to students. Since a large proportion of mathematics teaching is carried out in a lecture mode, Ausubel's procedures for structuring information so that it can be learned in an efficient and meaningful way can be very useful to secondary school mathematics teachers.

The various theories of teaching and learning can be used as a basis for designing and presenting mathematics lessons and also provide a rich background of information which teachers can use in developing and improving the effectiveness of their classroom strategies for teaching mathematics to students in secondary schools.

Things To Do

1. List and define the stages of intellectual development identified by Piaget and discuss the mathematical abilities which people can be expected to attain in each stage. What differences in learning abilities exist between junior high school and senior high school students? Discuss teaching strategies which would be appropriate to use with junior high school students; with senior high school students.

2. Define these terms which are used in Piaget's theory of intellectual development: *assimilation, accommodation, maturation, physical experiences, logico-mathematical experiences, social transmission, and equilibration.* Discuss each term according to its application to learning mathematics.

3. J. P. Guilford has identified five *operations of learning,* four *contents of learning,* and six *products of learning.* Define and give an example from secondary school mathematics of each of these fifteen characteristics of intelligence.

4. From the set of *operations, contents,* and *products* of learning identified in Guilford's Structure of Intellect Model, select ten specific intellectual aptitudes (ten ordered triples, each consisting of an *operation,* a *content,* and a *product*) which you think are important aptitudes for learning mathematics. Then, give examples of ten learning tasks in mathematics, each of which requires one of the ten intellectual aptitudes which you selected.

5. How can a mathematics teacher who is not a trained psychologist apply Guilford's Structure of Intellect Model in his or her own teaching?

6. The four direct objects of mathematics learning are facts, skills, concepts, and principles. Define and give several examples of each object. Choose and discuss four different teaching strategies, each one of which would be appropriate for teaching one of the four direct objects of mathematics.

7. Define each of the eight types of learning which Robert Gagné has identified, and give an example from mathematics education of each learning type. Suggest some teaching strategies which would be appropriate for promoting each one of the eight learning types.

8. Select a mathematical skill (for example, solving two equations in two unknowns) and write a list of steps required in applying the skill. Then, develop a learning hierarchy (see Figure 3.2 for an example of a learning hierarchy) for teaching and learning that skill.

9. Zoltan Dienes has categorized three types of mathematics concepts—pure concepts, notational concepts, and applied concepts. Define and give several examples of each type of concept, and suggest teaching/learning activities which would be appropriate for each type.

10. Analyze and illustrate Dienes' six stages in teaching and learning mathematics by selecting a secondary school mathematics topic and preparing a six-stage teaching/learning strategy which illustrates the applications of the six stages to classroom teaching.

11. Explain the relationship between Dienes' six stages in concept learning and his four general principles and five subprinciples for teaching concepts.

12. Discuss Ausubel's two preconditions for meaningful reception learning and explain how they can be applied to meaningful teaching and learning.

13. Select a topic from secondary school mathematics and, based upon Ausubel's strategies for meaningful verbal learning, design a teaching/learning plan for presenting that topic to students.

14. Choose a secondary school mathematics topic and develop an *advance organizer* for use in introducing the topic.

15. List and describe Bruner's six characteristics of intellectual growth, and discuss the implications of each characteristic for teaching secondary school mathematics.

16. According to Bruner, a theory of instruction should be both *prescriptive* and *normative*. Explain what he means by these two terms and why it *is* necessary for instructional theories to be both *prescriptive* and *normative*. Discuss the four major features which prescribe the nature of the instructional process, and which Bruner believes should be contained in any theory of instruction.

17. Explain the distinction between a learning theory and a theory of instruction. Why is it necessary for teachers to be familiar with learning theories and instructional theories? What is the relationship between learning

theories and instructional theories when they are applied to classroom teaching and learning of mathematics?

18. State the four general ''theorems'' about learning mathematics which were developed by Bruner and Kenneys and explain how these theorems can be used in teaching and learning mathematics.

19. Skinner uses the terms *respondent conditioning* and *operant conditioning* in his theory of learning. Define each of these terms and give an example of each type of conditioning in mathematics education.

20. Explain the difference between *positive* and *negative reinforcers* and give several examples of each type of reinforcement.

21. Discuss the difference between *forgetting* and *extinction*. Explain how extinction occurs. Give several examples of the operations of forgetting and extinction of previously learned mathematics facts, skills, concepts, or principles.

22. Discuss the relative advantages and disadvantages of *rewards* and *punishment* in a mathematics classroom. What do you consider to be appropriate methods of rewarding and punishing students?

23. Discuss the difference between Gagné's and Dienes' definitions of *concept* and the difference between their approaches to learning.

24. Show how Dienes' theories of teaching and learning mathematics are related to Piaget's theory of intellectual development.

25. Analyze and discuss the similarities and differenes between Gagné's and Skinner's theories of learning.

26. Select two or three of the theories presented in this chapter and research them in more detail. The **Selected Bibliography** for this chapter provides a good starting point for locating additional references for this activity.

27. Synthesize a composite theory of learning and instruction based upon the theories of teaching and learning which are presented in this chapter.

Selected Bibliography

Aichele, Douglas B. and Reys, Robert E. (Editors). *Readings in Secondary School Mathematics*. Boston, Mass.: Prindle, Weber & Schmidt, Inc., 1971.

This book of readings in mathematics education contains eight articles on contemporary theories about how people learn mathematics. Among the authors of these articles are Robert Gagné, Jerome Bruner, David Ausubel, and Zoltan Dienes.

Ausubel, David P. ''In Defense of Verbal Learning.'' *Educational Theory* XI (1961): 15-25.

———. *The Psychology of Meaningful Verbal Learning*. New York: Grune & Stratton, 1963.

A comprehensive exposition of Ausubel's theory of meaningful verbal learning through expository teaching, this book is useful to the person who wants to carry out an in-depth study of the work of Professor Ausubel.

————. *Educational Psychology, A Cognitive View.* New York: Holt, Rinehart and Winston, Inc., 1968.

A general work on the psychology of learning, this book is a presentation of learning psychology based upon Ausubel's theories of learning. Among the topics which Ausubel discusses are meaningful reception learning, retention, transfer of learning, practice, individual differences, motivation, personality, social factors in learning, discovery learning, concept acquisition, problem solving, and creativity.

————. "Facilitating Meaningful Verbal Learning in the Classroom." *The Arithmetic Teacher* 15 (1968): 126-32.

This article is recommended reading for the mathematics teacher who is concerned with improving his or her expository teaching.

Beard, Ruth M. *An Outline of Piaget's Developmental Psychology.* London: Routledge & Kegan Paul, 1969.

This book is a very readable discussion of the Piagetian stages of cognitive development with some implications for classroom teaching.

Bell, Frederick H. "Let's Make a Computer." *Model for Teaching,* a component of the Croft Teacher's Service, New London, Conn., February, 1973.

Brearley, Molly, and Hitchfield, Elizabeth. *A Guide to Reading Piaget.* New York: Shocken Books, 1972.

An interpretation of Piaget's research, this book is a good starting point for the novice to Piaget's developmental psychology. Several Piagetian experiments relating to each developmental stage are presented and discussed.

Bruner, Jerome S. "On Learning Mathematics." *The Mathematics Teacher* LIII (1960): 610-619.

In this article Bruner presents his thoughts about discovery learning, intuition, and readiness for learning.

————. "Observations on the Learning of Mathematics." *Science Education News* April, 1963: 1-5.

In this article Bruner states, discusses, and illustrates his four theorems about learning mathematics.

————. *The Process of Education.* Cambridge, Mass.: Harvard University Press, 1966.

This book is Bruner's synthesis of the themes which were debated by 34 educators and scientists from the fields of mathematics, science, history, education, psychology and medicine at a conference in Woods Hole, Massachusetts. The purpose of the conference was to discuss the basic processes involved in teaching the content and methods of science to school students. The major themes which were considered at the Woods Hole conference and which are presented in this book are (1) the importance of studying the structure of each subject, (2) student readiness for learning, (3) intuitive and analytic thinking, (4) motivation to learn, and (5) aids to teaching.

————. *Toward a Theory of Instruction.* Cambridge, Mass.: The Belknap Press of Harvard University Press, 1966.

This book which contains some of Bruner's views of teaching and learning has a chapter "Notes on a Theory of Instruction" which is of particular interest and use to mathematics teachers.

161

————. *On Knowing: Essays for the Left Hand*. New York: Atheneum, 1971.

A collection of Bruner's previous writings, this book contains Bruner's general thoughts on education and his paper "On Learning Mathematics" which summarizes some of his views that are related to mathematics education.

————. "The Process of Education Revisited." *Phi Delta Kappan* 53 (September, 1971): 18-21.

In this article Bruner reflects upon the views of education held in 1960 and finds his own earlier book, *The Process of Education,* lacking in relevance for education in the nineteen seventies. Any student of Bruner's works should read this article.

Dienes, Z. P. *Building up Mathematics* (Fourth Edition). London: Hutchinson Educational Ltd., 1971.

In this book Dienes presents his theory of mathematics learning and discusses specific techniques for teaching several arithmetic concepts, algebraic concepts, topics in linear algebra, and other topics in geometry.

Gagné, Robert M. *The Conditions of Learning* (Second Edition). New York: Holt, Rinehart and Winston, Inc., 1970.

A comprehensive presentation of his theories about the conditions under which learning occurs, in this book Gagné defines and gives examples of his eight types of learning. He also describes learning hierarchies, discusses procedures of instruction, and considers appropriate uses for various learning resources.

Guilford, J. P. *The Nature of Human Intelligence*. New York: McGraw-Hill Book Company, 1967.

This book is indispensable to the person who is undertaking an extensive study of Guilford's conceptual model of the structure of human intelligence.

Higgins, John L. *Mathematics Teaching and Learning*. Worthington, Ohio: Charles A. Jones Publishing Company, 1973.

In this book Higgins presents a discussion of several general theories of learning as they apply to teaching and learning mathematics. He organizes his material into five units—(1) intelligence and the structure of mathematical abilities, (2) Piaget's analysis of intelligence, (3) stimulus-response learning in mathematics, (4) Gestalt learning and heuristic teaching and (5) concept learning and cognitive structure.

Hilgard, Ernest R. (Editor) *Theories of Learning and Instruction* (Sixty-third Yearbook). Chicago: National Society for the Study of Education, 1964.

This yearbook contains articles on learning theories, psychology, motivation, learning readiness, theories of teaching and educational practice. It also has an article on stimulus-response learning and an article titled "Some Theorems on Instruction Illustrated with Reference to Mathematics" by Jerome Bruner.

Isaacs, Nathan. *Piaget: Some Answers to Teachers' Questions*. London: National Froebel Foundation, 1965.

In this pamphlet, Isaacs answers nine questions about Piaget's theory and its applications in teaching arithmetic.

Joyce, Bruce and Weil, Marsha. *Models of Teaching*. Englewood Cliffs, New Jersey: Prentice-Hall, Inc., 1972.

The authors discuss approximately fifteen general models of teaching, many of which are applicable to teaching mathematics. Each teaching/learning model is presented according to its nature and structure and its classroom applications. Chapter 10 is an excellent introduction to David Ausubel's advance organizer approach to meaningful expository teaching.

Klausmeier, Herbert J. and Harris, Chester W. (Editors). *Analyses of Concept Learning.* New York: Academic Press, 1966.

A general reference on concept learning, the book contains sections on schemes for classifying concepts, learning of concepts, teaching and learning processes, and teaching mathematics concepts. Included among the sixteen chapters are articles written by Gagné, Ausubel, and Howard Fehr.

Lamon, William E. (Editor). *Learning and the Nature of Mathematics.* Palo Alto, California: Science Research Associates, Inc., 1972.

This book is a collection of articles written by mathematics educators, learning theorists, and psychologists. Among the contributors to this work are Dienes, Piaget, and Gagné. A brief biography of each writer is included as an introduction to his article.

Martorella, Peter H. *Concept Learning: Designs for Instruction.* Scranton, Pennsylvania: Intext Educational Publishers, 1972.

A general work on concept learning, this book contains a chapter titled "Concept Learning in the Mathematics Curriculum, K-12: Issues and Approaches." Piaget's, Bruner's, Dienes', Gagné's, and Ausubel's contributions to mathematics education are presented in this chapter, and several important mathematics curriculum projects, such as the School Mathematics Study Group and the University of Illinois Committee on School Mathematics, are discussed.

Meeker, Mary Nacol. *The Structure of Intellect, Its Interpretation and Uses.* Columbus, Ohio: Charles E. Merrill Publishing Company, 1969.

Dr. Meeker's book describes and interprets J. P. Guilford's Structure of Intellect Model and explains how it can be applied in curriculum planning and classroom teaching. She also presents examples of most of the 120 factors in the structure of intellect cube and references tests and test items which can be used to assess students' capabilities on individual intellectual factors.

Milhollan, Frank and Forisha, Bill E. *From Skinner to Rogers: Contrasting Approaches to Education.* Lincoln, Nebraska: Professional Educators Publications, Inc., 1972.

This book contains an overview of B. F. Skinner's analysis of the process of learning and his scientific analysis of behavior. Skinner's theory of learning is contrasted to Carl R. Roger's humanistic approach to human psychology and learning.

National Assessment of Educational Progress. *NAEP Newsletter.* VII (August, 1975): 1, 3.

This pamphlet contains a summary of the findings of the NAEP study of consumer mathematics skills of 17-year-olds and young adults between ages 26-35.

Piaget, Jean. *Science of Education and the Psychology of the Child* (Translated from the French by Derek Coltman). New York: Orion Press, 1970.

This is a general child psychology book which deals with developments in

163

learning theory, adolescent psychology, teaching methods, teacher education and developmental psychology.

Raths, James, Pancella, John R., and Van Ness, James S. (Editors) *Studying Teaching* (Second Edition). Englewood Cliffs, New Jersey: Prentice-Hall, Inc., 1971.

> *Studying Teaching* is a collection of articles about teaching and learning which is organized into sections on teaching methods, interactions in classrooms, planning in education, testing, discipline, motivation, and other topics. The book contains articles by Bruner, Bloom, Gagné, Piaget, and Ausubel.

Rosskopf, Myron F., Steffe, Leslie P., and Taback, Stanley (Editors) *Piagetian Cognitive-Development Research and Mathematical Education.* Washington, D.C.: National Council of Teachers of Mathematics, 1971.

> This book is a collection of papers which were presented at Teachers College, Columbia University as part of a conference on Piaget sponsored by the National Council of Teachers of Mathematics and the Department of Mathematical Education of Teachers College. Many of the papers illustrate implications of Piaget's theory for teaching topics in secondary school mathematics such as mathematical proof, functions, proportionality, and probability. The book also contains lists of references related to Piaget's work and its applications to mathematics education. This book is recommended reading for all secondary school mathematics teachers.

Skinner, B. F. *Science and Human Behavior.* New York: The Macmillan Company, 1953.

> Skinner, in this book which is representative of his early work in human behavior, presents his analysis of the behavior of individuals and people in groups, and discusses problems in controlling human behavior.

———. *The Technology of Teaching.* Englewood Cliffs, New Jersey: Prentice-Hall, Inc., 1968.

> In this widely acclaimed book, Skinner presents his views on learning as a science and teaching as an art. He also discusses reasons for teacher failure and methods for motivating students. In this book, Skinner shows how his theories of teaching and learning can be applied in the classroom.

Weisgerber, Robert A. (Editor) *Perspectives in Individualized Learning.* Itasca, Illinois: F. E. Peacock Publishers, Inc., 1971.

> Here is a general reference book which describes how learning theories and teaching strategies can be used to promote individualized learning in students. This book contains chapters written by J. P. Guilford and Robert Gagné, and also has a chapter on Benjamin Bloom's cognitive and affective taxonomies.

Preparing to Teach Mathematics Lessons

In order to become an efficient and effective teacher, it is necessary to understand the relationships among the mathematics content that is taught, cognitive and affective learning objectives, and various teaching/learning strategies for presenting mathematics lessons. Unless both the teacher and each student know what the objectives of the lesson are and what type of student performance is required to demonstrate that the lesson has been mastered, teaching and learning may be inefficient and ineffective. Certain teaching methods may be quite effective for promoting learning of some mathematics topics, but may be very ineffective for other topics. Expository techniques where students memorize facts, symbols, and skills using drill, practice, and games can be a useful strategy for teaching facts and skills, but may not result in meaningful learning of complex concepts and principles.

This chapter, and chapters 5, 6, and 7, are concerned with the many variables which interact in a classroom teaching/learning situation, and these four chapters contain procedures for improving the teaching and learning of mathematics in secondary school classrooms. The topics presented in this chapter deal with activities which are necessary for planning lessons and preparing teaching strategies. Chapters 5 and 6 concentrate upon a number of teaching/learning strategies, called models, which can be used quite effectively to promote learning in different situations. Chapter 7 deals with techniques for developing and organizing resources for effective teaching and learning, and is also concerned with methods for evaluating both student learning and the effectiveness of different teaching methods.

In Chapter 3, the topics found in secondary school mathematics textbooks were classified into four categories—facts, skills, concepts, and principles—called the direct objects of mathematics. Each mathematical object can be assigned to one of these four categories. *Facts* are the arbitrary symbols and conventions of mathematics. For example, a^n means n factors of a, 2 is a symbol for the idea of two, and, in the absence of symbols of grouping, we agree to carry out multiplications and divisions before doing additions and subtractions. *Skills* are procedures or sets of rules which students learn and use in computing answers to mathematics problems. Mathematical *concepts* are abstract ideas which are used to classify events and objects and to determine whether events and objects are examples or nonexamples of various ideas. The idea of a mathematical function is a concept, because sets of mathematical relations can be separated into examples and nonexamples of functions. *Principles* are structured sequences of concepts together with relationships among the concepts. Since nearly all theorems in mathematics describe relationships among concepts, mathematical theorems are examples of principles.

Selecting and Classifying Educational Objectives

As mathematics teachers, our general objective is to help students learn important and useful facts, skills, concepts and principles. However, in teaching each topic in mathematics, we should formulate more specific objectives to describe the expected outcomes of student learning. There are three types of educational objectives—cognitive objectives, affective objectives, and motor-skill or manipulative objectives. *Cognitive objectives* specify behaviors that indicate the functioning of and changes in various mental processes. *Affective objectives* specify behaviors that indicate changes in attitudes. *Motor-skill objectives* specify behaviors which show that students have learned certain physical manipulative skills.

Two learning psychologists, Benjamin S. Bloom (1956) and David R. Krathwohl (1964), with the help of many other psychologists and educators developed two classification systems, called taxonomies, of educational objectives. These two taxonomies, which are logically-developed and internally-consistent hierarchical classification systems for the objectives of education, specify the cognitive and affective behaviors that students are expected to exhibit as a consequence of our educational system. Since little is done, except in special education programs, in secondary schools and colleges with respect to teaching motor skills, Bloom, Krathwohl, and their associates have not yet formulated a taxonomy of motor-skill educational objectives.

Bloom (1956) defines the cognitive and affective learning domains (areas) as follows:

> The cognitive domain . . .includes those objectives which deal with the recall or recognition of knowledge and the development of intellectual abilities and skills. . . .The affective domain . . .includes objectives which describe changes in interest, attitudes, and values, and the development of appreciations and adequate adjustment. (p. 7)

Cognitive Objectives

In 1956 Benjamin Bloom *et al.* published their now famous *Taxonomy of Educational Objectives, The Classification of Educational Goals, Handbook I: Cognitive Domain*. The purpose of this hierarchical classification system is to categorize the cognitive changes produced in students as a result of the goals and methods of our formal educational system. Only observable mental changes (that is, changes which can be inferred from problem-solving, testing, and observations) are included in Bloom's taxonomy. The taxonomy can be used by teachers as an aid in formulating instructional objectives, selecting teaching methods, and designing tests and activities to determine student learning. Bloom and his associates, after an exhaustive study of statements of educational objectives taken from many sources, listed the cognitive objectives of schooling according to the complexity of observable behaviors and developed a hierarchy containing six major classes. These cognitive classes, listed from the simplest to the most complex, are:

Cognitive objectives

1. *Knowledge*
2. *Comprehension*
3. *Application*
4. *Analysis*
5. *Synthesis*
6. *Evaluation*

This taxonomy of cognitive objectives was developed from lists of school and college objectives in many subjects; some of the six classes contain several subclasses. We will limit our discussion of the taxonomy to objectives and applications from secondary school mathematics.

Knowledge

Knowledge objectives emphasize the mental processes of remembering and recalling information in approximately the same form in which it was presented. In each secondary school mathematics course we want students to remember mathematical symbols, terminology, facts, skills, and principles. We expect our students to remember the symbols for addition, subtraction, multiplication, and division; to define natural, rational, and real numbers; to recall addition, subtraction, multiplication, and division facts for one-digit numbers; to remember the procedures for carrying out long divisions and extracting square roots; and to state such principles as the Pythagorean theorem, the factor theorem, and the distributive law for multiplication over addition. The knowledge category includes only recall of specific mathematical material in a form similar to the form in which the material was presented.

Recalling knowledge requires little more than bringing to mind the appropriate material. Unfortunately, at times, some knowledge may be meaningless and of no value to some students. It is not uncommon for students, on occasion, to devote their efforts in learning mathematics to memorizing knowledge which, for them, is little more than sequences of nonsense symbols, syllables, and activities. The knowledge category does not necessarily include any degree of understanding mathematics; although the five higher level cognitive educational objectives do require various degrees of understanding.

Comprehension

Comprehension is the lowest level of understanding for students. Students comprehend a mathematical idea if they can make some use of it without necessarily relating it to other ideas or understanding all of its implications. One subclass of comprehension in mathematics is the ability to *translate* verbal statements or problems into mathematical symbolism and vice versa. For example, to understand that sine $(90°) = 1$ means that there is a mathematical function called *sine* which maps the angle $90°$ into 1 is to exhibit the type of comprehension called translation. Many students have difficulty with verbal problems in algebra because they are unable to translate verbal expressions into algebraic expressions, which indicates that they may not comprehend the meaning of algebraic expressions and verbal statements.

Another type of comprehension is *interpretation* which is the ability to formulate new viewpoints of material. An example of interpretation is understanding that ordered pairs of numbers can be used to represent points in a plane and vice versa. Many of the behaviors expected of students in graphing functions involve interpreting data in different ways as well as *extrapolation,* which is extending trends beyond the given data. This ability to predict the continuation of trends, *extrapolation,* is another of the educational objectives falling under the major heading of comprehension. Activities such as sketching graphs, understanding graphs and charts and interpreting lists of data have as their objectives the comprehension activities of translation, interpretation and extrapolation.

Application

Students can demonstrate their comprehension of a mathematical abstraction by correctly using it when told to do so. Whereas, to demonstrate the ability to apply a mathematical abstraction, students must select it and use it correctly in an appropriate situation without being told to do so. Application of a mathematical abstraction is using the abstraction in particular, concrete situations without being prompted. The ability to select the appropriate mathematical techniques, postulates and theorems to prove a new theorem is an example of an application of mathematics. Selecting and using principles of ratio and proportion to construct a scale model of a house and revising a recipe for six people to make a meal for two people are also examples of applying mathematical abstractions. Since tests have shown that most young adults in America can carry out the four arithmetic operations on whole numbers, but only 20 to 40 percent of these people can solve consumer problems such as computing a taxi fare or unit pricing grocery store items, it appears that Americans comprehend arithmetic fairly well, but apply it badly.

Analysis

Analysis is the ability to subdivide an information structure into its components so that the relative hierarchy of ideas is clear and the relationships among the ideas are apparent. Bloom *et al.* have identified three types of analysis; they are analysis of elements, analysis of relationships, and analysis of organizational principles. Comprehension emphasizes understanding the meaning of mathematical material. In applications the emphasis is upon knowing appropriate and useful information and being able to select that material and use it in appropriate situations. Analysis deals with breaking material into its parts, finding relationships among the parts, and observing the organization of the parts. Analyzing a mathematical structure requires a higher order of comprehension than applying that structure.

Some examples of the *analysis of elements* are the ability to separate facts from hypotheses, the ability to recognize unstated, but implicit, assumptions, and the ability to separate hypotheses from conclusions. At times many students, when proving theorems in geometry, will use part of the conclusion of the theorem as an hypothesis. Many errors in all mathematical subjects occur because students fail to consider implied conditions when using techniques and theorems. Common factors, *not terms,* can be cancelled in fractions. Both numerator and denominator of a fraction can be divided by the same, *nonzero,* number. The sum of an infinite geometric progression is $S = \frac{a}{1-r}$ *if r^2 is less than one.* In a *right* triangle, $a^2 + b^2 = c^2$.

Analysis of relationships involves identifying the major relationships among the elements of a mathematical structure. In solving statement problems in arithmetic, algebra, trigonometry, and calculus, students must analyze the relationships among the unknowns (variables) and the given information (constants). Another example of analysis of relationships is the ability, when proving theorems, to organize hypotheses in their proper relationships to each other and to detect logical fallacies in completed mathematical "proofs."

The most complex and difficult type of analysis, *analysis of organizational principles,* is the ability to recognize all the elements and relationships of a complex structure such as a mathematical field, the real number system, or a complex mathematical proof. This type of analysis includes the ability to observe and understand mathematical techniques, to understand a writer's logical organization of a mathematical proof, and to comprehend the structure of a mathematical system.

Synthesis

Synthesis is the ability to combine elements to form a unique structure or system. In mathematics, synthesis involves combining and arranging mathematical concepts and principles to create distinctive mathematical structures. This cognitive category provides for creative behavior and includes activities such as formulating mathematical theorems and developing mathematical structures. According to the product which is being synthesized, there are three subclasses of synthesis—*producing a unique written or oral communication, developing a plan or a set of activities,* and *deriving a set of abstract relations.* Writing mathematical papers and producing speeches about mathematics are examples of the production of unique communications. Production of a plan or set of operations is illustrated by developing a plan for teaching a unit in mathematics or devising an algorithm for solving a particular type of mathematics problem. Many computer programs for solving complex mathematical problems are plans or sets of operations. Making mathematical discoveries such as discovering a new theorem or developing a generalized abstract mathematical system are examples of deriving sets of abstract relations. Newton's creation of calculus, and Gauss' development of differential geometry involved synthesis at its highest level.

Evaluation

Evaluation is making judgments about the value of ideas, creations, and methods. Evaluation is the highest type of educational objective because it involves using knowledge, comprehension, application, analysis, and synthesis before it can be accomplished. At times evaluation can lead to the acquisition of new knowledge, better comprehension, new applications, and unique methods of analysis and synthesis. There are two types of evaluation—*judgments in terms of internal evidence* and *judgments in terms of external evidence.* When a mathematical proof is judged according to its accuracy, logic, consistency, and clarity, it is being evaluated in terms of its internal structure. When major mathematical theories and systems are judged according to their contributions to mathematical progress, they are being evaluated in terms of external criteria.

Using Cognitive Objectives in the Classroom

Some mathematics educators think that there is an overemphasis on knowledge and comprehension in mathematics textbooks, teaching methods, homework assignments and tests. A fairly large proportion of textbook problems and standardized test questions in secondary school mathematics require only the lower level cognitive activities of knowledge and comprehension. Analysis of textbook problems and teacher-constructed test questions indicate that high school mathematics students are infrequently required to practice synthesis and evaluation, and that many tasks requiring application and analysis are somewhat contrived and lacking in relevance.

Knowledge and Comprehension in Learning Mathematics

The acquisition of mathematical facts and skills is usually accomplished through the cognitive activities of knowledge and comprehension. Lectures, demonstrations, drill sheets, work at the chalkboard, written and oral quizzes, and games are effective teaching/learning techniques for accomplishing knowledge and comprehension objectives. The following list contains cognitive objectives and corresponding test items for the cognitive activities of acquisition of mathematical knowledge and comprehension of mathematical skills and concepts from secondary school mathematics courses:

Knowledge of Arithmetic

Cognitive Objective	*Test Item*
1. Students will give the definition of an even number.	1. Define even number.
2. Students will state the product of any pair of single-digit integers.	2. What is the product of $(-3) \times (-7)$?
3. Students will identify the parts of fractions.	3. In the fraction $\frac{2}{3}$, which number is the denominator?
4. Students will explain the meaning of square root of a number.	4. What is the meaning of the square root of a number?

Comprehension of Arithmetic

1. Students will identify even and odd numbers.	1. Which of these numbers are even numbers? 8, 11, 19, 352, 781, 28, 1001, 998?
2. Students will compute the quotient of two fractions.	2. Find this quotient $\frac{7}{8} \div \frac{2}{3}$.
3. Students will approximate the square roots of numbers.	3. Find the square root of 398.43.

Knowledge of Algebra

Cognitive Objective	*Test Item*
1. Students will define the symbol a^n.	1. Explain the meaning of the symbol a^n.
2. Students will write the quadratic formula.	2. Write the quadratic formula.

Knowledge of Algebra (Continued)

3. Students will explain the symbol $\log_n a$.

4. Students will define ordinate and abscissa.

3. What is the meaning of the symbol $\log_n a$?

4. Define the terms ordinate and abscissa.

Comprehension of Algebra

1. Students will compute powers of the form a^n.

2. Students will compute logarithms.

3. Students will find the product of a monomial and a binomial.

4. Students will give examples of quadratic equations.

1. What number is represented by $(-2)^3$?

2. Find $\log_3 81$.

3. Find the product of $3x(2x^2 - 4y)$.

4. Give an example of a quadratic equation.

Knowledge of Geometry

Cognitive Objective

1. Students will define a circle.

2. Students will state the Pythagorean theorem.

3. Students will state the congruent triangle theorems.

4. Students will give the definitions of postulate and theorem.

Test Item

1. What is the definition of a circle?

2. State the Pythagorean theorem.

3. State two different congruent triangle theorems.

4. Define postulate. Define theorem.

Comprehension of Geometry

1. Students will identify geometric shapes.

2. Students will explain the distinction between postulates and theorems.

3. Students will use the Pythagorean theorem.

4. Students will show the difference between congruence and similarity.

1. Give the name of each of these geometric shapes: ○ ▽ □ ⬡

2. Give an example of a postulate and an example of a theorem and explain the difference between your examples.

3. Use the Pythagorean theorem to find the hypotenuse of this triangle: 2⊿5

4. Construct two triangles which are similar but which are not congruent.

Knowledge of Trigonometry

Cognitive Objective

1. Students will state the law of sines.

2. Students will define a radian.

3. Students will explain the difference between arcs and chords.

4. Students will give the values of the trigonometric functions of special angles.

Test Item

1. State the law of sines.

2. Define *radian*.

3. State the difference between an arc of a circle and a chord of a circle.

4. What are the values of: $\sin(30°)$, $\tan(90°)$, $\sec(45°)$?

Comprehension of Trigonometry

1. Students will explain why $\tan(90°)$ is undefined.	1. Explain why $\tan(90°)$ is undefined.
2. Students will show the relationship between radian measure and degree measure.	2. Convert 3 radians to degree measure. Convert 280 degrees to radian measure.
3. Students will describe the difference between a trigonometric equation and a trigonometric identity.	3. What is the difference between a trigonometric equation and a trigonometric identity? Give examples of each.
4. Students will explain the meaning of the symbol $\text{Tan}^{-1}(x)$.	4. Explain the meaning of the symbol $\text{Tan}^{-1}(x)$. What is the value of $\text{Tan}^{-1}(\sqrt{2})$?

Note that knowledge objectives and knowledge test items merely require students to state the meaning of a symbol or to define a term. Knowledge objectives are met when students can correctly recall information and definitions in nearly the same form as they were presented in the textbook or by the teacher. Many teachers tend to assume that if students can write the correct definition of a concept, they comprehend the concept in a meaningful manner. However, such is not always the case, because many students memorize definitions with very little, if any, understanding of the concept being defined. To be reasonably confident that students comprehend defined concepts may require asking them to use the definitions to classify examples and nonexamples of the concepts. Even then a teacher cannot be certain that students understand the concept. For example, a teacher might define a matrix as a rectangular array of symbols and use

$$\begin{bmatrix} a & b \\ c & d \end{bmatrix}, \begin{bmatrix} \bigcirc & \hexagon \\ \triangledown & \square \end{bmatrix}, \text{ and } \begin{bmatrix} 6 & 4 & 3 \\ -1 & 2 & 5 \\ 3 & 1 & 7 \end{bmatrix} \text{ as examples of matrices.}$$

When asked to define *matrix,* students who do not understand the meaning of the word *array* could have memorized the teacher's definition and could reproduce it on a test. They may even memorize the teacher's examples of matrices and reproduce them when asked for three examples of matrices. When testing for comprehension it is well to ask questions that require students to translate definitions into their own terminology and to interpret or construct unfamiliar examples and representations.

Application in Learning Mathematics

The next higher level cognitive learning objective, application, can be accomplished using such teaching strategies as lectures, demonstrations, class discussions, field trips, small-group projects carried out in class, individualized classwork and homework. We usually want students to apply their knowledge of mathematics to learning more advanced mathematics and to solving practical or interesting problems. For many students practical problems, such as balancing a checking account, are not very interesting, and interesting problems, such as arithmetic puzzles, are not very practical. Few mathematics textbooks have many problems which are both practical and interesting for most students; consequently teachers and students should work together to find such problems. Students' hobbies and part-time jobs, newspaper and magazine articles, radio news items, and special reports on television about consumer problems are good sources for applied mathematics problems. In fact, some experienced teachers make exclusive use of these sources in gathering materials for use in teaching consumer mathematics courses. A set of interesting and/or practical problems illustrating applications in mathematics is given below. These are problems that my students and I have considered in mathematics courses that were interesting and useful to us at the time. Although many of your students may also find these problems to be interesting and useful, it is well for you and your own students to locate applied problems in such current sources as those mentioned above.

Problems Requiring Cognitive Applications of Mathematics

1. *Arithmetic or Algebra.* A boy began walking down the street carrying a bag of apples. He met a friend and gave him half of his apples plus one-half of an apple. Continuing on, he met a second friend and gave her half of his remaining apples plus one-half of an apple. Later he met a third friend and gave her half of his remaining apples plus one-half of an apple, only to discover that his generosity was such that he had given away all of his apples. How many apples did the boy have when he started his walk? This problem can be solved simply by using a bit of arithmetic and a lot of "common sense," or it can be solved using a complex algebraic equation with many symbols of grouping.

2. *Arithmetic or Algebra.* If you are going to work for a company and plan to stay on for at least five years, would it be to your advantage to agree to accept a $500 yearly salary increase or a $200 semi-annual salary increase?

3. *Arithmetic.* A state-run lottery offers a grand prize of $1,000,000 to the winner. However, in order to help the winner "save" on his Federal Income Tax, the million dollars is paid at the rate of $50,000 for twenty years. The Federal Income Tax rate is approximately 65% on $1,000,000, and 40% on $50,000. If you could take the $1,000,000 and pay the taxes on it, you could invest the remaining money in tax-exempt bonds which pay simple interest of 8% per year. Would you obtain more dollars in interest and principle over a twenty-year period by taking the $1,000,000 and investing what remains after taxes or by taking the $50,000 per year for twenty years?

4. *Trigonometry.* Locate a large dead tree in a populated area and, on a sunny day, use trigonometry to calculate whether it can be felled without damaging other trees, flower gardens, or near-by houses.

5. *Algebra.* What rectangular shaped one-acre lot could be enclosed with the least amount of fencing?

6. *Algebra or Calculus.* The cylindrical can in which tomato juice is sold requires metal which costs much more than the tomato juice contained in the can. If a tomato juice can is to contain one liter of juice, how tall should it be to minimize the cost of the metal needed to manufacture the can?

7. *Arithmetic.* Take a group of students to a supermarket and have them calculate the following price comparisons (however, be sure to make advance arrangements with the supermarket manager):
   A. Cost per gram and cost per ounce for soap powder.
      Brand 1 _____ Brand 2 _____ Brand 3 _____
   B. Cost per gram and cost per ounce for tomato juice.
      Brand 1 _____ Brand 2 _____ Brand 3 _____
   C. Cost per gram and cost per ounce for corn flakes.
      Brand 1 _____ Brand 2 _____ Brand 3 _____
   Also prepare a shopping list for food and supplies for a family of four. Take it to the supermarket and compute the total cost of the items on the list if the least expensive brands are purchased, and the total cost if the most expensive brands are purchased.

Analysis and Synthesis in Learning Mathematics

The fourth level cognitive objective is analysis. This is the breakdown of a mathematical structure into its components so that the relative hierarchy and relationship of ideas becomes apparent. Somewhat the reverse of analysis is synthesis where the learner puts several mathematical ideas together to form a more complex mathematical structure. Analysis and synthesis are usually practiced in mathematics classrooms after students have attained knowledge and comprehension of basic mathematical concepts.

Solving mathematical word problems and studying completed proofs of theorems require the cognitive ability of analysis. Teachers can help students develop their own analytical abilities by explaining the reasons for each step in the solutions of various problems and by discussing the rationale for each statement in proofs of theorems.

Proving theorems, writing term papers, and formulating and testing hypotheses require the cognitive skill of synthesis. Students can improve their powers of synthesis by writing proofs of theorems, by communicating their interpretations of complex mathematical structures to the teacher and their classmates (either in written or oral form), and by teaching mathematical principles to each other. Effective synthesis of a mathematical communication such as a proof, an explanation, or a problem solving procedure usually must be preceded by an analysis of the components of the task that is to be synthesized.

One of the common, albeit inadvertent, errors that teachers make in trying to teach students to analyze problems and formulate proofs is overspecification of rules and procedures. Although specific lists of rules may be useful for solving certain types of problems, there are elements of trial-and-error, creativity, and insight involved in higher level analysis and synthesis. Even though it is usually desirable that teachers be well-prepared for class, overpreparation for problem-solving and theorem-proving can, at times, lead students to believe that such activities are really very easy, if they were only intelligent enough to learn how to do them. It is well to show students that the precise, orderly solutions to word problems and the detailed, logical proofs of theorems which are usually presented in textbooks required false starts, frustrations, and mistakes before the original author was able to prepare a coherent communication of his or her work. Both analysis and synthesis are difficult cognitive activities which can be learned and practiced through the instruction of patient teachers and the perseverance of well-motivated students over a period of years. Most students need to practice theorem-proving and problem-solving for several years before they become good at it. Even then, it is difficult to explain to someone else how to prove theorems and solve problems. Listed below is a set of cognitive objectives and corresponding test items which, respectively, describe and measure the cognitive activities of analysis and synthesis in secondary school mathematics:

Analysis in Arithmetic

Cognitive Objective	*Test Item*
1. Students will explain the reason why $\frac{a}{b} \div \frac{c}{d}$ is equivalent to $\frac{a}{b} \times \frac{d}{c}$, where a, b, c, and d are natural numbers.	1. Explain why the division problem $\frac{2}{3} \div \frac{7}{11}$ can be written as $\frac{2}{3} \times \frac{11}{7}$.

Analysis in Arithmetic (Continued)

2. Students will tell why the method of casting out nines is a valid procedure for checking the sum of a column of numbers.

2. Explain why the procedure of casting out nines shown below is a valid check for addition:

Addends		Excess of nines
389	→	2
964	→	1
791	→	8
Sum 2144	→	2 Excess of nines in sum

3. Students will explain why 2112 in base three is equivalent to 68 in base ten.

3. Why is 2112 in base three equivalent to 68 in base ten?

Synthesis in Arithmetic

1. Students will develop procedures for multiplying numbers in various bases.

1. Construct a single digit multiplication table in base seven, and write a set of rules and procedures for finding the product of two three-digit numbers in base seven.

2. Students will write computer programs which will convert numbers from one base to another base.

2. Write a computer program to convert any number in base ten to an equivalent number in base two.

3. Students will prove that the sum of two odd numbers is an even number.

3. Prove that the sum of any two odd numbers is an even number.

Analysis in Algebra

Cognitive Objective

Test Item

1. Students will state and explain the validity of Cramer's Rule for solving three equations in three variables.

1. State Cramer's Rule for solving three equations in three variables. Explain why Cramer's Rule yields a valid solution for a system of linear equations.

2. Students will state the postulate of mathematical induction and will discuss the validity of its application to proving theorems which hold for all natural numbers.

2. State the postulate of mathematical induction and explain why it is a valid technique for proving theorems which are true for all natural numbers.

Synthesis in Algebra

1. Students will derive the quadratic formula.

1. Derive the quadratic formula.

2. Students will state and prove the binomial theorem.

2. State and prove the binomial theorem.

3. Students will state and prove the formula for the sum of an infinite geometric progression.

3. State and prove the formula for the sum of an infinite geometric progression.

Analysis in Geometry

Cognitive Objective

Test Item

1. Students will discuss the relationships among the validity of a proposition

1. Analyze and discuss the relationships among the validity of a proposition and

177

Analysis in Geometry (Continued)

and the validity of the converse, inverse, and contrapositive of the proposition.

the validity of its converse, inverse, and contrapositive.

2. Students will describe the nature of geodesics (paths of least distance) on the surfaces of planes, spheres, cylinders, and cones.

2. Analyze and discuss the nature of geodesics on the surfaces of planes, spheres, cylinders, and cones.

Synthesis in Geometry

1. Students will prove theorems from plane geometry.

1. In the same circle or in equal circles, prove that equal chords are equidistant from the center.

2. Students will prove theorems from solid geometry.

2. Prove that the volume of a pyramid is equal to one-third the product of the area of its base and its altitude.

3. Students will explain the consequences of contradicting Euclid's parallel postulate for plane geometry.

3. Write a paper discussing the consequences of the two possible contradictions of Euclid's parallel postulate.

Analysis in Trigonometry

Cognitive Objective

1. Students will interpret the graphs of trigonometric functions of the form $y = a \sin(bx)$.

Test Item

1. Discuss the *relative amplitudes and periods of functions of the form* $y = a \sin(bx)$ for positive and negative values of a and b, and for all combinations of a and b such that
$$a < 0, \quad a > 0,$$
$$b < 0, \quad b > 0.$$

2. Students will explain the relationship between the graph of each circular (trigonometric) function and its inverse function.

2. Consider the graphs of the six circular (trigonometric) functions and explain the relationship between each function and its inverse function.

Synthesis in Trigonometry

1. Students will prove trigonometric identities over the set of real numbers.

1. Prove the identity
$$\frac{2\cos^2(4t)}{\sin(8t)} = \frac{\sin(8t)}{1 - \cos(8t)}$$
over the set of real numbers.

2. Students will prove that certain trigonometric functions are irrational.

2. Prove that $\sin(10°)$ is an irrational number.

Evaluation in Learning Mathematics

The highest level of cognitive activity, evaluation, is judging material with respect to its internal accuracy, consistency, and completeness or judging material according to generally accepted external standards. In its most complex form, evaluation requires the use of all the other levels of cognitive activities. Evaluation can be practiced by students through term papers and projects, class discussions, certain types of homework assignments and carefully prepared classroom games. Even though evaluation is an appropriate cognitive activity for students at all grade levels in secondary schools, it is seldom emphasized in most mathematics classrooms. The following list illustrates the types of evaluation objectives and corresponding student activities that are appropriate for secondary school mathematics:

Evaluation in Arithmetic

Cognitive Objective

1. Students will describe and compare the merits of the two standard algorithms for calculating square roots of numbers.

2. Students will compare and discuss the relative merits of arithmetic in a number system based upon powers of two and arithmetic in a number system based upon powers of ten.

3. Students will explain the value of arithmetic in every-day activities.

4. Students will explain the value of zero as a number in our number system.

Student Activity

1. Find the square root of 6342.173 using each of the two methods that were presented in class. Compare the two methods and discuss the advantages and disadvantages of each method.

2. Discuss the advantages and disadvantages of arithmetic in a base-two number system and arithmetic in a base-ten number system.

3. Of what value is arithmetic in "real life"? What are the disadvantages of not being able to add, subtract, multiply, and divide? Are decimal fractions of any practical value?

4. Suppose that, just like many of the people who lived many years ago, we had to use a number system that did not have a number zero. What limitations would this put on our number system and our methods of adding, subtracting, multiplying, and dividing?

Evaluation in Algebra

1. Students will assess the merits of solving systems of linear equations by the substitution method, the method of addition and subtraction, and Cramer's Rule.

2. Students will judge the value of extending our number system to include irrational numbers.

3. Students will explain the relative merits of comparing the cardinal numbers of sets by counting elements and by setting up one-to-one correspondences.

1. Discuss the relative advantages of the three methods of solving systems of linear equations—substitution, addition and subtraction, and Cramer's Rule.

2. Why is it necessary to include the set of irrational numbers in our number system?

3. At times we compare the number of elements in two sets (cardinal numbers of the sets) by counting the elements of each set, and at other times we compare the cardinal numbers of two sets by setting up one-to-one correspondences between the elements of the sets. Evaluate the relative merits of these two procedures for "counting" elements in sets.

179

Evaluation in Algebra (Continued)

4. Students will recognize the different techniques for the arithmetic of exact numbers and the arithmetic of approximate numbers, and will compare and describe the two sets of arithmetic processes.

4. Most of the numbers that we use in algebra are pure or exact numbers, and most of the numbers that are used in the sciences and engineering are approximate measurements. Compare and evaluate methods for dealing with the arithmetic of pure numbers and the arithmetic of approximate numbers.

Evaluation in Geometry

1. Students will judge the relative merits of the rectangular coordinate geometry of algebra and the synthetic geometry of Euclidean plane geometry.

1. In algebra, lines, curves, and plane figures are represented as functions of the form $y = f(x)$ which can be plotted on a rectangular coordinate system to aid in studying their properties. The approach to the study of lines, curves, and plane figures that is used in Euclidean plane geometry is quite different. Compare and evaluate the merits of these two approaches to the study of plane curves and figures.

2. Students will describe the relative merits of the methods of direct and indirect proof and discuss the conditions under which each method is appropriate.

2. Give an example of a theorem which is proved using the direct method of proof and an example of a theorem which is proved using the indirect method of proof. Discuss the relative merits of each of these methods of proof and the situations in which each method is appropriate.

3. Students will judge the value of learning how to prove theorems in geometry.

3. Of what value is it to be able to construct proofs of theorems in geometry?

4. Students will compare geometry on a plane to geometry on the surface of a sphere and will evaluate the usefulness of these two types of geometry.

4. Compare geometry on a plane to geometry on the surface of a sphere and discuss the value of each type of geometry.

Evaluation in Trigonometry

1. Students will describe the procedure for solving a trigonometric equation and the procedure for proving a trigonometric identity and will compare the two procedures.

1. Solve the equation $4 \sin^4(x) + 3 \sin^2(x) - 1 = 0$. Prove the identity $\tan(x) + \cot(x) \equiv 2\csc(x)$. Explain the difference between an equation and an identity, and compare the logical basis for solving equations to the logical basis for proving identities.

2. Students will explain the rationale for concluding that $\dfrac{0}{0}$ is undefined and the rationale for concluding that

2. From arithmetic we know that $\dfrac{0}{0}$ is undefined; however in trigonometry, where x is given in radian measure,

$$\lim_{x \to 0} \frac{\sin(x)}{x} = 1.$$

$\lim\limits_{x \to 0} \dfrac{\sin(x)}{x} = 1.$ Explain the reason for this seeming contradiction between the values of these two expressions.

3. Students will explain and compare the definitions of $\sin(x)$ as a wrapping function on a unit circle and $\sin(x)$ as the ratio of the leg of a right triangle and the hypotenuse of that triangle.

3. Explain how the sine function can be defined in terms of parts of a right triangle and also as a wrapping function on a unit circle. Which of these definitions is more useful? Could we eliminate one or the other or both definitions without any loss to mathematics or the applications of mathematics?

Summary

One of the initial activities in preparing to teach a lesson or topic in mathematics is setting objectives, and one of the final activities is measuring student learning of the lesson or topic. The objective of the lesson, and the test questions and activities used to evaluate how well students learned the lesson, should be closely related. It can be very frustrating to students to be tested on material that was not included in the teacher's lessons and which appears, to them, to be unrelated to the mathematics topics that were studied. Also, if a teacher concentrates on presenting facts and skills and if the students know and understand the facts and skills but are tested on questions which require analysis, synthesis, and evaluation, they can not be expected to perform well and to develop positive attitudes toward mathematics. Teachers should avoid putting students in the position of having to guess what type of questions will be on their mathematics tests. Such situations usually occur when the teacher has specific objectives but does not share them with students, or when the teacher does not have any specific objectives other than covering the material and giving a test which is somewhat related to the material.

Bloom and his associates have provided a useful taxonomy of cognitive educational objectives which mathematics teachers can apply in their own classes. When preparing to teach each mathematics topic or unit, mathematics teachers should set two types of objectives. First, the mathematical content which is to be taught should be decided upon, and second, appropriate cognitive objectives should be determined for students. Both the content objectives and the cognitive objectives should be explained to students as they prepare to study the topic or unit. Many research studies in mathematics classrooms have shown that students tend to learn mathematics better if they are told in advance, in terminology that they can understand, precisely what they will be expected to learn and the methods that will be used to measure their learning. Students should know in advance that they will be expected to define concepts (knowledge), master certain skills (comprehension), solve word problems (application), explain mathematical processes (analysis), prove theorems (synthesis), or compare mathematical methods or structures (evaluation). Then, the teacher should demonstrate examples, assign homework, and construct test questions which are closely related to the content and cognitive objectives of the topic or unit.

181

The lower level objectives of knowledge, comprehension and application, and the higher level objectives of analysis, synthesis, and evaluation, are equally important in secondary school mathematics. It is quite important that students learn the basic terminology and symbolism of mathematics (knowledge and comprehension) and basic computational and problem-solving skills (comprehension and application). Consequently, school teachers should not place a greater value on the higher level cognitive objectives of analysis, synthesis, and evaluation merely because they require more complex mental activities. The initial goal of mathematics education should be to teach basic skills which can be used to learn more complex mathematical concepts and principles, and which will support important, practical applications of mathematics.

Affective Objectives

Nearly all school systems have both cognitive and affective goals; however most school activities are designed to emphasize student mastery of cognitive objectives. Most testing and evaluation procedures measure, to a large extent, cognitive learning and there is a tendency to evaluate affective learning subjectively, if at all. This apparent neglect of affective learning, or at least the measurement of affective learning, has occurred for several reasons. First, one's attitudes, beliefs and values tend to be regarded as private considerations; whereas cognitive achievement is regarded as a public matter. Second, there are very few adequate appraisal techniques that can be used directly to measure affective learning. Third, it has been assumed, possibly incorrectly, that attitudes, beliefs and values develop relatively slowly and can be measured only over long periods of time. Fourth, affective educational objectives usually have been stated in such general terms that it has been difficult, if not impossible, to interpret them in any teachable and measurable manner. For example, the affective goal of "helping students appreciate their worthiness as members of society" is a difficult goal to operationalize. That is, to use this goal effectively in teaching it is necessary to restructure it into specific objectives for which instructional strategies and evaluation instruments can be developed.

The taxonomy of affective educational objectives, which was prepared by David Krathwohl, *et al.,* is an ordered classification system of interest, appreciation, attitude, value and adjustment objectives. This taxonomy contains five major affective objective categories with each category containing two or three affective levels. These major categories and subcategories are:

Affective Objectives

1. Receiving
   A. Awareness
   B. Willingness to Receive
   C. Controlled or Selected Attention
2. Responding
   A. Acquiescence in Responding
   B. Willingness to Respond
   C. Satisfaction in Responding
3. Valuing

    A. Accepting a Value
    B. Preferring a Value
    C. Commitment to a Value
  4. Organization
    A. Conceptualization of a Value
    B. Organization of a System of Values
  5. Characterization by a Value or Value Complex
    A. Generalized Set
    B. Characterization

Although studies such as the National Assessment of Educational Progress show that the majority of people in the United States do learn arithmetic skills in school, other studies such as those carried out by the School Mathematics Study Group indicate that many students, as well as adults, have developed negative attitudes toward mathematics. In addition to teaching students to know, comprehend, apply, analyze, synthesize, and evaluate mathematical facts, skills, concepts and principles, people who are concerned about mathematics education also want students to enjoy mathematics, view mathematics as an important human endeavor, and learn about the nature of mathematics and the work of mathematicians. While some people appear to have an inherent talent for and interest in mathematics, many students develop a rather strong dislike for the mathematics which is taught in school. In an attempt to increase students' interest in mathematics, many writers of mathematics textbooks have begun to include historical information about mathematics and mathematicians in their books, and show students the value of mathematics and some of its many uses. Some affective objectives are concerned with motivating students to learn mathematics, but the general purpose of such objectives is much broader than just student motivation. In addition to its many applications, mathematics can also be an interesting and enjoyable social and cultural activity for many people. Many fascinating books and articles have been written about mathematics and mathematicians. When teaching "mathematics", teachers should help students understand and appreciate the role of mathematics in both social and technological progress. The following discussion of affective objectives in mathematics and the examples of affective objectives are designed to help you in formulating affective objectives for your students. In subsequent chapters various teaching strategies for helping students meet both affective and cognitive objectives will be discussed and illustrated.

Receiving Objectives
At the receiving level, with its three categories of awareness, willingness to receive and controlled or selected attention, we want students to be aware of mathematical information, to be willing to learn about mathematics, and to consciously attend to observing and learning mathematics. If students are not aware of mathematical information and its importance, are not willing to learn mathematics, or will not turn their attention to learning mathematics, it is unlikely that they will be at all successful in their mathematics classes.

    The following list of objectives together with appropriate questions to evaluate students' success in meeting each objective contains examples from mathematics of the three categories of receiving objectives:

Receiving

Objective	*Measure*
Awareness:	
1. Students will identify the influence of science and scientists upon the development of mathematics.	1. Who were some scientists who developed new ideas in mathematics to help them in their scientific work?
2. Students will identify women mathematicians and their contributions to the development of mathematics.	2. Name three great women mathematicians and tell what were their contributions to mathematics.
Willingness to Receive:	
1. Students will describe the importance of learning about complex numbers.	1. Why do we need complex numbers in mathematics? What are some uses of complex numbers in the sciences?
2. Students will accept the fact that women, as well as men, should have the opportunity to become mathematicians.	2. Do you think that it is proper for women to work in industry as mathematicians? Why?
Controlled or Selected Attention:	
1. Students will express a preference for one of two methods for solving a class of problems.	1. Which method for solving systems of linear equations do you prefer—elimination or substitution?
2. Students will listen for the correct pronunciation of mathematical terms.	2. How is this word pronounced—RADIAN?

Responding Objectives

The three categories of responding to information and situations—acquiescence in responding, willingness to respond, and satisfaction in responding—go beyond mere receiving. The previous category of receiving requires only a passive involvement on the part of students; responding implies a level of active student involvement. At the lowest level of responding, student responses result merely from compliance or obedience. At the next level, students have some willingness or desire to respond. Finally, at the highest level of responding, students obtain pleasure or enjoyment from responding. Receiving is passive learning of affective behaviors which requires little effort on the part of the learner. Responding is active affective learning or "learning by doing." Following is a set of illustrative affective objectives and measures for the three subcategories of responding:

Responding

Objective	*Measure*
Acquiescence in Responding:	
1. Students will hand in completed homework assignments on time.	1. An assignment is given and students return it to the teacher when it is due.
2. Students will attempt to solve problems at the chalkboard.	2. Students go to the chalkboard when asked to do so by the teacher.
3. Students will not talk in class when another student is speaking.	3. Students speak only when recognized by the teacher.

Willingness to Respond:
1. Students will volunteer to answer questions in class.
2. Students will assist other students in learning skills and concepts.
3. Students will attempt to solve problems from the textbook which are not assigned by the teacher.

1. When the teacher asks a question, students raise their hands.
2. Students work together in small groups and explain ideas and procedures to each other.
3. Students ask the teacher to check their solutions to problems that were not assigned.

Satisfaction in Responding:
1. Students will enjoy playing mathematical games.
2. Students will enjoy finding examples of applications of mathematics.
3. Students will enjoy using the metric system of measurement.

1. Students make up games in arithmetic and ask the teacher to permit them to play the games in class.
2. Students voluntarily look for examples of consumer mathematics problems in magazines and bring their examples to class.
3. Students bring labels from grocery store items, which are marked in metric units, to class and show them to each other and the teacher. Students purchase metric measuring devices.

Valuing Objectives

The affective objective of valuing provides for students to see the worth of an object, idea, phenomenon, activity, or behavior. The three stages of valuing—acceptance of a value, preference for a value, and commitment to a value—exemplify the commitment that people acquire for their values. A student who merely accepts a value has little commitment to that value and will readily reevaluate his or her position and may replace the value with a different, or even contradictory, value. Preference for a value implies that the individual is sufficiently committed to the value to want to retain it. Commitment to a value involves a high degree of certainty regarding the retention of the value. A person who is committed to a value will reject it with considerable reluctance, if he or she will reject it at all, and may attempt to influence others to accept the value. Both political and religious values are usually held with a considerable degree of conviction and commitment. A set of example objectives and measures for each of the three valuing phases is presented below:

Valuing

Objective

Measure

Acceptance of a Value:
1. Students will accept the value of learning arithmetic.

1. Students attend all class sessions, ask questions in class, and attempt to complete all homework assignments.

2. Students will accept the values of organization and neatness as appropriate in solving mathematics problems.

2. Students complete homework assignments that are neat and well organized.

3. Students will value respect and consideration for other people's mathetical hypotheses and arguments.

3. Students show respect for the conjectures and opinions of other students and do not ridicule or attempt to embarrass slower students.

Preference for a Value:

1. Students will exhibit a preference for learning mathematics.

1. Students elect advanced mathematics courses, participate in mathematics clubs, and seek out challenging problems in mathematics.

2. Students will show consideration for slower students.

2. Students invite slower students to work with them on group activities in class, assist slower students in completing homework assignments, and help slower students prepare for tests.

3. Students will value the roles of people of various nationalities in the development of mathematics.

3. Students select and read history of mathematics books and biographies of well-known mathematicians and study the mathematical contributions of various nations.

Commitment to a Value:

1. Certain students will commit themselves to the study of mathematics.

1. These students will enter mathematics contests, will spend much of their free time in mathematical pursuits, or will major in mathematics in college.

2. On the negative side, certain students will value attention from their classmates to such an extent that their efforts to gain attention may interfere with the teaching and learning in the classroom.

2. Some discipline problems and lack of interest in mathematics are due to students' commitments to values which interfere with the development of more acceptable values.

Organization Objectives

Krathwohl, Bloom, and Masia (1964) explain the affective category of organization as follows:

> As the learner successively internalizes values, he encounters situations for which more than one value is relevant. Thus necessity arises for (a) the organization of the values into a system, (b) the determination of the interrelationships among them, and (c) the establishment of the dominant and pervasive ones. Such a system is built gradually, subject to change as new values are incorporated. In the adult, changes are made with much greater effort and difficulty than in the child; the organism becomes more rigid with age and less ready to accept a value inconsistent with those already embraced.
>
> *Organization* is intended as the proper classification for objectives which describe the beginnings of the building of a value system. It is subdivided into two levels, since a prerequisite to interrelating is the conceptualization of the value in a form which permits organization. Thus *Conceptualization* forms the first subdivision in the process, *Organization of a value system* forming the second (p. 154).

Consistency and stability are important characteristics of valuing; and abstraction, analysis, and differentiation of values characterize conceptualization of a value. In the organization of a system of values, the learner is required to order, structure, and accommodate a complex set of values which may be disparate. Examples of these two levels of organization are shown below:

Organization

Objective	*Measure*
Conceptualization of a Value:	
1. Students will attempt to identify the logical structure of mathematics.	1. Students will conduct a discussion on the nature of proof and the logical foundations of mathematics and will explain their value in the development of mathematics.
2. Students will determine the basic assumptions underlying the structure of the real number system.	2. Students will discuss the assumptions underlying the structure of the real number system and will explain the value of these assumptions.
3. Students will evaluate their own standards and goals through reading the biography of a great mathematician.	3. Students will discuss their own goals and standards and compare them to those of a famous mathematician.
Organization of a System of Values:	
1. Students will compare the social policies and practices regarding the role of women in mathematics throughout history to the social policies and practices regarding women in mathematics today.	1. Success in meeting this objective can be measured through a reading assignment on the history of mathematics followed by a class discussion.
2. Students will judge the contributions to mathematics which have been made by people of various national origins.	2. Reading assignments in the history of mathematics followed by a class discussion can be used to assess success in meeting this objective.
3. Students will form judgments regarding the positive and negative effects of mathematical and scientific progress upon society.	3. Students' performance can be measured on this affective objective by asking them to write a paper discussing the effects of scientific progress upon society.

Characterization By a Value or Value Complex

At this stage of value development, values are organized into an internally consistent structure, have been held by the individual for some time, and are firmly established as part of the individual's characteristics. The subcategory of generalized set is the predisposition of a person to act in a consistent way each time a certain set of circumstances is encountered. This generalized behavior pattern is so pronounced that it is possible to describe an individual as a person who has certain values and who can be expected to behave in consistent ways in specific situations. The highest level of affective behavior, which is the higher of the two subcategories within characterization by a value or value complex, is called characterization. At the level of characterization, values are so generalized that they tend to characterize the individual to a great extent.

Educational objectives in schools are usually not set at the level of characterization by a value or value complex; these types of affective behaviors develop slowly over a period of time, are difficult to control and predict, and can not be easily measured or evaluated. Illustrative objectives for this affective level are given below:

Characterization By a Value or Value Complex

Objective	*Measure*
Generalized Set:	
1. Students will readily revise their judgments and behaviors when presented with new evidence about the foundations of mathematics and the nature of proof.	1. Students accept axioms as a basis for mathematical systems and accept and use proof by mathematical induction and proof by contradiction.
2. Students are willing to accept conclusions which can be drawn logically from sets of axioms and hypotheses.	2. Students revise their intuitive opinions and conjectures concerning mathematical "truths" when presented with contradictory "truths" that can be demonstrated to be valid using accepted methods of proof.
3. Students are confident of their ability to succeed in learning mathematics.	3. Students exhibit positive attitudes in mathematics classes and exert substantial effort toward knowing and comprehending mathematical concepts and principles.
Characterization:	
1. Students will develop a consistent philosophy of life.	1. Progress toward this objective can best be measured through perceptive observations of students over a long period of time.
2. Students will develop the ability to consistently recognize right and wrong actions and will develop a conscience.	2. This objective is difficult to measure directly and students' progress toward developing a conscience must be observed over a considerable period of time.

Summary

Many of the measures for the sample affective objectives presented in the previous pages require subjective observations, interpretations, or evaluations of students' behaviors by teachers. Even so-called objective measures which require precise answers to specific test questions are subjective to a certain extent because the values and expectations of the test maker influence the selection of test items and the determination of "correct" answers. Measuring students' progress toward cognitive and affective objectives is usually imprecise and time-consuming; affective objectives in mathematics are more difficult to measure and document than are cognitive mathematics objectives. It is easier to measure and document the fact that a student doesn't know and comprehend a mathematical skill than it is to demonstrate conclusively that he or she has not organized an appropriate value system for the study of algebra.

Some secondary school textbooks are published with teacher's editions and supplements containing cognitive performance objectives and tests of cognitive mathematical abilities; however few textbooks come with supplements containing affective objectives and affective measures. In many school systems teachers have few guidelines for formulating and measuring affective objectives and do so in a very haphazard manner, if at all. Nearly all school systems require periodic summary evaluations of students' cognitive progress, which are usually carried out by computing six-week grades, and sending report cards to parents. Some schools use report cards that contain evaluations of affective student progress. Categories such as "ability to work with other students," "cooperation," and "attitude toward the subject" are included on some report cards, and students may be rated along a satisfactory-unsatisfactory continuum on such affective characteristics.

Regardless of the procedures used for setting objectives or the methods used in evaluating progress toward objectives, it is important that teachers set cognitive and affective objectives for their students, share these objectives with students, and select or develop fair and consistent methods for measuring student progress. Students tend to learn (in the cognitive sense) better if they have specific cognitive learning objectives, and they tend to develop and maintain good attitudes (in the affective sense) toward mathematics if they know what is expected of them and how they will be evaluated.

Several years ago I observed a situation in a vocational/technical school where an inexperienced teacher had to be replaced in a mathematics classroom because he could not maintain order in his classroom. Students were complaining to the school principal about their grades and were refusing to attend his class. The person who replaced this teacher at mid-term found that the previous teacher's grade book contained A's and B's for all students, which was surprising since the students were dissatisfied with the grading system. Further investigation showed that the ineffective teacher had no learning objectives of his own, had not told the students what was expected of them, and had an arbitrary and inconsistent student evaluation and grading procedure. The conclusion to this story is that every student in the class *earned* lower grades from the replacement teacher, had no complaints about these lower grades, attended class regularly, and was well-behaved in class. There were several reasons for this dramatic change. The replacement teacher told the students precisely what it was that they were expected to learn, set definite rules for classroom behavior and enforced them, and maintained a fair and consistent testing and grading policy which he explained in detail to the class.

As you may have observed, each higher level cognitive objective requires the use of lower level cognitive abilities; each higher level affective objective includes unstated lower level affective objectives. Cognitive and affective objectives are interrelated. One can neither receive, respond to, value, organize, nor characterize a vacuous phenomenon. Values, attitudes, appreciation, and interest must be directed toward something, which in mathematics classes may be the facts, skills, concepts, principles, processes, and structures of mathematics. In addition to acquiring specific cognitive abilities and affective behaviors related to mathematical content, students are expected to develop generalized skills and behaviors by studying mathematics. It is expected that general problem-solving skills, logical reasoning abilities, and personal values (such as cooperation, good work habits, and appreciation of mathematics) will be acquired in the process of learning the specific content of mathematics.

Although Bloom, Krathwohl, and others have structured their taxonomy of educational objectives into two separate taxonomies, cognitive and affective taxonomies, they do not intend to suggest that there is a fundamental practical separation between the two sets of objectives. In fact, as Martin Scheerer (1954) says in the *Handbook of Social Psychology:*

> Behavior may be conceptualized as being embedded in a cognitive-emotional-motivational matrix in which no true separation is possible. No matter how we slice behavior, the ingredients of motivation-emotion-cognition are present in one order or another. (p. 123)

However, in order to study behavior, it is necessary to separate the components of behavior while keeping in mind the interrelation among these components. Krathwohl, Bloom, and Masia (1964) describe the interrelation between the categories of the cognitive and affective domains as follows:

> When one looks for relations between the subcategories of the two domains one finds that they clearly overlap. This overlap is implicit in the following descriptions of roughly parallel steps in the two continua. · · ·

> 1. The cognitive continuum begins with the student's recall and recognition of *Knowledge,*

> 1. The affective continuum begins with the student's merely *Receiving* stimuli and passively attending to it (sic). It extends through his more actively attending to it (sic),

> 2. it extends through his *Comprehension* of the knowledge,

> 2. his *Responding* to stimuli on request, willingly responding to these stimuli, and taking satisfaction in this responding,

> 3. his skill in *Application* of the knowledge that he comprehends,

> 3. his *Valuing* the phenomenon or activity so that he voluntarily responds and seeks out ways to respond,

> 4. his skill in *Analysis* of situations involving this knowledge, his skill in *Synthesis* of this knowledge into new organizations,

> 4. his *Conceptualization* of each value responded to,

> 5. his skill in *Evaluation* in that area of knowledge to judge the value of material and methods for given purposes.

> 5. his *Organization* of these values into systems and finally organizing the value complex into a single whole, a *Characterization* of the individual. (pp. 49-50)

Planning Mathematics Lessons

The observations of many mathematics teachers and the systematic research findings of educational researchers show that teaching effective mathematics lessons requires careful attention to fourteen planning activities which should be considered in selecting mathematics topics and preparing lessons. These fourteen activities can be classified into six major topics—*Mathematics Content, Learning Objectives, Learning Resources, Preassessment Strategies, Teaching/Learning Strategies,* and *Postassessment Strategies.* This section on planning mathematics lessons deals with identifying and carrying out these fourteen activities which are listed below. Subsequent chapters will treat learning resources, assessment strategies, and teaching/learning strategies in more detail. Mathematics content has been discussed in detail in Chapters 1 and 2, and learning objectives have already been considered in this chapter.

Activities in Planning Mathematics Lessons

Mathematics Content
1. Selecting and naming the topic to be studied
2. Identifying the mathematics objects in the topic
3. Sequencing each topic in a hierarchy of topics

Learning Objectives
4. Identifying cognitive objectives
5. Selecting affective objectives
6. Sharing objectives with students

Learning Resources
7. Preparing materials for student use
8. Obtaining supplemental resources

Preassessment Strategies
9. Identifying prerequisite mathematics content
10. Assessing student readiness to learn the topic

Teaching/Learning Strategies
11. Choosing an appropriate teaching strategy
12. Managing the learning environment

Postassessment Strategies
13. Assessing student learning
14. Evaluating teaching effectiveness

Mathematics Content

In many schools the selection of mathematics content is predetermined for the teacher through the selection of mathematics textbooks. It is common practice for committees of administrators and teachers, and sometimes parents, to select mathematics textbooks. Textbooks are adopted for use for periods of four to six years, which is about how long it takes for a textbook to wear out. In many cases, once a mathematics textbook is selected for a certain course, teachers are expected to teach the topics from that textbook in approximately the order in which they appear. This does not mean that no attention is given to the proper sequencing of topics since textbook writers usually have a plan for organizing their textbooks. However, in some courses, usually courses such as consumer mathematics or advanced mathematics, teachers are relatively free to choose their own topics and to sequence them in the order that they think is appropriate. Although freedom of choice may be satisfying to teachers, it does require increased responsibility and extra work on their part.

After a mathematics topic has been selected, by whatever means, it is well to give the topic a verbal label and to have students use that label to identify the topic. Several research studies, some of which are reported in the School Mathematics Study Group *Newsletter No. 39* (August 1972), indicate that meaningful verbal labels do facilitate learning of skills, concepts and principles. There are also reports in the research literature indicating that verbalizing newly learned information facilitates learning, and that verbal definitions are more effective than numerical examples in explaining students' errors to them. Names that are given to skills and principles help students recall them for use in appropriate circumstances. For example, in mastering the skill of solving triangles, students are more likely to learn and correctly use the laws of sines, cosines, and tangents if these principles are identified by name rather than presented as three nameless algorithms for solving triangles. Whenever practical in teaching mathematical skills and principles, it is well to associate each topic with a meaningful name.

For the purposes of selecting teaching strategies and facilitating learning, it is also well to identify the mathematical objects (facts, skills, concepts, and principles) contained in the mathematics content of each topic and to share this information with your students. After the mathematical objects have been identified, teaching strategies appropriate for promoting students' learning of each object can be selected. In many cases discovery strategies are inefficient in promoting meaningful comprehension of facts and skills. It may be better to choose expository methods, demonstrations and drill strategies for teaching facts and skills. Effective strategies for teaching principles are group activities, class discussions and guided discovery techniques.

When the learning objective is high level comprehension of concepts, students should know that they are expected to learn concepts in enough depth to be able to explain them to others and to apply them in certain situations. If principles, such as theorems, are to be mastered at the higher cognitive levels of analysis and synthesis, students should be told that they will be required to prove theorems. Lower level learning objectives, such as knowledge, comprehension, and application of principles, may only require students to state principles and apply them in solving certain types of problems. Learning facts, skills, concepts, and principles requires the use of different teaching/learning models and progressively higher level cognitive, as well as affective, objectives.

Properly sequencing the teaching and learning of mathematics topics is an important job for teachers, especially when a textbook with specified topic sequencing is not used. Robert Gagné has demonstrated how hierarchies of mathematics topics can be constructed and used to promote learning of facts, skills, concepts and principles. In mathematics, more than in some other subjects, it is obvious that certain topics can not be learned until certain other topics have been mastered. One can not learn to solve trigonometric equations until he or she has mastered techniques for solving algebraic equations. The concept of square root and the skill of finding square roots of numbers must be learned before the Pythagorean theorem can be applied in trigonometry.

Even though it is obvious that certain prerequisites are required for learning each new mathematics topic, teachers, at times, tend to forget or disregard this important fact. The frustrations to the teacher, trying to teach students a new skill which they seem unable to learn, may cause the teacher to question the intelligence of his or her students, instead of first trying to determine whether they have failed to learn some prerequisite skills. A large proportion of learning problems in secondary school mathematics can be traced to lack of learning or confused learning of prerequisite topics. In preparing to teach new topics, good mathematics teachers usually determine the prerequisite topics, consider whether students have mastered the prerequisites, and whenever it is appropriate, design preassessment strategies and remedial teaching techniques. Both the real and imagined pressures to "cover material" tend to obscure the absurdity of teaching topics which students are not prepared to learn and can not be expected to learn with any degree of comprehension.

Learning Objectives

Once the mathematical content of a lesson has been determined, it is helpful, both for selecting teaching strategies and facilitating meaningful learning, to formulate cognitive and affective learning objectives and to discuss these objectives with students. Research studies, some of which are cited in the SMSG Newsletter No. 39 (August 1972) show that the students of teachers trained in writing behavioral objectives learn more. Having specific objectives and sharing them with students facilitates learning. The types of cognitive and affective objectives that teachers formulate for their students are related to four other variables—the mathematical objects to be learned, the grade level of students in the class, students' stages of intellectual development, and the teaching methods to be used. Figure 4.1 is a convenient reference for the following discussion of the interrelations among these six important teaching/learning variables.

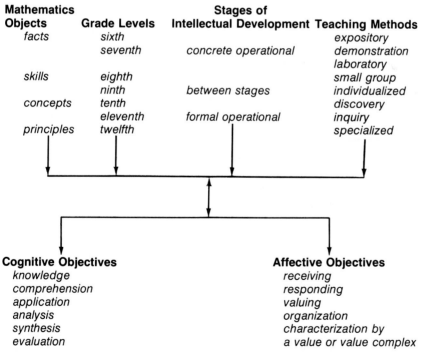

Mathematics Objects	Grade Levels	Stages of Intellectual Development	Teaching Methods
facts	sixth		expository
	seventh	concrete operational	demonstration
			laboratory
skills	eighth		small group
	ninth	between stages	individualized
concepts	tenth		discovery
	eleventh	formal operational	inquiry
principles	twelfth		specialized

Cognitive Objectives
knowledge
comprehension
application
analysis
synthesis
evaluation

Affective Objectives
receiving
responding
valuing
organization
characterization by
a value or value complex

Figure 4.1.   Some important variables in teaching and learning.

The objects of mathematics (facts, skills, concepts, and principles) are taught at all grade levels; however facts and skills tend to be emphasized in lower grades, concepts in intermediate grade levels, and principles in higher grades. Sixth, seventh, and even eighth graders tend to be concrete operational thinkers, and tenth, eleventh, and twelfth graders tend to be formal operational thinkers; although at times students at all grade levels will operate concretely. Most secondry school students will learn better if new concepts and principles are illustrated by concrete representations. Facts and skills are usually taught using expository methods, demonstrations and individualized models; concepts and principles can be approached through discovery, inquiry, and laboratory models. However, there are no hard and fast rules for matching mathematical objects, grade levels, stages of intellectual development and teaching methods.

After the mathematical objects have been selected for students at a specific grade level, who are assumed to have reached certain stages of intellectual development, the three variables of teaching method and cognitive and affective objectives should be matched to the other teaching/learning variables. Knowledge, comprehension, and application (with some degree of analysis) usually are appropriate cognitive objectives for learning facts and skills. Although concept learning does include knowledge, comprehension and application, analysis objectives are most appropriate for higher level concept formation. Appropriate cognitive objectives for principles are analysis and synthesis, and evaluation is an appropriate objective when sets of principles are to be compared or structured into mathematical systems. Whatever cognitive objectives are chosen, it is important to remember that these objectives are directly related to the depth of study of each topic, the nature of questions asked by the teacher, the type of homework assignments given to students and selection of examination questions.

As was shown on page 190, cognitive and affective objectives are interrelated. Nearly all school mathematics affective objectives are at least at the level of responding, and many are at the valuing and organization levels. Some affective objectives, especially for advanced mathematics courses, are at the lower stage of characterization by a value or value complex, which is generalized set; however few are at the higher level, which is characterization.

The following illustration of a mathematics lesson designed by considering the interrelations of mathematical objects, grade level, intellectual development, teaching method, and cognitive and affective objectives will help to clarify the relationships among these six teaching/learning variables.

The topic of this lesson is *Fourth-Dimensional Geometry*. The mathematical objects of the lesson are facts and concepts, although some students may formulate a principle or two during the lesson. This topic should be sequenced near the end of a high school geometry course since it requires some knowledge and comprehension of facts and concepts of trapezoids, cubes and frustums of pyramids. Consequently, this lesson is appropriate for eleventh or twelfth graders who are well into the formal operational stage. The purpose of the lesson is to encourage students to use inductive reasoning or spacial perception to determine the number of point vertices, line edges, plane faces, and solid cubes contained in a four-dimensional cube which is called a hypercube or tesseract. Although models of four-dimensional tesseracts obviously can not exist in our three-dimensional world, they can be studied mathematically and their three-dimensional projections can be represented. The specific observable outcome of this lesson is to have students fill in the body of the chart shown in Figure 4.2. The appropriate answers have already been included in the chart shown in this figure. The teaching strategy to be used in this lesson is a class discussion in which the teacher will employ a guided-discovery teaching model.

Geometric Figure	# of Point Vertices	# of Line Edges	# of Plane Faces	# of Solid Cubes	N-1 Dimensional Projection
Point	1	0	0	0	none
Line Segment	2	1	0	0	point
Square	4	4	1	0	line
Cube	8	12	6	1	*A* *B*
Tesseract	16	32	24	8	*C* *D*

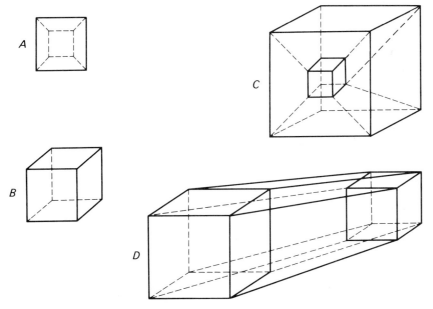

Figure 4.2.   Characteristics of some geometric figures, including a tesseract.

Cognitive performance objectives and corresponding evaluation items for this lesson are:

Objective 1. Students will know and comprehend the number of point vertices, line edges, plane faces, and solid cubes of a point, a line segment, a square, and a cube.

Measure for Objective 1. Ask each student to fill in the numbers for the first four columns and rows of the chart in Figure 4.2 and to give a reason for arriving at each number.

Objective 2. Students will analyze the information obtained for the first four columns and rows of the table in Figure 4.2 and will apply this information to completing column five and row five.

Measure for Objective 2. Ask each student to complete the fifth row and fifth column of Figure 4.2.

Affective student objectives and corresponding affective measures for his topic are:

Objective 1. Each student will be willing to participate in (respond to) the guided discovery discussion and will contribute ideas regarding appropriate data for completion of the chart. (This cognitive objective is willingness to respond.)

Measure for Objective 1. Observe the degree of participation of each student in the class discussion which is a part of this lesson.

Objective 2. Some students will express a preference for the method of observing numerical patterns to arrive at information for the chart; whereas others will show a preference for observing the characteristics of the geometric objects under consideration in order to fill in the table. (This objective is at the level of preference for a value, the value being one or the other mathematical method of approaching problems such as the one illustrated in this lesson.)

A summary of the six teaching/learning variables contained in this lesson is given in the following list:

Fourth-Dimensional Geometry

1. **Mathematical objects**—*facts* and *concepts*.
2. **Grade levels**—*eleventh* or *twelfth* grades.
3. **Stage of intellectual development**—high level *formal operational*.
4. **Teaching method**—*guided discovery*.
5. **Cognitive objectives**—*knowledge, comprehension,* and *analysis*.
6. **Affective objectives**—*willingness to respond* and *preference for a value*.

Learning Resources

After the mathematics content of a lesson and the learning objectives for the topic have been selected, the next important activity for the teacher is preparing instructional resources. In recent years many teaching and learning resources of varying quality have become available to mathematics teachers. Teachers no longer have to rely primarily upon chalk, a blackboard and the textbook. There are three general sources of instructional resources: commercially available resources which at times may be purchased out of the school system budget, resources prepared by the teacher and students and resources available within the community. Teaching and learning resources from these three sources can be used to improve students' interest in mathematics, to motivate drill and practice of skills, to illustrate and clarify mathematics concepts and principles and to provide remedial work for slower students and supplemental activities for faster or highly motivated students. Since learning takes place within each student, it is a highly individualized process. Consequently, teaching/learning strategies and activities should be individualized for students, as well. This means that the ideal teacher-student ratio is one teacher for each student or one teacher for a small group of several students. The cost of such an ideal system of public and private education is prohibitive, so most teachers usually carry out a considerable portion of their teaching with moderately large groups of students ranging in size from 20 to 40, or even larger. Consequently, the use of supplemental teaching/learning resources is, for many teachers, an excellent way to partly individualize instruction for many students.

In addition to a chalkboard, every mathematics classroom should be equipped with an overhead projector and a permanent screen, storage shelves and cabinets for books and resources, and several large bulletin boards. This is the minimal equipment necessary for a mathematics classroom, and additional equipment such as tape recorders, projectors for films, filmstrips, and slides, and duplicating or copying machines should also be available to teachers. Some schools have mathematics laboratories or resource centers, and a few schools have individualized student learning centers and computer terminals for the use of teachers and students.

There are a number of companies that distribute resources for mathematics education. Some of these resources are films, filmstrips, slides, audio and video tapes, models, sets of duplicator masters, mathematical games, individualized learning packets and materials for teaching the metric system. Information about commercially available teaching and learning resources can be obtained from current catalogs of companies distributing educational materials. Lists of these companies, as well as lists of textbook publishers who also may distribute other resources, can be obtained from high school librarians, high school administrators and public libraries. You can obtain catalogs of mathematics teaching resources by writing to each company (use school letterhead stationery if possible) and requesting a copy of their current mathematics education resources catalog. Mathematics education professional organizations such as the National Council of Teachers of Mathematics and the School Science and Mathematics Association publish resource bibliographies, which are either free or inexpensive; these bibliographies can be obtained upon request. Most schools have budgets for instructional resources (usually very limited budgets) and you may be able to have your school purchase some mathematics education resources each year. Many larger school systems and groups of school systems maintain centralized instructional resource facilities which contain resources for teaching mathematics.

Over a period of several years, you can build an adequate collection of mathematical games, models, posters, and handouts by developing them yourself and by encouraging students to produce mathematics learning resources as out-of-class projects. Many times groups of students enjoy constructing geometric posters and models or preparing attractive and informative bulletin boards on interesting topics in mathematics. Some schools have mathematics clubs for interested students, and the activities of a mathematics club may include locating and preparing resources that can be used in mathematics classrooms. The National Council of Teachers of Mathematics (NCTM) has several inexpensive publications to assist mathematics teachers in locating, developing, and using resources. Titles of some of these publications are *Instructional Aids in Mathematics* (1973), *The High School Mathematics Library* (1973), *Games and Puzzles for Elementary and Middle School Mathematics* (1975), *Mathematics Library—Elementary and Junior High School* (1973), *The Overhead Projector in the Mathematics Classroom* (1974), *Polyhedron Models for the Classroom* (1966), *Puzzles and Graphs* (1966), and *Topics for Mathematics Clubs* (1973). A complete list of NCTM publications can be obtained free of charge by writing to NCTM, 1906 Association Drive, Reston, Virginia 22091 and requesting a copy of their brochure "Current Publications."

Both human and inanimate community resources can, at times, be quite helpful to mathematics teachers. Some industries and businesses are pleased to conduct tours of their facilities for groups of students and, if given advance notice, your tourguide will usually point out mathematics in action. At times museums and other cultural centers create displays illustrating the historical development and applications of mathematics, and both public and private television present occasional specials about mathematics and science. Before scheduling a field trip for one of your classes, you should obtain approval from your school principal for the trip. He or she will assist you in making arrangements with the agency to be visited, will schedule necessary transportation, and will provide appropriate permission forms which must be signed by a parent or guardian for each student. In nearly all schools it is highly improper for a teacher to take a class on even a short field trip without clearance from the school administration. Many schools even require advance notice if a class is to be conducted outside the school building on school property.

At times it is more practical and less dangerous to invite a guest speaker from business, industry, a trade, or a profession to come to your school and speak to one or two of your classes. In fact, some professional organizations (the Mathematical Association of America is one of them) have established speakers bureaus and will provide guest speakers at no charge for school-wide programs or individual classes. Speakers can help motivate students to learn mathematics by illustrating useful and interesting applications of mathematics in their own work. It is usually well to inform your principal when you plan to have a guest speaker, and of course it is always appropriate to send a thank-you letter to your speaker shortly after he or she has addressed your class. To help your speaker prepare for his or her visit, it is well to discuss the topic, the ages of your students, their interests, and their mathematics backgrounds with the speaker well in advance of the scheduled visit.

Many communities have centralized educational resource centers which teachers and students can use to supplement their own resources. Libraries and other community agencies also may have teaching/learning resources for mathematics. Some community agencies even provide free tutorial services for students who need them. Students in local college and university teacher education programs sometimes are required, as part of their preparation for teaching, to work in schools assisting teachers and tutoring students. As a professional teacher, one of your responsibilities is to seek out and use community resources which can help you become a better teacher.

This brief discussion of locating, obtaining, and using resources for teaching and learning mathematics is by no means complete, and more will be said in Chapter 7 about this important area of mathematics education.

Preassessment and Postassessment Strategies

In planning mathematics lessons, it is important to consider methods for determining student readiness to learn the lesson and student mastery of new material after it has been taught. Since many of the same strategies are used in preassessment and postassessment, these two activities will be discussed together. The purposes of preassessment techniques are to review the prerequisite facts, skills, concepts, or principles of the lesson before it is presented and to determine whether each student has mastered the mathematical objects which will be required to learn the new material. Postassessment strategies are used to determine how well each student has learned each new mathematics topic and how effective the teaching strategy for that topic was in helping students attain the cognitive and affective objectives of the lesson. Nearly all mathematics teachers recognize the value of, and even necessity for, postassessment of learning; however many neglect the preassessment aspect of lesson planning.

Before selecting a preassessment strategy preparatory to teaching a new topic, it is well to analyze the topic for its prerequisite facts, skills, concepts, and principles. Once prerequisites have been identified, the necessary preliminary information should be reviewed with the class to find out if individual students will be able to apply the prerequisites to learning the new material. Sometimes students' performance on previous tests indicates their comprehension of prerequisites; however a brief written or oral quiz may be useful as a check. In addition to tests and quizzes, learning can be evaluated through teacher observations of student homework and classwork, class discussions, questions asked by students, students' attitudes, and group games. In most cases a brief review of previous material is a helpful preliminary activity before introducing a new topic. Some teachers begin each lesson by tying it to the previous lesson and end each lesson by introducing the following lesson.

Since preassessments are not usually used to determine grades, it is easy (but not wise) to forego them. However, very few mathematics teachers neglect postassessment; although some teachers use tests and quizzes as their only postassessment strategy. There are probably several reasons for this emphasis upon tests as a postassessment technique. First, testing students in large groups with everyone taking the same test is less time consuming than some other forms of evaluation. Second, test grades provide (or at least appear to provide) an objective measure of the relative performance of students. Third, written tests are a traditional part of our educational system and are widely accepted by students and parents as the proper method for assigning grades.

There are three types of tests in common use—norm-referenced tests, criterion-referenced tests, and domain-referenced tests. These test types vary according to the standards against which students are measured and, to some extent, the use that is made of the test scores. *Norm-referenced tests* are used to measure each student's achievement in comparison to other students. Norms are established and students are classified according to how far above or below average they are. Certain "rewards" such as high grades and approval are given to students who score well above the norm, and "punishments" such as low grades and disapproval are given to those people scoring considerably below the norm. Norm-referenced tests have been used nearly exclusively in the past and are still the predominant type of academic measure. Although student scores on norm-referenced tests can be used to determine if remedial teaching is necessary, such is not usually the practice. Unless it is obvious that hardly anyone in the class comprehended the material, teachers tend to forge ahead to new material, because they are usually required to cover a specified amount of material in each course.

Criterion-referenced tests measure each student's performance according to how close he or she comes to meeting a certain objective or achieving a certain standard. When criterion-referenced tests are used, it is usual practice to have those students who fall far short of the standard study the same material again. Students who meet or come close to the objective move ahead to new material. Criterion-referenced tests can be used to assign grades, but their primary purpose is to help determine the material that each student will cover next. So-called individualized instructional programs in mathematics usually contain criterion-referenced tests.

Recently, *domain-referenced tests* have been receiving an increasing amount of attention from some educators. This type of test evaluates students according to their absolute strengths and weaknesses. Students are not measured against each other, as they are in norm-referenced tests, and are not measured against an external standard, as is the case with criterion-referenced tests. With domain-referenced tests students are evaluated according to how well they do a task and are told which variables in the task are causing them trouble and which variables have been mastered.

Many competitive endeavors such as athletic contests or keeping one's job contain evaluation techniques of all three types. To win and keep a competitive position on an athletic team, a man or woman must be better than others competing for that position (norm-referenced evaluation), must have a high level of athletic ability (criterion-referenced evaluation), and must show proficiency on a number of variables related to that sport, work to maintain his or her strengths, and improve his or her weaknesses (domain-referenced evaluation). To play in the top professional tennis matches, Billie Jean King had to be better than other professional tennis players, had to be an exceptionally good athlete, and had to practice diligently to maintain her strengths and improve her weaknesses.

In mathematics, a report such as "you were slightly above average on this arithmetic test" indicates the use of a norm-referenced evaluation system. The statement "you solved 11 out of 17 of these problems correctly, but you should be able to get 15 out of 17 correct" probably came from a criterion-referenced evaluation system. The analysis "you found the correct sum of all of the fraction pairs that had the same denominator, but you missed most of the problems where the fractions had different denominators; it appears that you are having trouble finding common denominators; let's see what might be done about this problem" indicates a domain-referenced evaluation system.

Norm-referenced tests do require the least amount of teacher time to administer and grade; however they are also the least useful evaluation method for helping students improve their performance. Criterion-referenced tests require more individual attention for each student, but do contain a built-in provision for remedial work. Domain-referenced tests tend to be difficult and time consuming to construct and evaluate; however they are the most equitable and most helpful type of testing procedure for students. A good mathematics teacher should strike a balance among norm-referenced, criterion-referenced, and domain-referenced testing and evaluation procedures. Schools that use an *A, B, C, D, F* grading system (or a similar system) where *C* indicates average achievement, require teachers to report their evaluations of students according to a norm-referenced system. However, it is possible, although not ideal from the standpoint of student motivation, to determine norm-referenced grades by using criterion- or domain-referenced student evaluation systems in the classroom. Pass/fail and satisfactory/unsatisfactory grade reporting systems tend to be more supportive of criterion- and domain-referenced classroom evaluation procedures. Since preassessments are not usually used to determine students' grades, it is easier to justify the use of criterion- and domain-referenced tests here than it is in postassessment testing.

One should remember that tests are not the only form of student assessment. Based upon specific cognitive and affective objectives, class discussion, group work, boardwork, question-and-answer sessions, homework, students' facial expressions, term projects, class participation and mathematics laboratories are all valid and useful approaches to evaluating student mastery of mathematical facts, skills, concepts, and principles.

Not only is it necessary for teachers to evaluate students, but teachers should also evaluate their own professional development, their attitudes toward students and the appropriateness of their teaching methods. The first, and possibly best, evaluation of a teacher is the cognitive and affective performances of his or her students; but it is not adequate to use students' cognitive performances as the sole measure of their teacher's effectiveness. It is quite possible for a teacher who dislikes teaching and students to use authoritarian, fear-inspiring methods to effect oustanding mastery of mathematical facts and skills; however the affective consequences on some students exposed to such teacher personalities and methods can be devastating. There are many instances where inhumane or unfeeling teachers have distorted students' perceptions of education and their values toward learning. In the most extreme cases, "brainwashing" in war and politics has shown that tyrannical methods can produce rather dramatic cognitive outcomes, if one is not concerned with their affective consequences to individuals.

One good, informal way to evaluate your own professional development is to make a list of objectives together with evaluation questions for yourself and answer these questions at the end of each school week. Becoming an outstanding teacher requires a large number of small steps taken over a period of at least five years. Since the objective of excellence as a teacher is such a long-range goal, it is very easy to avoid or procrastinate taking those small steps one at a time. I have talked with several teachers who are aware of the value of individualizing instruction for each student, but who never attempt it because it would take so long to develop materials and the process would never be completed.

Some suggested activities containing implied objectives for improving your professional development are:

1. Prepare one "super lesson" each week, containing each of the fourteen activities in planning mathematics lessons which are listed on page 335.
2. Locate and obtain one good instructional resource each week and use it in one of your classes.
3. Prepare, either alone, with other teachers, or with students, one good teaching resource each week and use it.
4. Read at least three articles each week in a professional journal such as *The Mathematics Teacher, The Arithmetic Teacher,* or *School Science and Mathematics.*
5. Prepare one good student evaluation procedure each week and use it in one of your classes.
6. Participate in one extra-curricular activity each week.
7. Learn a new mathematics skill, concept, or principle each week.
8. Try one unique teaching/learning strategy each week, evaluate its effectiveness, and modify it if your evaluation indicates ways to improve it.
9. Assess your attitudes toward teaching and students each week. If you have any unprofessional attitudes (and you will at times when things go wrong) analyze their causes and consider ways to correct your negative attitudes.

You can also evaluate your teaching effectiveness more specifically on a day-to-day basis by observing student attitudes and behaviors in your classroom. If some students in your class consistently appear to be bored and unresponsive, you should attempt to involve them in classroom activities. The press of teaching five or six mathematics classes, each of which has 25 or more students, five days a week makes it very easy to avoid attending to those students who do not participate in classroom activities. Having a number of students working problems at the chalkboard at one time is an efficient way to observe error patterns of individual students and can indicate skills which few students have mastered. Checking and evaluating student homework assignments is another good way to observe the effectiveness of your teaching methods on a day-to-day basis. Of course students' test results should not only be used as a basis for calculating grades, they should also be used as an evaluation of the effectiveness of your teaching.

Even though student preassessment and postassessment strategies and self-evaluation procedures can be difficult and time consuming, they are very important activities in teaching and learning and should be an integral part of every lesson, topic and unit plan for teaching mathematics. Without systematic and perceptive evaluation of teaching and learning in the classroom, little can be done with respect to improving these very important human endeavors. More will be said in Chapter 7 about preassessment and postassessment strategies in mathematics teaching.

Teaching/Learning Strategies

Selecting mathematics content, setting learning objectives, obtaining resources, and preparing preassessment and postassessment strategies are important activities in planning mathematics lessons. As a group, these activities are factors in the selection of an appropriate teaching/learning strategy for each lesson. In planning teaching/learning strategies, consideration should be given to both the teacher's activities in teaching the lesson and managing the learning environment and the students' participation in classroom activities. A list of general teaching methods is included in Figure 4.1 on page 193. Expository, demonstration, laboratory, small group, individualized, discovery and inquiry teaching methods will be defined and discussed briefly in this section. Since the choice of a particular teaching/learning strategy is closely related to the mathematical objects that are to be learned, specific models for teaching facts, skills, concepts, principles and generalized problem-solving procedures will be discussed and illustrated in some detail in Chapters 5 and 6.

Planning Mathematics Lessons

Expository Strategies

Expository teaching methods (sometimes called lectures), which can be used to teach facts, skills, concepts, and principles, are teacher-centered or teacher-dominated approaches to instruction. Expository strategies are the most common of the various methods used to teach mathematics and are effective strategies when used properly. In fact, based upon their own research and reviews of other research studies, the School Mathematics Study Group (August 1972) claims that "no non-expository procedures have been demonstrated to be more effective, overall, than exposition." (p. 14) This is not to say that expository teaching is always the best method and should be used for all students in all mathematics classes. What is implied here is that when used properly in appropriate situations, expository methods can be effective methods for teaching mathematics.

Typical teacher and student classroom activities in expository teaching include short lectures by the teacher, teacher presentations of concepts and demonstrations of skills, questions directed from students to the teacher, teacher questions directed to students to determine if they comprehend mathematical objects in the lesson, and student note taking. Related activities include students' working on problems (either individually or in small groups) at their desks or at the chalkboard and an occasional class discussion of a concept or principle.

David Ausubel's advance organizer approach to introducing a new topic is a type of expository teaching technique. In this approach a new topic is organized at a high level of generality, abstractness, and inclusiveness and is presented to students in this highly structured form as an introduction to new material. It is thought that Ausubel's approach will help students formulate a high-level mental construct which will assist them in accepting, accommodating and assimilating the various elements of a new topic into a meaningful structure in their minds.

Demonstrations and Laboratory Strategies

Demonstrations and laboratory strategies are related to expository methods; however they usually result in a higher level of student involvement than is found in expository teaching. Demonstrations and laboratory methods are used to teach skills, concepts, principles and some problem-solving techniques.

When a demonstration strategy is used, in teaching a skill or a problem-solving technique, the teacher, or possibly a student, may use the chalkboard or transparencies on an overhead projector to illustrate the skill or technique. Teacher demonstrations of general strategies for solving word problems or for solving applied mathematics problems can result in a high degree of student involvement in the lesson and may facilitate learning of general and transferable problem-solving skills. Students can demonstrate the principle of mathematical induction, principles of geometric proof, and methods of doing geometric constructions to each other through group discussions and boardwork. Many mathematical principles can be demonstrated by using a variety of examples to deduce or verify general principles. Junior high school students can demonstrate many important principles of plane geometry to themselves by constructing and measuring geometric figures of varying shapes and sizes. The approximate value of *pi* can be demonstrated by constructing and measuring circles; the value of $(a + b)^2$ can be demonstrated geometrically by using squares and rectangles with dimensions *a* by *b, b* by *b*, and *a* by *a*; general ratio and proportion principles for similar triangles can be demonstrated by constructing and comparing the sides and angles of triangles; the Pythagorean theorem can be demonstrated geometrically; and formulas for the areas of triangles, trapezoids, and parallelograms can also be demonstrated geometrically. At times it is better to prepare demonstration activities that can be carried out individually by students, rather than relying solely upon teacher-conducted demonstrations.

Animated sound and color films can be used to demonstrate concepts and principles of continuity, and limiting processes in algebra, geometry and calculus. Films can also be useful in demonstrating properties of algebraic and trigonometric functions through animated representations of their graphs. Catalogs containing lists of mathematics films can usually be obtained from libraries and instructional resource centers. Most schools have copies of the catalogs of the larger educational film distributors. The National Council of Teachers of Mathematics sells a publication called *Audiovisual Material in Mathematics* (1971), which is a useful reference.

For many years science laboratories have been regarded as indispensable components of secondary school science programs; however mathematics laboratories have only recently been considered to be appropriate facilities for school mathematics programs. A growing number of schools, especially larger schools, are setting up mathematics laboratories which are usually called mathematics resource centers. Mathematics resource centers typically contain books on fascinating topics in mathematics, history of mathematics, mathematical games and puzzles, and methods for constructing plane and solid geometric figures. Resource centers may also have geometric models, measuring instruments, various types of audio/visual materials, educational games, construction materials, demonstration devices, and some even contain computer terminals. In schools that have mathematics resource centers, students are permitted to spend their free periods in the center and may work on individualized projects at the center during mathematics class periods or before and after school.

If your school does not have a mathematics laboratory or resource center, you can, over a period of several years, turn your classroom into a mini-laboratory by accumulating and using mathematics education resources of the types mentioned in the preceding paragraph. Even if resources for mathematics education are severely limited in your school, you can develop pencil-and-paper experiments and laboratory exercises. For example, data collection and evaluation experiments can be carried out through student surveys or coin-tossing and dice-rolling experiments; measuring activities for learning the metric system can be done in class; formulas for areas of geometric figures can be discovered by cutting geometric shapes into pieces and reconstructing the pieces into figures whose area formulas are known. More will be said about laboratory resources and activities in Chapter 6.

Individualized and Small Group Strategies

Although expository teaching and teacher-centered demonstrations are good strategies for introducing facts, skills and concepts, they are not particularly effective in promoting meaningful in-depth learning of mathematical skills and principles. At certain stages in learning some mathematics topics, students need to internalize and apply the mathematics they have been taught by working individually or in small groups. After the teacher has introduced a new topic, students should be permitted to work on problems or laboratory activities in small groups. Even though the statement ''the best way to learn something is to teach it'' has become a cliché, it is, nevertheless, at least partly true. Students can learn a great deal of mathematics from each other and can identify their own areas of confusion by attempting to explain skills, concepts and principles to other students. Many teachers like to prepare problem and activity sheets for students to work on in small groups. This strategy can help to identify specific problems that individual students are having and can give the teacher more time to spend with those students who are having learning difficulties.

In general, individualized instruction is instruction which attends to the distinctive learning styles, learning difficulties, and mastery levels of individual students. While most teachers know that they should give attention to the specific needs of each student, large classes and heavy teaching schedules can, at times, make individualized teaching a difficult concept to apply. A number of individualized instructional programs have been developed for school mathematics courses and are sold to school systems at costs ranging from $5 to as much as $100 or more per student per course. Although some of these programs are little more than programmed textbooks, others are complex and provide for sophisticated differentiation of activities from student to student. Among such programs, those which come closest to being truly individualized contain hundreds of branch points where students, depending upon their performances on tests, study different materials, engage in different activities, and use different instructional resources. Such programs contain sets of student workbooks and study guides subdivided into topics and units for several different student ability levels, lists of cognitive and affective performance objectives for each topic and ability level, pretests and posttests for topics and levels, guides for using the programs and selecting appropriate paths through each unit for various students, a small reference library containing multiple copies of each book, audio/visual materials, and sometimes even instructional hardware such as individualized audio/video learning carrels or computer terminals. Some of these programs are effective for teaching facts and skills and do an adequate job with some concepts and lower level principles; however some are not very effective and tend to dominate the learning environment to such an extent that activities outside the program are difficult to schedule. When the best of these programs are used intelligently, and not dogmatically, with provision for large and small group discussions, interactions, and demonstrations, they can be useful and effective approaches to teaching and learning most secondary school mathematics subjects.

For the majority of mathematics teachers who do not have access to a good commercial individualized instructional program, individualizing instruction can be accomplished, to a considerable extent, through intelligent and perceptive selection and management of learning resources and the use of diverse teaching/learning strategies. A judicious blend of lectures, group activities, individualized study, demonstrations and laboratory activities, selected according to students' abilities and personalities, can be used to provide a degree of individualization of teaching. Homework assignments and student work in class can be used by the teacher to identify learning problems. Small group activities can be used to permit students to assist each other and can provide extra time for the teacher to work with those students who may have serious learning problems. More about ways to individualize instruction will be said in Chapter 5.

Discovery and Inquiry Strategies

Discovery and inquiry teaching methods are more specialized teaching strategies than expository, group and individualized methods. Discovery lessons are usually carried out in an expository mode or a small group setting. Inquiry strategies can be employed with expository, group, or individualized methods. Discovery and inquiry strategies are related to the extent that both require students to find something out, formulate an hypothesis, or arrive at a conclusion more or less on their own. When a discovery lesson is used, the precise form of the mathematical object to be discovered is known to the teacher and he or she guides the students in discovering the object—guided discovery. A teacher using an inquiry strategy also wants students to discover a mathematical object; however the study of the discovery process itself is an important consideration in an inquiry lesson. One purpose of inquiry lessons is for students to learn scientific methods of inquiry and be able to apply them in other situations.

When teaching a guided discovery lesson, teachers often use a modified expository lesson, which is a class discussion, or laboratory lesson where students work together in small groups on an activity specified by the teacher. The teacher has predetermined a mathematical problem-solving skill, concept, or principle that he or she hopes to have the class discover, partly on their own, with the teacher directing the discussion, asking questions, and answering student questions. It is thought by some educators that this partially independent discovery of a mathematical truth will be interesting and even exciting for students, will increase their motivation to learn mathematics, and will result in more meaningful learning. A disadvantage of the discovery method of teaching is that it requires more time for an entire class or small group of students to discover a mathematical object than it does to present the object to them. Of course, a completely unguided discovery could take days to make or may never be made by a class. Teachers usually begin a discovery lesson by asking a question of the class or setting an activity for them. Then the students discuss the question or work at the activity with the teacher guiding the discussion or activity in the proper direction by asking pointed questions and supplying crucial information when it appears that students may not perceive its relevance to the task at hand. After the hoped-for discovery has been made, the next objective is to verify its validity, either by testing out a newly discovered method or proving a newly discovered theorem. Following is a list of topics from arithmetic, algebra, geometry and trigonometry that lend themselves to guided discovery lessons. Of course, in the interest of learning more than a few mathematical objects, it would not be wise to attempt to have students discover every interesting mathematical principle. However, occasional use of guided discovery is appropriate for promoting learning and increasing motivation.

Some Topics for Guided Discovery Lessons

Arithmetic

1. By being instructed to search for patterns which suggest a formula for summing number sequences, students can discover the formula $S = \dfrac{n(a + 1)}{2}$ for the sum of an arithmetic progression, which is a topic usually reserved for algebra classes.

2. Arithmetic students can discover the formulas for the area of a triangle, the area of a trapezoid, and the area of a parallelogram if appropriate guidance is given by the teacher.

3. Students can discover general principles about even, odd, prime and composite numbers if the teacher asks appropriate questions. For example, the sum of two prime numbers (excluding 2) is always a composite number and the product of two prime numbers (excluding 2) is always an odd number.

Algebra

1. When shown how to add and subtract in the set of integers modulo n (i.e., when taught modular arithmetic) students can discover the field properties of arithmetic in the integers modulo 3 or the integers modulo 5.

2. With quite a lot of assistance, students can discover the quadratic formula.

3. Students can discover the algebraic properties of matrix arithmetic for two-by-two matrices over the real numbers.

4. By studying graphs of quadratic functions, students may discover that the x-coordinate of the maximum or minimum point of the graph of a quadratic function $y = ax^2 + bx + c$ is $\dfrac{-b}{2a}$.

Trigonometry

1. By constructing and observing graphs of trigonometric functions of the form $y = a\sin(bx)$ students may discover that the period of this function is $\dfrac{2\pi}{|b|}$ and the amplitude is $|a|$.

2. With proper guidance students can discover the Law of Sines.

3. Students can discover a large number of trigonometric identities.

Geometry

1. By properly folding and cutting apart paper triangles, students can discover some of the triangle theorems of plane geometry.

2. Students can discover methods for bisecting angles, constructing perpendicular bisectors of line segments, and constructing a line tangent to a circle at a given point on the circle by using a straight edge and compass as tools.

3. Many interesting theorems from plane geometry and their proofs can be formulated through guided discovery lessons.

According to J. Richard Suchman (1962) the objectives of inquiry teaching/learning strategies are:

> to develop the cognitive skills of searching and data processing, and the concepts of logic and causality that would enable the individual child to inquire autonomously and productively; to give the children a new approach to learning by which they could build concepts through the analysis of concrete episodes and the discovery of relationships between variables; and to capitalize on two intrinsic sources of motivation, the rewarding experience of discovery and the excitement inherent in autonomous searching and data processing. (p. 28)

The procedures of an inquiry strategy reflect the general processes which people use in order to study their environment. In a classroom inquiry process four interacting, complementary activities are carried out: (1) The teacher presents students with a situation, question, puzzle, or seeming paradox. (2) Students, working individually, in small groups, or as a class, determine procedures and collect information that may be useful in studying the situation, resolving the question, or solving the puzzle or paradox. (3) Students reorganize their knowledge according to the information obtained in step 2. (4) The class conducts an analysis of their inquiry methods and procedures in an attempt to find generalized methods which can be applied in other inquiry situations. These four activities are an approximate model of the so-called scientific method of studying variables in our environment, and inquiry teaching/learning strategies may help students develop scientific inquiry skills.

In a guided discovery lesson, the teacher usually takes a major role in directing the discovery process; students rely partly upon their own initiative and partly upon direction from the teacher. In an inquiry lesson students are challenged to formulate and test their own hypotheses and to decide for themselves what additional information is necessary for resolving the issue at hand. No attempt is made by the teacher to pass judgment upon the students' hypotheses or volunteer useful information. Students quickly realize that they must decide for themselves what kind of data they need and determine how and where to get this data. The responsibility and control of the learning situation rests with the students; the teacher functions as a resource person who may be able to provide information when specifically requested to do so by students.

Step 1 in an inquiry lesson requires the teacher to present students with a problem which lends itself to study and resolution by methods of scientific inquiry. Questions such as "What is the population of the world?" and "How do you divide pairs of fractions?", which are fact and skill oriented do not lend themselves to study using an inquiry strategy. The following questions are more appropriate for consideration in an inquiry lesson:

1. We know that the formula for the distance between two points x and y on a straight line is $d_1 = \sqrt{(x - y)^2}$, and that the formula for the distance between two points (x_1, y_1) and (x_2, y_2) in a plane is $d_p = \sqrt{(x_1 - x_2)^2 + (y_1 - y_2)^2}$. Can you find a formula for the distance between two points in a three-dimensional space? Would it be possible to determine formulas for the distances between points in higher-dimensional mathematical spaces?

2. The problem of finding the number of point vertices, line edges, plane

faces, and solid cubes contained in a hyper-cube (tesseract) and a hyper-tesseract is an appropriate problem for an inquiry lesson, provided geometric models of cube and tesseract projections are available.

3. For an arithmetic class, the problem of estimating how much water flows from the Mississippi River in one year could be solved using an inquiry strategy.

4. After the trigonometric sine and cosine functions have been defined as functions on a unit circle, the activity of defining and determining the properties of two similarly defined functions on a unit square, which is formed by connecting the four points $(1, 0)$, $(0, 1)$, $(-1, 0)$, and $(0, -1)$ in pairs on a rectangular coordinate system, can be carried out using an inquiry approach.

5. Prepare four dice of different colors with the following numbers on their faces.

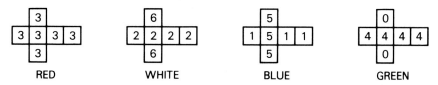

Ask students to determine the various probabilities of one die coming to rest with a larger number facing up than the number facing up on another die, when all combinations of pairs of dice are considered. Some students may decide to approach this problem empirically by tossing pairs of dice a number of times and tallying the results; whereas others may elect to consider the problem using the a priori approach of comparing the faces of pairs of dice. However, the class should be permitted to determine and apply its own approach to studying the problem.

In Step 2 students formulate procedures for solving the problem and collect the information that is necessary for finding the solution. It is the responsibility of the teacher to anticipate the resources that will be required by the class and to have them available in the classroom for use when students request them. For example, a large map of the United States and an almanac of geographic information might be requested by students who are solving the Mississippi River problem. The tesseract problem will require advance preparation of geometric models. In an inquiry lesson the teacher should not volunteer information and provide resources until the class requests them, and then only the specific data and resources asked for by students should be provided.

Step 3, reorganization of knowledge, is primarily an internal process; however the class may choose to verbalize their findings and conclusions as part of a brief summary of their solution to the problem.

Step 4 is the only teacher-directed step in the inquiry process. After the problem has been solved, the teacher should lead the class in a discussion of the general processes and procedures which were used in solving the problem; that is, students should consider the nature of the inquiry process itself. This step may help the class formulate generalized problem-solving strategies which can be applied to other mathematics problems and to problems outside the school.

Inquiry lessons are an appropriate means of teaching general problem-solving approaches; however many teachers who are accustomed to teacher-directed classes find inquiry lessons difficult to teach, or more appropriately, they find inquiry lessons difficult *not* to teach. It is hard for a teacher, who feels that his or her job is to *teach*, to refrain from participating in the Step 2 activities of formulating problem solving strategies, gathering information and solving the problem. This step can also be difficult for students who have been conditioned to regard the teacher as the primary classroom source of procedures and information.

Managing the Learning Environment

After the teaching strategy for a mathematics lesson has been selected, its success is dependent upon the teacher's skill in managing the classroom environment. Managing a classroom includes attending to the needs of individual students, using resources appropriately, asking good questions, observing students and their work for indications of confusion or error patterns, covering material efficiently but not so rapidly that students fall behind in assimilating information, holding the interest of students, and maintaining student discipline. Many, if not most, discipline or behavior problems occur among students because the teacher is ill-prepared for class, disorganized, lacking in self-confidence, pacing the lesson too slowly or too rapidly, appears to be uninterested in teaching the lesson, or does not provide activities to encourage each student to participate in the lesson. This is not to say that all discipline problems are inadvertently created by the teacher. Some behavioral problems are due to emotional disturbances of students, students' desire for attention, and other factors within students. Teachers who treat students respectfully, humanely, fairly, considerately, and consistently are usually not confronted with a large number of discipline problems. However, there are some schools and some classes where students are labelled as intellectually slow, troublemakers, unmotivated. Many of these students have poor self-images and even poorer images of the educational system in which they are forced to participate. A higher than average number of discipline problems and serious behavioral problems can be expected among these students and special methods may be required to deal with them. More will be said about motivation and discipline in Chapter 7.

Summary

Preparing to teach a mathematics lesson or topic, which includes planning the lesson and rehearsing the lesson, is not a distinctly separate act from teaching; it is an integral part of teaching. As you have probably observed, a large proportion of the information in this chapter about preparing to teach mathematics lessons and topics is concerned with procedures for teaching lessons. Some of this information will be discussed again in more detail in Chapters 5, 6, and 7 which deal with models for teaching, developing effective learning environments, and methods of evaluation.

This chapter concludes with a lesson plan illustrating the application of each of the 14 *Activities in Planning Mathematics Lessons* which are listed on page 191. The lesson plan presented below is considerably more detailed than reasonably could be expected from teachers who have to prepare several lesson plans each day. However, people who are preparing to teach should write several lesson plans containing this much detail, and experienced teachers should on occasion write a lesson plan as detailed as this one to be sure that they are attending to each one of the 14 planning activities. Many of these planning activities are done mentally by experienced teachers, whose written lesson plans may need to be only a few sentences or a brief outline. A lesson plan is much more a mental activity than a written script for teaching a class. After a more detailed mental lesson plan has been formulated, many teachers find that a few notes on a page are adequate memory-joggers for use in teaching the lesson. Inexperienced teachers usually need to prepare more detailed written outlines and sets of notes for use in the classroom. However, even a very inexperienced teacher will find that there is little time while teaching a class to sort through a dozen pages of notes to determine what he or she had planned to do next in class. Many journals such as the *Mathematics Teacher* contain articles that are tantamount to long lesson plans. These articles and the detailed lesson plans which you may have written can be reviewed shortly before you plan to use them in teaching a class. A brief review of a plan, together with making a few notes, usually is adequate preparation for a lesson which you have taught previously, evaluated, and modified based upon your evaluation.

A Lesson Plan for a Topic from Statistics

Mathematical Content: This lesson is appropriate for use in an advanced mathematics course or a probability and statistics course. The *name* of the topic is *using chi square to test a statistical hypothesis.* The *mathematical object* of this lesson is a *principle,* the principle of testing a statistical hypothesis. This topic could be sequenced near the end of a secondary school advanced mathematics course or near the middle of a probability and statistics course.

Learning Objectives: The *cognitive learning objectives* of this lesson are: (1) Students will *know* the principle of statistically testing hypotheses. (2) Students will *comprehend* the nature and structure of the chi-square statistical test. (3) Students will *apply* the principle of a chi-square statistical test to interpreting sets of numerical data which are organized in frequency counts.

The *affective learning objectives* of this lesson are: (1) Students will be willing to participate in the statistical experiment of this lesson; that is, they will be *willing to respond.* (2) Students will *accept the value* of a statistical test for interpreting sets of numerical data obtained by tallies.

Both sets of objectives, the cognitive and affective objectives, should be shared with students. The class should also be told that the goal of this lesson is for them to learn to interpret sets of information gathered through surveys, opinion polls, and observations.

Learning Resources: The learning resources needed for this lesson are (1) enough copies of a statistical chi-square table so that each student will have access to a chi-square table and (2) a standard die (a cubical die with the numerals one through six on the faces) for use during the lesson. Chi-square tables are found in most handbooks of mathematical tables and statistics textbooks. Inexpensive plastic dice can be purchased in toy stores or through the mail from suppliers of educational resources.

Preassessment Strategies: To participate in this lesson and comprehend the chi-square statistical test, students should understand the concept of probability. The following questions could be presented either orally or as a written quiz to determine whether students have the prerequisites for this lesson:

1. When a fair coin is tossed, what is the *a priori* probability that it will land with its head facing up?
2. If a fair die is tossed, what is the *a priori* probability that it will come to rest with a four facing up?
3. When a fair coin is tossed 10 times, how many times ''should'' it land head-up? Will it always land head-up that many times when tossed 10 times?
4. If a fair die is rolled 36 times, how many times would you expect *one* to come up? *two* to come up? each of *three, four, five* and *six* to come up? Will this *always* happen when a die is rolled 36 times? Will it usually happen?
5. How many times would a die have to be rolled so that it would come to rest with each face up exactly one-sixth of the time?

Teaching/Learning Strategies: Since this is an introductory lesson for an unfamiliar principle, an *expository teaching strategy* will be used.

Begin the lesson by presenting the following situation to the class:

Suppose that a crooked gambler, who is not a law-abiding citizen, was making her way through a dark alley to a clandestine dice game. Being a crooked gambler, she was carrying a crooked (loaded) die in her right hand while traversing the gloomy alley. All of a sudden, she tripped over a trash can and fell into a pile of empty orange boxes, which broke her fall. However, she nearly dropped her very expensive (and only) loaded die during her fall. Picking herself up, she put the loaded die into the right side pocket of her chartreuse motorcycle jacket and continued on. As she approached the site of the clandestine dice game she reached into the right side pocket of her chartreuse motorcycle jacket only to discover, to her horror, that there were two dice in that pocket. She had forgotten to remove her fair die from the jacket, and now she had two dice which looked exactly alike. However one was fair and the other was loaded. Having flunked arithmetic 101½ and dropped out of school at a tender age, she knew of no way to discover which die was loaded, so she took a chance and picked one die to use in the crooked dice game. The sad end of this story is that she picked the wrong die and lost all of her grocery money in the dice game.

Ask the class to suggest ways in which our heroine could have determined which die was loaded. Someone might suggest a strategy such as ''roll one of the dice 36 times and if each number doesn't come up six times, the die is loaded.'' If another student does not find the fallacy in this strategy, point out that we can not expect even a fair die to always land with six of each number showing when it is tossed 36 times. It is possible that another student may suggest rolling the die many times, for instance 3600 times. Even then we could not expect each face to show up exactly 600 times; also, by the time our heroine tossed a die 3600 times, the dice game would be over and she would have missed it.

After the students have had a few minutes to consider this problem, tell them that you will show them a mathematical strategy for resolving the loaded-die issue, which is called a chi-square test of a statistical hypothesis. Explain that a general strategy is to sample each die by rolling it a number of times and to compare the results; that is, compare the two sampling distributions. If the two dice have greatly differing distributions, then one is probably loaded. The statistical test called a chi-square test will give us the probability that the two dice are different. If we find a high probability that the dice are different, then we can conclude that the differences are probably *not* due to chance and can observe the two sampling distributions to determine which die is loaded.

Have students in the class take turns rolling a fair die and recording the results until they have made approximately 100 observations. Take the students' data and enter it into a table such as the one shown in Figure 4.3. This table contains a set of data for two dice; one die is known to be fair and the other is suspected of being loaded. Since you probably do not have a loaded die, use the data for the first die in Table 4.3 to represent the suspected loaded die; however use your students' data obtained from a fair die to replace the data for the second die in Figure 4.3.

Assist the class in formulating the following hypotheses about the data in Figure 4.3. The first hypothesis is that neither of the two dice is loaded; this hypothesis is called the *null hypothesis*. The second hypothesis is that one of the dice is loaded; this hypothesis is called the *research hypothesis*. Explain to the class that a *significant difference* between two sets of observed data is a difference that is probably *not* due to chance. A non-significant difference is one that probably *is* due to chance.

Next, discuss the chi-square data analysis table shown in Figure 4.4 with your students. Explain that the numbers in the cells labeled *Expected* are the frequencies that one would expect to find if the two dice behave in the same way. The chi-square test compares the combined differences between the observed number in each cell and the expected number in that particular cell. The corresponding expected number for each observed number in each cell is found by taking the product of the row sum and column sum for the respective row and column containing the observed number, and dividing this product by the total number of observations, which is 230 for this illustration. For example, the observed number 32 in the first row, third column has an expected number 26.1, which is calculated by $\frac{120 \times 50}{230} = 26.1$.

Dice	# of ones	# of twos	# of threes	# of fours	# of fives	# of sixes
First die	15	14	32	29	16	14
Second die	18	22	18	16	19	17

Figure 4.3. A sampling distribution table for two dice.

		#1	#2	#3	#4	#5	#6	Observed totals for rows
First die	Observed	15	14	32	29	16	14	120
	Expected	17.2	18.8	26.1	23.5	18.3	16.2	
Second die	Observed	18	22	18	16	19	17	110
	Expected	15.8	17.2	23.9	21.5	16.7	14.8	
Observed totals for columns		33	36	50	45	35	31	230

Figure 4.4. A chi-square data-analysis table for a sampling distribution of two dice.

Chi-square, the measure of the composite difference between each observed value and its corresponding expected value, is computed by squaring the difference between each observed and corresponding expected value, dividing the result by the expected value, and summing the results; that is, chi-square $= \sum_{i=1}^{n} \frac{(O_i - E_i)^2}{E_i}$ where n represents the number of cells (12 cells in this case), O_i an observed value, and E_i an expected value. Have the class compute chi-square for the data in Figure 4.4. The value of chi-square is given by:

$$\text{Chi-square} = \frac{(15 - 17.2)^2}{17.2} + \frac{(14 - 18.8)^2}{18.8} + \frac{(32 - 26.1)^2}{26.1} + \frac{(29 - 23.5)^2}{23.5}$$

$$+ \frac{(16 - 18.3)^2}{18.3} + \frac{(14 - 16.2)^2}{16.2} + \frac{(18 - 15.8)^2}{15.8} + \frac{(22 - 17.2)^2}{17.2} +$$

$$\frac{(18 - 23.9)^2}{23.9} + \frac{(16 - 21.5)^2}{21.5} + \frac{(19 - 16.7)^2}{16.7} + \frac{(17 - 14.8)^2}{14.8}$$

$$\text{Chi-square} = 9.68$$

Before using a chi-square table to look for the value 9.68, it is necessary to calculate the number of degrees of freedom for the table in Figure 4.3. The number of degrees of freedom for a table such as this is $(r - 1) \times (c - 1)$ where r is the number of rows of observations in the table and c is the number of columns. In this problem the degrees of freedom is $(2 - 1)(6 - 1) = 5$. A chi-square table shows that a chi-square value of 9.236 for 5 degrees of freedom has a probability of 0.10 of occurring due to chance. A chi-square of 11.070 has a probability of 0.05 of occurring due to chance. Since our value of chi-square is 9.68, we can reject our null hypothesis that neither of the two dice is loaded in favor of our research hypothesis that one of the dice is loaded. The value of chi-square is large enough so that the probability that neither of the two dice is loaded is less than 0.10. By examining the observed values in the cells in Figure 4.3, it appears that the first die is loaded to favor three and four. Our chi-square test does give statistical support for the observation that one of the dice is loaded.

Near the end of this lesson discuss with the class the logical nature of a chi-square test for significant differences among distributions. Also discuss some applications of chi-square hypothesis testing in analyzing and evaluting the results of opinion polls and surveys. Be sure to point out that even though we could observe the data for the first die in Figure 4.3 and conclude that the die was loaded, the chi-square test tells us how confident we can be in making that decision.

Postassessment Strategies: As a strategy to determine if students know, understand, and can apply a chi-square test of a statistical hypothesis, have your students choose an issue and survey other students on that issue. For example, the question ''who do you think would make the best president of the United States'' with the names of several public figures as choices could be asked. A null hypothesis such as ''there is no difference between males and females in preference for president of the United States'' could be studied using the chi-square test on the data collected in the survey. Permit the class to select its own research question, or small groups of students may choose to study different questions through a survey of students or even adults. Be sure that all students are involved in collecting data and analyzing the data using a chi-square test. Also, offer enough guidance to students when they are choosing a topic for their survey so that they will formulate testable null and research hypotheses.

Students' success in meeting the cognitive and affective objectives for this lesson can be verified by observing their postassessment data collection activities and by checking their chi-square analysis of the data that they collect. Students who successfully design a study, carry out a survey, and complete a correct chi-square analysis of data will have demonstrated their knowledge and comprehension of the principle of a statistical test and their ability to apply this knowledge and comprehension to interpreting sets of data using a chi-square analysis.

You can evaluate the effectiveness of this lesson, and your effectiveness in teaching the lesson, by observing students for indications of confusion while you are presenting the lesson as well as by evaluating their success in carrying out their surveys and data analyses. Some possible sources of student questions during this lesson are the meaning of degrees of freedom, the origin of the formula for computing the value of chi-square, and the correct way to interpret the chi-square table.

You might also point out that another strategy for determining the probability that a single die is loaded is to compare an actual distribution found by rolling that die many times to a theoretical distribution obtained by hypothesizing that each face on the die should come to rest facing up the same number of times as every other face. For example comparing the data for the first die in Figure 4.3 to a set of a priori data would yield the chi-square data analysis table shown in Figure 4.5. In this case the results of tossing a die suspected of being loaded are compared to a set of a priori expected values for a hypothetical die which is assumed to behave perfectly.

You might want to have your class formulate null and research hypotheses for the data in Figure 4.5 and use a chi-square test with five degrees of freedom to test this pair of hypotheses.

Dice	# of ones	# of twos	# of threes	# of fours	# of fives	# of sixes
Actual die	15	14	32	29	16	14
Hypothetical die	20	20	20	20	20	20

Figure 4.5. A sampling distribution table for a single die.

Things To Do

1. Benjamin Bloom's Taxonomy of Educational Objectives contains six cognitive objectives—knowledge, comprehension, application, analysis, synthesis, and evaluation. For all six cognitive objectives and for each of the subjects—arithmetic, algebra, geometry, and trigonometry—write two specific cognitive objectives with corresponding test items to measure each objective.

2. Develop two interesting and relevant applied problems for each of arithmetic, algebra, geometry, and trigonometry and several applied problems for higher level courses such as probability, statistics, and analysis.

3. Pages 175-176 contain a list of problems illustrating applications of matheics. Write an appropriate cognitive performance objective for each of these problems.

4. For each of the thirteen levels of affective objectives listed on page 182, write two specific mathematics objectives and corresponding measures which illustrate the application of that affective objective in teaching and learning mathematics.

5. Select a mathematics skill, concept, or principle and write a lesson plan which uses an expository teaching strategy for presenting that skill, concept or principle. Include each of the fourteen activities for planning a mathematics lesson, which are listed on page 191, in your plan.

6. Prepare a discovery lesson plan for teaching a specific mathematical principle which includes the fourteen activities for planning a lesson that are given on page 191.

7. Choose a topic from a secondary school mathematics textbook and plan an inquiry teaching/learning strategy for teaching that topic. Include each of the fourteen planning activities listed on page 191 in your lesson plan.

8. Suggest at least five different mathematics learning resources that would be useful in teaching each one of these subjects: arithmetic, algebra, geometry, and trigonometry. Write a cognitive learning objective and an affective objective that could be achieved through the use of each resource.

9. Write to at least five different textbook publishing companies and request a copy of each company's secondary school mathematics textbook catalog. After you have collected several different publisher's catalogs, compare the descriptions of each publisher's arithmetic, algebra 1, algebra 2, geometry, trigonometry, and higher mathematics textbooks. Do the descriptions reflect a modern mathematics orientation? What are the outstanding characteristics of each textbook? Do these characteristics appear to reflect sound teaching and learning principles?

10. Obtain a list of companies that distribute instructional resources for secondary school mathematics and write to each company requesting a copy of their secondary level resources catalog. Carefully browse through each resource catalog and select approximately $100 worth of ''the-most-for-your-money'' resources which you think would be appropriate for teaching and learning mathematics.

11. Prepare a list of resources that you believe would be appropriate for a mathematics laboratory. Write a brief rationale for your selection of each resource.

12. Suggest at least five pencil-and-paper mathematics laboratory experiments which require only ''scrap'' materials or very low-cost resources to carry out.

13. Prepare several mathematical models or attractive illustrations for use in a mathematics classroom or resource center.

14. Select ten topics from a variety of secondary school subjects and select an appropriate strategy, or several appropriate strategies, for teaching each topic.

15. What types of teaching/learning strategies are appropriate for teaching facts? skills? principles? concepts? problem solving?

16. Make up several different hypothetical discipline problems, ranging from minor to very serious, and discuss alternative procedures for dealing with each one. How could each of these discipline problems be avoided?

17. Suggest several student projects that would be valuable learning experiences for students and that would also result in the production of useful teaching/learning resources for use by other students.

18. Make a list of at least ten rules for student behavior in the classroom and

give a satisfactory and reasonable reason why students should observe each rule.

19. Prepare a five item test on learning facts for a specific mathematics topic, a five item skill test for another topic, a five item concept test for another topic, and a five item test of principles for yet another topic. Are your test items measures of cognitive objectives or affective objectives? What objectives are measured or evaluated by each test item?

20. Discuss the differences between norm-referenced tests, criterion-referenced tests, and domain-referenced tests. Select a topic from high school mathematics and write a five item norm-referenced test for that topic, a five item criterion-referenced test for the topic, and a five item domain-referenced test. Explain the differences in the manner in which you would report a student's performance on each of these three types of tests to that student.

21. List and discuss several strategies that you might use to analyze and evaluate your own teaching effectiveness.

22. Decide upon five mathematics topics that could best be approached through an individualized teaching/learning strategy, five topics to be taught using expository strategies, five topics that lend themselves to discovery strategies, and five topics that are appropriate for inquiry strategies. Tell why each topic can best be taught using the particular strategy that you selected for it.

Selected Bibliography

Aichele, Douglas B. and Reys, Robert E. *Readings in Secondary School Mathematics*. Boston: Prindle, Weber & Schmidt, Inc., 1971.

    This collection of articles on mathematics education contains a section titled "The Mathematics Teacher" which contains articles on goals and objectives, methods of teaching, and characteristics of good teachers. There are also sections titled "Materials, Math Labs, and Instructional Media" and "Evaluation." Many of the articles in this book contain useful information about considerations and activities in planning lessons.

Bloom, Benjamin S. (Editor) *Taxonomy of Educational Objectives, The Classification of Educational Goals, Handbook I: Cognitive Domain*. New York: David McKay Company, Inc., 1956.

    Bloom's *Taxonomy of Educational Objectives* treats the problems of classifying educational objectives and test exercises and contains definitions, sample objectives, and sample test items for each stage in the taxonomy of cognitive educational objectives. Although this book is concerned with general objectives as well as specific objectives from various disciplines, it does contain many examples taken directly from mathematics education or related to mathematics education.

Dunkin, Michael J. and Biddle, Bruce J. *The Study of Teaching*. New York: Holt, Rinehart and Winston, Inc., 1974.

This book treats research findings which have resulted from systemmatic and controlled studies of many variables in the teaching/learning process. It also contains interpretations of research findings together with their implications for teaching and learning practices in classrooms. Among the topics discussed are a model for classroom teaching, teacher behavior, classroom management and control, and knowledge and intellect.

Gagné, Robert M. and Briggs, Leslie J. *Principles of Instructional Design.* New York: Holt, Rinehart and Winston, Inc., 1974.

Gagné and Briggs in *Principles of Instructional Design* discuss outcomes of instruction, varieties of learning, performance objectives, instructional sequences, events of instruction, designing lessons, and assessing student performance, all of which are considerations in planning to teach lessons, topics, and units in secondary school mathematics.

Krathwohl, David R., Bloom, Benjamin S., and Masia, Bertram B. *Taxonomy of Educational Objectives, The Classification of Educational Goals, Handbook II: Affective Domain.* New York: David McKay Company, Inc., 1964.

This taxonomy of affective educational objectives is a companion volume to Bloom's taxonomy of cognitive objectives. It presents and defines each level of affective objectives and presents illustrative affective objectives together with illustrative test items for many objectives. These illustrations are taken from many different school subjects including mathematics.

National Council of Teachers of Mathematics. *The Teaching of Secondary School Mathematics* (Thirty-third Yearbook). Washington, D.C.: National Council of Teachers of Mathematics, 1970.

This 1970 yearbook of the National Council of Teachers of Mathematics contains sections about textbooks and supplementary materials, media systems, teaching for special outcomes (such as interest, concept formation, problem solving ability, and theorem proving), organizing classrooms, preparing plans for teaching arithmetic, algebra, geometry, and low achievers in various subjects.

National Council of Teachers of Mathematics. *The Arithmetic Teacher* (a monthly journal published eight times a year). Reston, Virginia: National Council of Teachers of Mathematics.

Current and back issues of this journal contain many helpful articles on planning and teaching a variety of topics in arithmetic. Any secondary school teacher who has classes in arithmetic or applied and consumer mathematics will find useful suggestions for preparing and teaching lessons for students studying these subjects. Every mathematics teacher should browse through back issues of this journal and should read each current issue as it is published.

National Council of Teachers of Mathematics. *The Mathematics Teacher* (a monthly journal published nine times a year). Reston, Virginia: National Council of Teachers of Mathematics.

Frequently articles about particular strategies for teaching secondary school mathematics topics appear in *The Mathematics Teacher*. This journal is a valuable resource for mathematics teachers. Each issue contains several articles that are concerned with improving teaching and learning in high school mathematics classrooms.

Raths, James, Pancella, John R., and Van Ness, James S. (Editors). *Studying Teaching,* Second Edition, Englewood Cliffs, New Jersey: Prentice-Hall, Inc., 1971.

This book is a collection of readings suggesting various ways in which teaching can be described and studied. Sections of the book treat planning for teaching, classroom interactions, methods of teaching, testing and grading, and motivation and discipline.

Scheerer, Martin. "Cognitive Theory," Chapter 3 in *Handbook of Social Psychology,* Volume I. Cambridge, Mass.: Addison-Wesley, 1954.

School Mathematics Study Group. *Final Report of the SMSG Panel on Research, Newsletter No. 39.* Stanford University: School Mathematics Study Group, August, 1972.

The final report of the School Mathematics Study Group deals with the SMSG findings concerning the structure of mathematics, the objects of mathematics learning, canonical instructional procedures for presenting mathematical skills, concepts, and principles, and research findings in mathematics education.

School Science and Mathematics Association. *School Science and Mathematics* (a monthly journal published October through May). Indiana, Pennsylvania: School Science and Mathematics Association.

Each issue of this journal contains articles which are of use to mathematics teachers in planning and teaching lessons.

Suchman, J. Richard. *The Elementary School Training Program in Scientific Inquiry,* Report of the U.S. Office of Education, Project Title VIII, Project 216. Urbana: The University of Illinois, 1962.

5

of 20

$$\frac{75}{100} \quad \frac{25 \times 3}{25 \times 4} = \frac{25}{25} \times$$

$$0 =$$

Models for Teaching and Learning the Direct Objects of Mathematics

In Chapter 4, the following 14 activities in planning mathematics lessons were discussed and illustrated:

Activities in Planning Mathematics Lessons

Mathematics Content
1. Selecting and naming the topic to be studied
2. Identifying the mathematics objects in the topic
3. Sequencing each topic in a hierarchy of topics

Learning Objectives
4. Identifying cognitive objectives
5. Selecting affective objectives
6. Sharing objectives with students

Learning Resources
7. Preparing materials for student use
8. Obtaining supplemental resources

Preassessment Strategies
9. Identifying prerequisite mathematics content
10. Assessing student readiness to learn the topic

Teaching/Learning Strategies
11. Choosing an appropriate teaching strategy
12. Managing the learning environment

Postassessment Strategies
13. Assessing student learning
14. Evaluating teaching effectiveness

Although each one of these 14 activities has an effect upon the manner in which a mathematics lesson is presented to students and how well they learn the lesson, the two activities under the topic *Teaching/Learning Strategies* are among the most important activities for teaching and learning in a mathematics classroom. Choosing an appropriate teaching strategy and managing the learning environment have a significant influence upon the success of a mathematics lesson. Even when appropriate learning objectives are set, classroom resources are abundant, and valid preassessment and postassessment procedures have been prepared, students may fail to learn the mathematical content of the lesson if inappropriate teaching/learning activities are used. Consequently, the purpose of this chapter is to present models for teaching and learning mathematics, to discuss situations in which the use of particular models is most effective, and to illustrate how each model can be used in teaching a mathematics lesson.

What is a teaching/learning model and do teaching/learning models differ from teaching/learning strategies? Although many people use the words "model" and "strategy" synonomously in every-day speech, in technical use the term "model" is usually reserved for generalized processes and "strategy" for more specific procedures. A *teaching/learning model* is a generalized instructional process which may be used for many different topics in a variety of subjects. A *teaching/learning strategy* is a particular procedure for teaching a specific topic or lesson. For example, individualized models, group models, discovery models, and inquiry models can be used for teaching and learning in many subjects; whereas a lesson plan that incorporates one of these models in a particular strategy for teaching a specific mathematics topic is only of use in teaching that topic.

This chapter considers the properties of several teaching/learning models and how these models can be used in developing strategies for teaching and learning particular topics in mathematics. For example, the *Lesson Plan for a Topic from Statistics,* which is presented in Chapter 4 beginning on page 211, is a strategy for teaching and learning how to test a statistical hypothesis by using a chi-square test. This particular lesson plan uses an expository strategy for teaching a specific mathematics topic; the expository strategy is based upon a general expository teaching model that can be used in teaching many subjects.

Although the appropriateness of a teaching/learning model is related to the mathematical object being taught and to cognitive and affective learning objectives, no one-to-one correspondence can be established between sets of models and sets of other learning variables. The selection of teaching models is both complex and imprecise; however certain models tend to be associated with certain types of objectives. Twelve different teaching/learning models that can be used effectively in teaching mathematics will be discussed and illustrated in this chapter and the following chapter. An example lesson plan for a specific topic in secondary school mathematics will be presented to illustrate how each model can be used to develop a strategy for teaching a lesson.

In teaching mathematics, intuition, trial and evaluation, and experience can be useful guides in selecting teaching models. You will discover that characteristics of individual students and classes are also factors in determining the success of particular teaching/learning models. Students who have been conditioned to learn mathematics through certain teaching methods may have to be reconditioned in order to feel comfortable learning in classrooms where different methods are used. Age, personality, and mental and emotional development are also factors that should be considered when choosing teaching/learning models.

In this book teaching/learning models are matched to either the direct or indirect objects of mathematics learning; however you should keep in mind that this structuring of models and objects is an oversimplification of the much more complex selection of models. Figure 5.1 contains a list of the direct objects of mathematics with appropriate models for teaching these objects, as well as a list of indirect mathematics objects with models for developing these objects. For most mathematics lessons, any one of several teaching/learning models may be appropriate and several direct and indirect objects of mathematics may be taught simultaneously.

The six teaching/learning models which are appropriate for teaching the direct objects of mathematics (see Part I of Figure 5.1) will be discussed in this chapter. The teaching/learning models associated with teaching the indirect objects of mathematics (Part II of Figure 5.1) will be discussed in Chapter 6.

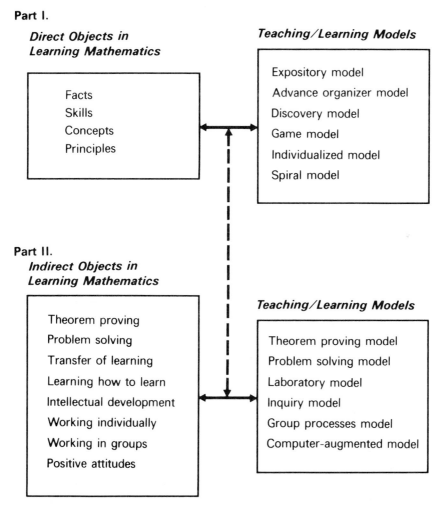

Part I.

Direct Objects in
Learning Mathematics

Teaching/Learning Models

Facts
Skills
Concepts
Principles

Expository model
Advance organizer model
Discovery model
Game model
Individualized model
Spiral model

Part II.

Indirect Objects in
Learning Mathematics

Teaching/Learning Models

Theorem proving
Problem solving
Transfer of learning
Learning how to learn
Intellectual development
Working individually
Working in groups
Positive attitudes

Theorem proving model
Problem solving model
Laboratory model
Inquiry model
Group processes model
Computer-augmented model

Figure 5.1.   Mathematics objects and related teaching/learning models.

Expository Teaching/Learning Model

Expository teaching/learning strategies for presenting skills, concepts and principles were discussed briefly in the context of planning lessons in Chapter 4. The distinguishing characteristic of the expository model is that it is teacher dominated; that is, the teacher controls the flow of the lesson by presenting information and demonstrating solutions to problems. This model is well-suited for teaching mathematics because material can be organized by the teacher and presented to the class in an efficient manner. When used by a perceptive teacher who provides for frequent interactions with students, the expository model can be very effective for teaching many topics in mathematics. Skills, concepts and principles can be presented and developed using the expository model; however some of the indirect objects in learning mathematics such as theorem proving and learning to work effectively in small groups or by oneself can sometimes be learned better when other models of teaching are used.

The expository model for introducing a mathematics topic that is unfamiliar to students should include from seven to nine teacher-directed activities which are discussed below. In teaching mathematics topics there are three variations of the general expository model which are used depending upon whether a skill, concept or principle is being presented. The expository model for presenting a skill contains eight teacher-directed activities; the model for presenting a concept has nine activities; the model for a principle consists of seven activities. These activities for expository teaching of skills, concepts, and principles are summarized in the following outline:

Activities in Teaching Skills, Concepts, and Principles

Activity	*Mathematical Objects for which the Activity is Appropriate*
1. Discuss objectives with students.	skill, concept, principle
2. Name the skill, concept, or principle.	skill, concept, principle
3. Identify and discuss prerequisite skills, concepts, and principles through a preassessment strategy.	skill, concept, principle
4. Develop the skill through an example.	skill
Define the concept.	concept
Deduce or demonstrate the principle.	principle
5. Demonstrate the skill, concept, or principle through several more examples.	skill, concept, principle
6. Have *students* develop the algorithm for the skill.	skill
Compare examples and non-examples of the concept.	concept
Apply the principle in several cases.	principle
7. Have students practice the skill on several exercises.	skill
Have students identify irrelevant dimensions of the concept.	concept
Evaluate student mastery of the principle through a postassessment strategy.	principle
8. Evaluate student mastery of the skill.	skill
Have students practice using the concept.	concept
9. Evaluate student mastery of the concept.	concept

Since these three variations of the expository model are similar in structure, they will be discussed together. Consequently, each of the following activities for teaching an expository lesson in mathematics is discussed in three contexts; that is, the context of teaching a skill, the context of teaching a concept, and the context of teaching a principle.

Activity 1. The teacher should begin the lesson by telling students what it is that they will be expected to learn in the lesson; that is, the teacher should share his or her cognitive and affective student performance objectives with students.

Activity 2. Whenever possible, the skill, concept, or principle that is to be presented in the lesson should be given a name which is shared with the class.

Activity 3. Immediate prerequisite skills, concepts, and principles should be identified by the teacher and discussed with the class. The teacher should list each prerequisite object and should prepare a preassessment activity that can be used to determine whether each student is prepared to learn the new material.

These three activities prepare students to learn a new topic by helping them understand what is expected of them, by providing a label that they can associate with the topic, and by tying the new lesson to mathematics skills, concepts, and principles that have been studied and that will be used in mastering the new mathematics objects.

Activity 4. If a skill is being taught, the teacher should develop that skill by applying it in a particular example. If the new topic is a concept, the concept should be defined using language that is appropriate for the age and maturation levels of students in the class. When a new principle is being taught, it should be deduced or demonstrated using a particular case.

When teaching mathematical skills and principles, it is important to begin with a particular example of the skill or principle rather than a general (and usually symbolic) representation. Mathematics teachers know that the skill of solving a linear equation in one variable with integer coefficients can be summarized as "the solution to a linear equation of the form $a \cdot x + b = c$ is $x = \frac{c - b}{a}$." However, few beginning algebra students would be able to solve a linear equation after being introduced to this skill through this general representation. Students are more likely to comprehend and apply the skill if it is presented through a specific example such as

$$3x + 4 = 2$$
$$3x + 4 - 4 = 2 - 4$$
$$3x = -2$$
$$\frac{3x}{3} = \frac{-2}{3}$$
$$x = -\frac{2}{3},$$

where the teacher discusses the steps with the class and explains the mathematical logic of each step.

While few teachers, experienced or inexperienced, would attempt to introduce a skill by using a generalized formula, some teachers do tend to present principles too abstractly. When teaching geometry, which contains many theorems, each one of which is a principle, many teachers fail to introduce theorems through specific representations. For example, instead of presenting the principle that in a circle equal arcs are subtended by equal central angles as a theorem to be proved, it would be well to have students draw circles of different sizes, construct equal central angles in each circle, and measure subtended arcs. When this approach is used, many students will discover the principle for themselves. Then the principle can be formalized as a theorem and the theorem can be proved. Some students who are chided by teachers for incorrectly using intuitive ideas and measurements as steps in proving theorems, decide that these imprecise techniques have no place in mathematics. Such is not the case. Intuition and measurement have been used by the greatest mathematicians throughout history to discover mathematical truths. Once a geometry principle has been discovered using imprecise techniques, it can be formalized as a theorem and the theorem can be proved using more rigorous mathematical procedures. Of course, the use of intuition and measurement will occasionally result in the "discovery" of incorrect "theorems;" however further measurements or attempts at a proof usually will show the fallacy of the "theorem."

One of the common hazards in defining a concept for students is the inadvertent use of terminology that is meaningless to some students. At times it is well to introduce a concept by using a definition that is not as precise, rigorous, and inclusive as desired, provided such a definition is meaningful to students. After students have used and comprehended the imprecise definition, the teacher can point out its shortcomings and can guide the students in formulating a more rigorous mathematical definition of the concept. For example, most students better understand the concepts of circle, ellipse, parabola, and hyperbola when these concepts are introduced as sections of a cone. After these geometric figures have been presented in this intuitive manner, each one can be defined as the locus of points, which is a more useful definition for mathematical applications.

Activity 5. After a skill has been developed using a particular case, it should be demonstrated through several other examples presented by the teacher. Likewise, a new principle should be demonstrated several times by the teacher using several different examples. These repeated demonstrations help students comprehend the skill or principle.

The various examples selected for demonstrating a skill should include representations of each type of prerequisite skill that might be encountered in using the new skill. For example, demonstrating the skill of solving a linear equation by using the equation $-3x + 7 = -5$ requires the use of the prerequisite skill of dividing pairs of negative integers. Principles should also be demonstrated through examples that require the use of various prerequisites and embody different representations of each principle. For example, when demonstrating the principle that in a circle equal arcs are subtended by equal central angles, acute, right, and obtuse angles should be used as examples.

After a concept has been defined, students should be shown several different examples of the concept and the teacher should demonstrate that each one is indeed an example. These examples should be chosen so that all of them do not contain an irrelevant property and so that every property embodied in the concept is represented. For instance, when demonstrating the concept of the graphical representation of pairs of linear functions, pairs of functions whose graphs are parallel lines, intersecting lines, and coincident lines should all be demonstrated. Also some functions whose graphs have negative slopes and some whose graphs have positive slopes should be represented, as well as functions whose graphs are parallel to one or the other of the coordinate axes.

Activity 6. After a teacher has developed a mathematical skill through the demonstration of several examples, students should develop the same algorithm using a new example. This step in learning a skill can be carried out by asking each student to develop the skill by solving a problem at his or her seat or by sending groups of students to the board to develop the algorithm from a particular case.

The sixth step in teaching a concept is to show the class several non-examples of the concept and explain why each one is a non-example. One of the important factors in concept learning is to be able to classify examples and non-examples of each concept. Being able to write the definition of a concept only shows that the student knows the concept. However, the ability to classify examples and non-examples of a concept indicates comprehension and application of the concept on the part of the student. Learning to classify the concepts defined by various mathematical relations and functions through studying their equations and constructing their graphs is a major activity in algebra and trigonometry.

In teaching a principle, the sixth step is to have students apply the principle to several different cases with immediate feedback from the teacher regarding the appropriateness and correctness of each application. In geometry the principle embodied in each theorem is applied in proving other theorems and in proving propositions following sets of theorems. Even though students may be shown a number of examples of a principle, many students will neither comprehend nor remember the principle if they do not apply it in several situations.

Activity 7. After a new skill has been developed by the teacher through several examples and each student has demonstrated the skill using a particular case, each student should practice the skill on several exercises. Since it is important that students do not practice *incorrect* procedures in using a new skill, immediate feedback should be provided to each student after each practice item. This can be accomplished by reserving time for student practice at the end of the class period in which a new skill is presented. The teacher should give one practice item at a time to the class, wait until each student has applied the skill to that item, and determine if each student has demonstrated the skill correctly. The teacher can check students' work by walking around the classroom or, in some cases, the correct solution can be put on the board and students can compare their work to it. Whichever method is used to immediately evaluate students' first attempts at using a new skill, this immediate feedback is important to assure that students are not practicing incorrect procedures which can be very difficult to extinguish after they have been learned through repeated practice.

In teaching a concept, it is so important for students to be able to identify irrelevant dimensions of the concept that the seventh activity of the expository model for teaching a concept emphasizes this process. In teaching the concept of parallelogram it is necessary to emphasize that squares and rectangles are also parallelograms, otherwise some students may infer that squares and rectangles are not parallelograms because they contain right angles. The concept of mathematical function is independent of the manner in which the function is represented. Functions can be represented by ordered pairs of objects or by mathematical formulas. The sine function can be defined as the ratio of two sides of a right triangle and the absolute sizes of these sides is irrelevant to the definition of this concept.

The seventh and final activity in the expository model for teaching a principle is a postassessment (which can be done as a homework assignment or an oral or written quiz) to evaluate each student's success in learning the principle and to aid in planning future teaching and learning strategies for the class as a whole and for individual students. Even though a principle has been taught by the teacher and applied by students, it may not have been learned by each student. The postassessment provides a measure of the degree to which each student comprehends the principle and is able to apply it in solving problems or proving theorems.

Activity 8. In teaching a skill, as well as in teaching a principle, the final activity should be an evaluation of each student's level of mastery of the skill. Students may differ in their ability to apply the skill in various situations and some students may have developed certain error patterns that interfere with their use of a new skill. In evaluating each student's ability to use a skill, it is not sufficient to identify correct and incorrect answers. Each incorrect application should be analyzed to identify the specific error or errors. The necessity for remedial arithmetic courses for high school juniors and seniors attests to the need for more careful evaluation of skill-learning. Until a student has mastered a skill, he or she should not be moved on to new skills that have the previous skill as a prerequisite; however in the press to cover material many students are left behind and merely "take" mathematics but learn very little of it.

The eighth activity in teaching a concept is providing each student with several practice items representing the concept. These practice items may include classifying examples and non-examples of the concept, making up examples of the concept, and applying the concept in solving problems or proving theorems. The practice items should be selected so that irrelevant dimensions are represented. An immediate evaluation of each student's success in meeting the objectives of the practice items should be carried out and students should be informed of their level of mastery of the concept.

Activity 9. Just as in expository models for teaching skills and principles, the final activity of an expository model for teaching a concept is a postassessment of students' knowledge and comprehension of the concept. In all teaching/learning situations the postassessment should be designed to measure students' success in meeting the cognitive and affective objectives. These should be shared with the class at the beginning of consideration of each new mathematics topic. Whenever they are appropriate, both higher and lower level cognitive and affective objectives should be included in expository models. Postassessment quiz items that are consistent with the learning objectives should be selected and developed to measure student achievement.

Even though the expository model is teacher-dominated, it can also be student centered if the teacher attempts to involve students in the lesson. Poor expository lessons can occur when the teacher concentrates upon mathematical content and lectures with very little interaction with students. Many inexperienced teachers, who are quite naturally concerned with their own teaching style and correct presentation of mathematical content, tend to lecture on mathematics while giving scant attention to any student reactions which are short of discipline problems. After a few weeks or months of teaching experience, most mathematics teachers overcome their self-centered teaching methods, become confident in their own knowledge and comprehension of mathematics, and develop a teaching style that permits them to concentrate upon students rather than upon themselves and the subject.

Good lecturers observe the facial expressions and other reactions of their students and make minute-by-minute adjustments in their lectures according to student behaviors. Boredom, confusion, and inattentiveness tend to be reflected in students' postures and facial expressions and the perceptive teacher can evaluate the effectiveness of his or her lecture by paying attention to these student behaviors.

An expository teaching strategy need not be a pure lecture and demonstration strategy. Teachers can ask questions, respond to student-initiated questions, and encourage class discussions and comments during each lesson. Although it may appear to be an effective procedure to pause occasionally during a lecture and ask ''Are there any questions?'' or ''Does anyone have a comment?'' these questions seldom elicit responses. The teacher's own attitudes and behaviors toward questions and discussions will tend to either generate or stifle student participation in an expository lesson. Frequent teacher responses such as ''You should know the answer to your own question.'' ''That's not a very good question.'' or ''That comment has nothing to do with the lesson.'' can cause most students to refrain from asking questions or participating in class discussions. Even negative facial expressions on the part of the teacher can discourage student participation. Students will learn to ask questions when they are confused if teachers react with sensitivity and empathy to each question. Teacher responses such as ''That's a good question,'' ''I'm sorry, I didn't explain that very well,'' or ''I'm glad you brought up that point'' tend to encourage student participation in lessons.

When asking students a question, it is usually well to phrase the question specifically and unambiguously. The following list contains pairs of questions, the first of which is a poor teacher question while the second is a better version of the same question:

Questions Asked by Teachers

1. *Poor question:* What do you do when you add fractions?
   Better question: When adding fractions with the same denominator, what is the denominator for the sum?
2. *Poor question:* Can you cancel anything in this expression?
   Better question: Is there a common factor that can be divided from both numerator and denominator of this fraction?
3. *Poor question:* What can be transposed in this equation?
   Better question: Could we add the same number to both sides of this equation to obtain a simpler equivalent equation?
4. *Poor question:* Can you simplify $\sqrt{4x^2 + 4y^2}$?
   Better question: Is there an algebraic expression with real coefficients whose square is $4x^2 + 4y^2$?
5. *Poor question:* What is a *contrapositive?*

**Models for Teaching
and Learning the Direct
Objects of Mathematics**   **Questions Asked by Teachers (Continued)**

	Better question:	What is the contrapositive of the theorem "if T is an equilateral triangle, then all of the angles of T are equal?"
6.	*Poor question:*	How do you compare degrees and radians?
	Better question:	What is the equivalent degree measure for one radian?
7.	*Poor question:*	Can you prove this theorem?
	Better question:	Would you suggest several theorems that might be of help in proving this theorem?
8.	*Poor question:*	In simplifying these problems, what do you do with the exponents?
	Better question:	When multiplying two powers with like bases how should you treat the exponents? Why?

Although it is important that teachers ask good questions, it is even more important that they listen to students' answers to questions and analyze and evaluate these answers before reacting. Teachers sometimes exhibit four common shortcomings when processing the information contained in students' answers to questions. First, some teachers know what they want for an answer and will not accept answers that deviate from their expected answer. Second, some teachers do not analyze and evaluate answers, especially wrong answers. Third, many teachers tend to reword or repeat students' answers to questions. Fourth, some teachers ask a question, call upon a student for an answer, then do not give the student enough time to formulate a response.

Many times students who are lacking in mathematical sophistication and vocabulary give conceptually correct answers to teacher's questions, but use imprecise or inappropriate terminology in their responses. Teachers should train themselves to analyze each answer for its correctness regardless of the vocabulary that students use in expressing answers. When answers contain particularly confusing or inappropriate terminology, an appropriate teacher response might be "You have the correct idea and I think you understand it; however a mathematician would probably word it as . . . ."

Teachers who ignore students' wrong answers are passing up an excellent opportunity to assess student learning. Many times incorrect answers not only indicate that students have not learned the material but also indicate specific sources of difficulty. Examples of appropriate teacher responses to wrong answers (and sometimes correct answers) are "What did you use to get that answer?" or "Can you give reasons for your answer?" At times when students explain their strategies for arriving at incorrect answers, specific misconceptions become apparent and can be corrected immediately. Sometimes when students attempt to explain their correct answers, it becomes obvious that they have merely memorized correct responses and have little comprehension of skills, concepts or principles.

Although rewording students' answers to questions can at times increase the precision of the answers, it can also discourage students from answering questions and can discourage them from listening to each other. When a student's correct answers are usually reworded by the teacher, that student may interpret the teacher's action as a criticism of his or her responses and may respond less frequently in class. Whenever students observe that the teacher usually repeats or rephrases their comments, they will tend to ignore each other's responses and regard the teacher as the only source of valid and useful information.

When a teacher asks a question, he or she nearly always has the answer in mind. Also when the teacher, or a student, is not talking during an expository lesson, that teacher tends to feel that time is being wasted. Consequently, it is not uncommon for teachers to expect students to respond to a question within two to five seconds after it has been asked. For most questions requiring higher level cognitive activities than knowledge, many students need ten seconds or longer to formulate a response. When a student remains silent after being asked a question, it may mean that he or she does not know the answer or it could also mean that the student is formulating an answer.

In spite of the fact that the expository teaching model has been losing favor among some educators during recent years, this model *is* a valid and practical model for presenting mathematical skills, concepts and principles to students. When used correctly, expository strategies are very effective in promoting meaningful learning in mathematics. As is the case with most other improperly used teaching strategies, expository strategies can also fail to achieve desired results. The expository teaching model is a valuable tool for mathematics teachers and can be used in combination with other teaching/learning models or can be modified to meet the requirements of specialized mathematics lessons.

The lesson plan for teaching the nature of a statistical test, which is found in Chapter 4 beginning on page 211, is an example of an expository strategy for teaching a principle. In reviewing this section of the present chapter, it might be useful for you to evaluate the expository lesson in Chapter 4 by comparing it to the seven activities which make up the expository model for teaching a principle.

Advance Organizer Teaching/Learning Model

The advance organizer teaching/learning model, which was developed and tested by the psychologist David P. Ausubel, is a teacher-dominated model closely related to the expository model. This model can be used as a supplement to other models or can be integrated with another model. Ausubel's model is based upon his theory of meaningful verbal learning, which is discussed in Chapter 3 on pages 130 to 135. The model, which uses an information-processing approach to learning, is concerned with the structure of subject matter and the structure of information in the mind. The advance organizer model is well suited for presenting facts, skills, concepts and principles based upon cognitive objectives at the knowledge and comprehension levels. Before reading the following discussion of this model, it would be well to review Ausubel's theory of meaningful verbal learning which is presented in Chapter 3.

Ausubel believes that each academic discipline can be uniquely structured into hierarchies of facts, skills, concepts and principles. General, inclusive concepts and principles that subsume less general and less inclusive facts, skills, concepts and principles are located at the top of each hierarchical structure. According to Ausubel, the objective of the educational system should be to identify and organize these information structures within each discipline and impart the structures in a meaningful manner to students. Teachers should organize infor-

Models for Teaching and Learning the Direct Objects of Mathematics

mation so that it will be related in a meaningful way to their students' existing cognitive structures.

The central strategy of the advance organizer model is the use of advance organizers. Advance organizers for topics in any discipline are introductory materials that are presented to students at a higher level of generality, abstraction, and inclusiveness than subsequent learning tasks. The advance organizer, when properly structured and received in a meaningful way by students, is designed to assist students to develop mental structures which will help them comprehend new learning material and integrate it with other material (within the same discipline) that they have learned previously. When using the advance organizer model, teaching methods which best enhance the formation of meaningful, stable, and integrated mental structures should be employed. The emphasis of this model is upon structure—both the structure of the discipline and the structure of information in the learner's mind. The structure of the discipline is relatively easy to determine; however the manner in which the learner structures information about the discipline in his or her mind is considerably more difficult to evaluate. Hubert Callihan (1975) has developed a procedure for measuring cognitive structure involving sophisticated statistical procedures to analyze the information contained in passages which are written by students. Students are given a randomly organized list of relatively familiar mathematical terms, which will be used in teaching and learning an unfamiliar principle; they are asked to write a passage using each word at least one time. After the new material has been presented and studied, the same students are asked to write a second passage using the same list of terms. The information and structure in each of these passages is analyzed and the two passages are compared. Callihan believes that his technique for measuring and evaluating the information contained in students' written passages provides before and after measures of students' cognitive structures. Although Callihan's method is a useful research tool for studying the nature of learning, it is not a practical procedure for classroom teachers to use in evaluating student learning. However, research studies have shown that advance organizers can facilitate learning; although most teachers must judge the effectiveness of their use of each advance organizer through standard postassessment techniques such as discussions and quizzes.

The advance organizer teaching/learning model can be characterized by the activities that are involved in preparing and using a teaching strategy based upon this model. The following outline contains the elements of the advance organizer model. These elements are activities which the teacher must carry out when using the model to present a new topic to a class:

Elements of the Advance Organizer Model

I. Attending to the basic assumptions underlying the model
   A. Progressive differentiation
   B. Integrative reconciliation
II. Developing the particular advance organizer
   A. Expository organizers
   B. Comparative organizers
III. Presenting the advance organizer to students
IV. Selecting activities to follow the presentation of the organizer

232

Assumptions Underlying the Model

The basic assumptions underlying the advance organizer model are embodied in two principles for organizing the content of a subject. Ausubel calls these principles progressive differentiation and integrative reconciliation.

The *principle of progressive differentiation* states that the most abstract, general, and inclusive concepts and principles contained in a topic from a particular subject should be presented first. After these higher level objects have been presented, less inclusive and more concrete facts, skills, and concepts should follow; that is, specific concepts and factual information should be presented following the presentation of general concepts and principles. Ausubel believes that this top-down approach to presenting a topic will help students organize and structure new information and will make learning more meaningful. The starting point for each mathematics course, unit, or topic should be a presentation and discussion of general principles followed by the presentation of specific facts, skills, and concepts. Most people use a form of progressive differentiation when assembling a jig-saw puzzle. They put the picture of the assembled puzzle, which is usually found on the puzzle's box top, in front of them and use this inclusive picture as a map in assembling the specific pieces of the puzzle. Some people do prefer the challenge of assembling a puzzle without using the picture as a guide; however this strategy is certainly less efficient and more difficult.

There are many situations in which mathematics learning can be facilitated by using a top-down approach and there are many other situations where a bottom-up strategy may be better. Younger students (sixth, seventh, and eighth graders) who tend to think in concrete terms may have difficulty comprehending high level abstractions and general principles. Perhaps advance organizers would not be as effective for these students as they would be for high school sophomores, juniors, and seniors. No doubt the principle of progressive differentiation is valid for some students in some mathematics courses; however it is not appropriate for all students in all mathematics courses.

The second assumption underlying the advance organizer model is the principle of integrative reconciliation. *The principle of integrative reconciliation* states that new information should be consciously integrated and reconciled with previously learned materials from the discipline. This means that teachers should purposely organize their courses, units, and topics so that subsequent learning is carefully related to previous learning. Teachers should also present material so that students recognize the relationships among various topics. These relationships should be explicitly identified for students and discussed with them.

Although many educators would argue this point, Ausubel thinks that integrative reconciliation should take place within each discipline and not among disciplines. He believes that each discipline has its own unique and distinctive structure and that the goal of the educational system should be to impart the structure of each discipline to students. Ausubel does not favor a principle of integrative reconciliation between two disciplines, even disciplines as closely related as mathematics and science.

Whatever one's viewpoint on integrative reconciliation among disciplines, most mathematics teachers will vouch for the importance of this principle within school mathematics. One source of learning difficulties in mathematics is the inability of many students to see the relationships among different mathematics courses and, even more important, the relationships among facts, skills, concepts and principles within each mathematics course. Many students regard algebra as a collection of unrelated facts and skills, and see few connections among algebra, geometry, and trigonometry.

These two principles (progressive differentiation and integrative reconciliation) form the conceptual basis for the advance organizer teaching/learning model and comprise the basic objectives of this model.

Developing Advance Organizers

The actual advance organizer, that is, the abstract, general and inclusive introduction to a new topic, can have many forms and can be presented in a variety of ways. Whatever the format of the organizer or method of presentation, the organizer should subsume the material to follow and aid the student in organizing it. Advance organizers are not merely outlines or summaries; even though some organizers are presented in these formats. Each advance organizer should be more abstract, general and inclusive than the content of the material that it is organizing.

Ausubel identifies two types of advance organizers, expository organizers and comparative organizers. *Expository organizers* are formulated to provide the learner with a mental structure to which he or she can relate unfamiliar material that will follow the organizer. Expository organizers are used to introduce material that is unfamiliar to students. *Comparative organizers* are used when relatively familiar material is being presented to students. Comparative organizers help students integrate new concepts and principles with concepts and principles that they have previously learned in the same subject. Comparative organizers also help students discriminate between familiar and unfamiliar ideas that are essentially different but which may be confused.

Since mathematics is a subject where unfamiliar information is usually related to familiar information, comparative organizers can be quite useful to teachers and students in mathematics courses. For example, 30 years ago, before the unifying concept of function was taught in most high schools, the transition from algebra to trigonometry was very confusing for many students. At that time, algebra was presented as a collection of skills and techniques relating to unknown quantities, expressions with unknowns, and equations containing unknowns. In trigonometry, sines and cosines were defined as ratios (fractions) of sides of triangles, and students were given no inclusive, subsuming concept to use in comparing the concepts of algebra to those of trigonometry. Now that most algebra textbooks use the function concept as a subsuming idea in algebra and many trigonometry books define sine and cosine as functions with respect to a unit circle, the function concept can be used as a comparative organizer in making the transition from algebra to trigonometry. Students, with the help of their teacher and textbook, can use the function concept to integrate familiar concepts and principles from algebra with unfamiliar concepts and principles from trigonometry.

Presenting Advance Organizers

Advance organizers have considerable versatility and can be used in teaching many skills, concepts and principles in mathematics. Advance organizers are also appropriate for use as introductions to lectures because they help both students and teachers organize and structure new material. Although the advance organizer was originally conceived as a verbal strategy for introducing new material in a lecture mode, it can also be presented in the context of a demonstration, a group discussion, a game, a laboratory exercise, a model or a film. The advance organizer illustrated on pages 136 and 137 is an activity-oriented student game for introducing a conceptualization of the operation of a computer system.

The length of an advance organizer can vary from a single sentence spoken in a few seconds to a series of classroom presentations lasting for several hours. It is doubtful whether very brief organizers fulfill the function of organizing students' cognitive structures for the incorporation and retention of the more detailed and differentiated material that will follow. Very long and complex organizers may cause students to form several mental structures that may interfere with each other or be forgotten before more specific concrete information is presented for assimilation into these structures. An intuitive guide for the length of an advance organizer in mathematics (which is neither contradicted nor supported by controlled research studies) is that the presentation of an organizer should last for at least several minutes but no longer than one class period. An exposure of several minutes duration should provide sufficient time for students to formulate a cognitive structure based upon the organizer before their attention is directed to more specific information. When the presentation of an advance organizer is interrupted by the bell ending the class and the organizer must be continued the next day in class, there is a risk that incompletely formed cognitive structures may be forgotten or may interfere with the mental structure that is formed when the organizer presentation is continued.

One potential hazard in using an advance organizer is that some students may not pay attention to the presentation of the organizer. Before presenting an advance organizer, the teacher should ensure that the class is quiet and that everyone is paying attention. It might be helpful to give a brief introduction before presenting the organizer in order to set if off from other classroom activities. It may also be helpful to refer back to the organizer several times at appropriate points during subsequent activities.

Activities Following the Organizer

Immediately following the advance organizer, the material that the organizer prepared students to receive should be presented. This material should be less abstract and more specific than the organizer itself; that is, subsequent subject matter should fall below the organizer in the subject hierarchy. Although the advance organizer must be highly structured and is usually teacher controlled, the presentation following the organizer can be less structured and the teacher and students can interact freely. Regardless of the instructional method used in presenting the organizer, the remainder of the lesson and subsequent lessons on the same topic can be taught using any appropriate teaching/learning model. Consequently, the advance organizer model may be incorporated into another model or may be used for only part of a lesson.

During the conduct of the lesson following the presentation of the organizer, the teacher may point out conceptual anchorages to the organizer and help students see how the material being studied fits into the structure developed by the organizer. When using advance organizers, it is critical that both the organizer and subsequent content are well organized by the teacher. Following the organizer, the teacher should take care to present material that fits into the organizer structure in a meaningful way.

Summary

In using the terms high-level of abstraction, generality, and inclusiveness to describe the content of advance organizers, one implies that students must be intellectually mature enough to deal with information requiring high-level mental processes. Ausubel does not discuss in any detail the stage of intellectual development that students must have attained in order to handle ideas near the top of a hierarchy within a discipline such as mathematics. However, Piaget's theory of intellectual development does indicate that students who have not reached the formal operational stage of intellectual growth can not handle lessons based upon Ausubel's advance organizer model for presenting unfamiliar material. This is to say that the use of teaching strategies centered around the advance organizer model should be reserved for students who have reached a minimum age of 12.

To conclude this discussion of the advance organizer teaching/learning model, the following advance organizer strategies for introducing topics from high school mathematics are offered. Since the advance organizer model has the specific objective of preparing students for meaningful learning of subsequent material, these strategies are not presented in the context of a complete teaching/ learning strategy containing the fourteen activities associated with a lesson plan.

1. *An Introduction to Algebra I.* For many students the first few weeks of a beginning algebra class are quite forbidding because the unfamiliar symbolism appears to be arbitrary and meaningless. To help make algebra more meaningful, a lesson near the beginning of an Algebra I course might begin with the following expository advance organizer presented in a lecture mode:

In algebra we are concerned with variables. A **variable** is a symbol that is used to represent any of the elements of a specified set of elements. In algebra the letters of the alphabet are used as variables and the sets of elements are sets of numbers. A set whose elements are represented by a variable is called the **replacement set** for the variable. This set is also called the **domain** of the variable. The elements of the replacement set for a variable are called **values** of the variable. A variable that has just one value is called a **constant.**

In algebra you will learn the arithmetic of variables; that is, you will learn how to add, subtract, multiply, and divide variables and how to find roots and powers of variables. In arithmetic a number represented by several numbers joined by the symbols for addition, subtraction, multiplication, or division or symbols of grouping is called an **expression.** An expression in algebra which contains a variable or several variables is called a **variable expression.** Any expression from arithmetic or any variable expression from algebra is called an **algebraic expression.**

This chart will help you understand these unfamiliar words which are used in algebra. (The teacher should write the following chart on the chalkboard or project it on a screen from a prepared transparency. It would also be well for the teacher to duplicate this chart on paper so that a copy can be distributed to each student at this point in the lecture.)

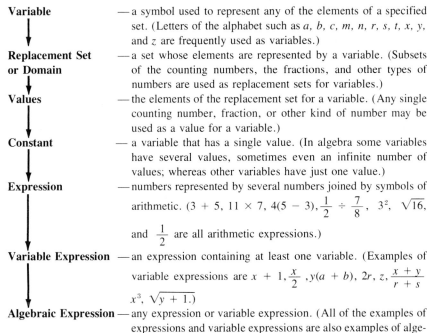

Some Definitions from Algebra

Variable ↓ — a symbol used to represent any of the elements of a specified set. (Letters of the alphabet such as a, b, c, m, n, r, s, t, x, y, and z are frequently used as variables.)

Replacement Set or Domain ↓ — a set whose elements are represented by a variable. (Subsets of the counting numbers, the fractions, and other types of numbers are used as replacement sets for variables.)

Values ↓ — the elements of the replacement set for a variable. (Any single counting number, fraction, or other kind of number may be used as a value for a variable.)

Constant ↓ — a variable that has a single value. (In algebra some variables have several values, sometimes even an infinite number of values; whereas other variables have just one value.)

Expression ↓ — numbers represented by several numbers joined by symbols of arithmetic. $(3 + 5, 11 \times 7, 4(5 - 3), \frac{1}{2} \div \frac{7}{8}, 3^2, \sqrt{16},$ and $\frac{1}{2}$ are all arithmetic expressions.)

Variable Expression ↓ — an expression containing at least one variable. (Examples of variable expressions are $x + 1, \frac{x}{2}, y(a + b), 2r, z, \frac{x + y}{r + s}$ $x^3, \sqrt{y + 1}$.)

Algebraic Expression — any expression or variable expression. (All of the examples of expressions and variable expressions are also examples of algebraic expressions.)

After this expository organizer is presented to the class and any questions that may arise are answered, students should be asked to give examples of each of the terms defined above. The class could also be given some simple algebraic expressions to evaluate by replacing variables with elements from various domains.

2. ***Introducing*** $(a \mp b)^2$ ***and*** $(a \mp b)^3$. Although most, but not all, algebra students accept and use the expansions for $(a \mp b)^2$ and $(a \mp b)^3$, many students have difficulty conceptualizing these products. The following introductory expository organizer, presented in the form of a demonstration, will make these products more meaningful for many students.

Begin the demonstration by selecting two arbitrary lengths a and b and demonstrating that the geometric representations of a^2 and b^2 are squares having dimensions a by a and b by b, respectively. Next, consider the length $a + b$, and construct a square of dimensions $(a + b)$ by $(a + b)$ as a geometric representation of $(a + b)^2$. Then compare the square having side $(a + b)$ to the two squares having sides a and b, respectively. The geometric representations of a^2, b^2, and $(a + b)^2$ are illustrated in Figure 5.2.

Next divide the class into small groups and ask each group to construct a geometric representation for $(a - b)^2$ and use their representation to find the algebraic expansion of $(a - b)^2$. Some students may prefer to draw their representations on paper, while others may want to cut out paper squares and rectangles. Be certain to have measuring sticks (metric rules are preferable) and scissors available in the classroom for this lesson.

After the expansions of $(a + b)^2$ and $(a - b)^2$ have been demonstrated, consider the geometric representation of $(a + b)^3$. This representation is shown in Figure 5.3.

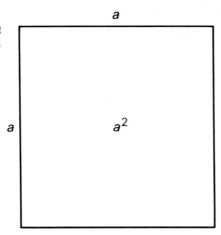

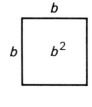

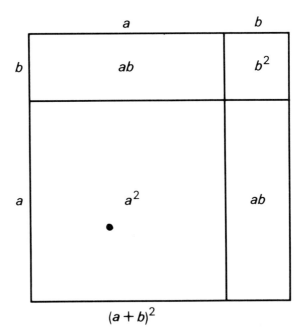

$(a + b)^2$

Figure 5.2.   A geometric model of $(a + b)^2$.

You may prefer to use wooden or plastic rectangular solids to demonstrate this expansion. Small wooden and plastic centimeter cubes can be purchased from several suppliers of mathematics education resource materials. These cubes can be glued together to form larger rectangular solids of various dimensions.

The geometric representation of $(a + b)^3$ can be separated into the four representations a^3, $3a^2b$, $3ab^2$, and b^3; these representations are shown in Figure 5.4.

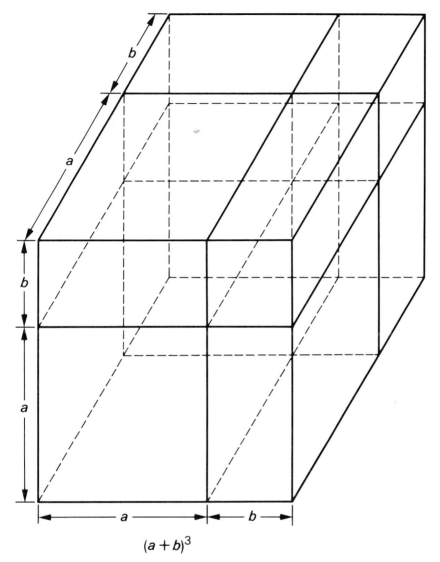

$$(a+b)^3$$

Figure 5.3.   A geometric model of $(a + b)^3$.

Each representation can be drawn on a separate transparency and the four transparencies can be overlaid, one at a time, on an overhead projector to illustrate
that $a^3 + 3a^2b + 3ab^2 + b^3$ does make up $(a + b)^3$.

    After you have shown a geometric representation of $(a + b)^3$ to the class, be
sure that each student does see that the sum of the parts a^3, $3a^2b$, $3ab^2$, and b^3 is
the expansion of $(a + b)^3$. Next discuss with the class ways in which $(a - b)^3$
might be represented geometrically. As an in-class or homework assignment,
you may want to have students attempt to construct geometric representations of
$(a - b)^3$, either as projections drawn on paper or as rectangular solids. Students

who are successful at completing this activity will discover that $(a - b)^3$ does indeed equal $a^3 - 3a^2b + 3ab^2 - b^3$.

Following the use of the advance organizer, ask students to calculate specific products such as $(11 + 4)^2$, $(16 - 3)^2$, $(x + y)^2$, $(3x - 2y)^2$, $(5 + 3)^3$, $(a + b)^3$, and $(2r - 3s)^3$ by using the appropriate product formula.

This advance organizer lesson, which will require one class period, will help prepare students to study special products in algebra and will set the stage for considering the binomial theorem. However, it is obvious that geometric representations can not be constructed for $(a \mp b)^n$ when n is greater than three. An approach to binomial expansions for n greater than three is to search for patterns, for instance the patterns found in Pascal's triangle.

Even though this organizer is of approximately the same level of abstractness, generality, and inclusiveness as the specific cases which follow it, it can help students formulate a cognitive structure to organize the concepts and principles involved in special products.

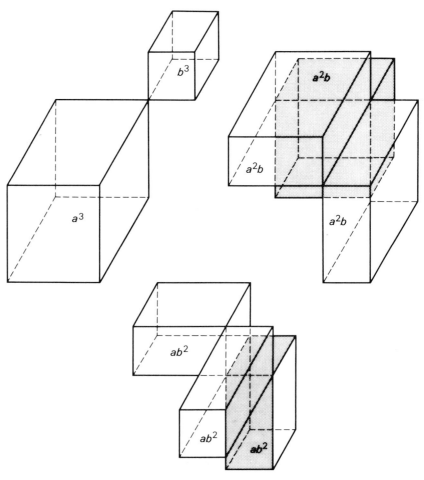

Figure 5.4.   Geometric models of a^3, $3a^2b$, $3ab^2$, and b^3.

Learning by Discovery

Teaching for discovery is more a range of teaching/learning strategies than a teaching learning model. Discovery teaching and learning are not yet well-enough defined to permit formulating an ordered sequence of activities called a discovery teaching/learning model. Consequently discovery learning will be presented here as a set of objectives, activities, and outcomes which are contained in a range of teaching strategies called the discovery method.

The discovery method of teaching, which was discussed briefly in Chapter 4, is a popular method among mathematics teachers. Several reasons for the popularity of the discovery approach are that it is related to the expository model, is appropriate for introducing unfamiliar skills, concepts and principles to class-size groups of students, permits considerable student initiative and involvement in lessons, and tends to be more interesting for students than a teacher-dominated lecture. Even though teaching for discovery has been criticized by some educators (David Ausubel is an outspoken critic of discovery learning) as an inefficient process for presenting material, it can be used effectively for a variety of mathematics topics.

Discovery Learning Defined

Discovery itself can be defined in general terms as any means of attaining knowledge for oneself by the use of one's own intellectual or physical resources. In a narrower sense, *discovery learning* is learning which occurs as a result of the learner manipulating, structuring and transforming information so that he or she finds new information. In discovery learning, the learner may *make* a conjecture, *formulate* an hypothesis, or *find* a mathematical "truth" by using inductive or deductive processes, observation and extrapolation. The essential element in discovering new information is that the discoverer must take an active part in formulating and attaining the new information. When a student who has not previously considered the matter is told by a teacher that multiplication of natural numbers is commutative, that student *has not* discovered the commutative property of multiplication. A student who has found by trial and observation that the roles of multiplier and multiplicand can be interchanged in a multiplication problem *has* discovered the commutative property. This discovery may have been planned by the teacher, who provided situations exemplifying this principle; or, the student may have made it with no prompting.

Teaching for discovery takes place through a range of learning activities which results in the learner making a discovery. These learning activities may be very structured and teacher-controlled or they may take the form of free play, unstructured manipulations of ideas and objects, or open-ended discussions. Discovery learning can occur in very structured situations such as a student/teacher or student/programmed-textbook sequence of interactions where the student is guided in a step-by-step, question-answer format to make a very specific and predictable discovery. At the other extreme of structure, unplanned discoveries may be made by students in open-ended discussions of problems which they formulate and consider with little or no teacher intervention.

Student discoveries can be made either inductively or deductively. *Induction* is the process of finding a generalization as a consequence of observing and manipulating specific instances which represent the generalization. Many arithmetic generalizations can be discovered by solving sets of problems and observing general properties and procedures embodied in all of the problems. *Deduction* is the manipulation of ideas through the use of logical rules in order to formulate generalizations, which later may be found to apply to certain classes of instances. In geometry, as well as other branches of mathematics, corollaries can be deduced by using logical rules to analyze certain implications of theorems. Theorem-proving, itself, is a deductive process because the proof of a theorem requires the selection and logical arrangement of definitions, axioms, and other theorems.

Purposes of Discovery Strategies

Before discussing the strategies and activities that teachers can use to guide students in learning how to make discoveries and in making discoveries, it is well to consider the purposes of learning by discovery. There are four general purposes of discovery learning. First, through involvement in discovery lessons students learn some of the procedures and activities that are necessary for figuring things out for themselves. Second, students will develop attitudes and practice strategies that are used in problem-solving, inquiry and research. Third, discovery lessons help students increase their ability to analyze, synthesize and evaluate information in a rational manner. Fourth, there are intrinsic rewards, such as interest in the learning task and satisfaction in making a discovery, that can motivate students to learn more efficiently and effectively in mathematics classrooms.

Among the more specific objectives of discovery-learning which are easy to observe and measure are the following:

1. In discovery lessons students have the opportunity of becoming actively involved in the lesson and many students do increase their level of classroom participation when a discovery teaching/learning strategy is used by the teacher.
2. Through discovery strategies students learn to find patterns in both concrete and abstract situations and also learn to extrapolate additional information by going beyond the given data.
3. Students also learn to formulate unambiguous questioning strategies and to use questions to obtain information which is useful in making discoveries.
4. Discovery lessons can help students develop effective ways of working together, sharing information, and listening to and using other people's ideas.
5. There is some evidence to indicate that skills, concepts and principles learned through discovery are more meaningful to students and are remembered for longer periods of time.
6. Skills learned in discovery-learning situations are, in some cases, more easily transferred to new learning activities and applied in other situations.

The Nature of Discovery Strategies

Classroom Situations for Discovery-Learning
Discovery-learning can occur during teacher lectures, in group discussions, through group activities, through mathematics laboratory experiments, and in

unstructured classroom situations. However the likelihood that students will make discoveries when the teacher is conducting an uninterrupted lecture or in completely unstructured classroom situations is small.

Students seldom make discoveries during a teacher's lecture because the responsibility for manipulating, transforming, and structuring information and ideas rests with the teacher who presents these ideas in final form to students. Student discoveries require active involvement on the part of students, and most students do not attempt to analyze and evaluate information presented in lectures. Lecture material may be ignored, written in a notebook, or committed to memory by students; however it is seldom restructured or extrapolated into new forms containing new information. At times some students do evaluate certain information presented during a lecture and do discover concepts and principles that were not specifically stated by the teacher. However, this type of activity usually causes a student to fall behind the lecturer and miss other information presented while the student is processing the information that results in a discovery. The penalties for missing lecture information encourage students to pay close attention throughout lectures and discourage the mind-wandering involved in making discoveries.

Unstructured classroom situations seldom result in discoveries, especially discoveries related to the mathematics content at hand, because students may not become involved in considering appropriate information. Even when students do attempt to make mathematical discoveries by discussing mathematics with no teacher intervention, the discoveries, if made at all, tend to require a large amount of time which may better be expended in other activities. Unstructured discovery-learning in classrooms tends to be inefficient on the few occasions when it does happen, because students may fail to formulate logical strategies for analyzing and evaluating information or may follow a reasonable procedure which leads nowhere but which is not rejected by the group. Some teacher intervention may be needed to encourage attention to the task at hand, to discourage spending too much time exploring procedures that the teacher knows will produce no results, and to encourage consideration of information and procedures which may lead to a useful mathematical discovery.

Student discoveries are more likely to be made in situations where the teacher begins the lesson by providing some guidelines and structure for the subsequent activities, monitors these activities during the lesson, and intervenes when appropriate or necessary. Consequently, strategies for promoting discovery-learning which lie between the extremes of total teacher control and total student control will be presented here.

Inductive and Deductive Discovery Strategies

Discoveries can be made by using either inductive or deductive learning strategies. When induction is used, generalizations such as problem-solving algorithms, concepts, and principles are discovered through consideration of a number of specific instances of each algorithm, concept, or principle. Deduction involves employing principles of logic to arrive at generalizations which may then be evaluated in order to find their particular instances or applications. In mathematics, definitions and axioms are combined using principles of logic to produce theorems. Searches are then made for applications of these theorems.

Procedures are also sought for ways to logically combine the theorems to produce new theorems which have their own specific representations and applications.

Inductive discovery strategies have been characterized as going from specific instances to generalizations and deductive strategies as going from generalizations to specific instances. Although these characterizations are not wrong, they do oversimplify the situation. The distinguishing characteristics of inductive and deductive strategies lie not so much in the objects with which one begins and ends as they do in the procedure used in going from starting objects to final objects. In using an *inductive discovery strategy,* the learner employs intuition (and some logic) to formulate a generalization of his or her observations of the common properties found in a number of related situations, techniques, or problem solving methods. When a *deductive discovery strategy* is used, the learner employs logic (and some intuition) to formulate a generalization based upon abstract ideas and other generalizations. Later (sometimes much later) examples and applications of the newly discovered generalization are found.

Even though, for the sake of clarity, inductive and deductive discovery strategies have been defined as distinct processes, most actual discoveries are made using a combination of both processes. This observation suggests that an inductive discovery strategy is one in which inductive processes predominate and a deductive discovery strategy is one in which deductive processes predominate. The following examples will help clarify the distinctions between these two types of discovery processes.

In the historical development of mathematics, the Pythagoreans (and probably others) discovered through many observations and measurements that the square of the hypotenuse of a right triangle is equal to the sum of the squares of the legs. This discovery was originally made using inductive strategies. However, the Pythagorean Theorem can be arrived at by using a deductive process. In the plane geometry described by Euclid in his *Elements* and the plane geometry taught in schools today, the Pythagorean Theorem is "discovered" by logically combining axioms, postulates and theorems. The Pythagorean Theorem can be deduced from other generalizations without ever observing a representation of a right triangle. When the Pythagorean Theorem was discovered inductively, observations of specific triangles led to this general and inclusive theorem. The deductive discovery began with some abstract and general definitions, axioms, and postulates and ended with the general theorem.

It is interesting to note that Euclidean geometry, based in part upon the postulate that through a point outside a line one and only one line can be constructed parallel to the given line, was known intuitively and used in land measurement before it was formalized as a deductive science. However, non-Euclidean geometries, based in part upon contradictions of the parallel postulate, were developed as deductive sciences many years before examples and applications of them were found.

Conducting Discovery Lessons

Discovery lessons can be conducted through teacher-directed expository methods or through student-centered laboratory activities. In some discovery lessons, the teacher may select activities that require the students to use inductive processes; other discovery lessons may require the use of deductive processes; whereas many lessons will require combinations of inductive and deductive processes.

Although pure lectures by teachers seldom encourage student discoveries, expository teaching with frequent teacher questions and student interactions can evoke student discoveries. When expository strategies are used to promote student discoveries, the role of the teacher should be that of monitor or discussion leader, but should not be that of presenter of knowledge. The teacher should encourage students to discuss ideas with each other, direct discussions toward useful outcomes, discourage discussions along unproductive avenues, and monitor the flow of ideas and activities within the classroom. When monitoring a discovery lesson, the teacher should not over-structure the lesson so that students merely sit back and wait for the teacher to progress step by step to whatever mathematical discovery he or she had in mind. Neither should the teacher permit the class to proceed unguided for long periods, which may result in no productive activities. The teacher may begin an expository discovery lesson by reviewing relevant information, presenting the situation that should lead to the desired discovery, and setting guidelines for the subsequent discussion. During the discussion, the teacher should answer students' questions and should ask a leading question or provide a piece of relevant information when the student-controlled discussion appears to be stalemated. After a discovery has been made by the class, the teacher should assist students in formulating an understandable and useful statement of it, encourage the class to test the validity of the discovery, and help students consolidate their discovery by incorporating it with related information. These activities should be followed by practice and applications of the discovery. If too much teacher control is exercised throughout a discovery lesson, student participation may be stifled or the class session may degenerate into a game to guess what the teacher is thinking. Too little teacher control may result in no progress toward a discovery. The ideal role for the teacher is that of monitor and not that of lecturer or non-participant.

As is discussed above, discovery lessons can be accomplished through an expository strategy with the entire class participating as one group. Mathematical discoveries can also be made by students working together in small groups or by students working individually on laboratory exercises. While the general advice, which is given above in the context of an expository discovery lesson also applies for a small group discovery lesson, the teacher's role is somewhat different in the latter case. Since the teacher can not exercise the same degree of intervention with each small group or individual student as he or she can exercise with the class as a whole, additional advance preparation is necessary in order to provide instructions which groups and individuals can follow mostly on their own. When discoveries are to be made through laboratory activities, it may be necessary to prepare student worksheets or sets of laboratory devices and materials. At times students may be required during the lesson to write answers to questions or to record data after each step of the laboratory activity is completed. The guidelines in the worksheets should be specific enough so that students do not become confused about what is to be done but they should not be so detailed that students automatically make the expected discovery. Worksheets should provide for student analysis of activities and evaluation of results in order to arrive at discoveries.

Either inductive or deductive procedures can be incorporated into an expository or a laboratory discovery lesson. When inductive processes are to be used for making discoveries, the teacher should make certain that all the necessary specific information is available to students so that they can discover the appropriate generalizations. Many and varied instances of each generalization should be provided so that the generalization is adequately exemplified. Negative instances should also be available in order to avoid over-generalizations which are not restrictive enough.

Deductive discovery lessons in high school mathematics are most appropriate for older students who are well into Piaget's stage of formal operations. These students are better equipped intellectually to synthesize known generalizations into unfamiliar generalizations. Deductive discovery lessons are useful when theorems are to be inferred from definitions, axioms and other theorems, or when proofs of theorems are to be constructed. Since deductive discoveries require the use of mathematical logic and abstract reasoning, they are more difficult to provide for than inductive discoveries, require more time, and are less likely to be made. More will be said about deductive strategies when problem-solving and theorem-proving teaching/learning models are discussed in Chapter 6.

The following list contains some considerations for conducting discovery lessons and some activities that may be selectively included in expository and laboratory discovery lessons involving either inductive or deductive processes:

1. Perplexing questions, problems, and situations can be presented to students in order to motivate activities that will lead to discoveries.
2. Mathematical algorithms and skills can be analyzed to discover general underlying mathematical concepts and principles.
3. Each discovery lesson should begin with known information and proceed step by step to new information and general discoveries.
4. Preassessment strategies should be used to find out if students possess the skills and knowledge required to make each expected inductive discovery.
5. Preassessments should also be used to be sure that students know the concepts and principles necessary for each deductive discovery.
6. The timing of teacher interventions in discovery-learning situations is important. Helpful information should not be presented before students are ready to use it; students should be given an opportunity to assess and reject each unproductive strategy before the teacher discourages its consideration; students should be permitted to formulate and test their own procedures; and the teacher should refrain from frequent intervention which may discourage participation or make the expected discovery transparent.
7. The teacher should permit students to make a discovery in several ways, and should provide for and accept alternative discoveries.
8. Definitions, axioms, postulates, symbols and arbitrary conventions are difficult to discover and lessons designed for their discovery are usually guess-what-I'm-thinking games.
9. Conceptual models, physical models, games and devices can be useful for motivating discoveries.
10. Do not overuse discovery strategies; they can be time consuming and frustrating for students if used frequently.

11. Leading questions and other cues can be used as prompts when discovery lessons become bogged down.

12. At times students should be permitted to select their own questions and activities which may be used for the discovery of mathematical generalizations.

13. Students should be encouraged to check their tentative discoveries against reality and against the opinions and knowledge of other students rather than relying upon the teacher as the source of knowledge and arbitration.

14. In most instances, group work, rather than individual work, is more appropriate for making discoveries because groups provide more ideas and more critics.

15. Too much help or too much information can result in overattention to details and may inhibit consideration of generalizations which are the elements of discoveries.

16. Even though a few students may consistently make the discoveries within a group, rewards and encouragement should also be given to those students who contribute ideas and information which may generate discussions leading to new ideas or discoveries.

Outcomes of Discovery Lessons

Not only does discovery-learning lack a standard definition which is commonly accepted in education but it also lacks a generally accepted set of outcomes. Some empirical studies have been conducted to compare the effects of discovery-learning upon student achievement to the effects of other methods; however, when considered as a group, the findings of these studies are inconclusive. (See Marvin Bittinger's article "A Review of Discovery," in McIntosh (1971), pages 76 to 83.) In his review of research studies on discovery learning, Bittinger feels that the findings of these studies are inconclusive. However, there is some evidence to indicate that students learn equally well through lecture and discovery methods and that the discovery method may increase motivation. It does appear that the discovery method can be an effective approach to teaching certain topics in mathematics but that it is not an educational panacea.

Some of the hypothesized disadvantages of discovery-learning are that the lack of structure imposed upon students results in errors, incorrect discoveries, or no discoveries at all. Discovery-learning usually takes more time than other methods such as lectures and demonstrations, and students who are used to teacher-centered approaches may be frustrated by the responsibility of discovering generalizations for themselves.

Robert B. Davis directed a project (called the Madison Project) at Webster College and Syracuse University which was designed to incorporate discovery into the school mathematics curriculum. Davis, in an article titled "Discovery in the Teaching of Mathematics" (which is included in Shulman and Keislar (1966)), presents the following goals of the discovery-oriented Madison Project. These goals may be regarded as a set of objectives for discovery teaching/learning strategies.

i. We want to give students experience in discovering patterns in abstract situations;

   ii. We want students to have experience in recognizing potentially open-ended situations, and in extending open-ended situations by original creative work;

  iii. We want the students to be familiar with the basic concepts of mathematics . . .;

  iv. We want the students to build up, in their own minds, suitable mental imagery . . .to permit them to perform mental manipulations involving the basic ideas of mathematics . . .;

   v. We want the students to acquire a modest mastery of the basic techniques of mathematics;

  vi. We want the students to know the basic facts of mathematics . . .;

 vii. We want the students to possess considerable facility in relating the various parts of mathematics one to another . . .;

viii. We want the students to possess an easy skill in relating mathematics to the applications of mathematics in physics and elsewhere;

  ix. We want the students to have a real feeling for the history of mathematics . . .;

   x. We want the student to know that mathematics really and truly is discoverable . . .;

  xi. We want each student, as part of the task of knowing himself, to get a realistic assessment of his own personal ability in discovering mathematics;

 xii. We want the students to come to value 'educated intuition' in its proper place;

xiii. We want the students to value abstract rational analysis in its proper place;

xiv. We want the students—as much as possible—to know when to persevere, and when to be flexible;

 xv. We want the students to have a feeling that mathematics is fun or exciting, or worthwhile. (pp. 126-127)

A Discovery Lesson Plan

Many modern arithmetic and algebra textbooks not only present arithmetic and algebraic skills but also deal with the structure of arithmetic and other mathematical systems. The structural properties of many mathematical systems can be discovered by students after they have been shown the elements and operations of the system. The following lesson plan outlines the activities of a discovery lesson for arithmetic modulo 12, which is sometimes called clock arithmetic. Most of the activities in this lesson require inductive strategies; although questions 11 and 12 on the "Activity Sheet" below do involve deduction.

Discovering the Mathematical Properties of Clock Arithmetic

Mathematics Content: This lesson is appropriate for many eighth grade arithmetic classes and most Algebra I classes. The *name* of the topic is *discovering the mathematical properties of clock arithmetic. The mathematical objects* of this lesson are principles, the principles of the system of arithmetic modulo 12. This topic should be presented after students have studied number bases. They should also know and comprehend the following concepts: mathematical operation, commutative, associative, distributive, additive and multiplicative identity and inverse, and closure. This topic could precede the study of the concept of a mathematical group.

Learning Objectives: The *cognitive objectives* are that students will know and comprehend the skills of arithmetic modulo 12; students will analyze and synthesize the addition and multiplication facts for arithmetic modulo 12 and will *discover* the general principles of this system of arithmetic. The *affective objectives* are that students will be willing to participate in this discovery lesson and will obtain satisfaction in their participation. These objectives should be discussed with the class at the beginning of the lesson.

Learning Resources: The only *resources* required for this lesson, in addition to pencils, paper, and a chalkboard, are a large poster or a transparency containing the diagram of the "clock" shown in Figure 5.5 and the "Activity Sheet," which is included in the ***"Teaching/Learning Strategies"*** topic.

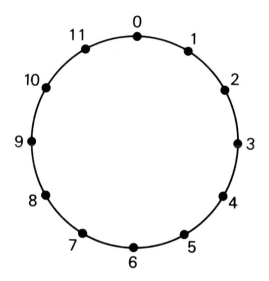

Figure 5.5.　　　A "clock" for arithmetic modulo 12.

Preassessment Strategies: Conduct a brief class discussion to review the concepts—mathematical operation, commutative, associative, distributive, additive and multiplicative identity and inverse, and closure. Follow this discussion with a brief oral or written quiz in which students are asked to define and give an example of each of these concepts.

Teaching/Learning Strategies: Begin the discussion of this lesson on clock arithmetic by showing the "clock" in Figure 5.5 to the class. Explain that the 12 on a standard clock has been replaced by the 0 on your clock so that clock arithmetic will contain an additive inverse of zero.

To be sure that the students know how to add and multiply the modulo 12 numbers on the "clock," conduct a brief question, answer, and discussion session containing questions such as: (1) What is $3 + 9$? (2) What is $9 + 7$? (3) What is 4×8? (4) What is 11×9? Be sure that each student understands the rules of clock arithmetic; that is, the only numbers available for use in this system are 0, 1, . . ., 11, and when you count past eleven you count zero, one, and so forth. Just like a clock, there is no 14 or 27 in this system of arithmetic.

Divide the class into groups of three or four students, and give each student in

249

each group a copy of the following activity sheet. Tell each group to complete the activities and questions on this sheet by working together within the group. Explain that you prefer that they work without assistance from you but if they encounter a problem which the group can not resolve, you will help out.

Activity Sheet

1. Fill in the following addition and multiplication tables for "clock" arithmetic:

+	0	1	2	3	4	5	6	7	8	9	10	11
0												
1												
2												
3												
4												
5												
6												
7												
8												
9												
10												
11												

×	0	1	2	3	4	5	6	7	8	9	10	11
0												
1												
2												
3												
4												
5												
6												
7												
8												
9												
10												
11												

2. Do you see any patterns in either of these tables?
3. Is the set of "clock" arithmetic numbers closed for addition? For multiplication? Why?
4. Double check your table to be absolutely certain that you haven't made any mistakes.
5. Is there an additive identity for clock arithmetic? A multiplicative identity? If so, what are they?
6. Is addition commutative? Is multiplication commutative? How do you know?
7. Is addition associative? Is multiplication associative? Why?
8. Does addition distribute over multiplication? Does multiplication distribute over addition? Give reasons for your answers.
9. Does each "clock" number have an additive inverse? Make a list containing each "clock" number paired with its additive inverse.
10. Does each "clock" number have a multiplicative inverse? Make a list containing each clock number paired with its multiplicative inverse.
11. Can you define subtraction for "clock" arithmetic? If you think you can, construct a subtraction table. Remember, there are no negative numbers on the "clock."
12. Can you define division in "clock" arithmetic? If your answer is yes, make up a "clock" arithmetic division table. Remember, there are no fractions on the "clock."
13. You might want to consider the properties of subtraction and division such as closure, commutativity, associativity, one operation distributing over the other, identities, and inverses.
14. Can you make any other discoveries about clock arithmetic?

As a note to you, the teacher of this lesson, most of these questions have positive answers; however several have negative answers. For instance, some "clock" numbers do not have multiplicative inverses; consequently division can not be defined for clock arithmetic. As an example, 6 has no multiplicative inverse because there is no clock number whose product with 6 is the multiplicative identity 1. Also, Question 14 is included to illustrate that discovery is an open-ended process and there may still be other discoveries to be made.

Postassessment Strategies: As a homework assignment ask students to consider arithmetic modulo 3 and arithmetic modulo 4 by answering the questions on the "Activity Sheet" for these two systems of arithmetic. In arithmetic modulo 3, every number does have a multiplicative inverse; however such is not the case for arithmetic modulo 4. (In general, when the modulus is a prime number p, the arithmetic system modulo p has all the properties of a mathematical field. When the modulus is a composite number c, an arithmetic system modulo c is not a field because there are elements that have no multiplicative inverses.) You can assess student learning by evaluating each group's answers to the questions on the "Activity Sheet" and by grading the homework assignments.

The evaluation of the success of the teaching strategy is obviously related to student success in completing the "Activity Sheet" and the homework assignment. In addition, a procedural evaluation of this lesson is that it may be too long to complete in one class period, and questions 11 through 14 on the activity sheet may be too difficult for slower students and students with limited mathematics backgrounds.

This discovery lesson is a *guided* discovery lesson and it is somewhat teacher-centered because the students do not formulate their own questions. The teacher-prepared "Activity Sheet" contains the questions that are to be answered and specifies the sequence in which the questions are to be considered. Although the groups are free to answer the questions in any order, most people do answer questions in the order in which they are listed on a paper. Each group is free to determine its own procedure for finding answers to each question.

Some other topics that could be studied through discovery strategies are Pascal's Triangle, the Euclidean Algorithm, casting out nines to check arithmetic, the game of Nim, and arithmetic systems in bases different from base ten.

The Use of Games to Learn Mathematics

Even though the procedures for using games in teaching and learning mathematics have not been well enough defined and structured to be given the technical status of a teaching/learning model, games are included here in our list of models because their use is prevalent in mathematics classrooms. Although the use of games is popular among mathematics teachers and students, in many instances games are used rather haphazardly and subsequent positive learning outcomes tend to be more serendipitous than planned.

The affective objective of *satisfaction in response* of most educational games is obvious; however the cognitive mathematical objectives of many games used by mathematics teachers are obscure or nonexistent. This fact is apparent from the status given to games by many mathematics teachers who use classroom games as rewards and time fillers. When a class has done well on a group project or test, students are permitted to play a game. Games are played on the day before a long vacation from school when students are excited and order is difficult to maintain in the classroom. When asked why they use games in their classrooms, most teachers respond that the use of games motivates students and helps them learn mathematics. However many teachers are unable to state cognitive performance objectives for the games that they use. In fact, perusal of catalogs of so-called mathematical games indicates that certain games are included for their popularity rather than their appropriateness for promoting mathematics learning.

The fact that little, if any, mathematics is learned through the use of some popular classroom games and some good games are used for marginal purposes is insufficient reason to indict all mathematics games. Games that are designed for specific learning objectives and used properly by teachers and students can be very effective resources for promoting learning. The hazard in using games occurs when teachers regard games as self-contained lessons and use them with little or no planning. A game lesson requires the same amount and quality of planning as any other mathematics lesson. In preparing to use a game, the teacher should carry out each of the fourteen lesson planning activities. The mathematics objects in the game should be identified. The game should be used in the appropriate place in the mathematics curriculum, which depends upon the mathematics topic embodied in the game. Cognitive and affective objectives should be determined for the game and these objectives should be shared with students. When necessary, resources to supplement the game should be prepared in advance. Preassessment strategies should be devised to assess student readiness to learn the game itself, as well as to learn the mathematical content to be taught during the game, because the rules of some games may be too complex for many younger secondary school students to understand. The teaching/learning strategies for using the game should be formulated; although in many cases the rules of the game are sufficient strategy for the lesson. Postassessment strategies should be used to assess the effectiveness of the game in helping students meet the learning objectives. In addition, the game should be evaluated for its appropriateness and efficiency as a mathematics learning resource.

Several considerations for using educational games in mathematics classrooms, which will be discussed below, are educational objectives and limitations of games, teaching/learning strategies for using games, evaluating the effectiveness of games as learning devices, different types of games, and sources of games. A sample lesson plan for using a game in teaching mathematics will also be presented.

Educational Objectives and Limitations of Games

Since the primary objective given by many educators for using games in mathematics is motivation, the affective objectives of educational games will be discussed first. Most students are willing to play games in their mathematics classes as an alternative to other less interesting activities, which means that they are *willing to receive* whatever mathematical information the game contains. In order to play a game students must become involved in the game; that is, they must be *willing to respond*. For students who enjoy playing games, and most students do, participating in games produces *satisfaction in responding*. The rules and strategies of many games are organized into hierarchies of values where some strategies are more valuable than others. Consequently, game players must be willing to *accept a value* and they usually learn to *prefer certain values*. Some more complex games require players to *organize a value system*. For example, playing games involves values such as individual initiative, working together, respect for the opinions of others, good sportsmanship, and competitiveness. Game playing can help students organize values such as these into *value systems*. An economics game, where winning requires bankrupting one's opponents, may over-emphasize the value of ruthless competition. A game which involves managing resources to build a balanced world economy can illustrate the importance of cooperation among people and countries, whereas the results of excessive competition may be war and economic ruin for everyone. Many educational games developed for the social sciences are designed to influence players' attitudes and values. Although it appears that some of these games are most appropriate for a history, civics, or economics course, many of them require the use of fairly complex arithmetic skills which makes them appropriate for courses in mathematics for two reasons. First, mathematics students can practice their arithmetic skills and, second, they can apply mathematics to solving problems in fields other than mathematics.

Mathematical games can also be used to meet a variety of cognitive objectives. Many games require the use of arithmetic, algebra or geometry skills and can be used to practice and reinforce these skills. Most mathematics teachers use one or two class periods immediately preceding a major test to review the material that will be covered on the test. The purpose of these review sessions is to recall and reinforce facts, skills, concepts and principles. Although review sessions can be useful learning strategies, they tend to be boring for many students. One good way to make a review session more interesting, and as a consequence more effective, is to incorporate the mathematical objects of the review in a game. The teaching/learning plan presented at the conclusion of this section is a general game that can be used to review a wide variety of topics from arithmetic, algebra, and trigonometry.

In general, games are appropriate aids for learning facts, skills, concepts and principles specified through a wide variety of cognitive objectives. Since games can be used to reinforce learning of facts and skills, knowledge and comprehension objectives can be met by playing games. Many commercially available games require the application of mathematics concepts and principles, so application cognitive objectives can be met using games. While many textbook problems neglect the higher level objectives of analysis, synthesis, and evaluation, some mathematical games require the analysis of game strategies and mathematical concepts and principles, as well as synthesis and evaluation of these concepts and principles, in order to formulate winning strategies.

Among the indirect mathematical objects contained in some games are improvement of problem-solving skills, transfer of learning, general intellectual development, and learning how to learn. Computer-based games and simulations can be effective in helping students improve their abilities with respect to these indirect objects of mathematics education.

Although games can be valuable activities for learning mathematics, they are not an educational panacea and do have some limitations. As is true of any teaching/learning model or strategy, games can be effective when judiciously selected and used in moderation. Involvement in mathematical games usually enhances learning for most students; however student involvement in games can become too intense. When playing a game results in winners and losers, unsuccessful students may avoid participating in the game or may participate half-heartedly. Also, the objective of winning may overshadow cognitive objectives and denigrate the value of these mathematical objectives. A few students just do not like to play games and the educational advantages of games for these people are limited. The strategies and rules of some games which do have good mathematical objectives may be too difficult for some students to understand or may be regarded as being beneath their consideration by older, more sophisticated students. Playing certain games may encourage inappropriate values such as winning at any price or refraining from cooperation.

Among the less tangible limitations of games is the fact that some students enjoy games so much that any other teaching strategy appears uninteresting when compared to game strategies. Probably the greatest intangible limitation of games results from the manner in which they are viewed in our society. Games tend to be regarded as diversions and not serious business. Work and education are serious activities because they lead to money, possessions, security and status. After serious business is finished, games can be used for fun and relaxation. Many teachers who use games regard them in this manner and use them as purposeless diversions. Even if teachers who do use good games to meet sound learning objectives rely too heavily upon games as a source of teaching strategies, their students, who have been conditioned to regard games as diversions, may feel that they are not learning any mathematics because the teacher is always playing games. At times it is necessary to educate students, parents and school administrators (as well as teachers) about the value of games as teaching strategies.

Strategies for Using Games

Although the heart of the teaching/learning strategy for a lesson centered around a game is the strategy or rules of the game itself, as a mathematics teacher you should carefully consider all of the activities in planning a lesson when you are selecting a game. It is important that you select or create games containing affective and cognitive mathematical objectives and use each game in the appropriate place in a mathematics course. If you would not follow an algebra lesson on solving two equations in two unknowns with a lesson on solid geometry, you should not follow that algebra lesson with a three-dimensional geometry game. Even though game playing can be an enjoyable diversion, it can also result in significant mathematics learning when appropriate games are selected and used at the proper time.

If you have purchased or created a game which you have not used before, carefully learn and evaluate the rules and play the game before using it in the classroom. This will help you determine whether the strategies and rules of the game are appropriate for your students, whether the rules make sense, and whether they can be learned in a reasonable period of time. There are a few excellent mathematical games that require several hours of practice in order to master their rules. There are other games which have rules that are more complex and abstract than the mathematical content of the games. It probably is well to avoid using games whose rules are harder to learn than the mathematical objects embodied in the games.

Modify the rules of a game, if necessary, to meet the particular requirements of you and your students. There is nothing inviolate about the rules of a game. Even the rules of standard card games, checkers, and chess are modified by players to suit their own purposes. It is also possible to make up an unlimited variety of games using parts of standard games such as boards, dice, spinners, decks of cards, and pieces according to your own rules and objectives.

Encourage students to make up their own games and to modify the rules of your games. You may want to require certain guidelines for student-authored games. Their games should be related to the mathematics topics which they are studying and should have rules and learning objectives subject to the constraints that you use in selecting and preparing your own educational games. In developing a game for particular mathematics learning objectives, students usually learn more about mathematics than they do in playing someone else's game. Herbert Kohl (1974) in his book *Math, Writing, & Games in the Open Classroom* discusses the important experimental, problem-solving and creative skills that children may learn by making up their own games.

Since you will have to teach the class how to play the game, you will need to prepare a mini-lesson plan for teaching the rules of the game. It is usually well to prepare copies of the game rules for each student in the class. If the rules are too long and involved for this to be practical, then they are probably so complex that the game is not appropriate for classroom use. Before beginning game play, make certain that each student understands the rules of the game. When students are confused about the game rules while playing the game, it is doubtful that they will attain the educational objectives of the game. When the game requires teams, you should assign students to teams that are well-balanced according to student abilities so that interest is maintained through fair competition. It is better not to let student team captains select their own teams because poorer students who are selected last may be embarrassed and may fail to give attention to playing the game.

During the course of a game, you should act as a moderator and referee so that game play progresses toward your learning objectives. Also encourage each student to participate in the game and discourage domination of the game by a few students. Game play should be structured and orderly; however students tend to move around and make noise while playing games, so be sure to keep the door to your classroom closed during a game. Unfortunately a few teachers and school administrators still equate movement and noise with discipline problems, so you may have to educate your colleagues to the learning value of games. This is no problem if you have well-defined learning objectives and use sound postassessment procedures.

Above all, treat classroom games as a serious, important and valid teaching/ learning strategy which also happens to be an interesting and enjoyable way for students to learn mathematics. Some people do contend that even though students may not learn any mathematics by playing a certain game, that game is still a good motivating tactic if students enjoy playing it. This argument is fallacious because students may only be motivated to play games and may not associate the enjoyment of game playing with learning mathematics when the games are not related to mathematics. There are many excellent mathematical games in use, as well as an unlimited number of ideas for other mathematical games, so games can be selected both for their motivational value and their value in learning mathematics. A cardinal principle for using educational games in mathematics is: **if the game does not have sound mathematics learning objectives and is not interesting and enjoyable, don't use it in your mathematics classroom.** Mathematics is an interesting subject and the occasional use of games can make it more enjoyable for many students.

Evaluating Games

Included in the previous discussion of games as educational strategies are several principles for evaluating games. Of course, as is true of all teaching/learning strategies, if students fail to attain the learning objectives of the lesson (that is, if they do not learn the material) then the lesson is a failure and the teacher should evaluate the lesson itself to find its deficiencies. However, even when most students are relatively successful in attaining the objectives of a lesson taught using a game strategy, the strategy should still be assessed for factors that could be improved. The following list of questions which should be asked and answered by the teacher when evaluating a game strategy provides a set of guidelines for postassessing game teaching/learning strategies:

1. Were the rules of the game clear to students?
2. Did it require too much time for the class to learn the rules?
3. Were the rules so involved or lengthy that they slowed the progress of the game?
4. Did the game appear to be either too silly or too sophisticated for the class?
5. Was the game structured so that all students had an opportunity to participate?
6. Did each student appear to be involved in the progress of the game?
7. Did the class enjoy playing the game?
8. Were there significant disruptions and minor discipline problems which interfered with an orderly classroom?
9. Did student over-involvement in the game strategy interfere with meeting the learning objectives of the lesson?
10. Were the mathematical objects of the game apparent throughout the game?
11. Did the students attend to the cognitive mathematical objectives of the game?
12. And most important, did the students do well on the postassessment of their learning of mathematics?

Types of Games

There are hundreds of thousands of games that are related to mathematics. In fact any game requiring a logical strategy, a random process, or computations could be considered a mathematical game. However, this definition of a mathematical game is much too general because it does not suggest how one might classify and select games based upon specific and measurable mathematics objectives. In this book a *mathematical game* will be defined as any source of amusement which has both specific, measureable mathematical cognitive objectives and specific, observable mathematical affective objectives.

Some commercial games, which can be purchased from distributors of learning resources, and many teacher-created games, which are described in mathematics education journals and books, have precisely stated learning objectives or learning objectives that can be easily inferred by most mathematics teachers. Unfortunately, many so-called mathematical games, which have become standard resources in mathematics education, appear to have few specific mathematics-related objectives. These games are interesting diversions, but have little to do with most of the objectives of learning mathematics. For example, number puzzles such as SEND multiplied by MORE equals MONEY and EVE divided by DID equals .TALK TALK TALK...are commonly used as mathematical games. In each case the student is to find digits to substitute for the letters so that the problems will be correct. These puzzles are interesting diversions, but considerable imagination is needed to find specific cognitive mathematics objectives in them. Although puzzles such as these are fun for students, when overused in mathematics classes they may give students a distorted viewpoint of the nature and applications of mathematics. A number puzzle such as "find a number so that the sum of the number plus the sum of its digits is 73″ is appropriate for a mathematics classroom because this problem is an example of Diophantine equations which are discussed in courses in number theory. Problems such as this can help students comprehend the concept of Diophantine equations and the principles involved in their solutions. While there is no harm in an occassional game for purely diversionary purposes, it is better, and just as easy, to find games which do have easily identifiable mathematics learning objectives.

There are many different definitions of the word *game*. A game can be defined as any source of amusement, a competition governed by specific rules, a contest among adversaries operating under constraints for a specific objective, etc. Games can also be classified in many ways. They can be classified according to the type of materials used for the game—board games, card games, dice games, etc.; the activities carried out in playing the game—random, probabilistic strategy, guessing, etc.; or the nature of the game—individual competition, team competition, non-competitive, etc. In our discussion of mathematical games, games will be characterized according to the learning objectives that students are to attain through playing each type of game. Some mathematical games involve individual or group competition but many games are non-competitive.

Games to Resolve Puzzles or Paradoxes
Some mathematical games require players to resolve a mathematics puzzle or paradox. In resolving the puzzle or paradox students either apply mathematical skills, concepts and principles, or discover new mathematical objects. Zeno's four paradoxes—the Dichotomy, the Achilles, the Arrow, and the Stadium—which were discussed in Chapter 1—can be resolved by applying appropriate definitions of the concepts of the infinite and the infinitesimal. A well-known

paradox in algebra is a "proof" that every number is equal to its negative which goes as follows:

Let x be any number; for instance, suppose x is equal to some particular number a. Then,

$$x = a$$
$$x - a = 0$$
$$(x - a)(x + a) = 0$$
$$\frac{(x - a)(x + a)}{(x - a)} - \frac{0}{(x - a)}$$
$$x + a = 0$$
$$x = -a.$$

But we assumed that $x = a$, so by substitution, $a = -a$. Of course, this paradox results from dividing both sides of our equation by $(x - a)$, which is equal to zero, yielding a dramatic illustration of the ambiguity of division by zero.

Games to Discover Why a Method Works

Closely related to games for resolving puzzles and paradoxes, which are cooperative rather than competitive, are games to discover why a rule, procedure, or algorithm works. These discovery games involve analysis of mathematical processes and require the application of mathematical skills, concepts and principles. For example, one discovery game involves an ancient algorithm which I call *The Game of Sheepherder Arithmetic*. This "discover-why-it-works" game can be presented to students in this manner:

A Lafamian sheepherder named Shep made his living by raising sheep and selling them to the butcher in his town. Having dropped out of school at a young age to work in the sheep fields, Shep didn't know much arithmetic, so the butcher named Butch had been cheating Shep on his sheep sales. Suspecting that Butch had been cheating him because he was not making any profit on his sheep, Shep, who could add, double, and halve counting numbers, devised a strategy for calculating the price due him from each sheep sale. His method goes like this:

Suppose Shep had 27 sheep to sell at 12 *fames* each (the unit of currency in Lafamia is the *fame*), then Shep would do this:

Sheep	*Price per Sheep*
27 sheep	12 *fames*
13	24
~~6~~	~~48~~
3	96
1	192
	324 *fames*.

Shep halved the number of sheep and doubled the number of *fames* until he could go no further, then he added the *fame* column to find the price he should receive from Butch for his 27 sheep. You will notice that Shep dropped the fractions when halving numbers of sheep. This is because he can not drive pieces of sheep to market, and he does not understand fractions anyhow. You will also notice that he crossed out the 6-sheep row. He did this because he has a superstition about even numbers of sheep, so he always crosses out the sheep and *fame* row when it contains an even number of sheep. Also notice that he did not include the number of *fames* in the row he crossed out as an addend in the sum of the *fame* column.

Why does Shep's method always work? The answer lies in the fact that he is using a strategy that combines a base-ten representation of numbers with a base-two method of addition. This can be seen from the following analysis of Shep's method.

27 Sheep in Base 10 Converted to Base 2		Base Two		Price per Sheep
1	27	1	×	12
1	13	1	×	24
0	~~6~~	~~0~~	~~×~~	~~48~~
1	3	1	×	96
1	1	1	×	192

Twenty-seven sheep in base ten is 11011 sheep in base two. Three hundred twenty-four *fames* in base ten is

$$(1 \times 12) + (1 \times 24) + (0 \times 48) + (1 \times 96) + (1 \times 192) \, fames.$$

Games to Find Rules or Patterns

An important part of the work of a professional mathematician is searching for generalizations and patterns which may lead to new mathematical discoveries. Mathematics students can better comprehend certain mathematics concepts and principles if they use analysis and synthesis to search for rules and patterns. For example, the concept of a mathematical function and the concepts of sequences and limits of sequences can be better understood if students search for generalizations in examples of these concepts. These searches can be motivated through the use of simple, teacher-prepared games. One simple game strategy is to divide the class into two teams and have each team take a turn at making examples of functions or sequences and presenting their examples to the other team. The job of the defensive team is to discover the function, the next term in the sequence, or the limit of the sequence. A point-scoring system can be decided upon to determine the winning team. A list of functions, and sequences is given below to illustrate the types of problems that students might make up for these games.

Discover Each Function

1.

x	1	2	3	0	−1	−2	−3
y	2	5	10	1	2	5	10

(The function is $y = x^2 + 1$.)

2. $(1, 0)$, $(10, 1)$, $(100, 2)$, $\left(\dfrac{1}{10}, -1 \right)$, $\left(\dfrac{1}{100}, -2 \right)$

(The function is $f(x) = \log_{10} x$.)

3. $(\square, \square)$, $(\triangle, \triangledown)$, $(\bigcirc, \bigcirc)$, $(\square, \square)$, $(\bigtriangledown, \bigtriangleup)$

(The function is "turn the first figure up-side-down.")

Find the Next Term in Each Sequence

1. $\dfrac{1}{2}$, $-\dfrac{1}{3}$, $\dfrac{1}{4}$, $-\dfrac{1}{9}$, $\cdots$ (Answer, $\dfrac{1}{8}$)

2. 2, $\dfrac{9}{4}$, $\dfrac{64}{27}$, $\cdots$ (Answer, $\left(1 + \dfrac{1}{4}\right)^4$)

3. $\begin{bmatrix} 1 & 0 \\ 0 & 1 \end{bmatrix}$, $\begin{bmatrix} 4 & 0 \\ 0 & 4 \end{bmatrix}$, $\begin{bmatrix} 9 & 0 \\ 0 & 9 \end{bmatrix}$, $\cdots$ (Answer, $\begin{bmatrix} 16 & 0 \\ 0 & 16 \end{bmatrix}$)

Find the Limit of Each Sequence

1. 1, 2, 1, 3, 1, 4, 1, 5, $\cdots$ (Answer, no limit)

2. $1 + \dfrac{1}{1}$, $1 + \dfrac{1}{2}$, $1 + \dfrac{1}{3}$, $\cdots$ (Answer, 1)

3. $(1 + 1)^2$, $\left(1 + \dfrac{1}{2}\right)^2$, $\left(1 + \dfrac{1}{3}\right)^2$, $\cdots$ (Answer, 1)

Games to Practice Skills

After skills are introduced to students by the teacher, they must be practiced by each student for complete mastery. Drilling and practicing skills by solving lists of textbook problems can be an effective way to master skills; however, it can also be routine and boring. One of the most useful purposes of mathematical games is practicing skills and many simple yet interesting games can be created by teachers and students to use in practicing skills. Games involving a moderate degree of competition can be used for learning skills; but over-competitiveness may interfere with skill mastery by evoking inappropriate attitudes and values. Games can promote comprehension, application, reinforcement and retention of skills as well as the affective objectives of willingness and satisfaction in responding. The majority of the games found in books and collections of mathematics games for secondary school students are designed for learning and practicing skills.

One arithmetic skills game having many variations is a grid game, where the objective is to work one's way from the center to the boundary of a number grid so that the product or sum of the numbers crossed will be either less than or greater than the opponent's product or sum. A grid similar to that shown in Figure 5.6 can be drawn on the chalkboard or projected from a transparency. Each student or group of students can attempt to proceed from the center through blocks to any block on the boundary to attain a certain numerical objective. In this case, the numerical objective is to get to the boundary by passing through five to eight blocks whose number product is smaller than the opponent's product. Moves can be made in any horizontal or vertical direction, but not diagonally; however once a block bordering the outer boundary is entered that player's move is finished. Two paths and the resulting products are shown in the figure.

Individual students or groups should be given a specified time limit of several

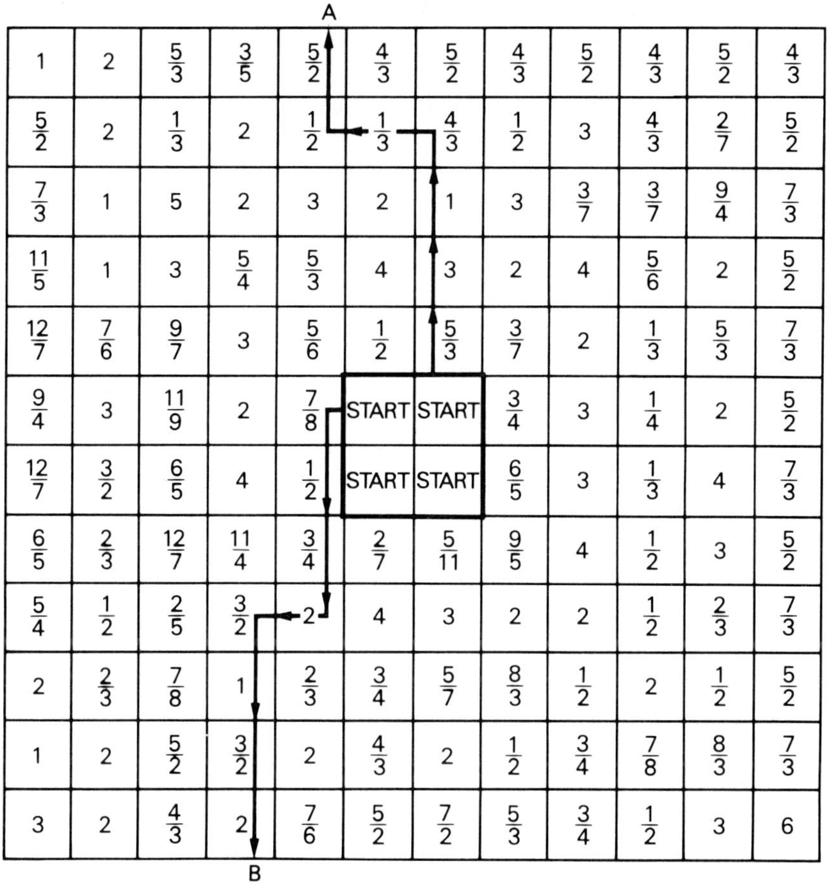

A (over col 5)											
1	2	5/3	3/5	5/2	4/3	5/2	4/3	5/2	4/3	5/2	4/3
5/2	2	1/3	2	1/2	1/3	4/3	1/2	3	4/3	2/7	5/2
7/3	1	5	2	3	2	1	3	3/7	3/7	9/4	7/3
11/5	1	3	5/4	5/3	4	3	2	4	5/6	2	5/2
12/7	7/6	9/7	3	5/6	1/2	5/3	3/7	2	1/3	5/3	7/3
9/4	3	11/9	2	7/8	START	START	3/4	3	1/4	2	5/2
12/7	3/2	6/5	4	1/2	START	START	6/5	3	1/3	4	7/3
6/5	2/3	12/7	11/4	3/4	2/7	5/11	9/5	4	1/2	3	5/2
5/4	1/2	2/5	3/2	2	4	3	2	2	1/2	2/3	7/3
2	2/3	7/8	1	2/3	3/4	5/7	8/3	1/2	2	1/2	5/2
1	2	5/2	3/2	2	4/3	2	1/2	3/4	7/8	8/3	7/3
3	2	4/3	2	7/6	5/2	7/2	5/3	3/4	1/2	3	6

B (below col 4)

$$A = \frac{5}{3} \cdot \frac{3}{1} \cdot \frac{1}{1} \cdot \frac{4}{3} \cdot \frac{1}{3} \cdot \frac{1}{2} \cdot \frac{5}{2} = 2\frac{7}{9}$$

$$B = \frac{7}{8} \cdot \frac{1}{2} \cdot \frac{3}{4} \cdot \frac{2}{1} \cdot \frac{3}{2} \cdot \frac{1}{1} \cdot \frac{3}{2} \cdot \frac{2}{1} = 2\frac{61}{64}$$

Figure 5.6. A grid game for practicing product skills.

minutes to select a path to the border and to compute the product of the numbers in the cells lying in the path. Scoring is as follows:

1. No score if the path is longer than eight steps or if diagonal steps are taken.
2. Each student or group gets the product obtained from multiplying the numbers in the cells traversed, provided the product has been computed correctly. If the answer is wrong, the score is zero.
3. Since the objective of this game is to find a product that is as small as possible, the student or group finding the smallest product is awarded ten bonus points.

After the game has been played several times, each player's or group's scores can be totaled to determine the winner.

The scoring rules for this game provide points for correct answers as well as for winning answers, and there is also some strategy involved. For example, it might be well to find a path yielding a large product even though it will not result in ten bonus points.

After the game has been played several times, someone may discover a path that will always be a winner. If this happens, the rules can be changed to make the largest product the winner, or diagonal moves can be allowed.

This game chart and the rules can be modified for practice of addition or multiplication skills for natural numbers, integers, fractions, mixed numbers, or decimal numbers. Game charts of different sizes and shapes can be used, and the game can even be modified for use in algebra or trigonometry. An element of chance can be added to games such as this by purchasing or constructing cards of standard playing card size and making up card decks with various types of numbers on each card. For example, a deck of sixty cards containing mixed fractions could be prepared and used in a manner similar to the grid game. Each student could be dealt five cards with the objective of selecting any three of his or her five cards to make the largest three-factor product possible from the hand. In fact there are nearly infinite variations on grid and card games for practicing skills in all mathematics subjects, and teachers and students can create any of these variations using very inexpensive materials.

Since commercial skill games tend to be expensive, it is better to purchase games that have many variations and that can be used to meet a number of different learning objectives. Mathematics game books also contain ideas for many games which can be modified for use in different subjects and for various learning objectives. With a bit of ingenuity and creativity, most games can be improved or modified for many learning objectives in a variety of mathematics topics. Although there are many good mathematics games on the market, a few inexpensive mathematical game books will provide enough good ideas for hundreds of games and modifications of games which can be used to practice and reinforce skills.

Guessing Games for Learning Concepts and Principles

Guessing games can be used to reinforce concepts and principles and can help students improve their ability to estimate and approximate. Cognitive objectives of knowledge, comprehension, application and analysis can be met through guessing games as well as the affective objectives of willingness to respond and satisfaction in responding. Mathematical concepts such as inequality, absolute value, solving equations and coordinate systems can be learned through guessing games. Guessing games can also be used to teach some of the skills of solving statement problems and proving theorems. Among the indirect objectives that can be met through guessing games are understanding the value of intuition, educated guessing, and approximation as useful strategies in mathematics.

The following coordinate game is an illustration of a guessing game which can be played by pairs or small groups of students. The game helps students understand the various concepts included in a coordinate system.

The only materials needed for this game, which is called **Snarf,** are pencils and rectangular (or polar) coordinate paper. The version of **Snarf** described here is a rectangular coordinate game. The simple but fascinating objective of **Snarf** is to guess the secret hiding place of a mythical bird called a snarf. One team competes against another by trying to guess the location of the snarf as the teams take turns hiding the snarf. The hiding team selects a hiding place for the snarf which is kept secret from the hunting team which asks questions that can be answered *yes* or *no* by the hiding team. The objective is to find the snarf using the fewest questions. As an illustration of the conduct of the game, suppose the hiding team has hidden a snarf at the point whose coordinates are $(-3, 2)$ and the hunting team is trying to guess the location. To keep the game manageable, integer pairs must be used as hiding places and the coordinate system has pre-determined dimensions for each game. In this game, the ten-by-ten coordinate system shown in Figure 5.7 will be used.

A typical questioning strategy that the hunting team might use on the hiding team to guess the location of the snarf is given below:

Hunting Team's Questions	**Hiding Team's Answers**
1. Is the snarf to the left of the y-axis?	Yes.
2. Is the snarf in the third quadrant?	No.

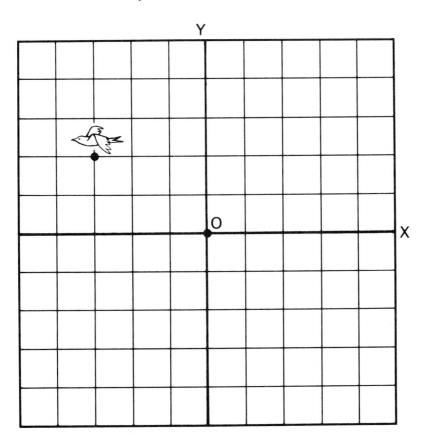

Figure 5.7.   **Snarf:** A guessing game for learning rectangular coordinates.

3. Is the snarf closer to the y-axis than the x-axis?   No.
4. Is the y-coordinate greater than 1?   Yes.
5. Is the y-coordinate 2?   Yes.
6. Is the x-coordinate less than or equal to negative 4?   No.
7. Is the snarf hidden at $(-3, 2)$?   Yes.

The rules of the game are:

1. The snarf must be hidden at a location whose coordinates are an integer pair.
2. The hunting team is given 20 points at the beginning of the game.
3. Each time the hunting team asks a question it loses one point.
4. If the hiding team should answer a question incorrectly, in the judgement of the teacher who is the referee, the hunting team is given one bonus point.
5. When the hunting team has guessed the location of the snarf its score is the number of points remaining from the 20 points awarded at the start of the game. (In this example, the hunting team took seven guesses to find the snarf, so their score is $(20 - 7)$, or 13 points.)
6. Each team is given an equal number of opportunities to hide and to hunt for a snarf and the team with the highest total score is the winning team.

Not only do students learn the properties of rectangular coordinates by playing **Snarf,** but they also learn to develop efficient questioning strategies. **Snarf** can also be played on a polar-coordinate system to help students learn skills and concepts of that method of locating points. More challenging versions of **Snarf** can be developed by using a three-dimensional rectangular-coordinate system or by having the hunters ask questions in rectangular-coordinate terminology and the hiders answer in polar-coordinate terminology or vice versa.

Many guessing games similar to **Snarf** can be created easily. For instance, games can be made for guessing the location of a point on a number line, for guessing a number by asking questions about its factors, and for guessing algebraic or trigonometric functions by asking questions about their graphs. In most cases where a specific mathematical object can be identified through information about its properties, guessing games such as **Snarf** can be used.

Problem-Solving Games for Learning Logical Principles
Two of the indirect objects of mathematics are learning general, transferable problem-solving skills and logical methods. Most mathematics game books contain several logical problems which have no observable cognitive objectives for learning specific mathematical facts, skills, concepts or principles. Although these logic problems, which appear to require many of the reasoning abilities found in television detectives, may be of marginal use for meeting cognitive objectives in mathematics, they are excellent motivational devices and do appear to involve the use of problem-solving and inquiry skills that have general applications. Since such problems are only several steps above the "SEND-MORE-MONEY problem" mentioned previously, they should be used sparingly in mathematics classrooms. Their benefits are maximized when teachers use them to analyze the generalizable inquiry and problem-solving procedures embodied in their solutions.

Miller and Henderson (1972) in their book *Let's Play Games in Mathematics* include the following game which is representative of this logical problem-solving type of game:

> Nine men, Brown, White, Adams, Miller, Green, Hunter, Knight, Jones, and Smith, make up a baseball team. Determine from the following facts the position played by each.
>
> 1. Smith and Brown each won ten dollars playing poker with the pitcher.
> 2. Hunter was taller than Knight and shorter than White but each of the three weighed more than the first baseman.
> 3. The third baseman lived across the corridor from Jones in the same apartment house.
> 4. Miller and the outfielders play bridge in their spare time.
> 5. White, Miller, Brown and the right fielder and the center fielder are bachelors and the rest are married.
> 6. Of Adams and Knight, one played in the outfield.
> 7. The right fielder was shorter than the center fielder.
> 8. The third baseman was the pitcher's wife's brother.
> 9. Green was taller than the infielders and also taller than the battery (pitcher and catcher), except for Jones, Smith and Adams.
> 10. The second baseman beat Jones, Brown, Hunter and the catcher at cards.
> 11. The third baseman, the shortstop, and Hunter each made one hundred dollars speculating on U.S. Steel.
> 12. The second baseman was engaged to Miller's sister.
> 13. Adams lives in the same house as his sister but dislikes the catcher.
> 14. Adams, Brown and the shortstop each lost money speculating.
> 15. The catcher has three daughters, the third baseman has three sons, but Green is being sued for divorce. (pp. 56-57)

Since very few people can read and analyze these fifteen statements about the players in a sequential mode to determine the position played by each man, use of an iterative strategy is required by most people. That is, a first reading of the statements will uncover certain obvious information and later readings will uncover less obvious information. There are also two strategies, direct and indirect, for solving problems such as this one. A direct strategy requires piecing together information that will indicate which position is played by each man. An indirect strategy involves using information to eliminate certain possibilities until eight of the nine possible positions have been eliminated for each man, leaving the set of correct positions as the only possibility. Most people find that problems of this type are easier to solve by using an indirect approach.

This problem and similar problems nearly always contain three kinds of information—direct information, indirect information, and misleading information. Direct information comes from inferences contained in the individual clues. For instance, Statement 4, "Miller and the outfielders play bridge in their spare time," directly implies that Miller is not an outfielder. Indirect information comes from combining several clues to discover inferences. For instance, Statement 6 eliminates one or the other of Adams and Knight as outfielders. But Statement 9 eliminates Adams as an outfielder, so Knight must be an outfielder. Statement 12 is subject to misinterpretation which makes it a misleading piece of information; however it is not incorrect or illogical. This statement says that "the second baseman was engaged to Miller's sister," which could be incorrectly

	C	P	1	2	3	SS	RF	CF	LF
Brown	10	1		10		14	5	5	
White			2				5	5	
Adams	13					14	9	9	9
Miller				12			4	4	4
Green	9	9	9	9	9	9	(5, 15)	(5, 15)	
Hunter	10	(2, 4, 5, 7, 9, 15)	2	10	11	11	(2, 4, 5, 7, 9, 15)		(2, 4, 5, 7, 9, 15)
Knight	(6, 9)	(6, 9)	(6, 9)	(6, 9)	(6, 9)	(6, 9)		(2, 4, 5, 7, 9, 15)	(9, 5, 15)
Jones	10			10	3		9	9	9
Smith		1					9	9	9

Figure 5.8. **Baseball players:** A game for learning a logical strategy for solving problems.

interpreted as meaning that the second baseman is single. He could now be married to Miller's sister or he could be married to someone else.

Figure 5.8 contains a chart illustrating part of an indirect strategy for solving this problem. The number written in each cell is the number of the clue that is used to eliminate that cell as a possible player/position combination. Sets of numbers in a cell indicate that combinations of clues were used to eliminate that cell.

The correct answers for the problem are: catcher—Smith, pitcher—Jones, first baseman—Brown, second baseman—White, third baseman—Adams, shortstop—Miller, right fielder—Knight, center fielder—Hunter, and left fielder—Green.

If you do plan to use games such as this one to teach logic and problem-solving skills, it is best to solve several such problems in class using a teacher-directed discussion so that each student will know that a good approach to these problems is to set up an elimination table similar to the one shown in Figure 5.8.

Games for Learning to Estimate

One skill that is neglected in many school mathematics programs is the skill of estimation. There are three mathematics-related types of estimation—estimating answers for word problems in arithmetic, algebra and trigonometry; estimating answers to computational problems; and estimating measures of physical objects. When solving computational problems in mathematics, many students do not know how to determine whether their answers make sense. In their minds the answer is either right or wrong and whether or not it is reasonable is of little consequence. When applying arithmetic skills to everyday activities such as shopping in a super market or department store, obtaining credit, and balancing a bank statement, many people are unable to make a quick, accurate estimate of the correct answer. A good shopper can mentally estimate the price of a basket of groceries or dry goods within a few dollars, which permits him or her to catch significant errors on cash register totals and bills. Many people are very poor at estimating lengths, areas, volumes, weights, and temperatures of physical objects. How good are you? Can you estimate your extended hand span, the width of your thumb, the weight of a pencil, or the Celsius temperature of a room? Although the inability to estimate length, weight, temperature, etc. within our United States Customary System of Measurement is a minor inconvenience, as more and more businesses, industries, and local governmental agencies adopt the Metric System of Units, the ability to estimate in both systems and to make comparisons between systems becomes an increasingly important skill.

Mathematics teachers can help students learn all three types of estimation by setting estimation tasks for students and by emphasizing the importance of sensible, if not completely accurate, computations through their methods of testing and evaluating students' answers on tests as well as assignments. At times it might be well to give partial credit for certain answers which are close to being correct. At other times, tests and quizzes can be given so that students are required to arrive at reasonable estimates to problems within a time limit.

One interesting approach to estimating is through games. Games can be used to improve students' speed and accuracy at estimating and to improve their ability to apply estimating skills to many out-of-school situations. The following game is designed to improve students' estimating skills in metric units of measure. The objective of the game is to be able to rapidly estimate the metric measures of a variety of common physical objects.

In preparation for this game, collect a large variety of common school and household items whose weights and measures can be estimated in metric units. Students may enjoy assisting in this activity. Some suggestions for your collection are:

1. Pencil
2. Chalk
3. Paper clip
4. Coins
5. Can of soup
6. Onion
7. Plastic cup
8. Plastic freezer containers
9. Pots and pans
10. Package of gum
11. Candy bar
12. Light bulb
13. Aspirin tablet
14. Dollar bill
15. Table spoon
16. Coffee cup
17. Empty boxes
18. Thumb tacks
19. Comb
20. Small pieces of scrap wood

The objective of the game is for students to estimate the mass (weight), length, area, or volume (whichever is appropriate) for each item that you take from a box. The class can be divided into small groups, with the group making the best estimate for an object being awarded a point. Even high school seniors enjoy this activity and competition can be lively. Be sure to have a variety of metric measuring devices available because the class will want to compare their estimates to the "exact" measures. Avoid telling your class the exact answers; students need practice in using metric measuring devices, so they should measure each item for themselves. You should have the following metric measuring devices available for student use during the game.

1. A 25 cm metric measuring stick for each student.
2. A meter stick for each student.
3. Approximately six metric scales.
4. Approximately six balances with sets of metric masses.
5. A Celsius thermometer for each student.
6. *Do **not** have any U.S. Customary/Metric conversion charts or devices in the classroom. The objective of this lesson is to estimate within the metric system, not to convert between the two systems of measurement.*

An alternative, individualized version of this game is to use your collection of objects for a quiz on estimating in the metric system. Show each object, one at a time, to the class and have each student write an estimate for its weight or measure. Give the class ten to thirty seconds between objects. After they have finished the quiz, let the students use the metric measuring devices to determine the precise weights and measures of the objects and to decide what range of answers constitutes a reasonable estimate for each object. Some sample quiz items are:

1. How long is this paper clip?
2. How thick is this dime?
3. What is the mass of a penny?
4. What is the temperature of this room?
5. What is the volume of this classroom?
6. What is the gasoline "mileage" of a typical automobile in kilometers per liter?
7. What is the area of the chalkboard?
8. How wide is your little finger nail?
9. How long is your arm?
10. How much do you weigh?

Be sure that each student uses the proper spelling for each metric unit, the proper symbol abbreviation for each unit, correct spellings for prefixes, and standard conventions for writing numbers and symbols in the metric system. For example, the symbol for centimeter is *cm*, not *Cm* or *cm* followed by a period. In the International System of Units (the modernized metric system) a number of standards for writing metric measures have been agreed upon. These standards are specified in some modern dictionaries and in metric instructional materials available from the United States Department of Commerce. Some commercially available metric resources do not use the standard symbols, so it is well to preview materials before they are purchased.

Sources of Mathematical Games

The best continuing sources of mathematical games are magazines and journals such as *The Mathematics Teacher, The Arithmetic Teacher, Creative Computing,* and *Scientific American.* Several of the recent yearbooks of the National Council of Teachers of Mathematics have a few mathematical games and lists of sources of many other games. The NCTM also has several inexpensive books containing mathematical games; these books are listed in their free brochure, ''Current Publications.'' Many publishers of mathematics textbooks for secondary schools also publish game books. Names and addresses of publishers can be obtained in most school offices.

Although there are many descriptions of mathematical games in print, not all games are good games. Some are too expensive or too complicated, others are too trivial, and still others have questionable objectives. However, many marginal games can be made into good games with minor modifications. Creative teachers find ideas in existing games which they use to develop new and improved games. It seems that every time a new game is created someone develops a better version of it.

A Lesson Plan for a Generalizable Game

To conclude this section on using games in teaching and learning mathematics, a complete fourteen point lesson plan for reviewing a topic from secondary school mathematics is presented below. The particular game strategy used in this lesson was chosen because it is generalizable to a number of topics in arithmetic, algebra, geometry and trigonometry as well as to other selected topics which are sometimes taught in high school mathematics courses. While this lesson plan illustrates how a game strategy can be used to teach a topic in mathematics, it is also an example of the application of the group processes teaching/learning model which is discussed in the following chapter.

A Game For Practicing Arithmetic Skills

Mathematics Content: The *topic* of this particular lesson is adding fractions; however the strategy of the lesson can be used in any drill and practice situation where the problems to be solved have numerical answers. The *mathematics objects* of this lesson are facts and skills. This lesson is appropriate for reviewing and practicing skills; that is, for adding various types of fractions and mixed numbers and for ranking fractions. The lesson should follow a unit on addition of fractions and mixed numbers. Since this is a review lesson, it would probably precede a topic test on addition of fractions.

Learning Objectives: The *cognitive objectives* of the lesson are: Students will know and comprehend the concepts of proper fraction, improper fraction and mixed number. Students will know, comprehend and apply the skill of adding fractions and mixed numbers. Students will know, comprehend and apply the concept of inequality. The *affective objectives* are: Students will be willing to respond during the individualized activities of the lesson and will obtain satisfaction in responding and contributing useful information during the group activities of the lesson. Students will also accept the value of practicing addition skills through structured group activities. Of course, these objectives should be shared with the students before the lesson begins.

Learning Resources: Prepare enough copies of the set of addition problems shown below so that *two* copies are available for each student. However, do not fill in the answers and ranks as is done in the problem list below; that task is to be done by the students.

Practicing Addition Skills

	Problem	*Answer*	*Rank*
A.	$\dfrac{2}{3} + \dfrac{5}{3}$	$\left(2\dfrac{1}{3} \right)$	(6)
B.	$\dfrac{8}{9} + \dfrac{2}{3}$	$\left(1\dfrac{5}{9} \right)$	(5)
C.	$\dfrac{1}{3} + \dfrac{1}{4} + \dfrac{1}{2}$	$\left(1\dfrac{1}{12} \right)$	(2)
D.	$\dfrac{2}{5} + \dfrac{3}{7} + \dfrac{1}{3}$	$\left(1\dfrac{17}{105} \right)$	(4)
E.	$1\dfrac{1}{2} + \dfrac{3}{4} + \dfrac{1}{8}$	$\left(2\dfrac{3}{8} \right)$	(7)
F.	$2\dfrac{1}{8} + \dfrac{1}{3} + \dfrac{1}{4}$	$\left(2\dfrac{17}{24} \right)$	(9)
G.	$1 + 1\dfrac{1}{2}$	$\left(2\dfrac{1}{2} \right)$	(8)
H.	$3\dfrac{1}{2} - 3 + \dfrac{1}{7}$	$\left(\dfrac{9}{14} \right)$	(1)
I.	$3\dfrac{1}{2} + 1\dfrac{1}{3} + 2\dfrac{2}{7}$	$\left(7\dfrac{5}{42} \right)$	(11)
J.	$\dfrac{7}{3} + \dfrac{5}{2} + \dfrac{15}{9}$	$\left(6\dfrac{1}{2} \right)$	(10)
K.	$\dfrac{1}{2} + \dfrac{2}{5} + \dfrac{1}{4}$	$\left(1\dfrac{3}{20} \right)$	(3)
L.	$2\dfrac{3}{4} + 1\dfrac{1}{6} + 3\dfrac{1}{3}$	$\left(7\dfrac{1}{4} \right)$	(12)

Preassessment Strategies: Since the purpose of this lesson is to practice and review addition skills, only a brief preassessment is necessary. Each student should be asked to give an example of a proper fraction, an improper fraction, and a mixed number. Each student should also be asked to rank the following numbers from smallest to largest:

$$2\frac{1}{3}, 1\frac{1}{3}, \frac{7}{8}, \frac{9}{11}, 1\frac{1}{5}, \frac{11}{7}, 1\frac{2}{5}, \frac{9}{4}, \frac{11}{5}.$$

Teaching/Learning Strategies: After the performance objectives have been shared with the class and the preassessment activities have been carried out correctly by each student, begin the lesson by giving each student one copy of the drill and practice sheet shown above. Tell the students to find the answer to each problem by working alone and to write each answer beside the problem in the *Answer* column. Also tell the students that after they have solved all the problems, they are to rank their answers from the smallest answer to the largest answer. This should be done by writing the rank of each answer beside that answer in the *Rank* column. The smallest answer should be assigned the rank 1, the largest answer the rank 12, and other answers should be assigned appropriate ranks between 1 and 12 with smaller answers being assigned lower ranks than larger answers. Tell the students to rank all the answers, and if there are some problems that a student is unable to solve, he or she should make a reasonable estimate of the answer and assign the proper rank to the estimate. Also tell the class that scoring will be done on ranks rather than answers, and that it is important to rank answers and estimates as accurately as possible.

After all the students have finished solving the problems and ranking their answers, ask each student to write his or her name on the paper and return it to you. When you have collected all of the students' papers, give each student a fresh copy of the problem sheet and tell the class that they are to work together to decide upon correct answers. Since you have collected the sheets containing their answers, the class as a group will have to solve each problem again. Not being able to refer to their individual answers will result in greater student participation within the group and will avoid having some students attempt to convince the class to accept the answers, right or wrong, from their own papers as the "correct" answers. After the class as a whole agrees upon a set of answers for the problems, have the group rank the answers from smallest answer (rank 1) to largest answer (rank 12) and write a list of their answers and ranks on the chalkboard or overhead projector. Since it is possible that the class may have agreed upon several incorrect answers and ranks, write a second list of your own correct answers and ranks beside the students' list as a comparison for later purposes.

Next return each student's original paper to him or her and have each student score his or her own work by comparing it to your list of correct answers. The scoring, which is done according to ranks rather than answers, is carried out as follows:

Step 1. Have each student calculate the absolute value of the difference between his or her rank and your correct rank for each problem.

Step 2. Ask each student to find the sum of the twelve differences calculated in Step 1. This sum is that student's score. Of course, the best score is the lowest score and a perfect score is a score of zero.

Step 3. Next, have the class use the procedures in Steps 1 and 2 to compare the set of ranks that they found by working together with your correct set of ranks. In nearly all cases, the score obtained in this step will be less than the score obtained by each individual student, which shows the value of working together to solve problems.

This procedure of scoring ranks instead of answers serves the purpose of showing students that accurate estimates and sensible answers, as well as exact answers, have a place in learning mathematics skills.

Postassessment Strategies: In the class session following the session in which the **Practicing Addition Skills** sheets are used, give the class a test or quiz containing questions and problems similar to those found in the preassessment strategies and the drill sheet. Student success in meeting the cognitive objectives of the lesson can be determined through their test or quiz scores. Success in meeting the affective objectives can be evaluated by observing the degree of participation and interest shown by each student during the group activities which are part of the teaching/learning strategies.

The strategy used in teaching this lesson can be applied in any drill-and-practice or review session on most topics in secondary school mathematics. However this particular strategy should not be used too frequently with any single class. Overuse of this, as well as most other teaching/learning strategies, can result in a decrease in interest and motivation for many students.

The Individualized Teaching/Learning Model

Students vary in stage of intellectual development, mathematical ability, problem solving skills, emotional and social maturity, learning styles, motivation to learn in school and background in mathematics. As a consequence of these many individual differences among students, the most effective mathematics teachers are those people who use teaching methods that provide for differences among students. Since students do differ in so many ways, teachers should vary objectives, homework assignments, classroom activities and evaluation criteria and methods for their students. Since most teachers are required to teach from 20 to 40 students simultaneously, it is seldom possible to provide a completely individualized mathematics program or course for each student. However, it is possible to make some limited but effective provisions for individualizing instruction in every mathematics classroom.

There are a variety of procedures to provide for individual differences in mathematics classrooms. These procedures range from system-wide programs initiated and supported by school districts to teacher-initiated, day-by-day classroom activities. In this section, a general individualized teaching/learning model will be presented, followed by a discussion of ways in which school districts and individual teachers can develop instructional programs and methods to provide for the many differences among students.

A General Model for Individualizing Instruction

The elements of a general model for individualizing instruction are similar to the activities in planning a lesson. The distinctive characteristic of an individualized instructional model, which is not usually found in other teaching/learning models, is that each student covers materials and learns at his or her own pace. In non-individualized programs, the teacher decides how rapidly material will be covered, when to give tests, when to review familiar information, and when to move on to new material. In an individualized program, each student, at least in theory if not always in practice, covers material at his or her own pace, takes tests when ready, reviews material when necessary, and moves on to new material when he or she has mastered the prerequisites for this material. Although individualized instructional programs differ from each other in many ways, this differentiated pacing of learning for each student is common to all such programs.

The elements of an individualized teaching/learning model are:

1. Individualized teaching and learning resources.
2. Individualized student learning objectives.
3. Individualized preassessment strategies.
4. Individualized learning activities.
5. Individualized postassessment strategies.

Individualized Teaching and Learning Resources

Most individualized learning programs contain a variety of teaching and learning resources which are selected according to the different learning styles of students. Some students are able to learn mathematics by reading textbooks; others need to work with concrete devices; still others learn by hearing lectures or seeing demonstrations. However, most students learn mathematics best through the use of special combinations of resources. Consequently, several different types of learning resources may be available to help students master a certain topic in mathematics. For example, the skills and concepts involved in graphing trigonometric functions could be presented in a textbook format, through a series of laboratory activities, by a tape-recorded lecture, through a filmstrip, or by a sound and color motion picture. Learning resources may be prescribed for each student based upon his or her individual preference, unique abilities and distinctive learning style. Learning resources are chosen so that each mathematics topic can be presented to students in several different formats.

Individualized Student Learning Objectives

When mathematics teachers are required to teach the same material to every student in the class simultaneously, they usually select the same learning objectives for every student; that is, the objectives are group objectives rather than individualized objectives. Even though a teacher might expect every student in the class to study the same mathematics topics, it can not be expected that all students will attain the same level of mastery in a specified time period. How well each student learns a certain topic is closely related to his or her special abilities, mastery of prerequisite topics, and rate of learning mathematics.

In individualized educational programs, student learning objectives are differentiated; that is, different objectives may be set for each student for a particular topic. Even when the same objectives are set for all students, each student is permitted to work at his or her own rate until he or she attains the objectives. Some individualized programs contain different tracks and students are assigned to tracks based upon their abilities and previous mathematics achievement. Students in lower tracks will not attain the same level of mastery as students in higher tracks. For example, some students may be expected to master more complex arithmetic skills than others; but all students should acquire the basic arithmetic skills. The objective for each student is to attain the highest mastery level that his or her ability permits for each topic. It is expected that some students will learn certain topics in more depth and will cover more topics than other students; however success and failure are based upon individual goals, not group goals. In this sense, each student is competing with himself or herself, not with other students.

Individualized Preassessment Strategies

In an individualized mathematics program, each student's level of mastery of prerequisite facts, skills, concepts and principles is assessed before he or she goes on to a new topic. When it is found that a student has not attained the prerequisites for a new topic, materials and strategies are selected to help him or her master those prerequisites before moving on to new material. Preassessment materials and activities are individualized, which means that there are several ways for a student to demonstrate mastery of prerequisites. Different levels of mastery may be acceptable for various students. Mastery of mathematics prerequisites may be demonstrated through written tests, oral quizzes, laboratory activities and discussions with the teacher.

Individualized Learning Activities

In an individualized instructional program, several different activities are available for students to use in learning each new topic. Physical devices and laboratory activities may be selected for those students who learn mathematical concepts and principles through concrete representations. Abstract thinkers, who are well into Piaget's stage of formal operations, may learn mathematics concepts and principles most efficiently by reading textbooks. Other students may understand certain concepts and principles better when they are animated in a motion picture or represented in a physical model.

When learning mathematics skills, some students need more practice than others. If a student can master a skill through several practice items, he or she should be permitted to go on to a new topic rather than being required to solve long lists of similar drill-and-practice exercises. Some students require a considerable amount of practice in order to master unfamiliar mathematical skills; these students should not be labeled as failures and moved on to a new topic before they have mastered the skill in question at an appropriate level. Since students' learning rates and learning styles vary, learning materials and activities should also be varied to meet the needs of individual students.

Individualized Postassessment

Just as preassessment objectives and procedures should be individualized, it is also appropriate to select and devise postassessment strategies based upon the learning characteristics of each student. At times certain students may not be able to attain the same level of mastery of a mathematics topic as other students. Also, students may demonstrate their levels of mastery in different ways. Every student should be expected to learn each topic to the best of his or her ability and at least demonstrate minimal competencies before proceeding to a new topic.

Since most individualized programs emphasize mastery rather than competition, postassessment testing situations in an individualized program do not pose the threat that they do in some other teaching programs. Each student knows that there is a second chance to learn a topic when he or she does poorly on the posttest. Since one does not have to keep up with the required pace of the class, as is true in group learning, students need not forge ahead to new material before they have learned prerequisite topics.

Specific Programs for Individualizing Instruction
In order to completely individualize a mathematics program, the decision to do so must be made by the school board members and school administrators who are responsible for providing the necessary funding. Implementing an individualized instructional model requires new and different instructional resources, inservice teacher education programs, and may even require alteration of physical facilities within the school. The additional cost of equipping and managing a completely individualized program may average out to as much as $100 per student per year. Many school districts that may not support the concept of a totally individualized educational program, or that may not have the funds required for such an endeavor, may take a partial approach to individualizing instruction.

Some partial approaches that school districts may take to individualize instruction are:

1. Providing accelerated classes for highly motivated students with exceptional mathematics ability.
2. Providing courses in remedial arithmetic for students who have failed to master basic arithmetic skills in elementary school.
3. Assigning students to differentiated sections of a mathematics course according to their ability levels and previous achievement in mathematics.
4. Providing for smaller classes or people to work as teacher aides in larger classes.
5. Using programmed textbooks in certain courses to provide for individualized pacing of learning.
6. Providing independent study courses and self-instructional materials for advanced mathematics courses which have limited registration.
7. Forming vocation-oriented courses where students must master the basic mathematics skills required for specific vocations.
8. Using computer-based programmed-instructional systems (which are an added expense) that can be appropriate for meeting certain objectives.

While these and other procedures do have the advantage of partially individualizing and differentiating instruction for some students, they may require extra money and have certain educational limitations. For example, leasing time on a computer which contains programmed-learning materials costs from two to five dollars per student hour, even though computer costs are decreasing rapidly. Tracking students into courses according to their ability levels may decrease motivation for lower-track students and may promote a mini caste system within the school. In general, however, these procedures are effective part-way measures for individualizing instruction.

Classroom Techniques for Individualizing Instruction
What can the teacher who works in a school that does not have an individualized mathematics program do about individualizing instruction in his or her own

**Models for Teaching
and Learning the Direct
Objects of Mathematics**

classes? There are many techniques that teachers can use to provide for individual learning differences among students. It is well to assess each student's level of mastery of prerequisite mathematics topics using teacher-constructed tests, commercially-available tests, or class question-and-answer sessions at the beginning of each course. It is also well to check students' records which contain information about their abilities, previous academic work, and motivation levels. Although this data will help you prepare teaching/learning strategies and instructional resources appropriate for your students, such information should be used with caution. Students may have matured since their records were last updated, their attitudes may have changed, and they may behave differently in your class than in previous classes. If you expect little from students whose records are poor, your attitudes, which are reflected in your treatment of these students, may cause them to fulfill your own low expectations. You should expect the best from each student; however, your initial evaluations of students may be useful later on if learning problems do occur for some students.

It is also well to set minimal and maximal cognitive learning objectives for a mathematics class. Every student should meet the minimal objectives before going to the next topic, and maximal objectives provide a learning goal that all students, especially better students, can aim for. For example, when teaching the topic of simplifying algebraic expressions containing radical signs, you might expect all students to handle expressions such as $\sqrt{128}$, $\sqrt[3]{-54x^4y^4}$, and $\sqrt{x^{-6}}$; however the maximal goal might involve simplifying expressions such as

$$\sqrt[5]{\left(-\frac{x^{-10}}{243x^2}\right)^{-4}}$$

Although you can not teach a lesson to 25 students and use optimal teaching strategies for each student, you can use a teaching strategy that is most appropriate for each topic and you can vary your teaching strategies. A well-mixed blend of teacher talk, student discussions, laboratory activities, etc. for each topic can facilitate learning for each student. When a variety of techniques, examples, activities, and resources are used in teaching each topic, it becomes more likely that the particular learning patterns of each student will be reached.

A variety of techniques should be used when assessing student learning. Many students become quite upset during tests; this may cause their test results to be a poor reflection of their learning. Teachers should use in-class practice sessions, laboratory work, class discussions, and homework assignments, as well as tests, to assess learning. You may want to establish a grading system that rewards relative individual improvement as well as absolute competitive standing in the class. Tests can be organized into sections so that each student can select and solve several problems from each section. A small bonus can be given for selecting harder problems; this may encourage better students to extend themselves. A similar system can be used when assigning homework problems.

Care must be taken in setting tasks for students when their learning is to be evaluated based upon their performance on the tasks. Lower ability students should be given many tasks that they can handle so that they do not become too discouraged and frustrated. Higher ability students should be assigned work that requires maximum use of their abilities.

Several additional suggestions for individualizing instruction in a mathematics classroom follow:

1. Ask students to write reports, conduct demonstrations, and carry out projects that are appropriate for many different learning styles.
2. Try to involve each student in a variety of classroom activities such as asking and answering questions, group discussions, and work at the chalkboard, so that each student feels that he or she has an important role in the classroom.
3. Provide time in class for supervised drill-and-practice work so that you can observe and assist individual students.
4. Permit small groups of students to work together on assignments in class so that students can teach each other.
5. Require a level and quality of work appropriate for each student's ability. Slower learners should be praised when their work is above average with respect to their abilities. More capable students should not be rewarded for mediocre work.
6. Accumulate a variety of books and other learning resources and use them to supplement the textbook.
7. Select and use good visual aids such as posters, bulletin-board displays, overhead projectors and films.
8. Accumulate a small library of interesting books about mathematics and mathematicians which students may use in class or take home to read.

Summary

Even though most mathematics teachers do not teach in schools that have the resources to completely individualize their mathematics programs, they should not regard this situation as a serious handicap to effective teaching and learning. Each of the individualized instructional programs for mathematics has its own limitations and all individualized programs have certain common limitations. Individualized programs tend to overemphasize the value of working alone and underemphasize the value of good expository teaching and group interactions in learning.

Good teaching is the key to effective learning, whether the teaching is conducted by a teacher, the writer of a programmed textbook, or the maker of a film. Each teacher can develop a number of excellent procedures for individualizing instruction which can be designed to capitalize upon each student's unique set of learning variables.

The Spiral Teaching/Learning Model

Facts and skills are usually learned by students several days after they have been presented by a teacher. Facts and skills are either learned shortly after they have been taught or they are not learned at all. Once a skill has been learned, repeated practice may facilitate remembering the skill for a long period of time and may help the learner improve his or her speed and accuracy in using the skill. If students fail to learn a skill the first time it is presented, reteaching the skill at a later time may still result in mastery of that skill. For example, many students fail to learn basic arithmetic skills even after these skills have been taught in several grades in elementary and junior high school. Consequently, most high schools offer remedial arithmetic courses so that these students will have a final chance to master the basic skills before they graduate.

Learning concepts and principles is a more complex mental process than mastering facts and skills. Many mathematical concepts can be correctly defined at several different levels of abstraction and generality. This means that even after a concept has been taught at one level it may be appropriate to define it in a more abstract and general manner in a later mathematics course.

For example, the concept of the area of a plane figure is defined for young children as the number of unit squares necessary to cover that figure. Although this definition is correct, it is not general enough to use in finding the area of most plane figures and it is too concrete to apply to more abstract representations of plane figures such as those in Euclidean plane geometry. In fact, this definition of area is of no use in finding the areas of circles. Later in school it is necessary to redefine the area of each particular class of plane figures by a formula. The area of a rectangle is the length times the width, that is $A = LW$, the area of a circle is pi times the radius squared, $A = \pi r^2$, the area of a triangle is one-half the base times the height, $A = \frac{1}{2} bh,$ and so forth. After functions have been studied in algebra and trigonometry, this second type of definition for areas becomes inadequate for finding areas bounded by the graphs of functions, and it is necessary to redefine area as a Riemann definite integral, which is still not general enough to handle certain classes of discontinuous functions. For these functions, area is once more redefined as a Lebesgue integral which is more general than the preceding three definitions of area. However, each succeeding definition of area is based in part upon its predecessors and includes the area representations and applications for which its predecessors were defined.

Since principles are relationships among sets of concepts, each principle can be restructured as a more abstract and general principle based upon each successive redefinition of its underlying concepts. The principle that the areas of two plane figures are equal if they contain the same number of unit squares must eventually be restated as: the areas bounded by two sets of functions are equal if the Riemann integrals over these functions are equal.

Although most mathematics skills are used in learning more complex skills and can be applied to solving progressively more difficult problems, mathematical skills are seldom reformulated into more abstract and general representations. They are merely applied to more abstract and general situations. Once a mathematical skill has been mastered, it can be applied to whatever situation necessitates its use; however, concepts may have to be completely redefined before they are applicable in new situations.

Most mathematical skills should not be taught to students until they have the mental maturity and mathematical knowledge to carry out the procedures involved in applying the skills. Students are not, or should not, be taught the skill of adding fractions until they can add, multiply, and divide natural numbers. Concepts and principles can be learned by students at various stages of development provided each concept and principle is defined and represented in a manner which is concrete and specific enough to be consistent with students' intellectual development and mathematical maturity. Reteaching mathematical skills in school is usually classified as a remedial activity; however redefining a concept is considered to be a new mathematical endeavor.

This sequential nature of concept development in mathematics is apparent in the structure and historical development of mathematics. The sequential nature of concept learning in students results from the chronological development of human mental processes. To take advantage of this sequential development of mathematical concepts and human intellect, the so-called spiral teaching/learning model has evolved as a useful, and even necessary, model for teaching and learning mathematical concepts and principles.

Spiral Teaching and Learning Defined

The *spiral teaching/learning model* can *not* be defined as a well-ordered sequence of teaching and learning acts for a particular lesson because the spiral approach to presenting a concept or principle may take place over a time span of several months or years. The *spiral model* is a model which subsumes the other models for teaching mathematics. It is characterized by a sequential procedure for teaching concepts and principles; each concept and principle is presented and represented to students as a series of progressively more abstract and general definitions, examples and applications. These presentations and representations are carried out intermittently over a long period of time. For instance, the concept of area is first presented in the initial three years of elementary school, is redefined in junior high school, is redefined again in high school or college calculus, and is defined once more as a Lebesgue integral in graduate school. When using the spiral model to present and redefine a concept or principle over a long period of time, any other appropriate teaching/learning model can be used as a source of strategies for presenting each lesson or set of lessons throughout the mathematics curriculum.

In summary, the essense of the spiral model lies in the fact that many mathematical concepts and principles are best learned by ''spiraling'' through them at various points in the curriculum. At each point in the spiral where the mathematics topic is touched upon again, the topic is presented at a somewhat higher level of abstraction and generality. Usually unfamiliar applications of the topic can be used to motivate the more abstract and general representation of the topic and the revised definitions of the concepts and principles can be learned through new examples and applications.

Examples of the Spiral Approach in Learning Mathematics

The concepts of *number, area, proof, counting, function* and *limit,* together with principles involving these concepts, are standard topics in the school mathematics curriculum. Each one of these mathematical concepts was developed by mathematicians in a progressive historical spiral going from very concrete and specific definitions and applications to progressively more and more abstract and general definitions and applications. As students mature intellectually, they become better able to comprehend and apply the more abstract and general representations of these concepts. The progressive development of these concepts in school is illustrated on the spiral shown in Figure 5.9. Each ring of the spiral represents a grade level between first grade and twelfth grade. The name of each

279

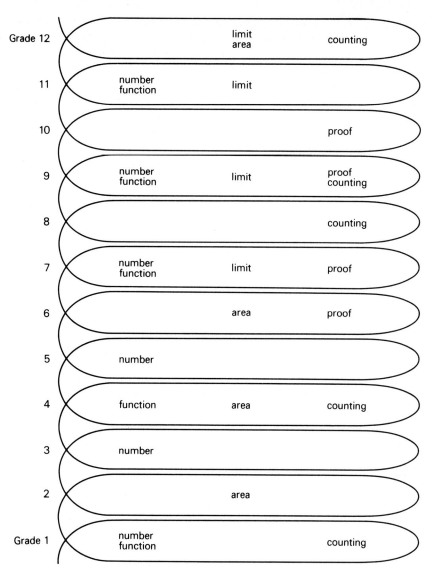

Grade 12		limit area	counting
11	number function	limit	
10			proof
9	number function	limit	proof counting
8			counting
7	number function	limit	proof
6		area	proof
5	number		
4	function	area	counting
3	number		
2		area	
Grade 1	number function		counting

Figure 5.9. A spiral teaching approach for six mathematical concepts.

concept is printed on the spiral near the rings representing the approximate grade levels in which that concept might be taught by teachers and comprehended by students. Most of these concepts have already been discussed in various contexts in previous chapters. If you would like to review the discussion relating to any one of them, refer to the Index to locate each concept.

Number

The concept of number is first presented in grade one where children learn to count, to recognize symbols for numbers, and to write number symbols. Later, in third grade, after students have learned about the set of natural numbers, the concept of a fraction can be presented and students can learn some of the properties of positive fractions. A year or two later decimal representations of fractions are presented as new representations of the concepts of whole numbers and fractions. About seventh grade, the number concept is generalized to include negative integers and fractions. Later, in algebra, the number system is further generalized to include the more abstract concept of real numbers. In algebra or trigonometry a further generalization of the concept of a number is made to include complex numbers. Some senior level courses also further generalize numbers through the concept of vectors. At each level, the number concept is generalized and the idea of a number becomes somewhat more abstract.

Function

The intuitive concept of a function is first presented in grade one; however the concept is not well-structured and the word "function" is not used. At this level, children pair husbands with wives, match people to their possessions, and partition objects into sets based upon the characteristics of each object. This matching and pairing process continues until fourth grade when the concept of a function becomes more abstract through its representations in mathematical formulas for finding areas and solving other types of arithmetic problems. By seventh grade the concept of a function is formalized and generalized as a relation, and the words "function" and "relation" may be explained and used. In ninth grade the concept of a function is defined using mathematical language and abstract symbols and functions are represented as special types of algebraic relations. In trigonometry the function concept becomes somewhat more abstract when trigonometric functions are defined as wrapping functions on a unit circle. The function concept becomes more restrictive and more abstract and its representations become more symbolic from grade one through grade twelve.

Limit

The limit concept tends to be neglected in schools; however this very important and useful mathematical concept can be introduced to students as soon as they enter the formal operational (abstract) stage of their mental development. Seventh graders can comprehend the limit concept when it is represented through infinite sequences and infinite decimal representations of numbers. In algebra, the limit concept can be further generalized when arithmetic and geometric progressions are studied. In geometry, the circle can be shown to be the limiting case of a sequence of regular polygons whose sides become increasingly numerous. Limits also arise in the study of the trigonometric functions as well as in the study of exponential and logarithmic functions. Of course a more general and abstract representation of the limit concept is given in high school calculus courses when the definite integral is defined as an infinite set of limits, which is to say "limits of limits." You may wish to refer back to pages 146-147 in Chapter 3, where a more detailed discussion of how limits can be represented in schools is presented.

Area

The concept of area is introduced early in elementary school where areas are represented as the number of unit squares needed to cover a plane figure. By fourth grade, students have matured mentally to the stage where they can comprehend the area concept when it is defined and represented by formulas for finding areas of certain types of plane figures. Sometimes the area concept is generalized to a limit concept by considering the area of a circle as the limiting value of a sequence of areas of regular polygons that are inscribed in a circle; this can be done in junior high school. Of course a much more abstract and generalized definition of area is found in calculus where area is represented as a definite integral.

Proof

One of the major stated objectives of geometry, if not *the* major objective of most high school plane geometry courses, is to teach students the ideas and procedures of mathematical proof; however most students begin to form their own unspoken concept of proof at an early age. Even though a young child's concept of proof is incorrect, it is acceptable to the child and he or she uses it to make generalizations. Younger children generalize principles, which may or may not be true, from a single instance or several instances of the principle. If the red figures on page ten of the workbook are called triangles, then the red figures on other pages must also be triangles. Even junior high school students tend to believe that if a generalization results in correct answers in the instances when they apply it, then that set of correct answers constitutes a proof of the generalization. Some geometry students fail to see the logic in many direct proofs of theorems and especially in the indirect method of proof. For these students proofs are by edict, not by logic; the teacher and the textbook are the authorities, and their proofs are to be accepted and memorized. Since the concept of a valid, logical mathematical proof is a difficult concept for many school students to comprehend, care should be taken not to force proofs upon students before they are intellectually prepared to accept them. As is true in learning many other concepts, the concept of proof should also be taught using the spiral approach of going from specific to general and from concrete to abstract. If you are not prepared to accept the less than perfect logic and validity of student proofs, it may be well to restrict your theorem-proving activities to the geometry classroom. Even there, a great deal of consideration and patience is required of the teacher.

Counting

Students learn to count even before they begin school; still a considerable amount of practice in counting sets of objects is needed before counting becomes meaningful to first graders. Probably by fourth grade most students are ready to understand the distinction between ten objects in a set (the cardinal number of the set) and the tenth object in a list (the ordinal number of that object); however, use of the words "cardinal" and "ordinal" should be reserved until later. By seventh or eighth grade most students are ready to comprehend and evaluate the two methods of counting—counting as an ordered sequence of natural numbers and counting by setting up a one-to-one correspondence between the elements of two sets. Many students may be in grade twelve before they can truly comprehend infinite sets, orders of infinity, and one-to-one correspondences for comparing the orders of infinite sets. The concept of counting should be generalized gradually from cardinal to ordinal numbers and from finite to infinite numbers. The abstraction of the counting concept to comparing orders of infinity through one-to-one correspondences should wait until students are well into the stage of formal operations and have developed sound abstract thinking processes.

As is true of many mathematical concepts, these six concepts—number, function, limit, area, proof, and counting—are interrelated. By presenting and discussing representations of several concepts simultaneously, mathematical principles can be formulated, from sets of concepts, at various levels of abstractness and generalization.

Whichever teaching strategies are selected for presenting mathematics concepts and principles, each mathematical object should be defined and represented at a level of abstractness and generalization appropriate for the stage of intellectual development of students. Concept formation is a gradual, long-term process which can best be carried out by using the spiral teaching/learning model.

Summary

The six teaching/learning models and strategies—the expository model, the advance organizer model, discovery strategies, game strategies, the individualized model, and the spiral model—presented in this chapter are appropriate for teaching and learning the direct objects of mathematics—facts, skills, concepts, and principles. Since facts are contained in skills, concepts and principles, all of these models and strategies can be used indirectly to teach facts. The expository and advance organizer models can be used in teaching skills, concepts and principles. The discovery model is appropriate for learning concepts and principles. Game strategies are most useful for practicing skills; however, concepts and principles can also be learned through games. The individualized model can be used to select resources and methods for individual students according to each student's unique learning characteristics. Individualized programs are most appropriate for teaching facts and skills, but can also be used to teach concepts and principles. The major purpose of the spiral model is to teach those concepts and principles which should be presented intermittently over a long period of time at progressively higher levels of generalization and abstractness.

Although they are not specifically designed for teaching the indirect objects of mathematics, each of these six models can be used for teaching and learning at least one of the indirect objects. Among the indirect objects of mathematics are theorem-proving, problem-solving, transfer of learning, learning how to learn, intellectual development, working individually, working in groups, and developing positive attitudes. Six models designed for teaching and learning the indirect objects of mathematics will be discussed in the following chapter.

Things To Do

1.   Choose a mathematics skill, concept, or principle and prepare an *expository teaching/learning strategy* for teaching the mathematics object that you selected. Include the seven to nine teacher-directed, expository activities in your strategy as part of the fourteen activities for planning a mathematics lesson.

2. Select a mathematical principle and develop a *comparative advance organizer* for introducing that principle. Suggest an appropriate follow-up strategy to use after the organizer has been presented.

3. Choose a mathematical skill and prepare an expository organizer for that skill. What activities should follow the presentation of the organizer?

4. Select twenty mathematics topics (five each from arithmetic, algebra, geometry and trigonometry) that could be taught using a *discovery strategy*.

5. Prepare a complete *discovery lesson* for teaching a specific topic in mathematics; that is, include each of the fourteen activities for planning a lesson in your lesson.

6. Use the various sources of mathematical games such as the journals, magazines, and books referred to in this chapter to locate:
   A. At least five games for resolving puzzles or paradoxes.
   B. At least five games for practicing skills.
   C. Several guessing games for learning concepts and principles.
   D. At least five problem-solving games for learning logical principles.
   E. Two games for learning to estimate.
   What are the cognitive objectives for each of these games?

7. Develop five original mathematics games, one for each of these objectives: (A) a game which resolves a paradox or puzzle, (B) a game for practicing a skill, (C) a guessing game for learning a concept or principle, (D) a problem-solving game for learning logical principles, (E) a game for learning to estimate. What are the specific learning objectives for each of your games?

8. Prepare a complete fourteen-point lesson plan containing a game strategy for teaching and learning a specific topic from secondary school mathematics.

9. List at least ten different methods that could be used to individualize instruction during classroom lessons in mathematics.

10. Specify at least five different types of individualized homework assignments for students in mathematics courses.

11. Discuss several different preassessment and postassessment techniques that could be used to individualize student evaluation.

12. Visit a secondary school that has an individualized mathematics program and observe several individualized classes. What are the different types of resources that are available for student use? What types of activities are students involved in during individualized classes? Do the students appear to be engaged in constructive activities and do they appear to be well motivated? Ask the teachers for their opinions and observations about the advantages and disadvantages of individualized programs in mathematics.

13. Select a concept from elementary and secondary school mathematics and prepare a series of teaching/learning activities for presenting the concept using a spiral model. Give progressively more general and abstract definitions of the concept for each higher level on the spiral and suggest specific student activities for learning the concept at each level.

14. For each of the six teaching/learning models and strategies discussed in this chapter, select two secondary school mathematics topics that could be taught effectively by using that model. Briefly present specific teaching/learning procedures that should be used in teaching each of these twelve topics.

Selected Bibliography

Gordon, Alice Kaplan. *Games for Growth.* Palo Alto, California: Science Research Associates, Inc., 1970.

This is a general book about the uses of educational games, the role of the teacher in games, methods of designing and modifying games and the problem of evaluating games. Although there are a number of principles in this book that are related to using games in schools (which may be useful to secondary school mathematics teachers), most of the games described in the book are for subjects other than mathematics.

Henderson, George L., and Glunn, Lowell, D. *Let's Play Games in General Mathematics.* Skokie, Ill.: National Textbook Company, 1972.

Motivation can be a problem for both teachers and students in general mathematics classes. This book contains 177 games and activities which can be used in teaching arithmetic. A set of general behavioral objectives for students is included for each game and activity. Many of the games can be adapted and modified to meet specific learning objectives.

Higgins, Jon L. *Mathematics Teaching and Learning.* Worthington, Ohio: Charles A. Jones Publishing Company, 1973.

In this book Higgins discusses five theories of learning and presents a specific teaching/learning strategy illustrating the application of each theory to teaching a topic in mathematics.

Howes, Virgil M. (Editor). *Individualizing Instruction in Science and Mathematics.* New York: The Macmillan Company, 1970.

This book is a collection of selected journal articles on programs, practices and uses of technology in individualizing instruction. Since all of the articles were first published prior to 1970, some of the information about instructional hardware is outdated. However, many of the concepts and principles presented here for individualizing instruction are still relevant for current practice. The articles in this book together with their bibliographies do provide a good reference for information about the use of technology in mathematics education before 1970.

Joyce, Bruce, and Weil, Marsha. *Models of Teaching.* Englewood Cliffs, New Jersey: Prentice-Hall, Inc., 1972.

This book contains discussions of 16 models of teaching. The models are categorized according to the theoretical sources underlying each model. These sources are social interaction as a source of models, information processing as a source, personal sources, and behavior modification as a source. About half of the models presented can be used in teaching secondary school mathematics.

Klausmeier, Herbert J., Ghatala, Elizabeth Schwenn, and Frayer, Dorothy A. *Conceptual Learning and Development: A Cognitive View.* New York: Academic Press, Inc., 1974.

A general, comprehensive presentation of the structure, sequence, and conditions of concept learning, this book discusses four levels of concept attainment—concrete level, identity level, classificatory level, and formal level. The mental operations involved in concept learning at each of the four levels of attainment are specified and described in detail. *Conceptual Learning and Development* is a book for the teacher or researcher who wants to engage in a detailed study of concept learning.

Kohl, Herbert R. *Math, Writing, & Games in the Open Classroom.* New York: Vintage Books by Random House, 1974.

The author discusses the similarities between the way theories are constructed in natural and social sciences and the nature of creating, exploring, and modifying games. When creating games, Kohl believes that children construct and explore theories, perform experiments, make appropriate modifications, and examine the consistency and applications of their theories. Creating, modifying, and playing games are shown to be good ways for children to learn how to work together and to make decisions. Although many of the games in this book were designed for younger students, the ideas are appropriate for developing games for secondary school students.

McClosky, Mildred G. (Editor). *Teaching Strategies and Classroom Realities.* Englewood Cliffs, New Jersey: Prentice-Hall, Inc., 1971.

The foreword to this book (page xix) describes the substance of its content as follows: "This collection of ideas for teachers, written by teachers, is a sensitive documentation of the joys and anguish of teaching and learning, especially of *learning to teach.*" (Italics mine.) This book contains a large collection of vignettes written by intern teachers. (Intern teachers are students who have finished most of their college teacher education program and are teaching under the close supervision of master teachers.) Most of the vignettes describe problems faced by intern teachers, the methods they used in attempting to solve the problems, and the joys of success and frustrations of failure that they experienced. A good resource to convince beginning teachers that their problems and frustrations are not unique and that teaching can be a very exciting and rewarding activity, this book is a good reference for student teachers and intern teachers.

McIntosh, Jerry A. (Editor). *Perspectives on Secondary Mathematics Education.* Englewood Cliffs, New Jersey: Prentice-Hall, Inc., 1971.

A collection of articles on a variety of variables in teaching and learning mathematics, this book contains a section on teaching methods with articles on learning mathematical concepts and discovery strategies for learning concepts and principles.

Miller, William F., and Henderson, George L. *Let's Play Games in Mathematics.* Skokie, Ill.: National Textbook Company, 1972.

A book of games and activities, with learning objectives for each game, this resource can be of use to teachers of middle school or junior high school students.

National Council of Teachers of Mathematics. *The Teaching of Secondary School Mathematics* (Thirty-third Yearbook). Washington, D.C.: National Council of Teachers of Mathematics, 1970.

286

This comprehensive work on teaching secondary school mathematics, which contains chapters written by many well-known mathematics educators, has a section on teaching methods for special outcomes. In this section various writers discuss the teaching of concepts, proof, problem-solving, generalizations and skills.

————. *The Slow Learner in Mathematics* (Thirty-fifth Yearbook). Washington, D.C.: National Council of Teachers of Mathematics, 1972.

This NCTM Yearbook describes special aids, activities, laboratory approaches, promising programs, teaching strategies and practices for teaching mathematics to slow learners. It also has selected bibliographies of games, enrichment activities, teaching aids and journal articles which are useful in helping slow learners learn mathematics.

Raths, James, Pancella, John R., and Van Ness, James S. (Editors). *Studying Teaching* 2nd ed. Englewood Cliffs, New Jersey: Prentice-Hall, Inc., 1971.

Studying Teaching has a chapter on teaching methods which contains articles about discovery strategies, advance organizers and inquiry learning.

Shulman, Lee S., and Keislar, Evan R. (Editors). *Learning by Discovery: A Critical Appraisal*. Chicago: Rand McNally & Company, 1966.

This book contains the proceedings of a 1965 conference on discovery learning, which was sponsored by Stanford University and the Social Science Research Council. The five sections of the book deal with the value of discovery learning, research pertaining to discovery learning, using discovery learning in the classroom, the implications of psychological theories and research for education, and a retrospective analysis of the conference. The book is a useful reference for the teacher who wants to study the theory and practice of discovery learning in some detail.

Stanford, Gene, and Stanford, Barbara Dodds. *Learning Discussion Skills Through Games*. New York: Citation Press, 1969.

This 75 page paper-bound book contains various game strategies to help students learn to listen effectively, participate in group discussions, and develop methods of logical reasoning. Although this general presentation of discussion skills was not written specifically for mathematics teachers, some of the games are mathematics oriented and most can be adapted for use in mathematics lessons.

Continuing sources of teaching/learning strategies for specific topics in mathematics. Among the best and most convenient continuing, current, and easily accessible sources of teaching/learning methods are journals such as *Creative Computing, The Arithmetic Teacher, The Mathematics Teacher,* and *School Science and Mathematics*. The latter three journals have been discussed before; however *Creative Computing* has not been mentioned previously. Although *Creative Computing* is a magazine about interesting educational applications of computers, many of its articles have fascinating ideas and methods which are useful to mathematics teachers. This journal is recommended for high school mathematics teachers, especially those who have computer access for their students.

Creative Computing is published bi-monthly by Creative Computing, P.O. Box 789-M, Morristown, New Jersey 07960.

6

Models for Teaching and Learning the Indirect Objects of Mathematics

The direct objects of mathematics—facts, skills, principles and concepts—can be taught using expository, advance organizer, discovery, game, individualized and spiral models. These models may also promote learning of the indirect objects of mathematics—theorem-proving, problem-solving, transfer of learning, learning how to learn, intellectual development, individual work, group work, and positive attitudes. However, theorem-proving, problem-solving, laboratory, inquiry, group-processes, and computer-augmented models, which are also useful in teaching the direct objects of mathematics, are especially appropriate for teaching and learning indirect objects of mathematics. Each of these models for teaching and learning the indirect objects of mathematics will be discussed and illustrated in this chapter. While reading this chapter, you should keep in mind that each of the models presented can be used in teaching several indirect mathematical objects as well as several direct objects.

A Teaching/Learning Model for Proving Theorems

Creating new mathematics and discovering relationships within and among mathematical structures is the most important activity of research mathematicians. Since the validity of new discoveries and new relationships must be demonstrated to the satisfaction of the mathematical community, theorem-proving is the second most important work of mathematicians. The importance of theorem-proving in mathematics is reflected in the emphasis placed upon learning some of the techniques of mathematical proof in high school mathematics. It is probably not inaccurate to say that the primary reason for teaching plane geometry in secondary schools is to teach students some of the elements of deductive arguments which are used in mathematical proofs as well as in everyday discussions.

Even though many school mathematics programs reserve the consideration of formal mathematical proof for their plane geometry course, nearly all students have an intuitive notion of proof before they study geometry. Students enter their plane geometry course with a self-centered idea of proof such as: ''If I am convinced, then the proposition is true or if the proposition is in the textbook, then it must be true.'' Few students begin their sophomore year of high school with a rigorous concept of proof, and many students complete plane geometry without comprehending the nature of a mathematical proof.

There are several reasons for students' incomplete or incorrect ideas about proofs. First, the development of the concept of proof is related to stages of intellectual development. Students who are in a relatively self-centered stage of mental development tend to accept the truth of a proposition if it appears to them to be true. Students who are concrete thinkers may accept a general proposition even if they have seen only a few instances of the proposition. Even formal, abstract thinkers may accept propositions based solely upon the textbook's or teacher's authority.

Second, students must have a genuine doubt of the truth of a proposition and must want to resolve this doubt in order for a proof to be meaningful to them. Whenever the truth of a proposition is obvious to a student, having to construct a valid proof may appear to be an exercise in pleasing the teacher. Even when a proposition is not obvious, a well-constructed proof may be ignored by students who have no interest in resolving a doubt about the truth of that proposition. Their attitude may be ''tell us what is true and how to use facts and skills to get answers in mathematics, but don't bother us with uninteresting proofs which don't make much sense.'' Contrary to what some educators and mathematicians believe, many secondary school students have little interest in learning why mathematical principles are true. A sense of curiosity about mathematics may have to be developed slowly in these students by using interesting questions and activities in mathematics classes.

A third reason for students' misconceptions about the nature of mathematical proof is that many teachers do not properly teach the various techniques of mathematical proof. Since many students have developed an incomplete and inaccurate concept of proof by the time they reach the high school plane geometry course, they need to be taught theorem-proving through a deliberate and well-organized presentation and analysis of various types of mathematical proof. Although teachers of arithmetic and algebra can help students formulate progressively more precise ideas about the types of arguments that constitute a valid proof, many students are not mature enough to comprehend the distinction between a valid mathematical proof and a persuasive, but invalid, argument until they are high school juniors. By age 15 or 16 most mathematics students have developed the mental maturity to permit them to comprehend formal and rigorous logical arguments. However, students will not cast aside their past misconceptions lightly and considerable patience on the part of teachers is required in teaching proofs. The concept of a formal and rigorous mathematical proof requires many years to develop in students' minds and should be taught using a long-term spiral strategy.

What Is a Proof?

Before discussing the reasons why theorem-proving should be taught in secondary schools and how students can learn to do valid mathematical proofs, it is well to consider the nature of proof and the different kinds of mathematical proofs. In general, a *proof* is any argument or presentation of evidence that convinces or persuades someone to accept a belief. At least six criteria can be identified for convincing either oneself or other people to accept an argument as a convincing proof. One type of proof is *personal experience*. In northern climates, the first snowfall of the year is a source of interest and excitement. When the first snowfall begins, it is a common occurrence in classrooms for a student to notice the initial snowflakes, and shout ''Hey! it's snowing.'' which causes all the other students to look out the window to verify that it actually is snowing. Personal experience can be a valid method for proving or verifying specific information, but is not usually valid for proving generalizations.

Acceptance of authority is another way to establish the truth of a statement. We accept the judgments of medical authorities that certain medicines are effective in treating specific illnesses and at times we accept the word of television personalities that the remedies they are promoting will cure our illnesses. There is also a certain aura of authority about the printed word and it is not surprising that most students accept as true whatever is printed in their textbooks. People also tend to accept the authority of statements printed in newspapers and magazines. In fact, one explanation for the success of some advertising is peoples' willingness to accept information presented by authorities or to accept the information found in someone else's personal experiences.

Some people accept *observations of instances* as proof of a generalization. For example, a proof of the untrue statement ''most teachers don't care about their students'' which is based upon the argument ''I know a teacher whose only concern about teaching is payday'' is an example of this type of proof. Younger students and even many high school students use observations of instances as proofs of generalizations. If in their limited experience a generalization holds, then they accept the generalization as being true.

The *lack of a counterexample* for a generalization is a fourth method that people use to establish the truth of statements or procedures. Students tend to use this method to justify their distinctive methods for solving certain types of skill-related problems. If no one is able to find a case where the method gives the wrong answer, then it must be a valid procedure. Even mathematicians tend to accept the validity of a conjecture when many other mathematicians are unable to find a counter-example over a period of years. The four-color-map conjecture that *four colors are both necessary and sufficient for coloring all plane maps so that no two regions with a common boundary are the same color* is an example of this situation. Since no one was able to construct a plane map to contradict this conjecture, many mathematicians thought that it was probably true.

A fifth method of proving an argument or proposition is by the *usefulness of results*. A part of the branch of mathematics called differential equations was developed in the early nineteen hundreds as a tool for science and engineering. Some of the procedures that were developed for solving differential equations were accepted and used because they provided appropriate mathematical solutions for physical problems. Even though there were no valid mathematical proofs for the principles underlying these procedures, they were considered to be true because they served useful purposes.

The sixth method of proof, *deductive argument,* is the acceptable method of proof in mathematics. A statement or belief based upon any one of the five previously mentioned types of proof—personal experience, acceptance of authority, observations of instances, lack of a counter-example, and usefulness of results—may possibly be untrue. However, a conclusion based upon a deductive argument is true, provided the assumptions from which the conclusion follows are true.

Many secondary school mathematics teachers tend to lead students to believe that deductive arguments are the only proper and worthwhile type of proof. Such is not the case; in fact, mathematics is the only field in which this type of argument is considered to be the only valid method of proof. Most of our social and political principles have their basis in personal experience and acceptance of authority. Observations of instances and lack of counterexamples are valid methods of verification in the physical sciences, and usefulness of results is a valid justification for principles in engineering. Rather than trying to promote deductive proof as the only proper way to reason, it is better to explain to students that the nature of mathematics and the way in which it is structured make deductive proof the acceptable method of proof in this field. The deductive method of proof, as well as the other five methods of proof, has its own limitations. Mathematical proof, while based upon logical arguments, does result in drawing conclusions from assumptions. If we assume the truth of hypotheses then we can use valid deductive arguments to prove the truth of conclusions. Euclid's formulation of plane geometry marks the time in history when deductive proof was set forth as the proper method of proof in mathematics. However, it is somewhat paradoxical to find that plane geometry also provides the prime example of the arbitrariness of basic assumptions. When mathematicians finally quit trying to prove Euclid's axioms and postulates and contradicted the parallel postulate, they created an internally consistent mathematical system which contradicts many of the important theorems of Euclidean geometry. Even as contradictory political systems can exist simultaneously in various countries without all but one system being false, so too can contradictory mathematical systems exist simultaneously.

Since deductive arguments are the arguments used in constructing mathematical proofs, they will be discussed in detail in this section. Before discussing the different types of deductive arguments, the term deductive argument must be defined. First, however, the terms truth and validity as they are used in mathematics must be explained. Truth is a characteristic of statements and validity is a characteristic of arguments. The truth values *true* and *false* are assigned to statements according to certain rules of logic or conventions. The value *true* is assigned to statements that are, in fact, the correct descriptions of reality or that, by convention, are agreed upon as acceptable descriptions of reality. As I sit in my study writing, I can look out the window and observe that the trees are casting shadows on the snow. The statement "the trees are casting shadows on the snow" is, in fact, a correct description of reality, so this statement is given the value *true*. Since it is not raining, the statement "it is raining" is assigned the value *false*. In Euclidean geometry, the statement "through a point not on a given line, one and only one line can be constructed parallel to the given line" is an agreed upon convention which is assigned the truth value *true*. In a mathematical system of non-Euclidean geometry, this same statement is given the value *false*. Every mathematical system is based upon a unique set of statements (axioms), each one of which is assigned the value *true*. Although *statements* are assigned the values *true* or *false,* they are not characterized as valid or invalid.

Validity is a characteristic of arguments, which are sets of statements. An argument is said to be *valid* if it is based upon accepted principles of implication which are contained in a formal system of logic. The following examples of arguments will help clarify these definitions. Argument 1 is a valid argument because it is an instance of the principle of formal implication called *modus ponens,* which is accepted in mathematics as a valid argument form. The modus ponens reasoning is: p is true, and if $p \rightarrow q,$ then q is true. Argument 2 is an invalid argument because it is not an acceptable form of argument in our logical system.

Argument 1

Statements	Truth Values
1. This geometric figure is a square. (*premise*)	true
2. If a figure is a square it has four right angles.	true
3. This figure has four right angles. (*conclusion*)	true

Argument 2

1. This figure is a rhombus. (*premise*)	true
2. If a figure is a rhombus it has four equal sides.	true
3. If a figure is a square it has four equal sides.	true
4. This figure is a square. (*conclusion*)	false

We are now in a position to discuss the sixth method of proof, the deductive argument, which is an accepted type of argument for proving theorems in mathematics. *A deductive argument* is a *valid* argument form which operates on a set of hypotheses that are assumed to have the truth value *true* until it terminates with a set of conclusions that follow logically from the hypotheses. For students, and even for mathematicians, the initial, difficult activity that precedes proving theorems is deciding what constitutes a valid deductive argument. There are two general categories of deductive proof—proof by direct argument and proof by contradiction. In the following discussion nine types of deductive proof, seven by direct argument and two by contradiction, will be presented. All of these types of proof, which are listed below, are used in secondary school mathematics.

Types of Deductive Proof

A. Proof by direct argument
  1. Modus ponens
  2. Transitivity
  3. Modus tollens
  4. Deduction theorem
  5. Contraposition
  6. Proof by cases
  7. Mathematical induction

B. Proof by contradiction
   1. Counterexample
   2. Indirect proof

Modus Ponens

Modus ponens is the easiest type of deductive proof for most students to understand because it has only three statements. The logical structure of modus ponens where p and q are statements is:

If p is true, and
if p implies q, then
q is true.

In symbols **Modus Ponens** is $\dfrac{p,\, p \to q}{q}$.

As an example of this type of proof, suppose that a student wants to prove that the graphs of the two functions $y = x + 4$ and $y = 2x - 1$ intersect. An imprecise and inelegant argument is to exhibit plots of the equations on a rectangular coordinate system and observe whether they cross each other. A more elegant argument, which is also a valid argument, is to use the modus ponens form of proof.

(p):   The slopes of these lines are 1 and 2, which are different numbers.
$(p \to q)$: We know that if two linear functions have different slopes, their graphs intersect.
(q):   Therefore, the graphs of these two functions intersect.

This particular argument is valid because it is an example of the general argument form called modus ponens which is a valid argument form.

Transitivity

Students also find the three-step proof based upon the valid argument form called transitivity to be logical and easy to understand because it is in common use outside mathematics. The logical structure of transitivity where p, q, and r are statements is:

If p implies q, and
if q implies r, then
  p implies r.

Transivity is represented as $\dfrac{p \to q,\, q \to r}{p \to r}$.

As an example of applying the general argument form of transitivity (which can be shown to be valid in our system of logic), assume that these two theorems have been proved:

If two angles of one triangle are respectively congruent to two angles of another triangle (p), *then all three angles of the two triangles are respectively congruent* (q);
If all three angles of two triangles are respectively congruent (q), *then the triangles are similar* (r).

Then, the following theorem holds:

If two angles of one triangle are respectively congruent to two angles of another triangle (p), *then the triangles are similar* (r).

The argument for this proof follows from the transitivity argument $p \to q$ and $q \to r$ implies $p \to r$.

Modus Tollens

The modus tollens argument form is somewhat more difficult for students to comprehend and apply than modus ponens and transitivity. This valid argument form is

If $p \to q$ is true, and
if the negation of q is true, then
the negation of p is true.

A symbolic representation of **Modus Tollens** is $\dfrac{p \to q, \ \sim q}{\sim p}$

As an example of the use of the modus tollens argument form in number theory (arithmetic) consider the following argument which uses this theorem:

If n is an even natural number, then n^2 is an even natural number.
$(p \to q)$: If n is an even natural number, then n^2 is an even natural number.
(true)
$(\sim q)$: It is shown that some number k^2 is not an even natural number.
(true)
$(\sim p)$: Therefore, the conclusion is drawn that k is not an even natural number.

One proof that $\sqrt{2}$ is irrational uses this particular argument about even numbers.

Deduction Theorem

The deduction theorem, which is seldom explained to geometry students, is used as a basis for most proofs in plane geometry. Even though this valid argument is the corner stone of much of plane geometry, many high school geometry teachers not only fail to explain it but also fail to even mention it. The deduction theorem can be stated as follows:

If from an assumption p and a
set of true statements $q_1, q_2, q_3, \cdots, q_n$,
it is possible to deduce r, then
it is possible to deduce p implies
r from $q_1, q_2, q_3, \cdots, q_n$.

In symbols, the **Deduction Theorem** is:

$$\frac{(p, q_1, q_2, q_3, \cdots, q_n) \to r}{(q_1, q_2, q_3, \cdots, q_n) \to (p \to r)}.$$

When applying the deduction theorem to the proof of a theorem in geometry, the following argument is used:

If the hypothesis of the theorem and a set of true statements (axioms, postulates, definitions, and other theorems), which are the statements of the proof, yield the conclusion, then the set of true statements alone yields the implication that the hypothesis of the theorem implies the conclusion of the theorem.

If the validity of the deduction theorem had not been established, most geometry proofs would be invalid. In a geometry proof one is not trying to prove the conclusion; it is the entire theorem that is to be proved. For example, consider proving the following proposition: If two legs of one right triangle are congruent, respectively, to two legs of another right triangle (p), then the triangles are congruent (r). To prove this proposition it is necessary to prove that $p \rightarrow r$. In order to shorten the discussion of the proof of this proposition, the two right triangles are represented in Figure 6.1.

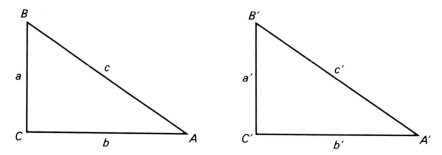

Figure 6.1.

The proof of this theorem is accomplished using the deduction theorem.

First, side a is congruent to side a' and side b is congruent to side b', which is assumed in the hypothesis. (This true statement is p in our symbolic representation of the deduction theorem.)

Next, angle C is congruent to angle C' because all right angles are congruent. (This true statement is q_1.)

Next, triangle ABC is congruent to triangle $A'B'C'$ because if two sides and the included angle of one triangle are congruent, respectively, to two sides and the included angle of another triangle, then the two triangles are congruent. (This true statement is $(p, q_1) \rightarrow r$.)

Finally, by the deduction theorem, the previous statement, $(p, q_1) \rightarrow r$, implies that if two legs of one right triangle are congruent, respectively, to two legs of another right triangle, then the triangles are congruent; that is $(p, q_1) \rightarrow r$ yields $q_1 \rightarrow (p \rightarrow r)$.

It is obvious that this final step is logically necessary to prove that p does indeed imply r. The previous step verifies that p and q_1, together, imply r, but not that p alone implies r. The deduction theorem permits one to make the final statement which is the proposition that we set out to prove.

A final step where the deduction theorem is applied should be included in proofs of this type, not as a hollow exercise in rigor but as a logical necessity and as an aid in helping students comprehend the logical foundations of proof.

Contraposition

The argument form of contraposition (or contrapositive) is sometimes taught as an indirect proof. This is incorrect. Contraposition is a valid direct form of deductive argument which can be stated as follows:

If the negation of q implies the negation of p, then p implies q. In symbols,

Contraposition is $\dfrac{\sim q \rightarrow \sim p}{p \rightarrow q}$.

Every proposition $p \rightarrow q$ has a contrapositive $\sim q \rightarrow \sim p$ and sometimes it is easier to prove the contrapositive than the proposition itself. Once the contrapositive of a proposition has been proved, the validity of the contraposition form of argument establishes the truth of the proposition. The contrapositive of the theorem "if both pairs of opposite sides of a quadrilateral are congruent, then the quadrilateral is a parallelogram" is "if a quadrilateral is not a parallelogram, then both pairs of opposite sides are not congruent."

As an example of proving a geometry theorem using the contraposition argument form, consider this theorem: If two lines form congruent alternate interior angles with a transversal, then they are parallel. This theorem can be proved directly by constructing an auxilliary line and using the deduction theorem; it can be proved by the indirect method, which will be discussed later; and it can be proved using contraposition. To illustrate the contraposition argument form, this theorem will be proved using its contrapositive.

Theorem: If two lines form congruent alternate interior angles with a transversal (p), then they are parallel (q).

Contrapositive: If two lines are not parallel ($\sim q$) then they do not form congruent alternate interior angles with a transversal ($\sim p$).

The contrapositive can be proved using the deduction theorem. To aid in the discussion, we will refer to Figure 6.2.

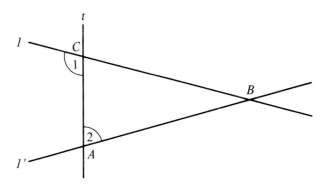

Figure 6.2.

Lines l and l' are not parallel by assumption ($\sim q$); consequently they will intersect according to the definition of parallel lines (r_1). Triangle ABC will be formed by the two nonparallel lines l and l' and the transversal t (r_2). But, angle 1 is an exterior angle of triangle ABC and angle 2 is an interior angle of triangle ABC (r_3). Angle 1 is larger than angle 2 (r_4). Angles 1 and 2 are alternate interior angles (r_5). Therefore, the alternate interior angles are not congruent ($\sim p$). Consequently, ($\sim q$, r_1, r_2, r_3, r_4, r_5) $\rightarrow$ $\sim p$. So by the deduction theorem, if two lines are not parallel, then they do not form congruent alternate interior angles with a transversal; that is, since ($\sim q$, r_1, r_2, r_3, r_4, r_5) $\rightarrow$ $\sim p$, then (r_1, r_2, r_3, r_4, r_5) $\rightarrow$ ($\sim q \rightarrow \sim p$). By contraposition, if two lines form congruent alternate interior angles with a transversal (p), then they are parallel (q); that is $\dfrac{\sim q \rightarrow \sim p}{p \rightarrow q}$.

The symbols used to represent statements and implications throughout this proof are included to illustrate the logic of the deduction theorem and contraposition. However, these symbols are not necessary for the proof and should not be required of students when they are writing proofs. The symbols are only helpful to students who are learning the various valid argument forms that are used (but not stated) in proving theorems.

Proof by Cases

Proof by cases is a relatively easy logical form for most students to follow because it appears to them to be related to the intuitive, but invalid, procedure of arguing from examples. There are a number of principles in arithmetic, algebra, geometry, and trigonometry that can best be proved by cases, which is a valid, logical form of argument. This argument form can be stated as follows: If each one of several hypotheses yields the same true conclusion, then the disjunction of all of the hypotheses yields the same conclusion. For example, if p_1 implies q, and p_2 implies q, and p_3 implies q, then $(p_1$ or p_2 or $p_3)$ implies q. **Proof by Cases** can be represented as

$$\frac{p_1 \rightarrow q, p_2 \rightarrow q, \cdots, p_n \rightarrow q}{(p_1 \vee p_2 \vee \cdots \vee p_n) \rightarrow q},$$

where "V" means "or."

Since $|x|$, where x is a real number, is defined by cases, it is not surprising that proofs of the properties of absolute value such as $|xy| = |x| \cdot |y|$, $xy \leq |xy|$, and $|x| - |y| \leq |x| + |y|$ involve using the deductive argument of proof by cases. In geometry, the proof of the theorem "the degree measure of an angle inscribed in a circle is one-half the degree measure of its intercepted arc" can be proved by considering three cases—the case where the center of the circle is within the inscribed angle, the case where the center is outside the angle, and the case where the center is coincident with a point on a ray of the inscribed angle. In trigonometry, the law of cosines is proved by cases. In general, most propositions in mathematics which are based upon a definition of a concept that is defined by cases are candidates for proof by cases.

Mathematical Induction

The term mathematical induction is misleading because the argument form underlying inductive proof is a deductive form. The valid logical form of mathematical induction is usually shown to students shortly after they have become convinced, either by authority or logic, that proof by example is an invalid form of argument. Even though an inductive proof is not a proof by example, it does appear to be so to many students when they see it used for the first time.

The principle of mathematical induction is used to prove that propositions are true for the entire set of natural numbers (and in some cases for an infinite subset of the natural numbers such as all natural numbers greater than six or all even natural numbers). An inductive proof of a theorem that is true for the entire set of natural numbers proceeds as follows: It is demonstrated that the theorem holds for $n = 1$; and it is demonstrated that the assumption that the theorem holds for k implies that the theorem holds for $k + 1$.

Some students fail to understand the validity of proof by induction because to them it appears that a theorem is being proved by looking at only two examples of the theorem, the example where $n = 1$ and one other example k, where k is greater than one. Some teachers have found that an analogy can make inductive proof appear to be more reasonable to students. Suppose that there is a ladder with an infinite number of rungs. We want to know if the spacing of the rungs is such that it is possible to climb to any height on the ladder. If we know for certain that the first rung is near enough to the ground to be reached and that it is possible to reach any higher rung from the rung just below it, then we can assume that it is possible to climb to any rung on the ladder. The argument form of **Mathematical Induction** for an ordered, infinite set N of natural numbers can be represented as:

$$\frac{P(1); \text{ and for every } k \in N, \, P(k) \to P(k + 1)}{P(n) \text{ for every } n \in N}.$$

That is, if the first natural number in the set has property P and if the implication *property* P *for the* kth *number in the set implies property* P *for the* k + 1 *number in the set* holds for every k, then every number n in the set has property P.

A recurring question asked by many students is: "Suppose k doesn't have property P, what then?" The answer is that one need not be concerned whether k has property P. What one is concerned with is to show that the implication *P(k) → P(k + 1)* holds for every k belonging to N.

Examples of proof by induction are found throughout mathematics, particularly in the second year of high school algebra, and an example of an inductive proof in algebra follows.

Prove that the solution set of $2^x > 1 + x^2$, where x is a natural number, is the set of natural numbers greater than four. By direct substitution we can easily show that 1, 2, 3, and 4 do not belong to this solution set.

If $n = 5$, then $2^5 > 1 + 5^2$.

Assume that $2^n > 1 + n^2$, then

$$2(2^n) > 2(1 + n^2),$$
$$2^{n+1} > 2 + 2n^2.$$

However, we must show that $2^{n+1} > 1 + (n + 1)^2$, which is equivalent to showing that $2^{n+1} > 2 + 2n + n^2$. But, if we are able to show that $2 + 2n^2 > 2 + 2n + n^2$ we will have demonstrated that $2^{n+1} > 2 + 2n^2 > 2 + 2n + n^2$. So by transitivity we will have proved that $2^{n+1} > 1 + (n + 1)^2$. To see that $2 + 2n^2 > 2 + 2n + n^2$, we need only simplify this inequality: Suppose that $2 + 2n^2 > 2 + 2n + n^2$, then

$$2n^2 > 2n + n^2,$$
$$n^2 > 2n,$$
$$n > 2.$$

But n *is* greater than 2 because we are considering the set of natural numbers greater than 4. Therefore, by the principle of mathematical induction, $2^x > 1 + x^2$.

Although there are other types of direct deductive proof, the seven types just discussed—modus ponens, transitivity, modus tollens, deduction theorem, contraposition, proof by cases and mathematical induction—are the major direct arguments used in proving theorems in secondary schools. It should be stressed that many, if not most, proofs of theorems in mathematics require the use of various combinations of these seven deductive argument forms within each proof. The purpose of presenting each argument form in its "purest" representation is not meant to suggest that each argument must be used exclusively in each specific proof of a theorem. Each argument was presented in relative isolation from other arguments in order to make its logical form apparent. Although this concludes our discussion of deductive proof by direct argument, two types of deductive proof by contradiction will be discussed and illustrated below—proof by counterexample and indirect proof.

Proof by Counterexample

In one sense proof by counterexample is a direct form of deductive argument. A counterexample may be used to demonstrate that a false generalization is indeed false. From another viewpoint, proof by counterexample is proof by contradiction because a general proposition is contradicted (shown to be false) by exhibiting a negative instance of the proposition.

> The argument form for proof by counterexample is the following: A conjecture is made that all elements of a specified set **S** have a certain property **P.** Then an element **x** belonging to **S** is found which does not have property **P.** Therefore, it is concluded that not all elements of **S** have property **P,** which is contrary to the conjecture, so the conjecture is false.

In symbols the **Counterexample** argument form is:
Conjecture: $\forall\, x \in S, P(x).$
Negative instance: $a \in S$ and $\sim P(a)$.
Conclusion: $\forall\, x \in S, \sim P(x)$

Many students question the validity of proof by counterexample after comparing this argument form to the direct deductive forms which they have used. Students will argue as follows:

> To prove that a theorem is true, we have to show that it holds for all examples. But, to prove that a proposition is false we only have to show that it isn't true for one example. That doesn't make sense.

The fallacy in this student argument lies in the fact that students who think that there is a logical contradiction between counterexample arguments and direct arguments have overlooked the quantifier "for every." This quantifier is easy to overlook in many propositions because it is implied but not actually stated. Consider the proposition "an exterior angle of **a triangle** is equal to the sum of the two opposite interior angles," which was copied from a plane geometry textbook. Since students have been told that mathematics is an exact science and that mathematical statements mean precisely what they state, it is not surprising that students want to prove this proposition by showing that it holds for one particular triangle. It does say "an exterior angle of **a triangle.**" It would be less confusing to students if this proposition had been stated "in **every triangle,** each exterior angle is equal to the sum of the two opposite interior angles." Since implied quantifiers are omitted from the statements of theorems in some geometry textbooks, it is well to have students rewrite the theorems so that quantifiers are explicitly stated.

Quantifiers should also be explicitly stated in propositions which are to be proven false and the set under consideration should be explicitly identified. For example, is this statement true or false? ''Addition distributes over multiplication.'' If the set being considered is the set of real numbers then the proposition is false. However, if the set is a set of sets then the proposition is true because set addition does distribute over set multiplication, where addition is defined as set union and multiplication as set intersection. While implied conditions and restrictions, such as those in the previous two examples, may be obvious to mathematics teachers, they are not obvious to many students.

To prove that every element of a set has a certain property, it must be demonstrated that each element has the property. But what is involved in proving that the elements of a set do not have a given property? There are two very different situations that could be inferred from this question, which accounts for much of the confusion students have about proof by counterexample. Students are correct in assuming that in order to prove that **each** element of a set does not have a specified property, it must be shown that every single element of that set does not have the property. However, to demonstrate that the **proposition** ''every element of a set has a specified property'' is a false proposition, one needs to find only one element of the set that does not have the property in question. The key to the issue of the validity of proof by counterexample lies in the fact that this argument form is used to demonstrate that a general proposition is false. The general proposition may be shown to be false because it is not restrictive enough. Proof by counterexample is not used to determine whether individual elements of the set under consideration have the property in question. Examples similar to the following example can be shown to students to help them understand why proof by counterexample is a valid argument form.

Read each of the following statements and decide whether it is *true* or *false*. The set in questions is **S** = { 1, 2, 4, 6} and the property under consideration is the natural number property of evenness.

Statement 1.   Elements of set **S** are even numbers.
Statement 2.   Every element of set **S** is an even number.
Statement 3.   Some elements of set **S** are even numbers.
Statement 4.   The statement ''If an element belongs to set **S,** then it is an even number.'' is a proposition.
Statement 5.   The proposition in statement four is true.

Whether Statement 1 is *true* or *false* can not be decided because it isn't quantified well enough.

Statement 2 is *false* because 1 belongs to **S** and 1 is not an even number.

Statement 3 is *true* because set **S** does contain the even numbers 2, 4, and 6.

Statement 4 is *true* because the statement in quotation marks which is part of Statement 4 **is** a proposition.

Statement 5 is *false* because the proposition in Statement 4 is not true. The proposition in Statement 4 is false because it implies that **every** element in set **S** is even. In fact, Statement 2 is equivalent to the proposition contained in Statement 4; however, the quantifier **every** is written in Statement 2 but is only implied in the proposition contained in Statement 4.

One point being made here is that sometimes it is necessary to decide what the implied quantifier is before attempting to prove or disprove a proposition. A second point is that proof by counterexample is an argument that a **proposition** is not true. The existence of a particular instance of a counterexample does not prove that the proposition fails to hold in all instances, but it does prove that the proposition is false. In mathematical logic, a proposition is labelled false if it is not true for **all** of the instances that it includes.

Indirect Proof

Indirect proof, which is one type of proof by contradiction, is a confusing argument form for many students. There are several reasons for this confusion. First, most students are not shown indirect mathematical proofs until they study plane geometry; consequently they have had few opportunities to formulate an intuitive conception of indirect argument. Second, many teachers treat indirect proof casually and do not explain the underlying logical form for this method of proof. Third, indirect proof should be used only when a proposition is either true or false. If a proposition is undecideable, one may arrive at a contradiction by assuming that it is true and also by assuming that it is false. Since secondary students seldom encounter undecideable propositions in their mathematics classes, undue caution in using this form of proof is unnecessary. However, some students justifiably feel uncomfortable about using indirect proof because in their words "just because we get a contradiction by assuming that the theorem is false doesn't necessarily mean that it is true."

There are several logical forms of indirect proof; however the form that is usually used in high school plane geometry will be presented here. Most propositions in geometry are "if/then" implications; that is $p \rightarrow q$. To prove that $p \rightarrow q$ indirectly, begin by assuming that p and the negative of q are true and deduce a contradiction that r and not r are both true for some statement r. That is,

$$\frac{(p,\ \sim q) \rightarrow (r,\ \sim r)}{p \rightarrow q}.$$

There are some propositions that are extremely difficult to prove by any method except indirect proof and others that can be proved using either direct or indirect methods. Several cases where indirect arguments are used are in proving that certain numbers are irrational, in proving that the set of prime numbers is infinite, and in proving that the cardinal number of the set of real numbers is larger than the cardinal number of the set of rationals. Some of the geometry theorems that are proved using indirect arguments can be proved using direct methods as well. In high school, indirect proof is certainly not limited to the geometry classroom as is shown in the following example:

An indirect argument can be used to prove the proposition that "if the product of two real numbers is zero, then at least one of the numbers must be zero."

First, let a and b represent two arbitrary real numbers. Assume that $ab = 0$, which is the hypothesis of the proposition. Also assume that $a \neq 0$ and $b \neq 0$, which is the negation of the conclusion of the proposition. Since the real number system is a field, a has a multiplicative inverse, $\frac{1}{a}$. But, $\left(\frac{1}{a}\right)(ab) = \left(\frac{1}{a}\right)(a)\,(b) = b$ from the fact that multiplication is associative and from the definition of multiplicative inverse. However $\left(\frac{1}{a}\right)(ab) = \left(\frac{1}{a}\right)(0) = 0$. Therefore $b = 0$ which contradicts our assumption that $b \neq 0$. We now have $b = 0$ and $b \neq 0$. We began by assuming that the product

$ab = 0$ and that $a \neq 0$ and $b \neq 0$ which led to the implication that $b = 0$ and $b \neq 0$. Therefore by the principle of indirect argument, if $ab = 0$, then $a = 0$ or $b = 0$.

Both direct and indirect argument forms are used to prove theorems in secondary school mathematics and a combination of direct and indirect arguments may be used in a single proof. For example, modus ponens, modus tollens, and the deduction theorem were used implicitly in the preceding proof. However, before students can comprehend mathematical proofs in a very meaningful way, they must understand each of the logical forms that are used as arguments in the proofs of propositions. Although some teachers prefer to teach a unit on logic as a separate topic in a high school mathematics course, many others prefer to incorporate principles of logic, argument forms, and their applications throughout the secondary mathematics curriculum.

Why Should Proofs Be Done in School?

Although mathematics educators have differing opinions about the amount of emphasis that should be placed upon proof in secondary schools, there are some compelling reasons for including a moderate amount of theorem proving in secondary school mathematics courses. Several of these reasons have already been stated or implied in the preceding discussion of the different types of argument forms and some additional reasons will be presented here.

An approach to deciding how much emphasis to place upon proof in high school mathematics is to identify the cognitive and affective objectives of theorem-proving, and then base the treatment of proof upon the importance of these objectives. We might begin by asking why mathematicians construct proofs. Since the work of research mathematicians is to extend mathematical knowledge as well as to reformulate and restructure existing knowledge, theorems are proved in order to resolve doubt and to permit continuing with confidence. After conjectures have been proved, mathematicians can continue their search for new mathematical principles, relationships and applications with increased confidence in the truth of their statements and the validity of their methods. Extending mathematical knowledge and resolving doubt are certainly important objectives of proof for mathematicians, but are these meaningful objectives for secondary school students? The answer to this question is "yes" for those very few students who will eventually become mathematicians. However, there are other reasons why theorem proving is useful to most students.

Most students have little doubt about the truth of propositions in their mathematics textbooks. They regard the mathematics classroom as a place to learn useful facts and skills, which indeed it should be, and expect that their teachers and the writers of their textbooks will have verified the truth of the facts and correctness of the skills that they present. Resolving doubt is not a very important objective for most students; however theorem-proving can be interesting and challenging when it is approached as a logical game, which is sufficient justification for some students. Since one of the objectives of school-based education is to develop an appreciation for various intellectual disciplines, theorem-proving can help students better understand the methods of mathematicians and the nature and structure of mathematics.

We also want our students to develop respect and appreciation for logical deductive arguments and to value and apply these argument forms after they finish their high school education. People who know how to use valid arguments are better able to participate in democratic institutions, can avoid being deceived by invalid arguments, and are better able to assist in solving some of the difficult problems of society. Theorem-proving in school provides a neutral situation in which newly-learned argument forms can be tested, practiced, applied and improved.

Proving theorems can also result in finding new conjectures and new arguments. Many people obtain a considerable amount of satisfaction and gratification from producing original work. Proving a theorem can be an interesting creative endeavor for some students.

Theorem-proving is an important type of problem-solving skill and one objective of mathematics education is to help students learn general, transferable problem-solving strategies. In general, it is thought that proving theorems, but not memorizing other people's proofs of theorems, can facilitate intellectual development and help people to learn how to learn.

Proofs not only verify principles but also yield new evidence which helps students assimilate logical principles and remember mathematical facts, concepts and principles by establishing relationships among them. Proving theorems may help students form unifying mental structures containing networks of mathematical objects and interrelations among the objects. In this sense proving theorems can serve as post organizers of previously studied mathematical objects and advance organizers for new objects.

Most mathematics educators do agree that these objectives of theorem-proving that have just been presented are important enough to justify proof as a valid activity in secondary school mathematics. How much time students should spend proving theorems and the degree of rigor required in proofs can be decided by each mathematics teacher for himself or herself. However, the types of proofs constructed by students and the degree of rigor expected in students' proofs does depend, to a large extent, upon the intellectual development and maturity of students.

G. Polya (1957) in answer to his own question, "Why Proofs?", says that:

If the student failed to get acquainted with this or that particular geometric fact, he did not miss so much; he may have little use for such facts in later life. But if he failed to get acquainted with geometric proofs, he missed the best and simplest examples of true evidence and he missed the best opportunity to acquire the idea of strict reasoning. (pp. 216-217)

Teaching Students How to Prove Theorems

Teaching students how to prove theorems is not unlike teaching them how to think. Since theorem-proving is a very individualized activity, which can't be accomplished using an algorithm, it is a difficult process to teach to students. Even though theorem-proving is difficult to teach and can be frustrating to learn, it should not be ignored in high school mathematics classrooms nor should it be approached haphazardly.

Before suggesting some useful strategies for teaching students how to construct proofs, it might be well to discuss some poor strategies which are in common use in mathematics classrooms. Since the central activity in many high school geometry courses is proving theorems and since geometry teachers feel obligated to cover a considerable amount of material, some teachers use poor strategies in attempts to speed up the learning of proofs. Students quite naturally learn how to construct proofs slowly and inefficiently. Many of their valid proofs are disorganized and messy, which is also natural. Mathematicians' proofs are also messy and disorganized until they write them up for use as lecture notes or publication in a book or journal. In an effort to have students write neatly organized proofs in a short time, some teachers require students to follow specific lists of instructions when proving theorems. An example of such a list is:

1. Draw a line down the middle of your paper and write statements on the left side and reasons on the right side.
2. Number your statements and reasons.
3. The first statement should always be the "given." The last statement should always be the "to prove."
4. Each reason should be either an axiom, postulate, definition, or previously proven theorem.

To assure that students will follow this set of instructions, the teacher may demonstrate the proofs of several theorems at the chalkboard by stating each theorem, drawing a line down the middle of the chalkboard, and writing statements and reasons to the left and right of the line, respectively. He or she may also use a questioning strategy such as: "What is the first statement? What is the first reason? What is the second statement? What is the second reason?...What is the last statement? What is the last reason?" This strategy usually causes students to memorize the teacher's and textbook's proofs in order to meet the teacher's conditions for proofs and to pass tests. While memorization is a useful activity in learning facts, it is a nearly useless strategy for meeting the cognitive and affective objectives of theorem-proving. The most serious limitation of using such a structured theorem-proving strategy is that students form completely incorrect ideas of the nature of mathematical proof and learn very little that can be applied outside the geometry classroom.

Even when such a misdirected approach is avoided, students can still fail to understand the logical argument forms used in proofs. It is well to teach the nine types of direct and indirect deductive argument forms concurrently with the geometric content in a geometry classroom. When each argument form is applied in a proof for the first time, that argument form should be discussed and illustrated until students at least understand the reasoning used in the form, even if they are not yet ready to agree that it is valid. Complete acceptance of some of the argument forms may come later after the form has been used in a number of proofs. Of course, these logical forms are used as a basis for argument in proofs and are not specifically written down as reasons each time they are used within a proof.

Since few proofs of mathematics theorems are written in outline form, students should be permitted to write proofs in prose in the form of paragraphs. The proof of the theorem that "if the product of two real numbers is zero, then at least one of the numbers is zero," which is presented on page 302, is an example of a proof written in paragraph form. If some students want to write proofs in an outline format, they should be permitted to do so, but this format should not be required.

Mathematicians do not produce polished proofs in their first attempts, and students should not be expected to do better than experienced mathematicians. When a student produces a poorly written but valid proof or presents a poorly stated but valid oral argument, his or her argument should be recognized as a sound mathematical proof. Since one of the goals of education is effective communication, students should be encouraged to rewrite their initial valid but messy proofs in a style that other students can understand. Students should first be encouraged to formulate sound, logical mathematical proofs and should be rewarded for doing so. The next activity in the theorem-proving process is communicating that proof to other people in a reasonably neat and coherent format.

Contrary to what some teachers believe, the best way to prove a theorem is not necessarily to begin with the hypothesis and work toward the conclusion. After a theorem has been proved, the proof is usually organized in this manner when it is written down; however when contemplating how to prove a theorem, one's thinking may go in many different directions. Proving a theorem and writing the proof on paper require different kinds of mental activities. Theorem-proving is a mental problem-solving activity and writing a proof is a form of communication. The former process may be disorganized and unstructured but the latter process requires organization, structure and explanation to assist the reader in understanding the proof.

Since proving a theorem requires showing why it is true, one should always convince himself or herself that the theorem is in fact true before attempting to write a proof. This can usually be done by constructing examples that are instances of the proof or by attempting to find counterexamples. After finding several examples of the theorem and failing to find any counterexamples, the person who is attempting to prove the theorem will have at least an intuitive understanding of the theorem. The procedure of searching for examples and counterexamples may also indicate a strategy for proving the theorem. In constructing examples one may find that all the examples are indeed instances of the proof because they have certain common properties which can be generalized into a proof strategy. Searching for counterexamples may indicate why the theorem can not be false and may also lead to a proof strategy. In any event, trying to find examples and counterexamples will help the student comprehend some of the implications of the theorem which may be useful in proving the theorem.

There is no best approach to proving theorems. Sometimes it is better to begin with the hypothesis, other times it is appropriate to start with the conclusion, and at times it may help to start in the middle. It is usually helpful to jot down definitions, postulates and other theorems that appear to be related to the hypothesis or the conclusion as well as any implications that follow from either. Notes such as these may suggest a strategy for proving the theorem.

Since there is no algorithm for proving theorems, teachers cannot teach students *the* method of proving theorems; however they can show students particular approaches that people have used to prove certain theorems. Theorem-proving skills are learned through practice and teachers can structure students' initial practice in proving theorems. Wickelgren (1974), in his book *How to Solve*

Problems uses a structured strategy for teaching his readers how to construct their own proofs of specific theorems. He begins by stating a theorem and suggesting an argument form that the reader can use in proving the theorem. Then, he says "stop reading and try to prove this theorem." If the reader is unable to prove the theorem and continues reading, he or she finds a hint about what type of strategy to use and is told to stop reading and try the proof again. If the reader is still not successful, he or she is given additional information such as another theorem or a proposition, which can be used in proving the theorem, and is told to stop reading and try again. This procedure can be continued until the reader finally comprehends the proof of the theorem. Wickelgren does not suggest this procedure as a strategy for proving theorems, instead it is a teaching strategy to help people learn how to construct proofs. The reader is involved in proving the theorem and is not merely trying to comprehend the steps in another person's proof. However, enough assistance is given to assure that the reader will end up with a proof of the theorem.

Teachers can use Wickelgren's strategy in the classroom when students are learning their own procedures for proving theorems. This strategy can prevent students from becoming discouraged because they do complete each proof with varying amounts of assistance from the teacher. The following example illustrates how this strategy can be used in a mathematics classroom:

Teacher: "Prove that two straight lines can intersect at no more than one point. This proposition can be proved using the indirect form of argument."

(Each student starts to work on a proof. After several minutes, a student becomes frustrated.)

Student: "I can't get started."

Teacher: "You might want to start with the assumption that two distinct points determine one and only one straight line."

(After several minutes the student is still unable to prove the theorem.)

Student: "I still can't prove it."

Teacher: "Did you begin by assuming that there are two lines which intersect in at least two points?"

Student: "No, I'll try that."

(The student is still unsuccessful.)

Student: "I can't prove it."

Teacher: "Do you know that if two straight lines intersect in two different points **A** and **B,** then there are two distinct straight lines passing through **A** and **B.**

Student: "O.K., but so what?"

Teacher: "Doesn't that contradict the assumption that two distinct points determine one and only one straight line?"

Student: "Yes it does, but how can two points make two different straight lines?"

Teacher: "They can't, which means that we have arrived at a contradiction."

Student: "Now what do I do?"

Teacher: "Try to figure out the remainder of the proof for yourself."

(A few minutes pass.)

Student: "I guess this contradiction means that the theorem must be true, because if it isn't we get something that doesn't make sense."

Teacher: "That's right! And that's what indirect proof is all about. To prove a theorem by this method, you assume the hypothesis is true and assume that the conclusion is false, that is, you assume the negative of the conclusion. Then, you try to find a contradiction. The contradiction verifies that the hypothesis and the negative of the conclusion are inconsistent. So by the logic of indirect argument, the theorem must be true."

Student: "I think I see what's going on."

Teacher: "Good, now try to write the proof so other people can understand it."

The advantage that this method has over demonstrating a proof at the chalkboard is obvious. When a teacher uses the "try-it-yourself-with-my-help" approach, students must take an active part in proving theorems; they don't sit back and watch the teacher demonstrate proofs.

Regardless of the methods which are used in teaching students ways to construct proofs, learning how to prove theorems requires intermittent practice over a period of years. Consequently, theorem-proving must be taught through a spiral strategy. Students should practice simple proofs in arithmetic using simple argument forms such as modus ponens and transitivity. Theorem-proving can be practiced in algebra using proof by cases and mathematical induction forms of argument. In geometry the more complex argument forms such as contraposition, modus tollens, the deduction theorem, and indirect proof can be used in practicing theorem-proving. Probably the best single piece of advice that teachers can be given about how to teach students to prove theorems is "be patient." Proving theorems is a complex, high level mental activity requiring the use of several different logical forms of argument and many mathematical facts, skills, concepts and principles as well as attention to the interrelationships among all of these argument forms and mathematical objects.

A Teaching/Learning Model for Problem Solving

One of the most significant characteristics of homo sapiens which distinguishes it from other species is the unique problem-solving ability of humans. A significant proportion of human progress can be attributed to the unique ability of people to solve problems. Not only is problem-solving a critical activity in human progress and even in survival itself, it is also an extremely interesting activity. Many pastimes such as games, puzzles and contests are in fact enjoyable tests of problem-solving abilities.

The importance of problem solving in mathematics and the fascination that mathematical problem-solving holds for many people have been illustrated throughout the history of mathematics and mathematics education. The problem of trisecting an angle led to important mathematical discoveries in the theory of equations. Attempts at squaring the circle led to the discovery of transcendental numbers. Numerous attempts to prove Euclid's parallel postulate of plane geometry influenced the development of important new geometries. Failure to find a general formula for solving fifth-degree equations led to significant developments in group theory. Even today, journals such as the *Mathematical*

Monthly and *The Mathematics Teacher* feature mathematical problems, games, and puzzles. The fascination of problem-solving in mathematics is also illustrated by the many high school and college students who participate in local, national and international mathematical problem-solving contests.

George Polya's books on general problem-solving strategies and problem-solving in mathematics (1957, 1962, and 1965) have become modern classics and other books and articles on problem-solving have used and extended Polya's ideas. For example, the discussion of problem-solving that is presented in this section is based upon some of Polya's ideas.

Since one of the major types of problem-solving in mathematics is proving theorems, many of the concepts and principles pertaining to theorem-proving, which were presented in the previous section, are also relevant for this section on more general problem-solving strategies.

What Is Problem Solving?

Before considering the educational objectives of problem-solving in mathematics classrooms, strategies for teaching and learning how to solve problems, and some examples of problem solving in mathematics, it is necessary to define general problem solving as well as problem solving in mathematics. The first step in defining problem solving is answering the question: "What is a problem?"

It is surprising to find that studying the characteristics of problems is of little assistance in defining the term "problem." The definition of "problem" is found in the attitudes of people toward situations which may or may not be problems for them. For example, the statement "find a number that can be placed in the box to make $3x \square + 7 = -5$ a true statement" could be a legitimate problem for many sixth or seventh graders, but is not a problem for most students in a second course in high school algebra. Finding a general formula that can be used to solve any quadratic equation is no longer a problem for any mathematician; however this could be a problem for most students who are just beginning to study high school algebra. A necessary condition for a problem is a situation (a question or issue) which needs to be dealt with; however whether or not a particular situation is a problem depends upon how the person who is confronted with the situation regards it. Writing with my right hand is no problem for me, but using my left hand to write could be a considerable problem because I don't even know how to hold a pencil in that hand. Writing with my left hand is currently no problem, because I don't need to use that hand to write and I don't care to learn how to write with my left hand.

These three examples suggest several characteristics of a problem. First, a person must become aware of a situation in order for it to be a problem for him or her. Second, he or she must recognize the fact that the situation requires some action. Third, the person must either need to or want to act upon the situation and must actually take some action. Fourth, the resolution of the situation must not be immediately obvious to the person who acts upon it.

As an example of a potential problem situation, suppose that a student is in her dormitory room studying for an examination when the electricity goes off in the room. Under what conditions is this situation a problem for her?

Condition 1. It is daytime and no lights or appliances are on. (The woman is not aware of the situation, so it is no problem for her.)

Condition 2. The radio goes off and she tries the light switch but the light doesn't come on. It is daytime, she decides that it must be a general power failure, and she continues studying. (She does not perceive that the situation requires any action on her part, so it is no problem for her.)

Condition 3. It is late at night when the light goes out. Even though she sees that lights are on elsewhere in the dormitory, she goes to bed. (She recognizes that the situation requires action but neither needs nor wants to take action, so the situation is not a problem for her.)

Condition 4. It is daytime, the radio goes off, and she wants to listen to the radio while studying. (She is aware of the situation, knows that it requires action, and wants to take action (although she doesn't need to), so she *may* have a problem.)

Condition 5. It is dark, she has not finished studying, but she must in order to pass her test. (She is aware of the situation, knows that it requires action, and needs to take action (although she doesn't want to) so she *may* have a problem.)

Condition 6. It is dark, she needs to and wants to continue studying, so she walks into her closet (as she has done before), flips the circuit breaker and the light comes on. (Even though she was aware of the situation, recognized that the situation required action, wanted to act, needed to act, and did act, the situation was no problem for her because its resolution was immediately obvious.)

Condition 7. It is dark, she needs to and wants to continue studying so she calls the main desk. The woman who answers tells her to try the circuit breaker. She does but the light still doesn't come on. She calls back and the woman tells her that she will send an electrician in the morning. After sitting in the dark for several minutes, she tries the radio and it works. Then, in a flash of insight, it occurs to her to replace the light bulb. She goes to the main desk, the woman on duty gives her a new light bulb, and her problem is solved. (This situation has all of the elements of a problem for the student, so, for her, this was a problem. However, if the same situation occurs again she will know how to resolve it immediately so it will not be a problem the next time she encounters it.)

In summary, *a situation is a **problem** for a person* if he or she is aware of its existence, recognizes that it requires action, wants or needs to act and does so, and is not immediately able to resolve the situation.

It is now obvious that *general problem-solving* should be defined as the resolution of a situation which is regarded as a problem by the person who resolves it. *Mathematical problem-solving* is the resolution of a situation in mathematics which is regarded as a problem by the person who resolves it.

If this definition of a problem is strictly adhered to, the sets of exercises in secondary school mathematics textbooks should be called "exercises," not "problems," as is the case in many textbooks. Whether or not an exercise in mathematics is a problem depends upon how the student regards it and how he or she goes about solving it. Many exercises in mathematics textbooks are designed for routine drill and practice; although some of the more difficult exercises are actual problems for most students. It is really not very important if we call drill and practice exercises problems and call procedures for solving them problem-solving skills. What is important is that students and teachers recognize the difference between learning mathematical skills by solving exercises and learning general approaches to problem solving by resolving situations that do have the characteristics which are used in defining an actual problem. The learning objectives that are met through practicing skills and by solving "real" problems are vastly different. It is certainly permissible for teachers and students to call all types of mathematical exercises "problems;" however drill-and-practice exercises are appropriate for learning facts and skills, and "real" problems are appropriate for learning discovery and inquiry strategies, for making original discoveries in mathematics, and for learning how to learn.

In the remainder of our discussion of teaching/learning strategies for problem-solving, we will use the terms "problem" and "problem solving" in the strict sense in which they are defined above.

Why Solve Problems in School Mathematics?

Problem-solving is an appropriate and important activity in school mathematics because the learning objectives which are met by solving problems and learning general problem-solving procedures are of significant importance in our society. Research findings indicate that general problem-solving strategies learned in mathematics classrooms can, in certain cases, be transferred and applied to other problem-solving situations. Principles that are learned and applied in classroom problem-solving sessions are more likely to be transferred to other problem-solving situations than principles that have not been applied in solving problems.

Mathematical problem solving can help students improve their analytic powers and can aid them in applying these powers in diverse situations. Solving problems can also help students learn mathematical facts, skills, concepts and principles by illustrating the applications of mathematical objects and the interrelations among objects.

Since problem-solving is a fascinating activity for most students, solving problems in mathematics courses can improve motivation; that is, it can make mathematics more interesting for many students. However, problem solving can also decrease motivation if speed, precision, format, neatness, and finding *the* correct answer become the objectives of problem solving in school. Problem solving is difficult and it can be very frustrating for students if their teachers do not exhibit patience and understanding, and offer unobtrusive assistance. When teachers approach problem solving by providing a relaxed, supportive classroom environment, students can have the satisfaction of finding creative and original solutions to mathematics problems.

Problem solving is a fundamental process in mathematics and constitutes a considerable portion of the work of mathematicians. Consequently, students can better learn about the nature of mathematics and the activities of mathematicians if they solve mathematics problems. Since passing on our cultural heritage is an important goal of our educational system, both the objects (facts, skills, concepts and principles) and the methods (problem-solving strategies) of mathematics, which are an important part of this heritage, should be transmitted to students in our secondary schools.

311

Strategies for Teaching and Learning Problem Solving

A general five-step problem-solving model is discussed briefly on pages 119-120. This general model subsumes the somewhat more specific strategies for solving problems and proving theorems in mathematics. The five steps of *the general problem-solving model* are:

Step 1. Present the problem in a general form.

Step 2. Restate the problem in an operational (solvable) representation.

Step 3. Formulate alternative hypotheses and procedures for attacking the problem.

Step 4. Test hypotheses and carry out procedures to obtain a solution or sets of potential solutions.

Step 5. Analyze and evaluate the solutions, the solution strategies, and the methods which led to discovering strategies for solving the problem.

An Explanation of the Problem Solving Model

Step 1 is the act of discovering the problem or becoming aware that a problem exists. For example, $1^3 = 1^2$, $1^3 + 2^3 = 3^2$, $1^3 + 2^3 + 3^3 = 6^2$, $1^3 + 2^3 + 3^3 + 4^3 = 10^2$, suggests that there might be a formula connecting cubes and squares; what is it? And, of course, our original example in Chapter 3 about the amount of water flowing from the Mississippi River in a year is a general presentation of a problem. When the student decided to take action after her light went out, she was confronted with a problem.

Step 2 involves stating the problem in better terms so that there is a chance of finding a method for solving it. Continuing with our three examples, is the proposition that $1^3 + 2^3 + 3^3 + \cdots + n^3 = (1 + 2 + 3 + \cdots + n)^2$ true? What is the approximate cross section of the Mississippi River near its mouth and what is its average rate of flow? What might have caused the light to go out?

Step 3 involves trying to find approaches to solving the problem. Maybe $1^3 + 2^3 + 3^3 + \cdots + n^3 = (1 + 2 + 3 + \cdots n)^2$ can be proved by looking at geometric representations of cubes and squares; possibly the equation can be simplified; mathematical induction might be a method to use in proving the conjecture; or maybe indirect methods would help. To find the amount of water flowing from the Mississippi River in a year we may need to locate a book of facts about rivers; we could also consider the watershed of the Mississippi, but we still need a data source. The woman might try a new light bulb.

Step 4 is actually solving the problem or testing one's conjectures. In this step, each of our several suggested approaches to solving each of our three problems might be tried. If none of the approaches works, we must search for other methods.

In **Step 5** the solutions are analyzed to determine whether they are reasonable. However, even more important, the solution strategies and the methods used in discovering these strategies should be analyzed; that is, we should attempt to discover generalizable problem-solving strategies. Although it is important to verify the correctness of a solution to a problem, it is even more important to analyze and evaluate general problem-solving methods to determine how efficient they are, whether they can be improved, and how they might be applied to solving entire classes of problems. If you used mathematical induction, ask yourself what caused you to think of using induction. In the Mississippi River problem, how did you arrive at your two approaches to solving the problem? Did you make false starts? Did you spend too much time going down a blind alley? Did you go away from the problem for a time? Did you have a flash of insight? What caused you to think of each method? The woman with the spent light bulb may ask herself why she didn't think to check the bulb in the first place. Why didn't she know about the circuit breaker? If the lights go off again are there any other easy and obvious possible solutions to the problem? Where were her blind spots? Why did she have blind spots? What can she do about them?

Now that these five steps have been briefly explained and illustrated, we will return to the general model and discuss techniques for accomplishing each step. After that, we will suggest strategies for teaching these techniques to students.

Techniques for Using the Problem-Solving Model

Step 1 of the model, presenting a problem in a general form, is an activity involving insight and discovery. For the mathematician, recognizing that problems exist and formulating conjectures are just as important as solving problems, maybe even more so. Even outside of mathematics, discovering problems and anticipating the occurence of problems are important and rewarding endeavors. Throughout the history of science, men and women have had to ask the right questions before solutions could be found. Questions such as the following led to solutions to important problems in science and mathematics: Does the sun revolve around the earth? Is it possible that the earth is not flat? What causes malaria? Can polio be prevented? How do birds fly? What causes the tides? Leaders of countries, managers of business, presidents of corporations, medical researchers, sociologists, educators, etc. must also ask the right questions before their problems can be understood and solved. As examples: What causes wars? Why do people purchase non-essential commodities? How can pollution be controlled without a subsequent loss of production? What causes cancer? What are the causes of crime?

Questions such as these lead one to ask how **Step 1** of the general problem-solving model can be accomplished. That is, how can general problems be found and more specifically for mathematicians, mathematics teachers, and students of mathematics, how can mathematics problems be discovered? As is illustrated above, the basic activity in finding problems is asking questions, but what types of questions can lead to the discovery of problems in mathematics?

1. One way to discover problems is to look for patterns. The patterns found in the coefficients of $(a + b)^n$ for $n = 1, 2, 3, \cdots$ lead to the binomial theorem.

2. Problems can be found by searching for relationships. The relationships among the sides of a right triangle and its area suggest the Pythagorean theorem.

3. Look for correspondences; that is, try to find similarities among different mathematical objects. Correspondences that have been discovered among the elements of different mathematical systems have led to important discoveries in group, ring and field theory.

4. Try to find variations in problems that have already been solved. Having proved that "the diagonals of a parallelogram bisect each other," one

might consider the converse of this theorem; that is, "if the diagonals of a quadrilateral bisect each other is the figure a parallelogram?"

5. Try to form generalizations. If the distance between two points, (x_1, y_1) and (x_2, y_2) in a plane is $\sqrt{(x_1 - x_2)^2 + (y_1 - y_2)^2}$, what might the distance between two points in three-dimensional space be?

6. Look for common properties in different problems. Some elements of rings do not have multiplicative inverses. Rings have divisors of zero; that is, there exist elements a and b in rings such that $ab = 0$ but $a \neq 0$ and $b \neq 0$. Is it possible that these two situations are equivalent?

In general, the best way to find problems is to speculate—be curious, ask questions, brainstorm, let your mind wander, think divergently. Of course speculation will result in the discovery of more false conjectures than true propositions, but this is natural. The set of false mathematical propositions is a larger set than the set of true propositions. Or is it? This statement is a speculation. Is it true? Can it be proved? Can it be disproved?

Step 2, restating the problem so that it is solvable, is also a difficult task. It has been said that any problem that is properly stated can be solved or if a problem can't be solved then it is improperly stated, which is the contrapositive of the first statement. A difficult problem, but one which was easier to solve than finding the cause of cancer, is the problem of determining whether cigarette smoking and air pollution can cause cancer. The problem of finding the causes of wars can be restated as a problem to determine the relationship between war and economic considerations. "Why do people purchase non-essential items?" can be restated as: "Are people more likely to respond to an advertisement if it is repeated many times?" Sometimes the restatement of a general problem in more specific terms can reduce the number of possible solution strategies from infinite to a finite number. Asking and answering the following set of questions can be helpful in formulating a "solvable" restatement of a problem stated in general terms. To illustrate how each of these questions can be used to restate a problem, the following general problem will be evaluated using each question: *When are two triangles the same?*

1. Does the problem make sense? It is reasonable to consider the meaning of "sameness" of triangles.

2. Is the problem worthwhile or interesting? This problem does appear to be worthwhile because triangular shapes are found in many types of architecture and have many applications in engineering. Whether or not this problem is interesting is up to the person who is considering it; however triangular shapes do interest some people.

3. Do I understand the problem? The statement of the problem is somewhat vague, but I do know the definition of "triangle." However, I am not certain that I understand what is meant by "same" in this question.

4. What does the problem mean? This problem means that we should try to determine which characteristics of triangles can be used to decide whether two triangles are the same.

5. Is the problem too general? In this example the problem is much too broadly stated.

6. What is known? We know the definition of "triangle."

7. What is unknown? We don't know the meaning of "same."

8. Is there enough information in this statement of the problem? The answer is no; our triangle problem is vaguely stated.

9. Can the problem be stated in a more meaningful way? Yes, we need to restate the problem so that the meaning of "same" is clear.

10. Can the problem be broken into subproblems? There may be several proper definitions of "sameness" for triangles; therefore there would be several subproblems.

A careful consideration of these ten questions might result in the restatement of this general problem into the following subproblems:

1. Under what conditions do two triangles have the same shape? That is, when are two triangles *similar?*

2. Under what conditions do two triangles have the same size? That is, find a formula for the *area* of a triangle and use it to define "having the same size."

3. Under what conditions do two triangles have both the same shape and size? That is, what are the conditions under which two triangles are *congruent?*

Even though it is still necessary to define *similar, area,* and *congruent* for triangles, we now have a set of more specific problems that appear to be solvable. The restatements of the vague, general problems are specific enough to suggest hypotheses, strategies and techniques for their solution.

In discussing **step 3,** the formulation of hypotheses and procedures for attacking problems, we will use the first subproblem of determining when two triangles are similar to illustrate particular strategies for carrying out this step.

1. What is given, that is, what do we know? Let us assume that we know the definition of triangle and the definition of similar triangles. We will say that two triangles are similar if the three angles of one triangle are equal (or congruent), respectively, to the three angles of the other triangle.

2. What is to be found? Since we are interested in finding conditions under which triangles are similar, we should look for relationships among the sides and angles of similar triangles.

3. What activities might lead to new information? In this case we could construct a number of similar triangles of different sizes and measure their sides and angles in an attempt to discover relationships.

4. What speculations appear to be reasonable? Based upon our observations of a number of similar triangles, we might conjecture the following propositions: Triangles are similar if their respective sides are equal (or congruent). Triangles are similar if their sides are proportional. Two triangles are similar if two angles of one are equal respectively to two angles of the other. Triangles are similar if their areas are equal.

5. What procedures might be used to prove or disprove conjectures? The nine types of valid deductive argument forms, which are discussed in the previous teaching/learning model for proving theorems, are candidates for proving or disproving our conjectures.

Step 4, testing hypotheses and carrying out procedures to obtain solutions to problems provides the actual solution to each problem which is solved. There is no algorithm or set of algorithms to use in solving problems. In fact, by our definition of problem-solving, if a general problem-solving algorithm were discovered, there would no longer be any problems, because the solution to every potential problem would be immediately obvious—use the algorithm. Fortunately for teachers and students, as well as for mathematicians, there are a number of general techniques that can be used to give some direction to the process of solving problems. Some of these techniques are listed below and each one is illustrated for the conjecture that "two triangles are similar if their sides are proportional."

1. Be sure that you know the correct definition of each concept used in the statement of the problem. What is a "triangle"? What do "similar" and "proportional" mean?

2. Be certain that you understand the problem. Could this proposition be stated more precisely so that there is no possibility of becoming confused about which pairs of sides are proportional?

3. Consider whether you may have solved a related problem. Have you ever proved another theorem about proportional sides of similar figures?

4. It may be possible that solving the problem for a special case will indicate a procedure to be used in solving the more general problem. Would proving the proposition for right triangles provide any useful ideas?

5. Consider which valid argument forms might be useful in solving the problem. Should a direct or an indirect method of proof be used here?

6. It might be easier to solve a more general problem which includes the problem under consideration as a special case. Is there a general theorem about similar figures which might apply here?

7. Be sure that you have not overlooked some of the given information which should be used to solve the problem. Are there any unstated assumptions in the hypothesis of this proposition which you have failed to consider?

8. Try to guess the solution. (This technique is more useful in solving logical puzzles and word problems in algebra than it is for proving theorems.)

9. Look for direct implications in the given information which could be useful additional information. Do the hypotheses of this proposition imply any relationships that may be of use in proving the proposition?

10. Try starting in the middle and working in both directions or start with the desired solution and work toward the given information. Could you start with the conclusion and work toward the hypothesis of this proposition?

11. Try breaking the problem into related parts and solving each part separately. Could this theorem be broken into several theorems?

12. Try making the problem into an ordered sequence of easier problems. Could this theorem be proved using a sequence of lemmas?

13. Consider using techniques from another area of study to solve the problem. Could this theorem be proved using techniques from algebra?

14. Try to locate additional sources of information which may be helpful in solving the problem. Have you reviewed the other theorems about triangles which you may have proved?

15. If the problem is proving a theorem, try drawing a figure or consider using auxiliary constructions. Did you draw a figure? Would auxiliary lines help?

16. Try restating the problem. Could you state this theorem in a clearer way?

17. See what conclusions can be drawn from the given information even though they may not appear to be related to the solution which you are trying to find. What other properties follow from similar triangles?

18. Try adding some additional conditions to the problem which may restrict it, but which may also make it easier to solve. Would adding an extra hypothesis be of any use here?

19. Try removing some of the conditions from the problem. What happens if part of the hypothesis is removed?

20. Take the opposite approach and try to show that the problem has no solution. It may be that the proposition is false.

21. If none of these previous 20 suggestions help, try explaining the problem to some other person. At times explaining a problem to another person will clarify it in your own mind and you will stop in the middle of your explanation with a clear idea of how the problem can be solved.

22. If nothing seems to help, leave the problem for a time and do something else. Your subconscious mind may work on the problem and all of a sudden a solution may come to mind. If nothing else, the rest may give you a fresh start on the problem.

23. Be careful not to develop a mental set and keep returning to a strategy that leads nowhere, but don't reject a strategy too quickly.

This list of suggested techniques could continue on and on; however there are sufficient activities here so that no student need read a problem and say: "I can't do it; I give up." You can find additional ideas for solving problems in Polya's books (1957, 1962, 1965) and in Wickelgren's book (1974).

Step 5 of the problem-solving model includes analyzing and evaluating the solution or alternative solutions to the problem as well as evaluating the problem-solving strategies that were used. The following list is a set of questions that can be used to evaluate solutions to problems or problem-solving strategies.

1. Is the solution correct?

2. How did you check your result?

3. If there are alternative solutions, is one more appropriate than the others?

4. Are there still other ways to solve the problem?

5. Did you use a valid argument in solving the problem?

6. What specific argument forms were used?

7. Did you use any unfamiliar argument forms which might be useful in solving other problems?

8. Can your problem-solving strategy be used to solve other problems of this type?

9. Can you use the same strategy to solve unrelated problems?

10. What did you learn about problem solving in general as a consequence of solving this particular problem?

11. What particular difficulties did you encounter in solving this problem and how can you avoid these difficulties when solving future problems?

12. Did you attempt any strategies that proved to be unsuccessful? Why were these strategies of little value?

These five lists, one for each of the five steps of the general problem-solving model, do provide an appropriate set of techniques which secondary school students can use as an aid in solving problems in their mathematics classes and in learning better problem-solving strategies. The five lists are too long for solving certain problems, because many problems can be solved using a small subset of the 56 techniques suggested here. In another sense, the list is not long enough because many people will find that they are unable to solve some problems even by using all 56 of the techniques. Although these 56 techniques were designed to help people solve problems in mathematics, most of them can be used in solving problems in other school subjects and in solving problems away from school.

Strategies for Teaching Problem-Solving

Since the best way for people to solve problems is to ask questions of themselves, a good strategy for teaching problem-solving techniques to students is to ask questions of them. Giving students a list of questions and telling them to ask themselves these questions when trying to solve a problem is a good first step in teaching problem solving but more must be done. Students also need to be shown how to use these questions; this can be done in three ways. First, teachers should demonstrate problem-solving methods to students by questioning themselves aloud as they solve mathematics problems. Second, teachers should conduct group problem-solving sessions with the entire class where both the teacher and students ask questions and offer suggestions which might be helpful in solving problems. Third, when a student is having trouble solving a problem, rather than suggesting a method of solution or telling the student an algorithm for solving that particular problem, it is well to help the student formulate questions which might be of use in finding a solution.

This indirect approach of helping students discover their own methods for solving each problem may appear to be less efficient than telling them a precise set of steps to carry out; nevertheless, in the long run, it is much more efficient because students will learn generalized approaches for solving entire classes of problems. After students have formulated their own algorithms for solving a particular type of problem, it is quite proper to permit them to write their algorithms as lists of steps and use them to solve other problems of the same type. In fact, this is a major objective of problem solving; that is, students should search for strategies that can be applied to solving entire sets of problems. However, if teachers prepare the lists of problem-solving steps without involving students, then students may learn the skill of solving certain problem types but may not learn much about problem solving. This is not to say that students should discover every mathematical skill or process for themselves. When the learning objective is comprehending and applying mathematical skills, these skills can be demonstrated to students without making them into problems and problem-solving situations. However, when the objective is to comprehend and apply principles and to learn general problem-solving techniques, students should be assisted in finding their own methods for solving problems.

To illustrate how a mathematics teacher might moderate a problem-solving lesson with an entire class, a strategy for helping students solve the problem of finding a formula for the diagonal of a rectangular solid will be demonstrated. The method used in ''teaching'' students how to solve this problem is the five-step problem-solving model, which involves asking many questions.

Step 1. Present the problem in a general form.

Teacher:	''I was making some braces for a platform last weekend and I encountered an interesting mathematical problem. I had to find the length of the diagonal of a parallelepiped.''
Note:	(Although this problem was not ''discovered'' by a student, the statement of the situation in which the problem did occur does suggest one source of mathematical problems to students.)

Step 2. Restate the problem in a solvable form.

Teacher: "How far is it from one corner of a rectangular parallelepiped to another?"

Note: (After the teacher asks this question there are puzzled looks on students' faces and a minute of silence.)

A Student: "I don't know what you mean."

Another Student: "Yeah, I don't understand it either."

Teacher: "Does anyone understand my question?"

Note: (The class indicates that they do not understand the problem.)

Teacher: "I guess I didn't state my question very well. What doesn't make sense?"

A Student: "What's a rectangular parallelepiped?"

Teacher: "A rectangular parallelepiped is a rectangular solid."

A Student: "What's that?"

Teacher: "An example of a rectangular solid is a shoe box."

Note: (Students now appear to understand the meaning of "rectangular solid.")

A Student: "Boxes have a lot of corners. Which corners do you want to find the distance between?"

Teacher: "I want to find a diagonal distance through space; for example, the distance from the left top corner of the front to the right bottom corner of the back."

A Student: "I still don't see it."

Teacher: "What could I do to help?"

A Student: "Why don't you draw a box?"

Another Student: "No, get a box and show us."

Note: (The teacher gets an open box and uses a metric ruler to represent one of the diagonals in question.)

Teacher: "Can anyone state my problem more clearly?"

Note: (Following a brief discussion, the class restates the problem as "Find the diagonal distance from a top front corner of a rectangular solid to the opposite bottom corner on the back.")

Teacher: "Now, is this problem stated in a way that is understandable to everyone?"

Note: (All the students indicate that they understand the problem.)

A Student: "What good is this problem?"

Teacher: "Can anyone see an application of this problem?"

Note: (Several students suggest applications.)

Step 3. Formulate hypotheses and procedures for solving the problem.

Teacher: "Our problem is to determine a method for finding a diagonal through the interior of a rectangular solid, such as a shoe box. Does anyone have an idea?"

Note: (A minute or two passes. Teachers should always provide time for students to think about answers to their questions.)

A Student: "Why not just take a meter stick and measure it?"

Teacher: "Is that solution general enough?"

A Student: "No, because how could you measure the diagonal of this room with a meter stick?"

Another Student:	"Get a long stick!"
Teacher:	"Where would we store the stick?"
A Student:	"I guess we would have to store it on the diagonal of the room; then it would be in our way."
Another Student:	"Why not use a string!"
Another Student:	"Because it would sag."
Another Student:	"We could hook it over a nail in the top corner and stretch it to a bottom corner and then measure the string with a meter stick."
Teacher:	"That's a good idea. Can anyone think of another way?"
A Student:	"The string's O.K., but is that the way engineers do it?"
Teacher:	"I doubt it, because I never saw a blueprint with a note telling the builder to stretch a string to find the length of a cross support."
A Student:	"What we need is a formula."
Teacher:	"That's another good idea. We'll try it! Does anyone else have another idea?"
Note:	(No more ideas were offered.)
Teacher:	"Now, let's summarize our methods and list the strengths and weaknesses of each method."
Note:	(The class lists the three methods—using a meter stick, using a string, and finding a formula—and discusses the advantages and disadvantages of each method.)
Teacher:	"Let's try to find a formula. What would we have to know about this classroom to find one of its interior diagonals?"
A Student:	"We should know the length, width and height of the room."
Teacher:	"Would these dimensions be easy to find?"
A Student:	"Sure, we could use a meter stick."

Step 4. Test hypotheses and carry out strategies to solve the problem.

Teacher:	"Suppose we let *l* represent the length of the room, and *w* the width, and *h* the height. Does anyone have a suggestion for finding the formula?"
Note:	(Two minutes of silence occur.)
Teacher:	"Have you ever found the diagonal of any figures before?"
A Student:	"The diagonal of a sphere is its diameter."
Teacher:	"That's right, do you see how we might use that fact here?"
Same Student:	"I guess we could put the box in a sphere."
Note:	(The class decides that this is an even more difficult problem.)
Teacher:	"Any other suggestions?"
A Student:	"We have found diagonals of plane figures."
Teacher:	"For example?"
Same Student:	"Squares, triangles, trapezoids."
Another Student:	"What's the diagonal of a triangle?"
Teacher:	"Maybe John was thinking about medians or bisectors of sides of triangles when he made that suggestion. Right John?"

320

Note: (John verifies that such was the case.)

A Student: "The sides of the room are rectangles and we know how to find the diagonal of a rectangle."

Another Student: "Yeah, use the Pythagorean theorem."

Teacher: "Will that help us here?"

Note: (After a discussion of several minutes, the class decides that a figure is needed and draws the rectangle shown in Figure 6.3, which contains a representation of the diagonal of the room. After ten minutes of discussion and work, with a few questions directed to the teacher, the students develop the formula $D = \sqrt{l^2 + w^2 + h^2}$, where D is the diagonal of the interior of the room.)

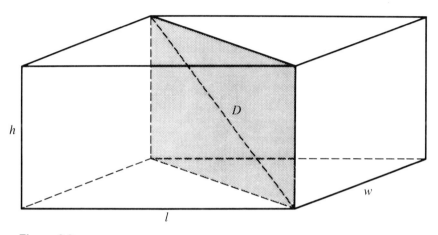

Figure 6.3.

Note: (In solving this problem, the class divided the problem into a sequence of two subproblems. First they used the length and width of the room to find the diagonal of the floor of the room. Next, they used the height of the room and the diagonal of the floor to find the interior diagonal of the room.)

Note: (It may be helpful for some students to find the interior diagonal of a particular rectangular solid (such as, $l = 12$ meters, $w = 8$ meters, and $h = 4$ meters) before trying to find the general formula. The concrete example may make the generalization easier.)

Step 5. Verify the solution and analyze the solution strategies.

Teacher: "Now that we have the formula, $D = \sqrt{l^2 + w^2 + h^2}$, how do we know that it is correct?"

Student: "Try it out."

Teacher: "How will we know if the answer we get by using the formula is correct?"

Student: "We could measure the diagonal and see."

Teacher:	"O.K., let's try the formula. Here's a box, find its interior diagonal. Also, find the interior diagonal of the classroom."
Note:	(The class uses the formula to find the length of the diagonal of the box and they also measure the diagonal using a meter stick.)
Teacher:	"Did you get the same answer by using the formula as you did by using the meter stick?"
Student:	"Nearly, but not exactly the same."
Teacher:	"Does that mean that the formula is wrong?"
Student:	"No, it means that our measurements aren't perfect."
Teacher:	"Now, let's try finding the interior diagonal of this room."
Note:	(The students measure the length, width, and height of the classroom and use the formula to calculate the interior diagonal. Then they use a string to measure the diagonal directly.)
Teacher:	"Are the answers the same?"
Student:	"Yes, they're very close."
Teacher:	"Do these two answers prove that the formula is correct?"
Student:	"No, just because it worked twice doesn't mean that it will always work."
Teacher:	"How could we prove the formula is true?"
Note:	(After a brief discussion the class concludes that the formula is true because the Pythagorean theorem, which was used in developing the formula, is true and because they used valid argument forms to develop their formula.)
Teacher:	"What general strategies did you use in solving this problem?"
Student:	"We used the Pythagorean theorem."
Another Student:	"We made a diagram."
Another Student:	"We tried the formula out."
Teacher:	"Anything else?"
Student:	"We had to put the problem in different words because we didn't understand the way you told it to us."
Another Student:	"We had to ask a lot of questions."
Teacher:	"Who answered these questions?"
Student:	"You answered some of them, but we answered most of them ourselves."
Teacher:	"Are these good strategies for solving other kinds of problems?"
Note:	(The class decides that their problem-solving method could be useful in solving other types of problems.)

Although in this hypothetical example, the teacher and students progressed in a well-ordered sequence from Step 1 through Step 5, such a situation is seldom found in an actual classroom. Some steps may be combined, the order of steps may be changed, and several steps may be carried out at once. The key principle to remember is that many of the activities contained in the five steps of the problem-solving model should be carried out during each problem-solving session. Some additional principles for teaching problem-solving to students are summarized in the following list:

1. Encourage students to use unique strategies.
2. Encourage divergent thinking.
3. A balance should be maintained between group problem solving and working on problems individually.
4. Give students plenty of practice in solving problems.
5. Encourage questions, questions, and more questions.
6. Be sure that students have mastered the prerequisite facts, skills, concepts and principles needed for solving a problem before it is given to them.
7. Encourage students to discover their own mathematics problems and find their own solutions.
8. Encourage intuition, creativity and logical analysis.
9. Create a relaxed, non-threatening atmosphere in which to solve problems.
10. When students get stuck in solving a problem offer suggestions *unobtrusively*.
11. Ask questions that are general enough to be applicable to solving various types of problems in addition to the present problem being considered.
12. Avoid offering suggestions to students which make the solution to a problem obvious.
13. Ask questions and offer suggestions that could have occurred to students themselves. If your questions and suggestions are so innovative that students would have had no hope of thinking of them for themselves, they may regard problem solving as a hopeless activity.
14. Reward students for using good problem-solving strategies as well as for obtaining correct answers.

This list of principles for teaching problem-solving suggests one question that teachers should ask of themselves: "How will I know if I am following these and other appropriate principles for teaching problem solving?" It could be that you are inadvertently offering so much help to students during problem-solving sessions that your assistance is akin to an algorithm for solving each problem. It may also happen that it is you, not the students, who are asking most of the questions and providing most of the answers.

A good technique for evaluating your own strategies for teaching problem-solving is to make occasional audio recordings of your problem-solving lessons. You can play these recordings at your leisure and analyze and evaluate your own success in teaching problem-solving and your students' success in learning problem-solving. A tape recording can be used to indicate how well you and your students are attending to each of the five steps in this general model for teaching and learning problem-solving. More will be said about evaluation techniques in Chapter 7.

The Laboratory Teaching/Learning Model

Research and observation in education show that many secondary school mathematics students need to work with concrete representations of concepts and principles before they can meaningfully comprehend abstract and symbolic forms of these mathematical objects. The work of Piaget, Bruner, Dienes, and others (see Chapter 3) supports the proposition that manipulating concrete objects is an important activity in learning mathematics. Not only does manipulating concrete representations of mathematical ideas make mathematics more understandable, it also helps students learn general problem-solving skills. In a mathematics laboratory students solve problems, explore mathematical concepts, formulate and experiment with mathematical principles, and make mathematical discoveries by manipulating concrete representations of relatively abstract mathematical ideas. The teacher's role in a school mathematics laboratory is to catalyze and facilitate student-centered inquiry and discovery activities. The teacher is a resource person who offers assistance when it is needed and who helps students become self-sufficient learners.

What is a *mathematics laboratory?* A mathematics laboratory may be an environment in which students learn mathematics by exploring mathematical concepts, by discovering mathematical principles, or by applying mathematical abstractions in concrete situations. It may also be a place where students go to study mathematical skills, concepts and principles as they are represented by physical objects, mathematical models, or manipulative activities such as games. In a mathematics laboratory students formulate and apply abstract concepts and principles by working with concrete examples of these mathematical objects.

What is the *laboratory model* for teaching and learning mathematics? The laboratory model is a set of teaching/learning strategies whereby students explore mathematical ideas through many types of student-controlled activities in a mathematics laboratory. These exploratory activities can be carried out through teacher or student demonstrations, individualized or group study procedures, discovery and inquiry methods, and various problem-solving activities. Although the teaching and learning strategies that are usually associated with the laboratory model are characterized as student-centered, activity-oriented, and concretely represented, these characteristics should not be regarded as necessary and sufficient conditions for a mathematics laboratory. The physical facility that is given the name "math lab" may be a section of a mathematics classroom, the entire classroom, a corner of the school library, a special room within the school, or a location away from the school such as a museum, resource center, or community center. The resources found in the "math lab" may include books, games, models, pictures, posters, bulletin boards, films, projectors, audio recordings, transparencies, inexpensive gadgets and materials, individualized learning carrels and computer terminals. The activities which students engage in while they are in the laboratory may be completing worksheets, using audio/visual resources, reading books, building models, playing games, solving problems, searching for patterns, discussing mathematical ideas, or writing and executing computer programs.

It is obvious from the descriptions of a mathematics laboratory and the laboratory teaching/learning model, which are given above, that the laboratory approach to teaching mathematics can not be neatly defined by a set of stages or activities. The three topics discussed below—*objectives in using mathematics laboratories, teaching/learning strategies for mathematics laboratories,* and *facilities and resources for mathematics laboratories*—will provide additional clarification of the laboratory model for teaching and learning mathematics.

Objectives in Using Mathematics Laboratories

Laboratory activities can help students learn and remember facts, apply skills, comprehend concepts, and analyze and synthesize principles, which are cognitive learning objectives for the direct objects of mathematics. Mathematics laboratory activities can also help students meet cognitive learning objectives for the indirect mathematics objects of problem solving, transfer of learning, and learning how to learn. Affective learning objectives of willingness and satisfaction in responding to mathematical activities, acceptance and preference for values in mathematics education, and conceptualization of personal values related to mathematics and education can also be attained through laboratory activities in mathematics. Certain types of laboratory methods help students learn how to work independently, while other methods assist them in learning how to work effectively with other people in group activities.

The laboratory model is specifically designed to capitalize upon secondary school students' preferences and intellectual requirements in learning mathematics through concrete physical activities. Students can discover mathematical principles by collecting information and studying properties of mathematical models. They can also search for mathematical patterns which can lead to generalizations of mathematical propositions and problems. Students can build mathematical models to illustrate and communicate abstract mathematical concepts and principles, which will prepare them to comprehend these concepts and principles when they are presented later in more abstract and general representations.

The five steps of the problem-solving model—discovering general problems, restating general problems in solvable forms, formulating problem-solving strategies, carrying out problem-solving procedures, and evaluating solutions and solution strategies—can be practiced in specific concrete situations in a mathematics laboratory. Students can discover interesting generalizations which lead to the formulation of mathematical problems and can try out scientific methods of inquiry in the laboratory. Conjectures can be offered and propositions can be set forth. These conjectures and propositions can be tested using valid logical forms and students can learn about the nature and methods of mathematical proof in the mathematics laboratory.

Some of the fascinating and useful applications of mathematics can be discovered and studied in the laboratory. Students will learn that many of the skills, concepts and principles of mathematics came from physical situations and that mathematical skills, concepts and principles are not merely arbitrary sets of rules for manipulating meaningless symbols. Laboratories can help students improve their understanding of the historical foundations and development of mathematics and the historical interrelations among mathematics and the other sciences.

Techniques of measurement, approximation and estimation can be learned and practiced through laboratory activities. Laboratory experiments can illustrate the inexact and imprecise nature of some of the applications of mathematics, the so-called exact science. With the gradual but certain adoption of the metric system of measurement in the United States, the need for all secondary school students (not just mathematics and science "majors") to learn and apply metric units is apparent. The best way to learn the metric system is to use it, and the best way to teach the metric system is to have students use it in laboratory activities.

Secondary school students are energetic and active people; however many, if not most, of the teaching/learning strategies that teachers regularly use provide few opportunities for students to become actively involved in their own learning in any ways other than mental and pencil-and-paper manipulations. Laboratory activities can provide a welcome break from teacher-dominated lecture and demonstration strategies, which may help students develop better attitudes toward learning mathematics. Many students who have little success dealing with abstract presentations of mathematical concepts and principles may have better results when they study mathematics through the less abstract representations which are found in mathematics laboratories. Their modest successes in the laboratory can help these "slower" students improve their self images and their attitudes towards mathematics.

In general, well-designed mathematics laboratory activities provide students with interesting problems to solve using newly learned mathematics objects, create a relaxed learning environment where students can learn at their own rate, and help teach students to be responsible for their own learning. The mathematics laboratory approach is one more model that teachers can use to help students meet some of the cognitive and affective objectives of mathematics education. It may well be that the most important function of the laboratory approach is that this method of teaching and learning can help students better understand the manner in which they learn mathematics; that is, students can learn how to learn by working in a mathematics laboratory.

Teaching/Learning Strategies for Mathematics Laboratories

Even though mathematics laboratory activities are student-centered, individualized, informal, and activity oriented, they should not be unstructured and disorganized; neither should they be overly structured and managed by the teacher. The teacher should specify the activities that students will be expected to carry out in each mathematics laboratory session and should help students set general learning objectives for each laboratory lesson. Although the lesson plan for a laboratory lesson may not need to be as detailed and structured as a plan organized around some of the other teaching/learning models, it should contain each of the fourteen **Activities in Planning Mathematics Lessons** which are subtopics of the following main topics: *mathematics content, learning objectives, learning resources, preassessment strategies, teaching/learning strategies,* and *postassessment strategies.*

In addition to the fourteen activities of any lesson plan in mathematics, there are three special activities which the teacher must carry out in preparation for a laboratory lesson. First, since most mathematics laboratory lessons center around student activities with laboratory resources, obtaining resources for students to use in the mathematics laboratory is an important responsibility of the teacher. There are many sources of laboratory resources; some of these sources were mentioned in Chapter 4 and other more specific sources will be discussed later in this chapter. For now, it suffices to say that four distinct types of laboratory resources are available—your ideas and those of your students, mathematics content, teaching/learning strategies and physical resources.

The second special activity in preparing a laboratory session is making plans for organizing and using resources during the lesson and supervising student activities in the laboratory. All of the materials that students will need for the lesson should be readily available in the laboratory. Care should be taken to choose materials that are representations of mathematical objects and that do have related cognitive and affective learning objectives. Resources should also be selected according to their suitability for the age and ability levels of the students that you teach and assurances that they can be safely used by students. Although students should have some degree of free choice in conducting laboratory experiments in mathematics, they also need judicious and unobtrusive direction from the teacher. Suggestions and assistance should be offered to students who appear to be having little success in working toward the objectives of the laboratory lesson and additional challenging activities should be provided for students who quickly and easily complete their laboratory tasks.

The third supplementary planning activity for mathematics laboratory lessons is teaching students to use mathematics laboratories effectively. Many students who are accustomed to well-structured expository lessons do not know what to do in a relatively unstructured laboratory situation requiring considerable student initiative. Conducting a "mathematical experiment" in a laboratory is similar to solving a problem and students who are going to be working in mathematics laboratories should be encouraged and, if necessary, assisted in carrying out these five general laboratory strategies:

1. Identify the problem; decide what you are going to do; state your objectives.
2. Think about ways to approach your problem; make a plan; find different ways to meet your objectives.
3. Obtain resources that may be of use in working on your problem; carry out your plan; look for patterns, relationships, and generalizations; try to make discoveries; search for alternative approaches; gather data.
4. Draw conclusions; answer questions; solve problems; analyze your conclusions; state your findings.
5. Analyze and evaluate your methods and procedures; compare different methods; evaluate your findings; look for relationships among your findings.

Many of the strategies for solving problems and for teaching students how to solve problems, which were discussed in the previous section of this chapter, can also be used in teaching students how to work in a mathematics laboratory. Most students do need some general preparation on how to use a mathematics laboratory before they undertake laboratory tasks.

Even if your school does not have a special room which is equipped for use as a mathematics laboratory, you can still use a corner of your classroom as a mini-laboratory where resources are stored and displayed. In some cases mathematics teachers may travel from room to room to teach their classes. If you are one of these teachers, careful planning for the movement of laboratory materials is necessary and you may even have to store some of your laboratory resources in your own home; however the school principal may be able to provide you with a storage closet. Although a well-equipped mathematics laboratory or resource room makes it possible to use a wide variety of laboratory teaching and learning strategies, it is not difficult to design interesting laboratory lessons which can be carried out within your own classroom with a few simple materials. In fact, most books and articles about mathematics laboratory activities contain mostly activities which can be carried out in a classroom with few resources.

There are several different techniques that you can use in conducting laboratory lessons. First, laboratory activities may be carried out in the classroom during regular class periods, assigned as homework, or completed as out-of-school projects. Second, mathematics laboratories may be very structured or may be quite unstructured. At times students may need a considerable amount of guidance in order to solve some problems or make certain discoveries in mathematics. In other situations where independent problem-solving strategies are being emphasized, it may be better to give very few directions and little assistance to each student. Third, laboratory sessions may be prepared according to the type and degree of direct participation required of each student. Several general techniques for conducting ''math lab'' sessions are listed below:

1. The teacher, a student, or a group of students may present a demonstration before the entire class.
2. Each student in the class may work individually on the same laboratory problem.
3. Students may work together in small groups on a common problem.
4. Each student may work by himself or herself on a problem that is different from the problem that each of his or her classmates is studying in the laboratory.
5. Small groups of students may select their own activities to carry out during a laboratory session.

Whether you are teaching arithmetic, algebra, trigonometry, geometry, or special topics in mathematics, there are many different laboratory strategies which you and your students can use in mathematics laboratories. Six general laboratory strategies, which are illustrated below through specific examples, are: (1) Discover theorems and relationships, (2) Find patterns, (3) Solve problems, (4) Explore concepts, principles, or applications of mathematics, (5) Develop methods of approximation, (6) Collect and analyze data.

(1) **Discover a Theorem.** Students as well as mathematicians find satisfaction in discovering theorems. With a few general instructions, most students can discover many theorems of plane geometry by measuring lines and angles, comparing geometric figures, and constructing and folding paper figures. For example, if students are provided with compasses, protractors and construction paper, they can discover the plane geometry theorems about parallel lines. General questions and suggestions such as the following can be given as guidelines for their explorations.

a. Consider the relations among the angles which are formed when two parallel lines are cut by a transversal.
b. You may want to compare angles by measuring them with a protractor, or you could construct parallel lines cut by a transversal and compare the angles by cutting them out with scissors and placing one over the other.

c. What conclusions can you draw when the transversal is perpendicular to one of the lines?

d. Suppose lines that are not parallel are cut by a transversal; what are the relationships among the angles formed?

e. Based upon your explorations, can you state any propositions which specify the conditions that must be met in order for lines to be parallel?

f. Do you think that the converse of each of your propositions is another true proposition?

(2) **Find a Pattern.** One of the most fascinating properties of numbers is the large variety of patterns that exists among sets of numbers and sets of geometric figures. Finding and examining number patterns can lead to the discovery of many important mathematical principles such as the binomial theorem, the Euclidean algorithm, the formulas for sums of arithmetic and geometric progressions, commutative, associative, and distributive properties, and conditions under which number series converge. Euler's formula—if V is the number of point vertices, E the number of line edges, and F the number of plane faces of a simple polyhedron, then $E = V + F - 2$—is an interesting example of a theorem which can be found by forming and studying number patterns. To assist students in discovering the number patterns leading to this theorem, have each student fill in the following table for the simple polyhedra shown in Figure 6.4.

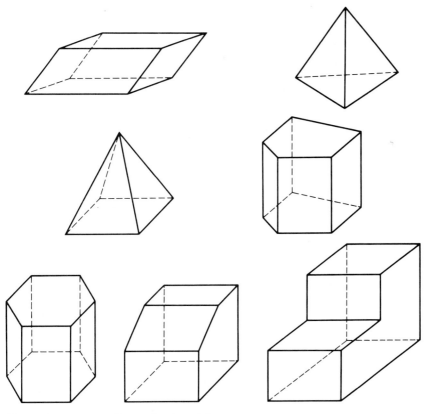

Figure 6.4. Some simple polyhedra.

Polyhedron	Number of Point Vertices	Number of Plane Faces	Number of Line Edges
Parallelepiped			
Tetrahedron			
Square pyramid			
Pentagonal prism			
Hexagonal prism			
Truncated cube			
Steps			

The following questions and suggestions could be used to guide students in discovering Euler's formula:

a. Can you find a pattern among the number of vertices, faces, and edges which gives a general relationship among these three characteristics for each figure?

b. If you can not find any direct relationship, you might see if one characteristic is the sum or product of the other two characteristics, plus or minus a constant.

c. When you think you have found this relationship, write it as a formula.

d. Construct some other plane polyhedra and determine whether they support your formula.

e. Can you think of a way to prove that your formula is correct?

(3) **Solve a Problem.** In the section on problem solving, we discussed a general five-step model for solving problems. The following problem can be solved in two ways; the first method is an experimental procedure which gives an approximate solution, and the second method is a deductive analysis which gives the exact solution. The problem is to find the probability that a dime tossed so that it comes to rest on a large 3-centimeter ruled grid will not fall on a grid line. This situation is represented in Figure 6.5.

You might want to offer the following suggestions to students:

a. Draw a 3-cm × 3-cm grid on a large sheet of poster board and toss the dime repeatedly so that it comes to rest several hundred times on the board. How can your results be used to find the probability that the dime will not come to rest on a grid line? Will the probability found in this way be exact? Why?

b. Use a valid deductive approach to find the exact probability by comparing the area of the dime to the area of a 3-cm × 3-cm square. Be careful, because the ratio of the area of the dime to the area of a grid square does not yield the correct probability. Why not?

The probability can be found by first assuming that the dime lands with its center anywhere within a specified square. The radius of a dime is 0.9 cm, so if its center is more than 0.9 cm from each side of a grid square, the dime will not be on a grid line. Therefore, the only possible positions for the center of the dime so that the dime itself is not on a line is within the small 1.2-cm square which is shown in Figure 6.5. The ratio of the area of this 1.2-cm × 1.2-cm square to the

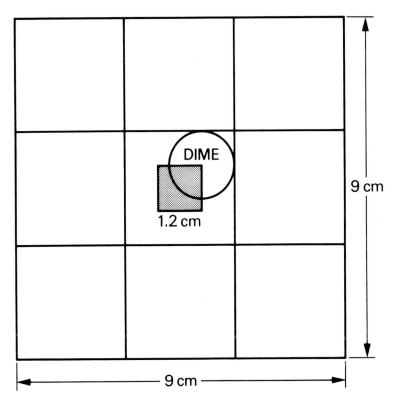

Figure 6.5.   A penny at rest on a 3 centimeter grid.

3-cm × 3-cm square is the probability that the dime will not fall on a grid line; that is

$$P \text{ (not on line)} = \frac{1.2 \text{ cm} \times 1.2 \text{ cm}}{3 \text{ cm} \times 3 \text{ cm}} = 0.16.$$

(4) **Explore a Principle through an Application.** Many mathematical concepts and principles become comprehensible and meaningful to most students only through practice with concrete representations and applications of these mathematical objects. The "math lab" is a situation in which students can explore and use mathematical concepts and principles. A principle which can be explored in a mathematics laboratory and which also combines elements of physical health, science, and mathematics is the principle that smoking cigarettes is harmful to the smoker's lungs. The objective of this laboratory demonstration is to simulate the effect of smoking a cigarette upon a person's lungs. Before starting this demonstration ask questions such as:

a.   What happens inside a person's lungs when he or she smokes a cigarette?
b.   How many breaths are required to clear the lungs of smoke after a cigarette is smoked?
c.   After the smoke has cleared from a person's lungs, are any residues left behind?

This laboratory experiment is found in Ralph Vrana's book *The Mathematics Laboratory: A New Teaching Approach* (1975) and it illustrates his approach to using "math labs" to help students understand principles of size and shape. His version of this demonstration, which is quoted below, simulates the effects upon a person's lungs of smoking a cigarette or a pack of cigarettes. The materials for this laboratory are shown in Figure 6.6.

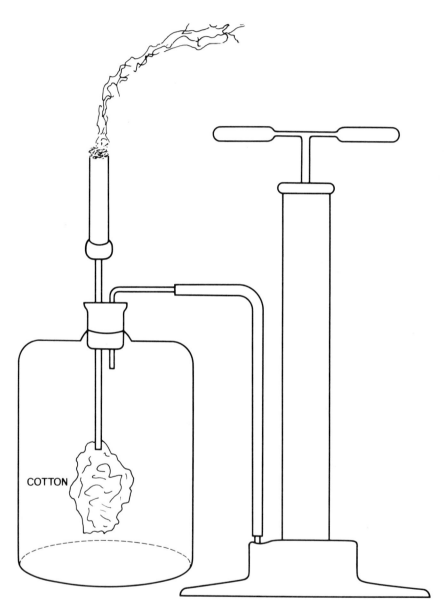

COTTON

Figure 6.6.   Apparatus for simulating the effects of smoking cigarettes upon one's lungs.

The by-products of a burning cigarette can be trapped in a filter and even weighed if a suitably delicate balance is available. In any case it is an instructive demonstration of the amount of smoke and tar given off when a cigarette is smoked. A hand vacuum pump is used to draw on the cigarette. If none is available a tire pump with leather piston reversed will work. . . .

A dense smoke fills the bottle and remains there a long time. The cotton absorbs some of the smoke, and the liquids from the burning cigarette roll down the tube into the cotton. A pack of cigarettes "smoked" this way will leave the cotton quite messy, and a weight measurement of the cotton before and after smoking will be more easily made than for one cigarette. The dense smoke in the bottle can be cleared by detaching the hose from the vacuum pump and blowing it out through the hose by mouth. The number of breaths required give some idea of how long after smoking one's lungs are cleared of noticeable smoke.

These experiments help the student visualize what happens when tobacco smoke is inhaled, a process otherwise concealed within the body. The notion that it is virile and romantic to smoke should be balanced with a little realism. (pp. 58-59)

(5) **Develop Methods of Approximation.** Although mathematics is called an exact science, methods of approximation which are used in the physical sciences, engineering, and computer science have played an important role in the historical development of mathematics and should play a role in secondary school mathematics education. The spiral teaching/learning model was discussed in the previous chapter and it was suggested that the concepts of successive approximations and limits should be "spiraled" throughout secondary school mathematics.

In calculus, the concept of the length of a curve can be defined as a limit of a sequence of successive linear approximations to the curve. A laboratory exercise to find approximations to various curves defined by mathematical functions could be carried out in high school algebra. To do this, give the class a list of functions and relations such as:

1. $y = x^2 - 2x$ 5. $y = x^2 + 2x + 4$
2. $y = x^3 - x$ 6. $y = x^4 - x^3 + x^2 - x$
3. $y = 2^x - x^2$ 7. $y = |x^3|$
4. $y = \log_{10} x$ 8. $x^2 + y^2 = 4$.

Begin the laboratory session by showing the class how to find a set of successive approximations to the curve defined by $y = \dfrac{x^2}{4}$ between $x = 0$ and $x = 3$. Draw the parabola represented by $y = \dfrac{x^2}{4}$ on the chalkboard and explain how the distance formula can be used to find three successive linear approximations to the length of this curve. These approximations are shown in Figure 6.7.

You may want to have small groups of students work together to find a sequence of approximations to the length of a curve defined by a specific function. Near the end of the laboratory session have each group explain its work to other groups and draw some general conclusions about strengths and weaknesses of

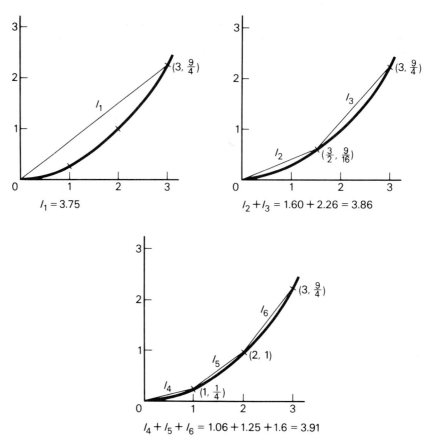

Figure 6.7. Successive approximations to the length of the curve defined by $y = \dfrac{x^2}{4}$ from $x = 0$ to $x = 3$.

their methods. Have each group consider questions and activities such as the following as they work on finding their approximations:

a. How well do your approximations represent the length of the curve?
b. Is each successive approximation better than the previous approximations?
c. Is it possible for an approximation made by using many line segments to be farther from the length of the curve than an approximation made with only a few line segments?
d. Are there any disadvantages to this method of successive linear approximations?
e. Can you think of other ways to find the lengths of curved lines?
f. Construct a graph to represent each of your approximations.
g. Since it is possible to approximate the length of part of a parabola using straight line segments, consider how lengths of graphs of higher degree equations might be approximated using segments of parabolas. What would one have to know in order to use segments of parabolas?

(6) **Collect and Analyze Data.** Coin-tossing, dice-rolling and questionnaires have been mentioned previously as methods of generating data for student con-

sideration. As an example of how students can collect and analyze data, and possibly discover a formula, a laboratory session for comparing Fahrenheit and Celsius temperature scales will be illustrated. This laboratory is most appropriate for algebra students who have had little experience with the metric system of units, who have not been given a formula for converting between Fahrenheit and Celsius measurements of temperature, or who have forgotten the formula. For this laboratory, the class should be divided into small groups and each group should have a Fahrenheit thermometer, a Celsius thermometer, a source of heat such as a small propane or gas burner, a flame-proof beaker, and some ice cubes. Each group should carry out these activities:

a. Fill the beaker partly full of ice and water, immerse the two thermometers in the beaker, and, after the readings have stabilized, record the Fahrenheit and Celsius readings on a chart.

b. Gradually apply heat to the beaker of water and record the readings from each thermometer on the chart. Temperature readings should be taken and recorded approximately every thirty seconds until the water boils rapidly.

c. Compare the ordered pairs of Fahrenheit and Celsius scale readings and analyze this data in an attempt to find a formula which relates the two scales.

d. Graph the ordered pairs of temperature readings on a rectangular coordinate system as an aid to guessing an approximation to the formula.

e. After arriving at a good guess for this formula, encourage the class as a group to consider a method for finding the precise formula if it is assumed to be a linear equation. Some classes may be able to carry out this step on their own; however other groups may need some suggestions from the teacher. One method for finding the formula is to assume that $F = aC + b$ where F is the Fahrenheit reading, C is the Celsius reading, and a and b are constants which are to be determined. Taking the two ordered pairs of (F, C) readings for freezing and boiling which are (32, 0) and (212, 100), respectively, the following substitutions can be made to find a and b:

First, $\quad F \quad = aC + b$
$\qquad 32 \quad = a(0) + b$
$\qquad 32 \quad = b$
therefore, $F = aC + 32$
then, $212 = a(100) + 32$
$\qquad 1.8 = a$
therefore, $F = 1.8C + 32$.

f. Determine whether this formula verifies some of the other (F, C) pairs which were obtained while the water was being heated from freezing to boiling.

These six examples of mathematics laboratory activities are included to illustrate six general types of laboratory strategies; however there are many other general types of laboratory strategies and thousands of specific "math lab" activities have been published in books and journals.

Facilities and Resources for Mathematics Laboratories

A mathematics laboratory activity can originate from an idea of a teacher or a student, in a segment of mathematics content, from a physical resource, or as a teaching/learning strategy. Consequently, the laboratory model for teaching and learning mathematics can be used in schools which do not have a mathematics resource room or many laboratory materials, devices, and other resources. The six laboratory strategies discussed above require few materials and those materials which are needed are inexpensive and readily obtainable. Free, inexpensive, and moderately expensive laboratory resources will be discussed below. In addition, for those mathematics teachers who do have a special room to use as a "math lab" and a moderate budget to equip it, facilities for mathematics laboratories will also be considered. However, it is well to keep in mind that pencil-and-paper explorations and discoveries can be just as interesting and useful in learning mathematics as information presented by an expensive resource such as a sound and color motion picture. In fact, good ideas are more important than expensive equipment when using the laboratory model.

Sources of Ideas

Good sources of ideas for mathematics laboratories can be found in a variety of books, journals, and magazines. The *Thirty-fourth Yearbook* of the National Council of Teachers of Mathematics (1973) contains ideas for a variety of "math labs" as well as book and magazine references for 67 different types of laboratory projects. The books by Vrana (1975) and Sobel and Maletsky (1975) also have many ideas for mathematics laboratories. The brochure "Current Publications" of the National Council of Teachers of Mathematics lists nearly a dozen books which can be used as sources of mathematics laboratories. Magazines and journals such as *The Mathematics Teacher, The Arithmetic Teacher, School Science and Mathematics,* and *Creative Computing* carry articles about activities for mathematics classrooms. When you do locate a good book or article on laboratory activities in mathematics, be sure to check its bibliography for other sources.

Books and articles about the content, history and development of mathematics can stimulate your thinking and catalyze ideas for mathematics laboratories. For example, Edna Kramer's book *The Nature and Growth of Modern Mathematics* (1970), which is available in a paperback edition, contains discussions of numerous topics in mathematics which lend themselves to a laboratory treatment.

As you read about models and strategies for teaching mathematics here and in other sources, you may think of ways in which certain strategies can be combined or modified to permit activity-oriented mathematics lessons. As you plan lessons and consider various teaching/learning strategies for use in each lesson, laboratory activities may come to mind for many topics in mathematics.

Audio-Visual Aids

Audio-visual aids can be used in mathematics laboratories to help students understand abstract concepts and principles, to illustrate applications of mathematics, to increase interest in mathematics, and to provide remedial and enrichment instruction. The following list of audio-visual aids serves as a check list for selecting audio-visual resources for use in a mathematics laboratory:

1. A chalkboard and colored chalk
2. An overhead projector and transparencies
3. Pictures, charts, graphs, posters and maps

4. Models made from paper, cardboard, wood, plastic and string
5. Bulletin boards
6. Books and magazines
7. Film strip projectors and film strips
8. Slide projectors and slides
9. Sound motion-picture projectors and films
10. Audio, video, and audio-video tape recordings and equipment for using them
11. Computer terminals such as hard-copy teletypes, cathode-ray-tube display screens, interactive graphic terminals and plotters
12. Closed-circuit television

Of course, few schools are able to equip a mathematics laboratory with all 12 of these types of audio-visual resources. However, every mathematics teacher can obtain and use the first six types of resources on the list in his or her own classroom as well as in a mathematics laboratory room. Nearly all schools have resources of the types listed in items 7, 8, and 9. Many schools have at least one of the sets of resources listed in items 10, 11, and 12; although very few schools have all of these resources.

Permanent Materials for the Mathematics Laboratory

Most of the audio-visual aids mentioned above are permanent resources for mathematics laboratories; however there are many other non-consumable materials which can be used by students to learn mathematics in a laboratory situation. Some of these materials are listed below; many of them can be stored and used in classrooms in schools that do not have special rooms to use as mathematics laboratories:

1. Metric and U.S. customary measuring sticks, scales, balances, masses, containers, and thermometers
2. Straight edges, compasses, protractors, T-squares, tape measures, plumb bobs, levels, templates for geometric figures and mathematical symbols and other drawing devices
3. Stencils for drawing rectangular- and polar-coordinate systems on paper or on the chalkboard
4. Building tools such as hammers, drills, screwdrivers, pliers, wrenches, saws and soldering guns
5. Mathematical games and demonstrations
6. Special devices such as dice of varying sizes and shapes, mechanical coin tossers, cardboard computers and "math-science gadgets"
7. Hand calculators, abacuses, and other computational devices
8. Scissors and other types of cutting tools
9. Special drawing and construction devices such as templates for drawing conic sections, parallel rulers, arc measuring tools and three-dimensional graphing devices
10. Binary counters, beam compasses, geoboards, instruments for determining *pi*, locus kits, mathematics design makers, geometric construction kits, and card and number games
11. Gravity protractors, isometric protractors, map measuring devices, sextants, mirrors, prisms
12. This list could go on for pages; however it need not, because pages 281-296 of the *Thirty-fourth Yearbook* of the National Council of

Teachers of Mathematics (1973) contain lists of demonstration devices, manipulative devices, computational aids, drawing and measuring instruments, learning kits, games and puzzles, and science apparatus, together with names of distributors of these materials for use in mathematics laboratories. In addition, descriptions and prices of these and other permanent laboratory materials can be found in current catalogs of distributors of mathematics resource materials, supplies, and equipment.

Consumable Supplies and Materials for the "Math Lab"

Not only can students learn about mathematical concepts and principles by working with prepared games, models and other devices, they can also better comprehend mathematics by applying concepts and principles in constructing their own physical representations of mathematical ideas. Like any other good laboratory, a variety of consumable materials and supplies should be available in a mathematics laboratory. Some of these construction materials must be purchased; however many can be accumulated by teachers and students by saving materials that are usually discarded. The following list of consumable materials contains items which can be obtained at no cost. In fact, most of these items can be classified as scrap:

1. Scrap paper, old posters, and cardboard boxes can be accumulated and used as construction materials for building models.
2. Empty cigar boxes, bandage boxes, pill boxes and other types of wooden, plastic, or metal containers can be used to store other laboratory materials.
3. Egg cartons, milk containers, empty cans and bottles and other types of food containers can be used as materials for the "math lab."
4. Discarded materials from the science laboratory can also be used to construct mathematics laboratory devices.
5. Resourceful teachers and students find uses in the "math lab" for bottle caps, corks, empty thread spools, plastic lids, coat hangers, mirrors, tongue depressors, pipe cleaners, wire, toothpicks, and dried beans and small pebbles.
6. Acoustical tiles, styrofoam packaging, linoleum blocks, wood, pegboard, and paneling can also be salvaged for use in the "math lab."
7. Discarded electronics equipment, old radios and television sets, and a variety of broken appliances can be salvaged for use in the laboratory. Even broken musical instruments can be used in a creative "math lab."
8. The best sources of laboratory materials are your students and yourself. Become a scavenger and encourage your students to be scavengers of laboratory resources. Don't throw anything away before considering whether it might be of use in the laboratory.

Of course some materials which can not be salvaged from the scrap heap are needed in the mathematics laboratory. Many of these materials are given in the following list of inexpensive "math lab" supplies:

1. Construction paper, poster board and graph paper
2. Colored pencils, crayons, colored marking pens, water colors, oil paints and acrylic paints
3. Index cards and storage folders
4. Glue, various types of tape, paper clips, staples, tacks, nails, nuts and bolts, screws and other types of fasteners

5. String, rope, wire, rubber bands, straws, and needles and colored thread
6. Various kinds of art-studio and science-laboratory supplies
7. Tape dispensers, pencil sharpeners and staplers
8. Paper towels, soap, cleaning cloths, paint brushes, sandpaper, solvents, and of course a first-aid kit for minor injuries

Permanent Laboratory Equipment

If a room within the school is set aside as a mathematics laboratory, it must be permanently equipped. The following examples of permanent equipment are representative of the kinds of equipment which may be found in a mathematics laboratory:

1. Book cases, storage shelves, storage cabinets and filing cabinets
2. Tables and chairs
3. A small library
4. A chalkboard and an overhead projector and screen
5. Bulletin boards and display cases to exhibit students' work
6. Folding screens to use as room dividers
7. Study carrels and work areas
8. Couches and lounge chairs for quiet study and thought
9. A copying machine
10. A typewriter
11. A sink with drains and sources of hot and cold water, natural gas and electricity
12. Projectors and screens for showing films
13. An audio tape recorder and player
14. Individual audio-video learning carrels
15. Electronic calculators
16. A computer facility with sound-proof carrels for teletype terminals

If you have to use your own classroom as a mathematics laboratory, you will only have space for the first six items on this list, which can be considered minimal permanent equipment for a mathematics laboratory. Schools that do have special rooms for use as mathematics laboratories will have varying amounts of the permanent equipment listed in items seven through sixteen.

Kidd, Myers, and Cilley (1970) in their book *The Laboratory Approach to Mathematics* present floor plans (pages 108-121) of the following types of mathematics laboratory rooms: (1) a mathematics laboratory for team teaching, (2) a conventional classroom adapted for laboratory activities, (3) one of two adjoining classrooms combined for laboratory activities, and (4) self-contained mathematics laboratories. Some schools, in order to save money by sharing resources, have one large laboratory/resource center which is shared by teachers of all subjects or they may have a common mathematics-science laboratory.

Even if you have to use your mathematics classroom as your "math lab," you can still use the laboratory teaching/learning model to develop interesting and informative laboratory activities for your students. While an abundance of resources and equipment can facilitate learning through the laboratory model, bountiful resources and equipment are neither necessary nor sufficient for a good "math lab." Energetic and creative teachers can develop excellent laboratories with minimal resources. At times, excellent resources go unused or are used improperly; as a consequence students meet few learning objectives in the mathematics laboratory which could not be met as well in a classroom where other teaching/learning models are used.

The Inquiry Teaching/Learning Model

The inquiry teaching/learning model was presented in Chapter 4 and the four steps of an inquiry lesson were discussed briefly (pages 208-210). The inquiry model is a special case of the more general problem-solving model; consequently many of the objectives and activities of the problem-solving model also apply to inquiry learning. *Inquiry* is the process of investigating and examining a situation in a search for information and truth. Inquiry processes are used in science and mathematics to extend and organize knowledge.

The four steps or stages of an inquiry into a situation are:

1. Formulating a question, encountering a puzzle, paradox, or inconsistency, or attempting to organize a set of facts, concepts and principles into a general and inclusive principle.
2. Developing procedures and collecting information which may be useful in resolving the situation under consideration.
3. Using the procedures and information from step 2 to reorganize and extend existing knowledge.
4. Analyzing and evaluating the inquiry process itself in order to develop general processes for investigating other situations.

As you can see these four stages of inquiry are similar to the five steps of the general problem-solving model—(1) Finding a general problem, (2) Restating the problem in a solvable form, (3) Formulating methods for attacking the problem, (4) Solving the problem, and (5) Evaluating solutions and solution strategies. However, the inquiry process is a specialized technique for extending knowledge through research and is sometimes called the scientific method of research. Inquiry is a self-initiated method of learning which can be carried out individually or in small groups. The ideal inquiry situation in a mathematics classroom occurs when students formulate new mathematics principles either by working alone or in small groups with minimal direction from the teacher. The main role of the teacher in an inquiry lesson is that of moderator.

Stages in the Inquiry Process

The first stage of inquiry, encountering a puzzling situation or attempting to discover a principle, is best approached by being curious; that is, by observing, analyzing, and evaluating situations and asking questions. The most proficient problem solvers in school mathematics and the most successful research mathematicians are those people who ask the best questions. Good questions lead to useful principles and asking good questions results in solutions to difficult problems. To find useful and interesting avenues of inquiry in mathematics, it is necessary to go beyond what is given and to do more than is required. Ask questions such as: Why does this algorithm work? Why doesn't this method give the correct answer? Is there a better way to do it? Are there any general patterns here? Does this theorem suggest other theorems? Is this problem one of a general class of problems? Can any generalizations be made? What are the differences between these two situations? What are the similarities among these mathematical systems? Is this particular observation always true? Is there a counterexample? Is there a better way to approach this problem? What would happen if these changes were made? Is this actually a paradox? Is there an inconsistency here? Can this information be reorganized? Can this principle be extended? What are some examples of this concept?

The second stage of inquiry, developing procedures and collecting information to use in studying various situations, can be carried out in two ways. First, the best way to find new procedures for solving problems is to be familiar with a variety of standard problem-solving techniques and common mathematical procedures. Many new problem-solving strategies are unique combinations or variations of familiar methods for solving problems. Throughout history, some of the most important problems in one branch of mathematics were solved by mathematicians who used techniques from another branch. When the obvious, standard methods for solving a certain type of problem do not work, it is well to consider procedures that are somewhat out of the ordinary and that are not usually used to solve other problems in the field in which you are working.

Second, solving problems and resolving situations usually requires locating and organizing information. The person who knows about a variety of information sources and who is adept at gathering, sorting, analyzing, evaluating and synthesizing information is likely to be a successful problem solver. In gathering and organizing information it is well to ask questions such as: What are the standard references in this area? Where are these references located? What are some other sources of information? How reliable are these information sources? How good is the quality of this information? Does this information source suggest other sources of information? How useful are these sources? How can this information be combined and organized? What concepts, principles, and methods are contained in this information? Is this information related to the problem under consideration? How might this information be used to solve the problem? Could this information or these procedures be modified for use in other situations?

The third stage of inquiry, reorganizing and extending existing knowledge, is the stage in which a discovery is made, a problem is solved, or a theorem is proved. At this point in inquiry, principles are formulated, relationships are established, structures are identified, and conclusions are drawn. New information has been generated and knowledge has been extended. For the person engaged in scientific inquiry, this stage is highly individualized and personalized, and here is where elements of genius (special abilities to analyze, synthesize, and evaluate) are exhibited. Reorganizing and extending existing knowledge requires activities such as these: Look for relationships. Search for patterns. Take a new viewpoint. Go beyond the data. Try a different approach. Reorganize your information. Use valid argument forms. Consider general problem-solving methods. Look for generalizations. Search for examples or counterexamples. State your conclusions. Establish the truth of your conclusions. Organize and communicate your findings.

The fourth stage of inquiry, analyzing and evaluating the inquiry process, is undertaken in order to better understand and improve methods of inquiry. At this point the focus shifts from resolving a particular situation to considering the inquiry process itself. Each discipline has its own inquiry methods and one objective of researchers in each discipline is to improve existing inquiry strategies within their discipline and formulate new inquiry processes which can be used to further extend and develop that discipline. As is the case throughout the inquiry process, an appropriate procedure for analyzing and evaluating an inquiry process is to ask and attempt to answer questions. Some questions that can be used in carrying out the final stage of inquiry are: What procedures were used to formulate the problem? What prompted the discovery of the generalization? How was the pattern found? What information and procedures led to the discovery of an inconsistency? Which information sources were most useful? What procedures were used to generate and collect data? Which logical argument forms were used in solving the problem? What thought processes were used to arrive at the conclusion? Can the methods used in solving the problem be generalized and applied in solving other problems?

Teaching and Learning Inquiry Methods

There are two general educational goals of each academic discipline; that is, teaching the facts, skills, concepts and principles of the discipline to students and imparting the general problem-solving and inquiry processes used in the discipline to students. In particular, one of the goals of mathematics education is to teach the distinctive methods of mathematical inquiry to students of mathematics. This means that the primary objective of the inquiry teaching/learning model in mathematics is to learn the methods of mathematical inquiry; that is, inquiry methods are taught so that students will learn how to inquire.

Some of the objectives of the inquiry model which are subsumed under this general objective are:

1. Students will develop the mental skills of searching for and processing information.
2. Students will learn principles of logic.
3. Students will understand cause and effect relationships.
4. Students will learn to inquire autonomously and productively.
5. Students will discover relationships among variables which lead to mathematical generalizations.
6. Students will value inquiry strategies as a means of making mathematical discoveries and solving problems.
7. Students will understand methods of mathematical proof and problem-solving procedures in mathematics.
8. Students will obtain a better understanding of the foundations of mathematics and the nature of learning.
9. Students will discover mathematical algorithms and principles.
10. Students will appreciate the methods of research mathematicians.

The first step in teaching students how to use inquiry methods and how to learn mathematics through inquiry is to present, explain, and discuss the four stages of the inquiry process. Students should discuss the questions and activities which are given under the four stages in the inquiry process. They should also formulate additional questions and activities to use in accomplishing each stage of inquiry.

In learning to carry out the first of the four inquiry stages, students should be encouraged to look for mathematical patterns, procedures, and generalizations and should be rewarded for offering conjectures and propositions. Curiosity and speculation should be valued characteristics of learning in the mathematics classroom. Teachers should ask questions that require students to suggest problem-solving algorithms and mathematical principles. Homework assignments in which students are asked to analyze algorithms, games, and proofs of theorems should be given. Students should be asked to compare different methods for solving mathematical exercises and to evaluate each method. Asking and attempting to answer questions should be an integral part of each mathematics lesson, and students' questions should be valued and discussed when they are asked. Students are naturally curious and mathematics is filled with facts, skills, concepts, principles, problems, and relationships which arouse curiosity. If students' questions are answered cursorily, postponed, or ignored, inquiry lessons will not be well-received by students and little will be accomplished when the inquiry teaching/learning model is used. Teachers must set an example for students by showing respect and appreciation for asking questions, which is a very important activity in learning mathematics.

Most students need assistance in carrying out the second stage of inquiry. Mathematics students are not very good at locating information and developing procedures for collecting data to use in mathematical problem solving. There are several reasons for their lack of skill in these endeavors. First, locating and using information is not usually regarded as an important activity in secondary school mathematics. The textbook and teacher are the primary, if not exclusive, source of mathematical information. Second, reading and library search skills are not promoted in most mathematics classrooms, and it does not occur to students to use library resources to learn mathematics. Third, even though mathematics laboratories are becoming increasingly common in schools, many students have had little experience generating, collecting, and organizing data in a mathematics laboratory. Library searches and laboratory data collections are too often left for English and science classes. Mathematics teachers should give reading and library research assignments to their students and should prepare laboratories and homework assignments which require students to generate and evaluate data and search for generalizations in their data.

In teaching students to carry out the third stage of reorganizing and extending existing knowledge, student independence should be required and individual initiative should be valued. Reorganizing and extending knowledge is a difficult activity which can only be learned through practice by using general problem-solving strategies. At this stage of inquiry students should work alone or in small groups with minimal assistance from the teacher. It is very tempting, and appears to be more efficient, for the teacher to do the reorganizing and extending of knowledge; however this tends to subvert the main objective of the inquiry model—learning how to inquire. This stage of the inquiry process will go slowly; but it is important for the teacher to avoid intervening and telling students what to do. The purpose of an inquiry lesson is not to cover material rapidly. When inquiry lessons are conducted the mathematics content is of secondary importance to the inquiry itself.

The fourth stage, analyzing and evaluating inquiry methods, may be the most important part of the inquiry process. It is in this stage that the researcher or the learner asks the question, "What have I learned about learning?" In this stage the student will better understand the methods of mathematics by evaluating his or her own inquiry methods. Questions such as those given on page 342 should be asked by the teacher and students, and students should attempt to answer each question. In this stage of inquiry, the teacher can take a more active role in the lesson by asking leading questions which may help students analyze and evaluate their methods of inquiry. Near the end of each inquiry session, students should attempt to answer the question, "What did I learn about mathematics and what did I learn about learning mathematics through my inquiry strategies?"

An Inquiry Lesson

A good way to learn methods of inquiry is to inquire, and a good way to learn the inquiry teaching/learning model is to observe it in use. Consequently, our discussion of the inquiry model concludes with an example inquiry lesson.

An Inquiry Lesson in Probability

Mathematics Content: The name of this mathematics topic is "an example of *random walk*." The mathematics objects are *concepts* and *principles* from probability theory. This is a special topic which can be sequenced anywhere in the senior year of high school mathematics. Few specific skills and little mathematical knowledge are required for this lesson; however some mathematical maturity is needed and students should be familiar with inquiry strategies.

Learning Objectives: The cognitive learning objective for this lesson is *application of a process;* that is, students will apply the inquiry process to a situation in probability theory which will lead to the development of many interesting questions as well as the resolution of some of these questions. The affective objective is *valuing;* that is, students will value the inquiry process as a means of formulating and resolving interesting questions, which is a process that leads to the discovery of even more questions.

Learning Resources: The only learning resources needed for this lesson are two pennies for each student, a copy of the diagram shown in Figure 6.8 for each student, and lots of scrap paper.

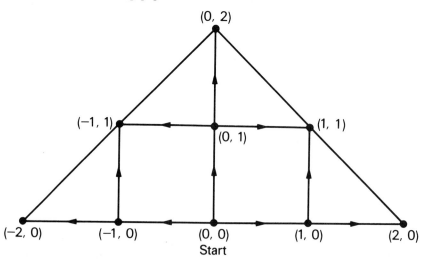

Figure 6.8.

Preassessment Strategies: In addition to mathematical maturity and knowledge of inquiry processes, students should know the probability of obtaining each of (H, H), (T, H), (H, T), and (T, T) when two coins are tossed simultaneously. They should also know that if the probability of event E_1 occurring is p_1 and the probability of event E_2 is p_2, then the probability of E_1 followed by E_2 is $p_1 \times p_2$, where E_1 and E_2 are independent events. In addition, the class should know that the probability of either E_1 or E_2 is $p_1 + p_2$. A brief class discussion can be used to verify that students do know and understand these principles of probability.

Teaching/Learning Strategy:

Begin the lesson by drawing the diagram shown in Figure 6.8 on the chalkboard and giving each student a copy of this diagram. Then give the following explanation of the problem that is to be considered in this inquiry lesson:

Suppose that a marker is placed on the point (0, 0) of the diagram and is moved according to these rules:

Toss two pennies simultaneously. If the pennies land (H, H) move the marker one unit to the right; if they land (T, T) move one unit left; and if they land with either (H, T) or (T, H) facing up, move one unit upward.

Toss the pair of pennies twice and make the two moves (right, left, or upward) according to these rules. After the pennies have been tossed two times, the marker may be at one of these points on the legs of the triangle—$(-2, 0)$, $(-1, 1)$, $(0, 2)$, $(1, 1)$, $(2, 0)$.

Ask each student or small groups of students to calculate the a priori probabilities that the marker will come to rest on each of the five points. They should find the following set of probabilities:

$$p(-2, 0) = \left(\frac{1}{4} \times \frac{1}{4} \right) = \frac{1}{16}$$

$$p(-1, 1) = \left(\frac{1}{2} \times \frac{1}{4} \right) + \left(\frac{1}{4} \times \frac{1}{2} \right) = \frac{4}{16}$$

$$p(0, 2) = \left(\frac{1}{2} \times \frac{1}{2} \right) = \frac{4}{16}$$

$$p(1, 1) = \left(\frac{1}{2} \times \frac{1}{4} \right) + \left(\frac{1}{4} \times \frac{1}{2} \right) = \frac{4}{16}$$

$$p(2, 0) = \left(\frac{1}{4} \times \frac{1}{4} \right) = \frac{1}{16}$$

At this point in the lesson, a class discussion should take place among the students. As the teacher, you should refrain from participating in the discussion unless it becomes apparent that the class is about to terminate its consideration of the coin-tossing situation. If the students do appear to be losing interest or are making little progress through the stages of inquiry, it may be necessary for you to ask a few leading questions. At times students may direct questions to you. If possible, respond to each student question with another question or a suggestion rather than a direct answer. One objective of an inquiry lesson is for students to make their own discoveries by engaging in an independent consideration of a problem; consequently teacher intervention should be minimized during an inquiry lesson.

The following dialogue simulates the dialogue that may take place in the classroom as students consider the coin-tossing situation:

A Student: "Hey, these five probabilities don't add up to one! I have $\frac{1}{16} + \frac{4}{16} + \frac{4}{16} + \frac{4}{16} + \frac{1}{16}$ which is only $\frac{14}{16}$."

Another Student: "That's what I got too."

Another Student: "Maybe we all made a mistake."

Another Student: "I doubt it; we couldn't have all made the same mistake."

Note: (Several students begin to check their computations and others discuss the situation. After several minutes someone finds the key to the puzzle.)

A Student: "I see what's wrong; you can get trapped inside the triangle."

Another Student: "What do you mean?"

First Student: (This student goes to the diagram on the board.) "Look, if you start here on (0, 0) and get (H, H), you move right. Then, if you get (T, T) you move left, which puts you back at (0, 0) after two tosses."

Another Student: "Then the probability of this happening should be $1 - \frac{14}{16}$, which is $\frac{2}{16}$." (The student then directs a question to the teacher.) "Am I right?"

Teacher: "Why don't you use probabilities to check yourself?"

Note: (Students begin working on this problem.)

A Student: "Sure, she's right! Look, the probability of starting at (0, 0) and going 'left-right' is $\left(\frac{1}{4} \times \frac{1}{4} \right)$, and the probability of going 'right-left' is also $\left(\frac{1}{4} \times \frac{1}{4} \right)$. Either of these could happen; so the probability of being trapped inside is $\left(\frac{1}{4} \times \frac{1}{4} \right) + \left(\frac{1}{4} \times \frac{1}{4} \right) = \frac{2}{16}$."

Another Student: "Maybe you could get trapped on the point (0, 1)?"

Another Student: "No, that's impossible; the only way to get trapped is to end up on (0, 0)."

Note: (The class agrees with this observation.)

Note: (The class appears to be satisfied with their "solution" of the problem and students begin to talk about other things. At this point some teacher intervention is needed.)

Teacher: "If you do get trapped inside the triangle after two tosses of the coins, why not toss the pair of coins one more time to try to reach a point on the side?"

A Student: "You can't get out by doing that because you're trapped on (0, 0), and one more toss won't get you out no matter what happens."

Another Student: "You could just keep tossing pennies until you finally got out."

Teacher: "I wonder what the probabilities would be if you did that."

A Student: "We could figure them out."

Another Student: "That would be impossible! We might have to keep tossing forever."

Another Student: "The probability of that happening is pretty small."

Previous Student: "Yes, but it could happen."

Another Student: "We could find the probabilities for three, four, five, and so forth tosses and maybe get a sequence of probabilities."

Another Student: "Yeah! Maybe we could find the limit of the sequence."

Another Student: "That sounds like mathematical induction to me. Maybe we could get a formula and prove it by induction."

Another Student: "Well, let's try it for three tosses."

Another Student: "We already decided that if you get trapped on two tries it will take at least two more tosses to get out."

Another Student: "Let's try to find the probability of still being trapped after four tries and then go on from there."

Note: (The class decides that the previous student's suggestion is a good one, so they begin to consider the case of two more tries after being trapped at (0, 0) following the initial two pairs of coin tosses.)

A Student: "When we get trapped inside after two tries, we are back at (0, 0), so two more tries would be the same as starting over."

Another Student: "That's right, so the probability of being trapped inside after four tries is still $\frac{2}{16}$."

Another Student: "No it isn't. Since the probability of not getting out after two attempts is $\frac{2}{16}$ and the probability of still not getting out after two more attempts is $\frac{2}{16}$, the probability of not getting out after four attempts is $\frac{2}{16} \times \frac{2}{16}$, which is $\frac{1}{64}$."

Another Student: "I don't see why."

Previous Student: "Well, not getting out the first time and not getting out the second time are independent events and the probability of one independent event following another independent event is the product of their probabilities."

Note: (Following a brief discussion of this situation, the class agrees that the probability of being trapped after four trials is $\frac{1}{64}$.)

Student: "O.K. Let's try it for five tosses."

Another Student: "We don't need to look at five tosses, because if you're still

Note:

trapped after four tosses you're at $(0, 0)$ and one more time won't get you out.''

(The class agrees with this student and decides to consider the case of six pairs of tosses.)

Student: "The answer is $\frac{1}{512}$.''

Another Student: "How did you get that?''

Previous Student: "It's $\frac{2}{16} \times \frac{2}{16} \times \frac{2}{16}$.''

Note: (Following a brief discussion the class agrees.)

A Student: "O.K. We have a pattern now. You just keep multiplying by $\frac{2}{16}$.''

Note: (The class agrees.)

A Student: "Maybe we can write a formula. We have $\frac{2}{16}, \frac{2}{16} \times \frac{2}{16}, \frac{2}{16} \times \frac{2}{16} \times \frac{2}{16}$, and so on, so the formula is $\left(\frac{2}{16}\right)^n$.''

Another Student: "Let's simplify it to $\left(\frac{1}{8}\right)^n$.''

Another Student: "What is n?''

Another Student: "n is the number of pairs of coin tosses.''

Another Student: "No it isn't, because $\left(\frac{1}{8}\right)^3$ is for six tosses.'' You can see it from this table.''

Note: (The previous student draws this table on the chalkboard:

Number of Tosses	2	4	6
Probability of being trapped	$\left(\frac{1}{8}\right)^1$	$\left(\frac{1}{8}\right)^2$	$\left(\frac{1}{8}\right)^3$

A Student: "Then the formula is $\left(\frac{1}{8}\right)^{\frac{n}{2}}$ where n is the number of tosses.''

Another Student: "That's right, and n has to be an even number, too.''

Another Student: "So, we're done.''

Note: (The class agrees that the problem has been resolved.)

Teacher: "What is the probability of not getting out after an even number of trials?''

A Student: "It's $\left(\frac{1}{8}\right)^{\frac{n}{2}}$.''

Teacher: (Directing the question to the entire class.) "Is that correct?''

Note: (The class agrees with the student's answer.)

Teacher: "What is the probability of not getting out in an odd number of trials?''

Student:	"Zero!"
Another Student:	"No it isn't."
Note:	(After discussing this question for a few minutes, the class decides that the probability of not getting out in $n + 1$ trials where n is even is also $\left(\dfrac{1}{8}\right)^{\frac{n}{2}}$.)
Teacher:	"Then, what is the probability of ending up on each of the points (2, 0), (1, 1), (0, 2), (−1, 1), and (−2, 0) after n or $n + 1$ trials?"
A Student:	"Well, since the probability of not getting out keeps decreasing, the probability of getting out keeps increasing, so it should always be a little more than $\dfrac{1}{16}, \dfrac{4}{16}, \dfrac{4}{16}, \dfrac{4}{16}$, and $\dfrac{1}{16}$, for each one."
Another Student:	"I think these new numbers should be proportional to $\dfrac{1}{16}$, $\dfrac{4}{16}, \dfrac{4}{16}, \dfrac{4}{16}$, and $\dfrac{1}{16}$ each time."
Note:	(After about five minutes of discussion, the class has not agreed upon an answer to the teacher's question.)
Teacher:	"All right, this appears to be a more difficult problem than finding the previous formula. Let's think about it overnight. Right now, let's look at the strategies that were used to get to this point in the problem. First, what are the four steps of the inquiry method of solving problems and making discoveries?"
A Student:	"Finding a problem, gathering information, solving the problem, and then looking back at the methods used."
Teacher:	"O.K., how did you find this problem?"
A Student:	"You gave it to us."
Another Student:	"Not really. You showed us how to move around in the triangle but we kind of figured out the problem as we went along."
Teacher:	"How did you do this?"
The Same Student:	"By asking questions and just talking about the problem."
Another Student:	"Yeah, we did most of the work ourselves."
Teacher:	"Is this question-and-discussion procedure a good way to find problems to consider?"
Note:	(The class agrees that it is.)
Teacher:	"How did you gather information to solve this problem?"
A Student:	"We figured it out ourselves."
Another Student:	"Yeah, you didn't help us, we just discussed things and figured out what to do next by ourselves."
Teacher:	"Is this a good way to develop methods for solving problems?"
A Student:	"It takes longer than having you tell us everything to do, but it's more fun."

Note: (The class agrees with this student's observation.)

Teacher: "So, you found your own problems by asking questions and you obtained data by discussing techniques and figuring things out for yourselves. How did you actually answer your own questions and solve your problems?"

A Student: "We did that ourselves."

Another Student: "Right, we discussed things, showed each other our mistakes, and explained our ideas to each other."

Another Student: "We kind of figured out ways to solve problems by asking a lot of questions, you know."

Teacher: "What general methods of inquiry did you use in this lesson?"

Student: "We asked questions."

Another Student: "We figured things out for ourselves."

Another Student: "We discussed things with each other."

Another Student: "We looked for patterns."

Another Student: "We tried to prove that what we were doing was right."

Teacher: "Yes, these are good approaches to solving problems. If you find time before tomorrow's math class, see if you can find the probabilities for ending up on each point on the legs of the triangle after a certain number of trials. You might want to try it for $n = 3, 4, 5, 6$, and so forth as special cases. Then, maybe, you can find a formula. In any case, bring your findings and conjectures to class tomorrow and we'll see what we can conclude from them. Oh, someone might want to consider a situation where the figure looks like this. (At this point, the teacher should draw Figure 6.9 on the chalkboard.) You could use (H, H), (H, T), (T, H), and (T, T) to determine whether to go up, down, left, or right after starting at (0, 0). You may want to use a penny and a dime, so that you can distinguish (H, T) from (T, H)."

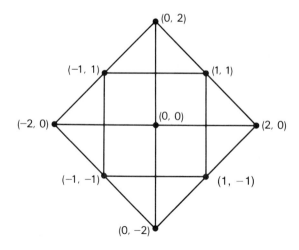

Figure 6.9.

Postassessment: The postassessment for this, as well as for other inquiry lessons, can be accomplished in part by teacher observations of the students' activities during the session. Were all students participating in the lesson? Did the students rely upon their own resources for information or did they depend upon the teacher? Did the students ask questions and generate their own problems? Did students use good methods of inquiry? What did the class learn about the inquiry process? Were you able to determine whether the students valued the inquiry process as a means of formulating and resolving interesting questions? The success that students had in carrying out the suggested homework assignment is also an indication of the types of cognitive and affective learning objectives which have been met through this lesson. What have students learned about random processes and what are their attitudes toward the procedures that were used in this lesson?

The Group-Processes Model

In most mathematics classrooms a considerable portion of instruction is directed toward a group of students and in many cases the group is the entire class. Even when the teacher is not using the expository model to teach mathematics to a large group of students, students may still work together in groups of varying sizes. Although the game model, problem-solving and theorem-proving models, the laboratory model, and discovery and inquiry models do require various kinds of teacher direction and intervention throughout the lesson, they also require many different types of student-to-student group interactions.

In one sense, the group-processes model of teaching and learning is an attempt to organize the classroom into a miniature functioning democracy. In order for the group learning situation to progress smoothy and effectively, each student must act in reference to his or her fellow students. Each student learns mathematical objects by contributing to the establishment and modification of social discussions, agreements and disagreements. According to Joyce and Weil (1972):

> The classroom is analogous to the larger society; it has a social order and a classroom culture and its students care about the way of life that develops there, that is, the standards and expectations that become established. Educational procedures should seek to harness the energy naturally generated by the concern for creating the social order. The [Group Investigation] Model for Teaching replicates the negotiation pattern of society. Through negotiation the students learn the academic domains of knowledge and ultimately to engage in social problem-solving. (p. 37)

Objectives of the Group-Processes Model

This quotation suggests that one of the objectives for using the group-processes model is to socialize students; that is, to help them learn to engage in activities that are appropriate for the needs of a group or society as a whole. Of course another major reason for using the group processes model in teaching and learning mathematics is to facilitate students' mastery of mathematical facts, skills, concepts and principles. When mathematical objects are learned through group activities, students also learn something about the social process by which mathematics is developed and organized. While learning how to learn effectively

351

as part of a group, students learn about how the methods and procedures for doing mathematics are developed.

With the exception of the individualized teaching/learning model, all of the models which have already been discussed in this chapter and the previous chapter have cognitive learning objectives that can be attained through the group-processes model. In fact, group activities not only help students to know and comprehend facts and skills, but they also lead to analysis, synthesis and evaluation of concepts and principles. It may be that the group processes model is most distinctive in its emphasis upon affective objectives of responding, preference for values, conceptualization of values, and organization of value systems. Stanford and Stanford (1969) believe that the discussions arising from group learning activities have the following objectives:

> . . .to solve problems, to air opinions, to find out what others think, to vent feelings, to clarify one's point of view, to reevaluate one's opinions, and to gain feelings of acceptance and belonging. (p. 15)

Characteristics of the Group-Processes Model

Classroom Discussions

The group-processes model centers around student discussions and there are several types of classroom discussions which can be distinguished by the degree of teacher intervention in the discussion. The first type of discussion is teacher-directed recitation whereby the teacher questions a particular student or the class as a whole to determine whether students have met specific learning objectives, have completed their homework assignments, or are prepared to move to a new mathematics topic. Although this type of "discussion" is quite teacher-centered, it does permit teachers to evaluate student mastery of mathematical content and students to review mathematics content.

A second type of classroom discussion which is still relatively teacher dominated is the guided-discovery dialogue. Here the primary objective is not only to determine how well students have mastered previous material, but also to guide students in discovering new mathematical principles. Although the teacher usually asks most of the questions and controls the direction of the discussion, there is more student-to-student interaction than is found in teacher-directed recitation. However, there is a special mathematical object to be discovered and the teacher carefully organizes and directs the discussion toward that object. Guided-discovery discussions usually involve inductive reasoning forms whereby students are encouraged to infer generalizations by observing and discussing specific examples of each general principle.

The third type of classroom discussion is a dialogue directed toward solving a problem presented by the teacher. After the teacher gives the problem to the class, the discussion is usually evenly balanced between student and teacher control of problem-solving considerations and activities. Both inductive and deductive strategies may be used in considering a particular problem; however the teacher may suggest the specific approach that students are to use. Many mathematics teachers use this type of classroom discussion to teach students how to solve mathematical word problems and prove theorems.

A fourth type of classroom discussion which may also be used to solve a problem is an inquiry-oriented discussion, in which students take an active part in formulating the problem to be considered and dominate the content and direction of the discussion. This type of discussion is student centered with the teacher acting as a facilitator but neither as a source of answers nor a judge of truth or falsity and validity or invalidity.

Each one of these four types of discussions, ranging from teacher dominated to student dominated, can be used in meeting mathematics learning objectives; however it is important for teachers to set objectives for each discussion type. If the objective of a class discussion is to test students' degree of mastery of a topic which has just been completed, an inquiry-oriented discussion would hardly be appropriate. Nor would a teacher-dominated guided discovery dialogue be appropriate for teaching students independent inquiry processes for discovering and solving general problems in mathematics.

Stages of the Group-Processes Model

Since group activities tend to be used in mathematics classrooms and laboratories to make discoveries, prove theorems, solve problems, and inquire into situations in mathematics, it is not surprising to find that the stages of the group-processes model are similar to the stages of problem-solving and inquiry models. The four stages of a group activity teaching/learning model are: (1) a situation which students can react to and discuss as a group, (2) a group diagnosis of the components of the situation so that students can understand the situation and consider alternative approaches to it, (3) a group discussion to formulate approaches to the problem, test hypotheses, evaluate and modify procedures, try out plans, and observe the consequences of various activities, and (4) a group reflection upon the strategies, purposes, and results of the first three stages. Since these four stages have already been discussed in the contexts of the problem-solving and inquiry models, further discussion of them is unnecessary.

Teaching Students to Work in Groups

It is a well-known fact that some people are quite proficient at group activities while others are not. Even in sports it is common to hear expressions such as "he's a real team player" or "he's a 'hotdog'." In classrooms some students tend to dominate group discussions and activities while others take a minor role, or no observable role at all, in group processes. Many students need to be shown how to participate effectively in classroom group activities and teachers must manage group work subtly and unobtrusively, so that each student can have an active role within his or her group. The group is both a place where students learn the objects of mathematics through inquiry and problem-solving activities and a situation where students must deal with potential conflicts between their personal desires and the social purposes of the group. Some students may strike a balance between their own emotional needs and the activities of the group; others may attempt to impose their own desires upon the group; whereas still other students may "mentally" drop out of the group by refusing to participate.

Many secondary school students are experiencing social desires, drives and frustrations which overshadow the importance of academic matters such as learning mathematics. When properly managed and moderated by the teacher, the social situations of group learning activities in the mathematics classroom can help students resolve these very real conflicts between immediate social needs and long-range academic objectives. The social involvement of group learning activities can be a means of promoting disciplined mathematical inquiry in a comfortable social setting.

Whether students work in groups with minimal teacher direction or interact with a teacher in a group setting, the groups should be small enough to encourage active participation by all students and large enough to provide a diversity of ideas. I have found that student discussion and problem-solving groups smaller than five people tend to function slowly and inefficiently and groups larger than fifteen students usually have several members who fail to involve themselves in the activities of the group. These observations indicate that the optimum size of a discussion group in a mathematics classroom or laboratory is ten students plus or minus five. However, this does not mean that certain group laboratory activities can not be accomplished with groups of students numbering fewer than five or that no group activities can be carried out with an entire class of 20 to 40 students. In order for very small or overly large groups of students to work together effectively, it may be necessary for the teacher to provide additional guidelines and instructions and to intervene frequently. When moderating large group activities, the teacher must take special care to assure that each student participates in the lesson. It may be necessary to ask questions of non-participants, to suggest activities to them, or to make statements, explanations, and clarifications directly to them. Students who hesitate to take part in group activities should neither be ridiculed, embarrassed, nor punished. Censure may only reinforce their determination to stay out of group discussions and activities. Usually it is possible to increase these students' participation within the group by offering encouragement and special rewards for their initial small efforts to become involved.

The teacher's function in a group activity is not that of a manager or resident expert who directs or passes judgment on each activity or each conclusion. Rather, the teacher's role may be that of adviser, consultant, questioner, or friendly and helpful critic. The teacher should take an active part in organizing the group work and in getting discussions or activities started. Once the group activities have begun, the teacher should refrain from intervening unless some type of direction or assistance is absolutely necessary for the progress of the group or the effective participation of individual students. Situations in which teacher intervention in a group's activities may be necessary are: (1) a case where a few students are dominating the group, (2) a case where one or two students are left out of group activities, (3) a group that is completely bogged down, (4) a group that is fooling around or creating a disturbance, (5) an activity where the group is consistently using its energies on inquiry strategies that prove to be unproductive, (6) an activity where a group is manipulating laboratory devices and mathematical symbols with little meaningful comprehension of underlying mathematical concepts and principles, and (7) a group whose members obviously lack prerequisite mathematical objects to complete the task that they are considering.

As has already been pointed out, students may not automatically work together effectively in groups and may need to be taught special skills for group work. Techniques for teaching students some of the special skills that are needed for working in groups will be presented below, and methods for dealing with some problems that may arise from having students study mathematics in groups will be discussed.

After a large group or several small groups of students are given a problem to solve or a situation to explore independently within the group, it is necessary for each group to organize itself, which may require some assistance from the teacher. The group may want to choose a moderator to monitor group activities and arbitrate disputes, or a recorder to keep a record of data generated by the group and make notes of the progress of the group. The group should also set guidelines for its activities. This may be a tentative plan for approaching a problem or activity or a set of rules specifying the degree and nature of the contributions expected from each group member. A group should be permitted to plan its own activities and determine its own pattern of organization; however the teacher should observe each group to be certain that some type of initial organization is agreed upon within the group. If a group appears to be having trouble getting started, questions from the teacher such as, ''What is the problem that you are going to consider?'' or ''Do you have a plan for working on the problem?'' may help the group in its initial planning activities.

Since a considerable proportion of classroom instruction in mathematics is teacher centered, students tend to regard the teacher as the primary source of important information and may have little confidence in each other's suggestions and contributions within a student-controlled group. When students are learning how to work in groups with minimal teacher assistance, they can be shown how to be attentive to each other's comments and how to value each other's suggestions by solving teacher-constructed ''mysteries'' where each student is given a clue to the ''mystery.'' The following mystery, which has enough clues so that each student in a class of 31 or fewer students can be given at least one important clue, can be used initially to demonstrate the importance of paying close attention to information presented by other students. This activity has no mathematical content objectives, but does serve as an ''ice breaker'' to show a class the value of each student's contributions in a group problem-solving session. This mystery-solving lesson for an entire class can be followed by teacher- or student-constructed ''mathematical mysteries'' which can be solved in smaller groups. This robbery mystery is a variation of one of many games contained in Stanford and Stanford's book, *Learning Discussion Skills Through Games*.

One dark and dreary night the Last National Bank in the city of Seldom Seen, Maine was robbed. After a thorough investigation, the police uncovered the following information about the robbery:

1. Ms. Moneypenny, an officer of the bank, discovered the robbery.
2. The robbery was discovered at 9:00 A.M. on Friday, December 12 when the bank opened.
3. The bank had closed at 4:00 P.M. on Thursday, December 11.
4. The bank vault had been blasted open with plastic explosives.
5. Jonathan Scrooge, president of the bank, was nowhere to be found when the robbery was discovered.
6. Later Scrooge was picked up by authorities at the airport in Mexico City at 1:00 P.M. on Friday, December 12.
7. When apprehended, Scrooge said that he was leaving his wife because she was spending him into bankruptcy.
8. Scrooge was the only person who had a key to the bank's vault.
9. Scrooge said that he had been at the airport in Chicago for 12 hours due to a snow storm before he continued on to Mexico City.

10. Leonard Lush, Scrooge's cousin, was very jealous of Scrooge.
11. Lush always became inebriated on Friday nights.
12. Leonard Lush showed up in Chicago on Monday, December 15 with a great deal of money.
13. Leonard Lush's wife, Sally, could not be located.
14. The robber or robbers opened the front door of the bank with a key.
15. The only keys to the front door of the bank belonged to the president of the bank, Mr. Scrooge, and the custodian, Elwood Turnkey.
16. Local police were unable to locate Turnkey.
17. Federal agents finally found Turnkey in Hideout, Virginia on December 12.
18. Turnkey said that he arrived in Hideout, Virginia on a commercial plane flight at 4:00 P.M., December 11.
19. The airline clerk confirmed the time of Turnkey's arrival in Hideout, Virginia.
20. There were no planes out of Hideout, Virginia between 3:00 P.M. and 9:00 A.M.
21. Turnkey's brother was an oil tycoon in Alaska.
22. Ms. Moneypenny said that Turnkey tried to flirt with her at the bank.
23. Ms. Moneypenny frequently borrowed Scrooge's key to the front door of the bank to open the bank early.
24. Scrooge said that Moneypenny had borrowed his key to the front door of the bank before closing time on December 11.
25. Moneypenny denied having borrowed Scrooge's bank key on December 11.
26. Some plastic explosives had been stolen from the Quicksand Construction Company on Wednesday, December 10.
27. Henry Moneypenny, a Quicksand employee, said that he saw Elwood Turnkey hanging around the Construction Company on Wednesday afternoon.
28. Ms. Moneypenny said that she saw Turnkey hanging around the bank on Thursday, December 11.
29. Ms. Moneypenny said that she saw Turnkey leaving the bank at 11:00 P.M. on December 11 while she was having coffee at the diner across the street.
30. Ms. Moneypenny and Henry Moneypenny said that they thought Turnkey robbed the bank.
31. The police confirmed Scrooge's story about being delayed in Chicago.

Write each of these clues on separate slips of paper and distribute all of the clues to individuals in the class so that each student has at least one clue. No other written record of the clues should be given to the class and each student is to hold his or her own clue but may read it to the other students. Tell the students to share their individual clues with the rest of the class by reading them aloud when they want to, and to try to solve the robbery mystery by discussing the clues. Allow students to read their clues to the class at any time, but do not permit the class to write a master list of clues on the chalkboard. In this way, each student will be forced to participate in the class discussion by contributing his or her clue and the class will see the importance of each student's participation in solving the mystery.

The class should conclude that Ms. Moneypenny and Henry Moneypenny conspired to rob the bank and tried to frame Elwood Turnkey, who unknown to the Moneypennys was not in town when the robbery took place. Mr. Scrooge was also out of town.

This lesson, which illustrates the value of each student's contribution in a group problem-solving discussion, can be followed by some small group considerations of "mathematical mysteries" such as the following whose objective is to find the name (equation) of a mysterious function.

A mathematical function "crawled around" on a sheet of rectangular-coordinate paper and the following clues are known about its graph:
1. It left at least one clue in each quadrant that it entered.
2. It went through the point $(1, 3)$.
3. No clues were found in the third quadrant.
4. It crossed the y-axis at the point $y = 1$.
5. It always traveled in straight line segments.
6. It passed through the point $(-2, 5)$.
7. It changed direction exactly once.
8. No clues were found in the fourth quadrant.
9. It never crossed the x-axis.
10. It came within one unit of the x-axis.
11. It crossed the point $(3, 7)$.
12. It crossed the point $(-4, 9)$.
13. It started at "infinity" in the second quadrant.
14. It stopped at "infinity" in the first quadrant.
15. Its minimum point was at $(x = 0)$.
16. It has a constant term of 1.
(Note: The "name" of this function is $y = 2|x| + 1$.)

The teacher could construct several mathematical mysteries such as this one and have students solve the mysteries by working in small groups or the entire class could discuss each mystery. Students may also enjoy developing mathematical mysteries while working in small groups, then exchanging mysteries with other groups and attempting to solve each other's mysteries. Guess-the-number mysteries can be constructed for arithmetic classes; guess-a-trigonometric-identity mysteries are appropriate for a trigonometry class; and theorems from plane geometry can be guessed from clues about their proofs or applications. Mysteries such as those suggested here are appropriate for meeting cognitive and affective mathematical learning objectives as well as for providing interesting problems to be considered in either large or small group problem-solving sessions.

In addition to assuming the responsibility to contribute to group activities and to pay attention to what other students have to say, students should also be taught to analyze, evaluate, and respond to other students' ideas and to synthesize the findings and conclusions from group discussions into unified sets of concepts and principles. Even though students may learn to be quiet while other students are presenting ideas, they may not be attending to these ideas, but may be daydreaming. Many times the excellent ideas of one student are ignored by the rest of the group because each member is thinking about something else. Students can be taught to attend to and respond to other students' ideas through teacher-moderated class discussions where the teacher regularly follows a student's comment with questions directed to other students such as: Do you agree with what he said? Why do you think her answer is wrong? Even if you don't agree with her suggestion, could you modify her ideas and use them? What do you think he means by that comment? How do you think she obtained that answer? Can you extend that idea? Can you use her idea to do what you suggested previously? If we follow that suggestion where will it lead us? How does her suggestion differ from yours? Are there similarities between his idea and your suggestion?

When working in groups, students should also learn to synthesize and summarize each other's ideas, suggestions, discoveries and conclusions. It is not uncommon for the members of a group to present a number of good ideas and conclusions which appear to lead nowhere, because no attempt is made to combine them into a coherent plan of action or set of general principles. At times it may be well for students who are working on group activities to select a "recorder" who takes notes during the group activities and periodically gives a summary of the group's progress and suggests alternative actions. Questions such as these might be asked by the "recorder" and answered by his or her group: What have we done so far? Have we made any progress? Do we have a plan? What are our findings at this point? What should we do next? Should we try a new approach? What's holding us back? Could we do better by approaching the problem in another way? What things do we all agree on? Where do we disagree?

Students should also be made aware of the different roles that members of groups can assume during group activities. There are various ways in which students can contribute to the progress of the group. In the beginning of a group activity certain students may initiate discussion, organize the group's activities, offer questions for discussion, and suggest plans for approaching the problem under consideration. Throughout group discussions certain students may challenge ideas of other students, request more information or better explanations, ask questions, or request clarifications of plans and ideas. At times during a discussion or laboratory activity, various students may summarize the group's progress and point out areas of agreement and disagreement. Other students may take the initiative in keeping the group informed about how well they are achieving their objectives, point out shortcomings in the processes used by the group, and attempt to lead the group into reaching a concensus about the usefulness of their problem-solving strategies, the validity of their arguments, and the truths of their conclusions.

A popular educational "game" in which group problem-solving processes and the various roles of participants in group discussions can be practiced and observed is a "moon-crash" situation based upon activities of the National Aeronautics and Space Administration. In playing this science-oriented game, the group is to arrive at a concensus by considering individual judgments, opinions, and information offered by members of the group.

The situation is to assume that you are a member of the crew of a space shuttle scheduled to rendezvous with a space laboratory on the lighted side of the moon. As a result of technical problems, the space shuttle is forced to land at an uncharted location approximately 200 miles from the space laboratory. During the forced moon landing most of the equipment and supplies aboard the shuttle craft are destroyed. Your survival and that of the rest of the crew depends upon reaching the space laboratory unaided. Listed below are 15 undamaged items which were salvaged after the unfortunate landing. The task of the discussion group is to rank these items according to their importance in helping the crew reach the moon laboratory. Place the number one beside the most important item, the number two beside the next most important item, and so on, until the number fifteen is placed beside the least important item:

The Group-Processes Model

A box of ordinary matches _____
Dried food concentrate _____
A 50 meter length of nylon rope _____
The silk from a parachute _____
A self-contained portable heating unit _____
Two .45 caliber hand guns _____
One case of powdered milk _____
Two large tanks of oxygen _____
A stellar map of the moon's constellation _____
An inflatable life raft _____
A magnetic compass _____
A box of self-contained signal flares _____
A first-aid kit _____
A solar-powered FM receiver/transmitter _____
Five gallons of water _____

It will take a group of high school students nearly one class period to reach a concensus for ranking these items. While they are discussing this problem they should also attempt to analyze and evaluate the group processes that they are using. The teacher should avoid offering suggestions, answering questions, or participating in the class discussion in any way. However, the teacher should make a list of notes describing the nature of the activities and group processes which students engage in during the discussion. In the class meeting following the "moon game" this set of notes can be used as a catalyst for discussing group problem-solving activities and processes.

A score for the group's rankings of the items can be obtained by taking the sum of the absolute values of the differences between the group's rank for each item and the "correct" rank for that item. The "correct" ranks which have been agreed upon by space experts are:

Matches	15	(Of no use on the moon)
Dried food	4	(May be needed for survival)
Nylon rope	6	(Useful in staying together and climbing)
Parachute silk	8	(Shelter against sun's rays)
Portable heater	13	(Useful only if crew landed on dark side of the moon)
Hand guns	11	(Could be converted to self-propulsion devices for use on the moon)
Milk concentrate	12	(Could be used for nourishment)
Oxygen	1	(Required for survival)
Stellar map	3	(Primary means of finding directions)
Life raft	9	(CO_2 cartridges could be used for self-propulsion across chasms, and other items could be loaded in raft to transport them)

Magnetic compass	14	(Of little, if any, use on the moon)
Signal flares	10	(Could be used as a distress signal)
First-aid kit	7	(Medicine valuable for sickness or injury)
FM transmitter	5	(Possible communication with space station)
Water	2	(Necessary for survival to replenish fluid loss from perspiration)

You might want to make up different situations with various items to be ranked in order of size (answers to mathematics exercises) or importance (mathematical discoveries throughout history). With a bit of ingenuity this game can be modified to contain cognitive mathematical objectives as well as the group-processes objectives that are contained in the original version of the game. In fact, the arithmetic lesson suggested on page 269 is a variation on the "moon-crash" game.

Special Problems Encountered in Group Activities

The Teacher's Role in the Group

Probably the most important function of the teacher during small group lessons is to observe the activities and progress of each group and keep students informed about the strengths and weaknesses of their procedures. At times it may be helpful to a group if the teacher interrupts their work and helps them evaluate their progress. The teacher can assist a group in evaluating how well members are progressing toward their objectives, the contributions being offered by each student, and special problems which may arise due to confrontations among group members. At times students may want to make audio tape recordings of group discussions which can be played back to assist in analyzing and evaluating the effectiveness of the group's activities. The teacher's role is that of monitor and facilitator and not that of group director and information source.

Argument and Conflict Within the Group

At times a group may become polarized into two competitive factions, each one of which attempts to impose its will upon the other. Rather than being a situation in which a mathematical activity is carried out rationally and objectively, a competitive group discussion can degenerate into a battle for dominance among group members. Sometimes when one student in a group attempts to impose his or her will upon the entire group, the other students in the group are able to control the situation. At other times, it may be necessary for the teacher to intervene in maintaining order within groups that have overly aggressive members. It may be necessary to remind students that the purpose of group activities in the mathematics classroom is to inquire into the nature of mathematical principles and not to win a debate. Often controlled and rational disagreement and argument can be quite useful activities in mathematical problem solving; however uncontrolled, irrational and disruptive conflict can only hinder progress toward meeting the mathematical objectives of group activities.

Unresponsive Groups

Not only can group members become overly aggressive, but they can also be inhibited and passive. A quiet, unresponsive group can be more frustrating to the teacher than a noisy, overactive group. The teacher can draw out one or two quiet members of a group by asking questions and offering suggestions; however it is difficult to deal with a totally unresponsive group. There are several reasons why groups may be unresponsive. First, if students are not well acquainted they may be reluctant to discuss mathematical problem-solving strategies within a small group. At the beginning of a new school year when students may not know each other very well and may not know the teacher, group activities can be unproductive. It is well to postpone using the group-processes teaching/learning model until students know you and each other quite well. Second, students tend to form social cliques and when students from different cliques are grouped for academic activities they may feel uncomfortable trying to work together. Although one solution to this problem is to group students according to their social preferences, such groupings tend to have affective disadvantages since certain students may not only be excluded socially but may also be excluded academically from associations with certain of their peers. Third, students may be unresponsive during group activities because they do not understand the task, are not interested in the problem, or do not have the prerequisites for meeting the mathematical objectives of the group's assignment.

The teacher may have to take an active part in an unresponsive group in order to get the discussion started. He or she can begin by asking questions to determine whether students do understand what it is that they are expected to accomplish as a group and do have the prerequisite skills for solving the assigned problem or carrying out laboratory activities. When tasks are beyond the ability of the group or are of little interest to most of its members, it may be necessary to modify the group's assignment and the objectives of the lesson. If groups are reluctant to act because of social considerations, the teacher can temporarily become a member of the group and get the discussion started through questions and suggestions.

Unproductive Groups

Groups may fail to obtain results for reasons other than over-aggressiveness or unresponsiveness. Unproductive groups may accomplish little because they are unable to stay on the topic, do not pay attention while the teacher is explaining the task, or fail to keep the objectives of the task in mind. The members of unproductive groups may fail to attend to each other's ideas and suggestions or may merely toss ideas around with little sense of direction or purpose. They may also fail to agree upon a plan, a set of strategies, or a goal; they may merely talk about details of the problem with little understanding of how to synthesize these details into a procedure which will lead to meeting specific objectives. Many unproductive discussions and arguments result from a group's failure to pay attention to definitions of mathematical terms, principles of logic, and valid argument forms. A group may become deadlocked because members are using different definitions of terms or interpretations of principles, and the group may not even realize the reason for its difficulties.

A teacher can usually find the source of a group's stalemate by observing the group members' activities for a few minutes. After the problem becomes apparent to the teacher, he or she can participate in the group activities for several minutes and assist in formulating plans, synthesizing details, defining terms, clarifying concepts and principles, or offering other suggestions to facilitate progress toward the objectives of the lesson.

Models for Teaching and Learning the Indirect Objects of Mathematics

Even though a primary objective of the group-processes teaching/learning model is to help students become independent inquirers and problem solvers, carefully planned activities, constant monitoring of student group work, and judicious participation within groups are a necessary part of the teacher's role in student-centered learning strategies. Since the teacher has less control of a group-activity lesson than an expository lesson, even more careful planning and anticipation of student difficulties must be carried out when the group-processes model is used.

The Computer-Augmented Teaching/Learning Model

Evidence reported from scores of studies designed to examine the effectiveness of computer-augmented teaching and learning indicates that computers can be used very effectively to enhance the learning of mathematics (Kieren, 1973). Many secondary schools have mini-computer systems, which cost from $5,000 to $100,000, and most of these schools use their computer facilities to support instruction in mathematics. Some school systems have even larger and more expensive computer facilities which are used to supplement instruction in various subjects from grades three through twelve. In some instances several school districts have combined their computing resources to form large regional computer networks to support classroom instruction in a variety of disciplines. Other schools which can not afford the cost and upkeep of their own computer systems lease time on a computer owned by another agency. The Federal Government has supported several large research and development projects to design computer systems for use in education and to develop computer-augmented curriculum materials for schools and colleges. The Federal Government, state and local governments, and other agencies concerned with education have also supported regional and local efforts to develop, disseminate, and implement computer-related curricula in secondary schools.

The hands-on use of computers by students in secondary school classrooms is a relatively recent phenomenon which shows promise of changing our approach to school-based education. However, irrespective of the educational benefits of computer-augmented education, there are several impediments to using computers in teaching and learning in schools. First, the cost of purchasing and maintaining a computer facility or leasing time on an educational computing system is still beyond the resources of many smaller school systems, in spite of dramatic decreases in the cost of computer technology. Second, many school systems do not have teachers who are trained to make effective use of computers in their classrooms. Third, since highly-touted educational technology such as closed-circuit television, teaching machines and programmed instructional systems have failed to fulfill their promise to revolutionize education in secondary schools; many school boards and school administrators are reluctant to spend taxpayer's money for yet another highly-acclaimed educational innovation. In spite of these serious impediments to the expansion of computer-augmented learning in secondary school mathematics, there are some compelling arguments for using computers in mathematics classrooms.

362

Why Use Computers in Teaching and Learning Mathematics?

It may be that the most dramatic influence that computers have upon learning in the mathematics classroom results from the significant increase in student motivation in a computer-augmented learning situation. The initial novelty of using a computer in the mathematics classroom can cause considerable improvement in many students' attitudes toward learning mathematics. Unlike some other educational innovations, the novelty of using a computer in learning mathematics doesn't seem to "wear off." There appear to be several reasons why many previously unmotivated students become "amateur" scholars in computer-augmented mathematics courses. First, many students who dislike mathematics and care little about learning mathematics do so because they have experienced only failure and frustration in this subject. Some of these same students can become "local" computer experts and their newly-found success and status can result in a welcome improvement in their attitudes. Second, learning is an active process; unfortunately many commonly used teaching strategies put students in passive, receptive roles; that is, students have very little, if any, control of the learning environment. Consequently, many students minimize their participation in a learning environment which they can neither control nor influence in any meaningful manner. When students use a computer to study mathematics, they are able to control what the computer does; that is, the computer responds to each of their actions. In this sense a computer-augmented learning environment permits each student to take an active role in his or her learning, while the computer is, or appears to be, a relatively passive part of the environment which is under the student's control. A third reason why computers serve as a motivational aid is found in the nature of motivation itself. People are motivated to learn in school and outside of school for four general reasons—to create things, to make things work, to obtain recognition, and to find personal satisfaction. Most students like to "create" computer programs and to make the computer "work" by either executing their own computer programs or running programs written by someone else. Students also find a considerable amount of pleasure and satisfaction in being able to cause a complex electronic computer to carry out their bidding and there is a certain amount of prestige in being able to operate the fictionalized "giant brain" which is an electronic computer.

If for no other reasons than these three—success and status for students, control of their own learning environment, and the motivational value of using computers in schools—it seems reasonable to expect that computer-related learning of mathematics will succeed in schools where other technology-based educational innovations have failed to have any really significant effect upon learning. Computer-augmented learning is effective and does justify the additional cost of computer hardware, software, and courseware. (Computer hardware is the wires, electronic components, and other physical parts of a computer system. Software is the set of programs, instructions, and procedures that are used to operate the hardware. Courseware is the set of teaching and learning resources such as computer programs and related workbooks, textbooks, journals, and other educational materials which are used for computer-augmented learning in the classroom.) When control of the computer and computer-related learning resources is shared with students in computer-oriented mathematics classrooms, they do perceive computer-oriented learning environments as being quite different from the traditional school environment; that is, classrooms arranged to accommodate lectures, teacher demonstrations, and control of students. A properly organized, student-controlled, computer-augmented learning environment is an effective learning situation because students can use the classroom as a learning laboratory to interact with a variety of interesting learning options. In this way even the somewhat artificial school-based learning environment can have many of the positive characteristics of a good non-school learning environment. In addition, the rewards, satisfactions, and other positive factors which can cause students to work very hard to learn mathematics in a computer-augmented mathematics classroom are similar to the positive factors that motivate people to learn outside of school. Consequently, learning in school becomes more closely related to "real-world" learning—a term students use in reference to non-school learning environments.

Ways in Which Computers Are Used in Mathematics Education

The computer-augmented teaching/learning model is composed of several modes of computer use for promoting learning in mathematics classrooms. These modes of educational uses of computers are characterized by the degree to which control of teaching and learning is shared by the student, the teacher, and the computer. Broadly stated, does the computer control the student or does the student control the computer? Of course, the computer has no control of its own over students; rather its control of instruction resides within computer programs which may be written by teachers, other students, or professional educational-computer programmers. To a large extent, what the computer programmer instructs the computer to do determines how it and a student working at a computer terminal will interact.

Computer-Managed Instruction

One mode of computer use in mathematics education which has not proved to be so successful as many of its proponents had expected is computer-managed instruction (CMI). Computer-managed instruction is an indirect mode of classroom use of computers, because students usually do not have much control over a computer operating in a CMI mode and may not even have much direct contact with the computer. The key descriptive word in computer-managed instruction is "managed." In the CMI mode the computer is used as a manager of the learning environment, and as a manager it may be used to carry out several or all of the following facets of teaching and learning:

1. Administering drill-and-practice skill exercises to individual students.
2. Evaluating, scoring, and providing feedback from students' answers to drill-and-practice exercises.
3. Administering pretests and posttests to individual students as well as evaluating and monitoring each students' work.
4. Keeping academic, personal, medical, and counseling records of students.
5. Setting cognitive (and occasionally affective) learning objectives for each student.
6. Prescribing learning activities for individual students by analyzing and evaluating each student's progress toward specified learning objectives.

7. Counseling students on higher education and employment opportunities.
8. Collecting data, keeping records, and averaging and reporting grades.
9. Managing and ordering instructional supplies and resources.
10. Handling teachers' bookkeeping chores.

It was thought that CMI systems would free teachers from many of the routine management and record-keeping activities of schools, so that they would have additional time to spend on individualized teaching, evaluation of students and other professional activities requiring human intellect. Although these reasons for using CMI appear to be sound, many teachers are reluctant to relinquish some of their traditional functions to a machine. Also, computer system failures which may last from several seconds to a few days not only disrupt planned activities but also, on occasion, result in the loss of irreplaceable data and student records. Although such failures seldom occur, many teachers who use CMI systems keep their own records, which makes many of the computer's functions redundant. Teachers have found that other modes of computer use in education can be modified to include CMI functions as well as to permit direct student control of the computer, which provides a means of attaining significant cognitive and affective learning objectives. CMI is still a viable mode of computer use in education; however it is doubtful that this mode will "revolutionize" our approach to mathematics education.

Computer-Assisted Instruction
The initial educational applications of computers in mathematics education were in the computer-assisted instruction (CAI) mode, which was being used experimentally to provide drill and practice in arithmetic skills as early as 1965. CAI has now been developed into a very sophisticated instructional mode which provides for complex evaluation of student responses, alternative branching of learning sequences, and significant student control of and interaction with the teaching/learning sequence. Students working in the CAI mode are ordinarily involved in drill, practice, and testing of skills, exploration of concepts, or demonstration of principles.

CAI programs in mathematics education have been written to provide students with a variety of learning options. For example, students can specify the type of problem or response that they want the computer to generate, can request special explanations of concepts, and can even communicate with teachers and students in remote locations via computer terminals. Students' responses to computer-generated questions and suggested activities can be stored in the computer and analyzed by teachers who can initiate appropriate changes in the computer programs which generated the questions and activities under consideration. Some relatively expensive CAI remote terminals have color graphics, computer-activated audio and video components, touch-sensitive viewing screens, and complex communication systems. (A remote computer terminal is a receiving and sending device which is used for communication between a student and a computer system. The student and the computer may be in the same room or thousands of miles apart, and the student may receive and send information as messages printed on paper by a typewriter-like device or as messages communicated on a television-like screen.)

CAI in mathematics education is used in teaching and learning many types of facts and skills, some concepts, and a few principles. The majority of the cognitive objectives met through CAI are at the knowledge and comprehension levels; however certain analysis and synthesis objectives may be met using CAI programs. In the CAI mode most of the control of the learning situation rests with teachers and computer programmers who write computer-based lessons; although the best CAI systems do provide for some degree of student control of the computer during most computer-based lessons.

Computer Simulations

A third important mode of computer use in education, as well as in business, industry and government, is to simulate complex systems in order to study their properties and the effects of modifying parameters upon each system. Computer simulations provide an inexpensive method of studying a variety of mathematical applications without having to be in contact with the physical situations and models that comprise the applications. Students can use computer-based simulations in applying mathematical principles to economic systems, businesses, industries, sciences, ecological systems, medicine, politics, and various types of social interaction systems. Mathematical applications that are too expensive to simulate in a secondary school laboratory, for instance problems in aerodynamics and thermodynamics, can be simulated using a computer. Many other mathematical laboratory experiments which might be too dangerous to attempt in a school; for example, nuclear reactions and environmental phenomena, can be simulated on a computer and studied by high school students. Both complex and simple computer simulations of mathematical phenomena can be presented as computer games. In fact, many of the common mathematical games found in books and articles can be programmed as computer simulations. Many students are fascinated by computer-based games and will spend long hours writing computer-game programs while learning mathematical facts, skills, concepts, principles and problem-solving methods in the process.

Well-constructed computer simulations can help students practice their skills of analysis and synthesis, since they must consider the properties of mathematical systems and mathematical applications as well as the effects of interactions among the components of a system. A considerable amount of analysis and synthesis is required in preparing a computer simulation. When computer programs don't behave as expected or when simulations go awry, students must evaluate the problem and synthesize improved procedures for modeling and simulating mathematics-related phenomena.

In using computer-based simulations and games, students do have much control over the parameters of the system being simulated. However, they may be constrained by the limited number of variables that can be built into any simulation and the values permitted for each variable. In most models and simulations, many of the facets of the real system must be omitted to make the problem manageable. A computer simulation also gives students some real control over the execution of the computer program and makes them feel that they are in control of the learning environment, which in this case is a computer.

Computer-Based Problem Solving

When studying mathematics in the computer-based problem-solving mode, students write, execute, and modify their own computer programs to solve specific mathematical problems. This is the first mode in which students are actually required to write their own programs. In the CMI, CAI, and simulation modes students nearly always interact with a computer program which has been written by someone else and is stored in the memory of the computer. However, in order to use the computer to solve problems students must learn a computer programming language, which most students enjoy doing. Although there are a number of excellent scientifically-oriented programming languages such as PL1, APL, FORTRAN, and ALGOL, the most frequently used programming language in secondary schools is BASIC. BASIC is easy to learn, is very much like English, and is a scientifically-oriented language. Most secondary school students can master the fundamentals of BASIC in 10 classroom sessions together with 20 hours of practice in writing BASIC programs. Among the many excellent books for teaching BASIC programming is Dwyer and Kaufman's book, *A Guided Tour of Computer Programming in BASIC* (1973). This book was written to be used by junior and senior high school students, but it is also a good book for adults to use in learning BASIC. The following issues of the magazine *Creative Computing* contain reviews and evaluations of nearly all of the BASIC programming books which were in print during 1975: Mar-Apr, May-June, Sept-Oct, Nov-Dec 1975 and Jan-Feb 1976.

Probably one of the best ways to learn how to solve problems is to solve problems by using a computer. In order to solve a mathematics problem using a computer, a student must take a general statement of the problem and translate it into a very precise and flawless algorithm. Next, the algorithm (which is sometimes represented as a flowchart) must be translated into a logically and syntactically correct computer program. Since the computer does precisely what it is told to do in the program, there is absolutely no margin for error or interpretation. This means that since most programs contain at least one error when first written, the student will have to correct (debug) his or her program based upon the problems that are encountered when the computer tries to carry out the instructions of the program (called executing the program). Consequently, if a program is ever going to execute properly, it must be analyzed, evaluated, and debugged—a critical step in any kind of problem-solving strategy.

Research and practice show that writing computer programs to solve mathematics problems is a good way to learn mathematical facts, skills, concepts and principles. Problem solving through computer programming can also be used to meet cognitive objectives of comprehension, analysis, synthesis and evaluation. The student who does not comprehend the mathematical objects of a problem can not even begin to write a computer program to solve the problem. Writing a computer program to solve a mathematics problem requires analysis of the problem and synthesis of an algorithm. Of course, debugging both the logical and syntactic mistakes in a computer program requires some very critical evaluation of the program as well as the problem-solving algorithm.

Those teachers who have had to chase students out of the computer center after school so that the custodian can lock up are well aware of the affective objectives which are met through computer-based problem solving. These objectives are at the levels of satisfaction in response, preference for a value, commitment to a value, and organization of a value system. Since students usually use the computer to solve teacher-assigned problems in this mode, with the teacher evaluating the students' work, control of the learning environment is shared by the teacher and students. However, each student who is using a computer to solve a problem by executing his or her own program does have considerable control of the computing system, which is an important part of this educational computing mode.

Student-Controlled Computing

The fifth, and most recent, mode of computer use by secondary school mathematics students is sometimes called student-controlled computing. Here a student not only writes programs to solve problems but also creates principles, extends knowledge, teaches other students how to solve problems, and learns how to learn. In this mode the student assumes most of the responsibility for organizing a significant segment of a mathematics course. The student may use the computer in all three of the CAI, simulation, and problem-solving modes to create a segment of a computer-oriented mathematics course which aids that student in learning mathematics and may be useful to other students, teachers, or professionals in the field of computer-related learning. For example, Michael Kaufman, the second author of the Dwyer and Kaufman book on BASIC programming (1973), did most of his share of the work on the book while he was a senior in high school. Dynamically involved in analyzing, synthesizing, evaluating, and applying mathematics concepts and principles, students working in the student-controlled computing mode become equal partners with their teachers in teaching and learning mathematics.

Because of its newness and complexity, student-controlled computing is difficult to characterize definitively. Some of the elements of student-controlled computing that we have observed in Soloworks (a computer-related learning project and laboratory at the University of Pittsburgh) are best expressed by these terms: open-ended learning, student-centered learning, truly individualized learning, powerful ideas, advanced laboratory environments, interdisciplinary learning, and zero failures. We have seen students who were called slow learners and who hated school suddenly blossom and achieve success in student-controlled computing environments. We have also seen these students learn mathematics, science, and programming by creating ideas, computer games and simulations, and physical devices—achievements that won for them the approval and respect of fellow students and teachers. It appears that many students are able to succeed in learning mathematics in a student-controlled computing environment because they can shape instructional procedures to their own learning styles.

An Approach to Computer-Augmented Learning

Between 1970 and 1977, people involved in a computer-augmented learning project called Project Solo experimented with various modes for using computers in high schools and developed computer-related curriculum modules for secondary schools. Project Solo, which was jointly supported by the National Science Foundation and the University of Pittsburgh, focused upon computer-augmented learning in secondary school mathematics and applications of mathematics in the sciences, engineering, and other fields. The primary objective of Project Solo was to stimulate students to analyze, synthesize, evaluate, and apply mathematics on their own by using algorithmic problem-solving and student-controlled computing as catalysts. The more than 100 computer-augmented curriculum modules produced by Project Solo are designed to help high school students use a computer as a tool in exploring concepts and principles from topics in high-school and college-level mathematics.

In the second phase of Project Solo, which is called Soloworks, five computer-related mathematics laboratories were developed and were used experimentally by secondary school students from grades six through twelve. The purpose of these laboratories is to develop interdisciplinary approaches to learning high-level mathematics concepts and principles using what is called a "top-down" approach to learning mathematics. This "top-down" approach begins by selecting significant mathematical ideas and identifying research skills and activities that can be used to motivate the study of these ideas in schools. Next, these high-level mathematical ideas are analyzed to determine the lower-level skills, concepts and principles that must be mastered while learning each higher-level idea. Finally, high school mathematics students study these powerful ideas and mathematical methods by applying them in interdisciplinary approaches to learning mathematics. The five laboratories which have been developed are called Computer Lab, Modeling/Simulation Lab, Dynamics Lab, Synthesis Lab, and Logical Design Lab.

The Computer Lab focuses upon computer applications in mathematics, computer programming, and algorithmic aspects of mathematics. In this lab students use computers and related technology to solve mathematical problems, write CAI curriculum modules, construct computer-based games, and write computer-based simulations of mathematical systems and applications.

The Modeling/Simulation Lab uses mathematics as a tool to create new physical or computer-simulated models of reality that can be manipulated and studied by students. One physical model which has been built by students and Project staff members is a computer-controlled lunar lander. Computer-simulations of probabilistic models, the dynamics of space flight, and other physical processes have been programmed by students.

The Dynamics Lab centers around mathematical methods for describing and studying physical processes that take place in space and time. This lab features an actual airplane flight simulator and a computer-operated plotter which students use to learn the mathematics and science involved in instrument navigation techniques. The flight simulator, which is a working model of the cockpit of a small airplane, can be "piloted" by a student who sits in the simulator or can be operated and charted by a computer program and a plotter.

The Synthesis Lab is concerned with studying the mathematics involved in producing complex effects by combining simple processes. One physical component of this lab is a pipe organ which can be played by people or by computer programs which were written by students and Project staff. The mathematics of music and the mathematics involved in coding computer-controlled music can be studied by students who work in this lab.

The Logical Design Lab was an outgrowth of the other four labs. In this lab the science, mathematics, and electronics principles needed in developing and operating the other labs are studied. Students not only study mathematical principles of logic in this lab but they also design and assemble the components of the devices used in the other labs.

Since the initial work of Project Solo and Soloworks was to discover the best ways of using computers and other forms of technology in teaching and learning mathematics, some of the Project Solo activities can be classified as laboratory-oriented research and development. However, many Project Solo ideas about using computers in mathematics education have been tested in several large schools in Greater Pittsburgh. Students in schools throughout the United States are using some of the Project Solo curriculum modules which have been published and are being distributed by Digital Equipment Corporation in Maynard, Massachusetts and the Hewlett-Packard Company in Cupertino, California. A computer resource book for algebra, which is authored by Thomas Dwyer, who was Director of Project Solo, and Margot Critchfield (1975), illustrates how the ideas for teaching and learning mathematics which have grown from Project Solo can be used in high schools that have access to a computer.

Computer Augmented Learning Resources

There are many fine resources available for use in computer-related mathematics laboratories; however few of these resources are found in mathematics textbooks and mathematics education journals. The best continuing sources of information about the uses of computers in mathematics education are the various journals which specialize in educational applications of computers and the computer hardware companies which manufacture and distribute computers designed for use in schools. Three of these companies are Digital Equipment Corporation, Hewlett-Packard Company, and Data General Corporation. There are a few books dealing with educational uses of computers and the ERIC Information Analysis Center has four papers on the uses of computers in mathematics education. You can keep abreast of developments in educational applications of computers and locate computer-related learning resources for mathematics education by doing the following:

1. Write to ERIC Information Analysis Center for Science, Mathematics, and Environmental Education, The Ohio State University, Columbus, Ohio 43210 and request information for ordering the following papers:
   a. Molnar, Andrew R. "Computer Innovations in Education," February, 1973.
   b. Hatfield, Larry L. "Computer-Extended Problem Solving and Inquiry," February, 1973.
   c. Suydam, Marilyn N. (ed.) "The Use of Computers in Mathematics Education: Bibliography," February, 1973.
   d. Kieren, Thomas E. "Research on Computers in Mathematics Education," April, 1973.
2. Obtain a copy of the algebra resource book by Dwyer and Critchfield, which is mentioned above, and see if you can locate some other books and resources about using computers to teach mathematics in secondary schools.
3. Write to the following computer companies and request information

about their newsletters for teachers and their computer-related curriculum materials for mathematics education:

a. Data General Corporation, Route 9, Southboro, Massachusetts 01772.

b. Digital Equipment Corporation, 146 Main Street, Maynard, Massachusetts 01754.

c. Hewlett-Packard Company, 11000 Wolfe Road, Cupertino, California 95014.

4. Subscribe to the following publications or read them regularly in a library:

a. *Creative Computing,* Box 789-M, Morristown, New Jersey 07960.

b. *People's Computer Company Paper,* P.O. Box 310, Menlo Park, California 94025.

c. *SIGCUE Bulletin,* Association for Computing Machinery, P.O. Box 12105, Church Street Station, New York, N.Y. 10249.

d. *The Mathematics Teacher,* 1906 Association Drive, Reston, Virginia 22091. (The "**New** Products, **New** Programs, **New** Publications" section of each issue of this journal contains information about computer-related resources for mathematics education.)

Each issue of *Creative Computing* and the *People's Computer Company Paper* contains listings of computer programs and sample computer runs, many of which can be used in computer-oriented mathematics classrooms.

The Future of Computers in Mathematics Education

Although computer-augmented learning does show promise of causing significant changes in mathematics education, there are no assurances that computers will become a necessary part of most mathematics education programs in secondary schools. It may be several years until we know whether computers in mathematics education will be just another educational fad, a limited part of a few mathematics programs in schools, or a revolutionary catalyst for change in our whole approach to teaching and learning mathematics. The following quotation from an article by Frederick H. Bell in *Educational Technology* (December, 1974) provides additional perspective on the uses of computers in education:

There is no particular magic about computers which makes them more effective learning devices than innovations that have failed. It is probable that any modification of the learning environment which is perceived by the learner as being different (in a positive sense) and which permits him to learn in modes similar to those that he uses outside of school in the "real world" would be quite effective in improving learning. For the child who is "turned off" by school, changing the content, style and design of the textbook, assigning different problems and presenting material in a different way is as meaningless as replacing a brown iron fence with a red steel fence—the fence is still there. Computer-related learning environments catalyze people to do outstanding work, because they provide a setting in which each student can create things, make things work (a computer, for example), obtain real recognition for work well done, and teach others how to do those things which he has learned to do well. (p. 18)

Things To Do

1. Use secondary school mathematics textbooks to locate examples of propositions and theorems which can be proved using various logical argument forms. Give examples from each of arithmetic, algebra, geometry, and trigonometry of propositions or theorems that can be proved using:
   a. modus ponens
   b. transitivity
   c. modus tollens
   d. deduction theorem
   e. contraposition
   f. proof by cases
   g. mathematical induction
   h. counterexample
   i. indirect proof

2. Select a theorem, from a high school plane geometry book, which has a relatively long and complex proof. Analyze each step in the proof to discover the underlying logical argument forms used in the proof. Next to each step, or set of steps, in the proof write the name of the argument form that justifies that step.

3. Outline several classroom methods that can be used to help students learn general strategies for proving theorems.

4. Make an outline of a general theorem-proving teaching/learning model which can be used to describe a spiral approach to teaching and learning theorem proving throughout secondary school mathematics.

5. Make a list of specific cognitive and affective student performance objectives which can be used to justify an emphasis upon proving theorems throughout high school mathematics.

6. Review the 56 techniques for using the five-step problem-solving model which are presented in this chapter and formulate several additional techniques for each of the five steps.

7. Review the dialogue, in this chapter, between a teacher and a class of students which is presented for solving the problem of finding an interior diagonal of a rectangular parallelepiped. Select another topic from secondary school mathematics and use the dialogue format of this chapter to write a hypothetical teacher/student interactive dialogue for solving the problem that you selected.

8. Obtain a copy of one of George Polya's three books on problem solving (1957, 1962, 1965) or Wayne Wickelgren's book on how to solve problems (1974). While reading the book that you selected, analyze and evaluate the following strategies presented in the book:
   A. General strategies for solving problems.
   B. General strategies for teaching problem solving.
   C. Strategies for solving specific types of mathematics problems.
   D. Strategies for teaching students how to solve specific types of mathematics problems.

9. Browse through recent issues of *The Mathematics Teacher, The Arithmetic Teacher, School Science and Mathematics,* and *Scientific American* and look for articles related to solving problems. Read the articles that you

locate and note special techniques for solving specific mathematical problems.

10. Make a list of laboratory resources which could be purchased for approximately $300. Give the price and distributor of each item and state a learning objective that can be attained by students who are using each resource.

11. Make a floor plan of a mathematics laboratory/resource room. Indicate where each piece of permanent equipment would be located and where consumable and non-consumable resources would be stored.

12. Write a 14-point lesson plan for teaching a topic in secondary school mathematics using the laboratory teaching/learning model.

13. Visit a secondary school mathematics department that has a special room designated as a mathematics laboratory. During your visit take notes about the nature and use of permanent facilities as well as the types of permanent and non-permanent resources. Try to write cognitive and affective learning objectives which can be met by students who may be studying mathematics in this laboratory.

    In addition, interview several students who are working in the "math lab" and ask them their opinions about learning mathematics in a laboratory. Also interview one of the mathematics teachers who uses the laboratory and question him or her about the nature and value of the laboratory resources, how the students use them, and what they learn about mathematics from working in the laboratory. Ask the teacher if there are other resources that he or she would like to have in the mathematics laboratory.

14. List the four stages of the inquiry teaching/learning model and suggest general teaching and learning strategies which could be used to help students carry out each stage in a mathematics laboratory or classroom.

15. Suggest and discuss methods for teaching students how to use inquiry strategies to learn mathematical principles efficiently and effectively.

16. Select a topic from high school mathematics and write a 14-point lesson plan for teaching and learning that topic through an inquiry strategy. You may want to use the "Inquiry Lesson in Probability," which is found in this chapter near the end of the section on the inquiry teaching/learning model, as a guide in preparing your lesson plan.

17. List and discuss at least 10 cognitive objectives that can be met using the group-processes teaching/learning model and at least 10 affective objectives that can be met through group activities.

18. Suggest five possible problem situations that could develop within a small group of students who are working on a task without assistance or supervision from the teacher. Suggest ways in which the teacher might intervene in the group to assist in resolving each of the problem situations which is impeding the group's progress.

19. A "moon-crash" group problem-solving activity is presented in this chapter in the section on the group-processes teaching/learning model. Modify this problem so that the fifteen items which are to be ranked in the

"moon-crash" activity are changed to mathematics items such as answers to exercises or mathematical principles. Then prepare a 14-point lesson plan centered around group activities for your "mathematical" modification of the "moon-crash" group discussion.

20. Read some of the articles in *Creative Computing* and other journals concerned with educational applications of computers and discuss various ways in which computers can be used to improve teaching and learning in secondary school mathematics classrooms.

21. Discuss the advantages and disadvantages of using computers in teaching and learning mathematics.

22. Visit a school that has a computer facility which students use in learning mathematics. Discuss with the mathematics teacher and students the various ways in which they are using computers to teach and learn mathematics and try to determine which of the following modes of computer use are found in the school mathematics program—computer-managed instruction, computer-assisted instruction, computer simulations, computer-based problem solving, student-controlled computing, modes of computer use not discussed in this chapter. Ask the teachers who are using computers in their mathematics courses to discuss the advantages and disadvantages of teaching and learning mathematics in a computer-augmented learning environment.

Selected Bibliography

Bell, Frederick H. "Why is Computer-Related Learning So Successful?" *Educational Technology* 12 (1974): 15-18.

    This article presents the case for using computers as an aid to teaching and learning in schools.

———. "Computers in the Schools: Catalysts for Learning." *Curriculum Trends*. Waterford, Conn.: Croft NEI Publications, December, 1974.

    This paper presents and answers several relevant questions about the uses of computers in education, discusses several modes of computer use in schools, and describes several large computer-augmented learning projects.

Dwyer, Thomas A., and Kaufman, Michael S. *A Guided Tour of Computer Programming in BASIC*. Boston: Houghton Mifflin Company, 1973.

    This book about how to program computers in the BASIC language was written for secondary school students. It contains sections about what to expect of computers, how to make the computer work for you, and how to use the computer for professional applications.

Dwyer, Thomas A., and Critchfield, Margot. *Computer Resource Book-Algebra*. Boston: Houghton Mifflin Company, 1975.

    The purpose of this book is to provide students and teachers with interesting things to do in algebra when a computer is available. It shows how the use of a computer can be combined with other activities in high school algebra courses.

Joyce, Bruce, and Weil, Marsha. *Models of Teaching*. Englewood Cliffs, New Jersey: Prentice-Hall, Inc., 1972.

Among the teaching/learning models discussed in this book are the inquiry model and the group-processes model.

Kidd, Kenneth P., Myers, Shirley S., and Cilley, David M. *The Laboratory Approach to Mathematics*. Chicago, Illinois: Science Research Associates, Inc., 1970.

This book contains information about planning, organizing, and supervising laboratory (activity-oriented) approaches for mathematics students in grades five through nine. Although most of the specific mathematics laboratory activities presented in this book were designed for students in these grades, many of the teaching concepts can be used by teachers of higher level mathematics courses.

Kieren, T. E. *Research on Computers in Mathematics Education*. Columbus, Ohio: ERIC Center for Science, Mathematics, and Environmental Education, April, 1973.

Kramer, Edna E. *The Nature and Growth of Modern Mathematics*. (Volumes 1 and 2) Greenwich, Connecticut: Fawcett Publications, Inc., 1970.

Many ideas for mathematics inquiry and laboratory lessons can be found in this fine book about the history and nature of mathematics.

National Council of Teachers of Mathematics. *The Teaching of Secondary School Mathematics* (Thirty-third Yearbook). Washington, D.C.: National Council of Teachers of Mathematics, 1970.

This NCTM yearbook contains two good articles on mathematical proof and problem-solving methods.

————. *The Slow Learner in Mathematics* (Thirty-fifth Yearbook). Washington, D.C.: National Council of Teachers of Mathematics, 1972.

The thirty-fifth yearbook of the NCTM contains a lengthy section on the laboratory approach to teaching and learning mathematics.

————. *Instructional Aids in Mathematics*. (Thirty-fourth Yearbook). Washington, D.C.: National Council of Teachers of Mathematics, 1973.

This book is an excellent source of information on planning mathematics laboratory activities and obtaining laboratory supplies, resources, and equipment. However, some of the information pertaining to resources and equipment is now somewhat out of date.

Polya, George. *How to Solve It* 2nd ed. Princeton, New Jersey: Princeton University Press, 1957.

A work that has become a classic in mathematics education, this book should be read by every mathematics teacher. Written by the well-known mathematician George Polya, the book contains a step-by-step discussion of problem solving and theorem proving with many examples from high school level mathematics. For the person who wants to improve his or her problem-solving skills or for the teacher who wants to help students learn good problem-solving strategies, this book is a must.

————. *Mathematical Discovery: On Understanding, Learning, and Teaching Problem-Solving*. New York: John Wiley & Sons, Inc., 1962 (Vol. 1), 1965 (Vol. 2).

These two small volumes contain general strategies for solving several different types of secondary school mathematics problems, procedures for learning through discovery, and principles for teaching and learning mathematics. The general problem-solving and discovery-learning principles presented in these books are illustrated by numerous high school mathematics problems. In discussing each problem, Polya explains the particular problem-solving procedure that is used in finding a solution. These two books should be read by every high school mathematics teacher.

Raths, James, Pancella, John R., and Van Ness, James S. (Editors) *Studying Teaching* 2nd ed. Englewood Cliffs, New Jersey: Prentice-Hall, Inc., 1971.

An article on inquiry strategies is included among the various teaching strategies discussed in this book.

Sobel, Max A., and Maletsky, Evan M. *Teaching Mathematics: A Sourcebook of Aids, Activities, and Strategies.* Englewood Cliffs, New Jersey: Prentice-Hall, Inc., 1975.

This book contains information on motivating mathematics learning, recreational activities in mathematics, mathematics laboratory experiments, classroom aids and models, and audio-visual facilities, resources, and references.

Stanford, Gene, and Stanford, Barbara Dodds. *Learning Discussion Skills Through Games.* New York: Citation Press, 1969.

This book contains several strategies for teaching students how to work effectively in groups.

Vrana, Ralph S. *The Mathematics Laboratory: A New Teaching Approach.* West Nyack, New York: Parker Publishing Company, Inc., 1975.

The Mathematics Laboratory contains a variety of applied mathematics activities and experiments, some of which are appropriate for class presentations and discussions; others involve small group activities; and still others are individualized projects. This book contains many fascinating and non-trivial applications of high school mathematics and is an excellent source of supplementary activities for standard mathematics topics. The projects and activities are organized under the following headings: (1) discovering patterns and cycles in mathematics, (2) understanding principles in size and shape, (3) measuring speed and strength, (4) understanding probability, (5) mathematics in simple machines, (6) mental exercises, (7) topology, and (8) establishing a classroom mathematics laboratory.

Wickelgren, Wayne A. *How to Solve Problems: Elements of a Theory of Problems and Problem Solving.* San Francisco: W. H. Freeman and Company, 1974.

The purpose of this book is to help people improve their abilities to solve many kinds of mathematics problems, including theorem proving. Although the book is intended to help college students solve problems in their own courses, most of the problem examples are from high school mathematics and the problem-solving strategies are certainly relevant for high school students. The author's sound, practical approach to problem solving makes this book a valuable resource for teachers who want to help students improve their problem-solving skills.

7

Developing and Maintaining an Effective Learning Environment

In addition to planning and teaching mathematics lessons, teachers must carry out many other activities that support their primary objective of helping students learn mathematics. In this chapter eight activities which are an important part of preparing and maintaining an effective environment in which students can learn mathematics will be discussed. In order to teach mathematics effectively, teachers must be able to:

(1) evaluate and use mathematics textbooks,
(2) select and use teaching/learning resources,
(3) assign and evaluate student homework,
(4) develop good questioning strategies,
(5) diagnose students' learning difficulties,
(6) maintain discipline in the classroom,
(7) test, evaluate, and grade students, and
(8) evaluate their own teaching effectiveness.

Evaluating, Selecting, and Using Mathematics Textbooks

Probably the most important teaching/learning resources for mathematics teachers are the textbooks which students use in their secondary school mathematics courses. Research has shown that one of the most effective ways to change what students learn in mathematics courses is to modify the content of their textbooks. In many school districts teachers have a major part in textbook selection; however whether or not teachers help to select the textbooks for the courses they are teaching, all teachers can improve their teaching effectiveness by making appropriate use of secondary school mathematics textbooks.

Purposes of Mathematics Textbooks

In a mathematics course the textbook can be a valuable resource to assist the teacher in teaching mathematics and to help students learn mathematics. For many courses the textbook provides most of the mathematics content and for some courses all of the content is taken from the textbook. In addition to the

primary objective of providing content for mathematics courses, texxtbooks are
also used for the following purposes:

(1) In the time between learning mathematics topics in high school and college
and teaching these topics to secondary school students, many teachers
forget some of the details. Teachers can use high school mathematics
textbooks to review mathematics topics that they have forgotten.

(2) Many textbooks are published in teachers' editions which present instructional strategies for teaching certain skills, concepts and principles.

(3) Textbooks assist teachers in organizing and sequencing mathematics topics
into appropriate teaching/learning hierarchies.

(4) Some textbooks contain supplementary materials which treat the history,
philosophy, and structure of mathematics.

(5) Many mathematics textbooks contain supplementary problems and exercises, some of which provide additional assistance for slow learners in
mathematics and others which provide advanced topics for students having
exceptional mathematical ability.

(6) The format and style of a well-written and well-illustrated textbook can
increase students' motivation to learn mathematics.

(7) A few mathematics textbooks contain cognitive and affective learning objectives for each topic.

(8) Textbooks contain examples and explorations of skills, concepts, and principles which help students master these mathematical objects.

(9) Some mathematics textbooks include applications of mathematical concepts and principles.

(10) A few textbooks contain problems and exercises designed for specific
higher-level cognitive learning objectives of analysis, synthesis, application and evaluation of mathematical ideas.

(11) Nearly all mathematics textbooks contain drill-and-practice exercises to
assist students in learning facts, skills, concepts and principles.

(12) Some textbooks contain problems and exercises differentiated according to
student ability levels.

(13) Many textbooks contain supplementary review exercises as well as topic,
chapter, and unit tests, and other instruments for evaluating student mastery of mathematics.

(14) Some textbooks offer several approaches to learning each topic; for example, content may be presented through both concrete and abstract representations.

(15) The textbook is a source of information about mathematics which students
can use to supplement the information presented by their teachers.

(16) In some schools, which have few instructional resources, the textbook may
be the only resource, other than the teacher, which most students can use to
learn mathematics.

(17) The textbook can be used as a reference book for students who may have
forgotten elements of previously learned mathematical objects.

What to Look for in a Mathematics Textbook

When selecting new textbooks or evaluating textbooks in current use in your
mathematics program, you can use certain specific and general guidelines, which

are presented below; however there is no absolute method for rating mathematics textbooks. Evaluation of a textbook is a subjective judgment which should be based upon careful consideration of criteria relevant to your teaching situation. Several important criteria in textbook selection and evaluation are the mathematical competence of the teachers who will be teaching from the book, the ability levels of the students who will be using the book, the degree of mathematical rigor preferred by teachers, the stage of intellectual development of the students, the relative emphasis upon basic facts and skills or high-level concepts and principles, the relative emphasis upon cognitive and affective objectives, and the value placed upon knowledge, comprehension, application, analysis, synthesis, and evaluation of mathematical objects. In general, the goals of your school's mathematics program, the specific cognitive and affective objectives of the mathematics course, and the learning-related characteristics of your students are the criteria against which a textbook should be evaluated.

In an article in *The Mathematics Teacher* (May, 1965), Philip Peak, Chairman of the Committee on Aids for Evaluators of Textbooks of the National Council of Teachers of Mathematics, describes an instrument that his committee developed to assist teachers in making qualitative judgments of characteristics of mathematics textbooks. His criteria are organized under two main headings—**"Criteria Relating to Presentation and Content"** and **"Criteria Relating to Physical Characteristics and Services;"** these headings will be used in our discussion of textbook evaluation. According to Peak, an instrument for use in evaluating mathematics textbooks should:

> . . .help the user in his decision-making process, but will not make the decision for him. It is not possible to use a single number to measure the quality of a textbook for use in a single institution. It is, rather, a subjective judgment based on careful consideration of criteria which are relevant to the evaluation. (p. 467)

The questions in the following outline can be used as a beginning point in evaluating secondary school mathematics textbooks. Additional questions that are related to specific objectives and criteria for a mathematics textbook to be used in a particular course should be added to the questions suggested in this outline. Be sure to keep in mind that there is no "right" nor "wrong" answer to many of these questions. If your answer to the question "Does the book contain...?" is "yes" and you want a book that contains what is asked in the question, then "yes" is the "right" answer for you. However, if you want a book that does not contain what is asked in the question, then for you "no" is the "right" answer.

Criteria for Evaluating Mathematics Textbooks

I. *Criteria Relating to Content and Methods*

    A. **Mathematical Content:** Not only should the mathematics in the textbook be correct, it should also be appropriate for the objectives of the course for which the book is to be used and the type of students who will take the course.

        1. Are the mathematics facts, concepts, skills and principles correct?

        2. Are standard mathematical symbols and other notation used?

        3. Does the book contain a number of printing errors and incor-

rect answers which interfere with comprehension of the content?

4. Is the presentation of content overly symbolic and abstract?
5. Are mathematical concepts defined correctly?
6. Are the underlying structures of the mathematical systems that are presented apparent?
7. Does the book deal with the history, philosophy and methods of mathematics and mathematicians?
8. Are the levels of rigor and precision appropriate for your students?
9. Does the book take a modern or a traditional approach to mathematical content?
10. Does the textbook emphasize mathematical facts and skills or does it emphasize concepts and principles?
11. Are valid logical forms used in proving propositions?
12. Does the book emphasize proof?
13. Is problem solving considered in the book?
14. Are the proofs, explanations and examples complete and understandable for the students who will be using the book?
15. As new topics are introduced, are their relationships to previous topics apparent so that the structure of mathematical systems is obvious?
16. Does the text point out common logical errors such as circular reasoning, assuming the truth of the converse of a theorem, and using unproven propositions to prove theorems?
17. Are mathematical terms defined correctly and understandably?
18. Are different meanings and uses of mathematical terms pointed out?
19. Is there a clear distinction between undefined terms, defined terms and theorems?
20. Is a clear distinction made between a proof and a reasonable conjecture?
21. Are all of the topics that you want to teach in the course included in the book?

B. **Teaching Methods:** It is also important to evaluate mathematics textbooks to ascertain the validity of the teaching and learning methods that are used and to determine whether the book is appropriate for the stage of intellectual development and ability levels of your students.

1. Are interesting examples and problems included to increase student motivation?
2. Are explanations, examples and problems for different student ability levels included?
3. Is a spiral approach used in developing concepts and principles at progressively higher levels of abstraction?
4. Are topics organized so that prerequisite topics precede the topics that depend upon them?

5. Is the content presented so that students have an opportunity to discover some mathematical principles?

6. Is each concept presented in various contexts?

7. Are examples, counterexamples, and irrelevant characteristics presented following the definition of each concept?

8. Are the teaching strategies suggested in the teacher's edition based upon sound principles for teaching and learning mathematics?

9. Are the questions, exercises and homework assignments based upon the topics and ideas presented in the body of each chapter?

10. Are the cognitive learning objectives for each topic and unit obvious to the teacher? to students?

11. Are advance organizers or outlines used at the beginning of each chapter or topic?

12. Are chapter and topic summaries given throughout the textbook?

13. Does the book overemphasize reliance upon rules? Does it underemphasize algorithmic approaches to solving problems?

14. Are general problem-solving methods presented?

15. Are relationships among various facts, skills, concepts and principles pointed out?

16. Are students given opportunities to apply, analyze, synthesize and evaluate mathematical concepts and principles as well as to know and comprehend facts and skills?

17. Are students given opportunities to make conjectures and generalizations?

18. Are inductive and deductive argument forms used?

19. Are reasons given for particular ''short-cuts'' and algorithmic procedures?

20. Does the book contain procedures which students can use for self evaluation?

21. Are the instructional strategies used in the textbook appropriate for the stage of intellectual development of your students?

II. *Criteria Relating to Physical Characteristics and Teacher Aids*

A. **Physical Characteristics:** The most important criteria in textbook evaluation are those judgments of the mathematical content and instructional methods contained in the book. After several books have been found that meet your particular needs in the content and pedagogical areas, the physical characteristics of these books should be evaluated. However, quality of paper and print and the physical appearance of the book should not be used as major factors in selecting a mathematics textbook.

1. Is the book well bound and is it printed on high-quality paper?

2. Is the title appropriate and will it appeal to students? (For example, a book titled *Remedial Arithmetic* is not the type of book that a senior would want to be seen carrying around.)

3. Are the pictures in the book current? (Pictures with people wearing out-of-style clothes or driving old automobiles indicate, especially to students, that the book is "old fashioned.")
4. Are the diagrams and pictures related to the textual material, are they interesting, and do they suggest mathematical ideas or questions?
5. Is the book well organized and are main headings and subheadings used to identify major ideas and topics?
6. Is the type size large enough to be easily read by students?
7. Are important concepts and principles highlighted in boldface type or in color?
8. Is the style of writing suitable for the students who will be using the book?
9. Is the reading level of the text appropriate for your students?
10. Is information easy to locate within the text?
11. Are examples, student exercises, and activities interspersed throughout the textual material?

B. **Teacher Aids:** Many secondary school textbooks have accompanying teachers' editions or teachers' manuals. Others have information and special sections such as mastery tests, performance objectives, appendices and chapter introductions which are useful to teachers in planning and teaching lessons. If the textbook has a teachers' edition or a teachers' manual, these special aids should be evaluated as teaching resources. If the book does not have a teachers' supplement, then the text itself should be evaluated for its assistance to teachers.

1. Does the publisher provide supplementary educational services?
2. Are special instructional resources needed to supplement the textbook?
3. Do the authors offer suggestions for using the textbook?
4. Are teaching/learning objectives included for the teacher?
5. Does the book contain a detailed and useful table of contents?
6. Does the book contain a complete index which is easy to use?
7. Do the authors specify the type of students for which the book was written?
8. Do the authors suggest supplementary materials such as films, games and books to use with the textbook?
9. Are interesting homework problems, student projects and laboratory activities included among the sets of exercises?
10. Do the authors suggest alternative sequences for presenting chapters and topics?
11. Is there enough material in the book for a complete course?
12. Is the material presented and explained so that you, the teacher, can readily understand it?
13. Do the authors specify where and how the book has been used and evaluated?

14. Are standardized tests available for use with the book?
15. For the teacher who teaches computer-supplemented mathematics courses, is this book computer oriented or does it have a computer-oriented supplement to use as a resource?
16. Is this a recent edition of the book? (It may be that a new and improved edition will be available shortly.)
17. Does the book contain answers to exercises or is there an accompanying answer book?
18. If there is an answer book, does it contain hints for solving the problems and proving the exercises in the textbook?
19. Are alternative problem solving-procedures and teaching/learning strategies suggested for certain topics?

The preceding set of 72 questions—under the headings *Mathematical Content, Teaching Methods, Physical Characteristics,* and *Teacher Aids*—which can be used to assist in evaluating mathematics textbooks may not cover all of the criteria that you believe are appropriate for judging textbooks. It may also be true that some of these 72 criteria are of little concern to you in selecting a textbook for a certain course. These questions are designed to serve as a guide, not a comprehensive standard, for textbook evaluation. When selecting or evaluating a textbook for a particular course, you may want to use some very specific criteria reflecting your particular requirements and the needs of your students.

Using Mathematics Textbooks Effectively

The most common fault of teachers in using a mathematics textbook in teaching a course is over-reliance upon the textbook. Some teachers "teach the textbook;" that is, they repeat the explanations and example exercises in the textbook in their lessons, use only exercises from the textbook as homework assignments, take all their test questions from the textbook, and never deviate from the topic sequencing of the textbook. Some teachers regard the textbook as a teaching resource for themselves but not as a learning resource for students; consequently these teachers teach from the textbook but students only use it to locate exercises that are assigned by the teacher. There are correct and incorrect ways for both the teacher and students to use textbooks.

When using a mathematics textbook as a teaching resource, teachers should read it carefully and consider rearranging topics, omitting topics and teaching topics that are not covered in the text. Most textbooks have several chapters and many topics that can be taught in various sequences, and the teacher should consider whether his or her students might better comprehend the material if it is sequenced differently from the arrangement used in the textbook. Some texts contain advanced topics and chapters that may be inappropriate for slower students and should be omitted. At times the teacher may feel that his or her students should study topics that are not included in the textbook and may prepare handouts and special student activities for these topics.

Most textbooks contain more material than it is possible for students to learn in a single course and teachers should not feel obligated to cover the entire textbook. Topics in the textbook should be covered at the rate at which students can master the mathematical objects and should not be rushed through in order to

cover material rapidly. At times it is appropriate to deviate from the textbook to
teach discovery lessons, problem-solving lessons and laboratory lessons which
are used to clarify and extend the topics in the textbook. The textbook can be a
valuable source of mathematical material and teaching techniques but it should
not be followed slavishly.

Nearly all mathematics teachers use the textbook as a source of classroom
exercises and homework assignments for students; unfortunately this may be the
only use that many students make of their mathematics textbooks. Before assigning exercises and problems from the textbook, teachers should read them carefully and select a sequence of problems which is most appropriate for helping
each student master the skills, concepts and principles that are contained in the
exercises. When teachers regularly assign the first 20 problems or all of the even
numbered problems at the end of a topic, students frequently regard homework
as something the teacher wants them to do, but fail to see much purpose in
completing homework exercises. Exercises should be selected and assigned so
that students begin with exercises that are easy for them and progress quickly
through a sequence of exercises which are progressively more difficult. It is
counterproductive to assign long lists of exercises to students who have already
mastered the content of the exercises and students can become frustrated if they
are assigned exercises that are too advanced and difficult for their mathematical
abilities and backgrounds. It is well to give ''open-ended'' assignments such as
''complete 20 of these exercises by starting with an easy set of exercises and
moving to a more difficult set after you think that you have mastered the easier
problems.'' With some judicious advice and assistance from the teacher, each
student will be solving those exercises that are most appropriate for him or her.

Students should be expected to use their mathematics textbooks as learning
resources; however they need advice and assistance in doing so. Many students
fail to use their textbooks because they do not know how to use them. At the
beginning of each course, the teacher should spend one class period introducing
students to the textbook and explaining how it is to be used. Students should be
shown how to use the index to locate definitions, examples, theorems, and
proofs in the textbook. Many textbook publishers use various formats, colors and
type styles to highlight different kinds of mathematical objects. Students should
be shown how to skim through a chapter and locate major topics, how to find
explanations of mathematical concepts and principles, and how to informally
outline topics and chapters. Have students practice using the index to locate
items in the textbook; select a topic and ask them to write a brief outline containing the main ideas; have them browse through several chapters and familiarize
themselves with the format of the book and the relative organization of information within each chapter.

Many teachers attempt to encourage students to read their textbooks throughout a course by giving reading assignments. However, reading assignments must
be treated by the teacher in a way that will make students aware of their value.
When students know that the teacher is going to ignore reading assignments and
repeat the assigned material in class, they are not likely to give much attention to
this type of assignment. In order to encourage students to read and study their
textbooks, teachers should give reading assignments that require supplementary

pencil-and-paper activities and should base each lesson upon the preceding textbook reading and study assignment.

When textbook reading and study assignments are made, the teacher should tell students to jot down questions that arise during their reading, to make notes about definitions, concepts, principles and examples that need to be clarified, and to use pencil and paper to work through example exercises in the textbook. As part of each reading assignment, several exercises based upon the readings should be assigned. When students attempt to solve the exercise problems, they will see the need to read, analyze and evaluate the textbook explanations and examples carefully. The teacher should begin each class session following a reading assignment by answering questions about the assignment, discussing the exercises that were assigned to supplement the readings, and pointing out the text materials upon which the solutions to the exercises are based. If these procedures are followed, students will quickly learn to value the textbook as a teaching/learning resource and will tend to refer to the textbook when they become ''stuck'' while trying to solve an exercise. Consequently, students will use their textbooks as information sources to supplement the teacher's presentations, and the teacher can build upon the explanations and examples in the textbook rather than repeating them in class sessions. Thus, students will see a greater variety of examples (the teacher's and the textbook's) and the teacher can present concepts and principles through representations that clarify those found in the textbook.

Obtaining and Using Teaching/Learning Resources

Different types of teaching/learning resources and a variety of sources for resources have already been discussed in Chapters 4, 5 and 6. As you have seen in these chapters, accumulating resources for use in mathematics classrooms is a continuing process which must take place throughout one's career as a teacher. Mathematics teachers should build a small personal library of resource books on mathematics and teaching mathematics and should accumulate mathematical models, games, demonstrations, audio-visual aids and teaching/learning supplements on a regular basis. Most schools have at least small library and mathematics department budgets which can be used by mathematics teachers to purchase resources. Many mathematics education journals and books about teaching and learning mathematics list sources of free or inexpensive teaching/learning aids. Some students enjoy constructing models, posters, and demonstrations as mathematics projects; these student projects are a good source of teaching/learning aids. Discarded household materials, building materials and appliances can be salvaged and used as materials for creating mathematics education resources. Creative lesson plans and student problem-solving and laboratory activities are also forms of learning resources, and particularly effective lesson plans and classroom activities should be retained for future use. Many teachers make collecting resources into a hobby and accumulate mathematics teaching resources much as one equips a home workshop.

When purchasing resources for use in mathematics classrooms or laboratories, four principles should be remembered and applied. First, there is little, if any, correlation between the cost of a resource and its effectiveness as a teaching/

learning aid. Sometimes a cardboard model can be just as effective in demonstrating mathematical concepts and principles as a $300 sound and color film. Second, before purchasing an expensive resource read and evaluate the advertisements for the resource. Do they describe the resource in sufficient detail so that you can see how to use it in the classroom? Are the cognitive and affective learning objectives to be attained by using the resource apparent? Is the resource too complex to be easily used by your students? Is it safe for student use? Is it sensibly priced? Many small, but expensive, resources such as films and games can be obtained on approval; after you have evaluated them, they can either be returned to the distributor or retained and purchased. When resources can not be obtained on approval, you may be able to preview them in a neighboring school, in a library, or in a college, university, or community resource center. The third principle for purchasing resources is to have your resource lists ready and your purchase orders completed. When funds are available in a school, the teacher who knows what he or she wants, why it is needed, what it will be used for, where to purchase it, and how much it costs tends to get a disproportionately large share of these funds for his or her classes. Fourth, after the school principal or curriculum coordinator has purchased mathematics education resources for use in your classes, use these resources, evaluate them, and report your use and evaluation to the person responsible for purchasing resources. Administrators are not likely to honor a teacher's requests for new resources if they have no information to show that he or she is making effective use of previously purchased classroom materials.

Mathematics education journals contain ideas for making your own classroom resources, reviews and evaluations of new resources, and information about distributors of resources.

The Arithmetic Teacher has sections in each issue called **What's going on . . ., IDEAS, Reviewing and Viewing, Let's do it!,** and **Books and Materials.**

What's going on . . . describes current activities in mathematics education which are being carried out by the Federal Government, state and local governments, school districts, agencies, publishers, projects, etc. and contains addresses to write to in order to obtain resources or additional information.

IDEAS contains suggestions for laboratory activities, resource centers, games, teaching strategies, etc. with information on preparing or purchasing resources.

Reviewing and Viewing contains descriptions and evaluations of new books, films, games, kits, gadgets and other resources that can be used in teaching mathematics.

Let's do it! has suggestions for activity-oriented strategies and resources for teaching arithmetic.

Books and Materials is a list of new books and other mathematics education resources. The list contains names and addresses of textbook publishers and distributors of educational resources together with the prices of many of the items listed. **Books and Materials** is a useful information source for preparing a list of suppliers of mathematics education resources and finding names and addresses of suppliers from which to request catalogs of instructional resources.

The Mathematics Teacher features sections in each issue titled **ACTIVITIES** and **NEW Products, NEW Programs, NEW Publications.**

ACTIVITIES contains suggestions for discovery lessons, problem-solving lessons, laboratory lessons and other student-centered activities for learning mathematics. Many of the suggested ideas contain instructions for constructing teaching/learning resources.

NEW Products, NEW Programs, NEW Publications contains descriptions and reviews of a diversity of resources for teaching and learning mathematics. In this section of *The Mathematics Teacher,* you will find names and addresses of publishers and other distributors of secondary-level mathematics education resources. You may want to write to some of these suppliers to request copies of their current mathematics education catalogs.

School Science and Mathematics contains features called **Math Laboratory Activity, Problem Department, Books and Teaching Aids Received, Book Vignettes,** and **Book Reviews** in each issue.

Math Laboratory Activity is a lesson plan for teaching a topic in mathematics by using a student-centered, activity-oriented approach. Some of these laboratory activities contain instructions for preparing teaching/learning resources.

Problem Department contains mathematics problems of varying degrees of difficulty which are selected for their appeal to both teachers and students of mathematics. Following the presentation of a problem, its solution appears in a subsequent issue of the journal.

Books and Teaching Aids Received contains a section listing recent books on mathematics and mathematics education. The size of the book, number of pages, publisher and price are given.

Book Vignettes contains brief descriptions and evaluations of recently published mathematics, science and education books.

Book Reviews contains longer reviews of mathematics, science, and related books.

The American Mathematical Monthly features a section on **Mathematical Education** and a section called **Reviews,** which deals with books on mathematics and topics related to mathematics, such as methods of teaching mathematics and types of instructional resources.

Mathematical Education contains one or two articles about methods of teaching mathematics. Although these articles are written to appeal to college teachers, they are also interesting and useful to high school mathematics teachers.

Reviews contains both detailed and brief descriptions and evaluations of books and other resources which may be useful to high school and college mathematics teachers.

Although published for teachers and students who use computers in their schools, *Creative Computing* is a magazine containing many useful ideas for mathematics teachers who do not use a computer to supplement their teaching. In addition to its many fascinating ideas about teaching and learning, *Creative Computing* features reviews of books on a variety of topics, including mathematics and education, which are of interest to mathematics teachers.

Most libraries have catalogs and indexes of teaching/learning resources and many of these references contain sections on mathematics education. Different types of teaching/learning resources are catalogued and names and addresses of publishers and suppliers are given. One good way to locate classroom resources is to browse through these catalogs. Writing to publishers and suppliers of mathematics education materials will provide you with a continuing source of current catalogs, and reading the journals described above will keep you well informed about the most recent teaching/learning resources for use in mathematics classrooms.

Assigning and Evaluating Homework

Many mathematics teachers assume that homework should be an integral part of each mathematics course and regularly assign homework to their students. In some schools administrative policy requires teachers to assign homework to students, and a few schools do have no-homework policies. Most students prefer not to be assigned homework, but many parents feel that teachers who do not give homework are shirking their responsibilities to students. There is some disagreement among teachers about the value of homework; although most mathematics teachers do believe that homework is a necessary activity in learning mathematics.

Although a few articles about the value of homework have appeared in the educational research journals, only a small amount of research into the value of homework has been carried out, and the findings are inconclusive. Some studies indicate that completing homework assignments has positive effects upon students' test scores, and other research studies have found no significant differences between test results of students who are assigned homework and those who are not.

Several factors may account for these inconclusive findings concerning the value of homework. First, the nature of the homework assignments that are given to students probably affects measures of the value of doing homework. Poorly chosen, routine exercises which are assigned because ''giving homework is the thing to do'' may be of little value to students. Second, students' attitudes toward homework and teachers' treatment of homework may be factors in determining its value. If students do not regard homework as a meaningful and useful activity, doing homework may have little effect upon learning. Also, teachers who have a casual attitude toward assigning, collecting and evaluating homework may inadvertently influence their students to regard homework in a similar manner. Third, since when, how, and by whom a student's homework assignment is completed is outside the direct control of teachers, they have no assurances that students will give proper attention to their homework.

Planning and Preparing Assignments

Objectives of Homework

For the teacher who does believe that homework is a valuable activity for students in learning mathematics, there are several ways to make homework meaningful to students which, hopefully, will have a significant positive effect upon learning mathematics. Homework assignments should be given the same consideration in lesson planning as each of the other planning activities. When homework assignments are included in mathematics courses, they should be made an integral part of teaching/learning strategies and postassessment activities, and they should be selected according to specific learning objectives.

Nearly all of the specific cognitive objectives that are formulated for each lesson can be met, in part, through homework assignments. Most mathematics teachers agree that mathematical skills can only be learned through practice, and the pressures to cover material in class sessions may not permit sufficient time in class for students to practice the skills that are introduced by the teacher. Consequently, one way to improve students' knowledge, comprehension and ability to use mathematical skills is to ask them to practice skills by doing homework assignments. Practicing and applying skills through homework assignments can also improve students' retention of these skills. Students can practice analysis, synthesis and evaluation of mathematical concepts and principles by completing carefully prepared homework assignments. Many teachers use homework assignments as a way of assuring that students will review topics and units in mathematics in preparation for quizzes, tests and other forms of evaluation. Homework assignments can also be used as advance organizers to prepare students for new concepts and principles which will be introduced in class the following day.

Since a large portion of class time must be used in presenting new material and assisting students with individual learning problems, little time may be available in class for student-centered laboratory activities. Many laboratory activities (which may improve student motivation) that require only common materials such as a pencil, paper, cardboard, scissors and glue can be completed as homework assignments. Some tasks which involve preparing concrete representations of abstract mathematical concepts and principles can be carried out through homework assignments.

Homework can, and should, be used as a diagnostic tool. During a class session where the teacher must attend to 20 or more students simultaneously, little time is available for assessing and assisting individual students. By assigning and evaluating homework which requires students to practice and apply new mathematical objects, the teacher can obtain a sample of each student's work and can use it to diagnose individual learning difficulties. Many teachers of large classes use homework as the primary method of individualized student evaluation on a day-to-day basis. Teachers can use their ''free time'' after classes to read students' homework papers and write comments, suggestions and corrections on student's papers. In this way students receive much of the individualized attention that they need but which teachers are unable to offer during class sessions.

Types of Homework Assignments
Student homework assignments can be classified according to two variables—the teaching/learning activities that students use in completing assignments and the degree of familiarity students have with material that is covered in assignments. Homework assignments which involve many of the following teaching/learning activities can be pepared by mathematics teachers and completed by students:

1. Many of the assignments given by mathematics teachers are exercises for the purpose of practicing and applying skills, concepts and principles.

391

2. At times homework assignments should be constructed so that students will discover mathematical principles while completing the activities specified by the teacher.
3. Since theorem proving and problem solving can best be done, at times, through solitary reflection, many teachers give theorems and problems as homework.
4. Incorporating laboratory activities in homework assignments has already been mentioned above.
5. Reading assignments to supplement and extend textbook materials and class sessions are frequently given as homework.
6. Special long-term projects such as designing and constructing mathematical models, collecting and analyzing data, and writing papers based upon library readings are occasionally given as assignments.
7. Some assignments are structured as advance organizers to introduce students to unfamiliar mathematics topics which will be covered in subsequent class meetings.
8. Other assignments are planned to assist students in organizing, synthesizing, and evaluating sets of mathematical ideas and topics.

With respect to the familiarity of material to students, the mathematics content that is included in homework assignments may be material from topics that were studied previously (*review topics*), the present topic under consideration in class sessions (*current topics*), or subsequent, unfamiliar topics that have not yet been presented in class (*unfamiliar topics*). Consequently, students may be given assignments containing any of the following mixtures of topics:

1. All of the topics are *review topics*.
2. All of the topics are *current topics*.
3. All of the topics are *unfamiliar topics*.
4. Both *review topics* and *current topics* are included in the assignment.
5. Both *current topics* and *unfamiliar topics* are contained in the assignment.
6. Both *review topics* and *unfamiliar topics* are included in the homework.
7. All three of *review topics, current topics,* and *unfamiliar topics* are a part of the homework assignment.

The choice of one of these seven mixtures of topics to be included in a homework assignment depends upon each teacher's preference and the purpose of the assignment. Homework assignments which contain all review topics are usually given to students to prepare them for a unit test or a final examination or to bring to their attention prerequisite mathematical objects that will be needed in learning new topics. Assignments limited to current topics are used to give students practice in analyzing, synthesizing and evaluating mathematical topics that are being covered in class sessions; the purpose of these assignments is to help students learn and retain the facts, skills, concepts and principles that are currently being presented by the teacher. Many teachers prefer that students first become familiar with new topics by reading about them in the textbook and considering them independently before they are presented and discussed in class. In this case activities to prepare students to learn unfamiliar topics are given as homework assignments.

Pairs of review topics, current topics, and unfamiliar topics are assigned as homework in order to emphasize the sequential nature of mathematics, the interrelationships among topics, and the structure of mathematical systems. Combining review and current topics in homework assignments may reinforce previously learned mathematical objects and highlight their relationships and applications to the current topic being considered in class. Current and unfamiliar topics usually are combined in assignments that are designed to help students use and extend familiar ideas in making discoveries of mathematical concepts and principles. Since review topics may have been forgotten by students, there is some risk in mixing review topics with unfamiliar topics in hopes of having students discover new concepts and principles. In most cases it is well to avoid giving homework assignments that involve a pure mixture of review and unfamiliar topics. The frustration and confusion of trying to discover the new while recalling the old may have a negative effect upon students' attitudes toward the mathematics course.

Possibly the most effective combination of topics for illustrating the hierarchic nature of mathematics is to include a blend of review topics, current topics and unfamiliar topics in each homework assignment. Many master teachers make a point of always tying yesterday's lesson, today's lesson and tomorrow's lesson together in today's homework assignment. Not only does this procedure highlight the sequential nature of mathematics, but it also is a sound teaching/learning technique. In each homework assignment students are simultaneously reviewing and reinforcing previously learned ideas, mastering the present material under consideration, and preparing for new material in somewhat of an advance organizer mode. This combination of review, current, and unfamiliar topics in homework assignments is an excellent way to help students meaningfully assimilate and accommodate a variety of mathematical objects into their cognitive structures.

Giving Homework Assignments to Students

How to Make the Assignment

There are correct and incorrect ways to give a homework assignment to students during the class period. Some teachers wait until the bell ending class rings, grab their textbooks, hurriedly find an exercise page in the textbook, glance at it briefly, and shout (while the students are heading for the door) "do the odd numbered problems." It is not surprising to find these teachers' students giving scant attention to homework assignments. When the teacher through his or her preparations and procedures for assigning and evaluating homework shows students how important homework assignments can be in learning mathematics, those students are likely to reflect the teacher's attitude toward homework as they complete their assignments. The following sequence of steps for giving homework assignments can be used as a guideline:

1. Before making the assignment be sure that you have each student's attention.
2. Always give a reason (or state objectives) for the assignment.
3. Give precise explanations of what is to be done in completing the assignment.
4. Tell the students when the assignment is due and what format is to be used in writing it up.
5. Allow time in class to answer students' questions about the assignment and to make appropriate clarifications and necessary modifications.

Special Considerations in Giving Assignments

The following list of special strategies and activities which should be considered when making assignments can be used as a set of suggestions for assignments. You may want to include some of these suggestions as a part of every assignment, while others may only be appropriate for certain types of homework assignments:

1. Never rush through the assignment; plan time at the beginning, middle, or end of the period to make the assignment and discuss it with the class.
2. Encourage students to ask questions about the assignment.
3. Include exercises and activities at the beginning of each assignment that can be completed successfully by every student. If a student can not do the first problem, he or she may not attempt any of the other problems.
4. Give answers to some of the assigned exercises so that students have a set of checks upon their work.
5. Offer hints and suggestions for harder activities and exercises.
6. Have students begin each assignment during the class period. This procedure permits every student to get started and also allows you to identify difficulties that particular students may have with the assignment.
7. Avoid giving all drill-and-practice exercises and other routine activities as homework assignments. Interesting games, puzzles and laboratory activities should be included in homework assignments.
8. Give some open-ended assignments where students select problems, exercises and other activities from lists of suggested work.
9. Permit the entire class and individual students to suggest some of their own homework assignments.
10. Some assignments may be made optional for certain students.
11. Give differentiated assignments to students according to their abilities and levels of mastery of previous mathematical materials.
12. At times students may be permitted and even encouraged to work on assignments in pairs or in small groups.
13. Try to encourage equal participation in group work on assignments and discourage copying.
14. Give some assignments that students will find interesting enough to share with their parents.

Evaluating and Grading Assignments

Regardless of how well homework assignments are planned and how conscientious students are in completing them, their full advantage is not realized if the teacher does not carefully evaluate students' work on their assignments by looking for error patterns and specific learning problems. Since teachers usually teach five or six classes of 20 to 40 students each day, it may not be possible to evaluate a set of homework papers from each class every day. Some teachers only give assignments every other day, give sequential assignments that are due at the end of each week, or only read and evaluate student work on selected assignments. None of these procedures is ideal, and it is usually better to give short daily assignments and evaluate students' papers each day by selectively reading and commenting on at least one activity or exercise that is representative of a problem type. In this way error patterns can be found and corrected before they are reinforced through repeated use. At times teachers discuss homework assignments in class the day they are due and students evaluate their own work and discover and correct their own mistakes during the discussion. This procedure permits the teacher to give individual assistance to those students who are having serious difficulties.

The teacher's evaluation of students' work on their homework assignments also serves as an evaluation of the effectiveness of his or her teaching/learning strategies. The fact that most students have trouble with a certain assignment indicates that they either have failed to master prerequisites or that the topic of the assignment should be taught again using a different strategy or a lower level of abstraction. Whatever the cause of the difficulty that students are having with the topic, it is counterproductive to continue on to new topics until they understand the current material.

Although the major reasons that most teachers give for assigning homework are that it helps students learn mathematics and provides information to the teacher about how well each student is mastering material, many teachers use homework, in part, to determine grades for students. Some teachers feel that grades provide an incentive for students to do homework assignments, and that they would have little reason to attend to homework in the absence of this type of reward-and-punishment system for homework. Even the threat of lower grades will not cause some students to do homework and it is hoped that students will learn to value homework for its intrinsic contributions to learning. While grades can be an effective incentive for doing homework, special recognition and privileges can also be used to encourage students to do their assignments. If the steps for assigning homework and the list of special considerations in making assignments, which are given above, are followed, it may not be necessary to use elaborate extrinsic reward systems to get students to do homework. Whatever the intrinsic or extrinsic outcomes from doing homework, students should be "rewarded" for attempting to complete their assignments and should not be "punished" for making errors on their work. These errors, while undesirable, do provide information to the teacher and the student about the nature of and reason for his or her difficulties in learning mathematics.

When homework assignments are included in a mathematics course, teachers should be able to justify their assignments to students, parents and school administrators. Since most parents value homework for their children, they will tend to support your giving interesting and purposeful homework to their children and will encourage, and at times even assist, their children in completing their mathematics homework assignments. However, it is well to remember that parents may have been taught different ways of solving mathematics problems than you are teaching their children; consequently a bit of good humor and diplomacy may be necessary when you are evaluating students' homework that has been done with the assistance of their parents. Rather than saying "your father's method is wrong," it would be better to say "there are several ways to approach most problems and I would prefer that you learn how to do these problems using this method."

Classroom Questioning Strategies

One of the most important activities in teaching and learning mathematics is asking questions. In Chapter 4 you have seen how questions can be developed and used to evaluate students' success in meeting cognitive and affective learning objectives. In Chapters 5 and 6 the importance of asking good questions was emphasized in the discovery, theorem-proving, problem-solving, laboratory, and inquiry teaching/learning models. In fact, questioning is the central activity in most strategies for teaching and learning mathematics and in many procedures for evaluating teaching and learning. George Polya's books on problem solving and mathematical discovery emphasize questioning strategies in learning mathematics and are an excellent source of good questioning strategies for teachers and students to use in the mathematics classroom.

Objectives of Classroom Questioning Strategies

Questioning strategies can be helpful in meeting a variety of learning objectives when using either group or individualized instructional strategies. Group learning activities involve discussions, inquiries and laboratory activities requiring student-to-student and student-to-teacher interactions in the form of questions and answers. In order for a group to solve a problem or arrive at a consensus, the people in the group must resolve general issues regarding procedures and strategies, and formulate and answer specific questions relating to the mathematical objects being considered. Most individualized instructional programs require frequent preassessments to determine students' levels of mastery of prerequisite mathematical objects and postassessments to measure students' progress toward specific learning objectives. These assessments are made by asking questions, either orally or in written form, and if higher level cognitive and affective learning objectives are desired, high level questioning strategies must be used to measure students' success in meeting these objectives.

In order to learn mathematics, students must take an active part in the teaching/learning process. Questions formulated by the teacher can encourage students to participate in class discussions and activities and can help students feel that they have an important and integral role in the classroom. One of the most common problems that teachers have in presenting mathematical objects to a large class of students is lack of student attention. Teacher-directed question, answer and discussion sessions can encourage students to attend to the learning objectives and activities which the teacher is presenting. Questioning strategies in the context of games, puzzles and discovery activities also make mathematics more interesting which, in turn, increases students' motivation to learn mathematics.

Many teachers use question-and-answer sessions very effectively to review topics and units immediately after they have been taught. These review sessions may be used to prepare students for tests or to assure mastery of prerequisites before beginning a new topic. If the teacher takes care to develop good questions, involve each student in asking and answering questions, and encourage class discussions, questioning strategies can be an excellent procedure for reviewing mathematical objects.

Questioning strategies are also used in presenting and discussing new topics. Mathematical facts, skills, concepts and principles can be learned through the use of appropriate questioning techniques. However, research indicates that most teachers emphasize knowledge of facts in their questions and give inadequate attention to higher-level learning objectives such as analysis, synthesis, application, and evaluation of concepts and principles. Questions reflecting each of the six levels of Bloom's Taxonomy of Cognitive Educational Objectives—knowledge, comprehension, application, analysis, synthesis, and evaluation—can and should be used in teaching mathematics and evaluating learning. Several examples of questions and activities for each of these cognitive levels are given in Chapter 4, and you may wish to review these examples at this time. Questions based upon affective educational objectives—receiving, responding, valuing, organization, and characterization by a value or value complex—should also be used in teaching mathematics. Examples of affective objectives, measures, activities and questions are also given in Chapter 4.

The use of good questioning strategies is imperative in discovery, inquiry, problem-solving and theorem-proving models for teaching mathematics. Questioning techniques for use in these models are presented and discussed in Chapter 6, and other questioning strategies can be found in Polya's book *How to Solve It* (1957). When using these teaching/learning models, it is just as important to teach students how to use questioning techniques effectively as it is for the teacher to use them in moderating lessons based upon these models.

Questioning techniques should also be used by teachers to diagnose students' learning difficulties and to evaluate students' mastery of mathematical content. Questions such as the following can help teachers determine whether students comprehend mathematical skills, concepts, and principles and are able to use them in various applications: Why did you set the factors $(x - 4)$ and $(x + 2)$ equal to zero in solving $(x - 4)(x + 2) = 0$? Why is the product of two negative numbers a positive number? Of what use are imaginary numbers? What are the reasons for proving theorems in geometry? Do trigonometric functions have any applications except for solving triangles? How can one determine the limit of a sequence of numbers when it exists? What do we mean by ''area'' in mathematics? What is the difference between algebraic and transcendental numbers?

Nearly all secondary school mathematics teachers use questioning strategies to determine students' grades through tests and quizzes; however some teachers use test questions to measure learning but fail to use them to diagnose error patterns. Questioning procedures for evaluating students' work in mathematics should not only be used to summarize their performances but should also be used to assist them in locating and correcting their error patterns and incorrect conceptualizations of concepts and principles. In addition, students' answers to teachers' questions serve as a means of evaluating the effectiveness of the teaching/learning strategies that are being used.

Types of Questions

The types of questions that teachers and students use in teaching and learning mathematics are closely related to the cognitive and affective learning objectives of lessons. In planning lessons teachers should prepare questions for students as part of their preassessment and postassessment activities and should develop alternative questions to use as part of their teaching/learning strategies. Also, while preparing a lesson, teachers should ask themselves questions relating to the

Developing and Maintaining an Effective Learning Environment

objectives of the lesson and the mathematical content of the lesson. Such questions will lead to the formulation of sound learning objectives, will aid in teaching the lesson, and will help teachers anticipate students' problems in learning the lesson. At times while preparing lessons, most teachers ask questions of themselves about the mathematical content of a lesson and find that they are unable to answer their own questions. An event such as this should cause a teacher to evaluate his or her own knowledge of the mathematics topic being considered and to take appropriate actions to improve his or her own understanding of that topic. Few secondary school teachers know everything about the mathematics topics that they are teaching; part of teaching, for a good teacher, is learning more about the mathematical concepts and principles which he or she is teaching. You will find that many of the questions that you ask yourself while preparing a lesson will also be asked by students in class when you teach that lesson.

The following list of questions illustrates the types of questions that can be used in teaching facts, skills, concepts or principles to meet knowledge, comprehension, application, analysis, synthesis or evaluation cognitive learning objectives:

1. *Knowledge of a Fact:* What are the three methods of representing "2 divided by 3?"
2. *Knowledge of a Skill:* What is the first step in rationalizing the denominator of this fraction— $\dfrac{3}{\sqrt{2}}$?
3. *Knowledge of a Concept:* What is the definition of a mathematical operation?
4. *Knowledge of a Principle:* What is the formula for the volume of a sphere?
5. *Comprehension of a Fact:* Why is x^0 defined to be one when x is not equal to zero?
6. *Comprehension of a Skill:* Why is the quotient $.34\overline{/9.46}$ the same as the quotient $34/946$?
7. *Comprehension of a Concept:* Why is $y = x$ a function while $y^2 = x^2$ is not a function?
8. *Comprehension of a Principle:* Why is division by zero undefined?
9. *Application of a Fact:* What is the product of $\dfrac{3}{4} \times \dfrac{1}{3} \times \dfrac{0}{2}$?
10. *Application of a Skill:* Which is the better buy, a pound of bacon for $1.79 or 12 ounces of the same bacon for $1.19?
11. *Application of a Concept:* Which of these figures are rhombuses? □ △ ○ ◇ ▭
12. *Application of a Principle:* Which lot contains the most land, a right triangular lot having legs 100 m and 80 m or an equilateral triangular lot 100 m on an edge?
13. *Analysis of a Fact:* Why are these statements equivalent? $\log_5 125 = 3$ and $5^3 = 125$
14. *Analysis of a Skill:* Why is the first step in finding the quotient $\dfrac{7}{8} \div \dfrac{3}{4}$ usually given as $\dfrac{7}{8} \times \dfrac{4}{3}$?

15. *Analysis of a Concept:* Why is every function also a relation?
16. *Analysis of a Principle:* Why is every equilateral triangle also equiangular?
17. *Synthesis of Facts:* Peggy is heavier than Mary. Mary is heavier than Susan. Who is heavier, Peggy or Susan?
18. *Synthesis of Skills:* Which is the better buy, ground beef that is 65% lean meat priced at three pounds for $2.00 or ground beef that is 85% lean meat that costs 89¢ per pound?
19. *Synthesis of Concepts:* Why are the integers modulo 5 under addition and multiplication a field?
20. *Synthesis of Principles:* Why does the graph of $y = x^3 - 1$ have only one critical value?
21. *Evaluation of Facts:* After having studied the contributions of the ancient Egyptians, Greeks, and Babylonians to mathematical progress, which civilization do you think made the greatest contribution to the development of algebra?
22. *Evaluation of Skills:* Which method for solving a system of linear equations is the most useful in algebra—graphing, addition and subtraction, substitution, Cramer's Rule?
23. *Evaluation of Concepts:* Mathematical concepts of shape, size, length, and area can be defined using facts and ideas from algebra or facts and ideas from geometry. Which of these methods of defining each of shape, size, length, and area are of the greatest value and utility in mathematics—algebraic definitions of concepts or geometric definitions? Which type of definition is most useful for applications of mathematics in the sciences and engineering?
24. *Evaluation of Principles:* We use several different logical principles to prove mathematical theorems—modus ponens, transitivity, modus tollens, deduction theorem, contraposition, proof by cases, mathematical induction, and indirect arguments. Evaluate and compare these logical principles as a basis of mathematical proof. Which methods are more useful and which are more rigorous? Why?

Many other examples of questioning strategies for teaching and learning mathematics are given in Chapter 6. You may wish to review that chapter as an aid in developing appropriate questioning strategies for use in proving theorems, solving problems, making inquiries and conducting laboratory experiments.

Developing Effective Questioning Strategies
In addition to the suggestions offered in previous chapters for developing effective questioning strategies, the following general principles are helpful in using questioning as a teaching/learning technique in the classroom.

If a student is unable to answer most of the questions put to him or her by the teacher, he or she will come to regard questions as a personal threat rather than a valuable learning aid. The questions that are directed to particular students should be at a level of difficulty appropriate for their mathematical abilities. Poorer mathematics students should be asked questions requiring knowledge of facts and skills before they are presented with questions dealing with higher-level cognitive objectives relating to concepts and principles. Better students should be asked frequent questions requiring the use of higher-level mental processes. One general question may elicit a high-level correct response from an outstanding mathematics student, while a sequence of more specific leading questions may be necessary to obtain a correct response from a less capable student of mathematics. For example, a better student might be able to give an immediate correct response to the question, "What are the solutions to the equation $2x^2 + 5x - 3 = 0$?" While a less proficient student may need a series of questions similar to the following in order to arrive at the correct answer: "To solve this equation we need to factor $2x^2 + 5x - 3$; what are the possible factors of 2, the coefficient of x^2, and of -3, the constant term? What are all of the possible pairs of factors for $2x^2 + 5x - 3$, which can be made from the factors of 2 and -3? Which of these pairs of factors gives the product $2x^2 + 5x - 3$? Now that you have found the factors of $2x^2 + 5x - 3$, what should you do next? After setting $2x - 1$ equal to 0 and $x + 3$ equal to 0, what are the solutions of the quadratic equation, which can be found by solving the linear equations $2x - 1 = 0$ and $x + 3 = 0$?"

When you are using questioning strategies during a mathematics lesson, try to involve each student in the classroom in giving answers. It is very easy to inadvertently permit the better and more extroverted students to dominate the classroom, while less competent or more introverted students are ignored. Direct questions to each student during the lesson and try to ask each student questions that he or she is likely to be able to answer. Also be sure to give each student enough time to formulate an answer before reacting to his or her failure to respond.

During a question-and-answer classroom session it is also well to encourage students to direct questions to you, the teacher, and to each other. This results in a more informal and open classroom environment and also gives you more information to use in evaluating students' knowledge and understanding of the topics being discussed. However, be sure that you do not let a few students dominate the discussion by talking to each other while others in the class are excluded from participating in the discussion.

Carefully consider your responses to students' answers to your questions and your answers to their questions before reacting. Thoughtless teacher responses, which are condescending or threatening, will discourage students from participating in question-and-answer lessons.

Ask questions that cover all types of mathematical objects and all levels of cognitive activities. Do not make the mistake, which some mathematics teachers make, of limiting all of your questions to knowledge and comprehension of facts and skills; although it is obvious that some questions should be asked about facts and skills at the lower cognitive levels. Also ask questions that relate to affective educational objectives which can improve students' attitudes toward mathematics.

In summary, questioning is an effective strategy to use in teaching mathematics and evaluating student learning. However, it requires careful planning before class and carefully considered teacher responses during the lesson so that each student will benefit from its use. Questioning by both the teacher and students is also an important activity in most of the 12 teaching/learning models that are discussed in Chapters 5 and 6.

Diagnosing and Resolving Learning Difficulties

One of the many day-to-day activities of a mathematics teacher should be diagnosing and resolving difficulties that individual students have in learning mathematics. Some students experience only infrequent and minor problems in learning mathematics, while others have continuing problems which are serious impediments to their learning. The large number of books and articles about teaching slow learners, teaching students with learning disabilities, teaching disadvantaged students, and remedial teaching certainly attests to the universality and significance of difficulties that students have in learning mathematics. In most mathematics classes of 20 or more students, the teacher will probably find at least one student who has a significant problem learning mathematics and several other students who have continuing minor problems. It is the responsibility of the mathematics teacher to identify the specific learning difficulties that a student may have and take actions which may be helpful in resolving these problems.

Students' learning difficulties can be classified into eight different categories—sensory problems, mental deficiencies, emotional problems, lack of motivation, cultural disadvantages, social problems, reading problems, and problems within the educational system. Specific problems in learning mathematics which fall under each of these categories will be discussed in this section. Some of these problems can be identified and resolved by the teacher, while others require the services of specially trained resource personnel such as psychologists, physicians, social workers and counselors.

The process of diagnosing and resolving learning difficulties is a problem-solving procedure that can be accomplished using a modification of the general problem-solving model which is discussed in Chapter 6. The steps in helping students resolve their difficulties in learning mathematics are:

1. Both the teacher and the student must be aware of the existence of a learning difficulty.
2. The teacher and the student should attempt to identify particular representations of the difficulty.
3. The teacher and the student should try to identify the causes of the learning difficulty, which may require generating and testing conjectures.
4. The teacher should solicit the assistance of the student in developing procedures for resolving the learning difficulty.
5. The student, with assistance from the teacher, must carry out the procedures that were developed to assist him or her in resolving the learning difficulty.
6. The teacher should evaluate the student's success in resolving his or her difficulty and should also evaluate the procedures that were used to help the student solve his or her learning problem.

In the remainder of this section causes of learning difficulties, techniques for diagnosing learning difficulties and procedures for resolving learning difficulties will be discussed. All of these activities are subsumed under the general six-step procedure, which is given above, for helping students to resolve their difficulties in learning mathematics.

The Causes of Learning Difficulties

Students may have problems in learning mathematics as a result of sensory, mental, emotional, motivational, cultural, social, reading or instructional deficiencies.

Sensory and Speech Related Causes

Some students fail to do well in mathematics courses because they have either visual, auditory or speech defects. A student who has poor eyesight, which is neither detected nor corrected, may fail to comprehend mathematical concepts and principles because he or she is unable to read the definitions, examples and diagrams which the teacher writes on the chalkboard or overhead projector. Students with hearing difficulties may appear to be dull and inattentive because they are unable to hear well enough to distinguish the instructions and questions that are presented by the mathematics teacher. Students who have speech defects may be shy and unresponsive because they are reluctant to answer questions and participate in class discussions for fear of being laughed at by other students or chided by the teacher for being slow in responding. Even though these fears may be unwarranted in many instances, they are, nevertheless, real fears for the student who has a speech defect and may also contribute to the defect itself.

Students who have any of these handicaps—auditory, visual, or oral—may appear to be slow, inattentive, introverted, unresponsive or unmotivated in the mathematics classroom. In fact, any apparent or hidden physical handicap may impair a student's ability or motivation to learn mathematics.

Mental Insufficiencies

A few students may be unable to master mathematical skills, concepts or principles because they have mental deficiencies due to birth defects, minor brain damage, or limited mental abilities for dealing with abstractions. Other students, especially junior high school students, may have problems learning abstract and general mathematical ideas because they have not reached the formal operational stage of mental maturation which is necessary for dealing with abstractions and generalizations.

J. P. Guilford's Structure-of-Intellect Model, which is presented in Chapter 3, hypothesizes 120 distinct intellectual abilities, some of which may be undeveloped in high school students who are experiencing difficulties learning particular mathematical topics. For example, a student who is unable to visualize sets of figures in various positions in space may have trouble with some of the topics in geometry. Teachers should expect even ''normal'' students to experience difficulties in learning certain topics in mathematics because all intellectual abilities do not develop simultaneously in people and some people may never attain certain of the 120 intellectual abilities.

Emotional Causes

All students experience minor emotional difficulties which may temporarily interfere with their learning of mathematics and a few students have serious emotional problems which have a significant and continuing effect upon their ability to learn in school. Increasing population density, environmental pollution, changing social values and loosely knit family patterns have all combined to create high levels of stress on many adolescents. As a consequence there appears to be a higher level of emotional maladjustment among students than was true several years ago. When a usually good student suddenly exhibits signs of poor motivation and inability to learn mathematics, the cause may lie in factors outside the classroom which are causing emotional problems for that student.

Motivational Causes

Lack of motivation to learn mathematics may be caused by other learning problems or may be the result of unpleasant experiences in attempting to learn mathematics. Students who are sound physically, intellectually and emotionally may do poorly in mathematics, even though they do well in other subjects. Some students find that other school subjects are more interesting than mathematics and others see little value in exerting the intellectual effort required to learn mathematics, a subject which doesn't appear to fit into their professional or vocational goals. Other students who do make an effort to learn mathematics may fail to master the subject because they have negative mental sets due to previous failures and frustrations in their mathematics classes. Punishment and other negative events associated with learning mathematics can make the mathematics classroom a distasteful place for even the most able students.

Cultural Causes

Recently governmental units and social, educational and cultural agencies have mounted massive efforts to attempt to remedy the disadvantages that young people born of parents who are unable to provide them with learning opportunities and resources have in our educational system. Some students have trouble learning in school because the culture reflected in their homes is not the same as the culture reflected in their schools. These students may experience barriers to learning mathematics as a consequence of their way of using the English language, the emphasis that their culture places upon formal education, and the resources available in their homes to supplement their learning in school. The goals, objectives and values of the educational system may differ from those found in their culture and in some cases the English language which is used in schools may not be their native tongue. Each teacher should understand that some of his or her students may have grown up in homes reflecting quite different cultural values than those learned by the teacher and reflected in the school system.

Social Causes

Some students may experience problems in learning mathematics because they are unable to adjust to the social system of the school or the classroom. Their friends may not be in their mathematics classes, may be in different schools, or may have dropped out of school. Other students may be social introverts who avoid group activities and other social interactions within the classroom. Students who have recently moved to a new school district may have trouble learning mathematics because they do not have any friends in the class and do not feel that they are part of the social structure of the classroom. Many students neither fit into nor care to participate in the social structure of the school or mathematics classroom, which can have a negative effect upon their progress in mathematics. Social factors can have a profound effect upon students' desire to learn mathematics and their attention to teaching/learning activities designed to promote mastery of mathematical objects.

Reading Difficulties

Although reading mathematics textbooks and other printed materials is only one of many strategies for learning mathematics, general reading problems and the inability to read and understand presentations and explorations of mathematical ideas can cause students to have trouble learning mathematics. The language used in presenting mathematical concepts and principles can have a significant influence upon students' ability to understand these ideas. The importance of reading in solving verbal problems in mathematics is apparent.

A number of research studies have been carried out to determine the effects of language factors upon mathematics learning and to measure correlations between reading ability and mathematical ability in students. Research shows that the choice of language and terminology does affect students' mastery of mathematics and that reading ability and mathematical ability are highly correlated. In other words, students with high reading scores tend to have high mathematics scores and students with low reading scores tend to have low scores in mathematics.

Instructional Deficiencies

While many sources of trouble in learning mathematics are the result of students' physical, mental, emotional, social, and motivational characteristics, the school system and the teacher may be the cause of certain learning problems. Poor physical facilities within the school and lack of instructional materials and resources can have a negative effect upon learning. Teachers who have little interest in teaching can contribute to students' learning difficulties, and teachers who use inappropriate teaching/learning strategies or set low-level learning objectives can expect that their students will experience problems in learning mathematics. When lectures are the primary teaching strategy and memorization is encouraged through objectives and testing, students are unlikely to understand the mathematical skills, concepts and principles that are being presented to them. In order to learn to apply, analyze, synthesize and evaluate mathematical ideas, students must be given practice in using these higher-level cognitive processes. Students will not learn to prove theorems and solve problems if their mathematics teachers treat these complex processes as algorithms to be memorized and applied to problem types. Most, if not all, high school students need to work with concrete representations of abstract concepts and principles in order to comprehend them in a meaningful way.

Techniques for Diagnosing Learning Difficulties

In general, alert, concerned and empathetic teachers who continually discuss learning problems with students and conscientiously develop and evaluate homework assignments, tests and quizzes are the teachers who are most likely to be successful in diagnosing learning problems in individual students. A teacher who "teaches to the class" or the hypothetical "average student," while paying little attention to individual students, is not likely to discover the sources of students' learning difficulties.

Some teachers expect that a percentage of the class should do well, a percentage should do average work, and a percentage should do poorly; these teachers through their teaching, testing, and grading techniques tend to assure that their students meet their performance expectations. Although it may not be possible to turn failing students into "A" students, each teacher does have the responsibility to help every student reach his or her potential and succeed in mastering mathematics at a level appropriate for his or her ability. If you do suspect that a student has some sort of learning handicap because of low achievement scores, you should observe that student for signs of any of the causes of learning difficulties which are discussed above.

Diagnosing Physical Handicaps

Visual, auditory and speech handicaps can be found by observing and working with individual students. If a student usually squints and cranes his or her neck toward the chalkboard or asks you to read what you have written on the board, he or she probably has a visual problem. Sight problems are also indicated by students who read with their noses close to the page or who hold the book at arm's length while reading. The student who always appears to be daydreaming and usually responds to your questions with "Huh?" may have a hearing problem. If you suspect that a student has either of these problems, speak to him or her privately, but phrase your questions diplomatically. Rather than asking public questions such as "Is there something wrong with your ears?" or "Can't you read what's in front of your face?", privately ask questions such as, "Do you have trouble reading my writing on the board?" or "Do you find that I don't speak loudly enough in class?" Questions such as the latter two do not pose a threat to the student and are not likely to elicit defensive responses. Speech handicaps are obvious and should be dealt with sympathetically and sensitively.

Diagnosing Mental Handicaps

If a student tries hard to learn mathematics and makes a sincere effort to do homework and participate in classroom activities but still is unable to master mathematics, it may be that he or she has a mental insufficiency. Students who have severe problems in mastering mathematics may require special instructional programs and resources. If the entire class fails to comprehend a new concept or principle, the cause may rest with your approach to the topic; however if only a few students have problems it may be because they do not have the specific intellectual ability to learn that specific topic in the manner in which you presented it.

The best way to diagnose the occasional and specific learning problems which all students have is through careful selection of homework exercises and test questions and careful analysis of each student's work which resulted in a wrong answer. Many error patterns can be discovered by analyzing students' incorrect algorithms as they are exemplified in the students' solutions to in-class and homework exercises. Try to find the exact cause of each wrong answer. You will usually find that one or two misconceptions or incorrect procedures will account for the incorrect answers to an entire class of problems. Another good way to discover error patterns which particular students are making is to ask students to solve problems at their seats or at the chalkboard. You can look over a student's shoulder and observe each specific error as he or she makes it.

Certain errors may be due to common misunderstandings, others may occur because the student lacks one of Guilford's 120 intellectual aptitudes, and still others may be due to serious mental handicaps. If a student continually makes the same type of error on a whole class of different but related problems or consistently fails to master materials requiring a certain type of mental operation, he or she is probably deficient in one or several of the aptitudes identified by Guilford. A student who appears to be at a total loss in learning mathematics, no matter how hard he or she tries, may have a more serious intellectual problem. The occasional, isolated learning difficulty is no cause for alarm and usually can be resolved through some individual teacher assistance to students when these minor problems occur.

Diagnosing Emotional Problems

While the occasional bad mood or misbehavior of a student is to be expected, prolonged depression, withdrawal, or misbehavior may indicate a more serious emotional problem. A serious emotional problem, which can interfere with a student's ability to learn in school, can be caused by a variety of situations. Among the situations that can cause emotional problems are ingestion of drugs, lack of sleep, improper diet, certain types of illness, a poor self image due to failure or criticism, serious personal problems, participation in too many activities, pressures to do well in school and home responsibilities. A radical change in behavior lasting for a period of a week or more may indicate a serious emotional problem in a student.

When a normally alert and active student becomes inactive or lackadaisical it may be a sign that he or she is emotionally disturbed as a consequence of either a physical or psychological problem. Taking certain prescription medicines for an illness, lack of sleep, improper diet, or experimenting with certain drugs can cause normally active students to become quiet and withdrawn. Hyperactivity in a student may be caused by using certain kinds of drugs, social pressures, a dietary problem, or a medical problem. In general, any significant and prolonged deviation from usual behavior may be a symptom of a serious emotional problem in a student.

Diagnosing Motivational Problems

Repeated absences from school, cutting class, failure to do homework assignments, and refusal to participate in class, while possibly being indications of more serious emotional or social problems, may be due to lack of interest and motivation in learning mathematics. If a student who does not appear to have a physical, emotional, or social problem indicates a lack of interest in learning mathematics, he or she probably lacks motivation. Motivational problems can be caused by repeated failures in trying to learn mathematics, unpleasant experiences in the mathematics classroom, personality clashes between the student and the teacher, or failure to see any purpose in learning mathematics. The student who lacks motivation to learn mathematics will indicate his or her disinterest by withdrawing from classroom participation and related teaching/learning activities.

Diagnosing Cultural Impediments to Learning

When a student has trouble learning mathematics but no physical, mental, emotional, social, or school-related factors appear to be the cause, it may be that the problem is caused by cultural factors reflected in the student's home life. The student may come from a disadvantaged home where the things that are taught in school are not valued and supported by his or her family. The culture of which the student is a part may not consider school in general and mathematics in particular as an appropriate way to prepare for life and earning a living.

According to John Wilson and Mildred C. Robeck in a chapter in *Diagnosis of Learning Difficulties* edited by Wilson (1971):

> Each ethnic group has cultural advantages that distinguish it as a group. These culture patterns are learned by the child before he enters school. The traditions of any people can become disadvantageous when new or different modes of life become desirable. Cultural disadvantage is the inhibition, reactive or proactive, of past acculturation on a present learning situation.
>
> Some culture-oriented learnings are more likely to become barriers to change than others. A mother tongue, when different from the national language, interferes progressively as the individual advances in age before beginning to learn a new language. Because of a passion to fulfill the "melting pot" interpretation of democracy in the United States, a temptation has persisted to eliminate or even destroy the assets of the first language in order to teach English. The compulsory discarding of a person's language, whether dialectic or foreign, may make him feel that his whole culture is being discarded and that he is being downgraded. . . .
>
> Some ethnic groups have desired integration and have themselves rejected "old country" ways. But others, most notably the American Indians, needed to retain their cultural identity in a hostile environment. Recently many Negroes have recognized their exclusion from the melting pot and have attempted to reconstruct a cultural identity that includes all black groups. An attendant hostility toward the central group is likely to interfere with otherwise effective reinforcement schedules in school.
>
> Cultural disadvantage can result from any marked deviation from the social or economic mainstream. (p. 190)

If you have students in your classes who are having problems learning mathematics and are also outside the "social or economic mainstream," there is a possibility that their problems may be caused, in part, by cultural influences. Even though these cultural influences may be largely positive and of value to the individual, they may be inadvertently having a negative effect upon that person's attempts to learn in a school which is based upon a different set of cultural values.

Diagnosing Social Problems in Learning

Adolescents in secondary schools are profoundly influenced by social interactions with each other; their quest for peer approval may, at times, interfere with their learning in school. Students who are unable to win the approval of other students and are not accepted as part of a social group in school may withdraw from classroom activities because they don't feel that they fit into the social structure of the school. Some students may become discipline problems in attempts to get attention from the teacher and other students, while others may purposely do poorly in mathematics because their friends are not good mathematics students. The desire to belong to social peer groups and to behave in the same manner as other students can influence students' attitudes toward learning mathematics and their performance in mathematics classrooms.

A student who has social problems may attempt to monopolize the teacher's attention during lunch periods, free periods, and study halls in order to become friends with the teacher to compensate for his or her lack of friends among fellow students. Students who brag about not doing homework assignments and not studying for tests are usually trying to win approval from other students. A student who tries to disrupt the class, get the teacher off the subject, or monopolize classroom discussions and laboratory sessions may be trying to gain attention and approval from other students through these actions rather than through academic achievement. Other students feel so many social pressures to excel academically that they push themselves for grades and teacher approval to the point that their studies can interfere with their social and emotional development, and in some cases their physical and mental health. Social considerations have considerable influence upon most high school students and can seriously interfere with some students' learning in mathematics courses. In general, students who are either overly extroverted or extremely introverted in mathematics classrooms may be reacting to social pressures from other students or, in some cases, from their parents.

Diagnosing Reading Problems

Although most secondary school students are able to read the words in their textbooks, some students do have trouble reading the words in their mathematics textbooks and others are unable to comprehend what they read. You can determine whether a student's difficulties in learning mathematics may be due, in part, to reading problems by asking him or her to read aloud textbook passages explaining skills, concepts and principles and to interpret each sentence as it is read. You will find that some students are able to read the words correctly but do not understand what they mean. When reading statement problems and explanations, either silently or aloud, some students will skip key words or phrases or add information which is not printed in the passages that they are reading. The best way for a mathematics teacher to determine whether students' difficulties in mathematics are caused by reading and comprehension problems is to ask students to read textbook passages aloud and interpret them line by line. In this way many reading and comprehension problems will become apparent to the perceptive teacher.

Diagnosing Instructional Deficiencies

When most of the students in the class have trouble learning a mathematics topic, the cause may lie in the instructional strategies that the teacher is using. Strategies for evaluating the effectiveness of one's teaching methods are discussed in Chapters 4, 5, and 6. Even when only a few students fail to learn a particular topic, the cause may still be found in the instructional strategies. It may be that the methods being used to teach the material are not appropriate for the particular learning styles of some students. Carefully constructed sequences of test questions and learning activities may give some information about interactions between student learning characteristics and teaching methods. Conferences with individual students may also aid in diagnosing instructional deficiencies. Questions asked by students in class and the oral answers that they give to your questions can also help to locate specific deficiencies in your teaching methods. When students continually request additional examples of concepts and principles, it may be that your explanations and examples are too abstract for them to comprehend. In general, when diagnosing learning difficulties, a teacher should search for causes in his or her own teaching techniques as well as in student characteristics such as attitudes, behaviors and ability levels.

Procedures for Resolving Learning Difficulties

Most school systems now employ specially trained personnel to deal with more serious learning difficulties which classroom teachers are not trained to handle. However, teachers are expected to diagnose serious learning handicaps in students and to request special assistance when it is needed. Many of the less serious learning problems that students have can be both diagnosed and resolved by secondary school teachers.

Dealing with Sensory and Speech Problems

Teachers can help students with minor visual or hearing problems by seating students with either problem near the front of the room. Teachers should speak loudly enough, and encourage students to speak loudly and distinctly, so that students with auditory problems will be able to hear what is being said in class. When the teacher finds that a student has a serious hearing problem, he or she should make a point to get that student's attention before asking questions and should speak directly toward the student who has this problem. A well-lighted room can help students with visual problems, and such students should not be seated in dark corners of the classroom. Teachers should also be certain that the comments which they write on students' papers and the information which is written on the chalkboard or overhead projector is large and clear. When using audio-visual resources, films should be sharply in focus and the sound should be distinct and relatively loud, although not so loud that it may harm the hearing of students who do not have auditory problems.

Minor speech problems should be handled with patience and understanding. Students who stutter or have trouble forming words will need additional time to answer questions and make comments in class. Trying to make such students hurry their responses will only increase their difficulties. If students who have speech defects appear to be embarrassed about their problem, it may be well not to force them to respond orally in class or to answer questions or participate in discussions when visitors are present.

Serious visual, auditory or speech problems should be called to the attention of the school counselor or principal, who will contact students' parents. Sometimes specialists in dealing with each particular problem may be able to alleviate the difficulty or help the student compensate for his or her problem.

Compensating for Mental Insufficiencies

Probably the best advice that can be given to teachers regarding their treatment of students who lack some of the mental abilities required in learning mathematics is not to blame the students for their intellectual limitations. Although modern society has learned to treat physically handicapped people compassionately, many people (even some teachers) still tend to deal with people who have limited intellectual abilities as though they are willfully slow in learning. Slow learners in mathematics should be given extra time to complete assignments, should be assisted in setting learning objectives that they will be able to meet, and should be given many concrete representations of abstract mathematical ideas. Individualized assignments, classroom activities, and preassessment and postassessment instruments may be necessary in order to help slower students attain minimal mastery of mathematics skills.

Guidance counselors, school psychologists and testing specialists will be able to help you locate and use tests designed to identify and measure specific mental abilities. After you have identified the specific intellectual problems which a slower student has, there are two general approaches for dealing with the situation. You can help the student improve his or her deficient abilities or you can design teaching/learning activities to compensate for or bypass the student's intellectual insufficiencies. In most cases a combination of these two approaches is the most effective way to help students overcome their learning difficulties. Special mathematics exercises and activities can be prepared to help students strengthen specific intellectual abilities while other activities can be designed so that students can apply their stronger mental abilities in learning mathematics. For example, students who have trouble dealing with several characteristics of a mathematical concept simultaneously should be given practice in identifying relevant and irrelevant dimensions of many different mathematics concepts. Students who are unable to deal with mathematical abstractions may be able to learn mathematics skills, concepts and principles by working with concrete representations of these objects.

Some people do have severe intellectual handicaps, and these students may be assigned to special courses and programs where specially educated teachers can help them learn basic skills. Other students who are quite intelligent in some areas may not possess some of the unique abilities required of the mathematician. It may be that such students need not and should not take a complete sequence of secondary school mathematics courses. Mastery of basic arithmetic skills may suffice for some students who are only unhappy, frustrated, and unsuccessful in higher-level mathematics courses.

Overcoming Emotional Difficulties

Students who are seriously disturbed emotionally may require special counseling and assistance outside the classroom; however there are many things that teachers can do to help students who have moderate emotional difficulties. Since most emotional problems are caused by stress, you should protect students from further stress in your classroom and provide interesting and satisfying activities for them. School-related problems and pressures will only increase a student's emotional disturbance. When you find that a student has an emotional problem, it may be well to permit him or her to hand in homework assignments late or take a test when he or she is ready. Do not press students to give a great deal of attention to learning mathematics when they are attempting to deal with the problems that are causing their emotional difficulties.

Disturbed students may need someone with whom they can discuss their problems. In many cases they will select a favorite teacher, who may be you, to help them deal with their stresses. You may be able to help emotionally disturbed students by merely being friendly, considerate and understanding. At times teachers can assist disturbed students by being a friend or counselor to them. A relaxed, friendly and cooperative mathematics classroom may be a haven for the disturbed student who can temporarily escape from troubles by involving himself or herself in interesting mathematical pursuits.

Motivating Students to Learn Mathematics

Many physically, emotionally, and intellectually able students do poorly in their mathematics classes because they are not interested in mathematics and do not see much value in learning mathematics. Although a few students have become so alienated from school that little can be done to motivate them to learn mathematics, most unmotivated students can be helped to learn to appreciate and value mathematics as an interesting and useful subject. Several specific techniques for motivating students to learn mathematics are discussed in Chapters 5 and 6 and many of the teaching/learning resources for mathematics classrooms and laboratories are designed to increase student motivation.

In general, most students can be motivated to learn mathematics if their teachers show an interest in each individual student, are enthusiastic about mathematics themselves, and select interesting problems and activities for students to use in learning mathematics. Teachers should show students interesting applications of mathematics, should use a variety of teaching/learning models in presenting lessons, and should give students some measure of control over the activities that are used in learning mathematics. Teachers who follow the suggestions for planning mathematics lessons that are presented in Chapter 4 and who make appropriate use of the teaching/learning models discussed in Chapters 5 and 6 will find that most of their students will be positively motivated to learn mathematics.

Responding to Cultural Influences upon Learning

Culture-related problems in learning in school are seldom caused by deficiencies in particular cultures; they are usually caused by teachers' failures to understand and value the cultures of their students. Mathematics teachers should accept the fact that people whose life styles reflect various cultures have different ways of expressing themselves, use different speech patterns, behave differently, and have different attitudes and values. Attempts by mathematics teachers to impose their cultural values upon their students can have serious negative influences upon students' attitudes toward learning mathematics. Teachers should respect cultural differences among students and should build upon these differences in teaching mathematics. Even though a mathematics teacher's prejudices and inappropriate generalizations about certain cultural or ethnic groups may remain unstated, his or her treatment of students who are "different" can result in mutual disrespect between these "different" students and the teacher, which can cause students to develop negative attitudes toward learning mathematics. The best way to avoid creating learning problems as a consequence of cultural and ethnic differences is to treat all students the same; that is, treat each student with respect, sincerity and concern for his or her welfare.

Certain federal, state and private agencies have developed programs to assist students from economically and socially deprived families and to aid students whose cultural differences, such as language, may interfere with their learning in school. Many schools whose students come from families with low incomes are entitled to funds to improve the quality of education for these students. You may be able to obtain such funds, through your school district, to purchase teaching/ learning resources for use in your mathematics courses.

Dealing with Social Problems

Students who are excluded by other students from the social structure of the mathematics classroom may be retiring and unresponsive in class, while students who are seeking attention will engage in various activities that disrupt the classroom learning environment. Students who are excluded or ignored by other students may benefit from special attention by the teacher. You should attempt to involve these people in class discussions by talking to them, asking them questions, encouraging them to respond to statements by other students and encouraging other students to respond to their statements. Be sure to give these students their share of public recognition for exceptionally well-done homework assignments or well-written examination papers. At times you may be able to encourage socially shy students to complete projects such as building mathematical models, solving logic problems, or constructing visual aids which other students will find interesting. Many of these quiet students have special talents, interests and hobbies in which other students may want to become involved. You should attempt to make these students feel that they do have a place in the social structure of the classroom.

In order to keep the socially over-active student from disrupting the orderly conduct of mathematics lessons, it may be necessary to speak with him or her privately. At times you may be able to direct this student's energies into constructive attention-getting activities such as special mathematics projects that will provide him or her with the approval of fellow students.

It may be necessary to seek help from the school counselor or psychologist to deal with a student who is severely maladjusted socially. Such students need understanding and counseling, and pressures to "fit in" or adjust will only aggravate their social problems.

Dealing with Students' Reading Problems

Occasionally students reach secondary school without having learned to read, and other high school students are poor readers. If you find that a student in one of your mathematics classes has a serious reading problem, you should seek assistance from a counselor, the school principal, or a reading specialist. Many schools have special remedial courses and programs to help high school students learn to read.

You will probably find that many secondary school students have difficulty reading mathematics textbooks and comprehending what they read. Not only does the teacher have the responsibility to teach mathematics to students, but he or she should also teach them how to learn mathematics through independent study of mathematics textbooks. You can help students learn how to read and comprehend mathematics textbooks by giving them time in class to read and discuss explanations and examples in their textbooks. At times it is also well to read to students from the textbook while interpreting each new idea and clarifying examples as you read them. You will also find that asking students to read explanations and statement problems aloud from their textbooks will assist them in locating their own particular difficulties in reading and interpreting mathematics textbooks. Tell students to read textbooks slowly, to pause and think about each new concept or principle, and to use pencil and paper to work out details of example exercises and proofs by supplying additional steps to clarify the textbook presentation. Some teachers find that a student's reading ability can be improved by giving homework assignments that require him or her to write an explanation of a mathematical idea, which other students could read to help them better understand the idea.

Correcting Instructional Deficiencies
The teacher who evaluates the effectiveness of each lesson will usually find deficiencies in his or her teaching methods as soon as they occur. Regular evaluations of lessons and adjustments of lesson plans are the most effective approach to correcting instructional deficiencies. Evaluating teaching effectiveness has already been discussed in Chapters 4, 5, and 6, and more will be said about evaluation later in this chapter. When students are unable to master a mathematics topic in your classroom, you should first ask the question, "What's wrong with my teaching methods?" before asking, "What's wrong with my students?"

Maintaining Discipline in the Classroom

An important consideration in teaching and learning mathematics is maintaining student discipline. Discipline problems are a major cause of teacher ineffectiveness and many teachers who leave the teaching profession do so because they are unable to maintain a disciplined classroom environment. One of the main concerns of inexperienced teachers is their ability to maintain student discipline in their classrooms; student teachers are particularly concerned with the possiblity of discipline problems. In general, classroom discipline involves conductng worthwhile activities in each class session so that students can learn mathematics in an efficient and effective manner. In his book *Teacher and Child,* Haim Ginott (1972) uses the following anecdote to illustrate a sound approach to handling potential discipline problems:

> A teacher was about to give his first lesson in a school for delinquent boys. He was very apprehensive. Success and failure hinged on this first meeting. As the teacher walked briskly to his desk, he stumbled and fell. The class roared in hilarious laughter. The teacher rose slowly, straightened up, and said, "This is my first lesson to you: A person can fall flat on his face and still rise up again." Silence descended. Then came applause. The message was received. (p. 147)

Approaches to Discipline
The immediate objectives to be met through a well-disciplined mathematics classroom are obvious. Very little learning will occur in a chaotic classroom and the learning that does take place is not likely to be related to the teacher's cognitive and affective objectives for the lesson. Learning mathematics requires attention, concentration and student involvement in each lesson. Extremely noisy, unstructured, and undisciplined classrooms are not good situations for students to learn mathematics.

There are also several general societal-related goals which can and should be accomplished through the enforcement of discipline in schools. Ausubel (1961) describes these goals of discipline as follows:

Discipline is a universal cultural phenomenon which generally serves four important functions in the training of the young. First, it is necessary for socialization—for learning the standards of conduct that are approved and tolerated in any culture. Second, it is necessary for normal personality maturation—for acquiring such adult personality traits as dependability, self-reliance, self-control, persistence, and ability to tolerate frustration. These aspects of maturation do not occur spontaneously, but only in response to sustained social demands and expectations. Third, it is necessary for the internalization of moral standards and obligations or, in other words, for the development of conscience. Standards obviously cannot be internalized unless they also exist in external form; and even after they are effectively internalized, universal cultural experience suggests that external sanctions are still required to insure the stability of the social order. Lastly, discipline is necessary for children's emotional security. Without the guidance provided by unambiguous external controls, the young tend to feel bewildered and apprehensive. Too great a burden is placed on their own limited capacity for self-control. (p. 28)

There are two distinct approaches to dealing with discipline. One school of thought which is exemplified by Haim Ginott (1972), advocates complete avoidance of punishment when dealing with discipline problems. Ginott has said that:

The essence of discipline is finding effective alternatives to punishment. To punish a child is to enrage him and make him uneducable. He becomes a hostage of hostility, a captive of rancor, a prisoner of vengeance. Suffused with rage and absorbed in grudges, a child has no time or mind for studying. (pp. 147-148)

David Ausubel (1961) has argued that negative forms of discipline are necessary in teaching children. Ausubel says that:

According to one widely held doctrine, only "positive" forms of discipline are constructive and democratic. It is asserted that children must only be guided by reward and approval; that reproof and punishment are authoritarian, repressive, and reactionary expressions of adult hostility which leave permanent emotional scars on children's personalities. What these theorists conveniently choose to ignore, however, is the fact that it is impossible for children to learn what is *not* approved and tolerated simply by generalizing in reverse from the approval they receive for behavior that *is* acceptable. Merely by rewarding honesty and good manners one cannot, for example, teach children that dishonesty and rudeness are socially unacceptable traits. Even adults are manifestly incapable of learning and respecting the limits of acceptable conduct unless the distinction between what is proscribed and approved is reinforced by punishment as well as by reward. Furthermore, there is good reason to believe that acknowledgement of wrong-doing and acceptance of punishment are part and parcel of learning moral accountability and developing a sound conscience. Few if any children are quite so fragile that they cannot take deserved reproof and punishment in stride. (pp. 28-29)

In teaching and learning high school mathematics, I have found that positive reinforcement of desired behaviors is a better way to maintain discipline than punishment for inappropriate behavior. However, there are many instances in schools when it is necessary to impose judicious punishment upon students who continually disrupt teaching and learning in the classroom. Unfortunately, Ausubel appears to be correct in his observation that some people "are manifestly incapable of learning and respecting the limits of acceptable conduct unless the distinction between what is proscribed and approved is reinforced by punishment as well as by reward."

In managing a mathematics classroom, there are two kinds of situations that can lead to discipline problems. A student may either become involved in undesirable behaviors or may refrain from participating in desirable activities. In either case a response from the teacher is needed. In the former situation the teacher's job is to cause the student to *desist* from what he or she is doing and in the latter case the teacher wants to *engage* the student in doing something that he or she is not presently doing. Educational researchers have identified six variables in teachers' responses to either desist or engage situations; they are clarity, firmness, roughness, intensity, focus, and student treatment.

Clarity refers to how much information the teacher provides in his or her response. A teacher should be careful to give a desist or engage instruction directly to the student or group of students for which it is intended. The teacher should also tell the student or students precisely what is to be done. An instruction such as, "Susan, would you please stop talking to Herb and begin working on your homework assignment," is usually more effective than saying, "All right, everyone get to work."

Firmness is the degree of definiteness and imperativeness that the teacher puts into his or her treatment of a behavior problem. A teacher's attitude, facial expression, or tone of voice indicates whether he or she really means what he or she is instructing students to do. Some teachers in trying to quiet a noisy class will say, "All right, let's be quiet," every few minutes with no noticeable effect upon the noise level. However, a direct statement such as, "Larry, if you don't turn around and begin working on your homework, alone, you are going to be in trouble," will usually cause Larry to be quiet, at least temporarily.

Roughness refers to the degree of anger, frustration, or exasperation expressed by the teacher in a desist or engage order. A stern facial expression, an angry voice, a threat, or an actual punishment are examples of different types and degrees of roughness. The degree of roughness used in reprimanding a student should depend upon the student's sensitivity level, the seriousness of the offense, and the nature of the response expected from the student.

Intensity is the attention-getting level of the teacher's action and its potential to intrude upon the awareness of the class. If the teacher's command can not be distinguished from ordinary classroom noises, the intensity of the command is low. If the teacher's response gets the immediate attention of the entire class, it is of high intensity. Low-intensity responses that will not disturb other students are most appropriate for disciplining a single student who has committed a minor infraction. High-intensity responses are most effective when dealing with a more serious discipline problem involving a large subset of the class.

Focus refers to the object that the teacher concentrates upon in his or her desist or engage order. Is the teacher focusing upon an action that is to be stopped or an activity that is to be started? Does the teacher direct attention to the situation resulting from a student's misbehavior or does he or she focus upon the student's personal characteristics? Ginott (1972) advocates focusing upon the effects of a discipline problem rather than upon the character of the perpetrator.

415

For example, when a student consistently talks in class and disturbs your lecture or other students' study activities, it is better to say, "Paul, please be quiet; you're disturbing my concentration and interfering with everyone else's attempts to understand this idea," rather than saying, "Shut up, Paul. You're an inconsiderate loudmouth." The former response concentrates upon the undesirable effects of Paul's behavior, while the latter focuses attention upon Paul's character which may only cause resentment and reinforce Paul's dislike for mathematics.

Student treatment refers to how the student was disciplined by the teacher. Did the teacher treat the child as a friend who is being corrected for making an error in judgment or as an unsavory troublemaker who is regarded as an enemy of the teacher? When disciplining students it is always well to avoid treating them as juvenile delinquents or incorrigible troublemakers.

As you can see, these six variables in teachers' responses to discipline problems are interrelated. The clarity, firmness, roughness, intensity, focus, and student treatment contained in a teacher's response to a behavioral misadventure will depend upon the seriousness of the discipline problem.

Causes of Discipline Problems

The previous topic in this chapter deals with diagnosing students' learning difficulties, and any of the eight learning problems that are discussed there could be a cause of a discipline problem. A student's sensory handicaps, mental deficiencies, emotional problems, lack of motivation, cultural disadvantages, social problems, or reading problems, as well as problems resulting from poor instruction, can interfere with his or her learning of mathematics. Students who are having trouble learning are likely candidates for discipline problems. A student who is frustrated because he or she is unable to learn in school may retaliate against the educational system by engaging in unacceptable behavior such as disrupting classes, abusing teachers, breaking rules and destroying school property.

Threats from a teacher or confrontations with a teacher may menace a student's ego which could trigger defensive reactions resulting in retaliation against the teacher. When accused by a teacher in front of other students, a student may feel that he or she must engage in and win an argument with the teacher in order to maintain stature in the class.

If a teacher does not set consistent rules and standards of conduct and enforce them fairly, students may react by constantly testing the teacher's rules and tolerance of misbehavior. If the teacher fails to use fair and consistent evaluation and grading procedures, an entire class may "rebel" against that teacher. Although students at times behave irrationally, inconsistently and improperly, they expect teachers to be controlled, consistent and fair at all times in their treatment of students. When minor discipline problems and violations of rules are not dealt with promptly, they may escalate into more serious behavioral problems which are difficult to correct.

The teacher is also looked to as an exemplar of behavior and standards; students can not be expected to refrain from activities that the teacher engages in or to do things that the teacher does not do. A teacher should not attempt to force dress codes or standards of behavior upon his or her students if he or she does not abide by the same codes or standards. The "do-what-I-say-not-what-I-do" approach to student behavior is not a very effective way of dealing with discipline problems.

In order for punishment and penalties to be effective in extinguishing undesirable behaviors, they must be appropriate for the misconduct. When a teacher overreacts to a student's minor infraction by handing out a severe penalty, that student may vent his or her anger and frustration through more serious infractions of rules of conduct. By the same token, teachers who set either academic or behavioral standards that are too high for their students to meet may cause anger and frustration in students which result in discipline problems. "Failure-oriented classrooms" usually are classrooms with discipline problems.

Be sure to differentiate between students who are merely being mischievous in order to attract attention and those few students who are serious troublemakers. The mischievous student can be dealt with lightly and with humor; however the student who has serious behavior problems may need professional assistance which is beyond your capability as a mathematics teacher.

Some discipline problems are caused by poor teaching and insensitive teachers; however other discipline problems result from personal problems and characteristics of students which are beyond the direct control of the teacher. The causes of most discipline problems are usually found somewhere between these two extremes—all students are basically good and only behave badly because they have poor teachers, and when a discipline problem occurs, the student is always at fault.

Preventing Discipline Problems

Although all teachers are confronted with occasional discipline problems in their classrooms, there are a number of techniques which can be used to keep these problems to a minimum. The first meeting of a new class is the best time to establish the pattern of behavior that you expect from students in your classroom. Since there are many non-instructional activities to attend to on the first day of school, some teachers do not attempt to teach mathematics. They spend the first class meeting handing out textbooks, collecting data from students, organizing the classroom, and filling out record books while the students have little to do. Energetic adolescents who are seated in a large group in a small classroom for forty-five minutes become restless and look for ways to occupy their time. They will talk to each other, shout across the room, create minor disturbances, try to annoy the teacher, and move around the room and in and out of the classroom. Although none of these activities need escalate into serious discipline problems, as a group they tend to establish a pattern of discipline which is not what you want in your classroom.

It is much better to spend the first class meeting teaching mathematics by presenting new mathematical ideas and by having students discuss mathematics and work on mathematics exercises at their seats or at the chalkboard. If you prepare and teach the first lesson in each course so that every student is kept quite busy doing mathematics, you will have established your classroom as a place where everyone is expected to work hard and attend to learning mathematics. It is also well to give a homework assignment which is due to be completed for the next class meeting. If you attend to teaching mathematics the first day of school, students will know that you are going to be well prepared for each class and that your classroom is a place where serious learning activities are expected. It is well to be very firm and businesslike for the first several weeks of each new mathematics course and to keep all of your students actively involved in learning mathematics so that they will get a sense of the importance that you place upon teaching and learning mathematics.

Do not attempt to make friends with your students during the first few class meetings by showing them that you are a "fun" person and that your classroom is a place to "mess around" or to "take a break." During the first week of school you should earn the respect of your students because you are a competent mathematics teacher; you will earn their admiration and friendship later. Sometimes inexperienced teachers think that they can "win the students over" by joking around, playing games and permitting them to set their own standards of classroom conduct. This laissez faire approach to teaching usually results in an undisciplined classroom, student behavior problems and a minimum of learning. Once you have allowed students to establish poor learning and behavioral patterns, much time and effort is needed to extinguish these inappropriate patterns and to replace them with disciplined patterns of behavior.

There are routine administrative matters which must be attended to in class sessions. You should handle announcements, data collection activities and record keeping quickly and efficiently so that students realize that you consider such work to be less important than the business of learning mathematics. In some classrooms it seems, unfortunately, that procedural matters take precedence over academic affairs and teaching and learning mathematics must be squeezed into the time remaining after attention is given to less important matters.

As a teacher you are not necessarily better than your students; however your role is different from the roles of students. Students expect you to be a leader, to exhibit exemplary conduct, and to set standards for student conduct. You are not just "one of the gang" in the classroom and you should not attempt to assume that role. In order for students to look to you for counseling, assistance in learning mathematics, and standards of conduct, you must accept a position of authority and earn the respect of your students. But you need not, and should not, become an inflexible dictator and act as though you consider yourself to be infallible. A sense of humor and a willingness to compromise, when a compromise is in order, are necessary characteristics for teachers who must maintain an orderly classroom and an effective learning environment.

You should also be thoroughly familiar with all of the rules and standards for teacher and student conduct which are set by the board of education and the administration of your school system. Most schools have a printed bulletin containing the rights and responsibilities of students and another bulletin describing the rights and responsibilities of teachers. If the teachers in your school are represented by a bargaining agent (teachers' union) in dealing collectively with the school board and administration, many of the regulations governing teacher behavior may be included in a contract between the school board and the teachers' organization. Not only could your failure to enforce and abide by school regulations meet with disapproval from your principal, it could also result in your dismissal from your teaching position.

In dealing with students, you should enforce the school's standards and permit students their rights as stated in the students' code of rights and responsibilities. You will also need to set specific standards of conduct and behavior for your own classroom but your particular rules should be consistent with school-wide regulations. For example, if school regulations permit students to wear hats in class and male students to have beards, then you should not forbid hats and beards in your classroom. However, you may want to set standards of social behavior and interactions which may be unique to your classroom. If you set fair and reasonable standards of conduct and enforce them evenly for all students at all times, you can prevent many potential discipline problems from occurring. If you set unreasonable standards for your students, continually change the rules of conduct, enforce standards unevenly, or give rewards and punishments inconsistently, you will no doubt create discipline problems in your classroom. Students are quite concerned with fairness and consistency and they need to know precisely what the rules are, how they will be enforced, and what penalties will be assessed when rules are broken.

While many discipline problems occur in students through no fault of teachers, others can be prevented if teachers follow a few simple rules of conduct in dealing with students. The following list of "dos" and "do nots" is of use to the teacher who wants guidelines for preventing discipline problems in his or her classroom:

1. Do be well prepared for each of your classes.
2. Do use student-centered teaching and learning activities.
3. Do make fair and sensible rules and enforce them.
4. Do share your rules with students and explain your rationale for each rule.
5. Do involve students in setting rules of classroom conduct.
6. Do be willing to compromise.
7. Do use a variety of teaching/learning activities in your classroom.
8. Do give students opportunities to talk, move about, and express themselves in your classroom.
9. Do engage in high-level professional conduct at all times.
10. Do learn your students' names quickly and address each student by name.
11. Do take a sincere interest in students' out-of-school activities.

1. Don't try to "kill" time in class by setting useless tasks for students.
2. Don't make arbitrary and useless rules to show your authority or to punish students.
3. Don't punish the wrong student for a classroom altercation.
4. Don't punish the entire class for the misbehavior of a few students.
5. Don't be a rigid and inflexible disciplinarian.
6. Don't be spiteful and hold a grudge.
7. Don't attempt to "get even" with students for things that they have said or done to you.
8. Don't lose your patience or self control.
9. Don't use corporal punishment. (Many schools forbid it, and parents object to it.)
10. Don't take yourself too seriously.

12. Do become involved in extra-curricular student-centered activities.
13. Do use sincere positive reinforcements.
14. Do be patient with students when they occasionally misbehave.
15. Do use a variety of positive reinforcements.
16. Do be consistent in your treatment of students.
17. Do remember that adolescents are energetic and can be overly exuberant at times.
18. Do tell students' parents about their children's successes.
19. Do establish routines and rules of conduct at the beginning of each course.
20. Do give individual attention to each student.
21. Do admit your mistakes.
22. Do be sure that each student has some measure of success and status in your classroom.
23. Do have a sense of humor and be able to laugh at yourself.
24. Do solicit your students' respect and cooperation.
25. Do keep your own temper under control.
26. Do enforce school regulations.
27. Do treat students with kindness and courtesy.

11. Don't expect the principal or guidance counselor to handle all of your discipline problems.
12. Don't make threats which you are not prepared to carry out.
13. Don't ridicule students.
14. Don't try to embarrass students.
15. Don't give punishments which students regard as rewards.
16. Don't get into involved arguments with students.
17. Don't give a penalty that is inappropriate for the misconduct.
18. Don't look for trouble.
19. Don't use tests and homework as punishment.
20. Don't be overly friendly or familiar with students.
21. Don't have "teacher's pets."
22. Don't scream and shout at students.
23. Don't expect that students will always be completely quiet while studying and learning mathematics.
24. Don't let yourself become overly tired and irritable.
25. Don't use fear as your sole means of controlling students.
26. Don't impose punishment when you are angry.
27. Don't expect students to treat you with respect if you do not respect their feelings.

How to Deal with Discipline Problems

In spite of your best efforts to prevent discipline problems, some students will occasionally misbehave and disrupt the orderly conduct of your mathematics classes. Simple measures can usually be employed in dealing with minor discipline problems; however serious problems may require dramatic forms of correction or punishment. Henry Batchelder (1964) in an article in the *Journal of Secondary Education* presents methods for dealing with discipline problems which he collected from various sources. He identifies the following types of corrective measures: simple control, individual conferences with students, home-school cooperation and coaction, restitution and reparation, loss of privilege, rewards and prizes, detention after school, dismissal from class and isolation, group punishment, extra tasks, enforced apologies, lowering grades, corporal punishment, suspension from school, and expulsion from school.

Simple control includes procedures such as staring at a student who is misbehaving, a disapproving frown, directing a question to the student, a mild rebuke, a moment of silence, standing beside the student, relocating the student within the classroom, and involving the student in other classroom activities. Techniques of simple control are useful in dealing with minor problems because they do not upset the offender and do not seriously interrupt the activities of the teacher and other students. However, the effectiveness of simple controls depends upon the personalities of the teacher and the misbehaving student and may have little permanent effect upon the behavior in question or may have no immediate effect upon more serious violations of standards of classroom conduct.

Individual conferences with students are private sessions between the student who is misbehaving and the teacher. This method of dealing with discipline problems is usually very effective because the student no longer has the other students in the class to react to or support his or her undesirable behavior. An open but serious private discussion between a teacher and a student is the best approach to dealing with a continuing minor discipline problem or the occasional more serious infraction. The teacher has time between the occurrence of the problem and the discussion with the student to think about alternative ways to deal with the student and to regain any lost temper or composure. The student is also able to discuss the problem without having to put on an act for other students in order to maintain his or her status in the classroom. A private conference may also bring to light the causes of the student's discipline problems; whereas public action on the problem may only treat the symptoms but not resolve the causes.

Home-school cooperation and coaction in handling more serious discipline problems may provide the teacher and parents with new information about the problem, and cooperative teacher-parent efforts may be more effective in resolving the issue. However, parents must be willing to accept the fact that their son or daughter is misbehaving in school and must support the teacher in his or her attempts to deal with the student. Some students are quite adept at convincing their parents that the discipline problem does not exist and that the teacher is just "out to get the student." A few parents also feel that the behavior of their children in school is the responsibility of teachers and refuse to cooperate with teachers in handling discipline problems. Unless the problem is fairly serious or you know the parents well, it is better to deal with discipline problems without involving parents. If you send notes to parents about their children's problems in school, you should also make a point of sending parents letters about their children's successes in school. Positive letters can counteract the notion that the "teacher is always against me." Some teachers deal with moderately serious discipline problems by sending a personal letter addressed to the student at home. The student's surprise and fear of involving his or her parents in the dispute may lead to a quick resolution of the problem. You will find that you can win the respect, gratitude, and support of most students if you deal with behavioral problems privately and publicize each student's successes to other students and parents.

Restitution and reparation are fair and effective ways to punish students for destruction of other people's property and to repay the victim of the offense. When a student has to repair the damages that his or her actions caused, that student learns to associate improper actions with fair, just, impartial and unemotional punishment. However, the long-term effects of restitution and reparation upon a student's behavior are more positive if the student is sincere in making restitution for his or her actions. Forced restitution may only lead to resentment and a determination to get even. Also, in some situations a student may be unable to restore the damages caused by his or her actions.

Loss of privilege is a generally accepted method of punishing minor or moderate forms of misbehavior in school. This type of punishment is familiar to most students because it is used at home by their parents. The teacher should be certain that the "privilege" being denied is actually viewed as a privilege by the student. Not being allowed to go to the math lab for a week may be of little consequence to certain students and denial of library privileges may be unimportant to other students. It is also well to avoid removing privileges that could interfere with the student's ability to learn mathematics. Such an action would be counterproductive.

Rewards and prizes are effective methods for preventing discipline problems because they promote positive attitudes in students. Rewards such as praise and special recognition should be sincere and should only be given to students who have earned them. However, those students who do not receive rewards may develop negative attitudes that could actually foster discipline problems. Since all students have certain areas of strength, you should make a point of rewarding various activities so that every student will, at times, benefit from your system of rewards and prizes. A note of caution should be added; some students may become motivated to learn mathematics only to get a prize and the intrinsic rewards of learning for the sake of knowledge and self-satisfaction may be lost.

Detention after school is used to punish students for repeated minor violations of rules or a single more serious misbehavior. It is usually best to combine detention with a teacher-student conference so that the discipline problem is discussed during the detention. When students are forced to stay after school to work on mathematics exercises, they may merely have their viewpoint that learning mathematics is a form of punishment reinforced. Keeping students after school may also interfere with their part-time jobs or with activities that their parents have planned for them. In most cases, parents who are expecting their children home from school should be notified when the child is being detained after school. Unfortunately, the fact that staying in school for an additional half hour is viewed as a form of punishment is a sad reflection upon our regard for our educational system. Ideally, extra time in school should be a privilege, not a punishment.

Dismissal from class or isolation has the effect of temporarily getting rid of the troublemaker so that he or she no longer interferes with teaching and learning in the classroom. In some situations dismissal from class may be the only immediate way to deal with a disruptive student. However, dismissing a student from class may give him or her the peer attention that was desired, will interfere with the student's mathematics education, and may call to the attention of the principal the fact that the teacher was unable to control the student in class. In some cases the teacher who dismisses a student from class may share responsibility for the student's out-of-class actions such as destroying property, harming another student, or accidentally injuring himself or herself when the student is supposed to be under the teacher's supervision. When a student is removed from class, he or she should immediately be placed in custody of another responsible school employee. Usually it is preferable to isolate a student at the back of the classroom rather than to expel him or her from class.

Group punishment has but one possible advantage; that is, the group's disapproval may be aroused against the student or students whose conduct elicited the punishment. There are so many possible negative outcomes for group punishment that it should nearly always be avoided. First, it tends to solidify the entire class in their opposition to the teacher. Second, group punishment is grossly unfair to students who were not involved in the misbehavior. Third, students who are unjustifiably punished as a result of an action taken against the entire class may report this action to their parents, who in turn may call the principal or the teacher. The ultimate result of this sequence of events may be deterioration of teacher-parent-principal goodwill. Fourth, group punishment usually results in loss of status and respect for the teacher. The only situation in which group punishment is justifiable is when every member of the group misbehaved in the same way, and even in this case the teacher is still pitted against the entire class.

Extra tasks are not very effective ways to deal with discipline problems. If a task is not related to school work, the student may find it to be a pleasant break from the routine of classes. If the extra task is related to mathematics, it may only reinforce the student's impression that learning mathematics is unpleasant.

Enforced apologies may satisfy the teacher's ego and reinforce his or her feelings of authority; but they also embarrass students, cause resentment among students and promote insincerity and hypocrisy in students. An enforced apology is a very poor way to deal with a discipline problem, and teachers should use other methods of handling misbehavior which may lead to sincere student apologies.

Lowering grades is a poor way to discipline students because it is pure punishment which has few corrective attributes. Lowering a grade for misconduct, other than cheating, is unfair and may only cause resentment and disinterest in learning mathematics in the student who is punished in this way. Many parents also frown upon lowering grades as a form of punishment because these lower grades may have an influence upon their son's or daughter's opportunities for admission to college or obtaining a job. Many school administrators and teachers regard a teacher who uses grades to discipline students as a weak teacher.

Corporal punishment includes grabbing, shaking, hitting, physically restraining, or paddling a student. Many schools absolutely prohibit any form of corporal punishment, and most schools that do permit it require that it be done in the presence of another teacher or a school administrator. Corporal punishment is dramatic, does embarrass certain students, and is sometimes effective in eliminating undesirable behavior. However, corporal punishment does have certain disadvantages: it may alienate parents; it may result in a personal attack upon the teacher as the student attempts self-defense; it may cause resentment and hostility against authority; and in some places certain types of corporal punishment are against the law. If it is used, corporal punishment should only be used to deal with serious offenses, should be done with parent's consent, should be administered in private with an adult witness, and should not be brutal.

Suspension from school or *explusion from school* are extreme measures which are used as a last resort in dealing with serious discipline problems or moderate behavioral problems that are repeated many times and can not be controlled in the student by using other less severe corrective measures. Suspension can only be carried out by school administrators or the board of education; most school systems require school board approval when a student is to be permanently expelled from school. Before a student can be suspended or expelled from school, his or her constitutional rights require that a hearing be conducted. In the case of expulsion, a hearing is required and the student may be represented by legal counsel. Students are expelled from public school when their presence seriously endangers school property or the welfare of teachers or other students. Expulsion does empower the school to get rid of students who exhibit serious behavioral aberrations; however such students usually require professional help in order to determine the causes of their behavioral problems and to correct them.

Batchelder (1964) gives an excellent summary of general considerations in dealing with discipline problems. Some of his principles regarding corrective measures which can be taken in schools are given below:

Corrective measures should be based upon understanding of the student and sound guidance procedures.

The purpose of any correctional device is the improvement of the adjustment of the individual or of the group.

Measures must be taken for the welfare of the individual and for the welfare of the group. A measure applied to an individual must be destructive neither of the individual's personality nor of the group climate. . . .

In using punishment, the simple measures should be used before resorting to the more severe ones.

Punishment should usually be administered impersonally, objectively, unemotionally and privately.

The corrective measure should fit the offender and the offense. Intent of the offender should affect the choice of the corrective measure. . . .

Punishment should be exercised swiftly, though at times a short delay may be effective to enable the pupil to consider his actions.

Teachers must remember that most offenses are *not* personally directed against them, though *it may seem so* on the surface.

Desirable corrective measures are simple classroom control, individual conferences, cooperation with parents, restitution and reparation, loss of privileges, and the use of rewards.

Undesirable or questionable measures are detention after school, dismissal from class, sending to the office, punishing the group, extra tasks, enforced apologies, lowering the marks, personal indignities, threats and warnings, humiliation, sarcasm and ridicule, satiation, nagging, scolding, and *demerits*.

Corporal punishment, suspension, and expulsion are to be used in extreme situations only, and then, with appropriate precautions and care by the school administrators. (p. 93)

Testing and Grading Students

Testing is an accepted means of evaluating students' learning of mathematics and nearly all secondary school mathematics teachers use test scores in determining students' grades. Testing and evaluation are considered briefly in Chapter 4, and in this section testing and grading will be discussed in more detail. In the following paragraphs we will consider the purposes of tests, types of tests and test items, procedures for selecting and constructing tests, methods of testing students, various marking and grading systems, and ways to evaluate and use test results.

Reasons for Testing Students

The major reason for testing students is for evaluation—diagnostic evaluation, formative evaluation, and summative evaluation. *Diagnostic evaluation of students* is used to determine learning characteristics of individual students, the presence of absence of prerequisite skills, prior levels of mastery of mathematical objects, and underlying causes of learning difficulties. *Formative student evaluation* takes place while students are studying and learning new material and is used to find students' error patterns, to inform students of their progress, and to suggest areas of remediation so that immediate and subsequent teaching and learning can be more effective. *Summative evaluation* occurs after students have finished studying a topic or unit and is used to certify student learning, judge teaching effectiveness, and evaluate teaching methods and mathematics curricula. Diagnostic evaluation usually, but not always, takes place before a new unit is taught. Formative evaluation usually occurs during the presentation and study of a unit. Summative evaluation is carried out at the conclusion of study of a unit in mathematics. However, there can be considerable overlap among diagnostic, formative, and summative evaluation and a single mathematics test may be used for all three kinds of evaluation.

In general, students are tested to measure their achievement, to assess their progress toward cognitive and affective objectives, and to determine how well they are remembering what they have learned. Tests are also used to encourage students to pay attention during class sessions, to get them to do homework assignments, and to encourage them to organize and review the mathematical objects presented in a unit of study. Test scores are major factors in calculating students' grades which are used by teachers, school administrators, and parents to determine each student's progress and to compare students to each other.

Types of Tests and Test Items

Tests and test items can be categorized in several ways according to the purpose of the test, the methods used to compare students, the learning objectives measured, the format of the test and test items, and the resources that students use in taking the test.

As is discussed above, the purpose of a mathematics test may be for diagnostic evaluation, formative evaluation, summative evaluation, to measure retention or performance toward learning objectives, to determine levels of achievement, or to obtain a grade for each student.

Tests are also categorized according to how they are used to compare students to each other and to themselves. *Norm-referenced tests* are used to determine where each student stands with respect to other students, and each student's test score indicates whether he or she is above or below average. The grade from a norm-referenced test may be reported as a letter grade where "A" indicates well above average and "D" or "F" indicates far below average. A score may also be reported as a percentile which indicates the percentage of students whose scores are below a particular student's score. If a student's test score falls at the sixtieth percentile, then sixty percent of students in the comparison group did not do so well as that student. Other comparative scales such as deciles, quartiles, stanines, etc. may be used; in each case a student's score is reported as being in a particular category either above or below the group median.

Criterion-referenced tests are used to assess students' levels of mastery or their progress toward a goal or standard. A student's test score may be reported as a percentage of correct answers on the test. A grade of 80% indicates that the student correctly solved 80% of the problems and exercises on the test. A student's performance on a criterion-referenced test may also be reported as a mastery level. For example, a particular eighth grader may only have reached a third-grade level of mastery in mathematics or a fourth grader may be able to handle eighth-grade level mathematics problems.

Domain-referenced tests emphasize diagnostic evaluation and to some extent formative evaluation. After taking a domain-referenced test, each student will be informed of his or her particular strengths and weaknesses and the progress that he or she is making. Here the objective is not necessarily to do better than other students or to meet some externally set standard of learning. The objective of a domain-referenced test is to assess one's strengths and weaknesses and to determine procedures for correcting one's weaknesses. A more detailed discussion of domain-referenced testing, as well as criterion-referenced and norm-referenced testing, is presented in Chapter 4, beginning on page 199.

Entire tests, and particularly individual test items, can be classified according to the cognitive or affective learning objectives which are to be measured on the test as well as the mathematics objects included on the test. Tests and test items can be constructed to measure mastery of facts, skills, concepts and principles at the cognitive levels of knowledge, comprehension, application, analysis, synthesis or evaluation. Test items can also be designed to evaluate the affective objectives of learning which are receiving, responding, valuing, organization and characterization by a value or value complex. Many examples of affective and cognitive test items in mathematics are given in Chapter 4.

Tests can also be classified according to the format of the items on the test. Among the many item formats for mathematics tests are true/false formats, multiple-choice formats, solving exercises, solving problems, proving theorems, defining mathematical terms and symbols, questions requiring either short or long written answers, and essay questions. Example test items to illustrate each of these formats are given below:

True/false test item: If x and y are real numbers, then $x^2 = y^2$ is a function over the real numbers.

Multiple-choice item: Which of these number pairs is a solution to the equation $2x + y = -1$?

    (a) $(3, -8)$ (c) $(-1, 4)$
    (b) $(2, -5)$ (d) $(0, 0)$

Solving an exercise: Factor the polynomial $3x^2 + 8x - 3$.

Solving a problem: Find the length of an interior diagonal of a room whose dimensions are 7 m by 8 m by 4 m.

Proving a theorem: Prove the law of sines.

Defining a mathematical term: What is a mathematical group?

A short answer question: Why is 32 in base five equivalent to 25 in base six?

A long answer question: Explain why the set of integers modulo 3 under addition and multiplication is a field.

An essay question: Discuss the differences and similarities between plane geometry and analytic (coordinate) geometry and the applications of each of these branches of geometry.

Finally, tests can be classified according to the resources that students are permitted to use while taking a test. Tests can range from "closed-book" tests where students are only permitted to use pencil, paper, and their memories and mental processes to "take-home" tests where students are permitted to work together and use any resources such as their textbooks, handbooks, the mathematics library, and the mathematics laboratory. Some teachers prefer to give "open-book" tests when their objective is to assess students' abilities to apply, analyze, synthesize and evaluate concepts and principles in solving problems. When the objective of the test is to determine students' knowledge and comprehension of facts and skills, most teachers prefer to give a "closed-book" test.

Selecting and Constructing Tests

Mathematics teachers usually construct their own tests; however there are sources of ready-made tests. Some publishers of secondary school mathematics textbooks sell unit tests for use with their textbooks. Many mathematics textbooks contain sample tests at the end of each chapter or tests at the end of each unit. Some publishers include tests in the teachers' editions of their textbooks. Several publishing companies also specialize in developing, standardizing and selling tests.

A *standardized test* is a test designed to sample specific kinds of individual performance which can then be interpreted in reference to certain normative data. The items on standardized tests are selected on the basis of experimental evaluation which yields data about their reliability and validity. The *reliability* of a test is a measure of its consistency in measuring whatever it purports to measure. One way to obtain a reliability coefficient for a test is to give it to a large number of students, having diverse abilities, who have studied the material covered on the test. A short time later the same test, or a different form of the original test, is given to the same students. A correlation coefficient is computed between the two sets of test scores for the same group of students. This coefficient is a measure, usually between plus and minus one, of the degree of relationship between the two sets of test scores. If the correlation coefficient is near one, the test is quite reliable, because students with higher scores on the first administration of the test tended to have higher scores on the second administration. Conversely, students with low scores the first time tended to have low scores the second time. If the correlation coefficient is near zero or less than zero, the test is not reliable because it is not consistent in measuring the skills or abilities that it was designed to measure.

The *validity* of a test is the extent to which the test does the job for which it is used. A test is not valid or invalid in itself, but is valid according to the purpose for which it is used. Three types of test validity are content or curricular validity, criterion-related validity, and construct validity. The *construct validity* of a test is the extent to which it measures some relatively abstract psychological characteristic called a construct. *Criterion validity* of a test is either the extent to which scores on the test agree with scores on other tests which measure the same thing or the usefulness of the test in predicting some specified criterion measure.

Mathematics teachers are primarily concerned with the content validity of the tests that they use. *Content validity* is the extent to which the test measures the content of the material that it is intended to cover. A test having high content validity for a particular unit of mathematics will contain a balanced and adequate representation of items from the unit. As an extreme example of invalidity of tests for certain purposes, a test on geometric proof would be invalid in assessing knowledge of arithmetic skills and an arithmetic skill test would be invalid for assessing the ability to construct geometric proofs. However, each of these two tests would be valid for testing the abilities that they were designed to measure. In selecting a standardized test for a specific purpose, you should compare the items on the test with the mathematics content that you intend to measure with the test. If the items on the test do not cover the appropriate material in an adequate manner or cover irrelevant material, then the test is not valid for your purposes.

Since teachers usually construct their own topic and unit tests, several procedures for designing valid and reliable tests will be discussed here. First, in order for a test to be valid it should be closely related to the mathematics content that it will measure, that is:

1. The terminology and symbols used on the test should be the same as those used in the textbook and by the teacher in teaching the material.
2. The items on the test should contain the same mathematics content that was studied in the textbook, presented by the teacher, and learned by the students.
3. The directions for solving problems and completing exercises should be the same as the directions that were given in assigning homework and setting other activities for students while they were learning the topic or unit.
4. The cognitive and affective objectives that were developed in teaching the topic or unit should be used in selecting test items. If knowledge and understanding were emphasized during teaching and learning of the materials, analysis and synthesis should not be emphasized on the test.

Second, test items should be selected to measure a variety of cognitive activities and mathematical objects. There may be times when you will want to design a test which only measures facts and skills at the knowledge and comprehension levels. However, when you are teaching concepts and principles at higher cognitive levels of analysis, synthesis and evaluation you should take care not to design test items that only require recalling facts and applying skills in solving exercises.

When you are constructing a test, it is well to prepare a three-dimensional matrix having mathematics objects, cognitive (and/or affective) levels, and mathematics topics as its three dimensions. Then you can construct a test item or set of items for each cell that is appropriate for your teaching/learning objectives for the unit being tested. Figure 7.1 illustrates a blank matrix to use in constructing a mathematics test for a unit which includes four mathematics topics. For a

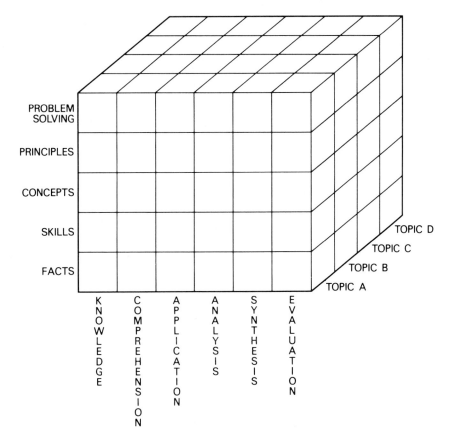

Figure 7.1.   A matrix for use in selecting test items.

particular unit, you could replace the letters A, B, C, and D in the figure with the names of specific mathematics topics and develop test items for appropriate cells in the matrix.

Finally, you should be sure that you have used correct mathematics in your test items, that each problem is solvable, and that your directions and instructions are clearly and consisely stated on the test. A hastily written test with sloppy directions, poor test items and no carefully considered objectives will no doubt be invalid and unreliable. The test will not measure students' mastery of the material that it is supposed to cover and each student's test score may be due, in large part, to chance.

In general, if you follow sound procedures for constructing valid tests (such as those discussed above) your tests will also be reliable. There are several simple statistical techniques for calculating reliability coefficients for tests and you may want to assure yourself that the major tests that you give students are reliable as well as valid. Bruce Tuckman (1972), in his book *Conducting Educational Research,* describes and illustrates several procedures for obtaining and interpreting test reliability coefficients as well as methods for preparing reliable and valid tests.

In her book *Evaluation in the Mathematics Classroom,* Marilyn Suydam (1974) offers the following suggestions for writing mathematics test items:

1. Select the measurement technique that is most effective for the specific objective.
2. Use clear, simple statements. Use language that students understand. . . .
3. Design each item so that it provides evidence that an objective has been achieved. . . .
4. Check items against [a] table of specifications [such as the matrix in Figure 7.1] to make sure that you have the desired emphasis on various content objectives at various levels of difficulty.
5. Work with another teacher or group of teachers in reviewing each others' items. . . .
6. Adopt the level of difficulty of a test item to the group and to the purpose for which it is to be used.
7. Initially, you may want to write more items than you will need on the final form of the test. Then you can discard weaker items. . . .
8. Have each student work from a separate copy of the test, rather than from a test written on the chalkboard.
9. Number all items consecutively from the first item on the test to the last.
10. Avoid putting part of an item on the bottom of one page and the rest on the top of the next page.
11. If the form of a test or a group of items is unfamiliar, use sample items to help clarify the directions. Spend some time teaching students how to take a test.
12. Precede each group of items with a simple, clear statement telling how and where the student is to indicate his answers.
13. When you want the student to show his computation, provide adequate space near each item. . . .
14. Begin a test with easy items. . . .
15. Many times you'll need to have more than one type of item on a test. . . . Place all items of one kind together. . . .
16. Avoid a regular sequence in the pattern of responses: students are likely to answer correctly without considering the content of the item at all.
17. Eliminate irrelevant clues and unnecessary or non-functional clues, but provide a reasonable basis for responding.
18. Make directions to the student clear, concise, and complete. . . .
19. Prepare a key containing all the answers that are to be given credit. . . .
20. After the test, go over questions with your students: they can point out ambiguities and other errors, helping you to improve items for future use.
21. Analyze student responses to each item, for diagnostic use. (pp. 23-25)

Giving Tests to Students

Some students become so upset about the consequences of doing poorly on a test that they are unable to concentrate upon answering the questions on the test. This fear of tests can cause students to do poorly on a test even though they may be well prepared for the test. Norm-referenced tests are a particular threat to students' egos because students are placed in a position of competing with each other. While it may not be possible to completely eliminate fear of tests, teachers can take several actions to reduce the threat of testing to a manageable level.

First, some tests should be given for diagnostic purposes and teachers should share this fact with students. Students may be permitted to correct their errors after the test has been evaluated or may be able to take a re-test after their error patterns have been identified on the first test and they have an opportunity to study the material again. Second, the sometimes irrational fear of tests is usually caused by fear of the unknown. When teachers design tests according to learning objectives that have been shared with their students and select test items based upon previous classwork, textbook material and homework assignments, students will know what to expect on each test. Consequently, much of the fear of the unknown will be removed from the testing situation. Third, if teachers regard testing as just another activity in the teaching/learning process, their relaxed attitude toward testing will be reflected by students as they take tests.

In order to do their best work on a test, most students need a quiet and comfortable classroom environment in which to take a test. Hot, noisy classrooms with poor ventilation can cause students to do less than their best work on a test. Before students begin a test, open the windows and let some fresh air into the classroom.

Frequent interruptions by the teacher or by other students may interfere with some students' concentration during a test. Such interruptions usually occur because the teacher has given poor directions on the test paper or has selected problems which are confusing, improper or incorrect. Teachers should solve each item on the test before it is typed to be sure that no impossible problems or ambiguous questions are included on the test paper. Students should also be discouraged from talking during tests, moving around the classroom, and making noises. If a student does have a question, he or she should raise a hand and wait for the teacher to go to the student's desk and confer privately and quietly about the question.

When space permits, students should be seated in alternate rows during a test or their desks should be spread throughout the room. This will improve ventilation, decrease noise, give each student a sense of privacy and make cheating difficult.

Since the desire to do well on tests can cause some students to forget their values, cheating can become a problem during tests—if the teacher fails to guard against it. Many students yield to the temptation to cheat on tests because teachers create situations in which cheating is easy. When students are seated far apart during a test, the opportunity to cheat is lessened. The teacher should also stand or sit in a conspicuous location where he or she can see each student's face. When a student looks up, for whatever reason, the teacher should look that student in the eye. This serves notice to the student that the teacher is aware of what he or she is doing throughout the test. A test period should not be used as a time for the teacher to grade papers or prepare lessons because the teacher's preoccupation with such activities only creates a situation in which it is easy to cheat. Neither should the teacher leave the room during a test nor confer with someone passing through the hall. The best way to handle cheating is to create a classroom situation in which it is extremely difficult for students to cheat.

Even though you may be certain that a student is cheating or attempting to cheat, it is well not to accuse the student directly. Once you have accused a student of cheating, you may have to prove to the satisfaction of the principal and the student's parents that the student did, in fact, cheat. You can use more subtle and effective means to stop cheating than direct accusation. Stand beside the student who is trying to cheat during a test. Before the test begins, seat any student who has tried to cheat on previous tests in an isolated location in the classroom or near your desk. Give very little partial credit for correct answers to test problems and exercises if the student's work is inconsistent with his or her answers.

In general, let the student who is trying to cheat know that you are aware of his or her attempts to cheat without directly accusing the student. Although in the past students may have been presumed guilty upon the word of the teacher, each student now has the right to a fair hearing when accused by a teacher, and the burden of proof rests with the accuser, that is, with the teacher.

Marking Tests and Assigning Grades

When marking test papers, teachers should attempt to find the source of students' errors on each test item and indicate, on the test paper, to the student why he or she made a mistake and what can be done to correct misconceptions and error patterns. If this procedure is used by teachers, even a test that is designed primarily for summative evaluation will also be diagnostic.

In grading tests some teachers give partial credit for partly correct solutions to exercises even though the student's answer is incorrect. This practice has both advantages and disadvantages. Partial credit can encourage students to attend to processes, procedures and algorithms as well as to getting the "right" answer. However, it is important to obtain correct solutions to problems and exercises and partial credit may underemphasize the value of correct results.

There are four generally used methods for assigning grades on tests—using percentages, using a "curve," using a continuum, and indicating levels of mastery. Each of these methods has both advantages and disadvantages.

Grading by Percentages

The method of grading by percentages is to assign a letter grade to each range of percentages or to report each student's percentage with an understanding that certain ranges indicate good work and other ranges indicate poor work. In any case, the student's percentage grade indicates the student's proportion of correct work and right answers on the test. Although this method of grading tests is probably the most common method used in schools, it does have several disadvantages. First, the standard against which each student is measured is the test itself. Whether the test is good, bad, indifferent, valid, invalid, reliable, or unreliable can be the most significant factor in determining each student's grade. Even good students may obtain a low percentage on an invalid test, and poor students may obtain high percentage grades on a test which is so easy that it does not discriminate among students having a wide range of abilities. Second, many teachers assign a letter grade to each percentage grade. It may be decided that 90% and higher are "A" grades, that 80% to 89% are "B's," etc. Few if any tests and scoring systems are so discriminating that a difference of one percentage point is in any way meaningful. This is to say that a student who obtains a score of 90% is probably no better or no worse than the student who obtains an 89%; however the former student gets an "A" and the latter student gets a "B." Consequently, the students with "borderline" percentage grades receive letter grades that are probably due to chance. Third, by writing easy or hard tests, the teacher can purposely or inadvertently influence the grade of each student and this grade may have little relationship to the student's knowledge and comprehension of the mathematics topics in the unit being covered by the test. Grading by percentages does have two advantages: Most people are familiar with the percentage grading system and few students, parents, and school administrations object to its use. Also, when the percentage system of grading is used, each student is competing against a fixed standard rather than against other students.

Grading on a Curve

Grading on a curve, which is usually an approximation to the normal bell-shaped curve, gives the illusion of being quite sophisticated because it involves using a statistical model. However, this method of grading is very unfair to students because it usually assumes that a few students will get failing grades irrespective of their abilities and knowledge of the subject, and that a large proportion of the class will be labeled as average. Grading on a curve also makes learning into a situation in which each student must compete with all of the other students in the class. A few students are destined to come out at "the bottom of the heap," and each student must try to compete with classmates to be sure that he or she is not one of these students. If an average student is assigned to a section of a course which has mostly poor students, then he or she may get an "A." If the same average student is assigned to a section of the same course which has mostly bright students then that student may fail the course. The only advantage to this grading system is that the teacher has a "nice" distribution of student grades to report to the office, which is hardly of interest to students who are trying to learn mathematics.

Grading Along a Continuum

Using a continuum to assign grades consists of placing raw scores along an ordered scale and using a combination of objective and subjective teacher judgments to determine a letter grade. For example, suppose the following scores were obtained in a class of 20 students taking a test having a possible maximum score of 110 points: 22, 35, 50, 53, 54, 62, 67, 67, 69, 70, 78, 80, 80, 81, 81, 82, 83, 89, 90, 91. On a continuum these scores group themselves naturally into five clusters, 22, 35 - - - - 50, 53, 54 - - - - 62, 67, 67, 69, 70 - - - - 78, 80, 80, 81, 81, 82, 83 - - - - 89, 90, 91. A teacher might fairly assign a letter grade of "F" to scores in the bottom cluster, "D" to the scores in the next cluster, "C" to each score in the 62 to 70 cluster, "B" to the 78 to 83 cluster, and "A" to the three scores 89, 90, and 91. If the test had been a particularly easy test, the teacher might subjectively assign "F" to the 22 to 54 range, "D" to the 62 to 70 range, "C" to the 78 to 83 range, and "B" to the 89 to 91 range. Or it could be that the two students who had scores of 22 and 35 did try hard and performed according to their intellectual abilities, so the teacher may want to assign a grade of "D" to these students. This system of grading objectively and subjectively on a continuum is both fair and flexible and students like a grading system such as this. However, the teacher should be certain that no student with a score higher than a second student's score is assigned a letter grade below that student's letter grade. For instance, if the student whose score is 82 is assigned an "A" grade, then the student whose score is 83 should also be given an "A" regardless of other circumstances such as relative ability levels or conscientiousness in doing homework. Students will object strenuously if they find that the teacher is inverting letter grades along the continuum.

Grading According to Mastery Levels

The method of grading tests according to levels of mastery is frequently used in competency-based programs in schools. Learning objectives are set for students according to each student's ability level and previous achievement in mathematics. Students may be given differentiated tests so that lower-ability students take easier tests than higher-ability students. Each student may be given a pretest before studying a unit in mathematics and a posttest after completing the unit. Then, each student is assigned a grade based upon his or her individual improvement. In an ideal educational system where the objective is to take each student at his or her individual level of mastery and help each student learn and achieve as much as his or her abilities permit, this grading system would be well received. However, in our less than ideal educational system, there is a blend of individualized learning and competitive achievement. While the brighter student may have compassion for the slower student, he or she may resent receiving lower grades for accomplishments that are superior to the achievements of the slower student who receives a high grade for improvement on easier tasks.

A Practical, Combined Grading System

A grading system that contains the advantages of both the continuum system and the level-of-mastery system is a combination of these two systems to determine individual test grades and final grades for each grading period. In this combined grading system, which I recommend to mathematics teachers, each test, quiz, homework assignment, term project and laboratory activity is assigned a maximum number of points. All students take the same tests and quizzes; although the teacher may prefer to give differentiated homework assignments, term projects, and laboratory activities while maintaining a constant possible number of total points for all students. In addition, each student is periodically assigned points based upon the teacher's subjective, as well as objective, assessment of his or her contributions in class, behavior, attitudes toward learning mathematics, improvement in achievement and mastery level relative to level of ability. At the end of each grading period, each student's points are totalled and letter grades, or absolute or relative percentage grades, are assigned to the point totals of students' scores along a continuum. The following example, shown in Figure 7.2, of three students' scores for a two-week period illustrates how this grading system can be used by teachers.

In the example shown in Figure 7.2, each activity resulting in a score for the students is weighted when it is assigned a maximum number of points. The *test* accounts for half of the two week grade because it was assigned the same number of points as the other activities combined. The *progress evaluation* is the teacher's partially subjective evaluation of each student's progress, attitudes, performance according to ability level, etc. Since Bob had the fewest points, his letter or percentage grade should be no higher than those grades assigned to Steffie and Joe. Since Bob's high progress evaluation already indicates that he is achieving according to his potential, no further adjustment is necessary or should be made for his total score.

Date	Activity	Maximum # of Points	Steffie Bell	Bob Jones	Joe Smith
1-17	homework	10	8	5	9
1-18	quiz	20	15	12	17
1-21	math lab	10	6	9	7
1-21	homework	10	7	7	9
1-24	homework	10	9	10	7
1-25	quiz	10	5	7	7
1-26	homework	10	5	9	6
1-28	test	100	83	61	94
1-28	progress evaluation	20	12	20	16
	TOTALS	200	150	140	172

Figure 7.2.   An illustration of an effective grading system that combines positive characteristics of several common grading system.

This grading system has the following advantages when assigning student grades:

1. It permits the teacher to make his or her own periodic evaluations of student characteristics which may not be reflected in tests, quizzes, homework assignments and laboratory activities.
2. It uses a simple and precise system of recording scores.
3. It is fair to all students—high-ability students, low-ability students, motivated students and unmotivated students.
4. Individual grades are totaled before they are converted to letter grades, which is more precise than attempting to average lists of letter grades that may have different weights.
5. Students can keep an ongoing record of their own scores, can total them at the end of the grading period, and can find their own letter grades on the teacher's continuum at the end of each term.
6. The teacher has a complete, accurate record of each student's scores and his or her relative standing in the class which can be used to justify letter grades should they be questioned by a student, parents, or a school administrator.

Evaluating Tests and Using Test Results

In addition to using test scores to obtain grades for students, teachers should use test results to diagnose students' learning difficulties and problems with their own teaching methods. A careful analysis of a student's errors on a test can help a teacher locate specific error patterns that the student is making. Analysis of the number of correct and incorrect responses to each test item will show areas of general difficulty for students and can indicate topics that should be retaught or presented in a different format. In carrying out an item analysis of a test and the students' results on the test, you should analyze the difficulty of each item and identify each student who responded incorrectly to each item. If a number of items were answered correctly by every student, these items are not discriminating among good and poor students. If none of the students were able to respond to certain items, these items may be either too difficult or poorly worded. You should consider modifying or eliminating items which are either too easy or too difficult when you revise the test for use the next time you teach the course.

Each test item should also discriminate between good and poor students. If a test item is missed by nearly equal numbers of good and poor students, that item does not discriminate properly.

If at all possible, a test should be graded the day that it is administered and should be returned and discussed during the following class meeting. Then the test questions will still be fresh in students' minds and they will be interested in finding out why some of their answers are incorrect. After you have discussed the correct methods and answers for the items on the test, you can have the students assist you in an item analysis of the test.

You can quickly determine the *difficulty* of each test item by going through a copy of the test while each student is reviewing his or her own paper. As you refer to each item, ask the students who had that item correct to raise their hands. Count the number of raised hands and record it on your copy of the test. This will give an indication of the difficulty of each test item, which you can use in modifying the test or preparing a new test when you again teach this course. It is usually well to include a few items on each test that nearly everyone will have correct and a few that most students will be unable to solve. The remainder of the items should vary in difficulty along an easy-to-hard continuum.

While determining the difficulty of each test item, you should also *identify* students who responded incorrectly to each item. Go back through the test item by item and assist students in finding and correcting their mistakes and in solving exercises that they did not attempt on the test. Students can assist you and each other in identifying and correcting errors.

If you find that most of the students missed a certain item, you should stop and review the skills, concepts and principles that are being measured by that particular item. In some cases you will find that a significant proportion of the class did poorly on a test and you may need to spend several days reteaching the material contained on the test. Although this may seem to be inefficient because you are repeating old material and losing time, it is much better than moving on to new material before the class has mastered prerequisite material. Since the objective of teaching should be for students to learn each topic and not merely to cover material, it makes little sense to move ahead regardless of how well students are mastering the mathematics content which you are presenting. When you do find that your teaching methods were ineffective for a certain topic, you should consider modifying your teaching/learning strategies when you reteach the material and when you teach the same material to a subsequent class of mathematics students.

Evaluating the Effectiveness of Instruction

Techniques for evaluating the effectiveness of instruction in terms of student learning as well as teacher behavior are discussed in various sections of this book. In particular, Chapters 4, 5 and 6 as well as this chapter contain a number of specific methods that mathematics teachers can use to evaluate the effectiveness of their own teaching methods. In general, teachers should evaluate their own teaching strategies in order to draw conclusions about the effects of their methods upon student learning outcomes and to improve their instructional strategies so that the attainment of positive learning objectives will be maximized for each of their students. In addition to self-evaluation, mathematics teachers can also solicit evaluations from other teachers, school administrators, parents and, most important, from their own students.

In this section we will present a general model for evaluating instruction; this model is based upon writings by Gagné and Briggs (1974) in their book *Principles of Instructional Design*. We will also look at some specific techniques that secondary school teachers can use to evaluate the effectiveness of the instructional strategies that they use in their classes.

A General Model for Evaluating Instruction

This general model for evaluating instruction includes two types of evaluation—formative and summative evaluation—and four variables related to learning—outcome, process, support and aptitude variables. An outline of this model is given below:

I. Types of Evaluation
    A. Formative evaluation
    B. Summative evaluation
II. Variables to be considered in evaluation
    A. Outcome variables
    B. Process variables
    C. Support variables
    D. Aptitude variables

Formative evaluation of instruction is undertaken during teaching and learning and is usually carried out while new teaching/learning strategies or new units or courses are being developed and used in a mathematics program. This type of evaluation is called "formative evaluation" because it is used while new teaching/learning approaches are being "formed." Formative evaluation is usually an informal and on-going process whereby evaluation of outcomes and modification of procedures are accomplished on a day-by-day basis. New ideas are tried out, evaluated immediately, and either retained, modified, or discarded according to their success in the classroom. In fact, the new teaching/learning procedures or mathematics programs may be loosely defined and structured and may be developed and modified while they are being used and evaluated. Formative evaluation is not used to compare one program to another; instead it is a procedure whereby an educational program is developed and evaluated according to internal standards which may be modified several times during program development.

Summative evaluation of instruction is undertaken to evaluate the effectiveness of a well-defined and structured educational program or to compare the relative effectiveness of two well-defined programs. It is used to draw conclusions about how well programs work in the classroom. This type of evaluation is called "summative evaluation" because it is used to "summarize" the effects of a new set of lessons and to decide whether the new program is better than the program that it replaced. Summative evaluation of a program is usually accomplished by using a research design in which specific evaluation instruments are developed and used to collect, analyze and interpret data. Specific educational objectives are formulated and summative evaluation methods are designed to measure the degree to which the objectives are met through the instructional program. Tuckman (1972), in his book *Conducting Educational Research,* discusses a number of research designs for carrying out summative evaluations of instructional programs.

The following example will help to clarify the distinction between formative and summative evaluation: If a school system wants to compare the effects upon teachers and students of using a particular "modern algebra" textbook to the effects of using a "traditional algebra" textbook, teachers and administrators could use a **summative evaluation** research design. Half of the algebra students in the school system would be randomly assigned to classes where the modern algebra book is to be used and the remainder would be assigned to classes where the traditional algebra text will be used. Algebra tests and attitude questionnaires would be developed and given to students at the end of the course, and statistical techniques would be used to measure the significance of the differences in test scores between the groups using the different textbooks. Statistical tests would also be used to determine the significance of differences in attitudes between the two groups as well as the degree to which attitudes towards mathematics changed within each group. Teachers would also be interviewed to assess their opinions about the two different algebra programs. However, if the school system had already replaced all of its traditional algebra books with modern algebra books, a **formative evaluation** of the newly developing algebra program would be appropriate. While teachers are using the modern algebra books in their courses, they may find that certain topics are presented too abstractly for their students and may decide to supplement the textbook with concrete examples of abstract concepts. They may find that the new book overemphasizes concepts and principles and neglects basic algebraic skills; in this case, teachers might mimeograph exercise sheets on algebraic skills which students would complete for homework. Teachers may also find that students are quite interested in the modern approach to algebra and are enthusiastic about their algebra classes and homework assignments.

Both formative and summative methods of evaluation are valid and useful means of assessing the effectiveness of instruction and educational programs. In many situations, mathematics teachers use informal combinations of both methods to evaluate the effectiveness of their own teaching strategies.

A combination of formative and summative techniques can be used to evaluate the four variables of instruction—outcomes, processes, support systems and student aptitudes.

The *outcome variables* of instruction are those variables that are affected by instruction; they are achievement, knowledge, skills, attitudes and various capabilities that are learned in school. Of course, the outcome variables which reflect what is taught and learned in school are also affected by the other three variables of instruction.

Process variables in instruction are those factors within the school environment that may influence the outcomes of instruction. Methods of instruction, procedures for student evaluation, homework, laboratory activities, learning objectives and the school curriculum itself are process variables. All of the procedures that teachers and school resource personnel use in teaching students are variables in the process of instruction.

Instructional *support variables* are the materials and resources that are used in teaching and learning. Physical facilities in the classroom, the mathematics laboratory, the school library, and the school building are support variables. The student's home and community, which influence his or her attitudes toward learning, are also support variables in the instructional process. The presence of adequate teaching and learning resources, a quiet and comfortable place to study, parents who value education, interesting learning activities, and pleasant schools and communities all support learning in school. Although support variables do not cause students to learn in school, they do have a significant effect upon the amount and quality of learning that does occur.

Aptitude variables are those innate abilities that students have which affect their learning in school. The general aptitudes and specific cognitive skills possessed by each student affect his or her ability to learn mathematics in school. Variables such as students' values, their previous learning in school, and their families' socioeconomic status, while not being aptitude variables, are closely related to aptitudes for learning mathematics.

Techniques for Evaluating Instruction

Self-Evaluation

As a consequence of their education, experience, training and interactions with students in their classrooms, teachers are in a good position to evaluate the effectiveness of their own instruction. Each mathematics teacher should systematically and periodically evaluate the outcomes, processes, supporting resources, and, in some cases, the student aptitudes which are part of the teaching/learning process.

The most obvious method of evaluating the outcomes of instruction is by evaluating and testing student achievement and attitudes. A number of specific techniques for evaluating the outcomes of instruction are given above in the section on **Testing and Grading Students.** In addition to using mathematics test results to evaluate student learning, teachers should periodically evaluate the outcomes of their teaching by reacting to the questions on a checklist such as the following:

Evaluating Outcomes of Instruction

1. Do my students appreciate and value mathematics as a consequence of my teaching?
2. Do my teaching methods cause my students to regard mathematics as an interesting and useful subject?
3. Are my students able to apply mathematics outside of school and in their other school subjects?
4. Are students persistent in trying to do mathematics exercises and solve problems, or do they give up when they can not solve a problem immediately?
5. Do my attitudes and actions in the classroom have the effect of preventing discipline problems?
6. Do students in my classes become involved in extracurricular mathematical activities such as reading books about mathematics, working on mathematics projects and participating in the school mathematics club?
7. Do any of my students go on to study mathematics in college?

8. Do any of my students want to become mathematics teachers and are some of my former students now teaching mathematics?

Although the outcomes of instruction are the most important variables in teaching and learning, the instructional process is also quite important because it has a significant effect upon outcomes. The items on the following list can be used to evaluate process variables in instruction:

Evaluating Process Variables

1. Do my students know what my objectives are for each lesson?
2. Do students know why each topic is being studied and the applications of each topic?
3. Do I involve students in setting learning objectives?
4. Do I give careful consideration to planning each lesson?
5. Do I teach students how to read and study their mathematics textbooks?
6. Do I use a variety of preassessment strategies to be certain that students have mastered the prerequisite mathematical objects for each new topic?
7. Do I use a variety of teaching/learning models?
8. Do I use teaching strategies that are appropriate for meeting the objecties of each lesson?
9. Do I use a variety of postassessment methods to evaluate student learning?
10. Do I periodically evaluate my own teaching methods?
11. Do I give interesting and useful homework assignments?
12. Do I involve my students in a variety of concrete laboratory activities to learn mathematics?
13. Do I use effective questioning strategies?
14. Do I encourage students to explore mathematics and ask questions?
15. Do I encourage high-level cognitive activities such as evaluation and problem solving?
16. Do I teach useful facts and skills?
17. Do I use fair and consistent grading methods?
18. Are my tests consistent with my learning objectives?
19. Do I make a point of getting to know each of my students well?
20. Am I able to create an effective learning environment in my classroom?
21. Do I handle discipline problems rationally, sensitively and effectively?
22. Do I make a point of learning new ideas about mathematics and new methods of teaching mathematics?
23. Are my students able to work effectively by themselves?
24. Are my students able to work together in groups?
25. Do I anticipate potential learning problems?
26. Am I able to resolve students' learning difficulties?
27. Do I teach my students how to evaluate their own learning progress?
28. Am I able to deal with routine administrative matters effectively and efficiently?
29. Am I able to work effectively with other teachers?
30. Am I able to intereact effectively with school administrators?
31. Am I able to work with parents and other people in the community to improve my capabilities in teaching mathematics?

It is also important for teachers to be able to evaluate and use teaching/learning materials, resources, equipment and support personnel. The following items can be used as a guide in evaluating instructional support:

Evaluating Instructional Support Variables

1. Do you have a variety of instructional materials available for use in your classroom?
2. Do you have access to adequate audio-visual resources such as tape recorders, various projectors, and different types of films?
3. Do you have a mathematics laboratory or laboratory resources for your own classroom?
4. Are your instructional resources adequate in meeting your learning objectives?
5. Can you identify the learning objectives that can be met by using each resource?
6. Do you have access to a typewriter and duplicating and copying machines?
7. Does the school furnish adequate supplies such as paper, drawing materials, posterboard, glue, staplers, etc.?
8. Does the school have a good mathematics library?
9. Does the school have the services of a counselor, a psychologist, or other resource people who can assist students in resolving their learning difficulties?
10. Are there any community agencies or resources that you can use to support your teaching?
11. Are the school administrators effective in supporting instruction through inservice teacher education programs?
12. Do you have access to a college or university where you can carry out graduate studies in mathematics and mathematics education?
13. Do you have a spacious and attractive mathematics classroom?
14. Does the school have a well-defined procedure for obtaining instructional resources?
15. Do you take your students on field trips or have guest speakers in your classes?

Evaluating students' general aptitudes for learning mathematics is usually not the primary responsibility of teachers. You may find that your students have already taken an IQ test, specific aptitude and attitude tests, and mathematics achievement tests and that their scores on these tests are on file in the school office. You may want to use such test scores as an aid in evaluating particular students' learning difficulties. You should also use homework assignments, classwork and diagnostic tests to evaluate students' aptitudes for learning mathematics. The following list contains items which you can use in evaluating your effectiveness in assessing students' aptitudes:

Evaluating Student's Aptitudes

1. Do you use general intelligence and aptitude test scores to help you in assessing students' learning problems?
2. Do you evaluate students' homework to assess their specific aptitudes for learning mathematics?
3. Do you use diagnostic tests to help in determining students' aptitudes?
4. Do you design instructional strategies based upon your assessments of students' learning abilities?
5. Do you use concrete representations when introducing new concepts and principles?
6. Do you apply sound principles of learning theory in preparing lessons and teaching your classes?

7. Do you evaluate your students' abilities to read and comprehend mathematics textbooks?
8. Do you observe students during your classroom activities in order to identify learning problems?
9. Do you attempt to identify the specific learning aptitudes that are causing a student's problem in learning a particular mathematics topic?

Student Evaluation of Instruction

Your own students can assist you in evaluating the effectiveness of your instructional methods. You can use private conferences with individual students, class discussions and questionnaires to help in assessing the effectiveness of your teaching. You will find that having students fill out a questionnaire can be an excellent way to discover problems with your teaching methods of which you are completely unaware. When you ask students to fill out a questionnaire, you should not require that they identify themselves on the questionnaire. If responses are anonymous, students will be more inclined to be candid in completing questionnaires.

After you have tallied students' responses to your questionnaire and identified specific criticisms of your instructional methods, you should discuss your findings with the class. You may find that students have contradictory opinions about the strengths and weaknesses of your teaching methods, and a group discussion may resolve these contradictions.

In order to keep students' responses from becoming too personal, it is well to phrase questions on questionnaires so that students are asked to evaluate procedures and situations rather than personalities. For example, the question, "Do you think that the teacher's methods of teaching are effective in helping you learn mathematics?" is better than the question, "Do you think that Mrs. Smith is a good teacher?"

The following student questionnaire contains example items which will be useful to you in evaluating the effectiveness of your teaching methods:

Student Course Evaluation Questionnaire

Please rate this mathematics course on each of the following items. Circle the code number that most closely represents your rating of the course for each item. Circle 1 if you rate the course as poor for an item, 2 if you rate the course fair, 3 if your rating is average, 4 if your rating is good, and 5 if you think the course was outstanding on an item. Remember, the codes are: 1—poor, 2—fair, 3—average, 4—good, 5—excellent

1.	New mathematical ideas were presented clearly and understandably.	1 2 3 4 5
2.	The examples, games, models, and class activities clarified the ideas presented in the course.	1 2 3 4 5
3.	The homework assignments were helpful in learning the mathematics topics.	1 2 3 4 5
4.	I knew what I was supposed to learn, why I should learn it, and how I could use what I learned.	1 2 3 4 5
5.	I was interested in learning the mathematics that was taught in this course.	1 2 3 4 5

6. Questions and opinions of each student in the class were respected and discussed. 1 2 3 4 5

7. The course stimulated my thinking about mathematics. 1 2 3 4 5

8. The course was well organized. 1 2 3 4 5

9. The tests were fair. 1 2 3 4 5

10. The grading system was fair and easy to understand. 1 2 3 4 5

11. The classes contained worthwhile and useful information. 1 2 3 4 5

12. Initiative and creativity were encouraged in this class. 1 2 3 4 5

Please answer these three questions:

13. What things did you like *most* about this course? _____

_____

_____

14. What things did you like *least* about this course? _____

_____

_____

15. Do you have any other comments about this course? _____

_____

_____

_____

Evaluations by School Administrators

In most schools, one of the responsibilities of the principal is to periodically evaluate each teacher. Most school systems have evaluation sheets which principals use to rate teachers, and many principals follow an evaluation by sending a written report to the teacher and the superintendent of schools and by having a conference with the teacher. In some schools, the mathematics curriculum coordinator may evaluate mathematics teachers and report his or her evaluation to the teacher being evaluated and the school principal.

Regardless of which administrator carries out an evaluation of a teacher, the written report and conference with the teacher usually are based upon an observation of the teacher while he or she is teaching a class. Many state departments of education and local school districts require periodic written evaluations of all teachers; beginning teachers may be evaluated monthly in order to be eligible for continuing certification and tenure.

443

When you accept a position in a school district, you should discuss the specific procedures that are used to evaluate teachers with your school principal as well as with other teachers. You should request a copy of the evaluation form from the principal so that you will know which variables are to be evaluated and as an indication of areas in which you may want to improve your teaching. In most schools, teacher evaluation is a joint activity between teachers and school administrators and is carried out in a spirit of cooperation and cordiality.

Parents' Roles in Evaluating Instruction

You may want to involve your students' parents in your efforts to evaluate and improve your instructional methods. If so, you will find that most parents appreciate your activities in trying to become an even better teacher and will be cooperative and helpful. You should attend joint meetings of parents and teachers (PTA meetings) and discuss your teaching/learning activities with your students' parents. You can also use school "open-house days" and "parents' evenings" to involve parents in your evaluations. Some teachers find that they can involve parents in evaluation by sending a questionnaire to each students' parents once or twice a year. You may want to prepare a questionnaire similar to the following and mail it to parents to assist you in evaluating the effectiveness of your teaching.

Parents' Questionnaire for Improving Teaching

Dear Mr. and Mrs. Jones:

As part of my continuing efforts to improve the effectiveness of my teaching and to help my students learn mathematics and enjoy studying mathematics, I would greatly appreciate your assistance. Would you please answer the following questions and return your answers to me? Your comments will be strictly confidential and will be used together with the comments of other parents to assist me in finding ways to help my students improve their knowledge and understanding of mathematics through my mathematics classes.

Are you aware of my specific problems that your son or daughter may be having in learning mathematics?

Do you find that the assignments that your son or daughter works on at home help him or her in learning mathematics?

Do you think that the textbook which we are using in your son's or daughter's mathematics course is a good textbook? Do you have any specific comments about the material in the textbook?

Do you think that the material that your son or daughter is learning in mathematics will be useful after he or she graduates from high school?

Do you see any ways in which we might improve our mathematics program?

Please make any other comments or suggestions that can help us better serve you and your son or daughter.

As you have seen in the previous discussion of evaluating the effectiveness of instruction, evaluation involves many people, includes a number of activities, and is an ongoing process. Evaluation of instruction is an important part of instruction, and all mathematics teachers should construct and use a variety of procedures for evaluating the effectiveness of their own teaching.

Things To Do

1. Select a secondary school mathematics textbook having a recent copyright date and evaluate it using the 72 "Criteria for Evaluating Mathematics Textbooks" presented in this chapter. Answer each of these 72 questions and include comments with your answer whenever appropriate. After judging the textbook according to these 72 criteria, write a brief evaluation of the textbook together with a recommendation for its use in a secondary school mathematics course.

2. Choose two textbooks designed for use in a secondary school mathematics course, evaluate them using the 72 "Criteria for Evaluating Mathematics Textbooks" and any other criteria that you feel are appropriate. Then decide which is the better book, and write recommendations regarding the use of each book in a secondary school mathematics program.

3. Select a particular secondary school mathematics course and write specific criteria that could be used to evaluate textbooks which might be considered for use in the course. You may wish to use the "Criteria for Evaluating Mathematics Textbooks" which are listed in this chapter as a guide in writing your own evaluation criteria.

4. Search through the two most recent issues of each of *The Mathematics Teacher, The Arithmetic Teacher, School Science and Mathematics, The American Mathematical Monthly,* and *Creative Computing* to locate new resources for teaching and learning mathematics in secondary schools.

Make a list of the resources that you have found which could be of use to a secondary school mathematics teacher. Include the name and address of the publisher or supplier of each resource and the current price of the item. Write to at least five companies that distribute some of these resources and request a copy of their current catalog of resources for teaching secondary school mathematics.

5. Choose a topic from each of arithmetic, algebra, geometry and trigonometry and prepare a good homework assignment for secondary school students who might be studying each of the topics that you selected. Be sure to include (1) the objectives of each assignment, (2) a precise explanation of what students are to do, (3) procedures for completing the assignment, (4) the amount of time that you think students will spend in completing the assignment, (5) specific difficulties that you anticipate some students may have with the assignment, (6) special considerations in completing the assignment.

6. Write a brief paper listing and discussing reasons for giving homework, problems that may occur in getting students to do homework, procedures which can be used to motivate students to complete homework assignments, and strategies for evaluating and marking students' completed homework assignments.

7. Make a list of at least 10 mathematics learning objectives that can be met by using questioning strategies in mathematics classrooms.

8. Discuss the advantages of using questioning strategies in mathematics classrooms and the problems that can arise if poor questions are asked or if improper questioning strategies are used.

9. Select a topic from each of arithmetic, algebra, geometry and trigonometry and discuss how each topic could be approached using classroom questioning strategies. For each topic list specific cognitive and affective objectives that can be met through questioning techniques and prepare a list of questions, together with anticipated student responses, that could be used in teaching each topic.

10. In this chapter under the heading *Diagnosing and Resolving Learning Difficulties,* eight types of learning difficulties were discussed—sensory problems, mental deficiencies, emotional problems, lack of motivation, cultural disadvantages, social problems, reading problems and problems within the educational system. Select several of these eight types of learning difficulties and carry out the following activities:

    A. For each learning problem suggest student behaviors that would indicate that a student may have that particular difficulty.

    B. Discuss possible causes of each of the learning problems that you selected.

    C. List and discuss techniques that you might use in diagnosing the *precise* causes of each learning difficulty.

    D. Suggest procedures that you as a mathematics teacher, in cooperation with the student, might use in resolving each learning difficulty.

11. Can you think of any learning difficulties, which a student could have in one of your mathematics classes, that may not be included under one of the eight categories listed in item 10 above? If so, state the difficulty and discuss how a student with that problem might behave, how you could diagnose his or her problem, and procedures for correcting the problem.

12. Make a list of strategies, activities, behaviors, etc. that you could use with your students so that you can minimize the occurrence of discipline problems in your mathematics classes.

13. List the possible causes (both teacher-centered and student-centered causes) of classroom discipline problems and suggest ways in which each could be removed as a factor contributing to ineffective teaching and learning in mathematics classes.

14. A list of 27 *dos* and 27 *donts* for preventing discipline problems is given on pages 419 and 420. Suggest a reason or several reasons why each of these *dos* and *donts* is an appropriate technique for preventing discipline problems from occurring in your classroom.

15. List effective and ineffective strategies for dealing with discipline problems once they occur. Explain why the effective strategies are good strategies and when and how each one should be used in handling discipline problems. What are the specific disadvantages that can occur when less desirable techniques are used to discipline students? Are there any situations in which these less desirable techniques can or should be used?

16. List and discuss reasons for giving tests to students who are studying mathematics in secondary schools.

17. List the different types of mathematics tests and discuss the uses, advantages and disadvantages of each type of test.

18. Use the three-dimensional matrix shown in Figure 7.1 as an aid in writing a mathematics test that could be used in a specific secondary school course. Be sure that your test covers a small unit of mathematics which contains at least three topics. State the learning objective that is to be measured by each item on your test.

19. Define each of these variables of instruction and give several examples of each instructional variable:
    A. Outcome variables   C. Support variables
    B. Process variables   D. Aptitude variables

20. Checklists for evaluating the outcomes of instruction, the processes of instruction, instructional support variables and student aptitudes are presented in this chapter. Study each of these four checklists and see if you can think of several additional items to include on each list.

21. Use the **Student Course Evaluation Questionnaire** which is presented in this chapter as a guide to develop your own student course evaluation instrument.

22. A **Parents' Questionnaire for Improving Teaching** is given in this chapter. Using this questionnaire as a model, prepare your own parents' ques-

tionnaire which you could use as an aid in evaluating your own mathematics courses.

Selected Bibliography

Aichele, Douglas B. & Reys, Robert E. *Readings in Secondary School Mathematics.* Boston: Prindle, Weber & Schmidt, Inc., 1971.

    This collection of readings contains articles on instructional resources, testing, student evaluation, and teacher and program evaluation.

Ausubel, David P. "A New Look at Classroom Discipline." *Phi Delta Kappan* XLIII (1961): 25-30.

    This article on historical and philosophic aspects of discipline in schools presents a strong case for firm but sensitive measures for dealing with discipline problems in classrooms.

Batchelder, Henry H. "Corrective Measures, Punishment and Discipline." *Journal of Secondary Education* 39 (1964): 86-93.

    This excellent article is a valuable source of information for teachers who want to learn more about dealing with discipline problems in their classes.

Bloom, Benjamin S., Hastings, J. Thomas, and Madus, George F. *Handbook on Formative and Summative Evaluation of Student Learning.* New York: McGraw-Hill Book Company, 1971.

    This handbook contains a general comprehensive treatment of evaluation of student learning as well as a more specific discussion of evaluation of learning in secondary school mathematics.

Braswell, James S. *Mathematics Tests Available in the United States* 3rd ed. Washington, D.C.: The National Council of Teachers of Mathematics, 1972.

    The purpose of this pamphlet is to provide a listing of sources of mathematics tests. The pamphlet lists arithmetic tests and senior high school tests in algebra, geometry, and trigonometry and gives the name and address of the publisher of each test.

Duncan, Michael J., and Biddle, Bruce J. *The Study of Teaching.* New York: Holt, Rinehart and Winston, Inc., 1974.

    This book, which discusses research findings and current educational practice, contains a section on management and control in the classroom which deals with teacher behavior and discipline problems among students.

Filbin, Robert L., and Vogel, Stefan. *So You're Going to be a Teacher.* Great Neck, New York: Barron's Educational Series, Inc., 1962.

    This book treats several of the topics presented in this chapter as well as other topics of interest to the college student who is preparing to become a teacher or the beginning teacher.

Gagné, Robert M., and Briggs, Leslie J. *Principles of Instructional Design.* New York: Holt, Rinehart and Winston, Inc., 1974.

    The concluding chapter of this book is a discussion of evaluating instruction, which is of use to secondary school mathematics teachers.

Ginott, Haim. *Teacher and Child.* New York: The Macmillan Company, 1972.

    This book, although written about younger students, contains advice for the secondary school teacher about ways to prevent discipline problems and deal with discipline problems which do occur in the classroom. It also treats homework, motivation, and other issues in teaching and learning.

Hunkins, Francis P. *Questioning Strategies and Techniques.* Boston: Allyn and Bacon, Inc., 1972.

This soft-bound book contains information about general considerations in developing questioning techniques. The topics covered in the book include types of questions, developing effective questions, questioning strategies, and methods of evaluation.

Index to Instructional Media Catalogs. New York: R. R. Bowker Company, 1974.

This index to various types of instructional media catalogs is intended as a guide to the suppliers of specific instructional media. It contains a section on suppliers of many different kinds of mathematics education resources.

Kounin, Jacob S. *Discipline and Group Management in Classrooms.* New York: Holt, Rinehart and Winston, Inc., 1970.

A comprehensive, research-oriented treatment of classroom management, this book is a good resource for the teacher who wants to study group management and classroom discipline in depth.

McIntosh, Jerry A. (Editor) *Perspectives on Secondary Mathematics Education.* Englewood Cliffs, New Jersey: Prentice-Hall, Inc., 1971.

This collection of articles on mathematics, which were first published in various journals, contains writings on classroom evaluation, testing, and textbook evaluation.

National Council of Teachers of Mathematics. *The Slow Learner in Mathematics* (Thirty-fifth Yearbook). Washington, D.C.: National Council of Teachers of Mathematics, 1972.

This NCTM yearbook about teaching mathematics to slow learners contains several chapters that are related to diagnosing and correcting learning difficulties.

Peak, Philip. "Aids for Evaluators of Mathematics Textbooks." *The Mathematics Teacher* LVIII (May, 1965): 467-73.

This article is a useful guide for assisting teachers in evaluating secondary school mathematics textbooks.

Polya, George. *How to Solve It* 2nd ed. Princeton, New Jersey: Princeton University Press, 1957.

This book contains many excellent suggestions for questioning strategies which can be used in solving problems and proving theorems in secondary school mathematics classrooms.

Raths, James, Pancella, John R., and Van Ness, James S. (Editors.) *Studying Teaching* 2nd ed. Englewood Cliffs, New Jersey: Prentice-Hall, Inc., 1971.

This collection of readings contains a number of articles on testing, grading, discipline, and motivation.

Suydam, Marilyn N. *Unpublished Instruments for Evaluation in Mathematics Education: An Annotated Listing.* Columbus, Ohio: ERIC Information Analysis Center for Science, Mathematics and Environmental Education, 1974.

This publication contains an annotated bibliography of mathematics tests which are found in research publications and doctoral dissertations produced between 1964 and 1973. To examine actual tests, the reader can refer to the original publication, article, or dissertation.

―――. *Evaluation in the Mathematics Classroom: From What and Why to How and Where*. Columbus, Ohio: ERIC Information Analysis Center for Science, Mathematics and Environmental Education, 1974.

This publication is a good source of information on testing and evaluation in mathematics classrooms. The author discusses the purposes of evaluation, evaluation procedures, and techniques for developing mathematics tests.

Swain, Henry. *How to Study Mathematics: A Handbook for High School Students*. Washington, D.C.: National Council of Teachers of Mathematics, 1970.

This 27-page booklet, written for students, contains suggestions about doing homework, using class periods effectively, and taking tests in mathematics courses.

Tuckman, Bruce W. *Conducting Educational Research*. New York: Harcourt Brace Jovanovich, Inc., 1972.

This practical book has many good suggestions for applying statistical procedures to testing and evaluation in education.

Weigand, James E. (Editor). *Developing Teacher Competencies*. Englewood Cliffs, New Jersey: Prentice-Hall, Inc., 1971.

Among the general teaching competencies discussed in this book are developing competencies for evaluating students, developing competencies in interpersonal transactions, and developing competencies in assessing teacher effectiveness.

Professional Considerations Outside the Classroom

In this chapter some of the non-classroom professional activities of teachers will be discussed and illustrated. Even though these duties do not involve teaching students, they do have a bearing upon each teacher's effectiveness in promoting student learning. Not only must teachers be able to work with students, but as professional people they should also be able to deal responsibly with their colleagues, school administrators and parents. Teachers as well as students have rights and responsibilities in school and away from school, and both groups should be aware of their prerogatives and their accountability to others. Good teachers will learn how to handle unexpected problems in school, accept and carry out directions from school administrators, react appropriately to criticism and respond in a reasonable manner to changes within their schools. They should also be able to evaluate educational systems and initiate desirable changes in education. Additional duties of professional educators may include directing extra-curricular student activities, advising and counseling students and participating in inservice professional improvement programs. As a mathematics teacher, you should be responsive to educational changes in general as well as specific changes in mathematics education. Each mathematics educator has an important stake in the future of school mathematics and should take an active part in shaping this future.

Working with Other Teachers, School Administrators, and Parents

Some classroom teachers have their professional effectiveness reduced through their inability to work with colleagues, school administrators and parents. A few teachers are so used to having their own way with students in their classrooms that they try to dominate colleagues, school administrators and parents. However, teachers must learn to deal with the fact that their role in the classroom is very different from their professional role outside the classroom. They must be able to work with other teachers as professional equals. They must be able to accept directions, advice, and in some cases orders from school administrators. They should exhibit a high degree of professional responsibility in interactions with parents.

Working with Other Teachers

Although a few teachers prefer to work in relative isolation from other teachers, most people find that they can be more efficient and effective professionals if they share resources, ideas and methods with others. Both students and individual teachers benefit from a school mathematics faculty who work together in developing and implementing the total mathematics curriculum and in sharing good ideas which will strengthen a school's mathematics program. Most schools can afford only a limited number of mathematics education resources and teachers must share those resources that are available. However, ideas for classroom methods, lesson plans and laboratory activities are limitless, and school personnel should meet on a regular basis to share their successes and evaluate their problems.

Since most secondary school teachers teach from four to six classes each day and have other duties such as supervising study halls, monitoring lunch rooms and directing extracurricular activities, there is little time in the school day to discuss curriculum and methods with other mathematics teachers. Such discussions usually must take place in small groups during lunch or during the occasional "free periods" that teachers have. Consequently, many of the professional relationships among the mathematics teachers in a school occur in a somewhat haphazard manner. Although it does require finding time in a busy schedule, the mathematics teachers in a school should meet regularly, on their own initiative, to discuss mathematics, the mathematics curriculum, methods of instruction and classroom problems. It may be possible to schedule an hour meeting after school every other week or at least once each month.

Some schools do adjust their class schedules so that teachers are freed from other responsibilities once or twice each week in order to meet in content groups to discuss professional concerns. Most school districts have one or more "inservice days" when students do not attend school but when teachers come together for professional meetings and other activities. Even though some of these inservice days may be planned for clerical activities or listening to lectures from experts in education, time can usually be found for a professional meeting of the mathematics faculty. Many school systems do allocate time so that the faculty can spend an entire day or several days preparing curriculum resources, modifying the curriculum, writing student performance objectives, planning lessons and sharing ideas.

Whenever a mathematics faculty meeting is scheduled, either after school or during an inservice day, activities should be planned in advance for the meeting and a printed agenda should be distributed to participants at least several days before the meeting. This will allow time for each teacher to prepare for the meeting and will help to assure that the meeting will have useful outcomes. When a professional meeting takes place with little planning and no agenda, it tends to become a general talk session which ends with few if any positive outcomes. Just as a lesson or unit plan for teaching mathematics should have specific, stated objectives, formulating objectives should be a part of the planning for a professional meeting. In addition to objectives, the expected outcomes of the meeting should be written down and shared with the participants. The objectives and planned outcomes given in the following three memoranda represent the types of activities that could be carried out by a group of mathematics teachers who are meeting for a day of professional activities:

1. The objective of the mathematics faculty meeting scheduled for Monday, January 24 is to evaluate the three new plane geometry textbooks which have been circulating among the mathematics faculty for the past month. Enclosed with this memorandum is a set of guidelines for evaluating textbooks. Please use these guidelines as a reference when you evaluate the geometry textbooks; however you are encouraged to use other evaluation criteria that you feel are important. Please come to the meeting prepared to discuss the appropriateness of each textbook for use in our plane geometry course. The outcome of our faculty discussions will be a recommendation to the school administration to purchase a set of one of these textbooks for use in our geometry course during the next five years.

2. Most of us are dissatisfied with the syllabus that is being used for the consumer mathematics course. During our mathematics department inservice day next Friday we will consider modifications for this course. Enclosed is a list of suggested topics for consumer mathematics. Please rank each topic according to how important you think it is. Use a rank of 1 to indicate that you think the topic is unimportant, 2 to indicate that it is somewhat important, 3 to indicate moderately important, and 4 to indicate very important. You are encouraged to add topics which you think should be included in the course to this list. When we meet Friday we will select topics and prepare a consumer mathematics course syllabus which will be used in teaching consumer mathematics next year.

3. As you know, the superintendent of our school district has requested that we prepare a list of general objectives for our secondary mathematics program and a list of specific student performance objectives for each of our nine mathematics courses. We will spend our two inservice days next month completing these tasks. Enclosed is a monograph containing sample objectives for a secondary mathematics program and a set of guidelines and procedures for writing both affective and cognitive mathematical objectives. Please read this monograph before our inservice workshop and begin to prepare objectives for each of the courses that you are teaching this year. Professor F. R. Hartman, the author of the enclosed monograph, will be here during our inservice days to assist us in developing and writing our objectives. Dr. Hartman, who is a mathematics education professor at State University, spent ten years teaching secondary school mathematics and is well qualified to assist us.

In addition to brief mathematics faculty meetings and mathematics faculty work sessions during inservice professional days, you will find that the teaching methods and learning resources used by non-mathematics teachers can be useful to you in teaching mathematics. Social studies, science, music, art, industrial arts and home economics teachers in your school can assist you in finding many interesting and useful examples and applications of mathematics. The ideas for some of the teaching/learning models, example lesson plans and learning activities presented in this book were taken from disciplines other than mathematics. Although mathematics and mathematics education do have their distinctive content and methods, they also contain content and methods that are shared with other disciplines. Do not become one of those mathematics teachers who thinks that the only sources of information about mathematics content and mathematics teaching are other mathematics teachers and books and journals about mathematics. Books, articles and people in the other disciplines are a rich source of ideas about teaching and learning mathematics. Make a point of reading books and articles about general principles and methods of teaching and discussing teaching and learning with non-mathematics teachers as well as with teachers of mathematics. You will find that you can learn a lot about your profession through general faculty meetings and through specific workshops and programs that include teachers of various subjects. It is unfortunate that in some larger schools few opportunities exist for planned meetings and workshops where teachers of different subjects can come together to discuss methods and resources.

One of our problems in mathematics education is that elementary teachers, who teach mathematics to children ranging in age from five to thirteen, have little contact with secondary school mathematics teachers, who teach mathematics to students ranging in age from thirteen to nineteen. Some teachers specialize in teaching either junior high school mathematics (grades seven through nine) or middle school mathematics (grades six through eight). In nearly all school systems, the elementary education program is in a building separate from (and in some cases miles away from) the secondary education program. Many times junior high school or middle school programs are also housed in separate school buildings While there are advantages to having separate schools for students in various grade levels, there is the disadvantage that communication may be limited among elementary, junior high school and senior high school teachers. In addition, most colleges and universities have separate teacher preparation and certification programs for elementary and secondary teachers, which compounds the communication problem between these two groups of prospective teachers. Since most elementary teachers are expected to teach a variety of subjects, including mathematics, elementary teachers are unable to study mathematics in depth as do secondary teachers. While some elementary schools do have mathematics specialists to teach their mathematics classes, many do not. Consequently, elementary teachers tend to be well prepared in learning psychology and methods of teaching, while secondary teachers are well prepared in the content of their subject specialty.

This segregation of elementary, middle school, junior high school and senior high school teachers of mathematics causes misunderstandings which can have unfortunate consequences for students. Elementary school teachers may not know what mathematics secondary school students are expected to study and what the prerequisites are for secondary school mathematics courses. Secondary school mathematics teachers may have only a vague notion about what mathematics is taught in elementary school and how it is taught. Consequently, many students finish elementary school poorly prepared to study mathematics in secondary schools, and many secondary school teachers are poorly prepared to help students bridge the content and methods gaps between elementary and secondary level mathematics education.

Elementary and secondary school teachers should make a point of getting together during professional meetings to discuss the mathematics content that they teach, their instructional methods, and the problems that students have in learning mathematics. As a secondary school mathematics teacher, you should encourage the administrators in your school system to schedule inservice programs where the secondary school mathematics teachers can come together with the elementary school teachers to discuss their common concerns. You should also read elementary education journals and journals such as *The Arithmetic Teacher,* and you should browse through the elementary school mathematics textbooks that are used in your school district.

Working with School Administrators

At times during your career, it may seem to you that your school administrators neither understand nor support what you are trying to do in your classes. You should realize that school administrators and school teachers have different responsibilities within schools; however both groups of people have a common objective—to provide a good education for each student. School administrators, in addition to being concerned about the quality of education in each classroom, must deal with school budgets, complex record keeping procedures, individual parents, the school community, the more serious student discipline problems, as well as a school filled with teachers and students who have a diversity of personal characteristics.

Most school administrators just do not have all the time that they would like to have to spend with individual teachers in discussing their needs and concerns. As a professional educator, it is partly your responsibility to see that your school principal and other school administrators are kept informed of your objectives, classroom activities and requirements for teaching/learning resources. You can help your school principal help you to become a more effective teacher by informing him or her of your objectives for each of your courses, by formulating a sound rationale when requesting teaching/learning resources for your classroom, and by communicating your specific needs in a concise and orderly manner. Don't expect results when you tell your principal that you need a new instructional resource for your classroom while you are both hurrying through the hallway to a meeting. When you want classroom resources, you should wait until you have a list of several resources, then send a written request to the principal containing the following information:

1. A catalog description of each resource that you need.
2. The address of the company that sells each resource.
3. The exact cost of each resource if you know it; if not, an estimate will do.
4. A description of the learning objectives that will be attained through the use of each resource that you request.
5. A sound rationale for requesting each resource and a brief description of the use that you will make of each item.

If you work with your school administrators in a spirit of understanding and cooperation, you will usually find that they will do their best to make your job easier and more pleasant. After all, all of you do have the welfare of your students as a common concern. More will be said later in this chapter about your rights and responsibilities in dealing with school administrators.

Working with Parents

Ways to involve the parents of your students in evaluating the outcomes of your teaching are discussed in the previous chapter; however there are other situations in which you may need assistance from parents, and parents may also call upon you for assistance. Parents are quite naturally concerned about the welfare of their children and you will find that many parents want to discuss their son's or daughter's progress in school with you. Hopefully all of your interactions with parents will be pleasant, but occasionally there may be some unpleasant confrontations between you and parents. These confrontations usually result from a student's low grades or a discipline problem. A few parents are so supportive of their children that they will always side with their son or daughter in a disagreement with the teacher. Other parents feel that the teacher has complete authority in the classroom and is always right. Most parents take a more moderate approach in their dealings with teacher/student relationships.

As is pointed out in the previous chapter, you can avoid many confrontations with students by concentrating on the consequences of their actions rather than verbally attacking their personalities or characters. If you refrain from accusing students of cheating in the absence of incontrovertible evidence and do not cast aspersions upon the character of a misbehaving student, you will avoid most confrontations with parents. You can also avoid confrontations with parents about the grades that you give students if you use a fair grading system, such as the one presented in Chapter 7, and explain it to your students at the beginning of each course.

In spite of your best professional efforts and ethics, there may be a time when you are confronted by an angry parent. If an obviously irate parent phones you either at school or at home, the best immediate strategy is to hear him or her out. If you listen a lot and talk little, the parent will usually clam down and you will not say something that you may regret later. Arguing with an angry person tends to increase the person's anger. If you are unable to resolve the situation over the phone, make an appointment to meet the parent at school during your free period or at the end of the day. **Never** meet an angry parent at his or her home or at your home. You have neither the assistance of your principal or guidance counselor nor the records of the student at your home. Before your scheduled meeting with the parent at school, apprise the guidance counselor or the principal of the situation and request his or her advice in dealing with the problem. When talking with an angry parent always maintain an objective but concerned posture. Even if the parent questions your teaching ability or character, you should still maintain an objective, professional attitude.

The overwhelming majority of your contacts with parents will be pleasant for both of you. Whether you speak with a parent at the supermarket, at a PTA meeting, or at a school open house, be cordial and emphasize the good characteristics of his or her child. This is not to say that you should "cover up" learning difficulties or behavioral problems. However, you will obtain more support from parents, as well as their goodwill, if you present a balanced picture of the strengths and weaknesses of their children. In general you should consider parents not as a threat to your professional stature but as concerned partners in the education of their children who are your students.

Rights and Responsibilities of Teachers

Most schools and school systems have written codes which specify the rights and responsibilities of teachers. In many cases where teachers are represented by collective bargaining agents in their negotiations with school boards and school administrations, these rights and responsibilities are written into contracts between school boards and professional bargaining organizations. In general, teachers have two kinds of rights and responsibilities in school—rights and responsibilities in dealing with students and rights and responsibilities in working with school administrators.

Although each school system and school building has its own standards of teacher conduct, there are certain universal standards which govern the rights and responsibilities of teachers in their interactions with students. The following lists of teachers' responsibilities and teachers' rights are common to most schools and school districts:

Teachers' Responsibilities in Dealing with Students

1. Teachers should respect the rights of students. In many schools these rights are specified in a written student code.
2. Teachers should enforce school regulations governing student conduct.
3. Teachers should set fair and reasonable rules for students conduct in their own classrooms, should make their rules known to students, and should enforce their rules evenly.
4. Teachers should set a good example for their students through their own conduct in school.
5. Teachers should always maintain high ethical and professional standards in their interactions with students.
6. Teachers should prepare written lesson plans for each of their classes and these plans should be available for the substitute teacher in case the teacher must be absent from school due to illness.
7. Teachers should be certain that they carry out their assigned teaching responsibilities. For example, teachers should not leave their students unattended during class periods, should meet their classes on time, and should be in specified locations during working hours.
8. Teachers should carry out their assigned non-teaching responsibilities such as supervising study halls, cafeterias, homerooms and student activities in a responsible manner.
9. Teachers are expected to act as counselors and advisors to students who request their assistance.
10. Mathematics teachers have considerable responsibility for the effectiveness of their teaching methods and the degree to which students learn mathematics in their classrooms.
11. Students should be evaluated and graded fairly and objectively.
12. Teachers should keep complete and accurate records on each of their students.
13. Teachers should use only those methods of disciplining students which are approved by the school administration.
14. In many schools, teachers are expected to supervise extracurricular student activities.
15. The confidentiality of students' grades, personal data and personal problems should be respected.

16. Teachers have the responsibility to teach the approved mathematics curriculum in their school districts.
17. Students should be treated with respect and dignity at all times.

Teachers' Rights in Dealing with Students

1. In most schools, teachers have the right to select their own teaching methods within certain general guidelines.
2. Teachers have the right to set standards of student conduct for their own classes and to enforce their standards.
3. Teachers usually have the right to design their own testing and measuring instruments for use in evaluating and grading their students.
4. Teachers have the right to enforce the school's standards of student conduct.
5. Within certain limits, teachers have the right to conduct their classes as they see fit.
6. Teachers have the right of privacy in the conduct of their personal affairs.
7. Teachers have the right to assign learning tasks and activities to their students.
8. In most schools, teachers have the right to select some of the resources and materials that are used in their classes.
9. In most schools teachers have *some* freedom to select the content which they cover in their courses; however this freedom is subject to certain limitations, because most schools have a specified set of topics to be covered in each of their mathematics courses.
10. Teachers have the right to protection from verbal and physical abuse by students.
11. Teachers have the right to a hearing if they are accused of unethical conduct by a student.
12. In general, teachers have the right to carry out their professional obligations to students in the manner in which they see fit, subject to the rights of students and school regulations, requirements and standards.

Since all teachers were students at one time, most of them are familiar with many of the rights and responsibilities of teachers and students. However, many teachers are inept in their interactions with school administrators, which indirectly influences their effectiveness in the classroom. In most school systems, teachers deal directly with their building principal and interact infrequently with higher-level administrators who may occasionally visit the school building and participate in professional meetings and inservice workshops. Teachers have certain rights and responsibilities in their work with school administrators; in situations where they are represented by a teachers' union in their negotiations with school officials, these rights and responsibilities may be included in a professional contract. The following lists of teachers' responsibilities and rights in dealing with school administrators will assist you in your interactions with administrators:

A Teacher's Responsibilities in Dealing with Administrators

1. You should respect the administrative "chain of command," and in most cases you should take your problems, concerns and grievances directly to your building principal.
2. If you teach in a school district that has a negotiated union contract, you

should study the contract to determine precisely what your responsibilities to the school administration are.

3. When you are ill and must be absent from school, it is your responsibility to notify the appropriate school official of your impending absence in time to arrange for a substitute teacher. You should also inform this school official of the location of your lesson plans, which the substitute teacher may use in maintaining the continuity of instruction.

4. You should report your grades, attendance data and other information about students in the proper format and on time.

5. You are responsible for seeing that information from school administrators, which is directed to you and which is meant for students, is communicated to your students.

6. You should refrain from publicly criticizing your school administrators.

7. In most school systems, you are required to attend certain teachers' meetings after school, to participate in inservice professional programs, and you may be expected to attend PTA meetings.

8. If you plan to resign your teaching position, you should give advance written notice to your principal and the superintendant of schools in order to allow adequate time for them to hire a replacement for you. Whenever possible you should terminate your employment at the end of a grading period or school year.

9. When seeking a new teaching position, you should not sign a contract with one school district, continue searching for a better position, and then break your first contract when you receive a better offer. Such an action is not only unethical, but it is also in violation of a contractual agreement.

10. You have the responsibility of coming to school each day at a certain time and staying in school until a certain hour.

11. You should always use high standards of courtesy, ethics and professional conduct in your dealings with school administrators.

12. You should attempt to understand the responsibilities of each school administrator and help him or her meet those responsibilities.

A Teacher's Rights in Working with Administrators

1. If the conditions of employment in your school district are covered by a collective bargaining agreement, you should read your employment contract to determine your specific contractual rights.

2. In many states the teachers in each school district have the legal right to organize and to bargain collectively with the school board and school administration in order to set the terms and conditions of professional employment.

3. All teachers have the right to employment in a school district without regard for their race, sex, age, national origin and religion.

4. Pregnant teachers have the right to continue teaching as long as they are able to carry out their professional responsibilities.

5. In many school districts a pregnant teacher has the right to a leave of absence during pregnancy and following the birth of her child.

6. Some school districts permit leaves of absence for additional study, illness, or personal reasons.

7. Some school districts permit teachers to take sabbatical leaves with full or part pay after teaching a specified number of years in the district. Sabbatical leaves may be granted for advanced study, professional activities, or illness.

8. Many school districts have "fringe benefits" such as medical and dental care plans; health, accident and life insurance coverage; pension plans; sick leave; and group purchasing discounts in local retail stores, which teachers are entitled to receive.

9. In most schools, teachers have the right to a "free period" each day—time during school hours to prepare lessons and grade papers—and a duty-free lunch period each day.

10. You have the right to come to school at a specified time each morning and to leave school at a certain hour each afternoon.

11. You have the right to fair and equitable treatment by school administrators.

12. The school district can not dismiss you from employment without just cause, and you have the right to a hearing if you are dismissed. The school district does have the right to reassign you to a different position within the school system.

The preceding lists of rights and responsibilities of teachers are not meant to include all situations and are obviously incomplete. However, they do cover many of the situations that are commonly encountered in schools. Many of your specific rights and responsibilities are not absolute, but are relative to the school district in which you teach. A good way to obtain more information about your general rights and responsibilities as a teacher is to read the publications of professional teachers' organizations such as the National Education Association, the American Federation of Teachers, and their state and local affiliates. You can also find information about the rights and responsibilities of students, teachers and administrators in journals which are published for school administrators. Some of these journals as well as other relevant publications are listed in the **Selected Bibliography** at the end of this chapter. Your state department of education may be able to supply you with information about the particular rights and responsibilities of teachers in your state. Most local school districts have specific information about teachers' rights and responsibilities in that district.

In a few school districts, which have an adversarial relationship between teachers and administrators, the rights of teachers and administrators are adhered to dogmatically and the responsibilities of both groups are strictly enforced. However in many schools, practical considerations result in a more flexible interpretation and enforcement of rules and regulations governing teacher/administrator relationships. If you teach in a relatively flexible school, you should realize that effective and cordial teacher/administrator interactions require give-and-take on the part of each group. For example, you may find that the fact that you were fifteen minutes late in reporting to school on a rainy day because your bus was late will be overlooked by the principal. Or you may need to leave school a half-hour early some day to attend to personal business and the principal will say, "Sure, go ahead." You should return favors such as these by occasionally agreeing to stay after school to supervise students when the school bus is late arriving, by giving up your free period to cover the class of a teacher who suddenly becomes ill during the school day, and by making other reasonable concessions.

In general, you will find that if you are flexible in occasionally giving up certain of your minor rights to assist your school administrators, they will in return overlook your occasional unavoidable infractions of minor regulations. However, if you are inflexible in insisting upon every one of your rights regardless of the situation, you should expect that your school administrators may become equally inflexible in enforcing each regulation that applies to you.

There are some situations in which you can be too accommodating in giving up your rights. For example, if you belong to a teachers' union, you may be censured by union officials if you volunteer to teach an extra course or supervise an extracurricular activity without extra monetary compensation. Your bargaining agent may regard such activities as a factor contributing to unemployment among teachers.

You should be aware of your rights and responsibilities and those of students and administrators within your school system. You should also be fair and flexible in exercising your rights and you should always exhibit high standards of professional ethics in carrying out your responsibilities. A spirit of cooperation among teachers, students, and school administrators will result in an effective learning environment where everyone involved will find their work rewarding and enjoyable.

Dealing with Changes in Educational Systems

It sometimes seems that a characteristic of human nature is resistance to change. Many people who have adjusted to the various routines in their lives are reluctant to accept changes in their patterns of living. We also know that human beings are quite adaptable to changes in their surroundings even though they may be reluctant to initiate such changes.

Teachers are no exception to these general observations of human nature. Many teachers are reluctant to accept changes in the school curriculum, methods of instruction and working conditions. However, most teachers are quite capable of adapting to a variety of changes in the educational system. During the past 20 years many mathematics teachers have adjusted to a new mathematics curriculum, adopted new instructional systems and teaching strategies, and accepted new theories of learning psychology and intellectual development.

Unfortunately, not all change is positive and some changes in mathematics education have not met the expectations of educational innovators. Programmed textbooks and instructional systems were not very successful innovations; some of the open-classroom approaches to teaching and learning confused and frustrated students; and some people believe that the modern curricula in several subjects, mathematics being one of them, have caused a decline in basic skills among students and young adults. Even though some of the educational innovations of the past 20 years have fallen short of expectations, the composite effect of all of the recent changes in teaching and learning has, in my opinion, resulted in an improvement in our educational system; although there are educators who disagree with me. Whether one favors or opposes change, it is a fact that changes have taken place in education and will continue to occur. Consequently, teachers should prepare themselves to respond intelligently and effectively to new developments in education and should also attempt to influence the directions of educational change.

In this section we will consider two kinds of changes which have an effect upon mathematics teachers—specific changes within one's school or school system, and general changes within the educational system. The specific changes which will be discussed are of three types—procedural changes, changes in course content and teaching strategies, and changing one's job. The general changes within the educational system which will be considered are changes in the mathematics curriculum and new roles and responsibilities for mathematics teachers.

Changes Within a School or School System

From time to time teachers can expect certain procedural changes within their schools. At times school administrators may adopt a more efficient and descriptive system of keeping records which may require teachers to learn how to fill out new attendance records, student data forms and grade reports. Although such changes can be bothersome, they usually can be accomplished with a minimum expenditure of time and effort and may, in the long run, make teachers' record-keeping chores more efficient and provide more useful data for students, teachers, parents and administrators.

At times a new contract between a teachers' organization and a school board will result in an agreement to change school working hours for teachers. Practical considerations such as extending daylight savings time, new school-bus schedules, or variable or split schedules for students may necessitate a change in school hours for reasons of safety or convenience for students. Although a change in working hours may inconvenience people, such changes usually must be accepted and teachers must adjust to their new schedules.

On occasion teachers can expect to have their teaching assignments changed or their other duties modified. Some schools rotate non-classroom assignments such as study-hall supervision, cafeteria duty, school-bus duty, hall monitoring, etc. among teachers term-by-term or year-by-year. Course assignments can result in disagreements among teachers and between teachers and school administrators. In some schools, people who have worked in the school system for the longest time have their choice of courses, while newer faculty members may be assigned several sections of remedial arithmetic or consumer mathematics, which can be difficult and frustrating courses to teach. Certain people may also have courses that they consider to be their own. For example, one teacher may teach all of the plane geometry sections and another may only teach senior analysis, probability and statistics courses. Many people find that teaching four or five sections of the same course each year becomes tiresome and boring, while other people prefer such a schedule because they have only one course preparation. However, most teachers like to have a variety of mathematics courses and two or three different course preparations each day. Many school administrators do try to arrange equitable assignments for all teachers by varying and rotating course and section responsibilities. While you may have some choice in your course assignments, this situation varies among schools. Your college or university teacher-education program should prepare you to teach mathematics courses ranging from sixth grade arithmetic to college-level calculus and probability courses.

If you teach in a school system that has a contractual agreement with a teachers' union, many of the conditions and terms of your employment will be specified in your contract. In some states and school districts, working hours, teaching loads, class sizes, non-teaching duties and other conditions of employment are negotiated between school boards and professional bargaining organizations.

Textbooks and instructional procedures are periodically changed in all schools. These changes may be initiated by teachers, school administrators, or committees of teachers and administrators which may, in some instances, include parents and students. The selection of a new textbook is usually made by a committee of teachers and administrators. However, any professional school system employee from a teacher to the superintendent of schools or a committee of teachers and administrators can modify instructional strategies.

Each mathematics teacher has the right as well as the responsibility to continually evaluate and adjust his or her classroom instructional strategies. Numerous techniques for evaluating and modifying teaching methods are discussed in Chapters 3, 4, 5 and 6. In some courses in certain schools, teachers also have the right and responsibility to select and modify the mathematics content of their courses; although in many school systems the content of most courses may be specified by school administrators.

Occasionally a school or school system may adopt a completely different instructional model such as a computer-managed instructional system, an individualized teaching/learning program, an open classroom concept, or a competency-based learning program. In such cases school personnel are required to use the new system and may be taught new methods and procedures through workshops during the school year or summer teacher-education programs. When a new instructional system is implemented in a school, teachers have little choice but to adopt the new system in their classes. Each teacher should monitor and evaluate a new system and use data collected through these activities as a rationale for recommending modifications of the system to the appropriate school administrators.

A few people regard periodic evaluations of their teaching by school administrators as a threat to their classroom independence; but these evaluations should be viewed as an opportunity to assess and improve teaching effectiveness. When an administrator observes you conducting a class and offers specific criticisms of your methods, it is quite natural that your first reaction will be to defend your instructional methods. The best approach in responding to such criticisms is to consider the criticisms objectively several hours or a day after they are made. Then your initial defensive reaction, hurt, or anger will be replaced by a more professional attitude and you will be able to react to the administrator's evaluation of your work in a rational manner. Your credibility and effectiveness in dealing with an evaluator will be enhanced if you attempt to find many points that you agree with in the evaluation and only a few points with which you are in complete disagreement. You should prepare a reasonable rationale to justify your disagreements and present it to your evaluator together with your plans for change in those areas that you both agree need to be improved.

In general, you will be most effective in initiating appropriate changes and resisting inappropriate changes in your teaching if you assume an aggressive, positive attitude rather than taking a defensive, negative approach. In most cases your arguments either for or against changes should be based upon your perceptions of what is best for your students.

Changing your job may or may not be a change within your school or school system; although it certainly does involve a change in your professional life. Although many secondary school mathematics teachers spend their entire professional careers as classroom teachers, others become department chairpersons, curriculum coordinators, principals, educational specialists, or college instructors. Some people find that teaching is the wrong profession for them and change careers after several years in a secondary school. There are a number of excellent positions within the educational system other than classroom instruction. Mathematics teachers are also partially prepared for many non-teaching occupations in fields such as social work, business administration, health-related professions, computer programming, science and technology. If you find that you do not care for teaching, you may do both yourself and your prospective students a service by changing to another profession.

General Changes in the Educational System

The past 20 years have witnessed dramatic changes in mathematics education in the United States as well as in other countries. An increased emphasis upon structure, rigor and proof has occurred in school mathematics; new instructional systems have been implemented in schools; and teachers are using new teaching/learning strategies in their classrooms. These and other changes in mathematics education are discussed in Chapter 2, and modern theories of how children learn mathematics are presented in Chapter 3.

Although the nature of future changes in mathematics education is difficult to predict, it is likely that the next 20 years will produce some very significant changes in our approaches to teaching and learning mathematics. Secondary school mathematics teachers should not only prepare to deal with these changes but should also assume considerable responsibility for determining the nature of changes related to their professional rights and responsibilities.

As a reaction to national, state and local test results, as well as the growing dissatisfaction with the new mathematics curriculum, it appears that the future may witness a renewed emphasis upon basic mathematical skills. As society becomes more aware of the importance and the consequences of individual's rights, responsibilities and values, it appears that there will be an increasing emphasis upon affective objectives in mathematics education. With the increasing cost of higher education, vocational skills are becoming more desirable as educational goals, and the value of college preparatory programs and courses in mathematics is being questioned by some people. Advances in technology, which have resulted in dramatic decreases in the cost of electronic equipment, have made digital computers and hand-held calculators common instructional resources in mathematics classrooms. Since the metric system of measurement is gradually being adopted in the United States, metric education is becoming a part of the school mathematics curriculum.

In addition to changes in the mathematics curriculum, mathematics teachers should prepare for new roles in schools. In the future, mathematics teachers may be expected to manage complex technological systems in support of teaching and learning and to use new instructional systems based upon modern theories of instructional management and learning psychology. Mathematics teachers can expect to function more as student counselors, instructional managers and resource personnel and less as dispensers of mathematical facts, skills, concepts and principles.

Individual teachers will be more effective in influencing the nature of changes in mathematics education if they make their desires known and influence felt through professional organizations such as the National Council of Teachers of Mathematics, the School Science and Mathematics Association, the National Education Association, and various other national, state, regional and local teachers' organizations. More will be said about changes in the nature of education, in general, and mathematics education, in particular, later in this chapter.

Working with Students Outside the Classroom

In addition to teaching mathematics and carrying out those functions directly related to the classroom, teachers are expected to work with students in a variety of non-classroom situations. As part of their responsibilities mathematics teachers supervise groups of students, offer special assistance to students when they have problems learning mathematics, advise and counsel students, help students prepare to take standardized tests, and direct extracurricular student activities. Many of the non-classroom duties of teachers are a regular part of their professional responsibilities to students; however a few are regarded as additional work for which teachers receive extra compensation in some schools. Since many of these non-classroom interactions between teachers and students occur on a one-to-one basis, they provide an opportunity for teachers to get to know each student personally and to learn about students' interests outside school. Non-classroom activities not only provide interesting and useful diversions for students but also provide teachers with enjoyable breaks from classroom routines.

Supervising Groups of Students

Adolescents can be exuberant, boisterous, rowdy and at times irresponsible. Since school administrators and teachers are responsible for the welfare and safety of students while they are in school, teachers are required to supervise students as they come together for various activities outside their classrooms. Most secondary school students have one or two periods each day when they are not assigned to a class. Many of these periods are to be used as study periods, and teachers can expect to be assigned study-hall supervision on a rotating basis. While supervising a study hall, it is the teacher's responsibility to see that students are relatively quiet and are engaged in useful learning activities. Since the teacher is not in direct control of students' learning activities in a study hall, many people find that student discipline is difficult to maintain during study halls. It is well to take several good books and educational games to a study hall to occupy those students who have nothing else to do during their study periods. In addition to maintaining order in study halls, teachers also assist students with their homework in mathematics and other subjects. If the students in a study hall do not appear to have work to do, you may want to turn the study hall into a classroom and present an interesting mathematical puzzle or paradox for student discussion.

You may also be assigned homeroom duty before classes begin each morning and after classes end each afternoon. Homeroom periods may last for a few minutes to a half hour. During homeroom periods you are expected to keep order, take attendance, read announcements, collect data from students and carry out various other administrative and clerical activities. In the morning, part of the homeroom period may serve as a waiting period for students as they arrive at school before classes begin. The homeroom meeting at the end of the day may serve as a final check on student attendance and as a waiting room for school bus transportation.

In some schools teachers are assigned supervisory duties as hall or cafeteria monitors one period per day. A person assigned to hall or cafeteria duty is expected to supervise students as they move through corridors or assemble for lunch in the cafeteria. In other schools, hall and cafeteria duties are regarded as inefficient uses of teachers' time and paraprofessionals are hired on either a full or part-time basis to supervise students in halls and cafeterias.

At times during school hours, special events such as field trips, concerts, plays, films and other forms of educational entertainment are scheduled for students. Teachers are expected to supervise students on field trips or during assemblies in school. Since most school assemblies are entertaining for students, teachers have little to do during these assemblies and can enjoy the scheduled activities. The school personnel in charge of a field trip are responsible for student safety; consequently field trips should be well organized and well supervised. Written permission from a parent or guardian of each student should be obtained before the field trip and a school bus or commercial transportation should be arranged in advance. Students should neither be taken on field trips in private automobiles nor permitted to drive their own cars, because the supervising teacher may be partly responsible for accidents or injuries that could occur.

Teachers may also be asked by students or school administrators to attend special student activities such as dances, proms, parties, plays, concerts and athletic events which take place in the school building after regular school hours. In such instances teachers act as monitors who are present to supervise students and assist in maintaing order. Most of these events are orderly and enjoyable; however athletic contests can pose problems because competition is keen and students may lose control of their emotions. Many schools hire uniformed security guards to maintain order during sports events. Unfortunately, in a few schools where fights, riots and injuries have occurred among spectators at athletic contests, some emotional games are played in unpublicized locations without spectators.

Tutoring Students

Some students need extra help from the teacher in learning mathematics and there is usually insufficient time during mathematics classes to attend to all students who need individualized assistance. Many mathematics teachers are able to help their students during study halls and most teachers assist students from time to time during their own preparation periods or after school. Nearly all students have occasional learning difficulties and some have persistant problems which may only be resolved through individual tutoring. Teachers should set aside regular times when they are available to students for individual help during the school day.

Some teachers earn extra money through private tutoring in their own homes

or in students' homes. However, there are ethical considerations in tutoring your
own students. If you do tutor students privately for pay, you should avoid tutoring students who are in your own classes. To do so could be regarded by parents as a conflict of interest, since it may appear that you are being paid extra to teach a student the mathematics that he or she should be learning in your classes. You should never suggest to one of your students or a parent that you should be hired as a mathematics tutor. If the parents of one of your students do ask to hire you as a tutor, you should check the policy of your school district and obtain the approval of your school principal before accepting. There are situations where students are ill or physically handicapped and need a tutor. In such cases your school district may pay you extra to tutor students at their homes after school hours. Tutoring for pay in these cases is ethical and professionally responsible.

Advising and Counseling Students

Even though your school district may have guidance counselors, learning disability specialists and school psychologists, some of your students will come to you for assistance in solving their problems. You will need to be able to help students who have learning disabilities (see Chapter 7) and to counsel students who have personal problems. Many times students need a sympathetic, "neutral" adult to talk with about their minor problems. When a student comes to you with a serious problem you can help him or her locate professional assistance which is needed but which you are not prepared to provide.

You should also be prepared to assist students in locating information about colleges, obtaining admission to colleges, learning about jobs available to high school graduates, and finding employment upon graduation from high school. Your school library, guidance counselor and local college library have current college catalogs and other information about colleges. Your local chamber of commerce and public employment agency have general as well as specific information about employment opportunities, and The National Council of Teachers of Mathematics has several publications about careers in mathematics. You can assist students in finding jobs, obtaining admission to colleges, and getting college scholarships and other types of financial aid for post-high school education by writing letters of recommendation for students and by counseling them about how to conduct themselves during interviews.

When writing a recommendation for a student, you should emphasize those characteristics of the student that may not be found in grade reports and other school records. You should also discuss specific characteristics of the individual that are relevant to the job or college program for which he or she is applying. Promptness, dependability, ability to work with others, initiative, industriousness, character and personality are some non-academic characteristics that employers and college admissions officers look for in candidates. You should also highlight a student's extracurricular school activities and those work and family responsibilities which are assumed in addition to his or her school studies. Special awards, honors and accomplishments should also be mentioned in a letter of recommendation.

You can also advise students about their conduct during an interview. A person should be sincere and honest during an interview, should answer questions thoughtfully, diplomatically, and truthfully, and should ask relevant and thoughtful questions of the interviewer. Before going for an interview, a student should be well groomed, neatly dressed and well informed about the company or college that is interviewing him or her for a job or admission.

Helping Students Prepare for Standardized Tests

In addition to helping students prepare for your own mathematics tests, you should also "teach" them how to take standardized tests. Although the value of standardized test scores is being questioned, many colleges and employers still consider scores on various standardized tests to be important factors when reviewing the credentials of candidates. Scores on the Scholastic Aptitude Test and other college entrance examinations are factors in obtaining admission to certain colleges and in being awarded scholarships. Scores on job aptitude tests are used in selecting people for employment.

Nearly all tests require a fairly good ability to read and if some of your mathematics students are poor readers, you should refer them to a reading specialist. Inability to read can be a greater handicap than poor arithmetic skills for many people. Some people do poorly on standardized tests because they become confused about the directions, are unfamiliar with certain test formats, or do not know how or where to record their answers to test items. You should gather a file of sample standardized tests which your students can review and practice taking in their spare time, so that they can familiarize themselves with various test formats and types of test items. Your school principal and guidance counselor can assist you in obtaining sample tests, and you can also obtain sample copies of tests from companies that develop and sell standardized tests.

Some of your students may also enter local, regional, state, national, or even international mathematics contests. Although it is unwise to center the teaching and learning activities in your mathematics courses around preparing to take various kinds of mathematics tests, it may be appropriate to conduct practice sessions for students who are going to compete in mathematics contests. Even students who are not going to compete in organized mathematics "olympiads" may enjoy an occasional mathematics contest during class, after school, or as an activity of the school mathematics club.

Directing Extracurricular Activities

With the exception of private tutoring after school hours, all of the activities discussed above are part of the teachers' regular professional responsibilities and teachers are not paid extra for these activities. Most schools pay teachers in addition to their regular salaries for coaching organized, competitive school sports and some school districts compensate teachers for sponsoring clubs within a school. When an extracurricular activity is scheduled during normal school hours, it is unlikely that a teacher will be paid extra for sponsoring or directing it. However, teachers may, in certain situations, receive extra pay for directing extracurricular activities after school. When after-school activities are considered as being part of a person's regular workload, he or she will not receive extra compensation. For example, an English teacher may sponsor the school newspaper or direct the senior class play as part of his or her workload. There are no general guidelines governing extra pay for extra work, and you should use the guidelines in your own school to determine which duties are included in your regular work load and which duties are not part of your professional responsibilities.

Among the extracurricular activities that teachers direct are various boys', girls', and mixed sports such as baseball, basketball, football, track, golf, volleyball, tennis and archery. If you were graduated from high school several years ago, you may be surprised to learn that many non-contact competitive athletic teams now contain young men and women on a single team and that women's athletics are on an equal or near equal basis with men's athletics. Teachers may sponsor student clubs such as future teachers' clubs, future farmers' clubs, nurses' clubs, art clubs, science clubs, mathematics clubs, chess clubs and service clubs. Teachers also direct student activities such as student newspapers, yearbooks, cheerleading, bands, choral groups, class plays, science fairs, honorary societies, athletic societies and student branches of professional societies.

As you have seen above, teachers have many duties in school other than preparing lessons, conducting classes and evaluating student work. As a professional, you should accept your share of these non-classroom responsibilities, many of which also involve important cognitive and affective student learning objectives. Many mathematics teachers find that some of their schools' extracurricular activities for students are consistent with their own hobbies and interests, and they obtain a great deal of enjoyment and satisfaction in sharing their non-mathematical knowledge and skills with young men and women after school.

Continuing Education and Professional Development

One of the most important, and sometimes neglected, non-classroom responsibilities of teachers is continuing self-directed professional development which can be accomplished through independent study; school or college programs, courses, and workshops; and professional education societies and organizations. A college degree and an intitial teaching certificate do not mark the end of a mathematics teacher's education but only the completion of the first stage of professional development. A suggested program of continuing education for mathematics teachers will be presented in this section.

Independent Study

Reading

Self-initiated independent study is an excellent way to keep abreast of developments in mathematics, mathematics education, and general education. You should regularly read several journals in mathematics and mathematics education. You should also read monographs and papers in your field as well as books about mathematics and mathematics education. Books and articles about general aspects of teaching and learning such as instructional strategies, learning theories, history and philosophy of education and educational psychology are appropriate materials for independent study. You should review new secondary school mathematics textbooks and keep informed about new equipment, resources, and materials for teaching and learning mathematics.

The following minimal reading program should be carried out by every high school mathematics teacher:

1. Each month during the school year you should browse through the current issues of *The Mathematics Teacher, The Arithmetic Teacher,* and *School Science and Mathematics* and read selected articles from each journal which are particularly relevant for your work.

2. You can keep abreast of recent developments in mathematics by reading selected articles in each issue of *The American Mathematical Monthly*. Although some of these articles are rather technical, you can learn about new mathematical discoveries by reading the text of some articles even if you do not care to follow the details of certain proofs.

3. You can learn about new research in mathematics education which has applications in classroom teaching by browsing through issues of the *Journal for Research in Mathematics Education* and the *International Journal of Mathematical Education in Science and Technology*. Many college and university libraries subscribe to these two journals as well as the journals mentioned above. You will probably want to obtain your own subscriptions to *The Mathematics Teacher, The Arithmetic Teacher,* and *School Science and Mathematics*.

4. *The Mathematics Student* which is published four times each year by the National Council of Teachers of Mathematics is a useful and interesting paper for secondary school students and teachers.

5. You should read at least one new book about mathematics each year, one book about mathematics education, and one book about general education.

6. Newspapers and news magazines contain regular features about current issues and developments in education and you can learn about general issues in education and specific happenings in mathematics education through these sources.

7. The Center for Science and Mathematics Education in cooperation with ERIC/SMEAC has a number of papers on issues in mathematics education and publishes several new papers each year. You can obtain an annotated bibliography of these publications by requesting it from:

   The Center for Science and Mathematics Education
   The Ohio State University
   Columbus, Ohio 43210.

8. You can find other journals and books about teaching, learning, mathematics and mathematics education which will be of interest to you by browsing through the book and journal shelves of a good college or university library.

9. The **Selected Bibliographies** at the ends of chapters in this book are another source of readings for mathematics teachers which will aid in your continuing professional development.

Writing

Although nearly all teachers are aware of the value of reading for their professional development, most overlook writing as a professional activity. Many of the articles that appear in the mathematics education journals mentioned above are written by secondary school teachers. High school teachers also contribute articles to state, regional and local journals and newsletters for teachers. You can obtain information about preparing an article for a specific journal or newsletter by writing to the editor and requesting a copy of the journal's guidelines for writers.

Even though you may not contribute articles to professional journals, you should write occasional course and topic supplements to distribute to your students. Many mathematics teachers prepare handouts for their students; these handouts may contain supplementary presentations of topics that are poorly developed in the textbook or may present a new topic in mathematics or applications of mathematics.

Writing is not only a means of communicating ideas to other people, but it is also a form of study and learning. In order to write a paper, one must read other articles related to the topic and analyze, synthesize, evaluate and organize information from these articles together with one's own ideas. A good way to learn how to write well is to read a lot. By reading articles in mathematics education journals, you will "absorb" the composite style of other writers which will assist you in your own writing.

If you do write an article and submit it to a professional journal, it will be evaluated by one or more reviewers who will either recommend that it be rejected or suggest modifications that will make it suitable for publication. In either case you will obtain a written evaluation of your work, which will help you become a better writer. Beginning writers may expect to have their work rejected for publication in a journal; however papers that are revised may be resubmitted to the same journal or sent to a different journal. Since it takes some practice together with informed, constructive cricitism to become a good writer, you should not be discouraged if your initial efforts are not appropriate for publication.

Effective writing, whether it is intended for your own students, a college course assignment, or a professional journal, requires attention to many grammatical and stylistic details. You must be concerned with limiting and developing your topic, breaking your topic into subtopics in the form of an outline, developing each subtopic, preparing coherent and unified paragraphs, writing clear and concise sentences, and using correct grammar, spelling and punctuation. It is beyond the scope of this book to teach you how to become an effective writer. You should refer to the *English Competence Handbook* by Kalkstein, Regan, and Wise (1974) and *A Manual of Style* (1969) for information about how to write well.

School Workshops and College Courses

Not only will continued education help teachers improve their instructional skills, but many states also require a specified number of postbaccalaureate credits before a teacher is awarded a continuing teaching certificate. Formal teacher education can be continued through programs and workshops sponsored by one's own school district or courses and programs offered by a college or university.

You may be able to obtain state-approved "credits" toward continuing teacher certification through your participation in inservice meetings, programs and workshops in your own school. Some school districts and colleges run joint inservice teacher education workshops which carry college credit. Certain states require a specified number of college credits in addition to a bachelor's degree for continuing certification; others accept a combination of approved inservice workshops and college courses; still others accept only college credits; and a few have no additional credit requirements for continuing teaching certification.

Many practicing teachers take additional college courses in evening school and summer school for their own professional development and for salary increases in school districts where salary incentives are offered for additional study. You may find that it is beneficial both professionally and financially to obtain a higher college or university degree or a special certificate relating to your professional duties. Some high school teachers go on to earn a master's degree in mathematics and others earn special certificates in curriculum development, instruction, supervision, counseling, or administration. A few teachers earn a doctorate in mathematics education or another field of education.

If you do continue your college studies after earning your bachelor's degree and mathematics teaching certification, your own professional goals should determine the courses you take and the college program in which you matriculate. Many secondary school teachers select a program of graduate studies containing courses in the following areas:

1. Mathematics
2. Teaching methods
3. History and philosophy of education
4. Educational psychology
5. Learning theory
6. Educational evaluation and research
7. Curriculum development
8. Special issues in education

You may be able to combine some of the independent study activities suggested above with a program of graduate studies in mathematics education. Regardless of the method that you use, it is important that you continue your professional development as a mathematics teacher throughout your teaching career.

Participation in Professional Organizations

Many teachers overlook the educational and professional benefits that are available to them through participation in professional organizations. Most educational societies publish journals or newsletters which can be valuable resources for teachers. These organizations also sponsor conventions, conferences, workshops and meetings where people can come together to exchange ideas and promote educational improvements. At times, most of us lose sight of many of the professional aspects of teaching as a consequence of heavy teaching loads and daily school routines. By attending local, regional, state and national meetings of mathematics and mathematics education societies, teachers can foster their own professional development and become revitalized.

National and regional meetings of professional organizations such as the National Council of Teachers of Mathematics and the School Science and Mathematics Association offer an opportunity for teachers to engage in a variety of activities which can improve their classroom teaching. For example, each annual meeting of the National Council of Teachers of Mathematics features commercial exhibits of textbooks and other instructional resources, viewing centers where one can preview educational films and filmstrips, exhibits of student projects, workshops on many different topics in mathematics education, free and inexpensive teaching/learning resources, and hundreds of lectures and discussions on interesting and useful topics in mathematics education. Regional and local meetings of the NCTM, as well as other mathematics education organizations, have many of these same activities on a smaller scale. Some schools provide time-off from school and travel money for selected teachers to attend one or two professional meetings each year. The cost in time and money of attending a large mathematics education meeting for several days is justified through the new ideas, materials, teaching methods and enthusiasm with which teachers return to their schools.

In addition to attending meetings of mathematics education organizations, there are many other ways of becoming professionally involved with such organizations. Many teachers evaluate books and instructional resources and write reviews which appear in mathematics education journals and newsletters. Some teachers serve on editorial panels of mathematics education journals or serve on policy-making boards and councils of professional societies. Teachers are also involved in planning professional meetings and conferences and most of the workshops, lectures and discussions at mathematics education meetings are conducted by teachers. Many teachers are able to obtain release time and funds from their school districts when they present a lecture or workshop for other people at a professional meeting. Even if you have to pay your own expenses (which may be "tax deductible") you should attend a large regional or national meeting of mathematics teachers every year or two. If you are unable to attend national meetings, you may be able to attend smaller regional and local meetings, many of which are held on weekends, and to become involved in other activities of professional organizations. As is suggested above, you may even want to write an article about a topic in mathematics or a particularly good teaching strategy that you have developed and submit your article to a mathematics education journal.

The Changing Nature of Education

Throughout the nineteen seventies a number of proposals for changes in the nature of our educational system have been made. The new models that have been proposed for education range from a business-management model for school administration to replacing schools with an apprenticeship system of learning. Even though it is not possible to forecast the long-term future of schools and educational systems, it is possible to make some short-term predictions concerning changes that appear likely in education. These predictions are based upon patterns of change in society and education during the past 200 years as well as recent trends in our social, economic and educational systems. Although they are at best tentative and in some cases contradictory, such predictions do have a reasonable probability of coming true. In this section we will consider the various social and economic trends in society that are having a significant influence upon educational policy, the direct results of these influences upon schools, our present and future educational needs and objectives, and changing roles for teachers.

Social and Economic Influences Upon Education

In the book *The Future of Education: Perspectives on Tomorrow's Schooling,* edited by Louis Rubin (1975), Daniel Bell identifies three social frameworks in American society that mark major structural changes in the lives of Americans. These social frameworks are the emergence of a national society, the emergence of a communal society and the emergence of a post-industrial society.

We have become a *national society* due to revolutions in communications and transportation which began about 50 years ago. Any significant event in one part of society now has immediate influence upon every other part of society. As a national society, the effects of a riot in New York City, a flood in Louisiana, or changing lifestyles on college campuses are immediately felt throughout the

United States. Even though the United States was a nation long before 1900, it was not a true national society, because it had many different regions, each with its own identity and little communication with the others. Recently issues of health, education and welfare have become increasingly national in their effects, but they are still handled largely by individual states or local organizations. Although the Federal Government influences health care, welfare and education, we have neither a nationally administered health care plan, welfare system, nor educational system.

During the past 20 years we have become a *communal society*. That is, we have shifted from private decision making in the marketplace to public decision making through governments. This change has occurred as a result of our increased awareness of the effects of private decisions upon public welfare and the increasing need to purchase public goods rather than private goods. The decision of a private industry to dump its waste materials into one of the Great Lakes has a direct effect upon an entire region and an indirect effect upon the entire country. As a communal society we are now aware of the consequences of such actions and react to them through public policies. The federal budget has increased to more than 500 billion dollars per year and state budgets run into the billions of dollars, which means that an increasingly larger portion of people's needs are being purchased through collective funds rather than by individuals for themselves. A large part of our education, all of our national defense, our fire and police protection, and, in some cases, our food and housing are purchased through public agencies and not directly by individuals.

Quite recently the United States has become a *post-industrial society;* that is, a society in which most of the labor force is engaged in services rather than manufacturing or agriculture. Before the Civil War, and even following that war, most workers in the United States were engaged in farming, by 1945 most workers were engaged in industrial production, and by 1970 well over half of the jobs in this country were in service occupations such as health care, education and other social as well as economic services. Since a majority of the work force is now engaged in providing human and professional services, Daniel Bell believes that a very important need of our society is for theoretical knowledge rather than experiential knowledge which was required in the past. Studying scientific, social, economic, political, and educational theories may now be more important in education than learning specific vocation-related facts and skills. Our communal needs and problems have grown in magnitude to a point where trial-and-error approaches such as "tinkering around until we find a way to do it right" are no longer viable problem-solving approaches. For example, Thomas Edison invented the electric light by tinkering around without benefit of theoretical physics and mathematical models; however this non-theoretical approach was of little value in developing the technology needed to put people on the moon.

In discussing the future of government and politics in the United States, which directly influences the future of education, Harold Lasswell (in Rubin, 1975) identifies 25 public policy clusters. These interdependent policy clusters which are subject to "authoritative and controlling decisions" from the political and economic sectors of the country are paraphrased below:

1. Governmental allocations of authority and control
2. International policies among countries

3. Supervisory and administrative policies
4. Policies for dealing with civil and criminal law enforcement
5. Policies in science and technology
6. Communication and public transportation
7. Economic policies
8. Budgetary policies
9. Population, health, and family policies
10. Policies affecting the nature of education
11. Art and culture
12. Human rights
13. Responsible conduct
14. Energy policies
15. Policies in using metals and other material resources
16. Policies concerning space exploration
17. Policies on air as a life supporting resource
18. Policies regulating climate and weather modification
19. Policies on water as a life supporting resource
20. Uses of oceans and seabeds
21. Policies for dealing with natural disasters
22. Food and population policies
23. Forest- and timber-management policies
24. Wildlife policies
25. Land-use policies

The manner in which national, state and local governments deal with this set of policy clusters will determine the quality of life and the types of lives that people will lead. An issue to be resolved in dealing with these policy clusters is whether our educational system will merely change to reflect the results of policy decisions or whether it will be a significant, albeit indirect, force in determining the nature of future policy decisions.

We must keep in mind that education results in both private benefits for the learner and public benefits for society as a whole. It appears likely that future changes in our educational system will continue to reflect these two goals of learning—private needs and public welfare—and that education may become increasingly more uniform through a degree of national standardization and control over educational policies. As it becomes more difficult for local communities and state governments to obtain sufficient public funds to meet the rising costs of education, the Federal Government may assume a larger share of the cost of education with a concomitant increase in the Federal Government's control of educational policies.

At present, research, experimentation, and the growth in our knowledge base have been outstripping public policies. Rather than setting governmental policies to determine the nature of changes in our society, we have used governmental controls as a means of responding to changes after they have already occurred. Whether government should cause the changes in society through a managed economy and society or react to changes which threaten the public welfare after they occur has recently become a much-debated issue.

It has become apparent that broad changes within society as well as specific changes in the educational system should be governed by a set of *principles for change:* First, change should be based upon present and projected practices, problems and needs. Second, changes should be formulated to meet both im-

477

mediate objectives and long-range goals. Third, as changes are effected they should be measured against these goals, objectives and needs. Fourth, after changes are implemented they should be continually evaluated and revised whenever necessary. Fifth, we do not yet know enough about the mechanisms for effecting change, and the processes and results of change should be studied in order to develop models and theories of change itself. Sixth, in general, history has shown that most permanent change is evolutionary, and we might expect future changes in society to be based upon our present social structures. All of the nine contributors to *The Future of Education: Perspectives on Tomorrow's Schooling* predict evolutionary changes for society in general and education in particular and reject the more dramatic "science-fiction" viewpoint of societal change.

Although far-reaching social changes have occurred since World War II, several factors have impeded corresponding changes in education. The scarcity of funds for non-salary purposes in schools has kept our educational system from responding more fully to new needs. Increased social awareness has resulted in increased educational expenditures to assure that all students will obtain equal treatment within the educational system. These necessary efforts and expenditures to assure relative educational equality have had a moderating effect upon efforts to improve the absolute quality of education. Historically, educational institutions have tended to be conservative in adapting their internal affairs to meet new external requirements of society. The tendency in society to maintain traditional attitudes, values, customs and institutional structures has also retarded schools (which reflect public attitudes) from taking the lead in social change.

In contrast to these factors that have impeded changes in the educational system, there are several recent developments which make significant educational changes very probable in the near future. New technological developments such as computer-augmented instruction and multimedia learning centers are already changing the nature of our "delivery system" for education. Research on the chemistry and functioning of the brain promises new implications for teaching strategies which will become increasingly more related to the nature of learning. New theories of learning and new models of instruction also promise to change our approaches to classroom teaching and learning. As the cost of education continues to rise and the demand for a better-educated citizenry increases, new pressures will be brought to bear upon our educational system and society may demand some significant changes in education in the interest of efficiency and economy. As traditional social values are replaced with new values, the resistance to social change, which influences educational change, may be replaced by more liberal attitudes toward all types of changes in society.

Some people have advocated "deschooling" society and replacing schools with informal "apprenticeship" approaches to education, such as open and flexible learning centers where people who want to learn about a specific topic can come and go at will. The fact that schools now serve a custodial purpose as well as an educational function for the children of working parents is a strong incentive not to turn the major responsibility for education back to the family. In addition, as families continue to become more loosely structured in our society, there will be an increasing need for schools to assume many of the responsibilities for education that previously rested with the family unit.

It has also been suggested that we need an educational system composed of alternative "delivery systems" so that parents and students can select among several educational options. Although the free-choice concept of this "supermarket" approach to selecting and obtaining one's schooling is appealing, this concept is not likely to be implemented. In spite of the advantages of a free-enterprise system, most Americans have accepted the fact that it is economically unsound to have competing public service systems in the communal sector of society. In the interest of efficiency, we have accepted the idea of "monopolistic" enterprises—such as our postal system, public utilities and public school system—being under strict public control. It is unlikely that the public will be willing to finance several alternative systems for public education. If it is found that the public school system is not able to assume the increasing number of non-cognitive functions that are being placed upon it, it is likely that other societal institutions will accept some of these new responsibilities.

In summary, according to Louis Rubin (1975):

> We can expect that—in the battle of conflicting aspirations and life-styles—the schools will become even more controversial than they now are, as the agents of competing philosophies attempt to "train up the young" in one particular set of beliefs or another. Hence, it seems likely that the schools will need to work zealously to maintain objectivity, to achieve public consensus as to purpose, and to help children ponder the values by which one should live and recognize that in a pluralistic society a tolerance for difference is indispensable. (p. 28)

Implications of Societal Changes for Schools

The rather rapid, recent evolutionary changes in society promise to have a significant effect upon schools. The future of schools is closely tied to our social, economic and political futures; our problems in one area of society are reflected in each of the other areas. Consequently, the social and economic influences upon education which are discussed above will play a large role in determining the future of schools.

Economic considerations are already resulting in some dramatic and unanticipated changes in schools. As local, state, and national governmental bodies assume additional responsibilities for the welfare of individuals (that is, as our society becomes more communal) a smaller percentage of financial resources may be available for schools. The rapid growth in the number of school-age people in the United States has leveled off and education is no longer a "growth industry." The median age of our population has begun to increase which means that the percentage of retired citizens is increasing; as a consequence, the percentage of people paying income tax will decrease while the percentage of citizens drawing Social Security benefits will increase. Some people have predicted that, as the over-sixty-five group becomes a powerful political lobby, fewer resources will be available to support schools. In general, as more and more services are being financed by various branches of government, less money will be available for each service—education included. The major local source of revenue for schools is the property tax and in many cities the property tax base is shrinking. Consequently, state governments, through their income taxes and sales taxes, and the Federal Government, through its income tax, are assuming more and more of the responsibility for funding schools.

As the state and national governments accept more of the costs of education, they also assume more control over educational policies in local schools. Thus, we can expect to see an increasing standardization of schools throughout the United States as the national government specifies common policies and practices for schools throughout the country. As a public endeavor, educational practice has always been subject to political pressures and we can expect political considerations to play an increasingly important role in schools. Already state legislative bodies are demanding greater accountability from schools and teachers. Part of the impetus for state and national testing programs, behavioral objectives, performance contracting, competency-based educational programs, and individualized instructional systems can be attributed to political pressures for greater accountability for learning from schools and teachers. Much is now being written about the need for a planned national economy and a national planning agency to set long-range national goals and see that procedures are designed and implemented to meet these goals. If such recommendations are adopted by Congress, we can expect that public education will be included in long-range national planning.

One of the reactions to increasing political and economic pressures in education has been the rapid increase in the number of teachers at all levels of education who are joining teachers' collective bargaining organizations such as the National Education Association and the American Federation of Teachers. Many teachers have found that their unions provide a means of collectively influencing politicians and governmental bodies to pass legislation favorable to education and to allocate more resources for education.

In addition to economic and political factors affecting education, social changes have a significant influence upon the nature of schools. If a society values vocational skills most highly, its schools will tend to be vocationally oriented. Conversely, if professional competencies which are traditionally attained through advanced study are valued, then schools are likely to emphasize academic, college-preparatory programs. As the United States continues to develop as a communal society, schools will be expected to offer programs to prepare people for more service occupations and fewer industrial and agricultural occupations. A society that is rapidly evolving, such as our society at this time, needs schools that will prepare students to influence change as well as adapt to change. Within the next few years we may see yet another swing of the educational pendulum away from specific basic skills toward concepts, principles and theoretical ideas. If the economic benefits of advanced college degrees decline, as many people believe they already are doing, we may find less emphasis in schools upon college-preparatory programs and a merging of vocational and academic objectives and programs.

Many people feel that schools do not reflect the realities of life outside school and we can expect that schools, teachers and students will become more involved in non-school modes of learning. In fact, this trend has already begun and many schools are now used as civic centers where community functions are carried out and where adults meet to study a variety of life-improvement and enrichment courses and topics. Many school students are now released from school for part of each day or for an entire semester to study and learn in various special programs in other community agencies, businesses, industries, professions and colleges.

Some people believe that, as a consequence of our service-oriented society with its many person-to-person relationships, we should emphasize human interactions such as negotiation, compromise and conflict resolution in school. Maybe schools should deal more with students' personal needs and less with vocational considerations? A few educators and philosophers argue for "educational interludes;" for instance, a school system based upon ten years of compulsory education from age seven to age seventeen followed by four to six years of voluntary school, college, or vocational education which one could elect to use as the need arises. It may be that schools should prepare students to use leisure time purposefully and enjoyably and that one of the functions of schools should be to provide a place where children and adults can spend their leisure time in constructive and interesting learning activities.

Some specific developments that we may expect to see in schools within the next 20 years are: (1) various attempts to control and quantify the outcomes of education, (2) removal of some of the categorization systems in schools such as tests, grade levels, report cards, diplomas and categories into which students are placed, (3) increased and more effective use of technology in teaching and learning, (4) the use of mass media to supplement school-based instruction, and (5) renewed emphasis on individualized instruction and learning outcomes. However, as we make more use of technology and increase our emphasis upon accountability for educational outcomes, we must guard against setting minimal educational expectations, geared to some hypothetical norm, which will quickly become maximal objectives for all, or at least most, students. We must take care to encourage every student to strive for open-ended, maximal individual goals as well as to see that all students attain predetermined minimal competencies.

In assessing the future potential demand for schooling, there are several factors which indicate that the demand for education may decrease and several others which indicate that it will increase. The demand for schooling may decrease due to the public's unwillingness to pay the increasing costs for education, especially since those who bear the immediate costs are those people who have already completed most if not all of their schooling. As the values and goals of society change, there may be a decreasing emphasis upon formal education, especially higher education, and school-based education may decrease in importance. It may be that new technology and knowledge about the nature of learning will result in a much more efficient educational system which will decrease the need for large numbers of teachers as more education can be obtained in less time with fewer teachers.

The demand for schooling could increase if new methods for funding education are adopted. Possibly a small federal surtax could be imposed upon one's income to repay society for the cost of each person's education. An increasing emphasis upon continuing adult education could increase the demand for schooling. The sheer growth in the quantity of knowledge could necessitate longer periods of schooling for each person in order to transfer this knowledge from generation to generation.

Educational Objectives for the Future

The numerous and rapid changes in society have caused a re-examination of the objectives of schools and subsequent modifications in the educational system. During the last two decades schools have been assuming more and more responsibility for the welfare of individuals and are taking a larger part in bringing about social change. Throughout the first half of the twentieth century schools were responsible for the cognitive development of individuals and the transmission of quite specific moral and ethical values. Schools transmitted the cultural heritage of society to young people, taught the basic reading, writing, and arithmetic skills, and attempted to prepare students for specific vocations or for college. As our society shifted away from individual decision making in the marketplace to public decision making, the claims upon a communal society were based more upon the rights and needs of groups and less upon private decision making. After various groups within society began demanding and obtaining group rights, these rights were translated into benefits for individual members of groups and some of the benefits were distributed through the nation's school system. Schools began to assume the responsibility for seeing that students obtain well-balanced meals, physical and mental health care, and various counseling services while in school. Schools are now being used as agencies to redistribute and equalize social benefits among people. Consequently, the objectives of our educational system have been extended to include much more than transmission of knowledge to young people. In the future interrelated social welfare, affective and cognitive objectives can be expected to have equal roles in education, provided that society is willing to assume the cost of these dual roles for schools.

Among the general goals of schools for the future should be to provide open and equitable opportunities for education, to develop and use new concepts in curriculum design and implementation, and to accommodate instruction to individual as well as societal needs. Those people who determine the objectives, curricula and policies of schools should assure equal educational opportunity for all people; however they should also, in the words of Harold Shane (pp. 112-113 in *The Future of Education*), "begin to concentrate on ways of changing markedly the differences we can create in learner's abilities to contribute.... This statement does not imply a lack of standards but an absence of standardization."

Changing Roles for School Teachers

Society is changing, the objectives of education are changing, and we can expect that the roles of school teachers will also change. As new forms of instructional technology such as educational-computing tend to be used more and more in schools, teachers will become planners and managers of instructional systems rather than stand-up lecturers. To suggest that a teacher will become a "manager of an instruction system" may sound to some people as though one is speaking about dehumanizing teaching; however the opposite situation is the case. Teachers are quite effective in teaching facts and skills to a few (one, two, or three) students at a time, but very few teachers are successful in simultaneously teaching a large group (25-35) of students these same facts and skills both effectively and efficiently. A moderate-size computer can simultaneously tutor up to 60 students at individual learning centers, which frees two teachers to plan instructional strategies, attend to the learning difficulties of individual students, and develop learning resources. Using technology in classrooms is not a case of replacing teachers with machines, but is a situation in which teachers are freed from machine-like teaching chores to function as professional learning diagnosticians and curriculum planners.

The future of learning in schools is bright because, in addition to better instructional technology, teachers now have new educational theories and teaching/learning models (which have been tested in laboratories and classrooms) for use in their own teaching. Teaching, which is, in part, a creative art is rapidly becoming a combined art and science. Scientific teaching and learning principles are now being applied in schools and teachers are becoming less like tinkerers and more like scientific professionals.

Better salaries and working conditions for teachers combined with an end to the teacher shortage of the nineteen sixties are viewed positively by certain analysts of education who think that people of exceptional ability will be more inclined to enter the teaching profession. Although these same analysts tend to be uncertain about the market for teachers, they do predict an encouraging future for education irrespective of the effects of declines or increases in numbers of students, schools and teachers in the future. It appears that as the quality of education improves the public may be willing to support increases in the quantity of education for people of all ages.

To conclude our discussion about the changing nature of education, the following speculations are offered concerning schools and teaching in the future:

1. New and spectacular forms of instructional technology will be used in learning—both in school and at home.
2. Scientific breakthroughs in our knowledge of the chemistry of the brain and the nature of learning will result in significant improvements in the quality and quantity of learning in school.
3. Schools will assume a large share of the responsibility for moral and ethical education of young people.
4. New educational delivery systems will be developed as alternatives to school-based learning.
5. Research will yield new knowledge about the nature of creativity and problem solving, and schools will concentrate upon teaching these high-level cognitive processes.
6. More emphasis will be placed upon learning basic skills in school; however better instructional methods will result in a significant decrease in the time required to learn the basic skills.
7. The rapid growth of knowledge and changing patterns of employment will cause a large increase in continuing adult education, much of which will be handled by public schools.
8. New forms of teacher-to-teacher, teacher-to-student, and student-to-student interactions in learning will be available through the development of computer technology.

9. The general level of education will increase to the point where educational norms will approximate the level of education now attained by those people who complete a master's degree.
10. Books will decrease in use as a means of disseminating information and learning will center around computer-generated audio-visual resources, rather than printed learning materials.
11. Improved computer technology will make it possible to store vast quantities of information in small spaces and instantaneous random retrieval of information will be possible through inexpensive computer terminals.
12. Schooling in the future will be closely related to learning in the "real world" and artificial barriers separating home, community, occupational and school-based learning will be removed.

Even though these predictions are based upon informed opinion and current trends, they are only predictions of events which may not come to pass. You are invited to add your own speculations about the schools of the future to the twelve presented above.

The Future of Mathematics Education

The numerous changes in society and education which were discussed in the previous section are having an effect upon the nature of mathematics education. Having passed through a period of curriculum revision and controversy in secondary school mathematics education between 1955 and 1975, we have now entered a period where the objectives and curriculum of school mathematics are once again being questioned. In this section we will examine the factors influencing changes in mathematics education, speculate about future content and methods in teaching and learning mathematics, and offer some recommendations for mathematics education in the future. One of the responsibilities of each mathematics teacher is to prepare for changes in mathematics education and influence the nature of these changes through participation in professional organizations of mathematics teachers.

Factors Influencing Mathematics Education

As is pointed out in Chapter 2, the various elementary and secondary school mathematics curriculum-development projects which were begun in the nineteen fifties and sixties have resulted in a new mathematics curriculum for schools. Although many of the nation's schools have adopted "modern" mathematics textbooks, it is difficult to determine the degree to which mathematics teachers are emphasizing new content and modern approaches in their classrooms. Examination of school objectives and standardized tests indicates that the school mathematics curriculum has been modified, but that there has been no dramatic revolution in mathematics education. While some new topics have appeared in many secondary school mathematics programs, little of the traditional subject matter has been eliminated in favor of these new topics. The National Advisory Committee on Mathematical Education, NACOME, (1975) concludes that "the principal thrust of change in school mathematics remains fundamentally sound, though actual impact has been modest relative to expectations." (p. 21) NACOME recommends that the term "new math" should now be used:

only as an historical label for the vague phenomenon or the very diversified series of developments that took place in school mathematics between 1955 and 1975. Reference to current school mathematics, its status, its trends, and its problems should be made only in such common-noun terms as the ''present mathematics program'', ''current school mathematics'', ''contemporary mathematics teaching'', etc. (p. 22)

National and state standardized testing programs are having an influence upon the content of school mathematics. Many of the tests used in these assessment programs contain mostly items from traditional topics in mathematics; few of the test items are written to measure the more recent secondary school topics of sets, functions, transformations, logic, etc. Although such tests are supposed to measure how well students are learning what is being taught in mathematics classes, they also influence the content of school mathematics courses. There is a tendency on the part of curriculum planners and teachers to emphasize those topics which are covered on the standardized tests taken by their students so that their students will perform well in relation to other students. Many schools tend to modify the content of courses to be consistent with the content of these standardized tests.

The public interest in accountability within the educational system for students' learning is influencing the content and methods of school mathematics. This increasing emphasis upon accountability of schools and teachers has caused a majority of the states to prepare lists of mathematics goals and objectives for school students. Such goals do have an influence upon the mathematics content and nature of instruction in schools. Many states are also promoting competency-based educational models for school students and for teacher education programs. Such models usually emphasize the use of specific performance objectives as a basis for selecting curriculum content and teaching strategies. This current interest in accountability and behavioral objectives is due in part to the conclusion that students are not learning as well as they should in school and that a new administrative/management system in education will improve this situation.

It is thought by some people that the use of competency-based teacher education models will prepare mathematics teachers to better teach mathematics to school students. At present there is no sound research base to support competency-based teacher education and there is little empirical support for the contention that competency-based teacher education programs will result in better teachers. Before this new concept of teacher education is either rejected or implemented on a large scale throughout the United States, studies should be designed and conducted to evaluate the relative effectiveness of teachers who are educated in competency-based teacher-training programs. NACOME believes that it is unlikely that one set of teacher behaviors promoted through a competency-based teacher education model will be found to be effective for teaching all of mathematics to all students.

The current surplus of mathematics teachers is another factor influencing mathematics education. On the one hand a teacher surplus could mean that only the best new teachers will obtain teaching positions. But on the other hand, it could also mean that poorer, dissatisfied teachers may be reluctant to leave the security of a ''tenured'' teaching position to try working in another field. In balance, these and other factors resulting from the current teacher surplus are not likely to have much immediate effect upon the quality of mathematics education. The reaction to the teacher surplus is causing many high school and college students to reject teaching as a career. Consequently, there may be a decline in the supply of new teachers throughout the late nineteen seventies and early nineteen eighties. In a study of the RAND Corporation in 1973-74 it was concluded that "if and when the [teacher] surplus ends, the inertia in the system will lead to the almost immediate onset of a substantial and lengthy teacher shortage." (p. 13)

During the "new math" period federal, state and local governments as well as private agencies provided large sums of money for mathematics curriculum development and the improvement of teaching. Since some people feel that mathematics education has already received its share of public resources for improvement, it is unlikely that the resources for another round of "new math" will be forthcoming. The overwhelming emphasis upon scientific and technical education during the nineteen fifties and sixties, as well as public support and interest, has now shifted to social programs and better education for students who have various social disadvantages or learning disabilities. The funds for research and development in mathematics education which were readily available 20 years ago probably will not be available during the next decade. NACOME (1975) takes the rather pessimistic, yet realistic viewpoint that:

> School mathematics is in an unusual state today. Long enshrined as a unique and well-supported discipline with a clear-cut and almost monolithic identity, it is suddenly beset with many troubles—an identity crisis brought on by the usual causes: internal confusion and loss of clear-cut direction and external changes in familiar support and status structures.
>
> Current cultural preoccupations no longer award mathematical, scientific and technological disciplines the first place of honor (and funding) that has been the case for many years. The centrality of mathematics to national needs triggered by the Sputnik launching is no longer felt. Young people who formerly flocked to mathematics because it was so important and had such national status now look elsewhere. The popularity of mathematics and its funding by public and private agencies has greatly waned. At the same time, a plateau has been reached in the two-decade series of developments referred to as the "new math." Whatever its achievements (and they were many), it also has enough problems and unfulfilled goals to generate a host of critics among educators, parents and even politicians. (p. 147)

Even though school mathematics no longer has the public interest that it once had, there are many reasons to be optimistic about the future of mathematics education. Mathematics teachers, at least at the secondary school level, are better prepared to teach mathematics than were teachers twenty years ago. Mathematics teachers at all levels have new, well-tested theories of teaching and learning to use in their classrooms. School administrations have become aware of the need for mathematics laboratory resources and are beginning to purchase such resources for teachers. Recent developments in educational technology promise to free teachers from some of their routine clerical and administrative chores. Elementary and secondary school teachers are becoming more involved in professional activities at state and national levels and are beginning to have a significant impact upon the nature of school mathematics. This increase in teacher involvement in determining the nature of school mathematics for the future is a positive reaction to some of the inadequacies of "new math" which were attributed to overdomination by college and university professors in the "new math" movement. Even though the issue over the educational value of competency-based teaching/learning systems has not been resolved, it has caused teachers to examine the goals and objectives of their courses. As compared to ten years ago, there has been a significant increase in the number of mathematics teachers who can justify the content and methods that they are teaching and using in their classes.

The "new math" movement did result in a modest modernization of the content of school mathematics; however a considerable portion of the content of present mathematics curricula is obsolescent. As we move toward adoption of the metric system and make more use of calculators and computers in schools and in society as a whole, many of the traditional skills learned in school mathematics are decreasing in relevance. How important are practicing skills for simplifying complex fractional expressions, learning dozens of manipulative skills in algebra, and studying various procedures for solving triangles in trigonometry? Will the metric system and hand calculators decrease the importance of studying fractions in school and result in greater emphasis upon decimal representations of numbers and the skills of estimating and approximating answers? Will computer-based algorithms from numerical analysis decrease the value of pencil-and-paper techniques for solving equations and systems of equations? Do we need to teach students how to compute using slide rules and logarithms? We can expect that practical considerations may have a greater influence in changing the content of school mathematics than did structural and philosophical arguments during the "new math" period.

Expanding mathematical knowledge and new applications of mathematics may also influence school mathematics in the future. As an example of the expanding applications of mathematics, René Thom and other mathematicians have developed a branch of applied mathematics called *catastrophe theory*. Catastrophe theory, which has its foundations in topology, is used to describe phenomena that jump abruptly from one state to a radically different state. At present it appears that catastrophe theory can be used to predict catastrophic events such as human nervous disorders, collapses of bridges, and abrupt natural changes. Thom has shown that the nearly limitless number of discontinuous scientific phenomena can be modeled using a small number of space surfaces. Catastrophe theory and other reserach developments in mathematics will have long-range implications for school mathematics.

Various innovations and panaceas in education have been consistently vying for the attention of teachers. One of the lessons that we have learned from the "new math" phenomenon is that innovations should be carefully tested and evaluated before they are universally implemented in the educational system. Teachers need to become much more critical before accepting educational innovations upon the say-so of an "authority." Before adopting new programs, teachers should demand solid empirical evidence based upon well-designed, longitudinal research studies such as the *National Longitudinal Study of Mathematical*

Abilities carried out by the School Mathematics Study Group. However, teachers should not let an irrational resistance to all change keep them from adopting proven curriculum innovations for use in their mathematics courses. Both "bandwagon" type promotion of innovations and dogmatic resistance to change can have serious negative effects upon our attempts to improve mathematics education in secondary schools.

The current teacher surplus has had the effect of moving the emphasis in teacher education programs away from preservice teacher preparation toward inservice teacher education programs. Various salary and professional incentives are prompting more and more mathematics teachers to continue their education beyond a bachelor's degree in college. The effect of this change in emphasis in teacher education is that mathematics teachers are more aware of new content, methods, theories and resources for school mathematics and are better able to assist students in attaining high-level cognitive and affective objectives in their mathematics classrooms.

It is difficult to predict the directions that mathematics education may take as a consequence of attempts to unify secondary school mathematics, to combine the teaching of mathematics with other subjects, to decrease emphasis upon college-preparatory mathematics programs, and to emphasize broad mathematics programs for career preparation and citizenship. One can expect that these efforts will have an influence upon the nature of mathematics in the future.

The Future Content of School Mathematics

Since the twenty-year "new math" period (when billions of dollars were spent to change the school mathematics curriculum) resulted in modest evolutionary changes in school mathematics, it is not likely that the next ten years will witness a revolution in school mathematics. It is more likely that the evolutionary changes begun in the "new math" era will continue during the foreseeable future. Throughout the "new math" period, issues were dichotomized as follows: old math versus new math, skills versus concepts, concrete representations versus abstract representations, intuitive concepts versus formal concepts, inductive reasoning versus deductive reasoning, mathematical structure versus applications of mathematics, and computation versus understanding. While this dichotomization of issues was useful in identifying the critical concerns of mathematicians and mathematics educators, it also served to obscure the real issues in school mathematics. The speeches, articles and books promoting and condemning certain practices seemed to indicate that the subsuming issue in mathematics education was the right way to teach mathematics versus the wrong way of teaching it, which is an inaccurate viewpoint of the issues in school mathematics.

At present we are faced with a choice among several right ways to teach mathematics and a problem of how to incorporate many good mathematics topics and teaching strategies into the mathematics programs of schools. Most mathematics educators agree that students should study some "old math" topics together with certain "new math" topics. Students need to learn both skills and concepts and should be able to perform computations as well as understand algorithmic procedures. Many students will find an understanding of the structure of mathematics as well as knowledge of the applications of mathematics interesting and useful. Certain mathematical concepts and principles should be introduced inductively and others should be presented deductively. Most school students learn mathematics best when new concepts and principles are introduced through concrete representations; but the power of mathematical ideas is best realized through subsequent abstractions. Both student intuition and formal, symbolic representations have their place in teaching and learning mathematics. Through hindsight, one can conclude that in nearly all cases the proponents of a certain method for teaching mathematics were at least partially correct in their beliefs and that in nearly all cases the critics were wrong in condemning them. It is very unlikely that a "best" way of teaching mathematics will be found within the next two decades. Until a best way is found, the most appropriate approach to mathematics education is to use a variety of tested methods which seem to work well in most instances and to use special techniques for special teaching/learning situations.

We can expect to see some modifications in the content of school mathematics within the next ten years. Specifically, we should anticipate the following changes in mathematics content and begin preparing for them:

1. As the use of computers and hand-held calculators becomes common in most schools, we can expect to see less emphasis upon pencil-and-paper arithmetic skills and more emphasis upon approximation techniques, estimation and evaluation of answers to see if they are reasonable.
2. As hand-held calculators become available to all school students, remedial arithmetic may disappear as a secondary school course. Those students, who for various reasons were unable to learn pencil-and-paper arithmetic skills in elementary school, will use calculators to do arithmetic calculations in secondary school. This will permit them to study some of the more interesting ideas in mathematics.
3. Computers in secondary schools with accompanying computer programs for carrying out various mathematical algorithms will result in discarding certain hand-calculation methods of algebra and trigonometry and replacing them with methods best suited for computer implementation.
4. Analyzing errors due to rounding, approximating and truncating may replace pencil-and-paper computations and become the new skills of a future mathematics curriculum.
5. Adoption of the metric system will decrease the time needed to learn measurement and will result in more emphasis upon decimals and less emphasis upon fractions.
6. For the next few years, mathematics teachers will have most of the responsibility for teaching computer literacy and computer programming courses in secondary schools.
7. School objectives and textbook exercises will begin to emphasize important applications of mathematics throughout society.
8. The teaching of skills and the teaching of concepts will assume equal importance in the school curriculum.
9. Although applications of mathematics will become more important in the school curriculum, there may be a renewed emphasis upon general mathematical structures and systems.

10. Formal mathematical abstractions will become an important part of the mathematics curriculum; however abstract concepts will be presented through a spiral approach beginning with concrete representations of each concept.

11. While proof will still be of concern in mathematics courses, the value of intuition and educated guessing will be highlighted in school mathematics. Both intuitive and rigorous methods of proof will be taught in mathematics courses other than plane geometry.

12. High school mathematics courses will be unified and the present categorization of courses into algebra, geometry, trigonometry, etc. may be eliminated.

13. Numerical analysis will become an important topic in high school mathematics.

14. Topics from probability, descriptive statistics, and inferential statistics will become part of the standard secondary school mthematics curriculum.

15. Special non-remedial courses will be developed for less able students. These courses will have their own distinctive learning objectives and content and will not be "watered-down" versions of topics from other parts of the mathematics program.

16. Practical, interesting, "real-world" consumer mathematics courses will be offered to all students, not only the less able students.

17. The so-called "new math" topics such as sets, functions, transformations and mathematical structures will be taught, not as an end in themselves, but as means to an end.

18. Euclidean geometry may be abandoned in favor of more general and inclusive approaches to geometry such as transformational geometry.

Teaching in the Future

In addition to changes in the content of secondary school mathematics, mathematics classes in the future will become more student centered. Teachers will spend more time diagnosing learning difficulties of individual students and prescribing individualized learning activities and less time lecturing to large groups of students. We can expect to find more teachers' aides in schools to handle many of the clerical and administrative responsibilities that teachers are presently expected to carry out without assistance. Aides will take attendance, gather personal data from students, order instructional resources, supervise students during non-classroom activities, and provide secretarial assistance to teachers. The use of teachers' aides will give mathematics teachers more time to plan individualized lessons and laboratories for students, evaluate student progress, and prepare a variety of instructional resources for use in classrooms. As computers and hand calculators become standard equipment in school mathematics programs, teachers' aides will assist students in learning how to operate these new electronic devices and will have the responsibility for the security of these and other forms of instructional technology.

In the future teachers and students will be less dependent upon their textbooks and will use a variety of supplementary books and articles in learning mathematics. Individual teachers and groups of teachers will write many of their own instructional units which will be copied in the school and distributed to students as supplements to commercial learning resources. Comprehensive textbooks

covering all of the material for an entire year of mathematics classes may be
replaced by paperback resource booklets covering individual topics in mathematics. Each mathematics program will have its own resource library and library
materials will be used as an integral part of the mathematics curriculum.

Schools will make more use of specialized resource personnel to assist teachers in diagnosing student learning handicaps, giving help to less able learners,
and handling discipline problems. Guidance counselors will work closely with
teachers in selecting course sequences and extracurricular activities for each
student.

Curriculum planners will make provisions for spiral approaches to teaching
and learning most of the content of school mathematics. This increased emphasis
upon spiral teaching/learning strategies will necessitate an integrated K through
12 mathematics curriculum. Each mathematics teacher, irrespective of the age
level of his or her students, may be expected to know the entire school mathematics curriculum and to be proficient in the entire spectrum of school mathematics.
If significant improvements in teaching and learning mathematics are to be accomplished, elementary school mathematics teachers must be specialists in
mathematics and teaching mathematics. This means that the gap between the
mathematical preparation of elementary and secondary school teachers must be
narrowed and probably should be eliminated.

We will see an even greater emphasis in the future upon teaching mathematics
according to specific student learning objectives. Students may be expected to
demonstrate minimum mathematics competencies before they are awarded a high
school diploma. The public will hold schools and teachers accountable for student mastery of basic mathematics skills in school. This emphasis upon minimal
mathematical competencies for all students could create a new problem in
schools. Unfortunately, there may be a tendency to teach for minimal objectives
and ignore the fact that each student is also entitled to achieve the maximal
amount of mathematical knowledge consistent with his or her distinctive
abilities. We must be certain that we do not permit minimal standards for less
able students to inadvertently become maximal standards for the most able
students.

It is unlikely that the several disciplines now taught separately in school will
be combined; however the increasing emphasis upon learning to solve difficult
"real-world" problems through interdisciplinary approaches will lead to new
interactions among teachers of various school subjects. We can expect to see
unidisciplinary classrooms and multidisciplinary laboratories in schools of the
future. In order to make school learning even more relevant to society, mathematics students will engage in multidisciplinary community learning programs
and will be released from school periodically to work and study in many different
types of public and private community agencies. In general, school learning will
be integrated with non-school situations for learning and applying mathematics.

Teachers should be expected to carry out ongoing, formative research and
evaluation in their classrooms in order to determine the most effective teaching/
learning strategies for themselves and their students. Unless a single best way of
teaching is discovered, which is unlikely, teaching and learning must be individualized according to characteristics of both teachers and students. Society has

accepted the fact that students have different learning characteristics and should
receive instruction appropriate for their individual learning styles. It should also
be realized that teachers have different teaching styles and that each teacher
should be permitted to develop and use his or her distinctive teaching strategies
in conjunction with the learning characteristics of students. Unless the future
brings some dramatic breakthroughs in our understanding of the nature of learning, it would be remiss to attempt to standardize teaching strategies. At present
there is no research evidence to suggest that there is one best model for teaching
all mathematics to all students.

The technology now exists to individualize a considerable portion of instruction in basic mathematical skills through educationally-sound, interactive computer programs. In the future computers can be used to teach routine facts and
skills in mathematics while teachers concentrate upon promoting inquiry and
problem-solving processes. As the relatively routine instruction in mathematical
facts and skills becomes more efficient, students can concentrate upon interesting
concepts, principles and applications of mathematics.

In general, as better methods are used in teaching a more relevant mathematics curriculum, we can expect students to be more successful in learning mathematics. Lack of motivation to learn mathematics, which is a serious problem in
today's schools, can be replaced by a fascination with the structure and uses of
mathematics. It is hoped that in the future the cycle of failure breeding disinterest
which breeds more failure can be replaced in school mathematics with a cycle of
success which increases motivation which leads to more success. The increasing
attention to affective learning objectives in education is an attempt to make learning in school a success-oriented endeavor for all students.

Recommendations for Mathematics Education

Although several predictions about the future of mathematics education are given
above, education is affected by so many factors that predictions about the future
of school mathematics are at best speculations. What we can do is analyze and
evaluate past trends and current practices in mathematics education to offer some
recommendations for the future. Many of the recommendations given below
reflect the NACOME recommendations found in *Overview and Analysis of
School Mathematics Grades K-12*.

The Content of School Mathematics

Changing goals and needs in society will have a significant influence upon the
content of school mathematics which will result in continuing changes in the
specific content of mathematics courses. Therefore it would be unwise to insist
upon adherence to specific long-range content objectives for school mathematics. What we can and should do is to set some general short-term content objectives for school mathematics programs. Some of these objectives are offered in
the following recommendations:

1. Numerical methods in mathematics which have evolved as a consequence of computer technology should be incorporated in the school
   mathematics program.
2. Various modes of computer-related instruction and learning should be
   used in mathematics classrooms.

3. In order to understand the uses and limitations of computers, students in mathematics courses should write and executive computer programs to solve applied mathematics problems.

4. School mathematics programs at all levels should include considerable instruction and practice in using the metric system.

5. Topics in probability and statistics should be "spiraled" throughout mathematics in elementary school programs, and inferential statistics and applications of probability theory should be emphasized in high school mathematics.

6. At least by seventh grade students should be encouraged to use hand calculators to do arithmetic calculations found in applications of mathematics. Schools should make calculators available to students for work in class and during mathematics tests.

7. The logical structural framework of mathematics should be used as a subsuming generalization in studying mathematical concepts and principles.

8. Concrete experiences and applications of mathematics should be an integral part of all school mathematics courses.

9. Topics in the history and philosophy of mathematics and biographical information about mathematicians should be included in mathematics courses so that students will appreciate the social as well as technological aspects of mathematics.

10. Abstractions and symbols should be introduced in mathematics courses when topics can not be further developed without such formalisms. However, abstractions, symbolism and structure should be regarded as a means to understanding and applying mathematical ideas and should not be taught as ends in themselves.

11. Intuition and rigor should be included in all mathematics courses and the role of each in mathematical progress should be demonstrated.

12. We should avoid the "all-or-nothing" controversies that were prevalent during the "new math" period and attempt to find reasonable compromises among conflicting sets of good ideas for the school mathematics curriculum of the future.

Student-Oriented Recommendations

One of the criticisms of "new math" is that the 20-year "new math" period was overly-oriented toward content with inadequate concern for the nature of student learning. We must take care in the future to see that a judicious balance is maintained between the integrity of mathematics content and the learning needs and characteristics of students. We can neither afford to permit the interests of professional mathematicians to dominate curriculum selection nor to include only those mathematics topics which are easy and popular among students in the school mathematics program. Based upon this premise of balance and moderation, the following student-oriented recommendations for school mathematics are offered:

1. Minimum skills should not be permitted to become performance ceilings for any student.

2. Every mathematics student is entitled to learn minimum mathematics skills necessary for intelligent consumerism and effective citizenship.

These basic skills include not only facts and computations but also concepts and principles.

3. Students should be given the opportunity to use and apply mathematics in the widest possible realm.

4. Students should learn logical reasoning and problem-solving capabilities in secondary school mathematics.

5. Students should learn to appreciate the uses and applications of mathematics outside the school curriculum.

6. Development of attitudes as well as cognitive abilities in students should be given continuing attention in school mathematics programs.

7. The unfounded assumption that mathematics is a subject more appropriate for males than females should be vigorously opposed by teachers and students.

8. Students are entitled to individual assistance in diagnosing and overcoming their difficulties in learning mathematics.

9. Fair and consistent policies for evaluating, testing and grading students should be used by all mathematics teachers.

10. Care should be used in constructing tests and interpreting test results in order to avoid potential cultural biases.

11. Evaluation instruments should be based upon both program goals and individual student learning objectives.

12. Vocational and college-preparatory objectives should be available to students during their school mathematics programs, and neither set of objectives in a mathematics program should preclude students from learning both vocational and college-preparatory mathematical skills.

13. Special high school programs should be available for less able students as well as for students showing unusual aptitude in mathematics.

14. Appropriate and sensitive measures of affective mathematics learning objectives should be developed.

Teacher-Oriented Recommendations

As we set out to improve mathematics education in the future, it is obvious that we must attend to the needs of students, but it may be less obvious that we must also attend to the needs of mathematics teachers. The following teacher-oriented recommendations are offered as a means of improving school mathematics by attending to teachers' needs:

1. In order to evaluate the effects of teacher education programs upon mathematics teachers and students, teacher education institutions should use follow-up studies of their graduates to evaluate and improve their programs.

2. Teacher education institutions should assess the inservice educational needs of teachers and prepare inservice programs to meet their needs.

3. Textbook publishers should be responsive to the needs of teachers by preparing special manuals and resources that teachers can use as supplements to student textbooks.

4. Better ways must be found to disseminate educational research findings to classroom teachers.

5. All mathematics teachers should take at least one computer-programming course in their college programs, a general computer-literacy course, and a course on educational applications of computers.

6. Professional organizations for mathematics teachers should take an ac-

tive role in determining educational and professional standards for teachers.

7. Professional organizations in mathematics education should take initiatives to insure that mathematics teachers have a voice in making decisions relating to all aspects of the school mathematics curriculum.
8. The backgrounds of college professors who are responsible for the education and certification of mathematics teachers should include relevant mathematical competencies and current experience with the school mathematics curriculum.
9. Agencies responsible for change in mathematics education should realize that teachers must accept new programs and methods and may need to be re-educated in order to implement educational innovations effectively.
10. School districts should support the inservice education and professional development of teachers.
11. School boards and administrators should assist teachers in obtaining the resources that they need in developing quality mathematics programs for all types of students.
12. Teachers need the interest, support and cooperation of parents in carrying out school mathematics programs.

A Final Note

In concluding our discussion of the future of mathematics education, we must be aware of the interest and influence of groups outside the educational system in the welfare of school mathematics. NACOME (1975) summarizes this relationship between educators and other citizens concerned about the future of school mathematics as follows:

> A positive side of the current wave of criticism is the evident interest and involvement in school mathematics of many important groups. This interest and even this criticism are welcomed, with the hope that they will be responsible and responsive to dialogue and interaction and will reflect the appropriate roles and competencies of the critical bodies. Legislative and governmental bodies have a legitimate interest in educational outcomes—but seldom the professional depth of educational expertise. Their voice is important—but should be raised with restraint and should remain in the policy sphere. Parents should remain interested and vocal—but should make every effort to become informed before becoming critical. Teachers, individually and through their various professional agencies, should have an increasing voice in determining the parameters of mathematical programs in the schools. (p. 148)

Things To Do

1. Make a list of your rights and responsibilities as a professional mathematics teacher. Discuss how your rights and responsibilities are related to and interact with the rights and responsibilities of other teachers, school administrators, students and parents.
2. Suggest ways in which you can work with other teachers, school administrators and parents to improve your capability to teach mathematics to your students.

3.   How do the rights and responsibilities of students affect your methods for maintaining a well-disciplined and effective classroom environment?

4.   Your professional rights and responsibilities as a mathematics teacher are not so well specified as to be completely and clearly defined. Suggest general areas and specific events in which your professional activities and responsibilities could conflict with the rights and activities of students, the professional activities of school administrators, or the prerogatives of the parents of your students. How could you resolve such conflicts in a professional and an equitable manner?

5.   Mathematics education has been and will continue to be in a state of change. Assess your own resistance to and acceptance of various changes in the school mathematics program. Outline some effective strategies for dealing with specific types of changes in mathematics education. Also, suggest inappropriate reactions to change and discuss why these reactions are neither desirable nor effective.

6.   If you should want to change teaching positions, what is the proper, professional and ethical way to go about seeking and accepting a new position and leaving your present position?

7.   Describe a number of non-classroom situations in which students might properly call upon you for assistance. Discuss how you might respond to each of these situations in which students need your professional services outside the classroom.

8.   What types of non-classroom duties might you expect as part of your regular professional assignment as a school mathematics teacher? What are some of the professional responsibilities that you will be asked to carry out in addition to your normal duties as a teacher?

9.   Outline a long-term program for your own continuing professional development as a mathematics teacher. Consider the importance of independent study, inservice programs within your school, college courses and programs, and participation in professional organizations as part of your continuing professional activities.

10.   Suggest a variety of ways in which you might participate in different educational organizations in order to foster your own professional development and benefit the students who will be studying mathematics in your classes.

11.   List, analyze and evaluate the influences of various social and economic changes upon the nature of education in the United States.

12.   Suggest how each of the 25 "public policy clusters" identified in this chapter may influence the nature of education in the future.

13.   Several general educational objectives for the future are presented and discussed in this chapter. Make a list of specific objectives which you think schools should attend to in the future.

14.   Present your perception of the role or various roles assumed by secondary school mathematics teachers. What changes in the roles of mathematics

teachers do you expect will occur in the immediate future? Ten years from now? By the year 2000?

15. List and discuss the various factors that affect the nature of mathematics education. What influence can you as, a secondary school teacher, have upon the future of mathematics education? Discuss specific ways in which you can have an effect upon future developments in teaching and learning mathematics.

16. Outline an ideal secondary school mathematics program for the future. Be sure to identify courses and specific mathematics topics that should be included in the curriculum.

17. Read the recommendations for mathematics education that are offered near the end of this chapter and add your own recommendations to the list. Give a rationale for each of your suggestions. Can you justify each recommendation that is made in this chapter? Do you think that any of the recommendations are inappropriate? If so, state your reasons.

Selected Bibliography

A Manual of Style. 12th ed. Chicago: The University of Chicago Press, 1969.
    This manual contains most of the things one needs to know about style and conventions in writing. It deals with punctuation, spelling, names, numbers, quotations, illustrations, tables, abbreviations, footnotes, bibliographies, citations and indexes.

American Teacher. Washington, D.C.: American Federation of Teachers.
    The *American Teacher,* which is the national publication of the American Federation of Teachers, is published monthly except July and August. Each issue of this publication communicates information about the policies and activities of the AFT to its members.

Carroll, Stephen J., and Ryder, Kenneth F. *The Supply of Elementary and Secondary Teachers.* Santa Monica, California: RAND Corporation, 1974.

Griffiths, H. B., and Howson, A. G. *Mathematics: Society and Curricula.* London, England: Cambridge University Press, 1974.
    Changes in mathematics education are discussed under the headings: *Determinants of Change: External, Determinants of Change: Internal,* and *Instruments of Change.*

Kalkstein, Paul, Regan, Thomas J., and Wise, K. Kelly. *English Competence Handbook.* Wellesley Hills, Massachusetts: Independent School Press, 1974.
    This handbook is a "recipe book" to help people learn how to write effectively. The authors discuss sentence structure, paragraph development, style and usage; they also present and evaluate many examples of written passages.

Morphet, Edgar L., Jesser, David L., and Ludka, Arthur P. *Planning and Providing for Excellence in Education.* Denver, Colorado: Improving State Leadership in Education, 1971.
    According to the *Introduction* to this book prepared by the project, *Improving State Leadership in Education,* its purpose "is to encourage and assist the citizens of each state to seek and utilize the most appropriate and

effective ways to improve all levels and aspects of education throughout the state—to become seriously and meaningfully involved in a continuing quest for excellence in education.'' (p. v) This book deals with the nature and process of change in education, forces and factors that influence educational change, and strategies for bringing about change.

National Advisory Committee on Mathematical Education. *Overview and Analysis of School Mathematics Grades K-12*. Washington, D.C.: Conference Board of the Mathematical Sciences, 1975.

This book contains a well-balanced, thorough analysis of current issues, policies and practices in mathematics education and a number of allusions to the future of mathematics education in the United States. The following topics in mathematics education are treated in this report of the National Advisory Committee on Mathematical Education (NACOME): mathematics curriculum reform 1955-1975, current programs and issues, patterns of instruction, teacher education, evaluation, and recommendations and perspectives on mathematics education.

NASSP Bulletin. Reston, Virginia: The National Association of Secondary School Principals.

This bulletin is published monthly September through May, and each issue contains articles about current issues and practices in secondary schools. Although published for secondary school principals, the *NASSP Bulletin* has articles of interest to teachers as well. Reading this publication will give you a better understanding of the work and concerns of school administrators.

NEA Reporter. Washington, D.C.: National Education Association.

The *NEA Reporter,* a paper published monthly September through June, is available to individuals only as a part of membership in the National Education Association. Issues contain information about collective bargaining in education and the rights and responsibilities of teachers, school administrators and boards of education.

Rubin, Louis (Editor). *The Future of Education: Perspectives on Tomorrow's Schooling*. Boston: Allyn and Bacon, Inc., 1975.

Among the papers contained in this collection are *The School of the Future: Adaptive Environments for Learning* by Robert Glaser, *The School of the Future: Technological Possibilities* by Patrick Suppes, and *The School of the Future: Needed Research and Development* by Ralph W. Tyler. This book is based, in part, upon a national invitational conference—The Alternative Futures of Education. I recommend this excellent book on the future of education and society to all secondary school teachers.

Schoen, Harold L., and Hunt, Thomas C. *The Effect of Technology on Instruction: The Literature of the Last Twenty Years*. Iowa City: The University of Iowa, 1975.

In this 15-page monograph the authors briefly review some of the literature and programs concerned with using technology in education during the previous 20 years. They discuss several technology-based instructional strategies and summarize trends in using technology in education. A brief bibliography is also included in the monograph.

Today's Education. Washington, D.C.: National Education Association.

   Today's Education is the journal of the National Education Association. It is published four times each year. Each issue of this journal contains a number of articles on current issues in education that are of interest and value to classroom teachers.

Turner, Nura D. (Editor). *Mathematics and My Career*. Reston, Virginia: National Council of Teachers of Mathematics, 1971.

   In this book seven people discuss the usefulness of mathematics in their widely differing careers.

Additional References: Occasional articles in issues of *The Mathematics Teacher* and *The Arithmetic Teacher* deal with non-classroom professional concerns of teachers.

9

The Slow Learner In Mathematics

Like a struggling plant, the slow learner needs a lot of light, nourishment, and care. The NCTM, your professional organization, has now published the 35th Yearbook, THE SLOW LEARNER IN MATHEMATICS. Editor William C. Lowry and twenty other outstanding educators have been working since 1967 on its development. This significant fully illustrated 530-page yearbook is organized into main parts.

part provides background information that teacher ful — characteristics and needs of slow lear rature, the advantages of stating student behaviors

Teaching Exceptional Students

For a number of years, many schools have offered special sections of mathematics courses for students who have greater than average difficulty learning mathematics. These students, who as a group exhibit a variety of problems in learning mathematics, are usually classified as underachievers, low achievers, or slow learners. In mathematics, the term slow learner has come to be used to identify this large group of students who do not learn mathematics as rapidly and as well as the school system and teachers expect they should.

More recently, an increasing number of school systems are offering special mathematics courses and programs for students who show outstanding mathematical ability. These students learn mathematics much more rapidly than other students in their classes and may have considerable interest in mathematics. Students with special talents for particular subjects are usually referred to as gifted students.

Since one goal of our educational system is to provide each person with the opportunity to develop his or her creative talents and intellectual abilities to their maximum extent, many state departments and boards of education mandate special programs for exceptional students. Slow learners are enrolled in appropriate courses designed to meet their special educational needs and gifted students are offered special courses to develop their exceptional abilities to their fullest. Ideally schools should not provide the same education for all students but should provide each student the opportunity to learn as much as possible at his or her own rate of learning. In mathematics education, we can not afford to ignore either the needs of the slow student or the requirements of the mathematically-gifted student.

Teaching Mathematics to Slow Learners

Probably the most dramatic characteristic distinguishing the student who does exceptionally well in mathematics from the student who does poorly is the speed at which these students are able to learn mathematics. While nearly all people do develop the mental abilities to learn much of school mathematics during the progressive stages of their intellectual development, there is considerable variation among students in the rate at which they are able to master mathematics skills, concepts and principles. Although a few slow learners may be unable to learn mathematics because they have severe intellectual handicaps or psychological problems, most poor students do not do well in the subject because they are (for various reasons) unable to learn new material at the rate the teacher presents it. Most teachers tend to present a subject so that the upper 60 to 70 percent of students in the class are able to master the material fairly well. So we see that the term "slow learner" best describes students who do poorly in mathematics because they do, in fact, learn more slowly than most of their classmates.

In this section we will discuss some of the characteristics and needs of slow learners, suggest ways of creating a favorable environment in which these students can learn mathematics, and examine those teaching/learning models and strategies that are most appropriate for helping slow learners learn mathematics.

Characteristics and Needs of Slow Learners

Richard Schulz, writing in the NCTM yearbook, *The Slow Learner in Mathematics,* has this to say about attempts to characterize slow learners:

> *Low achievers, underachievers, educationally disadvantaged, culturally deprived, emotionally disturbed*—with an alacrity and confidence betraying only superficial understanding, some educators apply these euphemistic labels to children and adolescents. Whatever term is used, there is little evidence that human beings can be so categorized with any degree of precision.
>
> Slow learners have been variously defined, in terms of IQ range, mathematical achievement, teacher grades, reading level, or various combinations of these. They do indeed demonstrate below-average intellectual capacity on the basis of at least one of these criteria and are likely to display mathematical atrophy, or arrested development. They thus have much in common. Nevertheless slow learners—by any definition—are not alike. Each has his own unique set of strengths and weaknesses, and each shares in the universal, though highly variable, attributes, concerns, and needs of other human beings. (p. 1)
>
> Slow learners, no less than other human beings, are unique individuals. Each has his own set of strengths and weaknesses; each defies a stereotype. Yet in some respects they are alike; for it is common to find them deficient in affective functioning as well as in cognitive functioning. In fact, if slow learners in mathematics do share any common characteristic, it is probably that of a poor self-image with respect to mathematics. (p. 22)

In general, a particular slow learner may do poorly in his or her mathematics classes as a consequence of any of a variety of learning difficulties or social, emotional and motivational problems. In Chapter 7 some of the more pronounced causes of learning difficulties are presented, and you may want to review the section "Diagnosing and Resolving Learning Difficulties" (pp. 768-794) before reading on.

Cognitive Difficulties of Slow Learners

Many slow learners in mathematics, especially those in junior high school, are mentally immature. That is, they have not yet progressed through the stage of intellectual development which permits them to reason abstractly and use formal logical processes when learning mathematical concepts and principles. Such students tend to have trouble dealing with several variables simultaneously, which is an important activity in learning mathematics. Students who reason from example to example and from specific instance to specific instance will encounter difficulties when they are expected to use inductive reasoning, to understand general, inclusive principles, and to use deductive processes in developing algorithms or verifying conjectures.

Many slow learners lack the ability to comprehend concepts and principles when they are presented and explained abstractly or symbolically. Even when they do understand mathematical ideas and relationships, they are unable to apply them in somewhat different contexts. These students also may be unable to transfer the mathematical facts and skills that they have learned in one situation to a new and less familiar situation. In general, many students who have not progressed well into the formal operational stage of intellectual maturity will be unable to apply the higher level cognitive skills of analysis, synthesis and evaluation in learning mathematical skills, concepts and principles.

Certain slow learners lack the ability to respond reflectively; that is, they jump to conclusions, guess at answers, or may not even try to solve mathematical exercises and problems. Students who lack the facility to respond reflectively will be unable to carry out complex problem-solving algorithms or construct proofs of theorems. They will tend to memorize definitions rather than try to understand concepts. They may memorize lists of procedures and steps for solving each type of exercise with little understanding of the reason for each step. And, they will memorize proofs of theorems with little understanding of the nature of proof and the reasons for constructing mathematical proofs of theorems.

Slow learners may also have a poorly developed sense of order, sequence and structure. They will use the wrong method for simplifying an algebraic expression; they may carry out the steps in solving an equation in the wrong order; or they may use a correct procedure on an exercise to which that procedure does not apply. For instance, slow learners who have an inadequate sense of structure will ignore the conditions under which a theorem is true and will use principles in situations where they do not apply. For them, mathematics appears to be an arbitrary collection of contradictory rules and procedures. At times one adds exponents, but at other times one multiplies exponents. Sometimes terms should be cancelled, but at other times they should not be cancelled. One should transpose variables and one should not transpose variables. Mathematics appears to be impossible because—for students with a poor sense of order, sequence and structure—it involves memorizing a plethora of definitions and algorithms which do not usually work in most situations. Without being able to understand some of the order, structure and relationships in mathematics, the subject is only meaningless and frustrating for these students.

Other slow learners in mathematics do poorly because they have developed a learning style which is slow. These so-called "plodders" will learn mathematics if they are permitted to learn in their own way at their own rate of speed. They are reluctant to take action on a problem or turn to new material until they know the reasons for and consequences of their actions and completely understand the old material. Consequently, as teachers move ahead rapidly due to the pressure to cover material, these overly reflective students are left behind and through little fault of their own are forced into the slow-learner category. Such students may become low achievers because they learn mathematics slowly even though they may be quite able intellectually. Unfortunately, these students become frustrated and develop a poor self-concept because they are not very successful in adapting their learning style to meet the expectations of the school.

Many students enter high school with a history of failure in mathematics. They have low achievement scores and do, in fact, lack many of the basic skills. Some of these students may do well in other subjects, but for them learning mathematics appears to be hopeless. It may be that a collection of minor learning problems such as somewhat slow intellectual and emotional development, failure to learn several basic skills, and a poor self-concept in a mathematics classroom have combined to culminate in a pattern of poor test scores for these students in their mathematics courses. Until teachers help such students diagnose and remediate deficiencies in their basic mathematical skills and help them develop a positive attitude about their ability to learn mathematics, there is little point in moving on to algebra and more advanced mathematics courses which have basic arithmetic skills as prerequisites.

Some students who find few successes in their mathematics classes may lack some of the expected academic skills. Such students may not have learned how to follow instructions, may work in a disorganized or haphazard fashion, and may have poorly developed study habits. They may also be unable to read and comprehend textbook explanations and examples and may have trouble concentrating upon teachers' lectures and demonstrations. Certain students have not developed enough self-discipline to be able to learn mathematics when working alone in the classroom or at home. Others may be unable to work effectively with other students during small group or laboratory lessons. In most classrooms order, neatness, punctuality and adherence to rules and conventions are expected and are rewarded; while divergent behavior, even though it may be creative and at a high cognitive level, is discouraged. So, some slow learners may not do well in mathematics because they have failed to formulate and demonstrate the type of learning behavior which is expected of and exhibited by the majority of students.

In addition to general reading problems and poor academic skills, slow learners may have poorly developed formal speech patterns and limited vocabularies. For students who use speech patterns, vocabularies and grammatical rules which differ from those of the teacher or other students, comprehending the teacher's explanations and the material in the textbook may be quite difficult. A limited mathematical vocabulary and inadequate knowledge and understanding of the symbol system used in school mathematics will also interfere with students' proficiency in learning mathematics. For many students, what appears to be an over-emphasis upon strange words and esoteric symbols will interfere with their mastery of mathematics and their interest in trying to learn the subject. Mathematics is a symbolic subject and for those school students whose formal operational mental processes are not well developed, the necessity to know, comprehend, and apply symbols in order to learn mathematics has a detrimental effect upon their achievement in mathematics.

Social, Emotional, and Motivational Difficulties of Slow Learners

In addition to cognitive difficulties which cause some slow learners to fall behind other students in mathematics classes, other slow learners' difficulties in school result from social, emotional or motivational causes. In some instances slow learners may be older and more physically mature than classmates because they have been held back a grade or two in elementary school. Such students may have different interests than the other students, may feel that they don't fit in with their classmates, and may attempt to avoid school by cutting classes or staying away from school, especially when tests are being given or when homework assignments are due.

Since most slow learners have few academic successes in school, some tend to display an indifference or even a contempt for school-based learning as a defensive mechanism. These students may give up trying to succeed in their classes and may concentrate upon gaining recognition through athletics, part-time jobs, hobbies and distinctive manual skills. For them, recognition and status come from non-academic pursuits which are much more satisfying than classes and coursework.

Some slow learners have limited attention spans and are unable to concentrate upon intermediate objectives or long-range goals. These people tend to display a live-for-today attitude and appear to give little thought to the future or at least to the value of school-based education in shaping their futures. Teacher-formulated objectives such as the following are of little relevance to students who don't care to think seriously about what they will do after leaving school: "Mathematics should be studied because it can help one get a good job. Mathematical skills are important in many trades and professions. If a person decides to attend college, he or she may need mathematics as an entrance requirement." Unless students who have short-range objectives find that learning mathematics is interesting and useful in achieving immediate objectives, and that mastering it provides recognition and status, they are not likely to devote much time to trying to learn mathematics facts, skills and concepts.

Since children obtain many of their attitudes and values from their parents, the value placed upon education by parents can influence students' attitudes toward school which in turn influences their behavior in school. In some cases, a parent who was able to achieve success in his or her vocation with a minimum of formal schooling may have little regard for school and the things that are taught in school. For these parents, school learning had little value and they may discourage their children from "wasting time" on "worthless" homework assignments. Working after school or learning a parent's trade will take precedence over homework and extracurricular school activities. Students whose parents place little value upon schooling may themselves have little regard for their school subjects and may do poorly in school because they don't care to "waste" time studying and completing assignments. This type of slow learner may value education but dislike school. He or she may find school learning to be uninteresting, irrelevant, and in some cases trivial and phony. In order to improve their learning skills and their interest in school mathematics, slow learners with attitudes such as these need to see reality reflected in the exercises and assignments which are given by teachers in their mathematics classes. Before students who have little regard for schooling can be expected to change their attitudes and values, they must be shown how their school subjects can be used in meeting their short-term goals and how they can be useful in after-school jobs and adult vocations.

Some students who do not do well in their mathematics courses may have minor, or in some cases quite serious, emotional problems. Students' emotional problems can be caused by cultural differences, poor social skills, or a great variety of personal problems either at home or in school. Slow learners whose learning difficulties are due in large part to chronic emotional problems may exhibit anti-social behavior. These students may be quiet and introverted or may become discipline problems and troublemakers in school. They tend to have a poor self image. They are unable to deal with teachers and other students in socially acceptable ways and either withdraw into themselves or become overly aggressive and disruptive in the classroom. In either case their behavior, which is an outgrowth of their emotional problems, will interfere with their mastery of mathematics which will cause them to fall behind the class in their studies.

In many cases, slow learners are unmotivated students. Whether or not this lack of motivation in school is the cause of learning difficulties or an outgrowth of learning problems can be difficult to determine. In most cases cognitive, social and emotional causes of learning problems for slow learners are closely linked to motivational causes. The student who is unable to do well in mathematics because he or she has cognitive insufficiencies will in most instances come to regard mathematics as frustrating, uninteresting and threatening. Conversely, a student who doesn't care for school in general and mathematics in particular is not very likely to do well in mathematics even though he or she may have adequate cognitive abilities. Students who lack motivation to learn mathematics tend to have short attention spans, see little use for learning mathematics, appear to lack initiative, and express a dislike for and disinterest in the subject.

In general, each slow learner is very much an individual and has a distinctive set of causes for his or her difficulties in learning mathematics. Unfortunately, in many schools students are categorized as slow learners and assigned to special class sections based upon their symptoms rather than the causes of their difficulties in learning mathematics. Chronic absentees, class cutters and students who are discipline problems may automatically qualify for placement in special courses for slow learners. Students who have low grades in previous mthematics courses, or who score below average on IQ tests or mathematics achievement tests may also be classified as slow learners. Some students who do poorly in several school subjects, even though they may have average or better mathematical ability, are placed in slow classes in all their school subjects, which has the effect of compounding their learning problems. Apathetic, antagonistic and disruptive students tend to be placed in classes for slow learners, and in some schools course sections for slow learners are used as holding areas for many of the school's discipline problems. Unfortunately, the student who really does work and learn mathematics slowly, and who should be in special classes for slow learners, may be kept in regular course sections, especially if he or she is personable, easy to get along with, and does put forth considerable effort toward trying to learn mathematics.

Since slow learners have special problems in learning mathematics, they also have special teaching and learning needs which must be met to attain an acceptable mastery level of facts, skills and concepts. These students may require special assistance from teachers, counselors and other resource personnel in the school. Before remedial tasks and procedures can be prescribed for slow learners, it may be necessary to give them a battery of tests to assess their current levels of mathematical mastery and determine the specific cognitive, emotional and motivational causes for their learning difficulties. While preassessment and postassessment activities are important parts of all lesson planning, frequent assessment of students' mastery of content is particularly important as slow learners move on to different mathematics topics. Most slow learners need to have mathematics presented to them in small segments and to be given a variety of learning tasks and activities. In general, slow learners need individualized attention and assistance from the teacher and need to be permitted to study mathematics at their own rates of speed consistent with their unique learning styles.

In secondary schools, lack of success in previous mathematics courses often results in negative attitudes toward the subject for most slow learners. Poor motivation to learn mathematics and lack of interest in mathematics dictate the use of special teaching/learning resources for slow learners. Many teachers have found that sets of drill-and-practice exercises which are given to slow learners in hopes of improving their scores on skill tests are of little use in resolving learning problems for students in remedial mathematics classes. Routine drill-and-practice exercises only reinforce students' boredom in the mathematics classroom and are not very effective in helping them achieve long-range learning objectives. Students who have been taught the same basic mathematics skills in the same manner in every grade from fourth through eighth, and who still have not mastered these skills, are unlikely to show much improvement as a result of one more course covering the same material taught in the same way. For students in high school mathematics courses such as senior mathematics, applied mathematics, or practical mathematics—euphemisms for remedial mathematics courses—basic skills must be presented in a new way using different classroom resources.

Textbooks and teaching strategies which concentrate upon routine drill-and-practice exercises should be used with caution. The ideal textbook or combination of textbooks and supplementary resources should present basic skills in the context of the history of mathematics, the work of mathematicians, relevant uses for mathematics, interesting mathematical concepts and principles, and student-centered classroom activities. That is, a good way to present fundamental arithmetic skills to slow learners in secondary schools is through courses with titles such as Number Theory, Probability and Statistics, Game Theory, The History of Mathematics, and Mathematics for the Professions. The need to learn and practice basic skills should arise naturally as useful and interesting ideas from mathematics and other disciplines are encountered. Drill and practice in arithmetic will still be necessary, but will be carried out by students because they need to master certain skills in order to achieve desirable objectives. Courses such as those mentioned above—where arithmetic is presented as a set of skills which are necessary in exploring interesting, intuitive concepts and principles from higher-level mathematics—can help remove the social stigma that may come from being assigned to remedial arithmetic courses.

It is obvious that slow learners with their many special problems need outstanding teachers. However, in many schools the newest and most inexperienced teachers are assigned to those courses containing the poorer students. Or, in other cases, experienced teachers who lack creativity, who are rigid disciplinarians, or who are regarded as the less able teachers in the school are assigned to class sections for slow learners. The best teachers, those people who have had many and varied teaching experiences, who are most knowledgeable about all aspects of learning and teaching, and who use a large variety of teaching strategies and learning resources, are in many cases given courses such as trigonometry, analysis and calculus which contain gifted or well-motivated students. It may be well to identify a special group of teachers (inexperienced teachers who show exceptional promise and the experienced, creative teachers in the school) to work as a team in teaching the classes for slow learners. Such special teams of teachers can use each other as resource people, share instructional materials, and work together on special problems.

Slow learners, who may have a poor self-concept and who have had few successes in their mathematics courses, need to have some measure of success in mathematics classes if their attitudes toward mathematics are to improve. The teacher should explain each particular learning objective to these students and give them some control over formulating certain learning objectives in their mathematics courses. Performance objectives for slow learners usually should be stated in tangible, concrete terms and should, in all cases, be shared with them by the teacher. Cognitive objectives should be closely related to homework assignments, term projects, classroom activities, and pre- and post-assessments of students' progress. These objectives, which may vary from student to student, should be realistic enough so that each student has a reasonable prospect of achieving most of his or her learning goals. This is to say that classes for slow learners should be success oriented and non-threatening. Students should not be placed in a situation where they will be competing with each other for grades. Instead, they should be encouraged to set realistic self-improvement objectives based upon their present level of mastery of each mathematics skill. With the teacher's assistance, students should also set affective objectives for themselves. They need to be shown the value of mathematics in their own lives and should be assisted in developing an interest in mathematics through activity-oriented lessons. Teachers should encourage slow learners to express their negative feelings about mathematics. This can provide the teacher with information to aid him or her in helping students improve their attitudes toward learning mathematics.

Success-oriented classrooms should be well-organized classrooms; yet they should also be flexible enough to provide various learning options for each student. Slow learners tend to become bored easily. They become bored with teacher-directed lectures on familiar topics, with work at the chalkboard, and with the same old drill-and-practice sheets. They need to be given new learning resources which contain new ideas in new settings. Attractive textbooks with better exercises and problems, audio-visual materials, models, books of games and puzzles, mathematics laboratories, class projects, and guest speakers are examples of resources and activities which can be used to supplement the drill and practice which is necessary for skill mastery. In order to reverse a pattern of failure and frustration among slow learners, the classroom environment may need to be changed. A bright, cheerful, attractive classroom can help to improve attitudes and enhance learning. Try rearranging the classroom; prepare colorful bulletin boards; put some posters on the walls; display books and models throughout the room; set off a section of the room as a math lab; give the students more control of the learning environment by permitting them to select some of their own learning activities. If you have computer terminals and calculators in your school, let students write computer programs to solve mathematics problems and use calculators to reinforce arithmetic skills. Encourage originality and creativity and reward them with the type of recognition that can provide status for each student.

Slow learners, in particular, need recognition and status. They are accustomed to feeling inferior in school because they are usually studying and learning topics and skills which the other students already know. Included in the material in each course for slow learners should be some high-status college-level topics (presented in an intuitive and concrete manner) such as orders of infinity, limits of sequences, group theory, etc. which even the students in classes for the gifted may not have studied. Slow learners need to study, and recognize that they are studying, mathematics which is just as important and sophisticated as that studied by other students in their mathematics courses. No high school student wants to think that all he or she is doing in a mathematics course is repeating the material that most other students learned in sixth grade—"the stuff that little kids learn." This is certainly not to imply that as teachers of slow learners, we should attempt to delude them into believing that the basic arithmetic skills which they are trying to learn are "high-powered" mathematics. Rather, what should be done is to help students practice these skills by imbedding them in interesting and important higher-level mathematical ideas.

As stated above, slow learners need some freedom of choice within their learning environment; but they also need discipline—teacher-imposed discipline and self-imposed discipline. Since many students in classes for slow learners are there because they are discipline problems to some extent, teachers of these classes should be particularly knowledgeable about alternatives for handling student discipline. A number of suggestions for maintaining discipline in the classroom and dealing with behavioral problems are given in Chapter 7, pages 413-424. Understanding, fairness, consistency and certainty are useful characteristics to aid in developing orderly and constructive classroom for slow learners.

In summary, just as slow learners have many different learning characteristics, so also do they have a variety of learning needs. It is quite important that slow learners in particular be dealt with as individual students rather than as groups of students. Since the past academic records of most slow learners indicate that they have had little success as students taught by teachers who use large-group instructional methods, individualized strategies usually prove to be somewhat more successful for these people. Irrespective of the individual characteristics and needs of slow learners, it is a fact that nearly all slow learners will not learn those mathematics skills which they failed to learn in the past by being given more of the same treatment. Different learning activities, teaching strategies and instructional resources are the best hope for meeting the needs of slow learners in their mathematics classrooms.

Teaching/Learning Strategies for Slow Learners

In Chapter 5, six models for teaching and learning the direct objects of mathematics are presented: expository teaching, advance organizers, discovery learning, games, individualized instruction and spiral teaching. Chapter 6 deals with models for teaching and learning the indirect objects of mathematics: theorem proving, problem solving, laboratories, inquiry learning, group activities, and computer-enhanced learning. As was noted previously in this chapter, slow learners need variety in the mathematics classroom; consequently teachers of slow learners should use a variety of teaching/learning models, strategies, and activities. Even though slow learners do need considerable practice in order to master basic skills, teachers should avoid overusing the demonstration/drill-and-practice/test strategy which can quickly become a boring routine for students. Although all 12 of the teaching/learning models listed above can be employed in courses for slow learners, some are more appropriate while others must be used with caution.

Expository Strategies

Since many slow learners in mathematics are also poor readers (or at least poor readers of mathematics textbooks) the teacher should use expository methods to introduce concepts and skills and to demonstrate mathematics skills. One should not expect these students to be very successful in reading and comprehending their mathematics textbooks. It is best to select textbooks which are written at an appropriate reading level, which present many concrete examples and illustrations, and which emphasize interesting activities and applications in mathematics. Considerable patience and persistence must be exercised by the teacher in helping slow learners read and comprehend textbooks and other books about mathematics. In addition, the teacher should prepare short (no longer than 15 minutes) expository lessons which cover the topics in the textbook in much the same manner as is done by the authors.

Most expository lessons should cover a single concept or a single skill algorithm; however some lessons will be needed to show the relationships among concepts (principles) as well as certain aspects of the structure of mathematical systems. Information and procedures should be presented in short units so that each student will be dealing with a small number of ideas and processes at one time. In most cases, slow learners need to work with each concept and practice each skill before additional concepts and skills are introduced. Many slow learners are poor listeners and have short attention spans, which are additional reasons for making moderate use of the expository model and for keeping lectures brief.

Advance Organizers

Advance organizers, as defined by Ausubel, are introductory materials that are presented to students at a higher level of generality, abstraction and inclusiveness than subsequent learning tasks. Since advance organizers are meant to help students formulate a cognitive structure to subsume subsequent information, they should be general and inclusive; however they need not be overly abstract. The advance organizer-lesson about how computers solve problems (pages 136-137) is certainly not abstract; yet it is general and inclusive, and most slow learners will have little trouble with this lesson. Advance organizers can be used to introduce certain topics in mathematics to slow learners, provided the topics are formulated in relatively concrete terms in the advance-organizer lesson. Post organizers, which are presented after a segment of material has been studied, are effective ways to summarize mathematical objects and their relationships and to help students reorganize these ideas and relations in their own cognitive structures. Since advance-organizer lessons tend to be expository lessons (but don't necessarily have to be), they should be used in moderation and in most cases should be relatively brief (5-20 minutes).

Discovery Learning

Discovery strategies are good teaching/learning strategies for slow learners because they tend to be used in the context of solving an interesting puzzle and require active mental involvement on the part of each student, as well as classroom discussions. While gifted students may be able to make mathematical discoveries with little help from the teacher, slow learners may need a considerable amount of direction and intervention. In order for students to make discoveries, resolve issues, or formulate conjectures, the teacher will find it necessary to ask leading questions, offer additional information, and suggest avenues for students to explore and procedures for them to carry out. Slow learners tend to make discoveries in small steps, so the teacher should structure learning activities to take the class step-by-step through several intermediate discoveries preparatory to making a more general discovery.

Since slow learners need to see many concrete representations of mathematical abstractions, they should be given physical models to manipulate in making their own discoveries. Gifted students tend to be adept at mentally manipulating abstract mathematical ideas and symbols to discover new mathematical structures, but slower students need to actually handle models and materials in order to formulte and test conjectures. For example, a gifted student may be able to discover relationships among the parts of similar triangles by logically combining known definitions, theorems and postulates. However, a slow learner may need to compare cardboard triangles to make the same discoveries. In both cases, the students will arrive at the correct conclusion, but they will use different procedures to make their discoveries.

Discovery lessons can be used to generate interest in mathematics and increase student motivation. But, you should keep in mind that it requires considerably more time for students to discover a relationship than it does for the teacher to state and demonstrate that same relationship. Since one objective in teaching slow learners is to help them catch up to other students in their level of skill mastery, time-consuming discovery lessons should be interspersed among other teaching strategies that are more efficient for transmitting facts and skills to students.

Games

Educational games with sound learning objectives, such as those discussed in Chapter 5, are excellent teaching/learning resources for slow learners. For high school students, mathematical games patterned after adult games such as those shown on television or played at home are most appropriate. Younger students (those in junior high school or middle school grades) also like to play adult games as well as children's games. If your high school students view a certain game as uninteresting, stupid, or beneath them, avoid using that game and attempt to obtain or create a more appropriate game for that mathematical topic. When you find several games that students like to play, suggest that they create variations of these games; you may also want to adapt these games for use in teaching several different topics in mathematics.

Good games generate interest in mathematics and increase motivation, but some games which appear to students to be trivial or childish can decrease motivation. If you insist that students play games which they regard as childish, you will only reinforce the poor self images which many slow learners have. Mathematical games should be easy enough so that students understand the rules but sophisticated enough so that playing them will enhance students' status. Remember that slow learners need to find status in the mathematics classroom and being forced to play "kiddie games" can be detrimental to students' images of themselves and their regard for mathematics. Game playing is an excellent way to turn drill-and-practice or review sessions into enjoyable learning experiences.

Individualized Instruction

Some of the individualized instructional programs which can be purchased for use with students who need remedial work on arithmetic skills are very boring for many slow learners. Individualized programs which center around programmed textbooks and drill-and-practice workbooks are not recommended for slow learners. Slow learners need a variety of interesting activities and teaching/learning models, and few individualized learning packages provide enough variety. However, many of these programs do have good diagnostic and mastery tests which can be useful to teachers and students.

Regardless of the materials which are provided by the school for use with slow learners, each teacher will have to take the initiative in finding and creating a large variety of lessons and student activities. For slow learners, individualized instruction should include differentiated assignments, different learning activities for selected students, individualized learning objectives for each student, and different expectations for individual students. An intelligent and creative teacher must be given the primary responsibility for individualizing instruction within his or her own classroom. Most individualized learning packages are useful in the classroom, but no one package can meet the diverse needs of a classroom filled with slow learners who have many different problems in learning mathematics.

Spiral Teaching

The spiral teaching/learning model, which subsumes other teaching/learning models, is a sequential procedure for teaching concepts, principles, and certain skills so that each mathematics object is presented to students as a sequence of progressively more general and inclusive definitions, applications and examples. For many secondary school students who have problems learning mathematics, the subject is viewed as a disconnected conglomeration of arbitrary facts and skills. They are unable to see much coherence and consistency in the mathematics which they have been taught. These students may have learned certain mathematical objects at one level in the cognitive spiral but may have failed to again learn these objects at a higher cognitive level. For them, the mathematical learning spiral is full of holes or has completely fallen apart. In many cases teachers of slow learners will have to recreate the learning spiral for certain skills, concepts and principles. For example, students who have a poorly developed concept of area may need to fill in rectangles with unit squares in order to understand the concept of area defined as length times width. Proper fractions may need to be represented as segments of pie graphs in order for these students to comprehend the algorithm for adding fractions and use it correctly.

When one uses a spiral approach to present mathematical objects to students who are seeing these objects for the first time, the spiral is a bottom-to-top spiral—concrete to abstract, exclusive to inclusive, simple to complex, intuitive to formal. For students who have gone through these mathematical spirals from grade one through seven and who have failed to master the mathematical content, a bottom-to-top or a top-to-bottom spiral may help them resolve some of their learning difficulties. These students may need to be shown how each simple mathematical idea or skill can be extended to create more complex ideas and skills. They may also need to be shown how the more inclusive ideas and skills which they are attempting to master can be separated into simpler ideas and skills as one progresses down the mathematical spiral.

For example, as one teaches the concept of number and the skill of adding numbers using an upward spiral, he or she can generalize the concept of natural numbers to the concept of integers to the concept of rational numbers. The algorithm (skill) used to add natural numbers can be generalized to the algorithm for adding rational numbers. In teaching a slow learner in high school, who is confused about the concept of number and the skill of adding numbers, a downward spiral could be used. That is, the student could be shown that the integers are a special set of rational numbers and that the natural numbers are a special set of integers. He or she could also be shown how the skill for adding rational fractions depends upon the skill for adding integers, which in turn depends upon the skill for adding natural numbers.

For some slow learners, the best approach to teaching or reteaching certain topics may be to use a bottom-to-top spiral. In other cases, the top-to-bottom approach may be most effective. In teaching some topics to certain students it may be best to use a bottom-to-top explanation followed by a top-to-bottom explanation or vice versa. In any event, one should recognize that certain learning problems of students occur because for them the concept/skill spiral has holes in it or has broken down completely. The teacher should help these students patch up the spiral or help them completely reconstruct it.

Theorem Proving

For slow learners, as well as for many other students, constructing proofs of mathematical propositions can be quite difficult. Since they have problems mastering mathematical skills, slow learners seldom spend much time trying to prove mathematical principles. In most instances they prefer to accept theorems as given facts or regard several instances of a theorem as an adequate justification of its truth. Many times slow learners have not adequately mastered the facts and concepts that are needed in proving particular theorems, or they have a poorly developed concept of proof as well as inadequate skills for proving theorems.

Becoming proficient in theorem proving requires years of practice and a sincere desire to demonstrate that conjectures about mathematical relationships are true. Since slow learners seldom have had much practice proving theorems, they usually dislike having to attempt proofs, because for them such activities tend to be unsuccessful and frustrating.

In order to assist slow learners in understanding the nature of mathematical proof, valid logical argument forms should be discussed with them and demonstrated intuitively. Rather than concentrating upon formal, rigorous and symbolic proofs, teachers should rely upon examples and convincing verbal arguments to demonstrate the truth or falsity of propositions. Resolving puzzles, finding the fallacies in arguments leading to paradoxes, formulating their own conjectures and verbal arguments are useful activities for helping slow learners improve their ideas about what constitutes a proof. Activities such as these will also help them develop positive attitudes about the value of sound deductive arguments.

Problem Solving

Many teachers use drill-and-practice exercise sheets as the main student activity for slow learners. Although slow learners do need to practice mathematical skills in order to master them, they should also be given bona fide problems to solve either individually or in groups. Solving interesting problems, either applied problems or pure mathematical problems, can be a good way to increase students' motivation and improve their attitudes toward mathematics. Teachers should be careful to select problems which will challenge students but which will not be so difficult that they have little chance of solving them.

The section on problem solving in Chapter 6 can be used as a model for teaching slow learners, as well as other students, some useful techniques for solving problems and for presenting some general problem-solving strategies. In addition to exercise solving, problem solving can be one of the best classroom activities for helping slow learners appreciate the value of mathematics and improve their mathematical skills.

Mathematics Laboratories

Many teachers have found that the laboratory approach to teaching and learning mathematics has a positive effect upon students' performance and mastery levels in mathematics courses. Using mathematics laboratories and laboratory activities are particularly good approaches to teaching slow learners for several reasons. First, slow learners need to be involved and intellectually active in school, and laboratories provide for student movement, interaction and mental focusing. Second, laboratory activities give individual students and groups of students more control over their own learning activities and the classroom learning environment than is permitted by some of the more teacher-centered models. Third, slow learners need to see concrete representations of mathematics concepts and principles and handle physical objects that illustrate the conceptual objects of mathematics. Math labs and lab activities are usually oriented toward physical materials and concrete representations of ideas. Fourth, slow learners need to improve their self images and become successful in their mathematics classrooms. The social interactions and peer teaching that occur in most mathematics laboratories can provide peer recognition as well as teacher recognition, and carefully formulated laboratory lessons can result in a measure of success for each student.

In previous chapters, resources and activities for mathematics laboratories are discussed, and reference books, materials, and other resources are listed and evaluated. Remember, as has been stated previously, that teachers can create excellent math labs in their own classrooms with inexpensive and readily obtainable resources. Good ideas and interesting things to do are just as important, if not more so, than large, specially-equipped rooms which are used exclusively as mathematics laboratories or resource centers.

Inquiry Learning

Many slow learners are turned off by school and care little about learning mathematics. Their primary form of inquiry in the mathematics classroom is, "How can I avoid doing mathematics?" and "Of what possible use is this stuff that the teacher is trying to force us to learn?" In order to inquire successfully about mathematical principles, the structure of mathematics, and the nature of the inquiry process itself, students must want to know why certain things occur in mathematics; that is they must be interested in learning mathematics and in learning how to learn. Uninspired inquiry lessons conducted with disinterested students are doomed to fail.

Before a teacher tries to involve the class in an inquiry lesson, he or she should select a puzzle, paradox, problem, or situation which will evoke sincere questions from the class. Statements and questions from students such as, "I don't think that's true. How could that happen? That's amazing! I'd like to see someone prove that! How could anyone do that? It's impossible!" can set the stage for an inquiry lesson. Some of the most productive inquiry lessons evolve from questions which one student or a group of students formulate on their own. In classes for slow learners, certain sarcastic or belligerent student questions about concepts, skill algorithms, or mathematical principles can lead to very enthusiastic, albeit serendipitous, inquiry lessons. A bored student's question, "Why don't you teach us some calculus like the other seniors get instead of this stupid arithmetic?" could be followed by an interesting inquiry lesson about orders of infinity and infinite sequences and series. Informed, perceptive teachers can teach a great many basic arithmetic skills in the context of some interesting, high-level, status-oriented mathematics concepts which can be presented in a student-centered inquiry lesson.

Group Activities

While individualized programs can help slow learners master the skills and concepts which they have failed to learn in large lecture-oriented classes, group activities can improve students' social skills and self-concepts. Most slow learners prefer working together in small groups of several students rather than being taught by the teacher as an entire class. By organizing heterogeneous student groups based upon ability and achievement levels, teachers can use students as peer instructors within each group. When teachers see to it that each member of each group contributes to the group, students may improve their self images and will be more likely to master basic skills and concepts. Students who work together in groups while solving exercises or problems tend to accomplish more through the peer teaching that usually takes place. The teacher can concentrate upon helping those students who have more serious learning problems, while students with less serious problems are teaching each other within their groups.

Some teachers like to give assignments which are to be completed in class by small groups of students and give tests and quizzes which are to be done by groups of students working together. Many teachers find that this form of group testing results in better grades for all students which does in fact reflect the mastery level of each student, even though he or she is assigned the test score obtained by the group. After students have taken a test (either by working individually or in small groups) and the teacher has graded and returned the test papers, students should work in groups to find and correct their mistakes on each item on the test. It seems to be a paradox that a good way to individualize instruction is by having students work together in small groups.

Computer-Enhanced Learning

A viewpoint supported by certain research findings and the opinions of many teachers who use computers to aid learning in their own classrooms is that computer-enhanced instruction is the best teaching/learning model for slow learners. When students learn to write computer programs (which is not at all difficult even for slow learners) and run their programs on a computer, they are engaging in a fascinating form of problem solving and learning. Hands-on student-controlled computing can help meet many of the diverse needs of slow learners who have different learning characteristics and difficulties. For students, using a computer as an aid to learning mathematics is a significant status symbol; not everyone can make a computer work! Many disinterested mathematics students are unable to concentrate upon learning mathematics and are easily distracted. But, when a person is writing a computer program or working at a computer terminal, interest is high and concentration is intense. It is a fact that some students, even slow learners, have to be chased out of the computer center at the end of the school day. Problem solving at a computer terminal, whether one uses his or her own program or a program prepared by another person, is an interesting activity for most students, and quickly resolves the motivational problems of many slow learners. Even solving computer-generated drill-and-practice exercises is more fun than most other kinds of drill-and-practice strategies. Computer-based games and simulations can be written (many are also available from various sources, e.g. *Creative Computing*) either by teachers or students to use in learning mathematical concepts and in practicing mathematical skills. Individualized instruction at a computer terminal is certainly more fun for most students than programmed workbooks and practice sheets.

Of course, the obvious disadvantage of computer-enhanced learning compared to the other teaching/learning models is that access to a computer is required. If, as a teacher, you do have access to a computer for use in your classes, be sure to permit your slow learners and your remedial arithmetic classes to use the computer. Some schools reserve the computer for instructional uses for ac-celerated classes, advanced mathematics courses, and gifted students. However, this exclusive use of computers for better students is a mistake. Slow learners can benefit greatly from computer-enhanced mathematics courses, and when com-puter use must be limited to certain students in certain courses, it may be well to give priority to slow learners in using the computer.

Reading Ability in Learning Mathematics

One of the factors contributing to the difficulties that some students have in learning mathematics is poor general reading ability or the specific inability to read and understand mathematics textbooks. Since many slow learners have little interest in mathematics, they have even less inclination to read mathematics books. Even when these students do read through the assignment they may do so in a superficial manner which results in little comprehension of the mathematics content. An erroneous assumption about teaching mathematics is that reading mathematics isn't a very important activity in learning the subject. Although most students can learn some facts and skills without ever opening their textbooks, concepts and principles (and also facts and skills) are best understood and mastered when teachers' lectures and students' exercise-solving assignments are supplemented with reading assignments. Richard Earle (1976, p. 5) states that "Most professionals agree that reading in any subject matter field cannot and should not be separated from concept development in that area."

In the International Reading Association publication, *The Evaluation of Chil-dren's Reading Achievement* (1968), Thomas Barrett defines reading as follows:

> Reading involves the visual perception of written symbols and the trans-formation of the symbols to their explicit or implicit oral counterparts. The oral responses then act as stimuli for a thoughtful reaction on the part of the reader. The type or level of thought induced by the stimuli is determined, in part, by the intent and the background of the reader and the nature of the materials. In addition, the effort expended in the perceptual act and the intel-lectual impact of the written materials on the reader are influenced by his interest in the specific selection and by his attitude toward reading in general. (p. 15)

One might ask the question, "What has been learned by reading Barrett's definition of reading?" First, if in reading the definition, one merely had a "per-ception of written symbols" (read the words) but did nothing else, then, for that person, Barrett's definition has very little meaning. That is, the person either had no "interest" in concentrating upon understanding the definition or was unable to understand it as a consequence of "the background of the reader" (his or her own reading ability and knowledge of the subject). Possibly, "the nature of the materials" (Barrett's use of the English language) may have interfered with the reader's understanding of the definition. If the reader had transformed the word symbols in the definition to their "implicit oral counterparts," which may be done through mental imagery, then this transformation would "act as a stimulus for a thoughtful reaction." In summary, Barrett is saying that the reader who has a positive attitude toward reading in general, wants to understand the definition, and has a good reading background will concentrate upon the words in the definition, will think about them in a meaningful way, and will understand the definition, provided Barrett himself knew what he was talking about and expressed himself clearly.

The preceding paragraph is an example of what one must do in order to read and understand written material in a meaningful way. By explaining my own thought processes relative to interpreting and understanding Barrett's definition of reading, I illustrated how one should read material for useful comprehension. When teaching students how to read mathematics textbooks, it is well to read passages to them from the textbook and then explain the mental imagery that you yourself used to understand each passage—much in the same manner as I have explained my mental perceptions of my reading of Barrett's definition to you.

Teaching Reading and Study Skills

An analysis of research reports and journal articles indicates that there is no single best method or combination of methods for teaching students reading and study skills to use in learning mathematics. However, most people do agree that teaching reading and study skills in mathematics will result in better student attitudes and improved test results. It appears that when students want to improve their study skills, instruction in reading and study methods may result in impressive gains in motivation and mathematics achievement. There is some evidence to indicate that slow learners benefit more from special courses and sessions on improving study skills than do gifted students; although research in this area is inconclusive.

Many mathematics teachers, by their own approach to giving study assignments, appear to think that study skills are learned without guidance. Such is not the case for most students, and in particular for slow learners. There are certain basic study skills which students need to master in order to learn mathematics, and these skills must be taught. High school mathematics teachers should not assume that students have already learned how to read textbooks and study mathematics, even though their students may have attained an acceptable level of general reading skills. Despite the fact that most students have been taught many good study skills in elementary school, they may fail to use them properly in secondary school mathematics courses. For some of these students, the reason that they don't use appropriate study skills in learning mathematics is that they have had little practice in reading and studying mathematics; although they have learned some mathematics by listening to a multitude of lectures, seeing many demonstrations of examples, and solving thousands of mathematics exercises. The efficient and effective use of study skills requires practice under the guidance of teachers until the use of these skills becomes routine and habitual.

According to Harold Herber in his book *Teaching Reading in Content Areas* (1970):

> [Some students] lack understanding of when to apply the skills they apparently know. It is, for example, easier to underline a sentence that appears to be important than it is to recognize how the sentence fits into the total organizational pattern of the content that is being studied. Such indiscriminate practices may prove to be more confusing than helpful. Most study skills courses are based upon the premise that students will benefit more from an orderly plan of learning than they will from a hit-or-miss approach. Some courses

place heavy emphasis on improving students' attitudes, motivations, and interests while others emphasize a particular technique or plan. Experience indicates that overemphasis on either the psychological aspects of learning or the skills is not the most fruitful approach. A successful study skills program is one in which a competent teacher has time to meet with students, provide extrinsic motivation when it is needed, supply students with numerous interesting materials at their own reading levels, and teach them the skills they need for learning. (pp. 71-72)

To consider study skills primarily as a set of mechanical procedures is to limit one's view of study, and to oversimplify; study skills, when properly taught, include a systematic, sequential approach to learning. (p. 70)

In summary, students should be taught reading and study skills, should practice these skills while learning mathematics, and should be given individualized activities and teacher assistance to help them improve their study skills. Reading mathematics textbooks and understanding what is read does not come naturally for most slow learners. These students need to be taught how to use printed materials efficiently and effectively as an aid in learning mathematics.

The Nature of Reading Mathematics

General reading is quite different from mathematical reading. Mathematical reading requires precision, orderliness, flexibility and concentration. When reading a newspaper or novel, one may pay little attention to details, may skip around, may read sequentially, or may let his or her mind wander. When reading a section of a mathematics textbook, the reader must know the precise meaning of each mathematical term and each mathematical symbol. There is little room for connotation, conjecture, and speculation. When a student attempts to understand a theorem or write a proof, he or she can not afford to ignore or skim over a word that he or she does not understand. Each mathematical concept has a precise meaning and plays a definite part in comprehending a principle or solving a problem.

In recreational reading, the reader may skip around, omit certain parts of the text, or skim uninteresting sections. When reading mathematics, each word and each sentence should be read carefully. Charts, tables, diagrams and examples should be studied thoughtfully. Steps in the solution of an exercise or problem and each part of a proof should be read and thought about until they are fully understood. Frequently it is necessary to use a pencil and paper to work out details that are omitted in the textbook examples and demonstrations. In some cases where material is not presented clearly, a note should be made and the student should request a clarification from the teacher.

Flexibility is required in mathematical reading. At times it may be useful to stop and look up the meanings of terms in the glossary. It may be necessary to read a passage several times before the author's intention becomes clear. Important mathematical objects may need to be reorganized or it may be useful to make an outline of a topic. It may be appropriate to return to early sections of the book in order to review materials which may have been forgotten. At times one should stop reading and look ahead to the chapter summary or to exercises at the end of a section. One can not usually study mathematics material sequentially—line to line, paragraph to paragraph, and page to page.

Concentration is crucial in order to comprehend written mathematics in a meaningful way. If a student becomes disinterested in the material or if his or her mind begins to wander, the sequence, structure and organization of the material will quickly be lost. Since subsequent mathematical skills and concepts are usually formulated from previous mathematical objects, a few misconceptions or omissions can result in complete confusion and lack of comprehension. Many of the specific cases where slow learners are unable to master new skills and principles can be traced back to a few omissions or misunderstandings of prerequisite mathematical materials. It is usually necessary to skim a section in a mathematics textbook in order to get an overview of the material and to see how it is organized and structured. Then, students should read and re-read the material slowly until they understand it, or at least until they are able to identify their specific points of confusion.

One of the most difficult aspects of learning mathematics for slow learners is being able to comprehend the complex relationships among the many facts, skills and concepts in each branch of mathematics. Those students who attempt to memorize mathematics as a collection of isolated facts and skills will be unable to comprehend written materials which require analysis, synthesis and structuring of a number of mathematics objects.

The Process of Reading Mathematics

Just as cognitive processes take place at different levels, so also do the processes of reading mathematics occur according to a hierarchy of psycholinguistic activities. In his book *Teaching Reading and Mathematics,* Richard Earle uses a classroom model of mathematical reading which contains four levels: perceiving symbols, attaching literal meaning to symbols, analyzing relationships among symbols, and solving mathematics exercises stated as word problems. In general, in order for a student to be successful at any one of these reading levels, he or she must achieve success at each of the preceding levels. For example, in order to solve word problems in mathematics students must be able to read each problem so that they perceive the symbols in the problem statement, attach literal meaning to each symbol, and analyze the relations among the symbols.

Perceiving symbols in mathematics is the ability to recognize mathematical terminology and symbols and pronounce them correctly. Little if any comprehension is implied at the symbol perception level. The reader simply recognizes words and symbols as being familiar and is able to say them correctly. In order for students to have success at higher-level reading tasks in mathematics, they must be familiar with the special vocabulary and symbols in the materials that they are studying. If a reader of mathematics is unable to recognize and pronounce symbols such as $x,\ a^n,\ \sqrt{(a+b)^3}$ and words such as *quadratic, equation, radical,* and *function,* he or she will probably be unable to understand much of algebra. Mathematics teachers should give students repeated practice in pronouncing the mathematical symbols that are necessary in meeting the objectives for each topic or unit.

To be sure that slow learners are able to recognize and pronounce mathematical symbols, a teacher might ask each student to occasionally read aloud appropriate textbook passages. When writing mathematical terms and symbols on the chalkboard, the teacher should ask students to pronounce them correctly. Tests

and quizzes can contain short multiple choice, matching, or identification sections where students are asked to match symbols with their correct names or
correctly identify symbols. A sample quiz of this nature is given below:

I. Select the correct written symbol for each of these mathematical
symbols:

1. $\dfrac{2+3}{5}$ is read ———?
   a. two-fifths of three-fifths.
   b. two plus three, divided by five.
   c. two-fifths of three.

2. $3x + y^2$ is read ——?
   a. three x y squared.
   b. three x plus two y.
   c. three x, plus y squared.

3. $\dfrac{3(5-7)}{2}$ is read ———?
   a. three times five minus seven over two.
   b. three times the quantity five minus seven, divided by two.
   c. three times five divided by two minus seven.

II. Match each mathematical symbol with its correct statement:

——1. $(x-y)^2$ a. x squared minus y squared

——2. $\dfrac{x-y}{2}$ b. two times the quantity x minus y

——3. $x^2 - y^2$ c. the quantity x minus y, divided by two

——4. $2(x-y)$ d. the quantity x minus y, squared

III. Write a correct statement for each of these mathematical symbols:

1. ab ——————————————————
2. $\dfrac{2}{3} \cdot \dfrac{1}{8}$ ——————————————
3. $\sqrt{3}$ ——————————————————
4. $5^{1/2}$ ——————————————————
5. 2^{-3} ——————————————————
6. $\sqrt{a+b}$ ——————————————
7. $a^3b^2 + 2ab$ ——————————————
8. $3\dfrac{2}{3}$ ——————————————————

After the reader is able to recognize and pronounce certain mathematical
words and symbols, he or she is ready to attach literal meaning to these symbols.
This is to say that understanding of words and symbols follows recognition and
pronunciation. Each reader should be able to locate and identify mathematical
words and symbols in different contexts and understand the significance of their
order. After readers are proficient at recognizing and stating mathematical objects, the teacher should explain their meanings in ways which students can
comprehend and apply. Students should be able to define mathematical words
and symbols correctly and in a manner which is understandable and useful to
them. A student could memorize the teachers' definition that the symbol a^n
means n factors of a, without understanding the definition or being able to apply
it. If understanding is to occur, the student must know that a is a symbol representing a real number and that n is a symbol representing a counting number.

He or she should also know and understand the meanings of the words *factor,*
real number, and *counting number.* A less precise but more meaningful definition (explanation) of a^n is to say that a^n means a times a times a and so forth,
until you have n of the number a in the product. Of course examples such as
$8^3 = 8 \cdot 8 \cdot 8$ and $\left(\dfrac{1}{2} \right)^4 = \dfrac{1}{2} \cdot \dfrac{1}{2} \cdot \dfrac{1}{2} \cdot \dfrac{1}{2}$ will help clarify this definition, and when students are able to find products such as $\left(-\dfrac{2}{3} \right)^3$ and $(4)^8$
they will have demonstrated an understanding of the symbol a^n. Just because a
student can reproduce the teacher's definition on a test is no assurance that he or
she understands and will be able to use a term or symbol in mathematics.

One approach to teaching meaningful definitions to students is to have each
student keep a notebook that is his or her cumulative mathematical dictionary.
Since some definitions given in the textbook or by the teacher will not make
sense to students, they should first write their own definitions of each term or
symbol in their notebooks. The teacher should read each student's definition of
each term or symbol to check its accuracy. However, when a student's definition
is incorrect, he or she should be assisted in modifying it so that it is both techni-
cally correct and meaningful to that student. As time permits, students' definitions can be read aloud in class, and other students can act as critics of each
student's individualized definitions. This activity will help students see the value
of correct and precise definitions and will give them practice in critically interpreting other people's definitions. Also, students will be given a major role in
making their own correct definitions with some help from the teacher. For the
sake of accuracy and consistency and as an aid in reading and understanding their
textbooks, students should write the textbook definition beside their own definition for each symbol or term in their notebooks. On tests and quizzes, students
should be permitted to use either their own approved definitions or those definitions given by the teacher or found in the textbook.

Important keys to students' abilities to attach literal meaning to mathematical
words and symbols are their involvement in formulating each definition, varied
examples to illustrate meanings of words and symbols, continued practice in
using each definition, and a flexible spiral approach to defining and redefining
mathematical terms. As students mature intellectually and become proficient
mathematically, they will be able to redefine terms and symbols in a more precise, abstract, inclusive and useful manner. Imprecise and inexact definitions
which students understand and which enable them to obtain correct and useful
results are preferable to memorized formal definitions which may be meaningless
to many students. In Chapter 4 of his book *Teaching Reading and Mathematics*
(1976), Richard Earle offers a number of suggestions for classroom activities to
help students attach literal meaning to words and symbols in mathematics. You
may want to refer to this book for additional ways to make symbols meaningful
for students.

Analyzing relationships among symbols is the ability to handle several stated
facts, ideas, terms and symbols simultaneously and to identify both stated and
unstated connections among them. As students read mathematical passages they
must perceive words and symbols individually, attach literal meanings to them,

and note common characteristics and relations among all the terms and symbols in each passage. They must also sort out irrelevant information and infer implied but unstated information. Varying degrees of analysis, synthesis, evaluation and interpretation are involved in reading mathematical materials that contain familiar words and symbols which have already been understood by the reader. In one sense, analyzing relationships is the process of structuring information as an interrelated set of outlines. Earle (1976) suggests that teachers use a *structured overview* as a guide to helping students learn how to analyze relationships when they are reading mathematics. His directions for preparing and using a structured overview are:

1. Analyze the vocabulary of the learning task and list all words that you feel are representative of the major concepts that you want the students to understand.
2. Arrange the list of words until you have a diagram which shows the interrelationships among the concepts particular to the learning task.
3. Add to the diagram vocabulary concepts which you believe are already understood by the students in order to depict relationships between the learning task and the discipline as a whole.
4. Evaluate the overview. Have you depicted major relationships clearly? Can the overview be simplified and still effectively communicate the relationships you consider to be most important?
5. When you introduce the learning task, display the diagram to the students and explain briefly why you arranged the words as you did. Encourage students to supply as much information as possible.
6. During the course of the learning task, relate the new information to the structured overview as it seems appropriate. (pp. 33-34)

Teacher-constructed structured overviews can be presented to students as advance organizer lessons; but in order for students to improve their ability to read and understand mathematics, they should prepare their own written structured overviews for short reading assignments in their textbooks. To prepare your students to write their own structured overviews, you should first construct several of your own overviews and share them with the class. Then, you should have the entire class read several pages of textbook material and work as a group under your guidance to prepare a structured overview. After students have worked together in constructing several structured overviews, they will have a model to follow in reading mathematics assignments. This model will help them know what to look for as they read, and will aid them in organizing and understanding material as well as in identifying areas of confusion. Earle (1976, pp. 38-47) also suggests additional classroom exercises and activities which can help students read, understand, and analyze relationships in mathematical passages.

The highest level psycholinguistic activity (which involves the lower level activities of perceiving words and symbols, attaching literal meaning to words and symbols, and analyzing relationships among words and symbols) is solving mathematical word problems. It is customary to think of word problems as the "story problems" in algebra, but here we use the term word problem in a much broader sense. In mathematics, word problems are any problems or exercises stated in prose. The standard story problems of algebra are word problems. In arithmetic, many of the application problems, such as those using mathematics to solve consumer problems, are word problems. The theorems and propositions in geometry textbooks are word problems and the statement problems about measurement, distances and angles in trigonometry are word problems. For our purposes, ''problems'' such as the following would **not** be considered word problems:

1. Simplify—$2(3 - 1) + 7(8 + 9)$.
2. Solve for x—$3x^2 + 2x - 1$.
3. Construct a triangle having the following sides—8cm, 7cm, 12cm.
4. Prove this identity: $(\tan x)^2 - (\sin x)^2 = (\tan x)^2 (\sin x)^2$

Solving word problems in school mathematics has as its objective the development of general problem solving skills which can be transferred to other mathematical, as well as non-mathematical, situations outside school. To read and solve a word problem, a student must perceive the relevant words and symbols in the problem statement, understand each word and symbol, and correctly analyze relationships among them. Finally, the reader must reconstruct the verbal problem into a symbolic mathematical relationship which can be solved using an algorithm.

Solving word problems is difficult to teach, difficult to learn for most students, and particularly troublesome for slow learners. Not only must the student operate at all four psycholinguistic levels, but he or she must also function at the higher cognitive levels of analysis, synthesis and evaluation. Most of the discussion and illustrations about problem solving in Chapter 6 are appropriate aids for learning how to solve word problems. You may want to review this section (pp. 308-323) and consider how the steps in the general problem solving model can be used to help students learn how to solve word problems. In general, the ability to read and understand word problems carefully and critically must be developed slowly in students over a number of years with the assistance of patient teachers. As a teacher of slow learners, one must be careful to select word problems which students can succeed in solving and provide appropriate assistance to assure a measure of success for all students.

Motivating Students to Read Mathematics

Many students in mathematics courses, especially students who are slow learners, do very little voluntary mathematical reading. In most cases slow learners do not even read the assignments in the textbook which their teachers may give. In mathematics, voluntary reading is reading which students do because they want to, not because they have to in order to satisfy their teachers. Even students who do complete assigned readings in their textbooks may do so in a very superficial manner if they are not interested in reading the material. Superficial reading of mathematics usually results in little student understanding, especially for slow learners. The question that will be considered in this section is, ''How can teachers motivate students to read mathematics—both their textbooks and other written materials in mathematics?''

Although some mathematics textbooks have sections in each chapter containing historical notes and applications of mathematics to stimulate student interest, by and large most textbooks are not very appealing to students. The first step toward fostering student interest in reading mathematics is to provide interesting things to read and display them in the classroom in an attractive manner. Magazines such as *The Arithmetic Teacher* and *The Mathematics Teacher,* although written primarily for teachers, contain some articles which may be of interest to students. Many slow learners in mathematics, who may also be slow readers, are reluctant to begin a book about mathematics because completing the book appears to be an insurmountable task. As a teacher, you can generate interest in books about mathematics and mathematicians by bringing a book to class occasionally and reading short, interesting passages aloud to your students or by telling "stories" from the book. Encourage students to browse through mathematics books and read chapters and passages which appeal to them. Activities such as these will help students realize that mathematical reading can be interesting and enjoyable and that one need not read the whole book once it has been started. For example, E. T. Bell's book *Men of Mathematics* is very formidable because of its size. However, it is a collection of essays about a number of mathematicians, and one can read all that Bell has to say about a single mathematician by reading a single chapter. Because students have been required to read entire library books and write book reports in some of their school courses, many students are not aware that it may not be necessary to read a book from cover to cover.

After you have read sections from books or magazines aloud in class or have told stories from them, place them on display in your classroom and permit students to borrow a book or magazine for a few days to read at home. A good way to encourage students to read mathematics is to fill your classroom with appealing materials about mathematics which are attractively displayed.

Once students discover that interesting things have been written about mathematics and begin to do some mathematical reading voluntarily, they will also begin to improve their reading skills and interest in mathematics. Consequently, when you give textbook reading assignments, more students will attempt them and be more successful in understanding the material, because mathmtical reading is no longer foreign to them. Even though the textbook assignments may not be as interesting as voluntary readings which students do in other books, they will be more likely to read the textbook assignment and will be better able to understand the material as they develop an interest in general mathematical reading.

As you teach students ways to read and understand their mathematics textbooks, be sure to follow up reading assignments with questions, discussions, and short, easy quizzes so that students will perceive that they have been successful in learning something as a consequence of reading their textbook assignments. If students do not perceive that reading textbook assignments has a payoff in terms of learning mathematics and teacher rewards, they will have little motivation to complete them.

In summary, motivating students to read mathematics requires helping them learn how to read and understand mathematics, providing them with interesting and appealing written materials, and rewarding them for their reading efforts. In addition, students must perceive that they have been successful in learning something about mathematics as a consequence of reading.

Assessing Reading Ability

In addition to oral question-and-answer sessions and classroom observations of students by the teacher, written quizzes and activities can be used as an aid in assessing students' reading abilities at each psycholinguistic level—perceiving symbols, attaching literal meaning to symbols, analyzing relationships among symbols, and solving word problems. For example, as students study a unit about the various types of real numbers and the operations on real numbers, quizzes and activities such as those presented below could be developed and used to measure each student's reading ability at each psycholinguistic level.

Activities such as the following can be used to aid in assessing students' abilities to **perceive symbols.** Each activity could be done orally or as a silent quiz.

Perceiving Symbols in the Real Number System

I. Directions: Tell whether you agree or disagree with each of these statements by writing either *agree* or *disagree* after each sentence.

1. $\frac{2}{3}$ is read either *two-thirds or two divided by three.* _____
2. 7 + 4 is read *seven before four.* _____
3. 3 − 2 is read *two minus three.* _____
4. $\sqrt{9}$ is read *nine squared.* _____
5. 3(5 + 9) is read *three fives and a nine.* _____
6. $\frac{1}{2} \cdot \frac{2}{3}$ is read *one-half times two-thirds.* _____

II. Directions: Carefully pronounce each term in the left-hand column to yourself, then match it with the statement in the right-hand column that best describes it.

_____rational   (A) begins with r, ends with l and contains a d.
_____fraction   (B) a mathematical word having two syllables.
_____radical   (C) begins with *rat.*
_____natural number   (D) is similar to *rational,* but has an extra syllable.
_____irrational   (E) isn't a word that is used to describe numbers.
_____fracture   (F) is two words.

III. Directions: Circle each term in the following list that is also found at least once in Chapter 4 of your mathematics textbook.

1. area
2. natural number
3. irrational number
4. rational
5. radical fraction
6. function
7. latitude
8. irrelevant number
9. radical number
10. volume
11. negative number
12. rational fraction
13. trigonometry
14. fraction
15. real number

The following activities are examples of strategies for assessing students' abilities to **attach literal meaning to symbols.** These activities could be done by students individually or in small groups.

Attaching Literal Meaning to Symbols in the Real Number System

I. Directions: Write a definition for each of these mathematical terms.

1. rational number
2. irrational number
3. negative number
4. natural number
5. integer
6. negative integer
7. proper fraction
8. decimal fraction
9. mixed number
10. whole number

II. Directions: Give one example of each of the types of numbers which are listed below.

_____1. fraction   _____ 6. rational number
_____2. proper fraction   _____ 7. irrational number
_____3. improper fraction   _____ 8. negative integer
_____4. decimal fraction   _____ 9. positive integer
_____5. real number   _____10. natural number

III. Directions: Using the hints given below, complete the spelling of each of these mathematical words.

1. O _ _ _ _ T I O N S
2. I _ _ _ T I O N _ _
3. _ _ _ _ T I O N
4. I _ _ _ _ _ _ S
5. _ _ _ _ R _ _ N U M B E R S
6. _ _ T _ _ _ _ N U M B E R
7. _ _ _ _ N U M B E R S
8. V _ _ _ A _ _ _

Hints

1. 2×7, $3 - 2$, $5 \div 8$, $6 + 5$
2. $\sqrt{3}$
3. $\dfrac{7}{11}$
4. $5, -3, 0$, but not $\dfrac{1}{2}$
5. $1, 2, +3$, but not $\sqrt{3}$
6. $\sqrt{9}$
7. $\sqrt{3}, -\dfrac{7}{8}, 3, 5\dfrac{1}{2}$
8. x

Students' abilities to **analyze relationships among symbols** can be evaluated by using techniques such as those illustrated below.

Analyzing Relationships Among Symbols in the Real Number System

I. Circle the number type in each column that contains all the other number types listed in that column.

Column A	Column B	Column C
positive	integer	pi
integer	rational	irrational
real	quotient of two	positive
whole	integers	negative
irrational	decimal fraction	$\sqrt{2}$
	mixed fraction	

II. In each column of numbers there is one number which does not belong in that column. Draw a line through the number that does not belong in each column.

A	B	C	D
$\sqrt{2}$	2	3	2/3
$\sqrt{9}$	7	-2	4/7
4	$\dfrac{3}{4}$	0	$-7/3$
$\sqrt{81}$	1/2	-4	$\dfrac{\sqrt{3}}{2}$
6	-1	2/3	$-3/5$

527

III.   Identify each statement as true or false by writing the word *true* or the word *false* in the blank before the statement.

_____1. All rational numbers are real numbers.

_____2. Zero is an integer.

_____3. Some real numbers are rational numbers.

_____4. All rational numbers are positive numbers.

_____5. Negative numbers are not real numbers.

_____6. Some rational numbers are natural numbers.

_____7. No rational numbers are natural numbers.

_____8. Decimal fractions are not real numbers.

Students' abilities, or difficulties, in solving word problems can best be discovered by asking questions about many different kinds of word problems. Although being able to find the correct answer to a word problem (or not obtaining the correct answer) is a gross measure of each student's ability to solve word problems, an incorrect answer tells little about the reasons why he or she has trouble with word problems. The following example questions illustrate the types of questions that teachers can ask students in order to assess their specific strengths and weaknesses in **solving word problems.**

Assessing Ability to Solve Word Problems

Problem: A local supermarket has three kinds of ground beef—hamburger at 99¢ per pound, ground chuck at $1.19 per pound, and ground steak at $1.39 per pound. The hamburger is 35% fat, the ground chuck is 20% fat and the ground steak is 15% fat. Since most of the fat will cook out of the ground meat when it is fried, which type of ground beef is the better buy in terms of edible lean meat?

Questions for Students to Answer:

1. How many kinds of ground beef does the supermarket sell?
2. What is the price of each kind of ground beef?
3. Which type of ground beef has the most lean meat?
4. Which type of ground beef has the least lean meat?
5. Which is more desirable, lean or fat ground beef?
6. What percentage of the hamburger is lean meat?
7. What percentage of the ground chuck is lean meat?
8. What percentage of the ground steak is lean meat?
9. How can we find the cost per pound for the desirable lean meat in each type of ground beef?
10. How many ounces of lean meat are contained in each pound of hamburger? of ground chuck? of ground steak?
11. What is the cost per ounce for the lean meat in the hamburger? the ground chuck? the ground steak?
12. How can we decide which type of ground beef is the better buy?

Questions such as these can be developed for a variety of word problems and can be used as a basis for class discussions, small group problem-solving sessions, or individual student work. Not only does this sequential questioning procedure help teachers and students analyze difficulties in solving word problems, but it also helps students learn strategies for solving various kinds of word problems.

The preceding quizzes, exercises and questions were designed to illustrate how abilities at each of the four psycholinguistic levels can be evaluated in students. However, a technique called the *cloze procedure* can be used to give teachers some idea of the general level of students' understanding of text material. This general information about students' reading abilities can be used to supplement information about their proficiency in using specific psycholinguistic skills. The cloze procedure is carried out by reproducing a passage from your students' mathematics textbook, with every fifth word left blank. The students' task is to fill in appropriate words for those which are omitted. Success in supplying the correct words is a measure of each person's ability to interpret and understand similar material in the textbook. The cloze procedure also indicates whether the level at which the textbook is written is consistent with the reading levels of your students. In addition, students' scores on cloze tests will indicate the range of general mathematical reading levels among the students in each of your classes and can be used to compare classes.

The following steps in the cloze procedure are given as a guide to carrying out this type of assessment of general reading ability in mathematics.

Directions for a Cloze Assessment of Reading Ability

Step 1. Select a running passage of approximately 300 words of prose from your mathematics textbook. Don't select material containing mostly formulas, examples, diagrams, exercises, and other types of non-prose materials.

Step 2. Type the first sentence in its entirety exactly as it appears in the textbook.

Step 3. Select at random one of the first five words from the second sentence, delete that word, and replace it with an underlined blank space, about 1½ inches long, when you type the sentence. From the second sentence on, beginning with the randomly selected first word deleted, delete every fifth word in the passage and replace these words with underlined blank spaces of uniform length until you come to the last sentence in the passage.

Step 4. Type the last sentence in the passage in its entirety with no omitted words.

Step 5. Give a typewritten copy of the cloze test (which was developed according to Steps 1-4) to each student in the class. Tell the class that each student is to read the passage and fill in each blank with a single word that he or she thinks makes the most sense. To illustrate the directions for this type of test, which will be unfamiliar to most students, write a cloze-type sentence (with blanks) on the chalkboard and have the class suggest words to place in the blanks.

Step 6. Give the class adequate time to complete the cloze test before collecting and scoring their papers.

Step 7. In scoring students' papers, mark as incorrect all words or symbols which are not duplicate replacements for the original words or symbols in the text. Even if a correct synonym is used as a replacement for the word used in the textbook, mark it wrong. (Since the cloze test will not be returned to the students and is not being used to determine a test grade, avoiding a search for synonyms makes scoring easier and still maintains relative rankings of students.) Compute the percentage of correct words for each student.

Step 8. Research studies of the cloze procedure have shown that it yields reliable and valid measures of reading comprehension in mathematics. As a rule of thumb, students who place the correct word in 55% or more of the blanks have a high understanding of the text material in question. Students who supply from 30% to 55% of the missing words correctly have adequate comprehension of the material. Students who have fewer than 30% of their words correct are likely to have trouble comprehending the textbook.

Step 9. After you have scored the cloze test and have identified students with scores lower than 30%, who may have reading comprehension difficulties, construct a frequency distribution of scores using 20 cells of 5 percentage points each from 0% to 100% correct answers. This frequency distribution will give you a good indication of the range of mathematical abilities in your class.

The following cloze test was constructed by modifying a passage from the textbook *Mathematics A Human Endeavor* by Harold Jacobs (pp. 372-373).

A Sample Cloze Test for Mathematics

A standard deck of playing cards consists of 52 cards which are divided into 4 suits of 13 cards each: spades, hearts, diamonds, and clubs. The cards in each _____ are: ace, king, queen, _____ , 10, 9, 8, 7, _____ , 5, 4, 3, and _____ .

Suppose a deck of _____ is shuffled and then _____ card dealt from it. _____ is the probability that _____ card will be a _____ ? Since there are 13 _____ ways of drawing a _____ compared to 52 ways _____ drawing any card, P(heart) _____ $\frac{13}{52} = \frac{1}{4}$. There _____ 1 chance in 4 _____ a heart will be _____ .

Now suppose that the _____ is put back into _____ deck where it is _____ with the others. If _____ card is drawn, what _____ the probability that it _____ also be a heart? _____ is the same as _____ : 1 chance in 4, _____ $\frac{1}{4}$.

If the dealer _____ at the beginning that _____ cards drawn will be _____ , what is the probability _____ this happening? To find _____ , we can multiply the _____ that each card will _____ a heart, in the _____ way that we have _____ the fundamental counting principle _____ many problems.

To find _____ probability of several things _____ in succession, multiply the _____ of each thing happening.

_____ the probability of drawing _____ heart from a full _____ is $\frac{1}{4}$, the probability _____ drawing 2 hearts in _____ row, the second one _____ the first had been _____ back, is $\frac{1}{4} \times$ _____ = $\frac{1}{16}$.

Since the _____ card was put back _____ the deck before the _____ card was drawn, what _____ in the first draw _____ no effect on what _____ in the second.

Events such as these which have no influence on each other are said to be independent.

The correct words and symbols in the correct sequence, as taken from the textbook from which this cloze test was made are: suit, jack, 6, 2, cards, one,

What, the, heart, favorable, heart, of, =, is, that, dealt, card, the, shuffled, another, is, will, It, before, or, claims, both, hearts, of, out, probabilities, be, same, used, in, the, happening, probabilities, Since, a, deck, of, a, after, put, $\frac{1}{4}$, first, into, second, happened, has, happens.

Although techniques for measuring and improving reading ability in mathematics have been discussed in the context of teaching slow learners, the suggestions for teaching reading in mathematics which have been presented here are relevant for all types of students—slow learners, average students and gifted students. Reading ability and mathematical ability are highly correlated, which means that many slow learners in mathematics are also poor readers. That is, they have various problems reading and comprehending mathematics textbooks. Facility in reading and understanding mathematics can increase students' achievement in mathematics classes as well as generate interest in the subject and increase their motivation in school.

Teaching Mathematically Gifted Students

Interest in the education of gifted students intensified during the nineteen fifties as a consequence of increased emphasis upon the importance of science and technology to society. During the nineteen seventies, an increasing awareness throughout society of the rights of individuals led some schools to offer special education programs for gifted students as well as slow learners. The need within society to develop people's talents in order to help solve serious social, political and technological problems, together with an emphasis upon the rights of individuals to have an opportunity to develop their particular abilities to their fullest in school, have prompted school systems to offer many more educational opportunities for gifted students.

Since people have many kinds of talents and abilities, there is no precise agreement as to who is a gifted student. Some people think of giftedness in terms of a high IQ. Others regard giftedness as the ability to do well in school. Still others consider giftedness to be a talent for music, art, writing and other creative endeavors. Another criterion for giftedness is the ability to reach the top in one's vocation or profession. Since IQ is a rough measure of both general intellectual ability and a combination of several particular mental abilities, many schools tend to classify students as gifted according to their scores on IQ tests. Some people consider IQ scores between 120 and 140 as an indication of a moderate degree of giftedness; scores between 140 and 160 as an indication of a high level of giftedness, and IQ scores above 160 as a measure of exceptional giftedness in people.

Even though IQ scores tend to be used as a first approximation to identifying gifted children, or as the sole criterion in some research studies, we will adopt the more inclusive definition of giftedness which is given by the National Society for the Study of Education. In its Fifty-seventh Yearbook, *Education for the Gifted, Part II* (1958), the NSSE defines giftedness as follows:

> The talented or gifted child is one who shows consistently remarkable performance in any worth-while line of endeavor. Thus, we shall include not only the intellectually gifted but also those who show promise in music, the

graphic arts, creative writing, dramatics, mechanical skills, and social leadership. (p. 19)

The NSSE Yearbook goes on to elaborate upon this definition by considering gifted people as "not...the 2 or 5 per cent with the highest intelligence quotients, but...the 20 per cent with promise of exceptionally good performance in a variety of areas of constructive activity."

Society has come to regard gifted people as a social resource that should not be wasted. Within the educational system, each student has the right, as well as the responsibility, to develop his or her gifts to their fullest extent. Consequently, special courses and programs have been developed and are being implemented for gifted students in elementary and secondary schools. It should be noted, however, that state departments of education and individual school districts use various criteria in defining giftedness and employ various procedures for identifying gifted students.

Characteristics of Gifted Students

Before discussing the intellectual, academic, physical and social characteristics of gifted students, it is well to dispel some common fallacies about gifted people. First, simply because a person is outstanding in one field such as mathematics does not mean that he or she will be inept in other fields. As is true of most people, a gifted student may be outstanding in many respects, average in other areas, and not particularly able in certain other endeavors. Second, gifted people do not as a group tend to have below average physical characteristics such as small size, poor eyesight or other physical deficiencies. In fact, gifted students tend to be somewhat above average with respect to physical characteristics as well as considerably above average in mental and creative abilities. Third, gifted students do not tend to be antisocial or emotionally immature. Research studies indicate that the gifted tend to be slightly more sociable and emotionally mature than other students in their age groups. In general, it is fallacious to think that because nature endowed a person with exceptional intellectual or creative abilities, it deprived that individual of certain other desirable characteristics in order to maintain a hypothetical balance among human traits.

Intellectual and Academic Characteristics of the Gifted

Gifted students tend to do well in most school subjects and exceptionally well in a few subjects. They score well on IQ tests, creativity tests, teacher-constructed mastery tests, and many other tests designed to measure particular academic attributes. Gifted students do well on most teacher-made tests because they have good memories; that is, they are able to memorize facts and skill algorithms quickly and remember them for a long time. They are also good readers and easily comprehend what they read. They retain much of what they read or hear with little drill and practice, and use a large number of words easily and accurately. They have little difficulty reading and understanding directions and instructions, which explains in part their ability to do well on tests. Most gifted students are able to read books which are several years in advance of their grade in school. There are many examples throughout the history of mathematics where mathematically gifted people in their early teens have read voraciously from books and articles written by research mathematicians and university professors—works written to communicate mathematical discoveries within the community of mathematicians.

Mathematically gifted students are quite good at the higher-level cognitive processes of analysis, synthesis and evaluation. They may enter the cognitive formal operational stage at an early age, and become quite proficient at abstract thinking and deductive reasoning. They are also good problem solvers because they can handle a number of variables simultaneously and can see complex relationships among mathematical concepts. The mathematically gifted are also able to understand mathematical concepts and principles by mentally manipulating and structuring sets of mathematical symbols. This is to say that they are good symbolic reasoners. Mathematically talented students are able to formulate conjectures, prove theorems and solve problems in mathematics because they tend to be both insightful and intuitive in their approach to mathematics. They can view problems from unique perspectives, have flashes of insight, and are able to engage in divergent as well as convergent thinking. They are creative and original mathematical thinkers.

In school, mathematically gifted students exhibit a considerable degree of intellectual curiosity. They are interested in a wide range of mathematical ideas, ask many good questions, come up with unusual and creative ideas, and always seem to want to know why things are the way they are. They want to know why algorithmic procedures yield the correct answer, why theorems are true, and how mathematical ideas were created or discovered. Gifted students are reluctant to accept "truths" based upon authority, and want to understand the mathematical concepts and principles underlying each mathematical process.

Since gifted students are able to read and understand mathematics on their own, they tend to work ahead in their textbooks and voluntarily find and read books and articles about mathematics. They look for challenging problems, interesting readings, and mathematical games and puzzles. Some gifted students like to ask difficult questions (the answers to which they already know) in class to see if they can trip up the teacher. As a result of the efforts of some gifted students to keep several steps ahead of the teacher, teachers of gifted students should themselves be mathematically talented, should be secure in their own knowledge of mathematics, and should have a good sense of humor. Since mathematically gifted high school students may quickly outdistance their teachers, teachers should avoid trying to enter into a oneupmanship contest with gifted students. The teacher will only lose the intellectual contest and will have to resort to authority to control the classroom situation. Attempting to compete in class with very talented students may result in loss of student respect for the teacher. Teachers who choose to settle mathematical arguments by using their disciplinary authority may generate a contempt for mathematics on the part of gifted students. A learning partnership should be established between the teacher and the gifted student, where each can learn from the other. The gifted student should recognize that the teacher is better educated and can help him or her learn even more about mathematics, and the teacher should recognize that the student has exceptional talent for mathematics and should help him or her develop that talent.

Gifted students are able to learn mathematical skills with little rote drill and can understand concepts and principles without seeing a large number of concrete examples. They are also alert and keenly observant which enables them to respond quickly in class. Consequently, teachers who have gifted students in their regular classes must be careful not to call on the better students consistently and, in effect, let them dominate the pace of the class to the exclusion of other students. Gifted students usually are well motivated and, if encouraged by perceptive teachers, will do a considerable amount of academic work on their own. Many mathematically gifted students can't get enough of mathematics and will spend much of their leisure time studying and learning mathematics. Gifted students do learn more rapidly than other students, and could be labelled "fast learners" in contrast to "slow learners," who are discussed previously in this chapter.

Physical and Social Characteristics of the Gifted

Since 1920 a number of people—Barbe (1965), Gallagher (1969), Laycock and Caylor (1964), Marland (1972), Martinson and Seagel (1967), Terman (1925-1959), Witty (1940), and others—have studied physical, social and emotional characteristics of gifted children. Between 1920 and 1955 Lewis A. Terman, a professor of psychology at Stanford University, collected data on 1,528 gifted people whom he identified as gifted children in 1920. He followed this group of people for 35 years, and many of the conclusions about characteristics of gifted people, which are given below, are based in part upon Terman's findings.

In terms of physical characteristics and general health, gifted students (those with high IQ's) tend to somewhat surpass general norms for American children. Such children are slightly larger and stronger at birth and learn to walk earlier. They have fewer health problems than average and have fewer than normal major and minor physical defects. The mortality rate of gifted people tends to be somewhat lower than that of the general populace. Since the gifted people who have been identified in research studies came from homes which were higher in socioeconomic level, it may be that the superior physical characteristics which were found are due in large part to better nutrition and health care rather than being directly related to the intelligence levels of the people studied. However, these studies of the physical characteristics of gifted people do refute the caricature of the puny, bespectacled, physically inept gifted student. Research studies indicate that as a group intellectually gifted students tend to be somewhat superior physically. Many gifted high school students have been found to be good athletes as well.

With respect to emotional maturity and social adjustment, the mentally gifted also fare well. Studies show that intellectually gifted children tend to have superior emotional adjustment. As a group, they tend to be more dominant, more self-reliant and less neurotic than their peers. However, as individuals, some gifted students have adjustment problems due to their frustrations in finding other children with similar abilities and interests and their heightened awareness of problems and injustices in society. Terman regarded the major emotional and social problems of gifted children as being due to their isolation from contemporaries, the frustration of being unable to meet their learning needs, boredom in school, and concern with moral and ethical problems.

In general, gifted children tend to be well accepted by other children. In school, they tend to be leaders and are frequently elected to school offices. They are active in student government, school clubs, athletics, creative endeavors and other extra-curricular activities. Although gifted students enjoy individual hobbies and solitary studies; they also enjoy playing games and engaging in other forms of group activities. In some cases, the desire for social acceptance and peer pressures have caused gifted students to neglect their academic studies in favor of social activities with other students. Since they perceive themselves as being intellectually and academically different, some gifted students purposely restrict their academic performance in order to be more like their classmates. In other cases, gifted students may regard themselves as socially superior to other students and seek out other gifted students for social interactions, while withdrawing from less academically able students in their age group.

In spite of a few contradictory findings in the research literature about the gifted and the few notable exceptions from the norm, intellectually gifted and creative students tend to be more similar emotionally and socially to other students than different from them. According to Ruth A. Martinson in the book *Exceptional Children in the Schools* (Dunn, 1973):

> In general, the pattern of postschool adjustment and productivity of gifted adults is excellent. Many gifted individuals find great satisfaction in their work and absorb themselves in their pursuits intensively by choice. They involve themselves in their work with greater intensity and dedication and often contribute far more to society than the average person. (p. 217)

The Needs of Gifted Students

Although mathematically gifted students may be able to learn the school mathematics curriculum rapidly with little attention from teachers, they do need guidance and direction to fully develop their mathematical abilities. Since slow learners tend to do poorly in school, it is obvious to most teachers that they need special assistance in learning mathematics. However, gifted students also have special needs; even though they may be able to obtain high grades with little assistance from their teachers. It is not correct, as some people believe, to assume that the best way to teach the gifted is to give them some textbooks and refrain from intervening in their learning. Gifted adolescents are first of all adolescents who have many of the problems and needs which are common to most teen-agers. In 1960, the National Education Association listed 11 general goals or needs of gifted students, which are still valid today. According to the NEA, gifted students need to:

1. Become intellectually curious, searching for meanings and seeking to find new relationships rather than old facts.
2. Improve the ability to do independent study and carry on research with attention to basic work habits, study skills, and methodology.
3. Learn to apply a wide range of knowledge and principles to the solution of many life problems.
4. Gain skill in self-evaluation.
5. Develop skills in critical thinking, gain a passion for truth, become open-minded with a sense of suspended judgment.
6. Realize the responsibilities as well as the power of knowledge.

7. Develop leadership ability including personal poise, respect for the worth of others, skill in group dynamics and person-to-person relationships.
8. Extend any tendency toward creativeness of various types.
9. Sense the implications of change.
10. Perfect skills in communication.
11. Develop the breadth of vision to see the possibilities of the future, the realities of the present, and the heritage of the past; to see in all this the continuing stream of man's ideas and question and concerns. (pp. 17-18)

While the general needs of the gifted, which are listed above, can be used as a set of goals for gifted students, these people also have certain specific needs in learning mathematics. Since many gifted students read mathematics books on their own and learn much more mathematics than their textbooks contain, they need to interact with teachers who know considerably more mathematics than they are presenting to their classes. They need knowledgeable teachers who can help them locate good books and articles about mathematics and who are sensitive enough to teach students who may be intellectually superior to themselves. Some gifted students will outstrip the teacher in their knowledge of certain mathematics topics, and teachers should feel that it is a compliment to their own teaching abilities to be able to assist gifted students in surpassing their own knowledge of mathematics. Teachers of the mathematically gifted should be interested in learning more mathematics themselves, so that they can aid students who are able to go beyond the standard school mathematics curriculum.

It is important for teachers to be able to recognize and nurture exceptional mathematical ability and adapt their teaching methods and the mathematics curriculum to meet the rapid pace at which these students learn mathematics. Gifted students, as well as slow learners, may need to spend extra time with their teachers outside class. They will need special assistance in understanding concepts and principles from the mathematical readings which they do independently.

Gifted students are able to learn school mathematics rapidly, but they still need to learn how to focus their attention and direct their efforts toward learning higher mathematics. Left to themselves, gifted students may spend many hours reading some of the poorest mathematical literature, playing irrelevant mathematical games, or working on trivial puzzles. They need help from teachers in finding and carrying out interesting and constructive activities in learning mathematics. As was noted in Chapter 5, many games and mathematics laboratory activities have questionable mathematics learning objectives. Unfortunately, if left to their own interest, some mathematically gifted students will waste many hours on trivial and unimportant pseudo-mathematical activities.

Since gifted students usually need to spend little time doing routine drill-and-practice exercises in order to learn mathematical skills, they should be permitted some flexibility in their classroom activities and homework assignments. But, they also need to be taught how to organize their time and discipline themselves. Some talented students become over-confident, fail to attend to learning facts and skills in class, and even become discipline problems in the classroom. They may fail to do homework assignments and take the attitude, "I don't have to pay attention in class or do homework assignments because I'm the best student in the class.'' Teachers should take care not to become so awed by a student's superior intellectual ability that the teacher permits that student to do as he or she pleases in the classroom. Gifted students also need to learn about rules of conduct and social conventions.

Gifted students should not be treated as superior human beings who are better than their classmates. They should be taught to respect people who may not have the specific intellectual abilities that they have, and should learn the value of non-cognitive abilities and competencies in our society. They should learn to use their superior knowledge of mathematics to teach and help students who are not doing very well in their mathematics courses. Gifted students in mathematics should also learn to respect and value the distinctive abilities and interests of their peers, which may be quite different from their own. In order to learn social skills, respect for others, and a degree of honest humility, gifted students should be included in homogeneous groups of students and should not be isolated from less able students for all their school studies.

Mathematically gifted students should be encouraged to do well in all of their school subjects and obtain a broad, liberal education in addition to developing their mathematical abilities. They should participate in extracurricular activities such as school clubs, athletics, music, dramatics and other creative endeavors. An over-emphasis upon mathematics in school may cause some students to develop into the false stereotype of a mathematician; that is, a person who is mathematically brilliant, but who can't deal with people and who is inept at most non-mathematical endeavors.

Gifted students need to be encouraged in their studies by being given sincere rewards and recognition. But since they have high abilities, high achievement should be expected of them. They should not be rewarded for merely good work when they are capable of excellent work. Gifted students should learn that they should use their special talents to do outstanding work. An exceptional ability in mathematics is a resource that should be developed and used, but not wasted. Gifted students need to learn that they have a responsibility to themselves and to society to use their gifts in a constructive manner.

In summary, gifted students have many of the same needs in school as other less gifted students. In addition, they have those special needs and responsibilities which have been discussed above. In particular, teachers should guide and counsel gifted students so that their talents are developed to their full potential.

Teaching/Learning Activities for Gifted Students

Gifted students tend to be well-motivated, have a wide range of interests, become fascinated with imaginative activities, and learn faster than most other students. In order to take advantage of their interests and abilities, gifted students should be taught by teachers who use a large variety of teaching/learning models. All 12 of the teaching/learning models discussed in Chapters 5 and 6 are appropriate for teaching mathematics to gifted students, but the inquiry, problem-solving and theorem-proving models are particularly well suited to gifted students.

Since most gifted students are fairly well motivated in school, the lecture-oriented **expository teaching/learning model** can be used effectively by teachers who are able to prepare and deliver interesting lectures. When using this model in teaching mathematically talented students, teachers are able to present new concepts and principles rapidly without the need for illustrating each idea with a large number of different examples. Although gifted students do need to work with concrete representations of mathematical ideas, they are usually capable of understanding many new concepts and principles through expository presentations by the teacher. The tendency for the gifted to develop large vocabularies makes them able to understand textbook definitions of concepts without having to reformulate each definition in their own words. Gifted students learn mathematics rapidly and are able to master new facts and skills by watching the teacher demonstrate several examples and by working a few exercises from the textbook. Even though lectures can be very effective strategies for teaching high-ability classes, they must be used with caution when teaching heterogeneous classes. Lecturing to a class containing gifted students and slow learners can cause either the gifted students to become bored because of the slow pace or the slower students to fall behind due to the teacher's rapid presentation of new ideas. In general, the expository teaching/learning model should be used in combination with other models when teaching gifted students, as well as other students. This model is especially appropriate for teaching gifted students because they are able to understand new concepts and principles more readily than most other students. When they don't understand a lecture, gifted students are likely to interrupt the teacher's presentation to ask questions and request explanations, clarifications and examples. As a consequence of their inquisitiveness, they are less likely to become confused and fall behind during a lecture where students are encouraged to interrupt the teacher with questions and relevant observations.

The **advance-organizer model** is a good model to use when beginning a new topic with a class of gifted students. Such students are able to think abstractly, can organize and structure information, and are able to see relationships among a number of concepts. Therefore, gifted students are usually able to prepare themselves for meaningful understanding of new information through teacher-presented, expository, advance-organizer lessons. Advance organizers are useful in helping gifted students assimilate and accommodate new information in their cognitive structures. Advance-organizer lessons require students to carry out the higher-level cognitive activities of analysis, synthesis and evaluation; and gifted high-school students tend to be well into the mental maturational level of formal operations, which permits them to use these high-level mental processes in learning new materials. Whereas slow learners tend to learn mathematics in small, relatively isolated segments, gifted students want to understand the relationships among mathematical facts, skills, concepts and principles, which can be facilitated through advance organizers. Well-organized, appropriately sequenced advance-organizer lessons are an excellent way to introduce new topics in mathematics and to show how new materials are related to topics learned previously.

Gifted students are naturally curious, are reluctant to accept new information based upon the say-so of an authority, and like to find things out for themselves. For these reasons, the **discovery teaching/learning model** is well-received by gifted students. While slow learners will need considerable guidance and teacher assistance in making mathematical discoveries, gifted students tend to make discoveries entirely on their own or with little direction from the teacher. In fact, mathematically-talented people seem to have flashes of insight which permit them to make broad, and accurate, generalizations based upon a few isolated and apparently unrelated instances of a principle. For example, a seventh grader may all of a sudden announce that, "Two consecutive whole numbers will never have a common divisor other than one," when studying common divisors. When a gifted student does suggest an unexpected proposition in class, perceptive teachers are able to use the discovery as a basis for an "off-the-cuff" problem-solving lesson by suggesting: "That's an interesting idea, can you convince the rest of us that it's true?" In heterogeneous classes, the conjectures of gifted students can be used as a focus for discovery and problem-solving lessons which can generate interest in mathematics for the entire class. Slower students can practice mathematical skills by finding examples or counter-examples of the proposition, while gifted students can attempt to formulate a proof. In fact, discovery lessons are an excellent medium for involving students of all ability levels in interesting and constructive mathematical activities.

Nearly all students like to play games, and **game-oriented teaching/learning models** can be effective approaches to drill-and-practice sessions and review sessions for classes containing a mixture of slow learners, average students and gifted people. Since gifted students require fewer drill-and-practice sessions to master skills and fewer review lessons to learn concepts and principles than other students, mathematical games can be used as a strategy to hold the interest of gifted students while the entire class is reviewing and practicing familiar ideas and skills. However, teachers should be careful to construct games that will involve all students in learning activities and that will not be dominated by gifted students due to their exceptional mathematical talents. Games for an entire class of gifted students should emphasize analysis and synthesis of concepts and principles, but games for groups of slow learners should usually concentrate upon knowledge and understanding of facts and skills.

In classes where students have a large variety of mathematical abilities, the **individualized teaching/learning model** may be one of the best models for attending to the needs of each student. Gifted students in the class may be able to work ahead of other students by studying alone or in small groups. Slow learners will need extra help from the teacher, and gifted students can test and strengthen their own understanding of mathematical objects by tutoring students who are in need of extra help. A good format for individualizing instruction for heterogeneously grouped students is to begin each lesson with a brief review of previous material and homework, followed by a teacher-directed introduction to new material. Next, students can begin work on differentiated homework assignments, with easier problems being assigned to slower learners and harder problems or projects being set for more mathematically talented students. When the better students are well along with their own work, they can be given supplementary readings and problems or can act as tutors for slower students who are having trouble with their work. This approach to instruction can be used to avoid the ploy of teaching to the "middle of the class," which can cause slow students to fall behind while gifted students become bored and restless.

The **spiral teaching/learning model** is a good general approach to use in teaching students of all mathematical ability levels. Slower students should be taken through each skill, concept, or principle spiral slowly and in small steps.

Gifted high-school students can progress rapidly from step-to-step in each mathematics spiral and can be expected to be able to handle abstract, formal representations of each mathematics object at a younger age than slow learners. Both slow learners and gifted students need to work with concrete representations of each concept and principle; although gifted students will be able to find many representations for themselves, while slow learners will be more dependent upon the teacher for their examples.

The **theorem-proving and problem-solving models** are quite appropriate for gifted students. Since gifted students want to know why things are as they appear to be in mathematics and enjoy solving challenging problems, they should be given many opportunities in their mathematics classes to make and prove conjectures and to formulate and solve problems. Since gifted students tend to be good problem solvers, their interest in mathematics and motivation to learn more mathematics can be increased by finding good problems for them to solve. For those few students who have truly exceptional mathematical talents, problem solving and theorem proving are critical activities in the development of their special abilities in mathematics. Many high school teachers find an occasional gifted student who is a much better problem solver than the teacher. In such a case, the teacher should encourage the student to read higher-level textbooks and magazines about mathematics and consult with college mathematics teachers and mathematicians working in industry whenever this is possible. While problem solving and theorem proving may discourage slow learners, who are not very successful at such activities, they can motivate gifted students to high levels of achievement in mathematics.

Mathematics laboratories and the laboratory approach to teaching and learning mathematics in the classroom are useful teaching/learning strategies for both gifted students and slow learners. While slow learners may practice skills and explore concepts through laboratory activities, gifted students are better able to formulate and test conjectures in mathematics laboratories. Teachers can expect gifted students to read and understand relatively difficult mathematical materials as part of their laboratory work. They are also able to manipulate and structure mathematical ideas in a manner which enables them to see complex mathematical relationships and formulate conjectures about mathematical structures. Although gifted students as well as slow learners need to work with concrete materials such as games, models and diagrams in mathematics laboratories in order to master concepts and principles, gifted students are better able to study mathematics using more symbolic and abstract representations of mathematical ideas. The main value of mathematics laboratories for gifted students is the opportunity which they have to explore, formulate and test hypotheses, which is the most important work of research mathematicians. In addition, applied mathematics laboratories or combined mathematics and science laboratories can help students understand the many uses of mathematics in our society and may prompt them to become interested in one or more of the many careers in mathematics.

Gifted students are more likely to become creative pure or applied mathematicians as adults than slow learners, so they, in particular, should be taught inquiry procedures through the use of the **inquiry teaching/learning model** in school. Gifted students, more so than other students, are able to develop general problem-solving and inquiry strategies and apply them in diverse situations. They also tend to have the ability to formulate problems and translate vaguely stated problems into terms which lead to their solutions. And, they are better able to analyze and evaluate the effectiveness of their own inquiry processes. As part of each teacher's responsibility to help individual students develop their abilities to the fullest extent, teachers should give gifted students many opportunities to inquire into the methods of mathematical problem solving and the nature of learning.

Because gifted students usually are able to study and learn mathematics independently, some teachers may be inclined to think that they should be excused from group activities in the classroom and be permitted to work by themselves. However, the **group activities teaching/learning model** can be used as effectively with gifted students as other students. Learning mathematics well and becoming a good mathematician require developing insight, intuition and communicative skills as well as becoming proficient at problem solving and theorem proving. One of the important objectives of our educational system is to help people learn how to work together for the common good. All learners, whether gifted or slow learners, can benefit from the social interactions that take place during group activities in mathematics. Isolating gifted individuals from less gifted students may create people who fit the false stereotype of a mathematical genius—a person who is self-centered, lacking in social graces, unable to communicate with others and barely able to function in any endeavor except mathematics. In order to become well-rounded human beings, gifted students need to be encouraged to play and work with other students in school. In addition to the socializing benefits of group activities, exchanges of ideas can foster mathematical learning. Even the best mathematicians throughout history were able to increase their mathematical productivity by exchanging ideas with each other and by discussing various techniques for proving theorems and solving problems.

The **computer-enhanced teaching/learning model,** when appropriately used, can develop and extend gifted students' interest in mathematics and their ability to produce high quality work in mathematics classes. Some gifted students who have access to computers in their mathematics courses are able to carry out mathematical research in a way that is quite similar to the manner in which mathematicians conduct their own research. By writing computer programs to test conjectures and solve problems, gifted students are able to greatly extend their analytical powers. When carried out by a gifted student, computer-enhanced problem solving can lead to the synthesis of new principles and the creation of unique problem-solving methods. When gifted students are given some degree of control over a computer as they study mathematics in school, they are able to learn a great deal about the nature of independent learning. Computer-enhanced instruction, when made available to gifted students is probably the most effective and efficient way to encourage these students to make the maximum use of their unique talents.

In summary, gifted students as well as less able students benefit most in school when a variety of teaching/learning models are used by their teachers. There is no single best model for teaching gifted students and helping them develop their talents. Using a variety of teaching methods is the best way to help students meet the specific objectives of the school mathematics curriculum and the general goals which we have set for students in our school systems. Teaching/learning activities which are best for each gifted student must be determined according to the needs of each student, the preparation of his or her teachers, and the resources which are available in the school.

Programs and Resources for Teaching the Gifted

In schools where mathematically-gifted students are provided special educational opportunities, two general practices are followed—either gifted students are placed in special programs and courses or they are given enrichment activities to supplement their work in standard courses. In addition, extracurricular activities such as mathematics clubs, fairs and contests may be available for gifted students who are encouraged to participate in these activities.

Special programs and courses for the gifted may be offered in larger schools having sufficient resources to implement such programs. Among the many adaptations that have been initiated by schools are:

1. Providing special advanced mathematics courses and projects through summer programs for gifted students.
2. Offering advanced placement courses which will permit students to skip a freshman course or several courses in college.
3. Permitting high-school students to get a head-start on college-level courses by taking a college course at a nearby college or university during the school year.
4. Permitting students to take one or two extra courses each semester in high school to accelerate their high-school graduation.
5. Running special sections of mathematics courses for gifted students who are able to cover more topics than are covered by students in other courses.
6. Giving high-school credit for extracurricular research projects, studies and other activities that students carry out in mathematics clubs, fairs, competitions, etc.
7. Making tutorial sessions available for students who are preparing a project for a mathematics fair or studying for a mathematics contest.
8. Permitting students to do independent study for school credit in special areas of mathematics under the supervision of a teacher.
9. Offering guidance and counseling services for gifted students.
10. Providing an "honors program" in school for those students who have demonstrated ability to achieve well beyond the standard requirements in their courses.
11. Allowing students to obtain course credit by examination and to enroll in correspondence courses or televised courses for school credit.

Even in schools where special courses, extracurricular activities, and programs are not provided for gifted students, teachers can provide a variety of opportunities to meet the needs of the gifted. When the 12 teaching/learning models are adapted for use with gifted students, in the ways which are suggested above, students will be able to develop their abilities whether they are grouped homogeneously in classes for the gifted or grouped heterogeneously. In either case (providing special courses for the gifted or placing them in regular classes with other students), exceptional textbooks and other learning resources should be available for use by the mathematically talented.

Some publishers of secondary-school mathematics textbooks have special textbook series for use in classes designed for gifted students. Several of the well-known mathematics curriculum projects have produced textbook series and supplementary books for high-ability mathematics students. There are also many excellent books about mathematics which, although not written as textbooks for particular courses, can be used by teachers and students as supplementary materials for high-school courses. In addition to books about mathematics, journals and magazines are published which are devoted exclusively to mathematics and mathematics education or contain regular features about mathematics.

The best way to find out if a textbook publishing company has a current mathematics textbook series for gifted students is to write to the publisher and request a catalog listing the company's secondary-school mathematics textbooks. Bookstores, school districts, colleges and libraries will have directories of publishers which you can use to find names and addresses of textbook publishers.

The *School Mathematics Project* (SMP) in England has prepared a set of textbooks and supplementary books for use in high-school classes with high-ability students. These books, which are titled *Advanced Mathematics,* are published by the Cambridge University Press: American Branch, 32 East 57th Street, New York, N.Y. 10022. The *School Mathematics Project* which prepared textbooks for students of various ability levels "was founded on the belief...that there are serious shortcomings in traditional school mathematics syllabuses, and that there is a need for experiment in schools with the aim of bringing these syllabuses into line with modern ideas and applications."

Among the many textbooks and supplementary publications of the *School Mathematics Study Group* (SMSG) are materials which can be used in mathematics classes for gifted students. The *Final Publication List* (Newsletter No. 43, August, 1976) of the *School Mathematics Study Group* can be obtained by writing to A. C. Vroman, Inc., 2085 E. Foothill Blvd., Pasadena, California 91109.

The *Comprehensive School Mathematics Program* (CSMP) has developed a set of mathematics textbooks for high-ability students in grades seven through twelve. This sequence called *Elements of Mathematics* contains books on logic and sets, fields, relations and functions, number systems, real analysis, geometry, trigonometry, linear algebra, groups, rings, probability spaces and measure theory. The developers of this program believe that "CSMP must be *discipline oriented.* By this they mean that, while all pedagogical aspects of mathematics education are of deep concern, priority is given to the selection and development of a sound mathematical content." The teaching methods used in the project emphasize multi-media activities, programmed instruction, independent but supervised study, and lectures. More information about CSMP can be obtained from CEMREL-CSMP, 610 East College St., University City Complex, Carbondale, Illinois 62901.

Another project which has developed mathematics curriculum materials for gifted students is the *Secondary School Mathematics Curriculum Improvement Study* (SSMCIS) which is discussed in Chapter 2. Additional information about the SSMCIS textbook series for the upper 20% of academic ability students in grades seven through twelve can be obtained from SSMCIS, Box 120, Teachers College, Columbia University, New York, N.Y. 10023.

Journals and magazines are another source of materials for gifted students. Many issues of *The Mathematics Teacher* and *The Arithmetic Teacher* contain articles about topics and teaching methods in mathematics which are of particular interest to well-motivated students. Issues of *School Science and Mathematics* contain articles about mathematics, mathematicians, and the history of mathematics; and a regular feature of this journal is a mathematics problem section. *Creative Computing* is a magazine which is especially appropriate for students who want to learn about applications of mathematics, mathematical games, and computer science. *The Mathematics Student,* which is published four times a year by the National Council of Teachers of Mathematics, is a good resource for gifted students and also for students who are not exceptionally talented in mathematics. A fascinating column written by Martin Gardner in each issue of *Scientific American* is devoted to mathematics and applications of mathematics. Each issue of *The American Mathematical Monthly* features a section called ''Elementary Problems and Solutions'' which will challenge even the most able high-school mathematicians. If the ''Elementary Problems'' section is too easy for some people, they can turn to the ''Advanced Problems and Solutions'' section for a real challenge.

Several publishing companies offer series of books about mathematics which can be used to supplement textbooks or as voluntary readings for gifted students. The L. W. Singer Company (249-259 West Erie Blvd., Syracuse, New York 13201) publishes a series of mathematics books called the ''New Mathematical Library'' which is appropriate for gifted high-school students. Blaisdell Publishing Company, a division of Xerox College Publishing, 191 Spring St., Lexington, Mass. 02173, has a series of books called ''Popular Lectures in Mathematics.'' Finally, Dover Publications, 180 Varick St., New York, N.Y. 10014, publishes a number of classics about mathematics, the history of mathematics, applications of mathematics, and games and puzzles in mathematics; many of these books should be in every high-school library.

The following list of books is a brief mathematical bibliography which can serve as a starter for a mathematics library for gifted students.

General Books About Mathematics Covering All Areas

Ball, W. W. Rouse. *Mathematical Recreations and Essays* (Revised Edition). New York: The Macmillan Company, 1960.

Caldwell, J. H. *Topics in Recreational Mathematics.* London: Cambridge University Press, 1966.

Gross, Herbert I., and Miller, Frank L. *Mathematics/A Chronicle of Human Endeavor.* New York: Holt, Rinehart and Winston, Inc., 1971.

Ogilvy, Stanley C. *Tomorrow's Math: Unsolved Problems for the Amateur.* New York: Oxford University Press, 1962.

Péter, Rózsa. *Playing With Infinity: Mathematics for Everyman.* New York: Atheneum, 1964.

Rademacher, Hans, and Toeplitz, Otto. *The Enjoyment of Mathematics.* Princeton, N.J.: Princeton University Press, 1957.

Rising, Gerald R. and Weisen, Richard A. (Editors). *Mathematics in the Secondary School Classroom: Selected Readings.* New York: Thomas Y. Crowell Company, 1972.

Sawyer, W. W. *Prelude to Mathematics*. Baltimore, Maryland: Penguin Books, 1955.

Singh, Jagjit. *Great Ideas of Modern Mathematics: Their Nature and Use.* New York: Dover Publications, Inc., 1959.

Steinhaus, H. *Mathematical Snapshots* (3rd Edition). New York: Oxford University Press, 1969.

Wren, F. Lynwood. (Chairman, Editorial Committee) *Insights into Modern Mathematics, Twenty-third Yearbook.* Washington, D.C.: The National Council of Teachers of Mathematics, 1957.

Books of Problems and Solutions

Charosh, Mannis (Editor). *Mathematical Challenges: Selected Problems from the Mathematics Student Journal.* Washington, D.C.: National Council of Teachers of Mathematics, 1965.

Dörrie, Heinrich. *100 Great Problems of Elementary Mathematics.* New York: Dover Publications, Inc., 1965.

Jones, Samuel I. *Mathematical Nuts.* Nashville, Tennessee: S. I. Jones Co., Publisher, 1932.

Kraitchik, Maurice. *Mathematical Recreations,* (2nd Edition). New York: Dover Publications, Inc., 1953.

Longley-Cook, L. H. *New Math Puzzle Book.* New York: Van Nostrand, Reinhold Company, 1970.

Phillips, Hubert. *My Best Puzzles in Mathematics.* New York: Dover Publications, Inc., 1961.

Polya, George, and Kilpatrick, Jeremy. *The Stanford Mathematics Problem Book.* Columbia University, New York: Teachers College Press, 1974.

St. Mary's College. *Mathematics Contest Problems for Junior and Senior High School.* Palo Alto, California: Creative Publications, Inc., 1972.

Applications of Mathematics

Amerongen, C. van. (Translator). *The Way Things Work, Vols. One and Two.* New York: Simon and Schuster, 1967, 1971.

Gray, William A. and Ulm, Otis M. *Applications of College Mathematics.* Beverly Hills, California: Glencoe Press, 1970.

Dantzig, Tobias, *Number: The Language of Science* (4th Edition). New York: Macmillan Company, 1954.

Logic, Philosophy of Mathematics, and the Nature of Mathematics

Abbott, Edwin A. *Flatland.* New York: Dover Publications, Inc., 1952.

Court, Nathan A. *Mathematics in Fun and in Earnest.* New York: The Dial Press, 1958.

Newman, James R. *The World of Mathematics, Vols. 1-4.* New York: Simon and Schuster, 1956.

Russell, Bertrand. *The Principles of Mathematics.* New York: W. W. Norton and Company, Inc., 1938.

Wylie, C. R., Jr. *101 Puzzles in Thought and Logic.* New York: Dover Publications, Inc., 1957.

Probability and Statistics

Mosteller, Frederick. *Fifty Challenging Problems in Probability*. Reading, Mass.: Addison-Wesley Publishing Company, Inc., 1965.

————, Kruskal, William H., et al. (Editors). *Statistics by Example: Exploring Data, Weighing Chances, Detecting Patterns, Finding Models* (4 Parts). Reading, Mass.: Addison-Wesley Publishing Company, Inc., 1973.

Tanur, Judith, Mosteller, Frederick, et al. *Statistics: A Guide to the Unknown*. San Francisco: Holden-Day, Inc., 1972.

Numbers and Number Theory

Davis, Philip J. *The Lore of Large Numbers*. New York: Random House, 1961.

Honsberger, Ross. *Mathematical Gems from Elementary Combinatories, Number Theory, and Geometry, Vols. I and II*. Washington, D.C.: The Mathematical Association of America, 1973.

Long, Calvin T. *Elementary Introduction to Number Theory*. Boston: D.C. Heath and Company, 1965.

Niven, Ivan. *Numbers: Rational and Irrational*. New York: Random House, 1961.

Ore, Oystein. *Number Theory and Its History*. New York: McGraw-Hill Book Company, Inc., 1948.

Geometry

Beard, R. S. *Patterns in Space*. Palo Alto, California: Creative Publications, Inc., 1973.

Greenberg, Marvin Jay. *Euclidean and Non-Euclidean Geometries: Development and History*. San Francisco: W. H. Freeman and Company, 1974.

Lindgren, Harry. *Geometric Dissections*. New York: D. Van Nostrand Company, Inc., 1964.

Manning, Henry P. (Editor). *The Fourth Dimension Simply Explained*. New York: Dover Publications, Inc., 1960.

Yates, Robert C. *Curves and Their Properties*. Washington, D.C., The National Council of Teachers of Mathematics, 1952.

Throughout the past 50 years, attention to educating the gifted and special programs for the gifted have run in cycles. Recently society has come to realize that gifted students as well as slow learners have special needs and that an equitable, democratic system of education must be concerned with the maximum development of all types of students. Ruth Martinson in *Exceptional Children in the Schools* (Dunn, 1973) says that:

> Progress in educating the gifted has been far less than spectacular during the past half-century. A good deal more is known about the problems of children with superior cognitive abilities than is being done to alleviate them. The educator who is sensitive to the problems and frustrations of the gifted is still the exception. Improvements and changes are occurring steadily, nevertheless, and growing numbers of educators and laymen are aware of the rights of the gifted and the contributions they make to humanity. A continued expansion of efforts made for them can produce untold benefits to both the individual and his society. (p. 236)

Things To Do

1. Define *slow learner in mathematics,* and list and discuss the various characteristics of students who are classified in school as slow learners. Which characteristics are common to nearly all slow learners in mathematics? Which characteristics are unique to each type of slow learner?

2. Define *gifted student in mathematics.* What characteristics do most gifted students have in common? What are some of the distinctive characteristics in a student which might indicate to a teacher that he or she is mathematically gifted?

3. Write a brief paper comparing the educational needs of slow learners and gifted students in mathematics classrooms. What educational needs do both the gifted and slow learners have in common? Which educational needs are unique for slow learners? For gifted students?

4. Which teaching/learning models do you think are most effective to use with slow learners? Why do you think these models are appropriate for slow learners? Are any of the 12 teaching/learning models discussed in this book particularly inappropriate for helping slow learners learn mathematics? Why?

5. Of the 12 teaching/learning models presented in this book, which are most effective for teaching mathematics to gifted students? Which are least effective? Give reasons to support your responses.

6. Select a topic from consumer mathematics and prepare a complete 14-point lesson plan (see Chapter 4) for teaching this topic to a class of slow learners who are not very proficient in arithmetic.

7. Choose a topic from college mathematics which is not usually taught to high-school students and write a complete 14-point lesson plan for teaching this topic to a small group of mathematically gifted students in high school.

8. Check through back issues of *The Arithmetic Teacher* and *The Mathematics Teacher* for articles about teaching slow learners. Read and summarize at least three such articles. You will find additional articles about slow learners in *The Phi Delta Kappan* journal as well as in other professional education journals.

9. Use books, journals, magazines, catalogs, etc. to find references to books, materials and other resources which can be used effectively in teaching mathematics to slow learners. Make a list of the resources that you have located and include the source of each resource, so that you will be able to locate it when you need it in your own teaching.

10. Go to the mathematics and mathematics education sections of a college or university library (or a good school library) and browse through the shelves looking for mathematics books which could be used as supplementary readings and references for gifted students in high-school mathematics classes. In particular look for good history of mathematics books, collec-

tions of problems, and mathematical games and puzzles, which are both interesting and valuable for learning mathematics. Make a list of the 20 best books which you find.

11. Write a short paper about methods for helping slow learners as well as other students improve their skills in reading and understanding mathematics textbooks. Describe each method in detail and discuss ways that it could be implemented in a secondary-school mathematics classroom.

12. Select a secondary-school mathematics textbook or a history of mathematics book and choose a 300-word passage from the book to make into a cloze test for assessing reading ability. Use the cloze procedure described in this chapter in preparing the test. Then, see if you can find about 10 people who are willing to take the test. Score each person's test, find his or her percentage of correct words placed in the blanks, and make a tally chart showing the range of reading and comprehension levels for the people who took the cloze test. Based upon your findings, determine which people in the group probably would have difficulty reading and comprehending the book which you selected. Which people would do adequately well? Who would do quite well?

13. If possible, work with a high-school mathematics teacher in preparing a cloze test to assess his or her students' ability levels in reading and comprehending each of the mathematics textbooks that the teacher is using in his or her classes. Help the teacher administer each test to the appropriate classes, score the test, and identify those students who probably are having trouble reading and comprehending their mathematics textbook.

14. Using the bibliography at the end of this chapter as a starting point, prepare three bibliographies of readings for secondary school mathematics teachers—one bibliography on teaching reading in mathematics, one on teaching slow learners, and one on teaching the gifted. Remember that each reference you locate on a particular topic will usually have a bibliography of other references on the same topic.

Selected Bibliography

Barbe, W. B. *Psychology and Education of the Gifted: Selected Readings*. New York: Appleton-Century-Crofts, 1965.

Dunn, Lloyd M. (Editor). *Exceptional Children in the Schools* (2nd Edition). New York: Holt, Rinehart and Winston, Inc., 1973.

This book contains 10 chapters, which were written by nine authors, pertaining to teaching exceptional children. The chapters deal with mild, moderate and severe general learning disabilities; superior cognitive abilities; behavioral disabilities; oral communication disabilities; hearing disabilities; visual disabilities; health problems; and major specific learning disabilities.

Earle, Richard A. *Teaching Reading and Mathematics*. Newark, Delaware: International Reading Association, 1976.

This 88-page monograph offers mathematics teachers ideas and methods for assessing students' abilities to read and understand mathematics books, and suggests ways for teachers to help students improve their reading skills. It is intended to provide the "what and how" of teaching reading in mathematics while teaching mathematics content. The book contains many specific activities for assessing and improving mathematical reading skills.

Gallagher, J. J. "Gifted Children." *Encyclopedia of Educational Research.* New York: Macmillan, 1969, pp. 537-544.

————. *Teaching the Gifted Child* (Revised Edition). Rockleigh, New Jersey: Allyn and Bacon, 1975.

An excellent resource for teachers who teach special classes for gifted students or who have gifted students in their regular courses, this book is recommended as a reference for mathematics teachers.

Hater, Mary A. and Kane, Robert B. "The Cloze Procedure as a Measure of Mathematical English." *Journal for Research in Mathematics Education,* 1975, Vol. 6, No. 2, pp. 121-127.

The article describes how the cloze procedure can be used to assess readibility of mathematical materials, and presents the conclusions from a study designed to "adapt the cloze procedure to the language of mathematics and to assess its behavior as a measure in that language."

Henry, Nelson B. (Editor). *Education for the Gifted. Fifty-seventh Yearbook, National Society for the Study of Education, Part II.* Chicago: University of Chicago Press, 1958.

This Fifty-seventh Yearbook of the National Society for the Study of Education contains 18 chapters on teaching gifted students. These chapters, which were contributed by 21 professional educators, are organized into three sections about gifted students—*Social Factors, The Gifted Person,* and *Education of the Gifted.* Included in the book are chapters about the nature of giftedness, identification of the gifted, secondary-school programs for gifted students, guiding the gifted, and preparing teachers for the education of gifted students.

Herber, Harold L. *Teaching Reading in Content Areas.* Englewood Cliffs, N.J.: Prentice-Hall, Inc., 1970.

A general book about the importance of reading in the content areas, this book contains a considerable amount of information which is related to teaching reading in the mathematics classroom. It also has an appendix titled "Reading and Reasoning Guides: Mathematics."

Jacobs, Harold R. *Mathematics A Human Endeavor.* San Francisco: W. H. Freeman and Company, 1970.

Although not designed specifically as a textbook for slow learners, Jacobs' book can be used quite successfully for junior high school courses, courses in high school for slow learners, and beginning general mathematics courses in college. The book contains many interesting mathematics topics and student activities. Whether or not it is used as a textbook for a mathematics course, it should be in the mathematics library and should be used as a resource by teachers and students.

Keating, Daniel P. (Editor). *Intellectual Talent: Research and Development.* Baltimore: The Johns Hopkins University Press, 1976.

This book of readings contains 18 chapters about research studies, findings, and conclusions related to the early childhood education of intellectually gifted people. The papers contained in the book are based upon the Sixth Annual Blumberg Symposium on Research in Early Childhood Education. The chapters are organized under three headings—*Identification and Measurement of Intellectual Talent, Programs for Facilitation of Intellectual Talent,* and *The Psychology of Intellectual Talent.*

Kirk, Samuel A. *Educating Exceptional Children* (2nd Edition). Boston: Houghton Mifflin Company, 1972.

This book is about many different kinds of exceptional children. It is intended to be the basis for a general, introductory course on the characteristics, needs, and education of exceptional children—slow learners, handicapped children, and gifted students. However, many teachers will find certain chapters to be useful references when teaching students with specific learning handicaps or students who are exceptionally talented. The book contains chapters about speech-handicapped children, the intellectually gifted, low intelligence, mental retardation, auditory handicaps, visual problems, neurologic and orthopedic impairments, and behavior disorders.

A very readable and useful book for teachers, *Educating Exceptional Children* contains an excellent chapter (pages 105-158) titled "The Intellectually Gifted Child." In fact, Kirk's book is a valuable resource for any teacher who encounters various types of exceptional children in his or her classes.

Laycock, F., and Caylor, J. S. "Physiques of Gifted Children and Their Less Gifted Siblings." *Child Development,* 1964. Vol. 35, pp. 63-74.

Love, Harold D. *Educating Exceptional Children in a Changing Society.* Springfield, Illinois: Charles C. Thomas, Publisher, 1974.

This book contains chapters about educating various kinds of exceptional children—mentally retarded, visually disabled, speech-handicapped, hearing impaired, physically handicapped, socially and emotionally maladjusted, learning disabled and gifted. Each short chapter contains a brief overview of several relevant factors in teaching a particular type of exceptional student.

Marland, S. P. (Submitter) *Education of the Gifted and Talented.* Washington, D.C.: U.S. Office of Education, 1972.

Martinson, R. A., and Seagoe, M. V. "The Abilities of Young Children." *CEC Research Monograph B4.* Virginia: Council for Exceptional Children, 1967.

National Council of Teachers of Mathematics. *The Slow Learner in Mathematics: Thirty-fifth Yearbook.* Washington, D.C.: National Council of Teachers of Mathematics, 1972.

An excellent resource on teaching mathematics to slow learners, this book contains 12 related sections written by classroom teachers and mathematics educators. The section titles are:

1. Characteristics and Needs of the Slow Learner
2. The Research Literature
3. Behavioral Objectives
4. A Favorable Learning Environment
5. Adjustment of Instruction (Elementary School)
6. Teaching Styles (Secondary School)

7. Aids and Activities
8. The Laboratory Approach
9. Diagnostic-Prescriptive Teaching
10. Classroom and School Administration
11. Promising Programs and Practices
12. The Training of Teachers
Appendix A: Activities, Games, and Applications
Appendix B: Sample Lessons

Project on the Academically Talented Student and National Association of Secondary-School Principals. *Administration: Procedures and School Practices for the Academically Talented Student in the Secondary School.* Washington, D.C.: National Education Association of the United States, 1960.

Even though it was published in 1960, this book still contains much relevant information about educating gifted secondary-school students in the nineteen eighties. The book has chapters about identifying gifted students, accelerating learning, ability grouping for students, enrichment teaching/learning strategies, and counseling and guiding gifted students.

School Mathematics Study Group. "Mathematics for Disadvantaged and Low Achieving Students: Newsletter No. 33." Stanford University, California: SMSG, September, 1970.

This newsletter contains a report and description of SMSG textbooks for slow learners in mathematics.

Shepherd, David L. *Comprehensive High School Reading Methods.* Columbus, Ohio: Charles E. Merrill Publishing Company, 1973.

Secondary school teachers will find among the 13 chapters in this book the following helpful topics for teaching students how to read and understand mathematics: *Effective Teaching Through Diagnosis, Vocabulary Meaning and Word Analysis, Comprehension of Reading Material, Reading Study Skills for the Student, Applying the Reading Skills to Mathematics.*

Shields, J. B. *The Gifted Child.* London: The National Foundation for Educational Research in England and Wales, 1968.

This 96 page soft-bound book contains summaries of research findings and conclusions about certain characteristics of gifted children. The five chapters in the book are titled *The Problem of Definition, A High IQ, Creativity, Logical Thinking,* and *Educating the Gifted Child.*

Sobel, Max A. *Teaching General Mathematics.* Englewood Cliffs, New Jersey: Prentice-Hall, Inc., 1967.

This book can be used by teachers as a source of topics and activities for slow learners in mathematics. It is intended for use as a teacher supplement for a standard course in general mathematics. Topics contained in the book are:
1. The Slow Learner
2. Survey of Related Curriculum Developments
3. Explorations with Numbers and Numerals
4. Explorations with Geometric Figures
5. Explorations with Computation and Mensuration

6. Explorations in Probability
7. Explorations with Mathematical Systems
8. Explorations with Mathematical Recreations

Stanley, Julian C., Keating, Daniel P., and Fox, Lynn H. (Editors). *Mathematical Talent: Discovery, Description, and Development*. Baltimore: The Johns Hopkins University Press, 1974.

Based upon the Third Annual Blumberg Symposium on Research in Early Childhood Education, this book contains sections about characteristics of mathematically precocious youth, methods for facilitating the educational development of the mathematically talented, a program for fostering mathematical achievement, and values and interests of the mathematically gifted.

Suydam, Marilyn N. *Teaching Mathematics to Disadvantaged Pupils: A Summary of Research*. Columbus, Ohio: ERIC Information Analysis Center, April, 1971.

This publication contains an annotated bibliography of research studies and conclusions relative to teaching mathematics to "disadvantaged pupils."

Swain, Henry. *How to Study Mathematics: A Handbook for High School Students*. Washington, D.C.: National Council of Teachers of Mathematics, 1970.

A good guide for both teachers and students, this monograph contains many practical suggestions about how to study mathematics reading assignments, how to use textbooks, how to do homework, how to make the most of the class period, how to take tests, and other "how to's" for studying mathematics.

Terman, L. M. (Editor) *Genetic Studies of Genius, Vols. I-V,* Stanford, California: Stanford University Press, 1925-1959.

The University of the State of New York. *Improving Reading-Study Skills in Mathematics Classes*. Albany, New York: New York State Department of Education, 1968.

This 25-page monograph contains some practical suggestions about how teachers can assist students in improving their reading and study skills in mathematics.

Travers, Kenneth J.; and others. *Teaching Resources for Low-Achieving Mathematics Classes*. Columbus, Ohio: ERIC Information Analysis Center, July, 1971.

According to the abstract, this booklet:

reviews teaching approaches and general resource materials for low achievers in both elementary and secondary mathematics classes. A survey of reported characteristics of low achievers is divided into two classes: (1) social and emotional problems, and (2) learning difficulties. . . . Teaching approaches which have been reported as being successful include the use of computational aids, manipulative devices, and laboratory techniques. Also reported was the development of individualized short-term curriculum units, emphasizing success and immediate reward. The two bibliographies included are: (1) a bibliography of general resource material, and (2) an annotated bibliography of articles which have appeared in *The Arithmetic Teacher* and *The Mathematics Teacher* which suggest lessons for low achievers.

Witty, P. A. "A Genetic Study of 50 Gifted Children." In Nelson B. Henry (Editor). *Intelligence: Its Nature and Nurture. Thirty-ninth Yearbook, National Society for the Study of Education, Part I.* Chicago: University of Chicago Press, 1940.

Index

Index

DATE DUE

AUG 1 9 1981			